Verse in English from Tudor and Stuart Ireland

Verse in English
from Tudor and Stuart Ireland

edited by Andrew Carpenter

CORK UNIVERSITY PRESS

First published in 2003 by
Cork University Press
Crawford Business Park
Crosses Green
Cork
Ireland

British Library Cataloguing in Publication Data
A CIP catalogue record for this book is available from the British Library.

Library of Congress Cataloging-in-Publication Data

Verse in English from Tudor and Stuart Ireland / edited by Andrew Carpenter.
    p. cm.
Includes bibliographical references and index.
ISBN 1-85918-354-9 (alk. paper)
1. English poetry—Irish authors. 2. English poetry—Early modern, 1500-1700. I. Carpenter, Andrew. II. Title.
PR8856.V48 2003
821'.00809417—dc21

                              2003011598

ISBN 1 85918 354 9 hardback
ISBN 1 85918 373 5 paperback

Typeset by Phototype-Set Ltd., Dublin
Printed by MPG Books Limited, U.K.

For Terence Brown,

Alan Harrison

and Tony Sweeney

CONTENTS

1. Poems are grouped by author and, except in the case of three poets who wrote poems
   about Ireland both when they were young men and again in later life (George Wither,
   Robert Boyle Earl of Orrery and Jonathan Swift), are placed chronologically according
   to the date of the earliest of the poet's verse included in this anthology – or by the date
   of the publication of verse which appeared posthumously. Three dates are given for each
   author: birth, date of appearance of the work in this anthology, and death.

Part II 1603–1641: Early Stuart Verse

Part III 1641–1660: From the Rising to the Restoration

Part V 1685–1701: Jacobite and Williamite Ireland

ACKNOWLEDGEMENTS

This book was planned three years ago and initial research was done in the years 1999–2001. But the completion of the book was only possible because I was awarded a Government of Ireland Senior Research Fellowship in the Humanities and Social Sciences for 2001–2. This enabled me to concentrate on the project full-time and I should like to record my gratitude to the Irish Research Council for the Humanities and Social Sciences through which I obtained the award, and to the staff of the council, particularly Dr Maurice Bric and Dr Marc Caball, for their help during the tenure of my fellowship. The UCD English Department also facilitated me with a semester's leave in the year 2000–01, and I am grateful to my colleagues in the department for this.

I should like to thank the following institutions for permitting me to use texts and readings from manuscripts in their care: The British Library, The Bodleian Library University of Oxford, The Library of Christ Church Oxford, The Board of Trinity College Dublin, the Trustees of the National Library of Ireland, the Council of the Royal Irish Academy, the Folger Shakespeare Library, Washington D.C. and the Trustees of the Osborn Collection, Beinecke Library, New Haven. My particular thanks to Stephen Parks, curator of the Osborn Collection at Yale University, for making the Ormond manuscripts available to me and for many acts of generosity.

The staff of the following libraries have been unfailingly helpful to me while I have been working on this book, and I would like to express my thanks to them: the library of University College Dublin, the library of Trinity College Dublin, the National Library of Ireland, the library of the Royal Irish Academy, Marsh's Library, The Gilbert Collection of the Dublin Public Library, the Bodleian Library University of Oxford, the Library of Christ Church Oxford, the British Library, the Library of the Royal Society of Antiquaries London, the Public Record Office London, Lambeth Palace Library, the libraries of Yale University, the Huntington Library, and the William Andrews Clark Memorial Library, Los Angeles.

Many people have been enthusiastic supporters of this project, particularly the three to whom I have dedicated the book, Terence Brown, Alan Harrison and Tony Sweeney. Terence Brown has given me invaluable help in various ways with this book and with its predecessor, *Verse in English from Eighteenth-Century Ireland*, while Alan Harrison's expertise in all things connected with the Irish language and Irish culture in the early modern period has saved me from innumerable errors. Tony Sweeney, the compiler of the indispensable bibliography of Early Modern Ireland, *Ireland and the Printed Word: A short descriptive catalogue of early books, pamphlets, newsletters and broadsides relating to Ireland, 1475–1700* (Dublin, 1997), has been particularly supportive of this project, always willing to share his encyclopaedic knowledge of sixteenth and seventeenth-century Ireland, to lend me books from his own collection and to point me in the direction of other promising material. His hope that this book might come out in folio format may yet be realised.

In addition, I should like to thank Eamonn de Burca and Fonsy Mealy for letting me examine their seventeenth-century Irish books, and to express my gratitude to several colleagues and friends who, once they had heard that I was working on this anthology, sent me transcriptions or photocopies of texts which might be suitable: these include Toby Barnard, Danielle Clarke, Alan Fletcher, Raymond Gillespie, Rolf and Magda Loeber, John McCafferty, Mary Paul Pollard, Clodagh Tait, Betsey Taylor, James Woolley and Andrew Zurcher. I much appreciate the fact that so many people went out of their way to bring to my attention material I would never have found without their help. In addition, Toby Barnard, Raymond Gillespie, John McCafferty and Clodagh Tait generously responded to many specific questions. I know that several aspects of the book have been greatly improved as a result of their help and I am very grateful to them.

As well as those named above, I should like to thank the following for help of various kinds: Bruce Arnold, Ray Astbury, Kevin Barry, Charles Benson, Nicholas Canny, Maurice Craig, Arch Elias, Neville Figgis, Anne Fogerty, Roy Foster, David Gardiner, David Hayton, Norma Jessop, Chris Johnston, Máire Kennedy, Muriel McCarthy, James McGuire, Robert Mahony, Christopher Murray, Tadhg Ó hAnnracháin, Hermann Real, Peter Reill, Peter Rowan, Andy Taylor, Anne Simmons, Andrew Smith, Annie Sweeney, Andy Taylor, Janet Todd and Nicholas Williams.

Sara Wilbourne, Caroline Somers and the staff at Cork University Press have been extremely helpful in seeing this book through the press, and my thanks to them. Jonathan Williams has been an exemplary proofreader and guide. Above all, I would like to thank my wife Dorothy Molloy, who has cheerfully put up with an anthologising husband for the last three years – in fact, for the last six years, since she had to endure

Verse in English from Eighteenth-Century Ireland before this book. She will be relieved to know that I shall not be doing *Verse in English from Nineteenth-Century Ireland*.

In addition, I acknowledge with thanks receipt of a grant towards the cost of publication from the National University of Ireland.

Andrew Carpenter

Dublin, September 2002

INTRODUCTION

I

When he was a young man in Dublin in the 1590s, James Ussher – later to be the famous archbishop of Armagh – declared himself 'addicted to Poetry', and though he afterwards 'shook it off, as not suitable to the great end of his more resolved, serious and profitable Studies', yet Ussher 'always loved a good Poem that was well and chastly writ'.[1] In fact, the practice of writing verse was not particularly out of the ordinary for educated men and women in early modern Ireland; its rhythm and rhyme made verse easy to understand and to remember and, as Roger Boyle, Earl of Orrery, explained in the introduction to his *Poems on Most of the Festivals of the Church* (London, 1681): '. . . it seems to be the Inherent Prerogative of *Verse*, above *Prose*, To be better Fancied; To be easier Learn'd by Heart; and to be Longer Retain'd in the Memory. . .'. A petition to a lord lieutenant or an archbishop, an account of a journey or a letter to a friend might well be in verse rather than prose and, of course, rhymes of all kinds permeated everyday life – rhymes to help in communal work, nursery rhymes, verses sung in the streets, verses repeated in church or chapel. It was an age much more accustomed to the sound of verse than our own and one in which verse was regarded as accessible to all, the illiterate and the literate.

If verse was written down at all, it might be designed to circulate in manuscript between friends, like the poems written in the coterie surrounding the Duke and Duchess of Ormond in Dublin Castle in the early 1660s, for example. Other verse was written for wider transmission, and for the printing press. In general, printed texts have a higher survival rate than manuscripts, and about two-thirds of the verse in this anthology is from printed sources; but the remainder comes from manuscripts of various kinds.

Few of the writers whose work is in this anthology thought of themselves as 'poets', though they were people who felt strongly and who put pen to paper with confidence. Some of what they wrote may sound a little stilted to modern ears and, in places, it is ingenuous; but, on the whole, the verse collected here is fresh and lively, giving the reader a clear impression of everyday life in sixteenth- and seventeenth-century Ireland,

---

1. Richard Parr, *The Life of . . . James Usher, late Lord Archbishop of Armagh* (London, 1686), pp. 3–4. See also Raymond Gillespie, 'The Social Thought of Richard Bellings' in *Kingdoms in Crisis: Ireland in the 1640s*; ed. Micheál Ó Siochrú (Dublin, 2001), pp. 212–28 (p. 213).

or of the views which outsiders had of the country during the period. Many of the voices which emerge from these pages have not been heard since their work first appeared, and a considerable number of them belong to that under-studied group which the Earl of Clanricard described as 'people of the middle rank'.[2] The lives and works of these people have not been investigated as much as have the élite of the age but, in this book at least, their views are given an airing.

As in my previous anthology, *Verse in English from Eighteenth-Century Ireland*, I have avoided using the word 'poetry' in the title of this book. All the material here is, however, in metre of some kind, and some of the seventeenth-century verse shows the prosodic ingenuity of the age. A few of the texts might, perhaps, be dismissed as 'rym dogerel' – the phrase used by Chaucer's host to describe Chaucer's own tale of Sir Topas[3] – and in some cases, the modern reader might wish that the writer had expressed things more succinctly. But I have not shrunk from making drastic cuts in poems, long or short, where necessary, and I believe that every one of the texts that has survived the selecting and cutting involved in making up this anthology will be seen to throw interesting light on the cast of mind of those living in Tudor and Stuart Ireland or on attitudes towards the Irish nation and its people. A few of the poems now rescued from oblivion will, I hope, bring real delight.

A surprisingly small amount of verse in English by women writers seems to have survived from early modern Ireland. As Jane Stevenson and Peter Davidson have demonstrated in their recent anthology, *Early Modern Women Poets* (Oxford, 2001), there were fine women poets writing in the Irish language in seventeenth-century Ireland, including Bríd Iníon Iarla Chill Dara and Fionnuala Iníon Uí Dhomhnaill. But I have been able to find little similar material in English. The work of some of the writers I have read, including Elizabeth Cary, Countess of Faulkland (*c*. 1585–1639), and female members of the Boyle family, did not seem to warrant inclusion (for various reasons) and, as it stands, the anthology provides examples of the work of only five women poets. This is less than I would have wished, but it seems to reflect what has survived. Perhaps the paucity of material may have something to do with the lack of education in English for girls in sixteenth- and seventeenth-century Ireland and with the fact that many Englishmen left their families at home

---

2. The earl used the phrase in a letter to the Marquis of Ormond (13 November 1643); see J. Lowe (ed.), *The Letter-book of the earl of Clanricard 1643–47* (Dublin, 1983), p. 16. The remark is quoted in T.C. Barnard, '"Parlour entertainment in an evening"? Histories of the 1640s', in *Kingdoms in Crisis*, p. 42.
3. F. N. Robinson (ed.), *The Works of Geoffrey Chaucer*, Second edition (London, 1957), p. 167.

in England while they served in Ireland. Few of the women who lived in Ireland at the time, therefore, were able to write verse in English.

Although there is a considerable amount of verse drama on Irish topics from England and Ireland in the seventeenth century, only dramatic prologues and epilogues which shed some light on the cultural world of seventeenth-century Dublin were included in the pool from which selections were made. In my view, the most important plays of the age, *Langartha: A Tragie-Comedie* (Dublin, 1640) by Henry Burnell and *A Tragedy of Cola's Fury, or Lirenda's Miserie* (Kilkenny, 1646) by Henry Burkhead, should both be edited and reprinted in full, with introductions which explain for a modern readership the complex political and cultural situation in which they were written; extracts of a few hundred lines would never do justice to either play. Dramatic prologues and epilogues, however, can shed interesting light on the world from which they come.

While there is some chronological overlap between *Verse from Eighteenth-Century Ireland* and this anthology, only two texts appear in both books: I have selected a different passage from *The Irish Hudibras* for this anthology, and have printed a different text of 'Lilliburlero'. In general, despite the fact that so many documents have been destroyed in Ireland over the last three hundred years, there exists a remarkable amount of material from which to make a selection for a book such as this. Even an anthology twice this length would have brought to light interesting, well-crafted poems which illuminate the age in which they were written. As it is, there is a wide range of poetic voices here, as well as many varieties of register and tone; some poets are deeply serious, others satiric or skittish; some are worried about propriety of language and correctness of rhyme, others throw themselves into complicated verse forms or outlandish rhyme schemes with reckless abandon; some hoped their verse would change the politics of the day, others merely needed to express private thoughts – though the sense of what was 'private' and what was 'public' was different, in early modern Ireland, from our own, and all private thoughts were, in a sense, relevant to the community.[4] Some felt they were at the centre of English or Irish culture, others knew they were on the margins; some wrote or composed verse because they were important people, others despite the fact that they knew they were not. From this large and varied body of work, I have selected material of all kinds and types which I hope reflects not only the diversity of the mass but also some of its intensity and its energy.

4. See David Cressy, 'Response: Private Lives, Public Performance, and Rites of Passage', in *Attending to Women in Early Modern England*, eds. Betty S. Travitsky and Adele F. Seeff (Newark, 1994), p. 187, quoted by Jane Stevenson and Peter Davidson, *Early Modern Women Poets: An Anthology* (Oxford, 2001), p. xxxviii.

II
The Rhymesters, Versifiers and Poets

Although this anthology includes only verse written or composed in the English language, that does not mean that its contents reflect only the views of English writers and English colonists in Ireland. Irish was far more widely spoken in early modern Ireland than English, and any assessment of the cultural or literary life of Ireland in the Tudor and Stuart period must take full account of writing in both languages; but the language of the coloniser was also widely understood and used outside the towns and cities, particularly for written communication, and much of interest can be found in English. Among those who spoke and wrote English, many were by no means Anglophiles; on the contrary, several of those whose work is included here believed that Ireland should be a sovereign kingdom and some were violently opposed to the forces of the English parliament in Ireland. In fact, there are almost as many political opinions expressed in this anthology as there are ways of expressing them and the poems included do, to a considerable extent, reflect the views of the four main ethnic or cultural groups living in, or connected with, Ireland in the early modern period: the unambiguously English, the New English settlers, the Old English settlers, and the native Irish. Though, as Raymond Gillespie has pointed out, defining these social entities in early modern Ireland has always been problematical, it is perhaps worth considering the contribution of each of these groups to this anthology in turn.[5]

The English

About half the poets whose work is in this anthology would have thought of themselves as English; however, if their verse is included here, it is because it is about Ireland or was written when they were spending time in the country. Writers in this category include John Bale, the fiercely protestant bishop of Ossory during the reigns of Edward VI and Queen Mary; the Elizabethan soldiers Barnaby Rich and Thomas Churchyard, who served in Ireland for many years; the shadowy John Derricke, who

---

5. Gillespie, 'The social thought of Richard Bellings', *Kingdoms in Crisis*, p. 228. The real complexities of the situation can be seen in many specialised studies of the period. A good example is in Appendix A of L. J. Arnold, *The Restoration Land Settlement in County Dublin, 1660–1688* (Dublin, 1993), where landowners in seventeenth-century County Dublin are listed under six distinct categories: Old English catholics, New English catholics, Old Irish catholics, Old English protestants, New English protestants and Old Irish protestants.

was attached to the household of Sir Henry Sidney; and administrators of various kinds, Barnaby Googe, Edmund Spenser, Francis Quarles, Sir John Davies and George Wither – all of whom wrote verse while they were living in Ireland. Anti-Irish feeling was most powerfully expressed during the Nine Years War at the end of the Elizabethan period by the anonymous 'J.G.E.', whose vituperative *England's Hope against Irish Hate* shows clearly the racist nature of some English writing about the Irish at the time. A generation later, the well-known London playwright James Shirley wrote revealing prefaces for the Dublin productions of plays in the 1630s, and Payne Fisher sent his friends vivid accounts of military life in Ireland in the 1640s.[6] English poets who are included from the period after the restoration of Charles II include Katherine Philips, who was at the centre of the coterie of those writing verse in Dublin Castle in the early 1660s, English ecclesiastics holding Irish appointments (such as William Fuller and Jeremy Taylor), and Englishmen who spent considerable periods in Ireland, Sir William Petty and the eccentric Colonel William Mercer. Some of the anti-Irish broadsides of 1687–91 are also the work of anonymous English poets.

The Old English

The second largest category is of poets from the Old English community in Ireland. By the end of the sixteenth century, these descendants of the knights who had come to Ireland in the reign of Henry II were thoroughly integrated into Irish life. They had long intermarried with the native Irish and were, many of them, substantial landowners. Despite being recipients of various titles and honours from the English crown, the largest Old English families remained catholic after the Reformation and, by so doing, set themselves apart from the other English in Ireland, military, administrative or adventurers. Though many of them retained close ties with family in England, they were proud to be catholic and Irish and, at various times, allied themselves with the native Irish, in opposition to the incoming New English, rather than with these Englishmen against the native Irish. During the early seventeenth century, it was the Old English who made up the Irish parliament and it was to this Irish, catholic group that Charles I was forced to make concessions in the 1620s. The Old English produced some fine poets, of whom Richard Stanihurst and Richard Bellings are the most considerable; but Richard Nugent and

---

6. Another interesting preface from this period is 'A Prologue and Epilogue at the "New house"' by John Clavell. See Alan J. Fletcher, *Drama and the Performing Arts in Pre-Cromwellian Ireland: A repertory of sources and documents from the earliest times until c. 1642* (Cambridge, 2001), p. 441.

Thomas Cobbes also wrote verse of great interest, while Bishop Luke Wadding's poetic laments for the plight of Irish catholics during the time of the Popish Plot have been unjustly neglected. Several of the Old English poets who were attached to the confederates in the 1640s sent copies of their verse to the Duke of Ormond, and the early songs in English in this anthology, for instance 'Ye merry Boyes all that live in Fingaule' of about 1636, reflect the life of the ordinary Old English of the period.

The New English

This term is used to refer to incoming English settlers who, on foot of grants of Irish land or positions, attempted to settle in the country during the later sixteenth and seventeenth centuries. Some of the poets among them, Spenser for instance, were chased out of Ireland. Others, like Lady Ann Southwell and the various members of the Boyle family, integrated into Irish society and lived lives not dissimilar from those they would have lived in England. Yet others, such as Sir Parr Lane and those he wrote about so effectively in 'Newes from the Holy Ile', felt vulnerable to attack by the native Irish they had dispossessed, and were distinctly uneasy living in Ireland. But the invasions of Oliver Cromwell in 1649 and of William of Orange in 1689–90 both strengthened the basis of power for the New English settlers in Ireland, and the second of these invasions allowed the New English to take over the Irish parliament in the 1690s and to create the protestant ascendancy of the eighteenth century. During the reign of James II, however, when it seemed for a short time likely that catholics would again hold the upper hand in Ireland, the New English voiced their fear and hatred of Irish catholics in satires such as the 'Purgatorium Hibernicum'. They may also have had a hand in the composition of the London-printed broadsides which calumniated Irish catholics in the early Williamite period.

The Native Irish

Since Irish was the language of most inhabitants of the island during the sixteenth and seventeenth centuries, little of their verse appears in this anthology. But stray glimpses of the life of the native Irish can be gleaned from, for instance, Edward Bletso's 'A dialogue between a traveller and a hermit . . . (c. 1622) and also from 'The Irish Exile's song' of about 1630.

One way of letting the invaders know how they were regarded was by writing in their own language – as did Cornelius Mahony in his 1642 'A kind of a Ballad' defying the English. Interest in Irish history could also stimulate the translation of Irish language material into English, as is the case with Michael Kearney's translation of the verse from Geoffrey Keating's *Foras Feasa ar Éirinn* of 1635. Equally, though Luke Wadding himself was from an Old English family, the voice of colonised and defeated native Ireland is reflected in his verse in the 1680s.

III
Sources, Manuscript and Printed

The most important material included here which has not previously been generally consulted is a collection of over fifty pieces of manuscript verse connected with James Butler (1610–88), twelfth Earl of Ormond, first Marquis of Ormond (from 1642) and first Duke of Ormond (from 1661). The verse, which dates from the early 1640s to the time of Ormond's death in 1688, was collected presumably by Ormond's secretary, Sir George Lane (later Lord Lanesborough), and kept in Kilkenny Castle until a few years ago; it is now in the Osborn Collection at the Beinecke Library at Yale University.[7] Most of the poets who sent work to Ormond are otherwise unknown, and their verse ranges from the pithy anagram to the extended, bombastic diatribe. Ormond was lord lieutenant for three terms, from 1643 to 1649, from 1662 to 1669 and again from 1677 to 1685, and much of the verse he collected can be dated to these periods. The material he received during his first two terms is the most fascinating. The complexities of confederate and royalist politics in the 1640s and 1650s are clearly reflected in the range and outspokenness of the material from that period, but the verse that circulated in Dublin Castle during Ormond's posting in the 1660s is of considerable importance also, and gives a useful indication of the state of cultural life in Restoration Dublin.

The most unusual piece in the Ormond collection is a long poem by an otherwise unknown poet called Thomas Cobbes, which he graphically entitled *A Poeme uppon Cromuell and his Archtrayterous Rabble of Rebellious Racailles[8] and Englandes Jaolebirdes, levelled and arraunged nowe togither with a compendious runninge over of greate Britaines present deplorable state, and a more ample description of Irelandes*

7. See Andrew Carpenter, 'A Collection of Verse Presented to James Butler, first Duke of Ormonde', *The Yale University Library Gazette*, vol. 75, nos. 1–2 (October 2000), pp. 64–70. For a note on 'Ormond' and 'Ormonde', see below, p. 33.
8. rakehells, scoundrels, rascals.

auncient, late, more moderne, and nowe imminent condition, if the Inhabitaunts thereof (as beneath exhorted) doe not unanimously and seriously addresse themselves to defende their auncient religion, theire kinge, theire countrey, the pristine Rights, Lawes and customes of their countrey, their wives, their cheildren and their owne Lands and Personall Estates. This remarkable piece – which Cobbes described in the prose address which accompanied it as 'this Poor Myte of a Poeme' – is a vituperative attack on the incoming Cromwellians and a stirring call to the catholics of Ireland, particularly the Old English catholics, to rise in arms against the 'hedge borne vagabondes' of Cromwell's army. Other poems in the Ormond collection repeat the call, and reflect the alarm felt by the still-powerful forces of Irish catholic royalists as they saw the New Model Army coming to force them to toe the English parliamentary and protestant line. The Ormond collection, as a whole, sheds remarkable new light on Irish cultural life in the seventeenth century and would repay further study.

Another manuscript which proved valuable in compiling this anthology was Thomas Crofton Croker's nineteenth-century draft of a never-completed 'History of Irish Poetry'. This volume, like Croker's other works, was to consist of a prose narrative interspersed with extended or complete quotations of relevant texts. Though Croker did not live to complete the work, his extensive manuscript notes found their way to the British Library. I owe the discovery of several of the more obscure texts in this anthology to Croker, who had read through scores of eighteenth-century English verse miscellanies looking for material which had any connection with Ireland. Among Croker's sources were the papers of what he described as a sixteenth-century English antiquary living in Ireland – now known to be Meredith Hanmer, historian of Ireland and rector of the College of the Blessed Mary at Youghal, County Cork. Though I have not used them myself, the Hanmer papers in the Public Record Office in London might yield more interesting early verse from Ireland.

Several other manuscripts have provided entertaining material for this anthology, including the verse epistles of Payne Fisher, who became Cromwell's poet laureate, and a miscellaneous collection of Restoration verse compiled by Sir William Petty – both of these manuscripts now in the British Library. A particularly useful source for later material is 'A Whimsical Medley', the four-volume collection of verse made between about 1682 and 1722 by Theophilus Butler, Lord Newtown Butler, now in the library of Trinity College Dublin. This manuscript has long been known to Swift scholars as an important source for some Swift poems, but it also contains a remarkable assortment of Irish material from the late seventeenth century, some of which is included in this anthology.[9] Another manuscript of interest, this time one which helped clarify the interaction between Irish and English culture in the middle of the seventeenth century, was Michael Kearney's 1635 translation of Geoffrey Keating's *Foras Feasa ar Éirinn* in the Royal Irish Academy.

As far as printed verse is concerned, the earlier material about Ireland comes, in the main, from descriptions of the country by English soldiers such as Barnaby Rich or Thomas Churchyard. Although much of this verse is directly concerned with Ireland, it was printed in London because of the lack of a printing or publishing industry in Ireland at the time – which was, itself, partly a result of the unsettled nature of the country and of the small number of people in Ireland likely to buy books in English. Spenser and other Englishmen writing in Ireland in the late sixteenth century would not have thought of publishing their work in Ireland: their audience was in London, even for as self-contained an account of an event in Ireland as Spenser's *Epithalamion*. Apart from 'Mount Taraghs Triumph' and the poetry of Richard Bellings, no verse was printed in Ireland until 1630, and not until about 1670 did the printing of verse occur in any quantity. Thus, much of the earlier printed material in this book bears a London imprint.

Many of the volumes from which I have selected verse for this anthology are exceedingly rare. For example, the only known texts of the 1630 Dublin printing of elegies by members of the University of Dublin for the Countess of Cork, *Musarum Lachrymæ*, and of the peculiar 1649 parliamentary poem *Ormondes Breakfast*, are in the library of Christ Church, Oxford. The Folger Shakespeare Library in Washington DC holds the only known copy of *Poems by Several Persons of Quality and Refined Wits* (Dublin, 1663), and the sole surviving copy of Bishop Luke Wadding's *Smale Garland of Pious and Godly Songs* (Gant, 1684) is in the British Library. The latter work was not rare in its own day – the bishop himself handed out scores of free copies in his diocese in the 1680s[10] – but, like almanacs and other popular, fragile books of the time, most copies fell to pieces over the years. It is perhaps more surprising that Richard Bellings's *A Sixth Booke to the Countesse of Pembrokes Arcadia*

9. For an assessment of this manuscript, see James Woolley, 'John Barrett, "The Whimsical Medley", and Swift's Poems' in *Eighteenth-Century Contexts: Historical Inquiries in Honor of Phillip Harth*, eds. Howard D. Weinbrot, Peter J. Schakel and Stephen E. Karian (Madison and London, 2001), pp. 147–70.
10. See Patrick J. Corish, 'Bishop Wadding's Notebook', *Archivium Hibernicum*, vol. 29 (1970), pp. 49–114.

(Dublin, 1624) should be so rare; this book, which contains eight occasional poems by Bellings, must have been fairly widely distributed in Dublin and London when it first appeared, but is now represented by a single copy in the British Library.

Irish material printed in London during the 1640s and 1650s and collected by George Thomason (now in the British Library) is fairly widely known to students of seventeenth-century Ireland, but surprisingly little attention has been paid to the Irish material in the great English ballad collections made after 1660 – for example, the Pepys Collection in Magdalene College, Cambridge. These texts reflect an exclusively English view of Irish affairs, but they still prove useful in providing the context for Irish poems published in London at the time, *The Irish Hudibras* in particular. Pepys collected nearly eighty ballads connected with Ireland in the period 1685–91, and other collections of ballads and street songs are equally rich in material of Irish interest. Much work remains to be done in this field.

IV

From the Spoken to the Written Word, and from Irish to English

In Ireland, as elsewhere in early modern Europe, most poetry was heard rather than read. The easy movement of material from the oral to the written and back to the oral in early modern England had been convincingly documented by Adam Fox, and there is no reason to assume that things were different in Ireland.[11] There must have been many songs like 'You and I will go to Fingall' sung in the Pale in the sixteenth century, but chance decreed that this is the one caught by Meredith Hanmer and written down. At other times, the words of printed broadside verses such as 'Mount Taragh's Triumph' were read or sung aloud and so migrated back into the oral tradition. 'Lilliburlero' belongs as much to the oral as to the written; in fact, it may well have originated as a marching song to which politically appropriate words were composed on the long roads between London and Chester or between Cork and Kilkenny; the song was then 'collected' and printed as a broadsheet.[12] Another example of the oral transferring to the written is the fragmentary lament 'Ribeen a Roon', collected in Fingal and written down by John Dunton in the 1690s.

The fact that this last text contains several words of Irish indicates the influence of the Irish language on the Hiberno-English spoken in Fingal,

---

11. Adam Fox, *Oral and Literate Culture in England 1500–1700* (Oxford, 2000).
12. See headnote to the song in the main text below, p. 504.

the area of the Pale just north of Dublin;[13] but few other texts in this anthology show any verbal interaction between English and Irish. However, the 1642 'true copy of most wicked verses written in forme of a Ballad defying the English', which were 'found in a Rebels pocket' and attributed to Cornelius Mahony, was certainly written by someone for whom Irish was a first language. The poem begins with the strange line: 'The mother of your evils your souls will receive'. This reads like an Irish curse, except that the future tense rather than the subjunctive is used. The phrase 'mother of your evils', awkward in English, reflects the Irish *máthair an oilc*. The poet's unfamiliarity with English has led him to select one of the two English meanings of the word *máthair*, 'mother', when he should have used its other meaning, 'source'. Later in the poem there occurs the phrase 'Our souldiers and male men'; here the poet, in translating the Irish adjective *fearga*, which signifies both 'male' and 'brave', has selected the first meaning rather than the second one.

This 'rebel' poem also contains an early example of comic interaction between the languages. An English planter's servant says to him: 'In troth good master of help is no way.' This almost unintelligible sentence is, in fact, a word-for-word translation into English of a sentence in Irish: *I bhfírinne a mháistir mhaith de chabhair níl aon tslí*. The poet is showing how ridiculous an Irish-speaker sounds when he thinks that all he has to do to communicate in English is to translate individual words into the new language. John Shank, an exiled Irishman who performed comic song-and-dance routines in England in the 1630s, made capital out of the faulty vocabulary and syntax of a native Irish-speaker attempting to speak English in his 'Irish Exile's Song'; Shank, though, added to the joke by putting in the line: 'None English could [I] speak'. Forty years later, when military defeats and wholesale confiscations had made the Irish far less of a threat to the English in Ireland, exaggerated Hiberno-English had become the main rhetorical strategy for ridiculing the native Irish, as the authors of the 'Puratorium Hibernicum' and 'To his Onor de Rit Onorable Richard Earle of Tyroincol' so vividly show.[14]

On the whole, there is far more evidence of interaction between the Irish and English languages in the verse of eighteenth-century Ireland than there is in equivalent verse from the Tudor and Stuart periods. After about 1760, chapbook verse from the Irish provinces shows Irish words,

13. For a study of the language of Fingal, see Alan Bliss, *Spoken English in Ireland 1600–1740* (Dublin, 1979). The spoken language in a manuscript considered by Bliss entitled 'The Fingallian Travesty' (BL. MS Sloane 900) is described in its introduction as 'Irish-English Hodge-Podge'.

14. On the development of the Irish joke in the English language in the seventeenth century, see Deana Rankin, '"Shet Fourd vor Generaul Nouddificaushion": Relocating the Irish Joke 1678–1690', *Eighteenth-Century Ireland*, vol. 16 (2001), pp. 47–72.

syntactical constructions and metrical patterns in verse in English. But the two literary cultures, Irish and English, did not exchange material with each other in the Tudor and Stuart period in the same way. Irish literature, though going through very hard times – particularly in the seventeenth century – was too self-confident to need to borrow from English.[15] It can be shown that some Irish poets of the seventeenth century, Dáibthí Ó Bruadair for instance, were familiar with the work of the poets of seventeenth-century England such as Abraham Cowley,[16] but they felt no need to make use, in their own poetry, of what they had read in English. They were working within a strong, if dying, tradition and were still honoured and, when possible, supported by the remaining Gaelic patrons. It was not until the Cromwellian plantations destroyed the social and educational structures of traditional Irish society that the world in which this culture could survive disappeared.

V

English Views of Ireland

Since this book collects material written in English, it is not surprising that Englishmen's descriptions of Ireland, as well as depictions of English attitudes towards the Irish, feature prominently in its pages.[17] In the early period, at any rate, these depictions are based more on prejudice and mythology than on observation. The generalised idea of the 'wild Irishman', familiar from classical times and reiterated frequently in the medieval period, lies behind Andrew Boorde's description of an Irishman in the first English poem about Ireland or Irishmen in this anthology. Boorde's main stress is on the Irishman's lack of civility; he has 'an angry hart', he is infested with lice, he eats his meat 'syttyng upon the ground'

---

15. As Alan Harrison points out in his essay 'Literature in Irish 1600-1800' in *The Field Day Anthology of Irish Writing*, 3 vols (Derry, 1991), I, 274–8, Dáibthí Ó Bruadair (c. 1625–98) referred to the period in which he lived as that of *briseadh an tseanghnáthaimh*, 'the break-up of the old custom'. See that essay as a whole, Marc Caball, *Poets and Politics: Continuity and Reaction in Irish Poetry 1558–1625* (Cork, 1998), especially pp. 83–143, and the introduction by Cecile O'Rahilly to her edition of *Five Seventeenth-Century Political Poems* (Dublin, 1952), pp. vii–ix. On Irish chapbook verse from the later eighteenth century, see Andrew Carpenter, *Verse in English from Eighteenth-Century Ireland* (Cork, 1998), pp. 6–23.
16. See Gerard Murphy, 'David O'Bruadair', *Irish Ecclesiastical Record*, vol. 78 (1952), pp. 340–57.
17. One of the few recorded Irish comments on England comes when Richard Nugent's lover Cynthia, bewailing the fact that he is to leave her in Ireland and go to England, regrets particularly that he will be buried in 'an uncouth land'. See below p. 125.

(implying that he has no proper house and no furniture), he boils his meat 'in a bestes skin' (implying that he does not even own a cooking pot) and he lives in poverty even in his 'owne countre'. Though Boorde does praise the Irishman's ability to make 'good mantyls' and 'aqua vitae', the main purpose of his verse description is to portray the Irishman as a barbarian, one who clearly needs 'civilising' by the English.

Boorde's vision was developed dramatically by John Derricke a generation later. In his *Image of Irelande*, Derricke portrayed Ireland and the Irish in a way which would allow any Englishman to feel justified in destroying them. Throughout the *Image*, the 'lothsome' manners of the Irish are constantly contrasted with the 'civill' behaviour of the English, and when Derricke criticises the Irish because they 'feare not God, nor honour yet their Prince', he touches a theme constantly repeated in Tudor writing about Ireland: the God the Irish should fear is the God of protestantism and the prince they should honour is the English sovereign. If they refuse to accept these badges of civility, the Irish deserve to be destroyed. Derricke's message is particularly effective since he describes in detail the activities in the household of one particular 'woodkarne'[18] whose 'rakehelly horseboys' (as Spenser was to call such camp followers) annoy 'true men'; the reader of Derricke's poem is clearly told that the Gaelic Irish are 'mortall foes unto the Common wealthe', bloodthirsty barbarians determined to attack godly, law-abiding citizens at every opportunity. As if Derricke's verbal descriptions were not enough, they were amplified with a set of twelve vivid woodcuts depicting Irish life which showed precisely the kind of uncivilised behaviour which is the subject of his vituperative poem.

An important theme in Derricke's poem – one which also concerned Spenser – was the deep-seated influence of the traditional Irish bards in the Gaelic world. A society where law was administered by hereditary brehons in the open air was threatening enough, but a society that held the bard and the harper in high esteem was even more alien – and could be dangerous; for the bard, by recounting Irish conquests of the past, encouraged rebellious behaviour. After an account of an Irish feast in the *Image*, Derricke describes how the 'Barde and Harper' stir up the rebels to attack the English: 'What greate renowne their fathers gotte, thei shew by Rimyng skill.' In a marginal note at this point, Derricke says that the bards and rhymers are as 'as holie as a Devill'. Equally dangerous are the priests attached to the household of the 'woodkarne' Derricke is describing; they tell the 'rebels' that it is 'an almost deede to God' to kill

18. = wood kerne. Though the word 'kerne' (Ir. *ceithearn*) means a band of footsoldiers, it usually refers, in English, to a single, Irish, armed foot soldier. Derricke's 'woodkarne' is a minor chieftain.

the English, and offer them 'heavenlie blisse' if they do so. The wise Englishman would have kept clear of the place.

Despite these descriptions, Ireland still appealed to any Englishman seeking to make his fortune and to better his social position. One such adventurer was Edmund Spenser who, fifteen years after the publication of Derricke's *Image*, made Ireland the setting for some of his most memorable verse. But he, with a bold and original stroke, chose to portray the country as a place of mystery and fascination as well as of danger. Like Derricke and others, Spenser stressed Ireland's beauty and her potential richness, but he chose to explain why it was full of savage beasts and the hostile, Gaelic Irish by imagining that discontented gods had laid 'an heavy haplesse curse' on the land so that 'all that goodly Chase, doth to this day with Wolves and Thieves abound'. Yet Spenser bestowed an almost magical significance on the hills and rivers around his castle at Kilcolman in County Cork when he made the area the setting for the grand trial in Book VII of *The Faerie Queene* between the claims of the present world order and those of 'Mutability'. Ireland becomes the arena where, before 'great Nature' herself, the values of a civilised, settled world are seen to be overwhelmed by those of instability and change. For Spenser, Ireland is the land where the great fight between good and evil comes to one of its climaxes.

The author of *England's Hope against Irish Hate* (London, 1600), however, had much less lofty thoughts on his mind. For him, nothing good could possibly come out of Ireland. Unlike many later anti-Irish poems which employ ridicule and parody to denigrate and satirise the Irish, this is a deadly serious text. Tyrone and his countrymen are no laughing matter: they are insinuating serpents, venomous toads, ravening wolves, traitorous outlaws, blind reprobates, dunghill gnats. There can be no compromise between the forces of civilised England and these blasphemous, blood-drinking savages. The 'lavish late expence' of English blood in Ireland 'incites revenge' till 'they goe downe, and we in conquest rise'. The poem is one of fear and loathing.

The defeat of the Irish and Spanish forces at Kinsale in 1601 and the subsequent Flight of the Earls, however, brought about considerable political and social change in Ireland and, as English law was gradually imposed throughout the more fertile parts of the island, so the English settlers sent by James I were able to establish themselves in reasonable security. Some of the defeated Irish co-operated with these settlers but others, as Sir Parr Lane pointed out in his fascinating long poem 'Newes from the Holy Ile', remained a threat. Lane drew a clear distinction between 'the best' of the Irish and 'crowes that cannot chaunge theire hew'. These are the ever-present 'kernes', ready to rise against the English and murder planters in their beds, given half a chance. To illustrate his point, Lane describes an Irishman who had 'latelie come from the Flemish warres, sparcklinge with silver as the night with starres'. 'But marke, within this yere', he warns,

> and you shall see
> a lowsy mantell will his wardroabe bee,
> and all the discipline that there he learnd,
> [in] the next rebellion, you shall see it kearnd.[19]

Like Derricke and Spenser before him, Lane lays much of the blame for the continuing threat on the Irish bards:

> Bard, Rimer, Harper with tale, rime and songe
> incite the rest, like boutefeux, to wronge.[20]

Equally pernicious is the influence of the catholic faith:

> For wee spoyle, rob, ravine, rape and kill,
> we pay the priest his due, and doe soe still.

These simple, clear verses convey a sense of ever-present danger – something with which many English settlers in early seventeenth-century Ireland had to learn to live.

The life of other, less threatened, settlers of the time can be seen in the poems of Edward Bletso and Lady Ann Southwell, though it was not long before the 1641 rising overturned what peace there had been and armies once more tramped over the countryside. An interesting, if jocular, account of contact between soldiers of different cultures, but fighting on the same side, comes in the anonymous *Account of an Irish Quarter* of about 1643. Here two English officers, who have been instructed by the Duke of Ormond, the lord lieutenant of the time, to carry a message to the high sheriff of the County of Waterford, John fifth Lord Power, describe the Power household. This consists of a series of thatched buildings looking so similar to each other that one officer takes his horse into the main dwelling mistaking it for a stable.

---

19. i.e. you will see him behaving like an Irish kerne.
20. boutefeux = firebrands, those who cause trouble.

Zownds, here's a Stable has no Rack nor Manger.
Peace, *Ned*, (quoth I,) prethe be not so hasty,
This room's no stable, though it be as nasty;
I see a Harp and chimney too, and dare
Say, there was fire in't before the war.

Later in the poem, there is a description of a typically robust Irish feast (at the end of which their host 'cross'd himself all o'er'), following which the guests are conducted to the chamber where they are to sleep.

But through the gaping wall came such a wind
That from my head my night-cap (this is true)
To th' farther side of all the room it blew.

This traveller's tale, which remained a popular poem throughout the seventeenth century, is one of the last descriptions of the traditional Irish way of life: the Cromwellian plantation would soon ensure that such things disappeared from everywhere but Connacht.

The wars of the 1640s brought soldiers to all parts of Ireland, and the poems collected here reflect both the military and the political side of Irish life at the time. Payne Fisher gives a vivid account of the day-to-day life of foreign soldiers in Ireland during the early part of the campaign, suffering from sea-sickness during a rough crossing of Lough Neagh or fortifying a ruined church on an island in Lough Beg. Most memorably, he describes the scene as the motley band of mercenaries and Scottish soldiers under his command takes part in the siege of an Irish town where the 'burgers' were 'now in Armes'. Fisher's portrayal of these horrible events is almost light-hearted – one young man's blustering account of a boyish escapade in a verse-letter to another – and his narrative seems designed, to use a phrase in one of Brendan Bradshaw's essays, to 'filter out the trauma of Irish history'.[21] Such events were real enough, however, for the anonymous author of A *Looking-Glasse of the World, or, the Plundered Man in Ireland* of 1644, who described what it was like to be a settler who had lost everything.

Some of the most interesting material from the war-torn middle years of the seventeenth century comes from the manuscript verse sent to the Marquis of Ormond at the time. The poems in the Ormond collection include attacks on parliamentary leaders like Charles Coote and Michael Jones, but also exhortations to confederates and other catholics to defend

21. Brendan Bradshaw, 'Nationalism and Historical Scholarship in Modern Ireland', *Irish Historical Studies*, vol. 26, no. 104 (November 1989), p. 338.

Ireland and her traditional faith against the incoming heretics. Once it was clear that there was no future for old-style royalism in Ireland after the execution of Charles I, one rather surprising voice was raised to welcome the parliamentary forces to Ireland, that of the Church of Ireland. Speaking through Edward Calver in his 1649 poem *Zions Thankfull Ecchoes from the Clifts of Ireland, Or the little Church of Christ in Ireland, warbling out her humble and gratefull addresses to her Elder Sister in England*, the church made specific appeals for generous treatment, *To the Parliament, to his Excellency, and to his Army, or that part assigned to her assistance, now in her low, yet hopefull Condition.* This fascinating poem, which contains sections addressed to Lord Fairfax (who was at that time expected to be leading the parliamentary invasion of Ireland) and 'To the English Commanders and Souldiers assigned for the reliefe of Ireland', was carefully crafted to impress on the English parliament and the incoming forces the need to move rapidly for the restoration of Ireland to the English protestant fold and the restoration of the Church of Ireland to its position as the church of the Irish state. Presumably whoever commissioned the poem must have thought that the message would get to Cromwell and his men more effectively in verse than in prose.

During the reign of Charles II, English verse representations of Ireland change markedly and become, almost without exception, jocose. Ireland is a place for endless drinking and whoring for the author of the 'Iter Hibernicum', which describes, in detail, the antics of early lager louts in language too disgusting to inflict on any reader.[22] The 1673 'Letter from a Missionary Bawd in Dublin to her cheif in London giveing an account of the propagation of lewdness and scandall in Ireland' is mild in comparison. Even Sir William Petty's heavy-handed 'Navall Allegory', addressed to the Duke of Ormond, is an attempt at wit.

The Popish Plot and its aftermath changed the mood considerably, and the battle lines were drawn once more between the English and the Irish, between protestant and catholic. The most memorable verse from this period comes in Luke Wadding's moving reflections on the sufferings of Irish catholics in a time of renewed persecution. The titles of his poems tell the tale: 'On Christmas Day the Yeere 1678, when the Clergy were Banish'd in the Time of the Plot'; 'Lines Presented to a Freind in her Garden, which Formerly was a Large Chapple'; 'The banish'd Man Lamenteth the 20th of November, the Day of his Parting drawing near', 'The banish'd Man's Adieu to his Country' and 'The Lamentation of the

---

22. The strong-stomached may find the whole text in the British Library at MS Sloane 360, pp. 54–142.

17

Scholars' of New Ross as their school was closed down. These verse lamentations provide the most extensive insight into Irish catholic life at the time, and deserve to be better known.

The accession of James II opened the floodgates again, this time for protestant verse ridiculing and abusing the catholics of Ireland, who seemed to be about to take command of the country. From 'Lilliburlero' to *The Irish Hudibras*, Irish protestant voices were raised to taunt the catholics,[23] while the streets of London were alive with mocking English voices telling the verse tales of 'The Lusty Friar of Dublin' or 'Poor Teague in Distress'. The tone of Williamite triumphalism is well heard in the title of one particular broadside: 'The Bogg-Trotters March, or, King Williams Glorious Conquest over the whole Irish Army'. As those who witnessed it could see, the Williamite victory over the Irish at Aughrim and Limerick in 1691 marked the beginning of a new era in Ireland. Irish armies were defeated, Irish culture and society were almost destroyed and Irish land was firmly in new hands. The country as a whole was to be ruled from London via Dublin and, in this context, Dublin Castle assumed an importance it had not had in Irish life for a long time. The wars were over and a period of peace and development was under way. The Stuarts were about to give way to the Hanoverians. The anthology ends, therefore, with three poems describing various aspects of life in the castle at the turn of the eighteenth century, one anonymous and two by Swift, the writer who was to dominate Irish letters in the first half of the new century and who, in 'Mrs Harris's Petition', wrote one of the finest poems to come out of Ireland in the early modern period.

VI

Humanism in Ireland: poets and translators

Despite the fact that conditions for reading or study were often difficult in sixteenth- and seventeenth-century Ireland,[24] writing verse in the classical manner or on classical themes, as well as translating or adapting the classics into English verse – both favourite pursuits of the gentlemen and scholars of Renaissance England – were surprisingly common in Ireland too. Dublin, although a small city, was the seat of English power in Ireland, the place where the English language was most widely spoken

---

23. For my remarks on the possible authorship of 'Lilliburlero', see the headnote to the poem, p. 504.
24. As Parr put it, late sixteenth-century Ireland was a country where there was 'a Scarcity of good Books and learned Men . . .' *Life of . . . James Usher, late Lord Archbishop of Armagh*, p. 4.

and the centre of an area which, on the whole, escaped the destruction wrought on the rest of the country during the last years of the century. It remained, throughout the late sixteenth century, a city under the distant but perceptible influence of English-language Renaissance culture. Several of its prominent citizens were habitual users of books, having spent time at English universities or inns of court. Some citizens owned collections of printed books and manuscripts, and there seems to have been, to a limited extent, the sort of intellectual interaction one would expect in an English city of comparable size at the time. Certainly Edmund Campion, used to life in Oxford, found much to praise about the quality of intellectual life he experienced during his stay in the house of James Stanihurst in Dublin in the 1570s.[25] His host, like many other citizens, was agitating for the foundation of a university in Dublin; this was a city which thought of itself as an intellectual centre.

The circle surrounding the lord deputy of the day always contained men used to the lifestyle of London, for whom reading and writing in English and translating from the Classics would have been perfectly normal activities. During periods when a Renaissance figure such as Sir Henry Sidney was in residence as lord deputy, Dublin Castle would have been a place for music, dancing and the reading of texts for pleasure. The earliest English verse known to have been printed in Ireland, the unique fragment of which is now unfortunately lost, was an adaptation into verse of a classical story entitled 'A most pithi and plesant history whear in is the destrouction of Troye gethered togethere of all the chyfeste autores turned unto Englyshe myttere'.[26] The tentative dating of this piece is 1558 and the fact that a typically Renaissance poem was printed in Dublin suggests that there were readers in the city in the 1550s prepared to purchase such a text.

Among these poets writing verse in English and translating from the Classics during the late sixteenth century in Ireland were Richard Stanihurst, who was beginning his writing life in Dublin, and Barnaby Googe. Googe spent the years 1574 to 1585 in Ireland managing the estates of Sir William Cecil (1574–85), during which time he accomplishing his translation of Conrad Heresbach's *Foure Bookes of Husbandrie* and completed a verse translation of a Latin poem on gout. He inserted translations from Virgil, among others, into his English version of Heresbach. When Edmund Spenser was in Dublin in the 1580s

---

25. Edmund Campion, *Opuscula Omnia*, ed. R. Turner (London, 1625), p. 208, and Edmund Campion, *Two Bokes of the Histories of Ireland*, ed. A.F. Vossen (Assen, 1963), pp. [6], [7] and [108]. Quoted in Colm Lennon, *Richard Stanihurst the Dubliner 1547–1618*, (Dublin, 1981), p. 28.

26. For details of this fragment, see the headnote to the text on p. 48.

as secretary to the lord deputy, Lord Grey, he became part of a circle of cultivated men living in the city at the time who were in the habit of meeting to discuss ideas and literary matters. A particular friend of Spenser was a young Italian named Ludowick Bryskett, a protégé of Sir Henry Sidney and close companion of his son, Sir Philip Sidney. Bryskett wrote two fine elegies on the death of Sir Philip Sidney which appeared in print with Spenser's own elegy on Philip Sidney, one of which is in this anthology. The circle in which Spenser and Bryskett moved in Dublin was similar to that which had earlier surrounded Sir Philip Sidney.[27] Bryskett gives a graphic account of a meeting of the group in his translation of the second part of Giraldi's *De gli hacatommithi*, which he published as *A Discourse of Civill Life*. This work is cast in the typical Renaissance form of a series of dialogues between three or four gentlemen, during which the text is presented and discussed. Bryskett stated that 'the occasion of the discourse grew by the visitation of certaine gentlemen comming to me to my little cottage which I had newly built neare unto Dublin',[28] and he printed his translation as if it had been the subject of discussion between his friends at a three-day gathering at his cottage. Among the company, he writes, were 'Doctor *Long* Primate of *Ardmagh*, Sir *Robert Dillon* Knight, M. *Dormer* the Queenes Sollicitor, Capt. *Christopher Carleil*, Capt. *Thomas Norreis*, Capt *Warham St Leger*, Capt. *Nicholas Dawtry*, & Mr *Edmond Spenser*, late your Lordships Secretary, & *Th. Smith*, Apothecary'.[29] When Spenser is invited by Bryskett to deliver to the gathering a dissertation on moral philosophy, he declines and suggests that Bryskett's own translation of Giraldi would be the ideal text to be read to the company. But Spenser also reveals something of the process of the writing of *The Faerie Queene* in his reply:

> For sure I am that it is not unknowne unto you, that I have already undertaken a work tending to the same effect, which is *heroical verse*, under the title of a *Faerie Queene*, to represent all the moral vertues, assigning to every vertue, a Knight to be the patron and defender of the same: in whose actions and feates of armes and chivalry, the operations of that vertue, whereof he is the protector, are to be expressed, and the vices & unruly appetites that oppose themselves against the same, to be beaten downe and overcome. Which work, as I have already well entred into, if

27. See H.R. Woudhuysen, *Sir Philip Sidney and the Circulation of Manuscripts 1558–1640* (Oxford, 1996).
28. Ludowick Bryskett, *A Discourse of Civill Life: Containing the Ethicke part of Morall Philosophie. Fit for the instruction of a Gentleman in the course of a vertuous life* (London, 1606 [facsimile London, 1972]), p. 5.
29. Bryskett, p. 6. The person to whom the whole document was addressed ('your Lordship') was Lord Grey. See Pauline Henry, *Spenser in Ireland* (Cork, 1928), p. 43.

20

> God shall please to spare me life that I may finish it according to my mind,
> your wish (M. *Bryskett*) will be in some sort accomplished . . .[30]

Though some doubt has been cast on the accuracy of the details of
Bryskett's account,[31] there is no reason to question the essential truth of
his story of a group of well-educated young men living in or near Dublin
in the late sixteenth century engaging in the exchange of ideas and
comments about literature and reading to each other their latest verses.
Passages at the beginning of Spenser's *Colin Clouts Come Home Againe*
suggest that a similar coterie formed around him and Sir Walter Ralegh
when Spenser moved to his newly acquired estates at Kilcolman, County
Cork in the mid-1580s.[32]

If Spenser was the most significant Renaissance poet writing in
Ireland, the most interesting Irish-born poet of the period was Richard
Stanihurst. Stanihurst, who came from a famous Old English family, was
a poetic theorist as well as a poet, translator, historian and alchemist. In
two prefaces to his translation of the first four books of the *Æneid*, he
defended his own use of English hexameters for the translation, and set
out his theory for the measurement of syllables in English verse.
Stanihurst combined a scholar's knowledge of the English language with
a poet's enthusiasm for it, and his verse was boldly experimental. He
measured English verse by quantity as if it were classical verse and
developed a way of writing verse in a style which combined rigidity of
metrical pattern with extreme flexibility in language. He coined new
words, amended old ones, mixed the colloquial with the stately, used
verbs as nouns and nouns as verbs. In the same way as James Joyce was
to do three hundred years later, Stanihurst also experimented with English
orthography, spelling words as his fancy took him or the logic of his
linguistic theories suggested. His trial pieces included translations of the
Psalms into various classical metres. A passage from his 'heroical and
elegiacal' translation of the second Psalm may give a flavour of the work:

> Wyth franticque madnesse why frets thee multitud heathen?
> And to vayn attemptings what furye sturs the pepil?
> Al thee worldlye Regents, in clustred coompanye, crowded,
> For toe tread and trample Christ with his holye godhead.
> Breake we there hard fetters, wee that be in Christian houshold,

30. Bryskett, pp. 26–7.
31. The earliest doubter was Professor John Erskine whose article in *PMLA*, vol. 30 (N.S.,
    xxiii, 1915), pp. 831–50 has been discussed and rebutted by several more recent
    scholars. See also Henry R. Plomer and Tom Peete Cross, *The Life and Correspondence
    of Ludowick Bryskett* (Chicago, 1927), pp. 77–83.
32. *Colin Clouts Come Home Againe*, line 17.

Also from oure persons pluck we there yrynye yokes.
Hee skorns their woorcking, that dwels in blessed Olympus:
And at theire brainsick trumperye follye flireth.
Then shal he speake too those in his hard implacabil anger,
And shal turmoyle theym, then, with his heavye furye . . .
. . . With the rod hard steeled thow shalt theyre villenye trample;
Lyke potters pypkin naghtye men easlye breaking . . .[33]

The modern reader may enjoy Stanihurst's uninhibited use of unconventional (if often basically phonetic) spelling, and will certainly agree that the verse sounds magnificent when the poet's love of rolling reverberation and extravagant onomatopoeia is given full rein and his work is read aloud. But the material does fall on the modern ear in a peculiar way. Unfortunately for Stanihurst, no other scholar or poet has ever agreed with his method of assessing the value and length of syllables or with his theories of stress in English verse, with the result that his verse remains, in appearance and sound, the most eccentric of the age.

Stanihurst was the first Irishman to assemble a collection of verse in English. The final thirty pages of his 1582 translation of Virgil contain what he calls 'Other Poetical Devices' and, though most of the verse is his own, he does include work by Lord Gerald Fitzgerald and what seems to be a parody of an epitaph such as might be written by 'oure unlearned Rythmours . . . upon thee death of every Tom Tyler . . .'. Though some critics have thought Stanihurst must have meant his verse to be comic, his prefaces show that he was trying to open up a new way of writing English verse, and that he saw this as a scholarly exercise in the highest humanist tradition.

Another interesting poet of the time was also from an Old English family, the Nugents in County Westmeath. Richard Nugent's slim volume of verse, *Rich: Nugents Cynthia. Containing direfull sonnets, madrigalls, and passionate intercourses, describing his repudiate affections expressed in loves owne language* (London, 1604), shows remarkable skill and poetic power, as well as an intimate acquaintance with the kind of verse being written at this time in London. His graceful sonnets tell of an unhappy love affair in County Westmeath and of his deep regret at having to leave Ireland. At about the same time, however, one of the few native Irish writers known to have written sonnets in English, the fourth Earl of Clanricard, was engaged in courtly dalliance at the English court in London, where he complimented the elderly Queen Elizabeth herself

33. Edward Arber (ed.), *Richard Stanihurst, Translation of the first Four Books of the Æneis of P. Virgilius Maro* . . . (London, 1895), pp. 127–8.

with the elegant lyric later scribally published under the title 'Of the last Queene'. That poem is included in this anthology not because there is unimpeachable evidence that it was written by Clanricard, but because, from the time of its appearance to the present day, it has been known as his, and no convincing evidence has been found to attribute it to any other poet.

There were several poets active in early seventeenth-century Ireland. George Wither spent a year or two in Dublin, probably as a retainer in the Loftus household at Rathfarnham Castle, during which time he wrote the words for a masque which was performed at the wedding of Sir Francis Willoughby and Lady Cassandra Ridgeway in October 1610. Francis Quarles was in Dublin as secretary to James Ussher, Archbishop of Armagh, in the late 1620s and, while in Dublin, completed *Argalus and Parthenia*, a poetic romance based on a story from Sir Philip Sidney's *Arcadia*. The Irish historian and poet Richard Bellings was, meanwhile, working on his addition to the *Arcadia* during his time as a student at Lincoln's Inn in London and, like many another young man about town, turning his hand to love poetry and occasional verse, a lively selection of which was collected by his friend, 'Sir R.C.', and printed at the end of the Dublin edition of Bellings's addition to the *Arcadia*. Bellings's love poetry and occasional verse is typical of that written by the London wits of the 1620s – witty, elegant and full of outlandish conceits – and its confident tone suggests that a catholic Irishman had little difficulty in integrating himself into the cultural life of early Stuart England. Bellings was a scholar and, as his addition to Sidney's *Arcadia* shows, a gentleman, quite at home in the humanist tradition of the age. His poetry should be edited and brought to a wider audience.

Humanism also flourished in the newly founded Trinity College, as can be seen in the extraordinary collection of verse produced by the scholars and fellows on the death of Katherine, Countess of Cork in 1630. This volume, entitled *Musarum Lachrymæ* and printed in Dublin, contains poems in English, Latin, Greek and Hebrew – a worthy exemplar of Renaissance learning. The antiquarian researches of two other scholars working in Dublin, Sir James Ware and Archbishop Ussher, were, directly or indirectly, responsible for the rendering of Geoffrey Keating's *Foras Feasa ar Éirinn* into English prose and verse by Michael Kearney in 1635.

During the twenty years of war that followed the rising of 1641, however, little original scholarship or translation could take place in Ireland. Once the Restoration had established some kind of peace in

Ireland again, poetry in English flourished almost at once, under the patronage of the new lord lieutenant, the Duke of Ormond. He and his wife numbered several writers among their friends, and these formed an active poetic coterie in and around Dublin Castle. The writers gave each other fanciful poetic names, exchanged poems, and behaved just as similar coteries had done in aristocratic circles in England since the time of Sir Philip Sidney. Irish writers in the group included members of the Boyle and Orrery families and the Earl of Roscommon; they were joined by the Welsh poet Katherine Philips, who spent some time in Dublin in the early 1660s. Many poems survive from this coterie, as does Katherine Philips's translation of Corneille's play *Pompey* into English, which was staged, with much pomp, in the new theatre in Smock Alley in 1663. Some of the verse of the coterie also spilled from the circle of intimates into the wider world when the Dublin bookseller Samuel Dancer somehow obtained copies of it, which he published.

His book, *Poems by Several Persons of Quality and Refined Wits*, was just one of many which began to appear in the bookshops of Dublin in the early 1660s as the more settled state of the country and the influence of a literary court led to an increase in the purchase and reading of books. There was also a surge of interest in the theatre, and prologues and epilogues were written for many Irish productions. Translation continued also and a powerful and urbane verse rendering of the tenth of Juvenal's satires appeared in Dublin in 1675. The author of this work was almost certainly the polymath orientalist and lawyer, Dudley Loftus,[34] and the fact that it was printed in Dublin suggests, again, a market for such work among the readers of the city.

Years of renewed political and military upheavals in Ireland between the Popish Plot and the battle of the Boyne put a stop to further writing of serious verse, but the Williamite victory brought about two early poems by Irish writers who were later to become famous. Both George Farquhar and Jonathan Swift celebrated the Williamite successes with Pindaric odes. Perhaps because both poems were intended to attract attention to their authors and so help them, in some way, to obtain jobs, they sound remarkably similar to each other. In Farquhar's 'On the death of General *Schomberg*',

> The *Hibernian* Harp in mournful Strains,
> Mixt with the *Eccho* of the Floud, complains,
> Round whose reflecting Banks, the grieving Voice,

---

34. For the reasons for this ascription, see the headnote to 'The Wish', p. 429.

24

Shakes with a trembling Noise,
As if afraid to tell
How the great, Martial, Godlike *Schomberg* fell.

In Swift's account of the battle of the Boyne in his 'Ode to the King on his Irish Expedition', the reader can hear almost the same voice:

For strait I saw the Field maintain'd,
And what I us'd to laugh at in *Romance*,
And thought too great ev'n for effects of Chance,
The Battel almost by *Great William's* single Valour gain'd;
The *Angel* (doubtless) kept th' Eternal gate,
And stood 'twixt Him and every Fate;
And all those flying deaths that aim'd him from the field,
(Th' impartial deaths which come
Like Love, wrapt up in fire;[35]
And like that too, make every breast their home)
Broke on his everlasting shield.

In these poems, derivative as they may be, Irish events are taken as a theme for serious verse for the first time since the 1660s.

The last years of the seventeenth century saw several Irish-born writers move to London and make a name for themselves as poets there. The best known of these was Nahum Tate, poet laureate and adaptor of Shakespeare's *King Lear*, a man much wronged by those who dismiss his work without reading it. Tate wrote an enormous amount of verse, some of it stylish and imaginative; examples of his work from the 1690s are included in this anthology. Three other poets of interest from the period were from Derry: the schoolmaster Ellis Walker, whose poetical paraphrase of the *Enchiridion* of Epictetus was, for many years, widely read, and the Hopkins brothers. The latter were the two sons of the Bishop of Derry, Ezekiel Hopkins; the elder, Charles, made a reputation for himself during the 1690s as a poet and playwright in London where he was friends with many writers, including Dryden. It seems clear that he would have become a considerable figure on the English literary landscape but for his fondness for women and the bottle. One or both contributed to his early death. His long poem, *A Court Prospect* (London, 1699), famous for its unflattering portraits of various court figures of the day, provided Alexander Pope with many ideas, some phrases and even a

35. i.e. bullets and mortars.

line or two for *The Rape of the Lock*. Charles Hopkins's younger brother, John, who had started translating Ovid into English verse while he was still in Ireland, also settled in London; he too published a large amount of miscellaneous verse – his *Amasia* (London, 1700) is in three volumes – and was well respected. His decision to translate portions of Milton's *Paradise Lost* into rhyming couplets was probably a mistake, and the result is more of a curiosity than a work of literature.

VII

Religious verse

There is some remarkable seventeenth-century religious verse[36] in this anthology, from Edward Bletso's strange little poem about the traveller and the hermit of 1622, to Nahum Tate's 'Upon the Sight of an Anatomy' of 1694. Two clusters of religious poems occur, one in the 1620s and 1630s and the other in the late 1650s and early 1660s.

The most impressive of the poems from the 1620s and 1630s is Lady Ann Southwell's 'Elegie ... to the Countesse of London Derrye'. Southwell was an unusual woman who, though she lived for many years at Poulnalong Castle in County Cork, managed to keep abreast of contemporary intellectual debate. Her commonplace book, now in the Folger Library in Washington DC, contains two ambitious poems, one of which is included in this anthology and the other of which is a verse letter addressed to Dr Bernard Adams, Bishop of Limerick from 1603 to his death in 1626. Both poems, but particularly that to Adams, show wide reading and detailed knowledge of Neo-Platonist philosophy, theology, cosmology, music, the Classics and alchemy. The verse itself shows Southwell's fascination with complex ideas and also the kind of delight in word-play normally associated with the work of the metaphysical poets. The passage which follows comes from her mock-elegy on the Countess of Londonderry and shows the level of esoteric knowledge Southwell expected in her reader. To make sense of the passage, the reader must be familiar with the details of the structure of the Ptolemaic universe – in which a series of concentric spheres, punctured by holes of different sizes through which shone the sun, the moon, the planets and the stars, were constantly moving, each in its own way, around the earth. As the soul of the Countess of Londonderry passes through the spheres on its way to the distant heavens, it gets a chance to see what happens on each level. The

---

36. I use the term to cover everything from private meditative exercises to philosophical or didactic verse.

first level encountered is that of Cynthia, the moon, who, personified as a goddess, controls the tides (the flood). The question is, are there men on the moon or, at least on the moon's sphere?

> Yet in thy passage, fayre soule, let me know
> what things thou saw'st in riseinge from below:
> Whether that Cynthia, regent of the flood,
> will in hir Orbe admitt of mortall brood?
> Whether the 12 Signes serve the Sun for state,
> or elce confine him to the Zodiaque,
> and force him retrograde to bee the nurse
> (whoe circularly glides his oblique course)
> of Alma Mater,[37] or unfreeze the wombe
> of Madam Tellus[38] – wch elce Proves a tombe?[39]
> Whether the starrs be Knobbs uppon the spheres?
> Or shredds compos'd of Phœbus goulden hayres?
> Or whether th'Ayre be as a cloudy sive?
> The starrs be holes through wch the good soules drive?
> Whether that Saturne that the 6 out topps[40]
> sitt ever eatinge of the bratts of Opps,[41]
> whose jealousye is like a Sea of Gall[42]
> unto his owne proves periodicall?[43]
> But as a glideinge star whoe falls to earth
> or lovers thoughts, soe soules ascend theyr birth,
> wch makes mee thinke, that thyne had noe one notion,
> of those true elements, by whose true motion
> all things have life, and death;[44] . . .

37. The ancient Romans gave this name, 'the white mother', to the nurturing goddesses, particularly Ceres. Here it is applied to a sign of the zodiac through which the sun has to pass on an oblique course so that, like a nurse, he can give life to the earth.
38. goddess of the earth. Some of the symbolism of the signs of the zodiac is linked to the seasons of the year, the ploughing of the land being associated with Taurus, the bull.
39. i.e. the earth would be a tomb if it were not warmed by the sun and if the seasons did not pass.
40. At the time this poem was written, it was thought that there were six planets, of which Saturn was the most distant from earth.
41. The god Saturn was in the habit of devouring the children born to him by his wife Ops, though she did manage, according to some legends, to save some of her children, including Jupiter, Neptune and Pluto, from their father.
42. See Job 16. 13.
43. This refers to the regular movements of the planet Saturn.
44. Like her contemporary John Donne, Ann Southwell was fascinated by the paradoxes inherent in a world where the facts and definitions of the new science came up against the poetic and symbolic ideas of the old world-view.

It is astonishing that such accomplished, metaphysical verse was being written by a woman in early seventeenth-century Ireland.

The most remarkable example of religious verse from the 1650s is *Ter Tria: or the Doctrine of the Three Sacred Persons, Father, Son, & Spirit* by Faithfull Teate. This very long poem – of which only a small extract is printed in this anthology – is a meditation on the Trinity which is divided into three sections, one on God the Father, one on God the Son and one on God the Holy Spirit. Each section is written in its own complex stanza form, to which Teate keeps with extraordinary fidelity. Though Teate's verse was clearly influenced by the metaphysical poetry of George Herbert and the rhetoric of early seventeenth-century divines such as Bishop Launcelot Andrews, *Ter Tria* is a poem of remarkable originality, freshness and wit. The opening stanzas from the first section of the poem may indicate the charm of this forgotten masterpiece and show Teate's infectious delight in word-play and metrical experimentation. He is addressing God the Father.

> Thou that begin'st All things, begin my verse:
> My words are wind:
> Thy words are works;
> Thou'lt lightness find
> Where darkness lurks:
> My Pen and Ink may me, not Thee, rehearse.

> My Pen is but a feather's vanity,
> Like me that write;
> Yet shall this feather,
> If thoul't indite,[45]
> Help me fly thither
> Where Angels wings make Pens beyond the sky.

> Father, mine Inkes dark hue presents[46] mine heart.
> Ink's not more dark,
> Ink's not more black;
> One beam, one sparke
> Supply this lack.
> Father of Lights, now shew thy perfect Art.

---

45. i.e. if thou wilt enable me to set this poem down in words.
46. i.e. brings my heart into your presence.

A contemporary of Faithfull Teate was John Perrot, the deranged Limerick Quaker who went to Rome to convert the Pope. This unfortunate, but dedicated, missionary spent several months in the 'Rome-Prison of Mad Men' where he wrote some extraordinary mystical verse, particularly 'A Song for that Assembly', which depicts all creation in its worship of God.

We have religious poems in English from both the protestant and the catholic side in Restoration Ireland. From the pens of Church of Ireland bishops such as Jeremy Taylor and Church of Ireland laymen such as Roger Boyle, first Earl of Orrery, came verse expressing their faith and exhorting others to follow them. These poems – particularly those of Bishop Taylor – were widely used in the protestant community. As much in demand in the catholic community was *A Smale Garland of Pious and Godly Songs* by Luke Wadding, catholic bishop of Ferns. Though Wadding's book includes many verses on the sufferings of catholics during the time of the Popish Plot, it also contains several simple carols – carols which are used in Wexford to this day – to help catholics in their devotions. The book was constantly reprinted and became the best-known manual for personal devotion throughout the eighteenth century in Ireland.

Towards the end of the century, Faithfull Teate's son, Nahum Tate, decided to make an annual compilation of sacred verse. Only the first issue of this projected set of publications appeared, but that volume contains two memorable religious poems. The first is a simple imaginary outburst or 'expostulation' by the Virgin Mary on her discovery that the twelve-year-old Jesus had stayed behind in Jerusalem after the family had left the city – a poem of remarkable power. The second is a witty and well-constructed meditation on mortality occasioned by the sight of an 'anatomy', that is a human skeleton with the bones wired together – such as was used for anatomy classes in a medical school. On the basis of these poems, the work of Nahum Tate is worth reconsidering – indeed, the religious verse of seventeenth-century Ireland as a whole would merit more attention.

VIII

Word-play, Wit and Parody

Although none of the examples of their verse in this anthology happens to illustrate this aspect of their output, several of the poets whose work is included, Francis Quarles and George Wither in particular, were famous in their day as emblem poets. For Quarles (particularly in his 1635 *Emblems*), the symbolic meaning of the picture which was printed facing each page of his verse was part of its meaning; Wither, like George Herbert, was fond of the pattern poem (the most famous example of which is Herbert's 'Easter Wings') and was well known in his day for a rhomboidal dirge that begins 'Ah me!' and was printed in his *Faire-Virtue* (1622). This kind of delight in word-play is seen in this anthology in several anagrams, in William Mercer's 'echo' poem and in John Booker's unambiguous 'Explanation of the Frontispeece' for his 1646 *Bloody Irish Almanack*. It is also at the centre of the work of two poets of the 1620s, Richard Bellings and Lady Ann Southwell.

Jousting with words can suggest whole new ranges of meaning. An anagram which converts the name 'Charles Coote' into the words 'Art hels cooke' (even if one letter is used elastically) opens up wild and unexpected connections; it yokes heterogeneous ideas together and plays straight into the seventeenth century's passion for 'wit':

> Since thou into Rebellion fell,
> Thou hast drest many [a] Dish for hell

the poem begins; and it ends with the memorable couplet:

> Now I see plaine the proverb's not mistooke
> God sendeth meat, the Divill sends a Cooke.

Rhyme, particularly in a rhyme scheme which encourages comic double and triple rhymes – like the rhyming tetrameter of the 'Purgatorium Hibernicum' and 'To his Onor de Rit Onorable Richard Earle of Tyroincol' – can also overturn expectations. Again it is an exercise of wit to be able to rhyme 'Unculpable' with 'fault ish able' or (as is done in the first few lines of the 'Purgatorium Hibernicum' included in this anthology) 'espied he' with 'Dydy', 'sences' with 'vench is' and 'butt itching' with 'a bit[c]hing'. The poet who ridiculed Petty's double-bottomed boat delighted in rhyming 'Aristotle' with 'twittle twattle' and 'Pythagoras' with 'was an ass'.

Near the centre of this anarchic world of words divorced from their normal contexts lies parody. Parody involves ridicule of the mindset of the victim through ridicule of his way of speaking. In the poem on Petty's boat, for instance, Petty himself appears ridiculous in his pompous appeal to the sailors' wives and in his attempts to bribe them to let their husbands sail on his ship. But most examples of parody in this book involve exaggerated mimicry of spoken Hiberno-English, and so suggest that the mindset of those who speak like this is worthy of nothing but ridicule. The burlesque or travesty of Virgil which lies behind *The Irish Hudibras* is not a criticism of genuine heroic behaviour but of the Fingallian 'Nees' who thinks himself heroic, who calls himself a 'prince' and who is proud of his grand Irish ancestry, but whose actions and words show him to be a buffoon who can not even speak English intelligibly. By calling Nees the Irish 'Hudibras', the author of the poem is making him an anti-hero in the tradition of the heroes of poems by Charles Cotton and Samuel Butler – figures whose zeal, though dangerous in real life, becomes merely ridiculous in the distorted world of the poem. In real life, Tyrconnell had been appointed lord deputy of Ireland and was a threat to the New English settlers; in the poem, the ridiculous 'Nees' and his exaggerated Fingallian speech is a parody of a leader and a leader's way of talking, a figure to inspire laughter rather than dread. Equally, the speech of the aspirant to a commission in the Irish army who signs himself 'Cromach O Rough' parodies what the New English would have seen as bog-Irish speech and ways, making what they feared most – an uneducated catholic Irishman in arms – into a joke. In general, playing with perspective and playing with speech – both common in seventeenth-century writing and both easier to accomplish in verse than in prose – provide much of the energy in some of the key texts in this book.

IX

Conclusion

One of the purposes of this anthology is to suggest that the widespread view that there was no verse of interest produced in Ireland before Swift should be reconsidered. The book aims to present a selection of the large amount of material which has survived from the Tudor and Stuart periods and, perhaps, to stimulate a re-evaluation of the culture which produced it. Those who wrote verse for public occasions, Richard Bellings or William Smith for example, must have possessed archives of hundreds of poems, all of which are now lost. Yet from what remains it is still possible to gain a fair idea of the world inhabited by these poets and versifiers, to judge what they thought of that world and to enjoy the verse in which they expressed their views. Other verse, more formal or more structured, gives an insight into the intellectual or spiritual world of the day.

One of the most impressive aspects of the verse composed in English in Ireland during the two hundred years during which English-speaking Ireland was transformed from the series of scattered settlements it was in 1487 to the centralised nation-state it was in 1701, is its range and variety. It is astonishing that so little attention has been paid to this material, and several of the writers whose work appears here would repay serious scholarly attention.

Above all, however, it is hoped that readers of this anthology will enjoy the verse it contains, much of which will be new to them. There may be no mute, inglorious Milton lurking undiscovered in its pages – though Faithfull Teate has a fair claim to be considered a fine poet – but still, readers may be able to catch some of the infectious enthusiasm for the writing and reading of verse which drove so many of those living in Ireland during the Tudor and Stuart periods to put pen to paper.

A NOTE ON THE TEXTS

The aim of this anthology is to present the reader with texts that are both true to their original sources, printed or manuscript, and yet readable. Thus the original spelling and capitalisation have been retained, even where there is inconsistency within a text, and proper names are given in their original forms. Obvious misprints and faulty transcriptions have been silently corrected, but I have not changed apostrophes in possessives since, though sixteenth- and seventeenth-century usage of apostrophes may be peculiar to modern eyes, it does not make the texts hard to understand.

However, some substantive changes have been made throughout: (1) the word 'least' is amended to its modern form 'lest' and (2) the words 'than' and 'then', often used interchangeably in the sixteenth and seventeenth centuries, are amended to their modern forms. The most considerable change, however, is in (3) punctuation. This is often erratic or nonexistent in manuscripts of the early modern period, and perfunctory and meaningless in some printed texts. I have therefore made such changes as are necessary to make the texts intelligible. In general, modern usage for question marks and inverted commas is followed, though passages of dialogue in which it is quite clear who is speaking have not been cluttered with inverted commas.

Since the only member of the Ormonde dynasty mentioned in this book, the first duke, always spelt his name 'Ormond', that spelling is adopted throughout.

The sources from which the texts have been taken are listed at the end of the volume.

PART I

1485–1603
Verse from Tudor Ireland

JOHN BUTLER, MAYOR OF WATERFORD, AND OTHERS
(1487)

During the chaotic period of the Wars of the Roses in England (1455–85), the English authorities paid little attention to Ireland. At the end of the wars, the English king's representative in Ireland was Gerald Fitzgerald, the great Earl of Kildare (1465–1513), but Kildare felt himself bound by few restraints and behaved, in many ways, like the king of Ireland. Though the Yorkist Richard III was killed at the battle of Bosworth in 1485 and Henry Tudor was crowned king of England as Henry VII, the Yorkist side was by no means defeated. They produced a young claimant to the throne, Lambert Simnel, and brought him to Ireland. Kildare, for a variety of reasons, decided to back the pretender and arranged for Simnel to be crowned king of Ireland in Christ Church Cathedral, Dublin. The coronation was probably performed by Kildare's ally, Walter Fitz-Simon, the Archbishop of Dublin. Most of the lords of the Pale backed Kildare and the new 'Edward VI'.

The city of Waterford, however, where many English merchants had settled, rejected Simnel and declared for Henry. The mayor and inhabitants sent a firm message to the Archbishop of Dublin protesting at his action in crowning the pretender and declaring their loyalty to Henry. The main plank of their argument was that of succession to the throne. The citizens sent their message in English and in verse. The stanzas are in a form known as rime royal, first used in English by Chaucer and so named because James I of Scotland chose it for his celebrated love poem *The Kinge's Quhair*; much sixteenth-century English and Scottish verse was in rime royal, which George Gascoyne considered suitable for 'grave discourses'.[1] About sixty years later, a poem praising the city, probably written by the then town clerk Patrick Strong and using the city's motto as a refrain, also used rime royal.

from: Letter sent by the Mayor and Inhabitants of the Citie of Waterford
unto Walter, Archbishop of the Citie of Dublin, the Mayor and Citizens of the same, in the tyme of their Rebellion

O thou most noble pastour, chosen by God,
    Walter, Archbishop of Dublin,[2]
Elect by th' Apostle, bearing the rodd
    Of perfect lief,[3] and also of doctrine
    To rule thy people by true discipline;
And if by custom men used[4] a cryme,
Thou shouldest correct them from tyme to tyme.

---

1. *Certain Notes of Instruction Concerning the Making of Verse or Rhyme in English* (1575), quoted by Thomas Crofton Croker, *Popular Songs of Ireland* (1866 ed.), p. 294.
2. Walter Fitz-Simon. See headnote.
3. i.e. having the rod (of authority) to lead us to perfect life, and also the rod of discipline ...
4. pursued, committed.

To thee we recommend us right humblie,
 And to all our masters of that citie,
Our neighbours of Dublin right hartelie,   10
 That be to us bound of old amitie,
 And we to them knitt both in one unitie,
Which restes with us by their seale and writing,
Not for a tyme, but perpetuall enduring . . .

O Dublin! Dublin! where be the jurours,
 Thy noble men of aureat⁵ glorie?
They be all passed by processe of yeeres;
 So is their renowne, worship, and victorie.
 Alas! therefore, thow maist be right sorie,
For thow hast made a plaine degression   20
From thy true leageance⁶ unto rebellion.

Moeses had of God, by commaundement,
 If a man died without issue male
His lands should, by lyniall discent,
 Descend to daughters, his heires generall;
 For fault of issue, his heires colaterall
Should have the same. Ye may read this story
Of Sulphact his daughters in the booke of Numery, 17°.⁷

Which was a figure of Christe's inheritaunce,⁸
 Descended to him by his mother Mary;   30
So that he, without doubt or variaunce,
 As man incarnat, I saie fynallie,
 And, as Scripture have it in memorie,
He was borne of the Virgin in Bethliem,
And, by her, true king of Hierusalem.

The actes of Christ, as saieth the Scripture,
 Is fynallie for man's instruction,
That wee his steppes should follow by nature,
 That everie man, without devision,

5. gold-coloured. This stanza follows several in which the poet has stressed the friendliness
between Dublin and Waterford and listed seven past mayors of Dublin by name.
6. allegiance.
7. The reference seems to be to Numbers 27. 1–11 where inheritance through the female
line is approved by Moses. The five women who asserted their rights were daughters not
of Sulphact but of Zelophehad.
8. i.e. this represents the way Christ obtained his inheritance . . .

By perfect law without conclusion,   40
Might be a king and have a monarchy
By his mother, as Christ had by Mary.

The figure and law is kept in generall;
   For the more perfeict among all other princes
Of Christe's faith, and in especiall
   In England, stabled with all sikernes,[9]
   As we shall shew you by divers chronicles,
And passed the tyme of man's memorie,
How, by a woman, descended that monarchy.

King Henry the First,[10] after the last conquest,   50
   He passed his traunce[11] without issue male.
Then entred King Stephen,[12] at the request
   Of the lordes spirituall and temporall,
   And raigned xix[th] yeeres, as telleth the tale.
He was this first Henry his sister's sonn,
And hereby had the title of his crowne.

And after him Henry, called Fitz Empres,
   The second Henry named by writing;
He was sonne to Maud, as I can devise,
   Daughter of the first Henry without leasing,[13]   60
   And by her title he married as a king,
Many yeeres, as telleth the story,
And was a prince of noble memory.

When he accomplished his yeeres of nature,
   His issue raigned King of England,
And sithen[14] that tyme have born the scepter,
   Having the governance of all that land
   From sonne to sonne, ye shall understand;
Till Edward the IIIIth most noble of fame,
Had the monarchie, and bare thereof the name   70

---

9. secured with all certainty; i.e. England is a place of civilised order where the true
   monarchy descends by inheritance through the female line, as decreed by God, and as
   exemplified by Christ.
10. i.e. Henry I of England (1068–1135).
11. passed away, died.
12. King Stephen of England (*c*. 1097–1154).
13. lying.
14. ever since.

This fourth King Edward his title and right
    Descended to him first by a woman,
The Duke's daughter of Clarence she hight,[15]
    Duke Leonell, called a noble man;
    His daughter Philippa, of whom began
This Edwarde's title of England and Fraunce,
And by her occupied as her enheritaunce.

Here may you see noble aucthorities,
    And first of Christ, which was made incarnate,
Whom he descended by many degrees   80
    Of that glorious Virgin immaculate;
    In his genelogie you maie read it algat,[16]
Whom he was king, by liniall discent
By his mother, without anie argument.

Theis[17] three princes, that we spake of before,
    Raigned in England, to everie intent
Trulie obeied; we can saie no more.
    The lordes and commons, by their whole assent,
    Were to them right humble and obedient.
This president[18] sheweth that th'eir female[19]   90
In England shall succeed for fault of the male.

By this processe unfayned we may shew
    That Stephen and Henry, before tyme of mind,
By both their mothers, as is well knowne,
    Were kings of England we can find;
    And also by Scripture Christ was betymde[20]
Of Hierusalem king, and of Juda:
So was the fourth Edward by the Philippa.

Which title is fallen to our soveraigne ladie,
    Queene Elizabeth, his eldest daughter liniall;[21]   100

---

15. was called.
16. everywhere.
17. these.
18. precedent.
19. the female heir.
20. = was betimed, betide; i.e. by this process, in time, in the scriptures, Christ became king of Jerusalem and Judea.
21. This is the key to the poem. Henry VII had recently married Elizabeth, eldest daughter of Edward IV, last legitimate king of England, according to the argument of this poem. Elizabeth's title to the throne was far stronger than that of Henry Tudor, so that Henry greatly strengthened his position by this marriage.

To her is com all the whole monarchie,
 For the fourth Edward had no issue male.
 The crowne, therefore, and scepter imperiall,
Both she must have without division,
For of a monarchie by no particion.

It is so that by Divine purveyaunce,
 King Henry the VIIth, our soveraigne lord,
And Queene Elizabeth, to God his pleasure,
 Ben maried both by amiable accord;
 Why should we speake more of this matter a word?   110
He is our true king without variance,
And to him by right we should owe our legeaunce.

Fortune on him have cast her lott and chaunce,
 That he by God is onely provided
Of England to have the soveraigne governaunce;
 And of the people chosen and elected,
 By grace in battaile he have obteyned;
The auncient right of the Brittons also,
Is cast on him with titles manie mo.[22]

First we saie that, by Gode's provision,   120
 This noble prince came by this his sceptor;
Second, by the common election
 Of the lordes and commons, he was made sure;
 The queene's title, by fortune's adventure,
He have theis three; the fourth by victorie;
And the fifth by the old Brittaine storie.[23]

Our holie father the Pope, our pastour,
 Of his certaine science and mere motion,[24]
Have written to all them that beare chardge and cure,
 By his bull papall, without exception,   130
 Affirming theis titles, with sharpe execution
Against all persons that will make debate
Upon King Henry the VIIth, his royall estate . . . .

---

22. more.
23. The reference is to prophesies about the future kings of England, perhaps by Merlin?
24. As T. Crofton Croker notes in his edition of this poem in *Popular Songs of Ireland*, this line translates the Latin phrase *Certa scientia et mero motu*, used in papal bulls and royal grants.

It is tyme for you to be reconciled,
    Of this matter now we will end;
Ye have ben to long[25] from trouth exiled,
        The tyme is now come for you to amend,
        A convenable[26] tyme is to you sent ;
The tyme of Lent, the mirrour of mercy,
For all them that will reverse their folie.   140

Retourne ones,[27] and forsake this folie,
    If anie there be revolved in your mynd;
Correct yourself, amend it shortlie,
        And to your soveraigne lord be not unkind:
        The people tongues no man can bind.
In such cases they saie, now and then,
The best clearkes be not the wysest men . . .

Reverend father, and our masters all,
    Wee make to you our protestation,
Not to offend one, nor you in generall,   150
        But for to represse your great rebellion,
        We send to you this our conclusion,
Hereby heartalie praying you that you applie;[28]
For your rather[29] dealing we be right sorie.

Thinke not in us no malice or envie,
    For of your honour we would be right faine,[30]
And of your reproche we be full sorie;
        We pray to God that we may once againe
        Your old worship, trouth, and manhood attaine;
So that ye please God and the kinge,   160
And eftsones[31] to keape you from all ill dealing.

Take the matter and leave the dittie, ⎫
For 'tis a cause of great pittie,   ⎬ quoth James Rice.
                                      ⎭

25. been too long.
26. convenient, suitable.
27. [at] once.
28. i.e. that you conform (to proper norms of conduct).
29. i.e. for your earlier actions . . . .
30. i.e. we would like you to think well of us.
31. afterwards.

Take no disdaine,
You to refraine,   to your soveraigne lord.
And to be plaine
Ye may be faine
So to attaine   with him to accord.
His grace againe,

JOHN BUTLER, Mayor of Waterford   170

Finis.   JAMES RICE

WM. LYNCOLLE

HENRY HOWARD, EARL OF SURREY
(*c*.1517–**1537**?–1547)

Though the love which the young Earl of Surrey professed for the celebrated Irish beauty Lady Elizabeth Fitzgerald in the sonnet which follows was used by Thomas Nashe, Michael Drayton and Sir Walter Scott as the basis for stories of an affair between the two, it seems more likely that Surrey was treating 'the fair Geraldine' as a Platonic love. Surrey first met Elizabeth Fitzgerald, youngest daughter of Gerald Fitzgerald, ninth Earl of Kildare, head of the family known as the Geraldines, when she was about ten years old, living in England with her mother while her father was detained in the Tower of London. In 1538, she was attached to the court of Princess Mary (later queen of England) at Surrey's grandfather's estate at Hunsdon in Hertfordshire. Two years later, Elizabeth joined the household of Queen Catherine Howard, Surrey's cousin, at Hampton Court near London and within a short while, when she was about fifteen years old, she was married to a sixty-year old widower, Sir Anthony Browne. After his death, she married the Earl of Lincoln. Surrey who, with Sir Thomas Wyatt, was heavily influenced by the Italian poet Petrarch in introducing the form of the sonnet into English, also followed Petrarch's lead in writing in the guise of a hopeless lover in pursuit of an ideal love.

Description and Praise of his Love Geraldine[1]

From Tuskane came my Ladies worthy race:
Faire Florence was sometyme her auncient seate:[2]
The Western yle whose pleasaunt shore dothe face
Wild Cambers clifs, did give her lively heate:[3]
Fostered she was with milke of Irishe brest:
Her sire, an Erle: her dame of princes blood.[4]
From tender yeres, in Britain she doth rest
With kinges childe, where she tasteth costly food.
Honsdon did first present her to mine yien:[5]
Bright is her hewe, and Geraldine she hight,[6]   10
Hampton[7] me taught to wishe her first for mine:
And Windsor, alas, dothe chase me from her sight,
Her beauty of kind,[8] her vertues from above,
Happy is he, that can obtaine her love.

1. This title was given to the poem by its first publisher, Richard Tottel (*d*.1594) in 1557.
2. The Fitzgerald family is said to be descended from 'Dominus Otho', from whom are descended also the family of Gherardini in Florence. Tuskane = Tuscany.
3. i.e. she was born in the island which faces the cliffs of Cambria (Wales).
4. Elizabeth's mother was Lady Elizabeth Grey, fourth daughter of Thomas Grey, Marquis of Dorset. Her grandmother, Elizabeth Woodville, was queen of England, having married, as her second husband, King Edward IV.
5. Hunsdon in Hertfordshire, the estate of Surrey's grandfather, Thomas Howard, second Duke of Norfolk; Surrey spent the summers there during his youth. yien = eyes.
6. i.e. Geraldine was her name.
7. Hampton Court which, like Windsor Castle in the next line, was a royal residence.
8. kind = nature.

ANDREW BOORDE
(*c*.1490–**1547**–1549)

Andrew Boorde, an indefatigable traveller as well as a skilled physician, gives vivid accounts of life in many parts of late medieval Europe in *The First Boke of the Introduction of Knowledge*. The chapters which describe individual countries begin with a verse purporting to be a self-portrait by a native of that country. Though it is not certain that Boorde actually visited Ireland, his chapter on the country shows extensive knowledge of it. It is preceded by a well-known woodcut of an Irishwoman removing lice from the head of a kern, and the verse which follows.

I am an Iryshe man . . .

I am an Iryshe man, in Irland I was borne;
I love to weare a saffron shert, all though it be to-torne.[1]
My anger and my hastynes doth hurt me full sore;
I cannot leave it, it creaseth more and more;
And although I be poore, I have an angry hart.
I can kepe a Hobby,[2] a gardyn, and a cart;
I can make good mantyls, and good Irysh fryce;[3]
I can make aqua vite, and good square dyce.
Pediculus[4] other whyle do byte me by the backe,[5]
Wherfore dyvers times I make theyr bones cracke.　　　　　10
I do love to eate my meate, syttyng upon the ground,
And do lye in oten strawe,[6] slepyng full sound.
I care not for ryches, but for meate and drynke;
And dyvers tymes I wake, when other men do wynke.[7]
I do use no potte to seeth[8] my meete in,
Wherfore I do boyle it in a bestes skyn;[9]

1. *Original note*: 'I wear a saffron shirt, and am hasty.'
2. small horse.
3. *Original note*: 'I make frieze and *aqua vitæ*.' frieze = woven cloth, tweed. mantyls = mantles, cloaks; *aqua vitæ* = whiskey. Dicing for money was common in sixteenth-century Ireland, and properly balanced dice were essential for fair play.
4. lice.
5. *Original note*: 'Lice bite me.' These lines explain the significance of the woodcut at the head of the chapter.
6. *Original note*: 'I squat on the ground, and sleep in straw.'
7. sleep.
8. boil, stew.
9. One of the woodcuts in John Derricke's *Image of Irelande* shows this custom, considered extraordinary by travellers, in which the skin of a calf is used as the container in which the flesh is stewed.

Then after my meate, the brothe I do drynk up,
I care not for my mather,[10] neyther cruse nor cup.
I am not new fangled, nor never wyll be;
I do lyve in poverty, in myne owne countre.   20

[*Irishwoman picking lice from the head of a kern*]

10 = meaddar = wooden drinking vessel; cruse = an earthenware drinking vessel.

JOHN BALE
(1495–**1553**–1563)

As a young man in England, John Bale was a member of the Carmelite order; however, once the Reformation took hold in England, he became one of its most enthusiastic supporters, favouring particularly the Calvinism of Edward VI. As well as many tracts against popery and a useful history of English writers, Bale wrote several plays on religious themes, three of which were performed in Kilkenny during his short residence in Ireland as Bishop of Ossory (see Alan J. Fletcher, *Drama, Performance and Polity in Pre-Cromwellian Ireland* (Cork, 2000), pp. 166–74). Bale was forced out of Ireland on the accession of the catholic Queen Mary, but his account of his time in Ireland, *The Vocacyon of Johan Bale to the Bishoprick of Ossorie in Irelande, his persecutions in the same & finall delyveraunce* (1553) is full of interest. The following verses reflect Bale's feelings when, as Bishop of Ossory, he learned of the death of the protestant Edward VI and saw the delight with which Irish catholics welcomed the return of a catholic monarch. He could see that all he had striven for might now be overturned.

Edward 6 *vel* Quene Marie[1]

Hospitals[2] pick't our purse, with Popish illusiõ,[3]
Purgatorie, Scala Caeli,[4] Pardons, cum Jubilio,
Pilgrimage Gate, where Idols sate, with all Abhominatiõ,
Channons,[5] Friers, common Liers, that filthie Generatiõ,
Nunnes hulinge,[6] pretty pulinge,[7] as Catte in Milke Pannio,[8]
See what knavery was in Monkery, and what Superstitiõ,
Becking, Belling, Ducking, yelling,[9] was then whole Religiõ,
And when Women, came unto them, fewe went sine Piliõ,[10]
But Abbeyes all, are nowe downefall, Dei Beneficio,[11]
And we doe pray, day by day, that all Abhominatiõ   10
May come to ——— Desolatiõ.

---

1. *vel* = or.
2. Foundations of the Knights Hospitallers or, in a general sense, pre-Reformation religious houses for rest or for housing the needy.
3. õ = 'ion' throughout the poem – left in contracted form here because lines 2, 5 and 9 end in 'io'.
4. The steps of Heaven. This might be a reference to the Holy Staircase, or Scala Santa – the staircase in Rome said to have been traversed by Jesus at the beginning of his passion, and a common place for devotion. Like the selling of pardons and a belief in purgatory, Luther specifically condemned as superstitious the practice of climbing these steps on one's knees.
5. Canons.
6. meaning unclear: probably equals 'howling'.
7. pretty [ones] whining or crying.
8. Probably refers to an obscure proverb about what happens if the cat takes milk from the pan.
9. bowing, ringing bells, plunging [people] into water, calling out loudly.
10. without a saddle, i.e. without being mounted.
11. through the goodness of God.

FRANCIS EDDERMAN (?)
(1558?)

This, as Tony Sweeney has written, is 'the most tantalising of all sixteenth-century fragments of a "lost" Dublin book'. In about 1934, the London bookseller Frank Marcham had in his possession two sheets of paper, apparently removed from a binding, on which were fragments of a poem printed in Dublin in the sixteenth century. The printer was probably Humphrey Powell, acting for the poet, whose name was Francis Edderman – at least, that is the name of the man who wrote the dedication. Since the poem was dedicated to Sir Henry Sidney, who acted as lord justice in the absence of the fourth Earl of Sussex in 1558, that year has been assigned as the year of printing. The subject of the poem is a typical renaissance one – the destruction of Troy – and the fragment represents by far the earliest example of a poetic text of this nature printed in Ireland. Unfortunately, the fragment has not been seen since 1934 and all that was recorded at that time was the title, the format and printing details, and the quatrain which follows.

from: A most Pithi and Plesant History

whear in is the destrouction of Troye gethered togethere of all the chyfeste autores turned unto Englyshe myttere[1]

> The Griekes to winn the flise of golde[2]
> To Colchoes[3] toke the waye:
> But on thyer Jornye very soare,
> waere tossede in the see.

---

1. metre
2. The Golden Fleece.
3. An ancient country at the eastern end of the Black Sea, now part of the Republic of Georgia.

ANONYMOUS
(*c*.**1560**)

This song celebrates three things: the accession of the protestant daughter of Henry VIII after the catholic Queen Mary (1558), the issuing of an Irish coinage, and the erection of public clocks in the city of Dublin (both 1560). In fact, three clocks were erected in 1560, one on the newly repaired Dublin Castle, one on St Patrick's Cathedral, and one for 'the City'. 'These,' notes Robert Ware in his translation of Sir James Ware's *Annals of the Affairs of Ireland* (Dublin, 1705), 'being a Novelty, [were] very pleasing to the common People.'

Song on Queen Elizabeth

Triumphant Joys may *Ireland* sing,
Of *Henry* the Eighth our gallant King:
For He has left us an Off-spring,
To be the Good Queen of *Ireland*.

Let Bonefires shine in every place,
Sing, and Ring the Bells apace;
And pray that long may live Her Grace,
To be the Good Queen of *Ireland*.

The *Gold* and *Silver*, which was so base,
That no man could endure it scarce,   10
Is now New Coyn'd with Her own Face,
And made go currant in *Ireland*.

She is the Nurse, that still doth rock
The Cradle of her loving Flock;
She held the *Diall* and the *Clock*,
Throughout the whole Realme of *Ireland*.

BARNABY RICH
(*c* . 1 5 4 0 – **1 5 7 9** – 1 6 1 7)

Barnaby Rich, a prolific writer on many subjects, spent much of his adult life in Ireland as a professional soldier. He reveals in *The Irish Hubbub* (1617) that he was in Limerick during the Desmond wars as 'an Officer of the field', and may have been close to Sir William Drury (1527–79) at a skirmish between English and Irish troops in October 1579 when Drury was mortally wounded. Drury had come to Ireland in 1576 as president of Munster after an energetic military career on the continent, in the north of England and in Scotland; he had been appointed lord justice of Ireland the year before his death.

This poem was probably written to order and is the first poem written in English about Ireland which makes use of classical references and poetic devices such as personification.

An Epitaph upon the Death of Syr William Drury, Knight,

Lord Justice and Governour of Yreland, deceased at Waterford the thyrd of
October. An. Do. 1579

> In place where wantes *Apollo* with his Lute,
> There peevish *Pan* may prease to pipe a daunce,[1]
> Where men of skill and learned Clarkes are mute,
> There Fools may prate, and hit the truth perchance;
> Why spare I then to speake,[2] when all are mumme,
> And vertue left forgot in time to come.
>
> Give pardon then to him that takes in hande,
> Though never taught, with Poets pen to write,
> Will yet presume, to let you understand,
> No straunge event, although a sieldome[3] sight,   10
> Which late I saw, a dolefull tale to tell,
> And followeth thus, then marke how it befell.
>
> I saw *Report* in mourning weede[4] arayde,
> Whose blubbered eyes bewrayde[5] some secret greefe,
> Besprent[6] with teares, with sighes and sobbes he sayd,

1. i.e. in a place which lacks Apollo (the god of music and poetry) with his (elegant) lute, peevish Pan (the shepherd god who can play only the rustic pipes) may try and pipe a dance tune.
2. Why do I hold back from speaking, when . . .
3. rare.
4. garments.
5. revealed.
6. sprinkled with.

You martiall wights[7] abandone all releefe,
Come wayle with me, whose losse is not alone,
When you your selves have greatest cause to mone.

For *Drurie* he, the choyse of all your trayne,[8]
Your greatest guyde, and lampe of clearest light,   20
The only man Bellona did retayne,
Her Champyon chefe, and made syr Mars his knight,[9]
Even he is now bereaved[10] of his breath,
Tis you, tis you, may most lament his death.

Then might I see a warlik crew appeare,
Came marching on with weapons traylde on ground,
Their outward show bewrayde their inward cheare,[11]
Their droms and tromps[12] did yeeld a dolefull sound;
They marched thus in sad and solemne sort,
As men amasde[13] to heare this late *Report*.[14]   30

And in the midst of this their heavy muse,[15]
I might perceive in sight a worthy Dame,
Who by her speech and tenure of her newes,
I knew her well, and saw twas Lady *Fame*,
With Tromp in hand, and this me thought she sed:
You worthy wights, your *Drurie* is not dead;

He liveth, he, amongst the blessed route,[16]
Whose noble actes hath purchaste endlesse fame:
Whylst world doth last, no time shall weare him out,
Nor death for all his spight[17] abridge his name,   40
But *Drurie* still for ever shall remayne;
His Fame shall live in *Flanders*, *Fraunce*, and *Spayne*.[18]

---

7. beings.
8. train, retinue.
9. Bellona was the goddess and Mars the god of war in Roman mythology.
10. deprived.
11. revealed their inward feelings.
12. trumpets.
13. amazed.
14. This stanza describes the soldiers presenting military honours at a funeral.
15. musing.
16. company.
17. spite.
18. Drury had served in many countries during his military career.

The *Germanes* eke,[19] *Italyans*, and the rest,
Can well discourse of *Druries* deedes at large,
With whom he servde, a Champyon ready prest,[20]
At all assaultes, the formost to give charge,
In many a fraye, himselfe he did advance,
Tweene *Charles* of *Rome*, and *Henrie* King of *Fraunce*.[21]

In vayne to vaunt the credite he attaynde
In native soyle, where he was knowne so well,   50
And *Brute* hath blowne what glory he hath gaynde,[22]
In Scotish Land, where they themselves can tell,
In *Edenbrough* he wan there Mayden tower,
By first assault, perforce the scotishe power.[23]

But *Ireland* thou, thou thrise accursed soyle,
Thy luck is losse, thy fortune still withstoode;[24]
What mischiefe more, to worke thy greater spoyle,
Than losse of him that ment thee greatest good?
Yet canst thou say, syr *Druries* noble name,
In *Ireland* still shall bide in lasting fame.   60

Wherefore you worthy wightes, leave of[f] to wrayle,[25]
Your *Drury* lives, his fame for aye shall last,[26]
His vertues byde, though wretched lyfe do fayle;
And taking then her Tromp, she blew a blast
Which sounded more his prayse than I can write,
Or with my tongue expresse in order right.

Then might I heare the Souldyers give a shoute,
The sounde whereof, redounded[27] in the skie,

19. also.
20. prest = pressed = pushing or straining forward (*OED* s.v. *press* III, 1, a).
21. Charles V (1500–58), Roman emperor and king of Spain, and Henry VIII (1491–1547),
    king of England, Ireland and, nominally, also of France, had jointly invaded France in
    1544. Drury had been in their army and present at the sieges of Boulogne and Montreuil.
22. i.e. and the chronicles ("bruts") have made public the glory he has gained.
23. Drury led the forces which besieged and took Edinburgh Castle in May 1573. His guns
    demolished David's Tower, Constable's Tower and (according to Barnaby Rich if not to
    the official history of the Castle) Maiden Tower. perforce = by force of – but here =
    against.
24. offering resistance; i.e. circumstances in Ireland still conspire against the country's good
    fortune.
25. (perhaps) = weep (from Middle English 'to rail' = to flow or gush down [of tears]).
26. i.e. his fame will last for ever.
27. reverberated.

Great joy was made amongst the armed route,
With streined throtes then all at once they cry,   70
He lives, he lives, our *Drurie* is not dead,
His vertues rare, by Fame shall still be spread.

In order then, themselves they did retire,
Their weapons vaunst, with Ensignes brave displayde,[28]
What would you more? Report is made a lyer;
Syr *Drurie* lives, sufficeth what is sayde.
What though his Corps entombed be in clay,
His vertues shyne, that never shall decay.

Vivit post funæra virtus.[29]

---

28. raised their weapons high with their splendid banners displayed.
29. Virtue lives after the grave.

THOMAS CHURCHYARD
(*c*.1520–**1579**–1604)

Thomas Churchyard wrote in a lively but – to use his own phrase – a rather 'plain' pen, on a wide range of topics throughout his long life. He was, for a time, a professional soldier and served in many European countries as well as Ireland. Churchyard wrote poems on each of the countries where he served, and published them as *The Miserie of Flanders, Calamatie of Fraunce, Misfortune of Portugall, Unquietnesse of Ireland, Troubles of Scotlande: and the Blessed State of England*. The first extract below shows Churchyard to have been one of the few English commentators who responded with sympathy and humanity to the sufferings of the Irish people during the wars of the latter end of the sixteenth century. The second extract, from a long poem included in his rambling *A Generall Rehearsall of Warres, called Churchyard's Choise* (London, 1579), gives Churchyard's view of the state of Ireland in the late 1570s. In particular, he objected to the self-interest of incoming English administrators and to the practice of 'coin (or 'coyne') and livery' – by which citizens were required to quarter troops free of charge.

from: Of the Unquietnesse of Ireland

> . . . To heare the people crie
>   and see their bare estate,
> Would sure move tears in any eye
>   that doth the countrey hate.
> I can but wishe them well
>   my duetie claims the same,
> For that thei are our neighbors nere
>   and ought, with equall name,
> Like subjects, live with us.
>   For since one Prince wee have,   10
> One minde & maner should we shew,
>   good order that doth crave.¹
> The hande doeth love the arme,
>   and arme with leggs agree,
> And all the joynts the bodie bears,
>   in perfite peace must bee:
> So head shall well bee servde;
>   but where those members jarre,
> There wil burst out some bold abuse,
>   some braule, or irksom warre.   20

---

1. i.e. we should show by our outlook and our behaviour that we seek good order.

54

Though Irelande hath bin long
   in most unquiet cace,[2]
It wil be well, when God shall plant,
   in peoples harts his grace.
I hope to see that daie,
   and that in season short
That my plain pen shall finde great cause
   to yelde them good report.

from: A Letter Sent from the Noble Earl of Ormond's House at Kilkennie

to the honourable Sir Henry Sidney, then Lorde Deputie, and lying at Korke
in Irelande

. . . Then why am I so long from Corke, you aske?[1]
The cause is knowne; when to the North we went,
I ever laie, like none[2] that tooke a taske[3]
Of corne to thrashe, and till the strawe was spent,[4]
I had no bed; yea twelve long weekes at least
I shifted out,[5] and laie as badde as beast.
Then drewe we home from savage countrey wilde,
But Harbenger[6] no better order tooke:
I durst not then complaine like little childe
That flings[7] from schoole, and madly burnes his booke.   10
So then for sleepe and ease I gan to looke
And left the streame, where fishe for place doeth strive,[8]
But lothe to part, yet glad to lye in sheetes:
Because with reste, our daies awaie we drive,[9]
And laisure finde, to charme and conjour spreets:[10]

---

2. case.

1. Churchyard's regiment was, presumably, quartered at Cork, but had undertaken a tour of duty in the north of Ireland.
2. i.e. I never lay, like one that . . .
3. a set quantity.
4. proved to be of good quality.
5. kept moving from one place to another.
6. the one who provided lodgings.
7. rushes.
8. i.e. the poet discharged himself from the regiment.
9. cause (the days) to pass.
10. i.e. conjure spirits. For a brief overview of Irish superstitions and magic practices in the Elizabethan period, see D.B. Quinn, *The Elizabethans and the Irish* (Ithaca, 1966), pp. 82–5.

A cunnyng knacke, for shreavde[11] and wicked heddes
That watche the Moone, and searche in gardein beddes
What herbs are good, to make a wilde Gose tame,
And where and how, the madde dogge must be cuerd:
That is no arte, but for old distaffe dame,[12]   20
That looks like witche, whose practise hath procuerd
A Horse or Mare, to swell and pine to death
Some saie for sport. These Callioghes[13] knowes a knacke
To blowe downe trees, thei have so strong a breath.
What needes more words? a plague take all the packe
That plaies foule plaie, in house, in holt,[14] or heath.
Let trifles passe, I use some houshold talke,
And write of state, and how the worlde doeth frame:[15]
Much shall thei heere that long abroad doeth walke,
And have some sight and skill to marke the same.   30
Thei saie this lande[16] hath many sores and greves,
That fewe, or none, doe seeke to salve a right,
And is so spoield by Rebells, Knaves, and Theves,
(And bareleggd Kerne,[17] whiche setts all goodnesse light)
That worse and worse the common wealth doeth waxe.
Why evry hedde should members badd reforme:[18]
And if men please to take the fire from flaxe,
The kirnell sweete, should soone be safe from worme,[19]
Though some have sought their onely private gaine,
And fedd on fleece that from the flocke did fall.[20]   40
Yet grace is lefte, and hope there doeth remaine
That some doeth live, to mend the mischieves all.
But to be plaine, I heare a wofull crie,
The noyes wherof resounds through starry Skie.
The poore that lives by toyle and sweate of browes
(And were good townes[21] where eche man knowes his own)

11. shrived, shriven; i.e. those whose sins have been absolved.
12. i.e. magic is an appropriate art only for an old woman.
13. Ir. *cailleach*, old woman.
14. wood.
15. i.e. what is happening in the world.
16. i.e. Ireland as a whole.
17. Ir. *ceithearn*, an Irish foot soldier, or (properly) a band of Irish foot soldiers.
18. This line seems to mean: That is why those in charge of the state should root out evil-doers.
19. the seeds of the common flax are used to make linseed oil, but they were also, sometimes, used as human food after they had been roasted. The exact meaning of the lines is, however, obscure.
20. Churchyard is highlighting the behaviour of the more rapacious planters.
21. i.e. and these people live in what were good towns . . .

Can not be free, nor well enjoye their plowes,
Thei are, in deede, with sesse[22] so overthrown.
In any place where proudest people dwell
Whose rule is mixt with rage and rigor still[23]   50
Was never seen, nor felt so foule an hell
As this, good Lorde, where waest[24] doeth what it will.
Suche as be borne as free as we our selves,
And tilles the ground, and dearely paies therefore,
(And for their babes, full truely diggs and delves)[25]
In their moste neede, we plague and scourge full sore,
Beyond the course of reason, law and right.
A cruel case, and twice as heavie a sight
To see the weake, with strongest,[26] thrust to wall,
And lose their goods – and not the halfe, but all.   60
The people saie, were coyne and livery gon,[27]
The lande would sure with Milke and Honie floe:
Their trust is now: redresse is commyng on
And havocke shall to hatefull harbour goe . . .

22. cess; specifically, the obligation to supply soldiers and the lord deputy's household with
provisions at prices 'assessed'.
23. i.e. whose conduct is a mixture of obedience to the law and rage at it . . .
24. *either* waest = woest, i.e. the greatest degree of woe or misery; *or* = waste.
25. to delve = to turn over the ground with a spade.
26. i.e. with the strongest . . .
27. coin and livery: Ir. *coinnmheadh* and Fr. *livrée*; coin was a prerogative of Brehon law by
which soldiers were permitted to take food and drink from those they protected without
payment: livery was the term for the same treatment for their horses. In addition to
feeding their unwelcome guests, the hosts often had to give money to the soldiers and
horseboys.

ANONYMOUS
(*c*.1580)

This is the most coherent of the fragments of popular song in English which survive from sixteenth-century Ireland. It was collected by Meredith Hanmer (1543–1604), rector of the college in New Ross, as part of the material he assembled while he was researching his history of Ireland. The cattle raids of heroic Ireland are here reduced to a rather pathetic meat-gathering foray by two hungry outlaws who clearly expect the expedition to end in their capture and execution.

You and I will go to Fingall

You and I will go to Fingall.[1]
You and I will eat such meats as we find there.
You and I will steal such beef as we shall find fat.
I shall be hanged and you shall be hanged.
What shall our children do?
When teeth do grow unto themselves, as their fathers did before.[2]

1. The prosperous area of the Pale, north of Dublin.
2. i.e. when they grow up, they will do as we do.

JOHN DERRICKE
(*fl*.1575–**1581**)

Nothing is known of John Derricke except that he was an Englishman and a follower of Sir Henry Sidney. His long verse description of Ireland, *The Image of Irelande*, reflects the crudeness of much Elizabethan English prejudice against the Irish, but his views would have been quite widely shared, in England at any rate. Derricke is remembered today not for his rather lumbering poem with its viciously anti-Irish notes, but for the twelve vivid woodcuts of late sixteenth-century Irish life which accompany the text. The selections from *The Image of Irelande* which follow comprise part of the second section of the main poem and two of the verses printed below the woodcuts.

Though the word 'kerne' (Ir. *ceithearn*) – which Derricke normally spells 'karne' – means a band of foot soldiers, it usually refers, in English, to a single, Irish, armed footsoldier. The kerne Derricke describes seems to be a minor chieftain, with a retinue consisting of family, friar, harper, bard, servants and lesser soldiers. The soldiers at the lowest level in such a group were 'daltins' (Ir. *dailtín*, fosterling, brat); above them were the 'horseboys' who were taken into battle by the kerns to look after their horses and to throw darts (see D.B. Quinn, *The Elizabethans and the Irish* (Ithaca, 1966), p. 41 and references). Derricke stresses the fact that this 'wild Irish' kerne and his company live in the woods, which heightens the contrast between them and the settled Irish or 'civil' English citizens of the towns. Because they reflect the venom of Derricke's view of the native Irish, his gratuitously insulting notes are included here.

from: The Image of Irelande, with a Discoverie of Woodkarne,
wherein is more lively expressed, the Nature, and qualities of the saied wilde Irishe Woodkarne . . .

from: *The second part of the Image of Irelande.*

[*A description of an Irish woodkerne.*[1]]

. . . Though that the royall soyle and fertill Irishe grounde,
With thousande sondrie pleasaunt thinges, most nobly doe abounde,
Though that the lande be free from Vipers generation,
As in the former parte[2] I made a perfecte declaration,
Though that the yearth, I saie, be bliste[3] with heavenly things,
And though tis like the fragrant flowre in pleasante Maie that springs,
Yet when I did beholde those whiche possesse the same,
Their maners lothsome to be told, as yrcksome for to name,

---

1. i.e. a kern or kerne [see headnote].
2. i.e. the former part of this poem.
3. blessed.

I mervailde[4] in my mynde, and thereupon did muse
To see a Bride of heavenlie hewe, an ouglie Feere[5] to chuse.   10
This Bride it is the Soile, the Bridegrome is the Karne,
With writhed glibbes[6] like wicked Sprits,[7] with visage rough and stearne;
With sculles upon their poules,[8] in steade of civill Cappes;
With speares in hand and swordes by sides, to beare of[f] after clappes;[9]
With Jackettes long and large, whiche shroude simplicitie,
Though spitfull dartes which thei do beare importe iniquitie.[10]
Their shirtes be verie straunge, not reachyng paste the thie:[11]
With pleates on pleates thei pleated are, as thicke as pleates maie lye.
Whose sleves hang trailing doune almoste unto the Shoe:
And with a Manttell[12] commonlie, the Irishe karne doe goe   20

Like as their weedes be straunge and monstrous to beholde,
So doe their maners far surpasse them all a thousande folde.[13]
For thei are tearmed wilde, Woodkarne thei have to name;
And mervaile not though strange it be, for thei desarve the same.
In maners thei be rude, and monst'rous eke in fashon,
Their dealynges also do bewraie[14] a crooked generation.[15]
For why, thei feare not God, nor honour yet their Prince:[16]
Whom by the lawes of mightie *Jove*[17] thei ought to reverence.
Eche theef would be a Lorde, to rule even by a becke,[18]

4. marvelled.
5. ugly companion.
6. Ir. *glibeanna*, long locks of hair allowed to fall over the eyes; the glib was considered a distinguishing mark of a native Irishman.
7. *Original note*: 'The discription of the Irishman, as well of the Lordes, as of the galliglasse and horseboy, fully set out.' Sprits = spirits. galliglass = gallowglass = Ir. *gallóglach*, heavily armed footsoldier, though the word was often used to mean Irishmen in arms.
8. with close-fitting caps on their heads. The dress described is shown in the woodcuts which accompany Derricke's poem. Town-dwellers ('civill' men) wore larger, broader caps. It is possible that the 'sculle' is the 'cap of steel' seen by Thomas Gainsford in 1601. See Quinn, *The Elizabethans and the Irish*, appendix, p. 169.
9. so that they can speed away after an affray(?)
10. i.e. they are intended to cause trouble.
11. *Original note*: 'The Irish Karnes apparell moste lively set out.' thie = thigh.
12. cloak.
13. *Original note*: 'Woodkarnes manners are more straunger than his apparell.'
14. betray (the fact that they are) . . .
15. *Original note*: 'The fruite sheweth the goodnesse of the tree – Approvyng all Woodkarne, strong theeves for to bee.' i.e. you shall know the tree by its fruit – which proves that all woodkernes are flagrant thieves.
16. *Original note*: 'Irishe Rebbelles feare neither god nor man.'
17. Jove, the chief god of the ancient world.
18. *Original note*: 'The hautie hartes of Woodkarne desire ruledome, but they shall have a rope.' beck = nod.

The faithfull subjectes often times, thei shorten by the necke.[19]   30
And those that would be true to God and to the Croune,
With fire and sworde, and deepe despight,[20] thei plucke suche subjects
    doune.[21]
Thus thei be mortall foes unto the Common wealthe,[22]
Maintainyng rackhells[23] at their heeles, through detestable stealthe.
Thei harpe upon one stryng, and therein is their joye:
When as thei finde a subtill sleight to worke true mens anoye.[24]
For mischief is the game, wherein thei doe delight,
As eke thei holde it great renowne to burne and spoile by night.[25]

[*A description of an Irish feast*]

Well, Beeves[26] are knocked doune, the Butchers plaie their parte,[27]
Who take eche one the intrails forthe, the Liver with the Harte;   40
And beyng breathyng newe,[28] th'unwashen Puddyngs thei
Upon the coales or embers hotte, for want of Gredyron[29] laie.
And scarse not halfe enough, (draffe[30] serveth well for Hogges),
Thei take them up and fall thereto, like rav'nyng hongrie Doggs,
Devouryng gutte and limme, no parte doth come amisse,[31]
Whose lippes & chappes with blood doe swim, moste true reporte is this.
As for the greatest Karne, thei have the cheefest stuffe,[32]
Though durtie tripes and offalls like please underknaves enoufe.

---

19. *Original note*: 'The Rebbelles envie towarde a good Subjecte, whereto many be joyned, the affection of a pernicious Papist, towarde a true Christian.'
20. feelings of contempt.
21. *Original note*: 'Marke the moste pestilent nature of the wilde villanous Woodkarne.'
22. *Original note*: 'Woodkarne are as Grashoppers, and Catterpillers to their countrey, and people.'
23. badly behaved young camp-followers. Spenser described the lowest grade of Irish footsoldiers as 'rakehelly horseboys, growing up in knavery and villainy'. *Complete Works of Edmund Spenser*, ed. William L. Renwick (London, 1934), IV, 98.
24. *Original note*: 'The joye of rebbelles is in plagyng of true men.'
25. *Original note*: 'Spoyling and burnyng is the Irishe karnes renoune.'
26. beef cattle, heifers.
27. *Original note*: 'A moste perfecte discription of Irishe horsboyes eatyng their meate.'
28. Breathing = the opening of a vein in order to let blood. The line seems to mean that, because the animal had been only freshly killed, its entrails are cooked in this way.
29. gridiron, griddle.
30. refuse, dregs.
31. *Original note*: 'The rudenesse of horsboyes is herein set open – Who fill them with driffe draffe, farwell the good token.' 'token' here probably means a stamped piece of metal, accepted for services, like a coin. A well-known sixteenth- and seventeenth-century phrase of contemptuous dismissal was 'Farewell forty pence!'
32. *Original note*: 'Beholde here the difference twixt Karne and their men – The Karne have the best meate, the horsboyes eate then – Of inmeates and puddings, which to lucke is imputed – Their lippes with greene oyntment beyng fouly poluted.'

Whereof thei parte doe roste, and other some thei boile:

Thus what betwene the sodde and roste, fearce honger thei assoile.[33] 50

No table there is spread, thei have no courtlike guise,[34]

The yearth sometimes standes them in steede whereon their victuall lyes.[35]

Their Coushens are of Strawe of Rushes or of Haye:

Made banckesetwise[36] with withies, their tailes to underlaie.

Their Platters are of wood, by cunnyng Turners made,

But not of Peauter,[37] (credite me), as is our Englishe trade.

Now ere the Lorde sitts doune with concubine or wife,

(Whereof he often makes exchaunge in compasse of his life),[38]

Before he takes his rome, a Frier doeth beginne[39]

To blesse the Rebell with his wife, the place and theeves therein; 60

Whiche when he blessed hath, in highest place of all,

The Cheeftaine then this traitrous knave, like honest man, doeth stall.

And next his Surgion he doth sette at Friar's side,[40]

And then himself his rome[41] enjoyth adorned with his Bride.

(In fine) the hellishe route like luckie fellowes mette,[42]

Doe sit them doune on strawe or grounde, their victualles for to gette . . .

. . . Now when their gutts be full, then comes the pastyme in:

The Barde and Harper mellodie unto them doe beginne.[43]

This Barde he doeth report the noble conquestes done,[44]

And eke in Rimes shewes forth at large their glorie thereby wonne.[45] 70

33. they set themselves free from their fierce hunger.

34. *Original note*: 'The very order of the wilde Irish, their sittyng, table, dishes, and cushens discribed.'

35. *Original note*: 'O brave swinishe fashion founde out emongst hogges – Deservyng for maneres to sitt amongst dogges.'

36. a misprint for 'basketwise'. Withies = flexible willow branches.

37. pewter.

38. *Original note*: 'Irishe Karne every yeare once or twise peradventure make exchaunge of their wives, as thei like them so will thei keepe them, for thei will not be bounde to them.' English propaganda often represented the native Irish as sexually promiscuous; Brehon law on marriage differed considerably from English law on marriage.

39. *Original note*: 'The order of Woodkarne is to have a Frier blesse hym and all his housholde before he sits doune.'

40. *Original note*: 'Friers have chiefest and hiest roomes at feastes amongst the Irishrie, and why should not we give them like honour at the gallowes.'

41. room, place.

42. *Original note*: 'Like unto like saide the Devill to the Collier.' A proverb first recorded in 1569 as 'Like will to like, quoth the devil to the collier.' A collier delivered coal and therefore looked as black as the devil.

43. *Original note*: 'The Woodthives love mirth after meate.'

44. *Original note*: 'A Barde and a Rimer is all one.'

45. *Original note*: 'The Barde by his Rimes hath as great force emongst Woodkarne to perswade, as the elloquent oration of a learned Oratour emongst the civill people.'

Thus he at randome ronneth, he pricks the Rebells on,[46]
And shewes by such externall deeds their honour lyes upon,
The more to stirre them up to prosecute their ill,
What greate renowne their fathers gotte, thei shew by Rimyng skill[47] . . .

. . . The Frier of his councells vile to rebelles doth imparte,[48]
Affirmyng that it is an almost deede to God
To make the Englishe subjectes taste the Irishe Rebells rodde.
To spoile, to kill, to burne, this Friers councell is,[49]
And for the doyng of the same, he warrantes heavenlie blisse.[50]
He tells a holie tale, the white he tournes to blacke: 80
And through the pardons in his Male,[51] he workes a Knavishe Knacke.[52]

[*The woodkerne with horse and boy*]

The lively shape of Irysh karne, most perfect to behold
Of man, the master, and the boy, these pictures doe unfolde,
Wherein is bravely paynted forth a nat'rall Irish grace,
Whose like in ev'ry poynt to vewe, hath seldome stept in place.
Marke me the karne that gripes the axe fast with his murd'ring hand,
Then shall you say a righter knave came never in the land.

46. he encourages the rebels.
47. *Original note*: 'The pollicie of the Barde to encense the Rebelles to doe mischefe, by repeating their forfathers actes. O craftie Appostle as holy as a Devill.'
48. *Original note*: 'A wicked man never wants ill counsell.'
49. *Original note*: 'The Frier perswades the Rebels that it is an high worke of charitie, to kill loyall Subjectes, which thyng they beleeve though never founde on scripture, O ghostly Frier as innocent as Judas.'
50. *Original note*: 'Beholde the plaguy counsell of a pockie Frier, the very fruite of Papistrye.'
51. = mail, a bag or travelling wallet. cf. Ir. *mála*, a bag.
52. *Original note*: 'This flatteryng Frier promiseth to the Rebels everlasting life, if they perceiver [persevere] in rebellyng against the Queene.'

As for the rest, so trimly drest, I speake of them no evil,
In ech respect, they are detect[1] as honest as the devil:
As honest as the Pope himself in all their outwarde actions,
And constant like the wavering winde in their Imaginations,   10
Which may be prov'de in sundry partes hereafter that ensue,[2]
A perfect signe for to define th'above additions true.

[*The MacSweeney at Dinner* [1]]

A) Now when into their fenced holdes[2] the knaves are entred in,
   To smite and knocke the cattell downe, the hangmen doe beginne;
   One plucketh off the Oxes cote, which he even now did weare,
   Another, lacking pannes, to boyle the fleshe his hide prepare.
C) These theeves attend upon the fire for serving up the feast.
B) And Fryer Smelfeast sneaking in, doth prease[3] amongst the best;
   Who play'th in Romish toyes the *Ape* by counterfetting Paull,[4]
   For which they doe award him then, the highest roome[5] of all.
   Who being set, because the cheere is deemed little worth
   Except the same be intermixt and lac'de with Irish myrth,   10
D) Both *Barde* and Harper is preparde, which by their cunning art
   Doe strike and cheare up all the gestes with comfort at the hart.

---

1. seen.
2. This line seems to mean: 'Will be proved true in various places by what is likely to happen'.

---

1. The letters correspond to letters on the woodblock illustration which depicts the chief of the MacSweeney (Mac Suibhne) sept.
2. = hole, secret hiding-place.
3. press forward.
4. i.e. who apes or copies St Paul with his Roman (catholic) nonsense.
5. place at the table.

LORD GERALD FITZGERALD
(1559–1580; pub. **1582**)

Gerald Fitzgerald, Lord Offaly, was the eldest son of the eleventh Earl of Kildare. He died in 1580 at the age of twenty, leaving a widow and a young daughter. Richard Stanihurst explained that the young lord, although possessed of many good qualities, was yet 'soomwhat wantonly geeven, where too *Youth*, *Nobilitee* and *lewd coompanye* dyd carrye him'.[1] However, before his death, Lord Gerald repented of his ways, 'in which tyme finding his conscience deepelye gauld with thee owtragious oathes hee used too thunder owt in gamening, hee made a few verses, as yt were his *cygnea oratio* . . .'[2] These verses were found among his papers, and Stanihurst, though he maintained that he copied them verbatim, amended the spelling of them to fit his own unusual practice.

A Penitent Sonnet written by thee *Lord Girald* a litle beefore his death

> By losse in play men oft forget
>   Thee duitye they dooe owe,
> Too hym that dyd bestow thee same
>   And thowsands millions more.
> I loathe too see them sweare and stare,
>   When they the mayne have lost;[3]
> Forgetting al thee byes,[4] that weare
>   With God and holye goast.
> By *wounds* and *nayles* they thinck to wyn[5]
>   But truely yt is not so;   10
> For al theyre frets and fumes in syn,
>   They mooniles must goe.[6]
>
> Theare is no wight[7] that usd yt more
>   Than *hee* that wrote this verse;

---

1. i.e. somewhat wantonly given, whereto youth, nobility and lewd company did carry him. Stanihurst is using his eccentric system of spelling English.
2. i.e. at which time, finding his conscience deeply galled with the outrageous oaths he used to thunder out when gambling, he made a few verses, as it were his 'swan song'. (The swan was reputed to sing only at the approach of death.)
3. In the game of 'hazard', the 'main' is the number called by the caster before the dice are thrown.
4. The opposite of the 'main' – so, in this case, a 'bye' is a number not called by the caster.
5. Common oaths included 'By God's wounds' and references to the nails by which Christ was fastened to the cross.
6. They must go without money.
7. man.

Who cryeth, *peccavi*,[8] now therefore
   His othes his hert doe perce.
Therefor example take by *mee*,
   That curse thee lucklesse tyme;
That eaver *dice* myn eyes dyd see,
   Which bred in mee this *crime*.   20
Pardon mee for that is past,
   I wyl offend no more:
In this moste vile and sinful *cast*,[9]
   Which I wyl stil abhore.

8. I have sinned.
9. cast = 1) the throw of dice; 2) that which is thrown out.

66

RICHARD STANIHURST
(1547-**1582**-1618)

Richard Stanihurst is the most interesting and significant Irish-born poet before Swift. His family was prominent in the Old English community in Dublin, and Stanihurst was educated at Peter White's famous school in Kilkenny, at Oxford and at the Inns of Court in London. (There was no university in Ireland when Stanihurst was young.) When he returned to Ireland, Stanihurst became, for a while, tutor to the children of the eleventh earl of Kildare. Though he is best known for his lively prose descriptions of Ireland, which were inserted into Holinshed's *Chronicles* in 1577, and for historical and philosophical tracts in Latin, Stanihurst also wrote a considerable amount of English verse, as well as a treatise on English prosody. He ended his life on the Continent, as a catholic priest, and as one of the most respected practitioners of alchemy of his day.

Stanihurst's English verse is all found in the volume which contains his translation of Virgil. The book begins with two prefatory dissertations in which Stanihurst sets out his views on how the English language should be pronounced and stressed in verse, after which he prints his lively translation of the first four books of the *Æneid* in hexameters. Following this is a thirty-page anthology of verse in English and Latin by Stanihurst and others in which, among other things, he parodies what he calls 'oure unlearned Rythmours' and tries out some of his own poetic theories; he provides, for example, psalms translated into English 'Iambical, Heroical, Elegiacal, Asclepiad and Saphick' verse. In a section called 'Poetical Devices', Stanihurst experiments with extended poetical conceits and elegies, using mimesis and onomatopoeia with an attractively reckless abandon. Throughout his English prose and verse, Stanihurst's highly developed, personal method of spelling gives the impression that what he is writing is even more peculiar than it actually is. For this reason, most modern readers do find Stanihurst hard to read, and his poems are here provided with prose paraphrases.

Stanihurst's contemporaries mocked his Virgil translations and his way of writing English, and their mockery has been repeated over the years, more by those who have not read him than by those who have. However, Stanihurst combined the scholar's knowledge of the English language with the poet's enthusiasm for it; he created striking effects by mixing words from the world of the epic with words from the street and by boldly employing nouns as verbs and verbs as nouns in a way later exploited by Lewis Carroll and James Joyce. Though some critics have thought that Stanihurst must have meant his verse to be comic, his scholarly prefaces show that he was trying to open up a new way of writing English verse, and that he saw this as a scholarly exercise in the highest humanist tradition. Stanihurst deserves to be remembered not just for his own lively verse and his enthusiasm for language but as the first Irish anthologist of verse in English.

Upon thee death of thee right honourable and his moste deere coosen, thee *Lord Baron of Louth*,

who was trayterouslye murthred by *Mackmaughoun*, an Irish Lording, about thee yeere 1577

Patrick Plunkett, third Lord Louth, was killed at Essexford, County Monaghan, in 1575 while trying to recover cattle stolen from him by members of the MacMahon sept. Stanihurst was related to Lord Louth through his wife's family, the Barnewalls.

Thus loa, thyne hast (coosen) bred waste too cittye, toe country.[1]
Thee bearbrat boucher thy corps with villenye mangled,
Not by his manlye valour, but through thy desperat offer.
As the liefe is lasting too sutch, as in armes ar heedye,
Evn so death is posting too those, that in armor ar headye.
Haulfpenye, far better then an housful cluster of angels,
Althogh habil, would not fro thye danger deadlye be parted.
Whom lief combyned, death could not scatter a sunder,
Sutch is thee fastnesse of foster brootherhod Irish.[2]
Thogh Sydny and Delvyn thee murther partlye revenged,[3]   10
A losse so pretiouse may not bee fullye requited.
Thee death of a thowsand Maghouns[4] is unequal amendment.
Thee nobles may not but a death so bluddye remember,
Thee Plunckets wyl not from mynd such boutcherye bannish.

1. A rough paraphrase of the text runs as follows: Thus, alas, cousin, your impetuousness has brought ruin to city and to country. The beastly butcher (who killed you) has grossly mangled your corpse, not because of his manly vigour, but because you attacked him so recklessly. As life lasts for those who are careful in battle, so death comes quickly to those who are headstrong. Halfpenny, a man better than a whole houseful of angels, though able to escape, would not be parted from the deadly danger you were in. Those whom life combined, death could not separate, such is the strength of relationships built through Irish fostering. Though Sydney and Delvin have partly avenged your murder, such a precious loss can not be fully paid for; the death of a thousand MacMahons would be an unequal payment. The nobles must remember such a bloody death, the Plunketts will not banish such butchery from their minds. Your wife and family miss your dear friendship, the city mourns the lack of a wholesome counsellor; the country bemoans the want of a zealous defender. Even virtue laments the lack of a holy penitent. Still, Dame Virtue does reward your goodness; your honour rests in our memories and your soul still rests in glory.
2. The Halfpenny or Halpenny sept (Ir. *Ó hAilpine*) inhabited an area now in County Monaghan, not far from Plunkett lands in County Meath. Clearly the young Lord Louth had been fostered to a Halpenny family and his Halpenny foster-brother had attempted to defend him in the skirmish in which both had been killed.
3. Sir Henry Sidney led an expedition against the MacMahon sept in the summer of 1578, and Christopher Nugent, fourteenth Baron Delvin (1544–1602) (the man who is said to have prepared the manuscript primer on the Irish language presented to Elizabeth I) was in command of the crown forces sent to the northern marches of the Pale against Turlough O'Neill in the autumn of 1579.
4. MacMahons.

Thy Ladye, thy kinred doo misse thy freendship aprooved;
Thee cittee mourneth the lack of a counsalor holsoom,
And thee countrye moneth thee want of a zealus upholder;
Vertu eeke lamenteth thee lack of an holye repentaunt.
How beyt, dame Vertu thy goodnesse kindlye rewardeth,
In memory thin honour, thy soul eeke in glorye reposing.   20

An Endevoured Description of his *Mystresse*[1]

Nature in her woorcking soomtyme dooth pinche lyke a niggard,[2]
Disfiguring creatures, lyms with deformitye dusking.
This man is unjoyncted, that swad lyke a monster abydeth;
Shee limps in the going, this slut with a cammoysed haucks nose,
And as a Cow wasted, plods on, with an head lyke a lutecase.
Theese faultes fond Hodipecks impute too Nature, as yf she
Too frame were not habil gems with rare dignitye lustring.
Wherefor in advis'ment laboring too cancel al old blots,
And toe make a patterne of price, thee maystrye toe pubblish,
For toe shape a peerlesse paragon shee mynded, asembling   10
Her force and cunning: for a spirt lands sundrye refusing,
And with al her woorckmat's travayling shee lighteth in *Holland,*
Round too the *Hage* posting, to the world *Marye* matchles avauncing.
In bodye fine fewterd, a brave Brownnetta; wel handled;

---

1. The woman celebrated in this poem may have been Stanihurst's second wife. Certainly he met her after he had moved to the Continent and long after the death of his first wife, Janet.
2. A rough paraphrase of the text runs as follows: In the way she works things out, Nature can be niggardly, sometimes making people misshapen or darkening limbs with deformities. This man's joints are loose, that one looks like a monster: that woman has a limp, this slut with the low, hooked nose plods like a cow and has a head like a lutecase. Silly fools impute these faults to Nature as if she were not capable of making gems of rare, shining beauty. Therefore, working under guidance, in order to cancel old mistakes and to create a prize-worthy ideal, to let her abilities be manifest, Nature decided to make a peerless paragon, and gathered to her all her force and cunning; because several lands refused her (being a spirit), she landed in Holland, with all the tools of her trade, went to the Hague and brought forth the incomparable Mary. She has a fine-featured body and brave brown hair; she is a good shape, a fine size, and not an inch too large. She has a gracious face and a pretty, quick, glancing eye; her lips are like ruddy coral and her lily white teeth are even. Though she is young, she remains wise and mature. She is bashful when she speaks, not rash, but careful in her answers. Good breeding sweetens her looks, her smile and her words. She is kind but also modest, linking attractiveness with chastity, and in all her gestures observing comely decorum. But why am I working away here, pressing myself down as if I were trying to move mount Etna or to count the stars – trying to do the impossible? Hush! not a word! Such an impossible task calls for silence. Her virtue merits more praise than any words can utter.

Her stature is coomly; not an ynch toe superfluus holding;
Gratius in visadge; with a quick eye prittelye glauncing;
Her lips lyke corral rudye, with teeth lillye whit eevened.
Yoong in age, in manners and nurture sage she remayneth;
Bashful in her speaking, not rash; but watchful in aunswer;
Her look's, her simpring, her woords with curtesye sweetning;   20
Kynd and also modest; lyking with chastitye lyncking;
And in al her gesturs observing coomlye *Decorum*.
But toe what eend labor I, me toe presse with burden of Ætna
Thee stars too number, poincts playnely uncounctabil opning.
Whust: not a woord: a silence such a task impossibil asketh.
Her vertu meriteth more prayse than parlye can utter.

from: Thee First Booke of Virgil his Æneis[1]

[King Æolus releases the storm winds which will scatter the Trojan fleet.]

This sayd, with poyncted flatchet thee mountan he broached;[2]
Rush do the winds forward through perst chinck narrolye whizling,
Thee land turmoyling with blast and terribil huzing;
They skud too the seaward, from deepe profunditie raking

---

1. Stanihurst spent some time in late sixteenth-century England when a lively debate was
   in progress between those who believed that English verse should be written according
   to the accentual rules of classical prosody and those who felt that end-rhymes and
   flexible rhythms suited the language better. Even as the debate was lumbering on, poets
   such as Surrey, Sidney, Spenser and Shakespeare began to demonstrate the power which
   lay in the rhythms and rhymes of the emerging language. The direction in which English
   verse was set to go became clear, and verse written according to the classical rules of
   accidence and scansion soon fell out of fashion. Unfortunately for his long-term poetic
   reputation, Stanihurst belonged to the old, classical school; in the treatise on the writing
   of verse which precedes his Virgil, he expressed his contempt for rhyming verse and
   explained that the verse he wrote was based on 'observation of quantitees of syllables'.
   The reader who approaches Stranihurst's verse today has, therefore, two hurdles to
   overcome: it sounds alien to the modern ear, and the author's eccentric spelling makes it
   look alien to the modern eye. The secret is to read Stanihurst aloud so that his bold and
   imaginative use of words is given free rein; the torrent of words and sounds, the irregular
   grammar, the use of nouns as verbs, alliteration, mimesis, onomatopoeia, surprising
   changes of register (as when words of slang are intermixed with epic and heroic
   language) all conspire to create a unique poetic effect. Stanihurst is the most remarkable
   Irish writer of the age.
2. A rough paraphrase of the text runs as follows: This said, he split open the mountain with
   his sharp pointed weapon and forth rush the winds, whizzing through a narrow chink; the
   land is in a turmoil with the blast and the terrible shaking. The winds scud to seaward,
   raking up waves from the profound depths to the sky – east and west winds
   struggle with each other, and both skirmish with the south wind; the angry, flooding
   water is hurled up onto the coast. [On the ships,] torn rigging crashes down: the men

Too the skye thee surges, the east west contrarie doe struggle
And southwind ruffling: on coast thee chauft flud is hurled.
Crash do the rent tacklings; thee men raise an horribil owtcrye.
Thee clowds snach gloomming from sight of Coompanie Trojan
Both Light and welken: thee night dooth shaddo the passadge.
Thee skyes doo thunder, thee lightnings riflye doe flush flash,   10
Noght breeds theym coomfort, eeche thing mortalitye threatneth.
Æneas (his lyms wyth sharp cold chillye benummed)
Dooth groane, then to skyward his claspt hands heavelye lifting,
Thus spake: O Trojans, ô thrise most nobil or happye
That before eine the parents wyth byckring martial ended
Your lives at townewals: of Greekes ô woorthye, the strongest,
Stout Diomed: bye the filds of Troy what fortun unhappye
Mee fenst from falling wyth thy fierce slaughterus hand stroke,
Wheare lyes strong Hector slaughtred by manful Achilles,
Wheare stout Serpedon dooth rest, where gauntlet or helmet   20
In water of Simois, wyth souldours carcases harboure.
This kyrye sad solfing, thee northen bluster aproching,
Thee sayls tears tag rag, to the sky thee waves uphoysing.
The oars are cleene splintred, the helme is from ruther unhafted,
Theire ships too larboord doo nod, seas monsterus haunt theym.

---

raise a horrible cry; the clouds sullenly snatch light and the sight of the sky from the Trojan company, night shadows their passage. The skies thunder and continuous lightning flashes around; nothing gives them comfort, everything threatens death. Æneas, his limbs numb with the sharp, chilly cold, groans and then, lifting his clasped hands to the heavens, he cries: O Trojans, O thrice noble and happy ones, who even before the eyes of your parents, ended your lives at the walls of Troy in the warlike encounters; O worthy, brave Diomede, the strongest of Greeks, what unlucky fortune defended me so I did not fall at your fierce, deadly stroke on the fields of Troy, where lies strong Hector, slain by manly Achilles, where noble Sarpedon rests, or where, in the waters of Simois, lie gauntlets and helmets with the corpses of soldiers? As this sad complaint is uttered, the blustering north wind approaching, tears the sails into shreds and lifts the seas up to the sky; the oars break in splinters, the helm is parted from the rudder; the ships dip to their larboard sides, monstrous seas keep at them; some ships hang perilously on the tops of the billows, some sink to the hollow between waves, driving furrows in the surges, mounting the sand [at the bottom of the sea]. The merciless, eager south wind forces three gallant vessels onto the craggy, jagged rocks (the Italians call these lines of rocks 'the Altars'). Likewise, the east wind overwhelms three ships and they disappear into quicksands – a sight to make one weep! The ship on which the Lycians had set the sails, with faithful Orontes, is swept away by a violent, huge flood of water, within sight of the captain [Æneas]. Headlong, the pilot [of that ship] tumbles down with a terrible splashing plunge; three times the [ship spins round?], then is plunged, pulled down into a whirlpool; some men appear floating on the waves in their armour; foam, froth and Trojan treasure come to the surface . . . The storm has won: the ships put up a weak resistance . . .

In typs of billows soom ships wyth danger ar hanging,
Soom synck too bottoms, sulcking thee surges asunder:
Thee sands are mounted: thee southwynd merciles eager,
Three gallant vessels on rocks gnawne craggye reposed,
(Theese rancks the Italian dwellers doo nominat altars)   30
Lykewise three vessels the east blast ful mightelye whelmed
In sands quick souping (a sight to be deepelye bewayled).
One ship that Lycius dyd shrowd, with faythful Orontes,
In sight of captayne was swasht wyth a roysterus heape-flud.
Downe the pilot tumbleth wyth plash round soommoned headlong.
Thrise the gravel thumping in whirkpoole plunged is hooveld.
Soom wights upfloating on raisd sea wyth armor apeered
In foame froth picturs, wyth Trojan treasur, ar upborne . . .
Thee storme dyd conquoure, thee ships scant weaklye resisted . . .

BARNABY GOOGE
(1540–**1586**–1594)

Barnaby Googe, sonneteer, translator and writer of eclogues, was a kinsman of Sir William
Cecil, who employed him on his Irish estates from 1574 to 1585. While he was in Ireland,
Googe undertook his translation and adaptation of Conrad Heresbach's influential treatise
on farming *Foure Bookes of Husbandry* . . . . – a book he might well have been consulting
for guidance on estate management since he was, himself, more of a courtier than a farmer.
The translation contains Googe's own versions of several passages from Virgil's *Georgics*,
including long verse descriptions of the behaviour of bees and the following spirited
description of a horse.

[A good horse described]

With head advaunced hie at first, the kingly Colt doth pace;
His tender limmes aloft he lifts, as well beseemes his race;
And foremost still he goeth, & through the streame he makes his way,
And ventures first the bridge, no sudain sound doth him affray.
Hy crested is his necke, and eke his head is framed small;
His belly gant,[1] his backe is brode, and brested big withall.
The bay is alwaies counted good, so likewise is the gray,
The white, and yellow worst of all, besides, if farr away
There happen a noise, he stampes and quiet cannot rest,
But praunceth here and there, as if some spirite were in his brest.   10
His eares he settes upright, and from his nose the fiery flame
Doth seeme to come, while as he snuffes, and snorthes at the same.
Thicke is his mane, and on the right side downe doth hanging fall,
And double chinde upon his loines, a gutter runes withall.[2]
He scraping standes and making deepe a hole, he pawes the ground,
Whiles as aloud his horned houfe,[3] all hollowed seemes to sound.

1. gaunt, slim.
2. The horse has a strong, broad back; he has a backbone of double width ('double-chined')
   with a 'gutter' or groove running between the two 'chines' or backbones.
3. hoof.

LUDOWICK BRYSKETT
(1546-**1595**-1612)

Ludowick Bryskett (Lodovico Bruschetto), an Italian who was attached to the London household of Sir Henry Sidney, spent much of his adult life in Ireland. In his youth, Bryskett accompanied Sidney's son, Sir Philip Sidney, on a three-year tour of Europe, but by 1571 he was in Ireland with Sidney himself. Bryskett stayed on in Ireland after Sidney's departure and held a variety of government positions, including clerk of the Irish council. He became close friends with Edmund Spenser when the latter came to Ireland with Lord Grey in 1580; Bryskett taught Spenser Greek, and Spenser mentioned Bryskett, as 'Lodwick' and under the poetic name of 'Thestylis', in his own work. In addition, the two poets formed the core of a coterie of writers working in Dublin in the 1580s; a meeting of this coterie is described in detail by Bryskett in the early part of his translation of Giraldi's *A Discourse of Civill Life* (London, 1606).

For the two men, as for the rest of the English-speaking world, the early death of Sir Philip Sidney in 1586 came as a huge blow, and Spenser and Bryskett both wrote elegies for the young soldier-poet; the elegies, with those by Fulke Greville, Sir Walter Ralegh and possibly the Countess of Pembroke, were published in 1595 in a volume entitled *Astrophel* – the most famous of about two hundred such volumes of elegies on the young Sidney. It is perhaps a reflection of the fact that Bryskett, like Spenser, had chosen to spend his life as an administrator in Ireland that the nymphs he calls upon for poetic inspiration at the beginning of this typically Renaissance elegy are the nymphs who live in mossy caves beside the river Liffey.

from: The mourning Muse of *Thestylis* [1]

Come forth, ye Nymphes, come forth, forsake your watry bowres,
Forsake your mossy caves, and help me to lament:
Help me to tune my dolefull notes to gurgling sound
Of *Liffies* tumbling streames: Come, let salt teares of ours
Mix with his[2] waters fresh. O come let one consent
Joyne us to mourne with wailfull plaints the deadly wound
Which fatall clap[3] hath made, decreed by higher powres,
The dreery day in which they have from us yrent[4]
The noblest plant that might from East to West be found.
Mourne, mourne, great *Philips*[5] fall, mourne we his wofull end,   10
Whom spitefull death hath pluct untimely from the tree,
Whiles yet his yeares in flowre, did promise worthie frute.

---

1. The poetic or coterie name for Bryskett. Spenser described Bryskett as 'Of gentle wit and daintie sweet device' and wrote that Sidney had held him 'in passing price'. *The Shorter Poems of Edmund Spenser*, ed. William A. Oram *et al.* (New Haven, 1989), p. 581.
2. i.e. the waters of the Liffey.
3. stroke.
4. taken away.
5. Sir Philip Sidney (1554–86), soldier, scholar, statesman, poet, killed at the battle of Zutphen.

Ah dreadful *Mars*[6] why didst thou not thy knight defend?
What wrathfull mood, what fault of ours hath moved thee
Of such a shining light to leave us destitute?
Tho with benigne aspect sometime didst us behold,
Thou hast in Britons valour tane[7] delight of old,
And with thy presence oft vouchsaft to attribute
Fame and renowne to us for glorious martiall deeds.
But now their ireful bemes[8] have chill'd our harts with cold,   20
Thou hast estrang'd thy self, and deignest not our land:[9]
Farre off to others now, thy favour honour breeds,
And high disdaine doth cause thee shun our clime (I feare);
For hadst thou not bene wroth,[10] or that time neare at hand,[11]
Thou wouldst have heard the cry that woful England made,
Eke[12] *Zelands* piteous plaints, and *Hollands* toren haire[13]
Would haply have appeas'd thy divine angry mynd:
Thou shouldst have seen the trees refuse to yeeld thir shade
And wailing to let fall the honor of their head,[14]
And birds in mournfull tunes lamenting in their kinde.   30
Up from his tombe the mightie *Corineus*[15] rose,
Who cursing oft the fates that this mishap had bred,
His hoary locks he tare, calling the heavens unkinde.
The Thames was heard to roare, the *Reyne* and eke the *Mose,*
The *Schald,* the *Danow*[16] selfe this great mischance did rue,
With torment and with grief; their fountains[17] pure & cleere
Were troubled, & with swelling flouds declar'd their woes.
The *Muses* comfortles, the Nymphs with paled hue,
The *Silvan*[18] Gods likewise came running farre and neere,
And all with teares bedeawd, and eyes cast up on hie;   40

---

6. fearsome Mars (god of war).
7. taken.
8. these (?) angry beams.
9. i.e. you have estranged yourself from us and do not think our land worthy of you.
10. very angry.
11. i.e. the fated time of Sidney's death.
12. In addition.
13. At the time of his death, Sidney was serving as colonel of the Zeeland regiment of horse in the protestant army (formed of Dutch and English regiments) which was trying to throw the Spanish out of the Netherlands. Holland and Zeeland would be in mourning at the loss of their soldiers.
14. i.e. their leaves.
15. Corineus = Corinnus, an ancient Greek poet who wrote a poem on the Trojan war.
16. The rivers affected by the conflict: the Thames, the Rhine, the Mosel, the Schelde and the Danube.
17. waters.
18. sylvan, of the woods.

O help, O help ye Gods, they ghastly gan to crie:
O chaunge the cruell fate of this so rare a wight,[19]
And graunt that natures course may measure out his age.[20]
The beasts their foode forsooke, and trembling fearfully,
Each sought his cave or den, this cry did them so fright.
Out from amid the waves, by storme then stirr'd to rage
This crie did cause to rise th'old father *Ocean* hoare,
Who grave with eld,[21] and full of maiestie in sight,
Spake in this wise; Refrain (quoth he) your teares & plaints,
Cease these your idle words, make vaine requests no more.   50
No humble speech nor mone, may move the fixed stint
Of destinie or death:[22] Such is his will that paints
The earth with colours fresh; the darkest skies with store
Of starry lights: And though your teares a hart of flint
Might tender make, yet nought herein they will prevaile.

    Whiles thus he said, the noble knight,[23] who gan to feele
His vitall force to faint,[24] and death with cruell dint
Of direfull dart[25] his mortall bodie to assaile,
With eyes lift up to heav'n, and courage franke as steele,
With cheerfull face, where valour lively was exprest,   60
But humble mynd he said: O Lord, if ought this fraile
And earthly carcasse have thy service sought t'advaunce,[26]
If my desire have bene still to relieve th'opprest,
If Justice to maintaine that valour I have spent
Which thou me gav'st; or if henceforth I might advaunce
Thy name, thy truth, then spare me (Lord) if thou think best.
Forbeare these unripe yeares.[27] But if thy will be bent,
If that prefixed time be come which thou hast set,
Through pure and fervent faith, I hope now to be plast,[28]
In th'everlasting blis, which with thy precious blood   70
Thou purchase didst for us. With that a sigh he set,[29]
And straight a cloudie mist his sences overcast,

19. being, man.
20. i.e. that he may be allowed to live out his natural life span.
21. old age.
22. i.e. no lowly complaint can change the prescribed time of death or the shape of destiny.
23. Sir Philip Sidney, just wounded on the battlefield.
24. i.e. who began to feel his life force growing faint.
25. i.e. with a cruel stroke of his dreadful arrow.
26. i.e. if in any way this frail and earthly body has sought to advance thy cause . . .
27. show mercy to these unripe years, i.e. to me who am still young.
28. placed.
29. With that, he suppressed a sigh.

His lips waxt pale and wan, like damaske roses bud
Cast from the stalke,[30] or like in field to purple flowre,
Which languisheth being shred by culter[31] as it past.
A trembling chilly cold ran throgh their veines,[32] which were,
With eyes brimfull of teares to see his fatall howre,[33]
Whose blustring sighes at first their sorrow did declare,
Next, murmuring ensude;[34] at last they not forbeare
Plaine outcries, all against the heav'ns that enviously   80
Depriv'd us of a spright[35] so perfect and so rare.
The Sun his lightsom[36] beames did shrowd, and hide his face
For griefe, whereby the earth feard night eternally:
The mountaines eachwhere shooke, the rivers turn'd their streames,
And th'aire gan winterlike to rage and fret apace:
And grisly ghosts by night were seene, and fierie gleames,
Amid the clouds with claps of thunder, that did seeme
To rent the skies, and made both man and beast afeard:
The birds of ill presage[37] this lucklesse chance[38] foretold,
By dernfull[39] noise, and dogs with howling made man deeme[40]   90
Some mischief was at hand: for such they do esteeme
As tokens of mishap,[41] and so have done of old . . .

---

30. like the bud of a damask (pink) rose which has been violently separated from its stalk.
31. coulter, the iron blade set at the front end of a ploughshare.
32. i.e. the veins of those standing by.
33. hour.
34. ensued; i.e. next they began to murmur . . .
35. being.
36. enlivening.
37. birds, the appearance of which is an indication of future evil, i.e. crows or ravens.
38. unfortunate event.
39. dreary.
40. conclude, guess.
41. signs of bad luck.

EDMUND SPENSER
(c.1552–**1595**–1599)

Edmund Spenser was born in London in about 1552. Though his father was a man of few means, the young Spenser was well educated and distinguished himself as a classical scholar at Cambridge. In 1579, he was adopted into the household of the Earl of Leicester where he became associated with Leicester's nephew, Sir Philip Sidney, and friendly with Sidney's Italian companion, Ludowick Bryskett. Another contact from Leicester's household was Lord Grey who, when he came to Ireland as lord deputy in 1580, brought Spenser with him as his secretary. Spenser was appointed to official positions in Dublin and in Munster and, in the late 1580s, successfully claimed a forfeited estate at Kilcolman, in north County Cork. Spenser moved to this estate and attempted to settle it. He married a kinswoman of the great Earl of Cork in 1595 and started a family. He also wrote an enormous amount of verse while in Ireland, including most of *The Faerie Queene*; in fact, Spenser's reputation as one of the greatest poets of the English Renaissance rests on work written, substantially, in Ireland.

As one of the hated settlers, Spenser encountered understandable hostility from the indigenous population in north Cork, and his strong views on how to settle 'the Irish question' are set out in his prose tract, *A View of the State of Ireland* (a text which circulated widely in manuscript but was not printed until 1633). Spenser also found it hard to retain the attention of literary patrons in England, including Queen Elizabeth herself, despite the fact that *The Faerie Queene* glorifies England and presents the queen as an almost divine figure. Spenser and his family fell foul of a renewed rising in Munster in 1598, during which his house was burned and one of his children is said to have been killed. He himself returned to England, where he died in 1599.

The relationship between Spenser and Ireland has become an important focus for recent Spenser scholarship, and the significance of Ireland in everything he wrote after 1580, including much of *The Faerie Queene*, is now beyond dispute. For this anthology, passages with Irish settings have been selected; in two of them, an early section of *Colin Clouts Come Home Againe* and the middle portion of the *Epithalamion*, Ireland is an idyllic setting; in the passage from the Mutability Cantos of *The Faerie Queene*, however, the mountains near Kilcolman are depicted as a wild and dangerous place.

from: Colin Clouts Come Home Againe

The passage which follows comes near the beginning of this autobiographical pastoral, and emphasises its setting in Ireland. The shepherd Colin (representing Spenser himself) has agreed to tell the other shepherds (his Munster planter friends) about his recent visit to England, and they gather round to hear his tale. Colin recounts how, before he left for England, he had been visited at his home at Kilcolman by the 'shepherd of the Ocean', Sir Walter Ralegh, the famous Elizabethan adventurer and poet who himself owned land in Munster. Colin/Spenser recounts the mythological story, which he says he had told Ralegh at the earlier meeting, concerning the rivers of north County Cork.

... One day (quoth[1] he) I sat, (as was my trade)[2]
Under the foot of *Mole*[3] that mountaine hore,[4]
Keeping my sheepe amongst the cooly shade,
Of the greene alders by the *Mullaes*[5] shore:
There a straunge shepherd[6] chaunst to find me out,
Whether allured with my pipes delight,
Whose pleasing sound yshrilled[7] far about,
Or thither led by chaunce, I know not right:
Whom when I asked from what place he came,
And how he hight,[8] himselfe he did ycleepe,[9]   10
The shepheard of the Ocean[10] by name,
And said he came far from the main-sea deepe.
He sitting me beside in that same shade,
Provoked me to plaie some pleasant fit,[11]
And when he heard the musicke which I made,
He found himselfe full greatly pleased at it:
Yet æmuling[53] my pipe, he tooke in hond
My pipe before that æmuled of many,[13]
And plaid thereon; (for well that skill he cond)[14]
Himselfe as skilfull in that art as any.   20
He pip'd, I sung; and when he sung, I piped,
By chaunge of turnes, each making other mery,
Neither envying other, nor envied,
So piped we, untill we both were weary,

1. said.
2. custom.
3. 'Mole' and 'Old Father Mole' are Spenser's names for the Ballyhoura and Galtee mountains near Kilcolman. The highest peak in the mountains is Galtymore.
4. hoary, grey or white with age.
5. by the shore of the river Mulla. In the personification of the poem, 'Old Father Mole' (the mountain range) has a beautiful daughter named Mulla (the Awbeg river, which rises in the Ballyhoura mountains).
6. Sir Walter Ralegh (*c*. 1552–1618).
7. shrilled: the obsolete y- prefix attached to a past participle is one of the many archaisms Spenser employed to invest his verse with a sense of mystery and antiquity.
8. what his name was.
9. called.
10. See headnote. Ralegh had many links with the ocean, including the title Vice-Admiral of the West.
11. urged me to play part of a song. Spenser seems to be suggesting that Ralegh asked him to read part of *The Faerie Queene*.
12. emulating (a Spenserian coinage), striving to equal or surpass.
13. he took up my pipe (i.e. poetry) that many had previously attempted to rival.
14. knew.

There interrupting him, a bonie swaine,
That *Cuddy* hight,[15] him thus atweene bespake:[16]
And should it not thy ready course restraine,[17]
I would request thee *Colin*, for my sake,
To tell what thou didst sing, when he did plaie.
For well I weene[18] it worth recounting was,   30
Whether it were some hymne, or morall laie,[19]
Or carol made to praise thy loved lasse.

Nor of my love, nor of my losse (quoth he)
I then did sing, as then occasion fell:
For love had me forlorne, forlorne of me,
That made me in that desart chose to dwell.[20]
But of my river *Bregogs*[21] love I soong,
Which to the shiny *Mulla* he did beare,
And yet doth beare, and ever will, so long
As water doth within his bancks appeare.   40

Of fellowship (said then that bony[22] Boy)
Record[23] to us that lovely lay againe:
The staie whereof, shall nought these eares annoy,
Who all that *Colin* makes, do covet faine.[24]

Heare then (quoth he) the tenor of my tale,
In sort as I it[25] to that shepheard told:

---

15. a lively young shepherd named Cuddy (not definitely identified).
16. i.e. he spoke what follows between Colin's speeches.
17. hold back your narrative.
18. know.
19. song.
20. i.e. for love had abandoned me, who had abandoned it. (Colin had previously appeared in *The Shepheard's Calendar* and he here refers to his lovelorn state in the eclogue *June* in that work.)
21. The Bregoge river flows around what used to be Spenser's land (hence "my" river) and joins the Awbeg river (Mulla). The Bregoge used to appear to dry up in summertime near the confluence but, in fact, the water flowed underground and rose again farther down its course to join the larger river. Spenser plays upon this natural phenomenon in this fanciful love-story about the two rivers. The Allo (now known as the river Blackwater, and the large river into which all these smaller ones eventually flow) is cast as the husband intended by Old Father Mole for his daughter Mulla. Her lover, Bregoge, outwits Father Mole by intertwining with Mulla before either river gets to the Blackwater. This tale, typical of topographical myths in Renaissance literature, exists in several forms in Irish folk sources.
22. bonny.
23. repeat.
24. i.e. we will not resent the time it takes to tell the story since we love to hear every tale Colin tells.
25. in the way I told it.

No leasing new, nor Grandams fable stale,[26]
But auncient truth confirm'd with credence[27] old.

Old father *Mole* (*Mole* hight that mountain gray
That walls the Northside of *Armulla* dale)[28]   50
He had a daughter fresh as floure of May,
Which gave that name unto that pleasant vale;
Mulla the daughter of old *Mole,* so hight
The Nimph, which of that water course has charge,
That springing out of *Mole,* doth run downe right
To *Buttevant*[29] where spreding forth at large,
It giveth name unto that auncient Cittie,
Which *Kilnemullah* cleped is of old:[30]
Whose ragged ruines breed great ruth[31] and pittie,
To travailers, which it from far behold.   60
Full faine[32] she lov'd, and was belov'd full faine,
Of her owne brother river, *Bregog* hight,
So hight because of this deceitfull traine,[33]
Which he with *Mulla* wrought to win delight.
But her old sire[34] more carefull of her good,[35]
And meaning her much better to preferre,[36]
Did thinke to match her with the neighbour flood,
Which *Allo* hight,[37] Broad water called farre:
And wrought so well with his continuall paine,
That he that river for his daughter wonne: 70
The dowre[38] agreed, the day assigned plaine,
The place appointed where it[39] should be doone.
Nath lesse[40] the Nymph her former liking held;
For love will not be drawne, but must be ledde,

---

26. i.e. no new falsehood or stale traditional tale.
27. trustworthiness.
28. Now known as the vale of the Blackwater.
29. Buttevant, a town in County Cork.
30. Spenser seems to be referring to the ruins of the Franciscan friary at Ballybeg near Buttevant. cleped = called.
31. sorrow.
32. willingly.
33. deceitful stratagem. The name 'Bregog' means deceitful.
34. i.e. Father Mole, the mountain range.
35. well-being.
36. to improve her rank or station – in this case by marriage.
37. so named. The Allo river was also known as the Broadwater; its modern name is the Blackwater. See above note 21.
38. dowry.
39. i.e. the marriage between the two rivers.
40. nevertheless.

And *Bregog* did so well her fancie weld,[41]
That her good will he got her first to wedde.
But for her father sitting still on hie,
Did warily still watch which way she went,
And eke from far observ'd with jealous eie,
Which way his course the wanton *Bregog* bent,   80
Him to deceive for all his watchfull ward,[42]
The wily lover did devise this slight:[43]
First into many parts his streame he shar'd,
That whilest the one was watcht, the other might
Passe unespide[44] to meete her by the way;
And then besides,[45] those little streames so broken
He under ground so closely did convay,
That of their passage doth appeare no token,
Till they into the *Mullaes* water slide.
So secretly did he his love enjoy: 90
Yet not so secret, but it was descried,
And told her father by a shepheards boy.
Who wondrous wroth[46] for that so foule despight,[47]
In great avenge did roll downe from his hill
Huge mightie stones, the which encomber might
His passage, and his water-courses spill.[48]
So of a River, which he was of old,
He none was made,[49] but scattred all to nought,
And lost emong those rocks into him rold,
Did lose his name: so deare his love he bought.[50]   100

from: Epithalamion

Ye learned sisters which have oftentimes[1]
Been to me ayding, others to adorne:

---

41. fasten to himself.
42. care.
43. trick.
44. unseen. See note 21 above.
45. side by side.
46. angry.
47. insult.
48. destroy. Boulders and rocks still obstruct the riverbed.
49. he was a river no more.
50. i.e. this was the high price he paid for his love.

---

1. Spenser wrote this wedding song to celebrate his own marriage to Elizabeth Boyle, an event which took place on 11 June 1594, certainly in Ireland and probably in Cork city.

Whom ye thought worthy of your gracefull rymes,
That even the greatest[2] did not greatly scorne
To heare theyr names sung in your simple layes,[3]
But joyed in theyr prayse;
And when ye list[4] your owne mishaps to mourne,
Which death, or love, or fortunes wreck did rayse,
Your string[5] could soone to sadder tenor turne,
And teach the woods and waters to lament   10
Your dolefull dreriment.[6]
Now lay those sorrowfull complaints aside,
And having all your heads with girland crownd,
Helpe me mine owne loves prayses to resound,
Ne[7] let the same of any be envide:[8]
So Orpheus did for his owne bride,[9]
So I unto my selfe alone will sing,
The woods shall to me answer and my eccho ring . . .

This introductory invocation to the muses is followed by five stanzas which describe, in detail, how the bride is awoken in the morning by muses and nymphs. Then the wedding day itself begins:

Now is my love all ready forth to come,
Let all the virgins[10] therefore well awayt,   20
And ye fresh boyes that tend upon her groome
Prepare your selves; for he is comming strayt.[11]
Set all your things in seemely good aray[12]
Fit for so joyfull day,
The joyfulst day that ever sunne did see.

In its form, the poem is based on the Italian *canzone* and, in its subject matter, Spenser combines traditional classical motifs for a wedding song with details of the Irish world in which the marriage took place. The poem has twenty-four stanzas, apparently representing the twenty-four hours of the wedding day; each stanza, except the final one, ends with an echoing refrain. The poem, which is among the highest poetic achievements of its age, begins with a conventional invocation of the muses of poetry.

2. i.e. rhymes so graceful that even the greatest (Queen Elizabeth) . . .
3. songs.
4. want.
5. The string of harp or lyre. The line means that the muses could also make sad music.
6. dreriment, dismal condition.
7. nor (used throughout the poem).
8. envied.
9. The legendary Greek poet and musician, a symbol of poetic power.
10. the girls attending the bride.
11. immediately.
12. array, order.

Faire Sun, shew forth thy favourable ray,
And let thy lifull[13] heat not fervent[14] be
For feare of burning her sunshyny[15] face,
Her beauty to disgrace.
O fayrest Phœbus,[16] father of the Muse,   30
If ever I did honour thee aright,
Or sing the thing, that mote[17] thy mind delight,
Doe not thy servants simple boone[18] refuse,
But let this day let this one day be mine,
Let all the rest be thine.
Then I thy soverayne prayses loud wil sing,
That all the woods shal answere and theyr eccho ring.

Harke how the Minstrels gin to shrill aloud[19]
Their merry musick that resounds from far,
The pipe, the tabor, and the trembling Croud,[20]   40
That well agree withouten breach or jar.[21]
But most of all the Damzels doe delite,
When they their tymbrels[22] smyte,
And thereunto doe daunce and carrol[23] sweet,
That all the sences they doe ravish quite,
The whyles the boyes run up and downe the street,
Crying aloud with strong confused noyce,
As if it were one voyce.
Hymen ô Hymen, Hymen they doe shout,[24]
That even to the heavens theyr shouting shrill   50
Doth reach, and all the firmament doth fill,
To which the people standing all about,
As in approvance[25] doe thereto applaud

---

13. life-giving.
14. fervent, burning.
15. bright and happy. A weather-beaten complexion was considered far less attractive than one shaded from the sun.
16. god of the sun. (It is more normal for Zeus to be considered the father of the muses.)
17. might.
18. favour.
19. i.e. begin to make loud sounds with . . .
20. Three traditional Irish musical instruments, the pipe (whistle or flute), the drum (perhaps the *bodhrán*) and the crowd or Celtic fiddle.
21. disharmony.
22. tambourines.
23. sing.
24. A ritual chant at Roman weddings – unlikely, in fact, to be what the boys of Cork were shouting as they ran up and down the streets beside the wedding procession.
25. approval.

And loud advaunce her laud,[26]
And evermore they Hymen Hymen sing,
That all the woods them answer and their eccho ring.

Loe where she comes along with portly[27] pace,
Lyke Phoebe[28] from her chamber of the East,
Arysing forth to run her mighty race,
Clad all in white, that seemes[29] a virgin best.   60
So well it her beseemes, that ye would weene[30]
Some angell she had beene.
Her long loose yellow locks lyke golden wyre,[31]
Sprinkled with perle, and perling flowres a tweene,
Doe lyke a golden mantle her attyre,
And being crowned with a girland[32] greene,
Seeme lyke some mayden Queene.
Her modest eyes abashed to behold
So many gazers, as on her do stare,
Upon the lowly ground affixed are,   70
Ne dare lift up her countenance too bold,
But blush to heare her prayses sung so loud,
So farre from being proud.
Nathlesse[33] doe ye still loud her prayses sing,
That all the woods may answer and your eccho ring.

Tell me ye merchants daughters[34] did ye see
So fayre a creature in your towne before?
So sweet, so lovely, and so mild as she,
Adornd with beauties grace and vertues store:
Her goodly eyes lyke Saphyres shining bright,   80
Her forehead yvory[35] white,
Her cheekes lyke apples which the sun hath rudded,
Her lips lyke cherryes charming men to byte,

---

26. praise.
27. stately.
28. The moon goddess, associated with virginity.
29. becomes.
30. think.
31. wire. The lines suggest that the bride's hair is as exquisite as spun gold thread; it is
decorated with pearls and flowers, the flowers being entwined (perling) in the hair.
32. garland.
33. nevertheless, still.
34. i.e. daughters of the shopkeepers of Cork.
35. ivory.

Her brest lyke to a bowle of creame uncrudded,[36]
Her paps[37] lyke lyllies budded,
Her snowie necke lyke to a marble towre,
And all her body like a pallace fayre,
Ascending uppe with many a stately stayre,
To honors seate and chastities sweet bowre.[38]
Why stand ye still ye virgins in amaze,   90
Upon her so to gaze,
Whiles ye forget your former lay to sing,
To which the woods did answer and your eccho ring.

But if ye saw that which no eyes can see,
The inward beautie of her lively spright,[39]
Garnisht with heavenly gifts of high degree,
Much more then would ye wonder at that sight,
And stand astonisht lyke to those which red[40]
Medusaes mazefull[41] head.
There dwels sweet love and constant chastity,   100
Unspotted fayth and comely womanhood,
Regard of honour and mild modesty,
There Vertue raynes as Queene in royal throne,
And giveth lawes alone.
The which the base affections[42] doe obay,
And yeeld theyr services unto her will,
Ne thought of thing uncomely ever may
Thereto approch to tempt her mind to ill.
Had ye once seene these her celestial treasures,
And unrevealed pleasures,   110
Then would ye wonder and her prayses sing,
That all the woods should answer and your eccho ring.

Open the temple gates[43] unto my love,
Open them wide that she may enter in,

36. uncurdled.
37. nipples.
38. i.e. the head (where dwell the higher faculties of reason).
39. spirit, soul.
40. saw.
41. bewildering. Medusa, one of the Gorgons in classical mythology, has snakes instead of hair on her head. Anyone who saw her head would not only be bewildered by it, but turned to stone.
42. lower instincts.
43. i.e. the doors of the church.

And all the postes adorne as doth behove,[44]
And all the pillours[45] deck with girlands trim,
For to recyve[46] this Saynt with honour dew,
That commeth in to you.
With trembling steps and humble reverence,
She commeth in, before th'almighties view: 120
Of her ye virgins learne obedience,
When so ye come into those holy places,
To humble your proud faces;
Bring her up to th'high altar that she may,
The sacred ceremonies there partake,
The which do endlesse matrimony make,
And let the roring Organs loudly play
The prayses of the Lord in lively notes,
The whiles with hollow throates
The Choristers the joyous Antheme sing,   130
That all the woods may answere and their eccho ring.

Behold, whiles she before the altar stands
Hearing the holy priest that to her speakes
And blesseth her with his two happy hands,
How the red roses flush up in her cheekes,
And the pure snow with goodly vermill[47] stayne,
Like crimsin dyde in grayne,[48]
That even th'Angels which continually,
About the sacred Altare doe remaine,
Forget their service[49] and about her fly,   140
Oft peeping in her face, that seemes more fayre,
The more they on it stare.
But her sad[50] eyes still fastened on the ground,
Are governed with goodly modestie,
That suffers not one looke to glaunce awry,
Which may let in a little thought unsownd.[51]
Why blush ye love to give to me your hand,

---

44. i.e. as is proper. The entrance to a church was often decorated with flowers for a
wedding.
45. the pillars in the church.
46. receive.
47. red.
48. = grain, a scarlet dye.
49. i.e. the angels forget their duty, which is to guard the high altar.
50. serious.
51. unsound, inappropriate.

The pledge of all our band?[52]
Sing ye sweet Angels, Alleluya sing,
That all the woods may answere and your eccho ring.   150

Now al is done; bring home the bride againe,
Bring home the triumph of our victory,
Bring home with you the glory of her gaine,[53]
With joyance[54] bring her and with jollity.
Never had man more joyfull day then this,
Whom heaven would heape with blis.
Make feast therefore now all this live long day,
This day for ever to me holy is,
Poure out the wine without restraint or stay,
Poure not by cups, but by the belly full,   160
Poure out to all that wull,[55]
And sprinkle all the postes and wals with wine,
That they may sweat, and drunken be withall.
Crowne ye God Bacchus with a coronall,[56]
And Hymen also crowne with wreathes of vine,
And let the Graces[57] daunce unto the rest;
For they can doo it best:
The whiles the maydens doe their carroll sing,
To which the woods shall answer and theyr eccho ring.

Ring ye the bels, ye young men of the towne,   170
And leave your wonted[58] labors for this day:
This day is holy; doe ye write it downe,
That ye for ever it remember may.
This day the sunne is in his chiefest hight,
With Barnaby the bright,[59]
From whence declining daily by degrees,
He somewhat loseth of his heat and light,
When once the Crab behind his back he sees.[60]

52. the sign of our bond.
53. i.e. the glory of gaining her hand in marriage.
54. joy.
55. want it.
56. i.e. crown Bacchus, the god of wine, with a garland of flowers.
57. The sister goddesses of classical mythology.
58. accustomed.
59. St Barnabas's day, 11 June, was in Spenser's time, at the summer solstice, the longest day of the year.
60. i.e. the constellation Cancer (the crab). As the sun passes through the zodiac (and the days get shorter), it leaves Cancer behind and progresses to Leo.

But for this time it ill ordained was,
To chose[61] the longest day in all the yeare,   180
And shortest night, when longest fitter weare:[62]
Yet never day so long, but late[63] would passe.
Ring ye the bels, to make it weare away,
And bonefiers make all day,[64]
And daunce about them, and about them sing:
That all the woods may answer and your eccho ring.

The next eight stanzas recount the evening and night of the wedding day, and the poem ends with a brief 'envoy', expressing the hope that this poem may be "a goodly ornament" and an "endlesse moniment" to Spenser's love.

from: The Faerie Queene

from: The Mutabilitie Cantos[1] (written before 1699, published 1611)
[Book VII, Canto VI, stanzas 36–55]

. . . Eftsoones[2] the time and place appointed were,
Where all, both heavenly Powers, & earthly wights,[3]

61. have chosen.
62. i.e. it would have been better to hold the wedding at a time of year when the nights were longer.
63. at last.
64. Bonfires were traditional at midsummer, and at weddings.

1. Although it is one of the longest poems in English, *The Faerie Queene*, as we have it today, is only just over half of the poem originally projected by Spenser. The six completed books are an enormous pageant of heroic and fairy tales woven around the adventures of simple, allegorical figures which represent Christian virtues. A belief in ultimately stable moral, political and religious values seems to underpin each of the six books. But in the short 'Mutability Cantos', generally printed as fragments of an otherwise lost seventh book, the reader is presented with a challenge different from that in the rest of the book. The theme of the Mutability Cantos is change, and they explore the very Renaissance paradox that man needs to accept both the idea of permanent perfection and the reality of often casual change and decay.

The main event of the Mutability Cantos is a grand trial at which the claims of the present world order – as presented by the existing gods – are challenged by a new, upstart goddess named Mutability, who wishes to supplant Jove as chief of the heavenly hierarchy. In the passage below, Spenser sets the scene for this contest in the mountains above his estate in County Cork, creating, as it were, an Irish Olympus. It is significant that he chose Ireland – a wild and dangerous place in which, Elizabethans believed, nothing was certain – for a contest between settled, civilised values as represented by the existing gods, and the instability represented by Mutability. As Spenser himself was to find out with a vengeance, the area around Kilcolman was subject to violent change, and he and his family were burned out of Kilcolman during the Munster rising of 1598.

2. Soon afterwards.
3. creatures.

89

Before great Natures presence[4] should appeare,
For triall of their Titles and best Rights:
That was, to weet,[5] upon the highest hights
Of *Arlo-hill*[6] (Who knowes not *Arlo-hill*?)
That is the highest head (in all mens sights)
Of my old father *Mole*,[7] whom Shepheards quill
Renowned hath with hymnes fit for a rurall skill.

And, were it not ill fitting for this file,[8]   10
To sing of hilles & woods, mongst warres & Knights,[9]
I would abate the sternenesse of my stile,
Mongst these sterne stounds[10] to mingle soft delights;
And tell how *Arlo* through *Dianaes* spights[11]
(Beeing of old the best and fairest Hill
That was in all this holy-Islands hights)[12]
Was made the most unpleasant, and most ill.
Meane while, ô *Clio*, lend *Calliope*[13] thy quill.

Whylome,[14] when *IRELAND* florished in fame
Of wealths and goodnesse, far above the rest   20
Of all that beare the *British* Islands name,
The Gods then us'd (for pleasure and for rest)
Oft to resort there-to, when seem'd them best:
But none of all there-in more pleasure found,
Then *Cynthia*; that is soveraine Queene profest[15]
Of woods and forrests, which therein abound,
Sprinkled with wholsom waters, more than most on ground.[16]

But mongst them all, as fittest for her game,[17]
Either for chace of beasts with hound or boawe,

---

4. Nature is the goddess who will decide whether Mutability should reign in heaven or not.
5. in fact.
6. Galtymore, the highest peak in the mountain ranges near Spenser's estate at Kilcolman, County Cork.
7. Spenser gave the name 'Old Father Mole' to the Ballyhoura and Galtee mountain ranges.
8. tale.
9. The main subjects of *The Faerie Queene* have been chivalry and feats of valour.
10. clashes.
11. spights = spite. Diana, goddess of hunting and forests, is also known as Cynthia in the poem.
12. i.e. that was previously the best and most beautiful hill in this holy island (Ireland) . . .
13. The muses of history and epic poetry, respectively.
14. In former times.
15. acknowledged. Cynthia = Diana.
16. ground = earth.
17. recreation.

Or for to shroude in shade from *Phoebus* flame,[18]   30
Or bathe in fountaines that doe freshly flowe,
Or from high hilles, or from the dales belowe,
She chose this *Arlo*; where shee did resort
With all her Nymphes enranged on a rowe,
With whom the woody Gods did oft consort:
For, with the Nymphes, the Satyres love to play & sport.[19]

Amongst the which, there was a Nymph that hight[20]
Molanna;[21] daughter of old father *Mole*,
And sister unto *Mulla*,[22] faire and bright:
Unto whose bed false *Bregog*[23] whylome stole,   40
That Shepheard *Colin* dearely did condole,[24]
And made her lucklesse loves well knowne to be.
But this *Molanna*, were she not so shole,[25]
Were no lesse faire and beautifull than shee:
Yet as she is, a fairer flood[26] may no man see.

For, first, she springs out of two marble Rocks,
On which, a grove of Oakes high mounted growes,
That as a girlond[27] seemes to deck the locks
Of som faire Bride, brought forth with pompous showes
Out of her bowre, that many flowers strowes:[28]   50
So, through the flowry Dales she tumbling downe,
Through many woods, and shady coverts flowes
(That on each side her silver channell crowne)
Till to the Plaine she come, whose Valleyes shee doth drowne.

In her sweet streames, *Diana* used oft
(After her sweatie chace and toilesome play)

18. from the heat of the sun.
19. Diana's nymphs are the (classical, mythological) goddesses of streams and trees, and the 'woody Gods' are satyrs, the goat-footed, half-human gods of the woods: satyrs were said to be addicted to wine and all sensual pleasures.
20. was named.
21. This is the name Spenser gave to the Behenna river, a shallow rocky river which rises in the mountains above Kilcolman Castle.
22. The Awbeg river.
23. Spenser is referring to the myth of the rivers told in *Colin Clouts Come Home Againe*. See note 21 to that poem above. whylome = whilom = once upon a time.
24. earnestly lamented.
25. shallow.
26. river.
27. garland.
28. brought forth from her flower-strewn bower with stately ceremonies.

To bathe her selfe; and after, on the soft
And downy grasse, her dainty limbes to lay
In covert[29] shade, where none behold her may:
For, much she hated sight of living eye.   60
Foolish God *Faunus*,[30] though full many a day
He saw her clad, yet longed foolishly
To see her naked mongst her Nymphes in privity.[31]

No way he found to compasse[32] his desire,
But to corrupt *Molanna*, this her maid,
Her to discover for some secret hire:[33]
So, her with flattering words he first assaid;[34]
And after, pleasing gifts for her purvaid,[35]
Queene-apples,[36] and red Cherries from the tree,
With which he her allured and betraid,   70
To tell what time he might her Lady see
When she her selfe did bathe, that he might secret[37] bee.

There-to hee promist, if shee would him pleasure
With this small boone, to quit[38] her with a better;
To weet,[39] that where-as shee had out of measure
Long lov'd the *Fanchin*, who by nought did set her,[40]
That he would undertake, for this to get her
To be his Loue, and of[41] him liked well:
Besides all which, he vow'd to be her debter
For many moe good turnes then he would tell;   80
The least of which, this little pleasure should excell.

The simple maid did yield to him anone;[42]
And eft him placed where he close might view

---

29. hidden.
30. An invented god (cf. 'faun') who, in this reworking of the classical story of Diana and Actæon, plays the part of Actæon.
31. privacy.
32. accomplish.
33. to reveal her (Diana), for some secret bribe.
34. tried.
35. brought her pleasing gifts.
36. crabapples.
37. hidden.
38. repay.
39. that is.
40. i.e. since, for a long time, she had been deeply in love with the river Funsheon, who cared nothing for her . . .
41. by.
42. in due course.

That never any saw, save onely one;[43]
Who, for his hire to so foole-hardy dew,
Was of his hounds devour'd in Hunters hew.[44]
Tho, as her manner was on sunny day,
Diana, with her Nymphes about her, drew
To this sweet spring; where, doffing[45] her array,
She bath'd her lovely limbes, for *Jove* a likely pray.[46]   90

There *Faunus* saw that pleased much his eye,
And made his hart to tickle in his brest,
That for great joy of some-what[47] he did spy,
He could him not containe in silent rest;
But breaking forth in laughter, loud profest
His foolish thought. O foolish *Faune* indeed,
That couldst not hold thy selfe so hidden blest,
But wouldest needs thine owne conceit areed.[48]
Babblers unworthy been of so divine a meed.[49]

The Goddesse, all abashed[50] with that noise,   100
In haste forth started from the guilty brooke;
And running straight where-as she heard his voice,
Enclos'd the bush about, and there him tooke,
Like darred Larke;[51] not daring up to looke
On her whose sight before so much he sought.
Thence, forth they drew him by the hornes, & shooke
Nigh all to peeces, that they left him nought;
And then into the open light they forth him brought.

Like as an huswife,[52] that with busie care
Thinks of her Dairie to make wondrous gaine,[53]   110

43. and immediately placed him where he might secretly view that which only one creature had ever seen before – i.e. Diana naked. The one creature who had previously seen this sight was Actæon, who, as a punishment, was turned into a stag, pursued by his own hunting dogs and devoured.
44. hue, i.e. pursuing him with the cries of hunting dogs.
45. taking off.
46. According to classical mythology, Jove (chief of the gods) was inclined to chase and ravish maidens of all kinds, earthly or heavenly, if he caught sight of them.
47. something.
48. i.e. declare what you were thinking.
49. Babblers are unworthy of so divine a reward.
50. disconcerted.
51. i.e. cast her hunting-net over the bush and caught him, like a cowering lark . . .
52. housewife.
53. profit.

Finding where-as some wicked beast unware
That breakes into her Dayr'house, there doth draine
Her creaming pannes, and frustrate all her paine;[54]
Hath in some snare or gin[55] set close behind,
Entrapped him, and caught into her traine,[56]
Then thinkes what punishment were best assign'd,
And thousand deathes deviseth in her vengefull mind:

So did *Diana* and her maydens all
Use silly *Faunus*, now within their baile:[57]
They mocke and scorne him, and him foule miscall;[58]   120
Some by the nose him pluckt, some by the taile,
And by his goatish beard some did him haile:[59]
Yet he (poore soule) with patience all did beare;
For, nought against their wils might countervaile:[60]
Ne ought he said what ever he did heare;
But hanging downe his head, did like a Mome[61] appeare.

At length, when they had flouted him their fill,
They gan to cast[62] what penaunce him to give.
Some would have gelt him, but that same would spill
The Wood-gods breed, which must for ever live:[63]   130
Others would through the river him have drive,[64]
And ducked deepe: but that seem'd penaunce light;
But most agreed and did this sentence give,
Him in Deares skin to clad; & in that plight,
To hunt him with their hounds, him selfe save how hee might.

But *Cynthia's* selfe, more angry then the rest,
Thought not enough, to punish him in sport,
And of her shame to make a gamesome jest;
But gan examine him in straighter sort,[65]

54. effort (to make butter).
55. trap.
56. snare.
57. custody, charge.
58. reviled him.
59. pull.
60. reciprocate.
61. fool.
62. deliberate.
63. i.e. some wanted to castrate him, except that this would destroy the race of wood gods, who must live for ever.
64. driven.
65. more strictly.

Which of her Nymphes, or other close consort,   140
Him thither brought, and her to him betraid?
He, much affeard, to her confessed short,
That 'twas *Molanna* which her so bewraid.[66]
Then all attonce their hands upon *Molanna* laid.

But him (according as they had decreed)
With a Deeres-skin they covered, and then chast
With all their hounds that after him did speed;
But he more speedy, from them fled more fast
Then any Deere: so sore him dread aghast.[67]
They after follow'd all with shrill out-cry,   150
Shouting as they the heavens would have brast:[68]
That all the woods and dales where he did flie,
Did ring againe, and loud reeccho to the skie.

So they him follow'd till they weary were;
When, back returning to *Molann'* againe,
They, by commaund'ment of *Diana*, there
Her whelm'd with stones.[69] Yet *Faunus* (for her paine)[70]
Of her beloved *Fanchin* did obtaine,
That her he would receive unto his bed.
So now her waves passe through a pleasant Plaine,   160
Till with the *Fanchin* she her selfe doe wed,
And (both combin'd) themselves in one faire river spred.[71]

Nath'lesse, *Diana*, full of indignation,
Thence-forth abandond her delicious brooke;
In whose sweet streame, before that bad occasion,
So much delight to bathe her limbes she tooke:
Ne onely her, but also quite forsooke
All those faire forrests about *Arlo* hid,
And all that Mountaine, which doth over-looke
The richest champian that may else be rid,[72]   170
And the faire *Shure*,[73] in which are thousand Salmons bred.

66. betrayed.
67. i.e. so terribly did they frighten him.
68. burst.
69. overwhelmed her with stones. The river is still shallow and rocky.
70. trouble.
71. The rivers mentioned all become part of the river Blackwater.
72. the richest countryside which might, otherwise, be cleared.
73. The river Suir.

Them all, and all that she so deare did way,[74]
Thence-forth she left; and parting from the place,
There-on an heavy haplesse curse did lay,
To weet, that Wolves, where she was wont to space,[75]
Should harbour'd be, and all those Woods deface,
And Thieves should rob and spoile that Coast[76] around.
Since which, those Woods, and all that goodly Chase,[77]
Doth to this day with Wolves and Thieves abound:
Which too-too true that lands in-dwellers[78] since have found.[79]   180

74. weigh, i.e. esteem.
75. roam.
76. land.
77. hunting-ground.
78. inhabitants.
79. This stanza reflects the view of Spenser and other English planters that it was almost impossible for them to settle the beautiful and potentially rich Irish countryside while savage beasts and the native Irish remained.

SIR JOHN HARINGTON
(1561–**1599**–1612)

Sir John Harington, Queen Elizabeth's godson and the translator of Ariosto's *Orlando Furioso*
into English heroic verse, served as a commander of horse in the army which came to Ireland
with the Earl of Essex in 1599. In his account of his time in Ireland (in *Nugæ Antiquæ*, ed.
Henry Harington, 2 vols [London, 1769]), Harington showed more generosity and sympathy
for the people of Ireland than did most of his English contemporaries; 'I think my very genius
doth, in a sort, lead me to that country,' he wrote, though as the poem which follows shows, he
clearly found the life of a soldier in Ireland less attractive than that of a courtier in England.

Of the warres in Ireland

I prais'd the speech,[1] but cannot now abide it,
That warre is sweet to those that have not try'd it,
For I have prov'd it now, and plainly see't
It is so sweet, it maketh all things sweet.
At home, Canarie wine and Greek grow lothsome:
Here milk is nectar; water tasteth toothsome.
There without baked, rost, boyl'd, it has no cheere:
Bisket we like, and Bonny Clabo[2] here.
There we complaine of one rare roasted chick:[3]
Here viler meat worse cook't ne're makes me sick.   10
At home in silken sparvers,[4] beds of downe
We scant can rest, but still tosse up and downe:
Here we can sleep, a saddle to our pillow,
A hedge the curtaine, canopy a willow,
There if a child but cry, O what a spite!
Here we can brook three 'larms[5] in one night.
There homely rooms must be perfum'd with roses:
Here match[6] and powder ne're offende our noses:
There from a storme of raine we run like pullets:
Here we stand fast against a showre of bullets.   20
Lo then, how greatly their opinions erre,
That think there is no great delight in warre.
    But yet for this (sweet warre) Ile be thy debtor,
    I shall for ever love my home the better.

1. i.e. the speech of those who talk of war.
2. Bonnyclabber (Ir. *bainne clabair*), thick, naturally soured milk, a common food in
   Elizabethan Ireland.
3. i.e. an under-cooked chicken.
4. canopies at the top of a tester or four-posted bed.
5. put up with three alarms . . .
6. short ropes dipped in melted sulphur, used to fire cannons.

J.G.E. [ANTHONY NIXON?]
(1600)

This is one of the most interesting of the poems about the Irish wars written in England at the time of the rebellion (1596–1603) of Hugh O'Neill, second Earl of Tyrone (1540?–1616). In the single printed copy which survives, the author is given as 'J.G.E.', but a manuscript dated 1602 which has recently come to light is in the hand of Anthony Nixon, a prolific versifier of the time, who might well be the actual author.[1] The poem vividly presents the English view of Ireland and the Irish rebels and suggests, through energetic language and unrestrained imagery, that their treachery threatens civilisation itself.

from: England's Hope against Irish Hate

The *Serpents* sly insinuating course,[2]
Is farre below most opposite to sight;[3]
His practize deadly, his desier worse:
The fairest greene conceales his hidden spight,
Nothing lesse feared than to shunne his force:[4]
Yet nothing sooner doth beget mishappe,
    For worst insnares the suddaine unseene trappe.

Such are those creeping *Machavils*[5] of late,
Those eves-dropping Heralts[6] listning spies,
That come to prye into our Countries state;   10
To hide their Treason, Vizards[7] they devize,
That so they may our purposes relate:[8]
With us they walke, they laugh; with us they eate
    Yet in their hartes hath *Judas* ta'ne his seate.

But if their falsehood, *Trueth* hath open laide,
If younger wits, their elder shifts[9] have seene:

---

1. I am grateful to Andrew Zurcher for this information and for invaluable help in deciphering this text.
2. The poem begins by attacking Irish 'spies' in England.
3. i.e. far lower than one expects to see.
4. Nothing is less feared (i.e. more attractive) than to keep away from the serpent's power.
5. Machiavells – i.e. examples of political cunning.
6. messengers.
7. masks, disguises.
8. i.e. so that they may tell others [catholics in general, and those in Spain, France and Italy in particular] what our intentions are.
9. stratagems, subterfuges.

If their close meeching[10] providence displaide,
And all their councels have confounded been:
If Trecherie have Treasons selfe betraide,
And not our selves do laugh at them alone,   20
    If all miscarry: Why not then *Terone*?[11]

What venome beast compared to the Toade,
Doth better picture malice of the minde?
Hee stripes so long his rancor to unloade,
As coveting an equall pitch to finde
With him whose cloven hoofe is scarce so broade;
In puft presumptuous humor glowting sitts,
    Untill his carcas quite in sunder splitts.[12]

Such is the broody monster *Rome* containes,[13]
His eyes he straines untill they sparkle fire: 30
His handes are fatted with continuall gaines:
Each howre against the annoynted[14] hee conspires;
His hart a thousand stratagems retaines,
And downe his throat he needs wil swallow *Spaine*
    With *Fraunce* and *Italy*,[15] to worke our paine.

But if this dyet have distemper wrought,[16]
If this huge glutton surfettor on hate,
In striving to be greater than he ought
Hath still been crost with death, a boading fate,
That his disseevered members fly about,   40
And some of them unto our gates ar blowne,
    For Crowes to feed on:[17] Why not then *Terone*?

---

10. a variant of 'mitching'; i.e. skulking, lurking out of sight.
11. i.e. if we have seen through these infiltrators and their treason, why can not Tyrone be defeated?
12. A rough paraphrase of this stanza would be: What venomous beast gives a better picture of mental maliciousness than the toad? When he wants to release his poison, he strives so long at it that he seems to want to equal the devil [the one with the narrow cloven hoof]; he sits gloating, puffed up with presumption until his body splits open [as he voids his poison].
13. i.e. the Pope.
14. i.e. the anointed monarch of England and Ireland, Queen Elizabeth I.
15. The three catholic countries most feared in England.
16. i.e. has made him ill.
17. i.e. if the Pope, in trying to increase his dominions, has been defeated and his power has been scattered (so that crows can peck at his body), why can this not happen to Tyrone too?

The Shepheards dread, the silly flockes annoy,
The ravening Woolfe, is ever knowne to be;[18]
His thirsty stomacke slaughter must injoy,
And naught but blood allayes his tyrannie:
The more he hath, the more he will destroy,
Nor is it soveraintie, but beastiall lust:
    For who knowes not the sillie *Lambe* is just?[19]

Such[20] is the sterne *Iberian Monarchy*,   50
Whose fingers dipt in ill effused gore
And hartes ybath'd in neighbor Tyranny,[21]
Lift up their snowts into the West for more,
And nought may staunch their bloody penury,
But wrongfull massacre of Gods elect,
    The more their proude ambition to detect.

But if the sinnewes of their strong assaultes,
The just revenger[22] have in sunder crackt:
If so their huge *Armados* in the vault's
Of vast *Oceans* kingdome have been wrackt,[23]   60
Leaving the world to descant on their faults:
If all their boasting threates away were blowne,
    And they supprest: then why not now *TERONE*?. . .

If *Rory Oge*,[24] a pillor of that crew
Of glib-pate Karne, and breechles pedigree,[25]
Presuming of a Scepter to ensue[26]
Fell headlong into cureles[27] miserie,
Cursing the time of treading thus awry,

---

18. i.e. The ravening wolf is always known to be the dread of shepherds and the molester of defenceless flocks . . .
19. i.e. the defenceless lamb is innocent?
20. i.e. like a wolf.
21. Probably a reference to the Spanish invasion of Portugal in 1581.
22. Presumably the English navy under Sir Francis Drake.
23. The reference is to the loss of the ships of the Spanish Armada in 1588.
24. Rory Oge O'More (Ruaidhrí Óg ua Mórdha) (*d.* 1578), a scion of an important Irish sept who had considerable success in various attacks against the English in the 1560s and 1570s. The stanza refers to an occasion in December 1575 when Rory Oge submitted to Sir Henry Sidney in the cathedral in Kilkenny.
25. of kerne (Irish foot soldiers) with glibs (long locks of hair) on their heads and with ancestors who wore no breeches . . . (i.e. armed, uncivilised Irishmen)
26. to succeed to a sceptre, i.e. become a king.
27. irremediable.

And with his blood powrde foorth repentant teares,
  To shew his sorrow, for mispence[28] of yeares: 70

If *Feaghe Mackhugh*[29] an other out-law carle,
Stampt of the same rebellious up-start moulde
With those, against the regall guidance gnarle,
Not enterprizing what they should, but would,
Receav'd his hire, for being over bould,
And for adulterat Nobilitie,
  Was taught the studie of Astronomie:[30]

If sterne *Mackshaw*[31] irregular and bloody,
That likewise gave us base[32] upon the bogges,
In treasons pursute, obstinate and moody,   80
Trayning with him a number such like dogges,
Performd at last his currish obsequie,[33]
A halter destin'd to his mankind necke,
  That gave the lusty gamester mate and checke:[34]

If great *Oneale*,[35] sole great in his abuse,
Rich in the want of true humilitie,
A pigmie punie for the spirits infuse,
And *Irus*[36] poore for his fidelitie,
Was forst to see his naked Trecherie,
And stealing foorth to finde the Figtree-shade,[37]   90
  Could no way shrowd th'offence his soule had made:

28. the misspending of . . .
29. Fiach McHugh was leader of a band of kerne based in County Wicklow, and a regular harrier of English settlers and forces. After his death, his head was pickled and sent to Queen Elizabeth before being spiked and displayed, like that of other traitors.
30. This reference is obscure, but may be a grim joke about those whose heads are spiked being able to study the stars.
31. Mackshaw is obscure: however, it may be a misreading by a copyist or compositor of 'Macshane', in which case the reference may be to one of the O'Neill sept, many of whose leaders were called Shane. In Ulster and Louth, the MacShanes were a branch of the O'Neills.
32. A reference to an old chasing and catching game called 'base' or 'prisoner's base'.
33. funeral rites.
34. A reference to the 'checkmate', a position which forces the end of a game of chess.
35. Shane O'Neill (1530–67). The reference later in the stanza is to the famous scene which took place in 1562 when Shane O'Neill, in London to sue for pardon for having rebelled against Queen Elizabeth and to plead for his rights of inheritance, appeared before her and the court in the full regalia of an Irish chieftain.
36. as poor as Irus, a beggar in Homer's *Odyssey*.
37. References to nakedness and fig trees suggest that O'Neill's crime is as great as that of Adam and Eve.

If *Desmond*,[38] that Hereditary Lord,
Like *Naball*[39] vaunting his large Seigniorie,
Thousandes depending on his ill drawne Sword,
Payde dearely for his damned perjurie,
His House attaint with lasting infamie,
And his cropt head advanct' in deathes pale throne,
    For men to gaze at:[40] Why not then *Terone*?

If Deitie the righteous cause upholde,[41]
And wrong be still the Jewell of his hate: 100
If band coale blacke, their Princes love have solde,
And blest that sticke unto their countries state:[42]
If death the one doe never subjugate,
But spight of Destinie, his fame shall flourish,
    Where as the other eternally shall perish:

If Traytors though immur'd in walles of Brasse,
And lockt in Armour of the strongest proofe,
In courage still, are brittle as the Glasse,
Their conscience telling how they keepe aloofe:[43]
If they are but a bubble, smoake, a puffe,   110
Afrayde to looke upon the rysing Sunne,
    And dreading more, when he his course hath runne:

If every scowlyng cloud aloft doth glaunce,[44]
And some times but the shadow of a *Tree*,[45]
Make them[46] conjecture some suddaine wrackfull[47] chaunce,

---

38. Gerald Fitzgerald, Earl of Desmond (*d.* 1583), fierce leader of resistance against the English during the Desmond rebellions of the 1570s and early 1580s, but also a famous foe to other Irish chieftains.
39. Nabal was a very rich man; see I Samuel 25. 3.
40. After his death, the Earl of Desmond's head was sent to Queen Elizabeth in London before being impaled over London Bridge with those of others who had defied her.
41. The next three stanzas assert that, since good triumphs over evil, Tyrone's defeat can be confidently foreseen.
42. If the band who have sold their prince's love are coal black, and those who have been loyal to their country's rulers are blessed . . .
43. i.e. their courage no longer active, are as fragile as glass, with their conscience telling them to keep themselves aloof . . .
44. glances off them, i.e. they are affected by every passing dark cloud . . .
45. i.e. which reminds them of the gallows.
46. i.e. the frightened traitors who are the subject of these stanzas.
47. disastrous.

Leading their senses to an extasie:[48]
If multitudes and many handes they bee,
But hartes to guide those handes but few or none:
    Who sees not then the downe-fall of *Terone*?

A Traitors Cognizaunce to know him by[49]   120
Are his leawd[50] deedes, and successe therein;
To finde them such, peruse their villany,
Unrippe the fardle[51] of their mouldy sin,
Describe the puddle they do wallow in,
The haynous theftes, the massacres of ruth,[52]
    Wherein they have bin nouzled from their youth.

As they are rude, and strange in their attyre,[53]
Portrayted in an Anticke fashion,
So all their dispositions, all desire,
Bewrayes[54] a crooked generation,   130
Uncivill in their first creation:
Each channell begger[55] needs[56] will be a Lord,
    Although his honors purchace be a cord.

Those civill hartes that stoope to just commaund,
Allow Religion, and imbrace their God,
They[57] seriously with all their might withstand,
Afflicting them with warres deepe wounding rod,
Accounting still the number to be od,
Untill such Subjectes they have overthrowne,
    As are unfaigned friendes unto the Crowne.   140

---

48. state of frenzy.
49. i.e. you can know a traitor by . . .
50. lewd = wicked.
51. bundle.
52. pity, compassion; i.e. *either* pitiless massacres (of people) *or* 'they have been nuzzled from their youth [like pigs] in a culture devoid of compassion'.
53. These stanzas are heavily influenced by (and sometimes quote directly from) the text of John Derricke's *The Image of Irelande* (see pp. 59–64).
54. Betrays.
55. i.e each beggar in the gutter thinks he should be a lord.
56. text reads 'needy', clearly a compositor's error.
57. i.e. the rebels.

Banquets wherein their appetites may broach
The crymsen veynes of kinne,[58] to quench their thirst,
In rage they wrecke[59] not Natures neare approach;
Who is the last, appeareth to be first[60]
If he can glory most of deedes accurst:
All their delight is generall annoy,
    And by most harmes acrues theire greatest joy.

Fruite Fieldes ore-runne, and stately Cities burning,
Order disordered, Justice in the wayne,[61]
The current of sweete *Peace*, to discord turning,   150
Women lamenting, Children cryes in vayne,
Where ere is got, accounted honest gayne,
Blasphemie to God, to Men a scandall,
    This *Irish* Kerne allowes, else they condemne all.

Their will submits not to their Princes will.
Obedience is a word, they never heard:
Their hope is for to be magnifide for ill.
The Law's a chastitie, a taske too hard.
Prayer, and all good exercise, is bard:[62]
And sooner they will lift a hand to kill,   160
    Than once intreat remission of that ill . . .

Obedience Joynes: Disorder seperates.
Obedience pitties: but Disorder scornes.
Obedience plantes vineyardes of sweete Grapes:
Disorder[63] planted with sharpe pricking Thornes,
This many cut-throate Ministers subbornes,
That styrres direct *Astras* golden Helme,[64]
    And makes a peacefull want, excluding Realme.

---

58. kine, cattle. The description of the feasting echoes that in Derricke. The sentence makes more sense if the phrase 'They take part in' is inserted before 'Banquets'.
59. wrecke = reck, to take heed of. i.e. Full of rage, they do not heed the natural order near them . . .
60. cf. Derricke's complaint that due hierarchy was not observed in the seating arrangements at an Irish feast.
61. in decline.
62. barred.
63. i.e. Those of disorder are planted with . . .
64. i.e. That (disorder) immediately turns the golden helm of justice, and brings about a lack of peace, preventing the establishment of good government. In Greek mythology, Astræa, a daughter of Jupiter, was goddess of justice.

Yet these blind reprobates, *Megara*'s brats,[65]
These Safforne[66] shirts, these party-pleited Jackes,[67]   170
These wod[68] borne Savages, these dunghill Gnats,
Had rather beare war-armour on their backes,
(So they may practise rapes, and tru-mens wrackes)
Than freely take fayre Mercy by the hand,
 To glad themselves, and dignifie their land.

But if the end of Theft be Jebbet-capering,[69]
Or if the Scorpion have a glosing[70] face,
Yet in her tayle conceale a deadly sting,
If Judgement do a while give Ryot place,
And in the end, pay home[71] with deepe disgrace,   180
If Treasons period be confusion,
 Quelling the proudest: Why not then *Terone*?

The valiant hand of *ESSEX*[72] honored line,
Already once displayde great *Mars* his Banner,
Ringing the snowtes of these rebellious Swine
Within their Confines, teaching them the manner
Of mylde obedience, humbly to surrender
Their necks to yoak,[73] though fircely they withstood
 And know the penalty of sheddyng blood.

A Vollume would but serve a readyer Pen,   190
Than my slow feathered *Muse,* to celebrate
The golden Trophies were erected then,
When that renowned Knight uphelde the state,
Sir HENRY SIDNEY[74] gratious by his fate;

---

65. According to Greek legend, Heracles rescued his wife Megara from rape, but afterwards, in a fit of delirium, killed her and her three children.
66. = saffron. The Irish were said to dye their shirts in saffron to discourage lice.
67. knaves. 'Party-pleated' is obscure but may mean 'double-sided' or treacherous.
68. = wood, again emphasising the contrast between settled, civil people who live in towns and outlaws who live in the woods.
69. gibbet-capering, hanging.
70. = glozing, flattering or deceitful.
71. The image is of pulling in an anchor rope, and the line means 'haul in the rope' (which has allowed this licence). In the next line, 'period' = conclusion.
72. Walter Devereux, first Earl of Essex (1541–76), renowned for savagery and treachery during his Irish campaigns.
73. yoke.
74. Sir Henry Sidney (1529–86), three times lord deputy of Ireland.

A throng of Rebels to his mercy crowched,
    And who refus'd, the scaffold dead avouched.[75]

The Bogges yet tremble, and the leaved Trees
Shake their high branches in memoriall
Of his sharpe censure, and severe decrees.
The warlike *GRAY*,[76] whose actions Tragicall,   200
Did likewyse curbe their mindes Imperiall,
Gives document; *Fitzwilliams*,[77] and the rest,
    In those proceedinges ever highly blest.

Prevaylde they then? Our quarrell's still the same,
Our wrong no lesse; nay rightly understood,
Who sees not merite of farre greatere blame,
By lavish late expence of English blood;
This joyned with th'abuse of Traytor-hood,
Incites revenge, deafes heaven with clamorous cryes,
    Till they goe downe, and we in conquest rise.   210

For this vile ribble rabble up-start crew,
Mis-led by Treasons treacherous commaunde,
And that rebellion teacher, that late drew
His Countrey gainst their head to lift up hand,
Will know what 'tis to dwell in warres false band,
And will with cause cry woe, woe, one by one:
    Woe to thee that misled'st us: woe *Terone*.

Fall then, thou worker of such misery,
Thou base abuser of sunshyning favours:
Fall, thou untimely-borne *Apanthropy*,[78]   220
Stiflying thy Countrey with ill smelling savours:
Never mayst thou have good successe in warres,
That guerdonst mylde aspecting Majestie[79]
    With such sanguinolent[80] hatefull villanie.

---

75. guaranteed.
76. Arthur Grey, fourteenth Lord Grey de Wilton (1536–93), lord deputy of Ireland 1580–82; the 'action tragicall' to which the poet refers is presumably the notorious massacre at Smerwick, for which Grey was responsible.
77. Sir William Fitzwilliam (1526–99), lord deputy of Ireland 1572–5. Gives document = gives instruction.
78. a form of melancholy characterised by a dislike of society (*OED*).
79. that rewards mild-looking majesty.
80. bloodthirsty, tinged with blood.

CONCLUSION

Fall then ingratitude; decline Terone,
That tearst thy Countrey with unnaturall fanges,
Hoping to wound the whole, by wounding one;
But feele thy body first deathes lingering panges,
And sound warres last retreat with thy last grone:
So begges my soule; so all true subjectes pray,   230
   Expecting howerly thy funerall day.

GERVASE MARKHAM
(1568-**1601**-1637)

Gervase Markham, who was born in Nottinghamshire, started life as a soldier, serving in the Low Countries and Ireland during the 1590s. After this, he turned to writing and soon proved to be one of the most prolific writers of his age. His best-known works are on horses and horsemanship, but he also wrote on agriculture, animal husbandry, household matters, horticulture, angling, fowling, hawking and hunting as well as on warfare. He wrote a considerable quantity of verse, including sonnets and religious verse as well as several substantial translations from Italian, and some plays. In addition – like Richard Bellings – Markham wrote a continuation for Sir Philip Sidney's unfinished *Arcadia*. Markham was so prolific a writer and so adept at recycling his own material in books of apparently different titles that, in 1617, the London booksellers made him sign an undertaking not to write any more books on diseases of horses or cattle.

Soon after he returned from military service in Ireland (where he had held a captaincy under the Earl of Essex), Markham wrote a long, rambling poem about Ireland entitled 'The Newe Metamorphosis'. An assortment of mythological figures moves through this multifaceted, allegorical text, and various elements of Irish history and topography undergo complex changes. The poem is so verbose and its plot so tortuous that it has proved almost impossible to make coherent extracts for this anthology. However, two short passages are printed below, the first of which comes at the moment when Apollo, who is a horse at this point in the story, is transporting a goddess called Calvina to Ireland so that she can establish the town of Galway. Apollo has a vision of a utopian Ireland.

from: The Newe Metamorphosis

> . . . Together let us pass
> Into the bordering land of Bernia,
> There to the kingdom of Connaught,
> Which opposite doth lie, on th'other side
> The sea. No hissing serpent there doth bide,
> No toad, nor spider, adder, nor yet snake,
> No stinging venom'd thing may there partake
> The sweets and pleasures of that happy soil.
> There they do live without tare[1] or toil:
> They neither plant nor sow, nor till the ground,   10
> Nor with a hedge their own encompass round.
> All things are common: there they nothing want;
> They feel no penury or pinching scant . . .

1. any harmful or noxious plant.

108

However, such a vision of perfection is soon shattered and much of Markham's poem describes a more violent and brutal Ireland. The Irish kern or fighting man aroused his particular ire, and, in an extended episode in the poem, Markham imagines that the Irish kern had originally been the inhabitants of a town called Kerne, a place of such wickedness that it was no better than an Irish Sodom. For its licentiousness, the town had been submerged beneath the waters of Lough Erne, and the town's inhabitants had been metamorphosed into wolves. In Markham's poem, however, Irish wolves have the ability to resume human shape and, as 'kern', to prey on the English inhabitants of Ireland again.

> The kerns sprung from this prodigious brood
> Are still as lewd as when their city stood.
> Fraught with all vice, replete with villainy,
> They still rebel and that most treacherously.
> Like brutish Indians these wild Irish live;
> Their quiet neighbours they delight to grieve.
> Cruel and bloody, barbarous and rude,   20
> Dire vengeance at their heels hath them pursued.
> They are the savagest of all the nation;
> Amongst them out I made my peregrination,
> Where many wicked customs I did see
> Such as all honest hearts I hope will flee . . .

RALPH BIRCHENSA
(*fl*.**1602**)

Nothing is known of Ralph Birchensa, whose only recorded work is the long, vitriolic, anti-Irish poem he wrote to celebrate the English victory at Kinsale. The family of Burchinshaw, Burchinsa, Byrchinshaw or Byrchinsa was Welsh, and Ralph Birchensa probably came to Dublin as a government official from Wales in the late sixteenth century. A musician called John Birchensa (*fl*. 1664–71), who lived in the household of the Earl of Kildare in Dublin in his youth, may have been his son. Birchensa's poem shows considerable first-hand experience of the native Irish, but no sympathy for them at all. He presents the Irish 'rebels' as worse than pagans, as traitors to Christ, as the imps of hell; they have forfeited the right to be treated as human beings, and are pursued like animals after their defeat at Kinsale in 1601. The reason for their suffering is plain: they have refused to become protestants. The poem begins with a catalogue of the villains of the Old Testament and then passes to the situation in Ireland.

from: A Discourse occasioned upon the late defeat, given
to the arch-rebels, Tyrone and ODonnel, by . . .
Lord Mountjoy . . .
the 24 of December 1601 . . . and the yeelding up of Kinsale shortly after by
Don John to his lordship[1]

. . . Most wicked then are Irish rebels breed,
Whose lawlesse lives weaves on their web of woe,
Whose wicked facts *Moab* and *Ammon* passe,[2]
Farre worse that heathen Pagans of the earth,
    The onely monsters that the world containes,
    And cursed crue whome all good men refraines.[3]

Rebels to God, despisers of his lawes,
Traitors to Christ, deprivers of his right,
Refusing still the gifts of holie Ghost:
Breakers of peace, rejecters of the Truth,   10
    Contemners[4] of Gods word and holy writ,
    That guides mens lives the perfect path to hit.[5]

---

1. The references are to Hugh O'Neill, Earl of Tyrone (1550–1616), Hugh Roe O'Donnell, Lord of Tyrconnell (1571?–1602), Charles Blount, Earl of Devonshire and Baron Mountjoy (1563–1606) and Don Juan de Águila (*d.* 1602).
2. i.e. whose wicked deeds [facts = deeds] surpass those of Moab and Ammon – two enemies of the Israelites who were defeated by Saul. I Samuel 14. 47.
3. either 'whom all good men shun', *or* 'whom all good men restrain'.
4. Condemners.
5. i.e. that guide men so that they choose the perfect path.

Rebels to Prince, rebels to native home,
Traitors to Prince, traitors to countries due,
Supplanters of all rule and government,
Infringing lawes, the waste of Common-weale:[6]
 The brood of wolves, the elder sons of *Cain*,[7]
 The impes of hell, and very markes of shame.

Champions of hell, borne with bloodie hand,
Haters of truth, sworne slaves to rape and spoyle,[8]   20
Authors of mischiefe: all on murther set,
Masking with faces like strong plates of brasse:[9]
 Furies of hell, shaking their dog-eard locks,[10]
 Like damned slaves sprung from most cursed stocks.

Breakers of wedlocke, wantons in their lives,
Most bred up bastards from their very birth:[11]
Lovers of theft, living by theeving trade,
Idle in life, like beasts fed in the stall:
 False lying mates, deceitfull and unjust,
 Whom God nor man, nor divell cannot trust.   30

Idolators, superstitious men,
False worshippers, sworne slaves unto the Pope,[12]
Trusting to dreames and fained prophesies,[13]
Observers of old writs that have no ground:[14]
 More ignorant than beasts are in their kinde,
 Willing to lose what chiefe they ought to finde.

Open maintainers of all runnagates,[15]
As peevish priests and filthie begging Friers,

---

6. the general good.
7. Cain, son of Adam and Eve, murdered his brother Abel: he and his sons were cursed by God. Genesis 4.
8. i.e. slavishly committed to rape and plunder.
9. bewildering (their enemies) with a show of bold effrontery.
10. their 'glibs' or long locks of hair.
11. A common English reference to the perceived laxity of Brehon law in family and sexual matters.
12. i.e. they have sworn to obey the Pope slavishly.
13. Irish hopes of defeating England were encouraged by prophecies throughout the early modern period.
14. Incoming English administrators refused to acknowledge any existing titles to land.
15. renegades, deserters.

Sold Seminaries to[16] the Romish Church,
False traitors to their soveraigne Prince and Queene: 40
    Vilde[17] lothsome locusts crawld from yond the seas,
    Whose stinking breaths ingenders sore disease.

That this is true, view Ireland's present state,
Which whilome[18] sate in faire and rich attire,
Which whilome flow'd in plentie of the earth,
But now growne naked, feeble, weake and bare:
    Who lately held sweete peace both neere and farre,
    But now in every place at deadly jarre.

View now their houses wasted as they lie,
View now their fields all barren round about,   50
View now their medowes overgrowne with weedes,
View their high waies untroden as they are:
    All honest trades are ceased very nie,
    And plague on plague you perfectly may spie.

The old men wander like as men forlorne,
And women faint for want of some reliefe;
Yong children starve and pine for bread we see,
Most of the poore resemble death in shew;
    In stinking holes and vilde unseemly place,
    Are Cels for such in this their dolefull case.   60

View well their bogs furd[19] all with bloodie hew,
View well their fastnes of the selfsame stampe,[20]
View well their hedges sprinkled all with red,
View well their brookes how bloodie they doe looke:
    The blood that Ireland sheds from day to day,
    For vengeance cries to God without delay.

What is the cause this land in such termes stands?
But only that the people fell from God,

16. betrayed sowers of the seed of . . .
17. vile.
18. in earlier times.
19. furred, covered over.
20. strongholds, similarly tainted.

And brake God's Sabboths with a mightie hand,
Forsooke the Preachers of his blessed word: 70
    Apostates the most of them have plaid,[21]
    And will not turne for ought that may be said.

Seminarie priests and lying Friers,
First sware[22] them that God's word they shall not heare,
And teach them their oath unto their Prince
May lawfully be broken when they will:
    And swears them, that devoutly they shall keepe
    What so[23] the Pope of Rome and themselves like.

These are the grounds from whence all mischiefe spring,
These are the causes that rebellion is: 80
These are the reasons Spaniards invade,
This is the matter no amendment comes:
    For why, the devill now is busie still,
    To draw all men to chuse what best he will.

O famous Queene,[24] who holds this land by right,
Whose care that been and is, to cure their sore:
What loving favours hath her Grace bestowd,
On mightie men, and subjects of this land,
    Whose wise foresights in time might stop full well
    The streames from whence these mischiefes so do swel.[25]   90

But well her Highness hath from time to time
Observed still this nations wandring thoughts,
And seene into their natures and their lives,
Who like young colts and heifers love to fling,
    That without bits and bridles and strong hand
    Will not be held in peace or rest to stand . . .

---

21. i.e. most of them have renounced protestantism and returned to the catholic church.
22. make them swear not to hear God's word i.e. not to attend protestant worship.
23. whatever.
24. i.e. Queen Elizabeth I.
25. i.e. whose wise provision for Ireland might well cease because of the growing mischief which flows from her.

Birchensa then considers Tyrone and his rebellion, and gives a detailed account of the battle of Kinsale. As the English forces under Mountjoy triumph at the end of the battle, the poem continues:

> . . . They[26] being broke, God so did strength *Mountjoy*,
> And blest the labours of his worthy men,
> That they with speed pursu'd the Rebell slaves,
> And in a moment had twelve hundred kild,   100
> > Nine Colours won, and many captives tane;[27]
> > Two thousand armes they lost unto their shame.

> In their pursute the rivers plaid their part,
> And rising up against such wicked imps,
> Their mounting waves did sinke them to the deepe,
> As most unworthie to enjoy the land:
> > Happie was he could shun that bloodie day,
> > And stoutest man that made most haste away.

> There might you see a just revenge for blood,
> Blood cries for blood, for in each dike and gap,   110
> They groveling lay, besprinkled all with blood:
> One leglesse lay, another wants his arme:
> > Some all to[28] cut and mangled back and face,
> > That streames of blood were shed in every place.

> There might you see from East, West, North and South,
> The Ravens, Crowes and fowles in flockes to come:
> There might you see from every den and bush,
> The greedie wolves and ravening beasts make haste:
> > As welcome guests unto so fat a feast,
> > They cheer'd themselves as well the most as least.   120

> Besides all this, above seaven hundred men,
> Were wounded sore and hurt in grievous wise:
> There might you heare them howling with loude cries;
> There might you see them stampe and stare apace,[29]
> > There might you see them languish and make mone,
> > Yet little helpe or succour to them showne.

26. i.e. the Irish forces at Kinsale.
27. taken. Colour = the regimental standard; the taking of a colour was tantamount to the defeat of the regiment.
28. i.e. so.
29. immediately.

114

Thus by Gods helpe *Mountjoy* was the meane,[30]
To daunt the pride of those Arch-rebels all;
And that same pit which they for others made,
Their cursed feete lay caught in the same gin.[31]   130
    And as this fell, so Lord let be thy will,
    When next they meete like hap,[32] send Rebels still . . .

30. means.
31. snare or trap.
32. fortune.

ANONYMOUS
(1602)

Once the news of an English victory over the combined forces of Ireland and Spain at Kinsale reached England early in 1602, the streets must have been alive with the strains of ballads celebrating the event. Only one of these ballads seems to have survived, however, and that by accident, preserved in a contemporary transcript. The text of the ballad contains several details which suggest that it was the work not of a professional balladeer but of someone who was present at the battle. Though the notes which accompany the text in the transcript are clearly by a later hand, those of interest are included here. As in the previous poem, the references are to Hugh O'Neill, Earl of Tyrone (1550–1616), Hugh Roe O'Donnell, Lord of Tyrconnell (1571?–1602), Charles Blount, Earl of Devonshire and Baron Mountjoy (1563–1606), and Don Juan de Águila (*d.* 1602), commander of the Spanish forces at Kinsale.

from: A joyfull new ballad of the late Victory obtain'd by my Lord *Mount-Joy* . . .[1]

England, give prayse unto the Lord thy God,
The which in mercye doth with hold his rod
    From us, whose synnes deserved have the same,
    Yet we continewe, *Sodome*-like, past shame.[2]

Oh, let us now returne unto the Lord,
And to his prayse singe Psalms with one accord,
    Which hath defended little England's right
    From forraigne foes, their cruelty and might.

Oh, give Him thanks for that which He hath done!
In *Ireland* through Him hath *England* won   10
    A victory, which doubted was of all,
    Till through God's help they saw the rebels fall.

For on the xx of *December* last
Tyrone with many Spaniards hyed fast:[3]

1. The full title of the ballad is as follows: 'A joyfull new ballad of the late Victory obtain'd by my Lord *Mount-Joy* and her Majesties forces in *Ireland* against yt arch-traytor *Tirone* and his confederats, upon the 24 of *December* last [1601]. Also of the yeelding of the towne of *Kingsale*, with 3 or 4 other houldes, by *Don Jhon* at *Aquila*, Generall of the *Spanish* army which was yeelded up the 9 of *January* last, 1602'.
2. When this ballad is sung in performance, the last two lines of each stanza are repeated.
3. *Note in transcript*: 'Hugh O'Neill'. During the autumn of 1601, O'Neill and O'Donnell

116

Syx thousand foote, five hundred horses, in all,
With courage bold, to work L[ord] *Mountjoy*'s fall.

Who had layd syedge that time unto a Towne,
Kinsayle by name, with hope to beat it downe,
   Or els to force them for to yeelde at last,
   Which to effect his Ordinance[4] plyed fast.   20

Kinsale that time the *Spaniards* did defende,
Till they were forced for more succour sende,
   Which came in number, as before is tolde,
   With hope to beat our forces from their holde.

It was agreed, the *Spanish* Captaine[5] should
Out of the towne yeeld all the force they could
   Against the Trenches, which we did defende
   And many *Spaniards* to their fellowes send.

While we our foes with valour did annoye,
Sir *Richard Wingfield*[6] came to L[ord] Mountjoye   30
   Saying: 'Tirone with many rebels more –
   The number I reported have before –

Are moving hither, and are very neare.'
Quoth L[ord] Mountjoie: 'And they shall buy it deare.
   Yf God assist me, I will them with stande,
   Hoping he will defend me with his hand.

Courage, brave Marshall, for our Queene we fight[7]
Let us goe forward; 'tis for *England*'s right,
   "God and S. *George* for *England*," still we crye;
   "Let us proceed: methinks the cowards fly!"'   40

---

led their forces south through Ireland to join the Spaniards who had landed at Kinsale; at the same time, Lord Mountjoy laid siege to the Spaniards in Kinsale. hyed fast = hastened.

4. artillery.
5. Don Juan de Águila.
6. *Note in transcript*: 'W of Kimbolton, afr. Visc. Powerscourt'. Sir Richard Wingfield, first Viscount Powerscourt (*d.* 1634).
7. *Note in transcript*: 'Wingfield'.

My Lord gave order to his forces straight
Some should the trenches and the townsmen wait;
    And he himselfe, with fifteen hundred more,
    March to the army, which was fled before.

And when my Lord did see them to retier
In such bad order, he had his desire:
    For presently he followed them soe fast
    That he enforced them to stand at last.

Then settinge all his men in order right,
He presentlye gave onset to the fight;   50
    Which was perform'd with valour and with skill,
    Forceing the *Irish* dearest bloud to spill.

The fight did not continue very longe,
Although *Tirone* with *Spaniards'* help was strong:
    Yet did our men behave them selves soe well
    That many *Spaniards* gayned heaven or hell.

The Rebels, fearing for to lose the daye,
Threw down their Armor, and ran all awaye,
    Which we perseivinge, followed them amaine,[8]
    Almost two miles, ere we returnde again.   60

Tirone the Rebell thought yt noe disgrace
To take his horse, and ride away apace:
    No more did *O'doneall*,[9] which ran awaye,
    Knowing it folly longer for to staye.

Chiefe of the *Spaniards*, *Allonso* by name,[10]
Was taken prisoner, unto *England*'s fame,
    Six *Allfaris*,[11] and forty Souldier's more:
    They that were *Irish* hanged up fo[u]r score.

Three Captains taken prisoner in that fight,
Eight hundred hurt, twelve hundred slain outright: 70

8. at full speed.
9. *Note in transcript*: 'Hugh O'Donnell aft. E. Tyrconnel'.
10. Captain Alonzo del Campo, whose 200 soldiers (the only Spaniards actually in the battle) fought valiantly.
11. Spanish officers. cf. Sp. *alférez*, second lieutenant, ensign.

Two thousand armes, their drums and powder-store,
The Rebels left, the which they had before.

Nine Ensigns there were taken at that time;
Six were the *Spaniards*, whose disgrace did clime
    A higher pitch th[a]n willingly they would:
    Thankes be to God, which have their courag[e] coolde.

Hurt of our side was fowre of account,[12]
Whose deeds that day in valour did surmount:
    Syxe common souldiers in that fight were slaine,
    Some horses kilde, and some still hurt remaine.   80

There was not one that on that day did fight
But gave the Rebels that which was their right;
    Chiefly my Lord *Mountjoy* perform'd that day
    Such warlike deeds as never will decaye.

The Earle *Clanrickard*[13] at that same place
Did through his valour purchase so much grace,
    That my Lord *Mountjoy* knighted him even there,
    Whereas[14] the bodyes kilde and mangled were.

The fighte endinge, he cal'd his forces all,
And willed them upon their knees to fall,   90
    Praysing the Lord for this great victorye;
    The which they did, kneeling immediatlye.

'Glory and prayses be gyven to thee, O Lorde!
Thy holy name we prayse with one accorde:
    The which hast kept us from our enemies all,
    And gyven us victorye, with their downefall.

Oh God, continue this thy favour still,
To us thy servants, yf yt be thy will,
    That *Pope* and *Spaine*, with all their *Irish* rout,
    May alwayes say, "The Lord for *England* fought!"'   100

---

12. i.e. four men of importance.
13. *Note in transcript*: 'Richard de Burgh, 4th Earl, surn. of Kinsale. Ob. 1635.' Richard
    Bourke, fourth Earl of Clanricard (*c*. 1580–1635), author of the next poem in this
    anthology.
14. where.

Then riseing straight, and takeing up the spoyle,
They left the place where Rebels had the foyle,[15]
    And to their trenches came in all the haste,
    The which they found in order, none displast . . .

The poet gives further details of the aftermath of the battle and then describes the surrender of the Spaniards (2 January 1602)

They had not stayed there full yet syxe dayes,
Eare *Jhon Aquila*[16] did our Generall prayse,
    Saying he was an honourable man,
    Who sayd for him, 'I'le doe the best I can:

For I do love him, though mine enemye,
And hate *Tirone*, for all his flatterye: 110
    Who being come with all the force he had,
    To take their heels, the cowards! all were glad.

Wherefore, upon condition that you will
Our [own] condition[s] with consent fulfill,
    We straight will leave this town, with many more
    That any *Spaniard* had in hould[17] before;

And we will leave the traytor Earle *Tirone*
In *Ireland* with grief to make his mone.'[18]
    They did agree, and *Spaniards* all depart,
    Which was great joye to good Lord *Mountjoye*'s hart.   120

Thus hath my Lord, to Earl *Tirone*'s disgrace,
Possest those houlds,[19] and *Spaniards* are defast,[20]
    To *England*'s comfort and Lord *Mountjoye*'s prayse.
    To God above be glory gyven alwayes.

To God [give praise, for He] doth still defende.
Lord, on [t]his [people still] thy blessinge send.
    Preserve our Queen, her Counsayle grave and wise,
    Confound her foes that doth the truth despise.[21]

---

15. were defeated.
16. Don Juan de Águila.
17. i.e. held.
18. *Note in transcript*: 'He fled to France, 1607.'
19. forts or fortresses.
20. i.e. they have 'lost face', lost their good name.
21. The paper on which the final stanza is written is decayed and the text is only partly legible. The stanza is given here as reconstituted by the editor of the Roxburgh Ballads. See *The Roxburgh Ballads*, ed. J. Woodfall Ebsworth, vol. VIII (Hertford, 1897), part 2, p. xiii***.

RICHARD BOURKE, EARL OF CLANRICARD
(*c*.1580–**1602**(?)–1635)

Although many Irish noblemen frequented the court of Queen Elizabeth – and some must, from time to time, have tried their hand at the writing of verse in English – the only surviving courtly Elizabethan lyric by an Irishman seems to be the one that follows. The fourth Earl of Clanricard was an enthusiastic supporter of English rule in Ireland and is perhaps best known for the fact that he was knighted on the field of battle at Kinsale in 1601 where he killed, according to contemporary reports, at least twenty men with his own hands. Clanricard was also an accomplished courtier in London, not only a favourite of ageing Queen Elizabeth but also the successful suitor of Frances Walsingham. She, daughter of one of the most powerful men in England, had been married twice before, first to Sir Philip Sidney and subsequently to the ill-fated second Earl of Essex. The poem which follows was presumably written when Clanricard was enjoying the queen's special esteem in the autumn of 1602,[1] though the title seems to date from after the death of Elizabeth in 1603.[2]

Of the Last Queene

My love doth flye with winges of feare
And doth a flame of fire resemble
Which mountinge highe, and burninge cleare
Yet ever more doth move and tremble.

My love doth see and doth admire
Admiring breedeth humbleness
Blinde Love is bold but my desire
The more it Loves presumes the less.

---

1. John Massingham recorded in 1602 that 'The Irish Earle of Clanrickard is well esteemed of by her Majestie, and in speciall grace at this tyme; hath spent lavishly since he came over, yet payes honestly.' John Bruce (ed.), *The Diary of John Massingham*, Camden Society (1868), p. 59.
2. Though early manuscripts credit the poem to the Earl of Clanricard, it has sometimes been said to be the work of Sir John Davies – on the peculiar grounds that it would be unlikely that Clanricard, who is not known to have written anything else, would have been capable of a poem of such delicacy. However, Davies's modern editor, Robert Krueger, acknowledges that the ascription to Davies is mere supposition, and suggests that 'If the poem is not by Davies, then probably Clanricard wrote it, copying from Davies.' *Poems of Sir John Davies*, ed. Robert Krueger (Oxford, 1975), p. 424. See also Katherine Duncan-Jones, '"Preserved Dainties": Late Elizabethan poems by Sir Robert Cecil and the Earl of Clanricarde', *The Bodleian Library Record*, vol. 14, no. 2 (April 1992), pp. 136–44.

My Love seekes not reward nor Glorye
But with it selfe, it selfe contentinge   10
Is never sullen, never sorie
Never repininge, never repentinge.

But who the Sunn beames can behoulde
But hathe some passion, feeles some heate?
For thoughe the Sunn himselfe be coulde,
His beames reflectinge fire begett.

O that mine eye, O that mine hart
Were both enlardged to containe
The beames and joyes she doth impart
While she this love doeth not disdayne.   20

This bowre unfit for such a gueste,
But since she makes it now her Inn,
Would God twere like her sacred breast
Most faire without, most rich within.[3]

---

3. The last stanza comes from the Burley or Burley-on-Hill manuscript, a commonplace
book belonging to Sir Henry Wotton. See Herbert Grierson, *Donne's Poetical Works*
(Oxford, 1912), II, 267–8.

PART II

1603–1641
Early Stuart Verse

RICHARD NUGENT
(*fl*.**1604**)

Richard Nugent was a member of a prominent Old English family based in County Westmeath. His only published work was a volume which appeared in London in June 1604 under the title *Rich: Nugents Cynthia. Containing direfull sonnets, madrigalls, and passionate intercourses, describing his repudiate affections expressed in loves owne language.* Though Nugent (like many other poets of the time) was heavily influenced by Petrarchanism in general and by the sonnet sequences of Spenser and Sir Philip Sidney in particular, his account of his unsuccessful wooing of his Irish love, whom he called Cynthia, contains some fine sonnets. Rejected in love, Nugent felt compelled to leave Ireland, and he writes of his feelings at the enforced exile in the first sonnet below. In the second sonnet, he describes the final meeting between him and Cynthia, and in the third sonnet he explains the situation to his cousin, another Richard Nugent. The fourth sonnet puts a paradoxical, witty spin on the whole sequence when the cousin is made to suggest that the poet is not suffering from love at all, but from lust.

Fare-well sweete Isle

Fare-well sweete Isle, within whose pleasant Bowres
I first received life and living ayre;
Fare-well the soile, where grew those heav'nly flowers
Which bravely decke the face of my fierce faire;
Fare-well the place, whence I beheld the towres
With pale aspect, where her I saw repaire;
Fare-well ye floods, encreased by those showres
Wherewith mine eyes did entertaine despaire;
Fare-well cleare lake, which of art made the glasse
To rarest beautie, of mine ill the roote,   10
When she vouchsafes upon thy shores to passe,
Blessing thy happie sand with thy[1] faire foote;
Fare-well faire *Cynthia*, whose unkind consent
Hath caus'd mine everlasting banishment.

His leave-taking of Cynthia, *wherein his owne death is presaged*

Comming to take my last leave of my Love,
(Oh that I then leave of my life had taken,)
I told her how I now my chance would prove
Abrode, since home-borne hopes had me forsaken.

---

1. a misprint for 'her'.

125

She then, in whom my piercing griefe did waken
Some spark of ruth,[1] too late alas, assayes
To crosse this course which I had undertaken.[2]
Now she perswades, now weepes, now sweetly prayes;
But neither reasons, teares, nor prayers could raise
The siege that honour to my heart had layd,   10
When with a deep-fetcht sigh, the lovely Maid,
The horror of her breast thus out bewrayes:[3]
Wo worth,[4] quoth she, must that deare head and hand
Lie lowly earthed, in an uncouth land.

To his Co[u]sin Master Richard Nugent of Donower[1]

Mine owne *Dicke Nugent*, if thou list[2] to know
The cause that makes me shun my westerne home,
And how my tedious time I here bestow,
Where angry *Thetis*[3] gainst her bounds doth fome,
Weet[4] that to ease that never-healing wound
Which now foure sommers heate hath made to fester,
By time, by absence, or by counsell sound,
I flee the soile where my sweete foe doth rest her.
I sojourne here, where I remaine so easde,
By this my flight, of the tormenting blow   10
As doth the deare on whom the shaft hath seazde[5]
By late unbending of the deadly bow;
And since, I have this cursse ev'n fatall proved,[6]
That I am borne to love, and not be loved.

The answer of M. Richard Nugent of Donower

Mine owne dear Dicke, whom I love as my life,
And ever shall, whiles I in life remaine,

---

1. pity, compassion.
2. tries to prevent me from doing what I had undertaken to do.
3. reveals.
4. This phrase, which means 'a curse upon the fact that . . .', was already archaic in 1604.

1. A village near Multyfarnham, County Westmeath.
2. wish.
3. In classical mythology, Thetis was mother of the sea-nymphs – so the poet is living beside the sea.
4. know.
5. As does the deer on which the arrow-shaft has fastened (i.e. not at all).
6. i.e. I have proved that this curse is even fatal to me.

I thee advise to leave this lingring strife
Betweene thy love and thy loves hope so vaine,
And for those yeares, wasted so long in vaine,
To shed some teares, with full remorse of minde,
And to be rid of thy tormenting paine,
To shun the path, misguided by the blind,
As for to flee the place of thy decay.
I ne mistake, (if that may worke thine ease)   10
Yet better were, this weede to root away,[1]
Which so infects and fils thee with disease;
For lust it is, not love, that doth torment;
Where love is just, there still is found content.

---

1. i.e. I am not mistaken (if that may make you feel better) that it would be better to root out this weed . . .

THOMAS SCOT (?)
(*fl*.**1605**)

This poem is unusual among accounts about great feasts in Ireland since it describes not the excesses of the native Irish but of members of the English-speaking settler community in Youghal, County Cork. The poem is found in the *Philomythie or Philomythologie: wherein outlandish birds, beasts, and fishes, are taught to speake true English plainely* (London, 1616), in a section entitled 'Certaine pieces of this age paraboliz'd'. The author of the whole book, which is a political and social satire, is given as 'Thomas Scot, gent.'; Thomas Scot is not known to have had any contact with Ireland but, since the poem occurs in a section of the book dedicated to the Cecil family, it is possible that Scot inserted into his book a poem by someone connected with the Cecils – who did have estates in Ireland, though not near Youghal.[1] In any case, the poem seems to be the work of someone who was present at an actual mayor's banquet which took place in Youghal between 1603 and 1607, i.e. between the time Ruardhí O'Donnell was made Earl of Tyrconnell (the title by which he is referred to at line 100) and the 'flight of the earls' (when he and Tyrone, among others, left Ireland for the Continent). This is perhaps the first poem in English about a gathering in Ireland where the women triumph over the men.

An Irish Banquet, or the Mayors Feast of Youghall

Tales many have been told by men of yore,
Of Giants, Dragons and of halfe a score
Worthies save one,[2] of Castles, kings and knights,
Of Ladies loves, of Turnaies,[3] and such sights
As *Mandevile*[4] ne'er saw; yet none like this
Which my Muse howles: then listen what it is.

Saturne[5] grew old, and the gods did agree
That *Jove*[6] should him deprive of Soveraigntie,
And become chiefe himselfe. A solemne day

---

1. Detailed municipal records of Youghal are available from 1610, but there is no mention of anyone called Scot or Cecil in the early years. See *The Council Book of the Corporation of Youghall*, ed. Richard Caulfield (London, 1878).
2. *Marginal note*: '9 Worthies.' The reference is to the ever-popular tales of 'The nine worthies', Joshua, David and Judas Maccabæus from the Bible, Hector, Alexander and Julius Cæsar from ancient history, and Arthur, Charlemagne and Godfrey of Bouillon from the more modern world.
3. tourneys, knightly jousting.
4. Sir John Mandeville (*d*. 1372) was said to be the author of a famous book of travels.
5. *Marginal note*: 'The old Maior.' The poem assigns classical names to the protagonists and assumes an extensive knowledge of the mythology surrounding the supreme classical deity, Zeus/Jupiter/Jove. The first reference to the myths concerns Jove supplanting Saturn as chief of the gods, in the same way that the old mayor gives way to the new one.
6. *Marginal note*: 'New Maior.'

Appointed was, when all the Gods[7] most gay, 10
Attired in mantles fayer, and truses strange[8]
Came to beholde the Lecher-like[9] lov'd change.
The frie[10] of all the Gods was there beside,
And each his Bastard had, his Whore and Bride.
The milk-white path that to *Joves* Pallace[11] leades,
In comely order all this rich troope treades.
Ceres[12] threw wheate upon *Joves* face most daintie,
Presaging and forespeaking future plenty.[13]
The well-instructed swine did follow after,
And for the wheate left something that was softer, 20
Civet,[14] like Irish sope. Sweete naturde beasts,
Fit waiters at such civill solemne feasts.
At length the traine reach't the high hall of *Jove*,
The Gods sat downe, the Goddesses[15] then strove
For place and state: but *Juno*[16] most demurely,
Plac'de and displac'de that day, as pleasde her surely.[17]
The tables stood full crownde with daintie dishes,
Enough to satisfie the idle wishes
Of longing Wives, or Maides growne greene and sickly,
With eating fruite, and doing nothing quickly.[18] 30

7. *Marginal note:* 'Aldermen.'
8. Mantles (or cloaks) and trews (or tight-fitting trousers) were clothes normally worn by native Irish rather than the planters. This may refer to particular clothes worn by the aldermen on the day of the installation of a new mayor or, more probably, it is a joke.
9. meaning obscure: was one of the protagonists a leech or doctor?
10. fry, i.e. children.
11. presumably the building in Youghal where the council chamber was.
12. *Marginal note:* 'An old wife.' Ceres was the classical goddess of the harvest. See the next note.
13. In the 1830s, Thomas Crofton Croker had intended to compile and edit an anthology of Irish poetry, which would have included this poem (see his notes for the project at British Library Add MS 20091). His note on this line is as follows: 'This Custom, which is called powdering the Mayor, was practised in Cork as late as the year 1809. It is the subject of a picture by Grogan. In the *Pacata Hibernia*, it is mentioned on the occasion of the young Earl of Desmond's visit to Kilmallock in 1600: ". . . every one throwing upon him wheat and salt (an ancient ceremony used in that province upon the election of their New Mayor and Officers as a prediction of future peace and plenty)." The Custom is also mentioned in *A Tour thro' Ireland by Two English Gentlemen* printed in the year 1748, page 56.'
14. *Marginal note:* 'Smell out the meaning.' It is impossible, now, to work out the significance of this remark. 'Civet' was the strong-smelling, brown, unctuous substance obtained from the anal glands of the civet-cat, and used in perfumery. Here the word is probably a euphemism for excrement. sope = soap.
15. *Marginal note:* 'Aldermens wives.'
16. *Marginal note:* 'Mistres Maiores.' Juno was wife to Jove.
17. i.e. the mayor's wife decided on the seating arrangements.
18. The reference is to green-sickness, an ailment suffered by anaemic girls; also known as chlorosis.

Huge hands[19] of butter not yet fully blew,[20]
With quivering custards of a doubtfull hue.
Stewde prunes, and bread that passeth Malahane,[21]
And honny sweeter farre then sugar cane.
Greene apples and such plenty of small Nuts, ⎫
That therewith safely one might fill his guts, ⎬
Though he were sure the Cooks were Irish sluts. ⎭
The goblets sweld with pride, themselves to see,
So full of French and Spanish wines to be.
Nectar-like Usque-bath, or Aqua-vitæ,[22]   40
And brown Ale growne in yeeres and strength most mighty
Was there as plentifull as Bonniclabbar,[23]
That every guest his cleane-lickt lips might slabbar
In full satiety, til they were crownde
With *Bacchus*[24] wreathes, and in still slumber drownde.
The fidling Spheeres[25] made musicke all the while.
And riming Bardes[26] brave meeter did compile
To grace this feast: When *Phœbus*[27] standing up
Tooke in his greasie fist a greasie cup
And drunke to *Daphnes*[28] health. *Bacchus* replide   50
And straightway quaft another to the bride
Of *Mulciber*.[29] This health past all along.
Then *Mars* his feather wagde[30] amongst the throng
Carowsing *Pallas*[31] health (brave wench and wise)

19. *Marginal note*: 'So they call their butter cakes.' 'Hands' probably means huge quantities, i.e. handfuls, of.
20. Luke Gernon also described Irish butter as being 'blew' in his manuscript 'Discourse of Ireland' written in about 1620 (British Library, Stowe MSS, vol. 28, folio 5, edited by C. Litton Falkiner, *Illustrations of Irish History and Topography* ... (London, 1904), pp. 345–62, p. 360); it is not clear what these references mean, although fresh buttermilk can look blue.
21. *Marginal note*: 'Bread of cruds', Ir. *mulcán*, buttermilk cheese.
22. Ir. *uisce beathadh*, whiskey; *aqua vitæ* = water of life, whiskey or other distilled liquor.
23. *Marginal note*: 'Common Irish drink', Ir. *bainne clabair*, thick, naturally soured milk.
24. The god of wine.
25. *Marginal note*: 'Two fidlers and a blind boy with a bagpipe.' There is an ironic echo of the medieval belief in the music of the spheres in the phrase used.
26. *Marginal note*: 'Their Poet Chroniclers.' A low grade of Irish poets, *aos dána*, specialised in praise poems – presumably, in this case, in English.
27. *Marginal note*: 'One of the Aldermen.'
28. Daphne was a goddess whom Apollo failed to seduce since she was turned into a laurel tree at the critical moment. There may be a local reference here.
29. Another name for Vulcan, the god of fire; here, presumably, the health is being drunk to the wife of another alderman.
30. waged his feather, staked his honour.
31. Pallas Athene, one of the twelve great gods of antiquity.

Which draught cost bonny *Cupid*[32] both his eyes,
Straining to pledge it. *Maias* sonne[33] stood still,
And slily mark'd how *Gamined*[34] did fill
The severall healthes, which swiftly past arownd,
Till all the Gods and Goddesses had bound
Their browes with wreaths of ivy leaves and vines,[35]   60
And each his forehead to his knee enclines.
Apollo then slipt thence,[36] and being halfe drunke
His burning bonnet doft, and slily sunke
His head in *Thetis* lap. So heaven lost light,
And cheerefule day was damp't with irksom night.
Jove yet disposde to mirth,[37] had *Juno* spread
Her Starry mantle or'e the worlds black head.
But she[38] inrag'de with plumpe *Lyæus*[39] juice
And mad with jealousie, without excuse,
Refusde to guild the then unspangled sky,   70
With th'eyes of *Argus*, her cow-keeping spie,[40]
And aided by Necessitie and Fate,
And all the shrewder Goddesses, *Joves* state
She durst assume,[41] and boldly presse as farre
As all the Gyants in their civill warre.[42]
They first bound *Jove*, then all the other Gods,
Who were constrain'd by darknes, drink and th'ods[43]
Of this conspiracie, to condescend
To hard conditions for a quiet end.[44]
Jove granted *Juno* power of all the aire,   80
Her frowne or smile makes weather fowle or faire.[45]

---

32. *Marginal note*: 'The fidlers boy.' Presumably the boy was blind – but it not possible to understand the exact meaning of these lines.
33. Hermes was the son of Maia – but the reference is obscure.
34. A beautiful boy kidnapped by the gods and taken to Mount Olympus to act as cup-bearer to Zeus. The reference is obscure here.
35. *Marginal note*: 'They were almost all drunke.'
36. *Marginal note*: 'The sun went downe.'
37. *Marginal note*: 'Master Maior cald to his wife for candles.'
38. *Marginal note*: 'She was drunke and would none', i.e. she refused to get candles.
39. Lyæus was a surname of Bacchus.
40. In Greek mythology, Argus, who had one hundred eyes, was set to watch Io, who had been turned into a heifer.
41. i.e. the mayor's wife usurped his position as ruler of the event (and the household).
42. *Marginal note*: 'She took Master Maior a box on the eare.'
43. the odds, i.e. the inequalities.
44. The references in the previous lines are to stories of the gods rising in rebellion against Jove.
45. *Marginal note*: 'Mistris Maioris might do what she would.'

His thunderbolts and lightning she may take,
And with her tongue the worlds firme axtree[46] shake.
From hence do women their free charter hold,
To rule gainst reason, or else cry and scold.
Proserpina obtained of her *Pluto*,
That such should only speed, who she-saints sue to,
That all affaires of man in state or purse,
His wife should sway, or women that are worse.[47]
From whence this custome springs in towne & city,   90
The wife growes rich, the banker out begs for pitty.[48]
Venus got leave to lie with all that love her,
And that no sawcy god should once reprove her,
That *Mars* and she might dally, whilst *Don Vulcan*
Should freely to their pleasures drinke a full can.[49]
From whence this use proceeds, that wives once wantons
Wage servants, as the French the Swizzers Cantons.[50]
You that are Statists[51] looke onto this geare,[52]
Do not *Tyrone* and his rash striplings[53] feare;
Feare not *Tirconnel*, nor those *Galliglasses*[54]   100
That cut, and hacke, and carve men as it passes;[55]
Feare those which all these feare, those fathers holy[56]
Which make the whole world their sole monopoly:

46. axtree = axle-tree = axle.
47. Proserpina or Persephone was wife of Pluto and queen of the underworld. It was maintained that no one could die unless the goddess herself consented to the death and cut off one of the hairs of the head with her own hand. The poet is interpreting the story liberally. speed = speed to their death. 'women that are worse' could mean mistresses.
48. This rather obscure line may mean that, once the wife becomes rich, she is more powerful than the banker.
49. Vulcan was the god of fire and metalwork and could therefore make the can out of which to drink healths. He was represented as the great cuckold of the ancient heavens and had to put up with the many infidelities of his wife Venus, including her dalliance with Mars, the god of war.
50. i.e. once wives become wanton in their behaviour, they bribe servants to keep silent, in the same way that the French bribe the Swiss cantons. During the late sixteenth and early seventeenth centuries, the French (among others) used various means to extend their influence in the western cantons of what is now Switzerland.
51. politicians.
52. rubbish, 'this lot', i.e. a deprecatory way of referring to all those attending the banquet.
53. young fellows.
54. Even though the Irish had been defeated at the battle of Kinsale in 1601, Hugh O'Neill and Ruardhí O'Donnell posed at least a potential threat to English planters and settlers in Ireland until 1607 when they and their followers left Ireland in 'the flight of the earls'. Galliglasses = gallowglasses (Ir. *gallóglaich*) were heavily armed infantry, originally mercenaries from Scotland, who were integrated into the marauding bands of Tyrone, Tyrconnell and others, and were widely feared.
55. i.e. as they pass.
56. i.e. the Pope and the cardinals in Rome.

That crowne & uncrowne Kings, when as they please,
Play fast and loose like Juglers with slight ease;
Dissolve all othes, though made with hand & heart,[57]
And pardon all sinnes, yea an Irish fart.[58]
Feare these, and those they joyne with,[59] lest too late
We finde our Ile an Amazonian state,
Where none but women, Priests and Cocknies[60] keepe   110
As close as young *Papirius*,[61] and as deepe,
And none but these state mysteries may know,
Lest they to more fooles than themselves should show
The treasons,[62] stratagems, and golden fables,[63]
Which are projected at their councell tables.
If this advice be good, crie, *Jove* be thanked,
And with that short grace close my Irish banquet.

---

57. a reference to the Pope's excommunication of Queen Elizabeth in 1570.

58. *Marginal note*: 'The eighth deadly sin; and more shunned of the Irishmen than the other seven.' Throughout the early modern period, the extraordinary belief that Irishmen had a rooted objection to farting is regularly repeated in English accounts of Ireland.

59. *Marginal note*: 'Their crosses, their wives.'

60. Cockneys, those born in London. As early as 1600, cockneys were famed for their contemptuously bantering ways. Here the word refers in general to low-class New English adventurers.

61. *Marginal note*: 'His historie is well knowne.' Papirius was a young man who, improperly, was allowed to attend a meeting of the Roman senate. Pressed by his mother to tell her what had been discussed there (though it should have been kept secret), Papirius made up a story that the senators had been discussing whether it would be better to permit one man to have two wives or one wife to have two husbands. Papirius's mother told this to the matrons of Rome, who then rushed to the senate to seek permission for a wife to have two husbands. The astonished senators forbade young men to attend the senate in future. The point of the reference is that, if things go on as they seem to be going, only women, priests and cockneys will have access to secrets of state, as did Papirius.

62. *Marginal note*: 'They plot and consult of nothing else.'

63. *Marginal note*: 'Stories out of the Legend, which they beleeve above Gods Word.' The reference seems to be to the fact that catholics paid attention to church history and doctrine rather than accepting, as did protestants, the supreme authority of the Bible.

SIR JOHN DAVIES
(1569-**1606**-1626)

Sir John Davies, one of the most famous lawyers of his age, was a prolific poet in his youth. Today, he is particularly remembered for *Orchestra* (1596), a wonderful poem on music and dancing, for *Hymnes of Astræa* (1599), a poetic sequence in praise of Queen Elizabeth, and for *Nosce Teipsum* (1599), a long poem on the immortality of the soul. He also, with Christopher Marlowe, wrote some epigrams so indecent that the church authorities had them burned. After he came to Ireland as solicitor general in 1601, Davies seems to have written almost no poetry, although the epitaph which follows is accepted as his work.[1] Davies's two lasting contributions to Irish writing – both of them designed to further the English colonisation of Ireland and the extirpation of the native Irish – are his law judgments (published in 1615) and his famous tract *A Discoverie of the True Causes why Ireland was never entirely Subdued* . . . (1612). The child commemorated in this poem was that of the lord deputy, Sir Arthur Chichester, Davies's immediate superior.[2]

On the Deputy of Ireland his Child

As carefull mothers doe to sleepinge lay
Their babes which would too longe the wantons play,
So to prevent my youthes approaching crymes,
Nature, my nurse, had me to bedd betymes.[3]

---

1. Davies's most recent editor, Robert Krueger thinks the attribution to Davies is 'probably correct'. *Poems of Sir John Davies* ed. Robert Krueger (Oxford, 1975), p. 303.
2. Arthur Chichester, only son of Sir Arthur, born 26 September, died 30 October 1606; buried in St Nicholas's Church, Carrickfergus.
3. early, speedily.

GEORGE WITHER
(1588–**1610**–1667)

George Wither was a prolific English poet who is thought to have spent some time in Ireland during his early manhood, perhaps attached to the Loftus household at Rathfarnham Castle, near Dublin.[1] The poem which follows is of considerable cultural interest since it is less a poem than a masque, the text being clearly intended for recitation as part of a dramatic performance which involved the participation of noble guests. The verse was obviously spoken by a narrator and provides cues for dramatic events typical of a masque, such as the interlude for music and the entrance of the page with wine in a cup of massy gold. The event at which the performance took place was the wedding between Sir Francis Willoughby and Lady Cassandra Ridgeway, which took place at Rathfarnham Castle on the last Tuesday in October 1610.[2]

Clearly a large contingent of nobles, soldiers and their ladies, led by the lord deputy, Sir Arthur Chichester (later Baron Chichester of Belfast), came out to Rathfarnham from Dublin Castle for the wedding. The text specifically addresses not only the viceroy himself and other nobles, but the 'brave Martialists' fresh in from skirmishes in the bogs; the wedding masque was intended to provide a short period of peaceful fantasy in the midst of an unsettled and martial world. The poet assures the lord deputy that 'all are good friends' here and that it is safe for him to play, dance and sing since his enemies are 'quelled'. The heavenly music and the appearance of 'lovely Ganimead' as well as the constant mention of parallels between what is going on in the performance and the life of the classical gods build up a dreamlike atmosphere typical of the court masque. This text is strong evidence for the existence of a court culture in the circle surrounding the lord deputy in early seventeenth-century Ireland.

[Poem for the marriage of Sir Francis Willoughby and Lady Cassandra Ridgeway]

When Pyrrhus did wed Hipodama,[3]
And to his nuptials did invite the gods,
Just such a train did follow Jove;
So sate he, and even so attended on
By his whole state, even as, great Viceroy,[4] now,

---

1. There are no records, apart from this piece, to explain where Wither spent the years between 1606, when he left Oxford, and 1612, when he was living in London.
2. There is a long and vivid description of the ceremony – mentioning 'maskings, feastings, fireworks and presents' – in a letter sent by Thomas Ridgeway, father of the bride, to the parents of the groom, Sir Percival and Lady Willoughby. See David Cressy, *Birth, Marriage, and Death: Ritual, Religion and the Life-Cycle in Tudor and Stuart England* (Oxford, 1997), pp. 290–1. The letter is in the Huntington Library, Stowe MSS. STB Box 2(1). My thanks to Danielle Clarke for this reference.
3. In Greek mythology, Pirithous (not Pyrrhus) invited many of the gods to his wedding with Hippodamia. The reference is somewhat unfortunate because the guests at Pirithous's wedding got violently drunk and attempted to carry off the bride.
4. Sir Arthur Chichester (1563–1625), lord deputy of Ireland 1604–14, created Baron Chichester of Belfast 1613.

Thou sit'st amongst the worthy statists[5] here,
Hem'd in with noble spirits, on whose brows
Me thinks I see the glorious characters
Of Victory and Fame so deep imprest,
As if they would out last the date of Time,   10
And out brave Mars, the Bloody God of War.
And then, Fair Cinthia[6] never had a train
Of such choice nimphs as these, which like bright stars
Yield such a glorious luster, that weak eyes
Grow dym with looking on such heavenly objects.

But, Honour'd and Right Worthy, since you dain
So worthyly to come and testifie
The knittings of this sacred Gordian Knot,[7]
Which policy nor force shall ne'r untie,
Since you have lain aside your conquering arms   20
And are invested[8] in your noble robes of Peace,
To grace the unitings of this noble pair
With your long wish'd for presence, ye are welcome,
With the best kind of welcome from the heart,
The worthy master of the feast says so.
The Bridegroom and the Bride say welcome too.
And now me thinks ev'n all the Palace rings
With welcomes, and the very walls do sound.
And with redoubling echoes answer it,
That I assure my self you know you are welcome.   30
Be frollick[9] then, and to your best content,
Use any thing that may content you best,
Play, dance or sing, you may do what you will.
Apollo[10] once a year would smile, and so may you
Once in a twelve-month lay your state a side.
You need not fear, your enemies are quelled
And lye like captives at your conquering feet,
The Furys are lock'd up in iron chains[11]

5. politicians, statesmen.
6. the moon; the poet suggests that the bride's attendants are brighter and more glorious than those of the moon herself.
7. The Gordian knot was an intricate knot, and the phrase 'to cut the Gordian knot' means to unravel a great difficulty; again, the poet may have misunderstood his mythology in his eagerness to stress that this marriage knot will be impossible to untie.
8. dressed.
9. merry.
10. The principal classical god of the arts, especially music.
11. The three goddesses of retribution and vengeance, in classical mythology.

And cannot come to disturb the feast,
They shall not trill the ball of discord here   40
That sate[12] the three fair Goddesses at odds;[13]
All are good friends, here's none that thinketh ill,
But loves, and by God's favour shall do still.

Brave Martialists[14] that in your Prince's service
Have all the long day pas'd a weary march
Through mountains, woods and boggs, and then at night,
Either kept watch, or on the cold bare ground
Took an unquiet sleep, and for your musick
Had thundring clamours or the rattling drum,
Co'mixt with fearfull grones of dying men;   50
You that instead of delicate perfumes
Have been nigh choaked up with the smothring shott,
All mask'd in blood and dust, and have endured
Heat, hunger, thirst and cold, that have sought
Great Mars his tryumphs, 'twill not be a miss
To do fair Celia one small courtesie.

But Ladies, as for you,
Vouchsafe to bend your gentle ears a while,
And you shall hear what heavenly harmony
The Muses send you from Parnassus Hill,[15]   60
Sweeter than that which antient Midas heard
When great Apollo did contend with Pan.[16]

Enter Musick,[17] Pause a while . . .

'Tis come . . . sweet Melody
'Tis yours to command; but worthys all,
Think not your hearty welcomes do consist
In this, or in these cates;[18] wer't in our power
We would have fetch'd Ambrosia down from Heaven,[19]

12. set.
13. The reference is to the golden ball inscribed 'for the fairest' for which the three beautiful goddesses Hera, Athena and Aphrodite had to compete.
14. soldiers.
15. The mountain of the gods. The muses were the goddesses of the arts.
16. Midas, king of Phrygia, was said to have been present at a music contest between Apollo and Pan – so the music he heard then came from heaven.
17. i.e. musicians.
18. food and drink.
19. The food of the gods was ambrosia.

Enter a Page with wine in a cup of massy gold.

That sweet celestial food; but see how Jove,
Willing to grace this worthy company,
Sends his cup-bearer, lovely Ganimead,[20]   70
With cup of Nector[21] to the brim
For to carouse a health to you, fair Bride,
Whose nuptials to solemnise you have dain'd
To make of this, God Hymans[22] Holy-day.
Then take it, noble Chichester, begin,
And those that pledge in love this new made wife
Let it be so much blood unto their life.

---

20. Ganymede was a youth of great beauty who was abducted by the gods to be cup-bearer to Zeus.
21. The drink of the gods was nectar.
22. Hymen was the goddess of marriage.

SIR PARR LANE
(*fl*.**1621**)

Sir Parr Lane, who was born in Northamptonshire, came to Ireland at the time of the Tyrone rebellion.[1] He served as captain of a company of English soldiers and was knighted for bravery in 1604. He settled in Munster and wrote, in addition to the poem which follows, a short 'Character of the Irish'. His main written work, however, was 'Newes from the Holy Ile', a poem on life in Ireland during the reign of James I, written from the point of view of an ordinary – if aggressively protestant – English settler. The text ranges over matters political, religious, social and military and is particularly valuable for the insight it gives into the fears and hopes of planters at this time. The poem, which remained in manuscript until 1999 when it was edited by Alan Ford, seems to be addressed either to the lord deputy, Viscount Grandison of Limerick, or to some statesman in London (see line 38 below). As Ford has pointed out,[2] Lane was heavily influenced by Spenser's views on Ireland in *A View of the Present State of Ireland*, which he must have read in manuscript since it was not printed until 1633.

from: Newes from the Holy Ile

My silent Muse which noe man yet did knowe
that shee had tonge to speake or feete to goe,
like Croesus sonne,[3] whoe dombe[4] burst fourth for feare
and told his father of a mischeeife neere,
craves pardon now if shee abruptlie tell
of daungers growinge while we thinke alles well.
The pietie that savde his father then
helpe now our Mother[5] and descry the den
where Erroure lies[6] and lives in spite of Lawes,
and subjectes hartes from due obedience drawes.   10
I speake not of the best[7] – I am theire freind –
nor of the rest that doe begin to mend;
I tell of crowes that cannot chaunge theire hew

1. For an account of Sir Parr Lane's life and an assessment of his poem, see Alan Ford, 'Parr Lane, "Newes from the Holy Ile"', *Proceedings of the Royal Irish Academy*, vol. 99C (1999), pp. 115–20, and references.
2. Ford, p. 116.
3. Croesus was the immensely wealthy king of Lydia. Lane seems to be mistaken in linking this story – of a son who had been dumb regaining the power of speech to warn the father of danger – to Croesus.
4. dumb.
5. i.e. the church and state.
6. cf. Edmund Spenser, *Faerie Queene*, Book I, canto I, the description of the den of the dragon Error. Parr's readers would have remembered that the dragon's vomit includes catholic books and pamphlets.
7. i.e. native Irish favourably disposed to the English settlers.

and meanes, but those that alls bad, thats new;[8]
nor doe I purpose to defame a Lande
where profitt walkes with pleasure hand in hand;
but to epitomise all in a woord,
I sing of beastes that made the wolfe their Lord
and lett the lion goe;[9] but would he rore,
Ceres might keep that kingdom for hir store,   20
and banish Bacchus with his forraine ware,[10]
which makes them idle, fugitife and bare,
that honnest paines and spendinges might enlardge
theire hopes at home, and ease the Lyons charge[11]
which soone would be if they had handes to gett
in some proporcion to the mouthes that eate . . .

Ask a Divine[12] whie kearne[13] still rebells be:
whoe feares not God, cares not for man, sayth he.
Men borne neere hill, neere rock, neere bog, nere wood
the statesman[14] saith, have quick and stiring bloud.   30
Aske one whoe reades old stories to discearne
manners and men; from Crete (saith he) came kearne.[15]
Whence they inferr that natures workes explore
the less in beastes, in men they venome more;[16]
and soe for kearne, whoe doe deserve the blame,
the rest whoe well deserve, have an ill name.[17]
Take measure of these kearne by that lyne there
which you may take of Irish footemen here.[18]

---

8. i.e. but those for whom everything new is bad.
9. i.e. the Irish have chosen to worship the wolf of barbarous crime rather than the (English) lion of order and civility.
10. i.e. but if only the English lion would roar, Ireland would become a grain-producing country (Ceres being the goddess of the harvest) and it would be possible to banish the foreign god of wine . . .
11. i.e. reduce the amount of money which England has to spend on Ireland . . .
12. clergyman, minister.
13. *Marginal note*: 'Why kearne rebells.' Like almost all English commentators of the time, Parr has a particular hatred and fear of the Irish kern or light-armed foot soldier.
14. MS. reads 'state man'.
15. Various theories about the origin of the Irish race were current at the time. See Andrew Hadfield, 'Briton and Scythian: Tudor Representations of Irish Origins', *Irish Historical Studies*, vol. 28, no. 112 (1992), pp. 390–408.
16. i.e. in a place where nature is less venomous (e.g. in Ireland, from which St Patrick had banished venomous beasts), men have more venom in them.
17. i.e. the rest (of the native Irish) also get an evil reputation, though they deserve a good one.
18. i.e. think of those kerne *there* as you think of Irish footmen *here*. This line suggests that Lane is writing for an audience in London rather than in Ireland.

Th'are the best slaves and will the least complaine
yf you can keepe them under, and restraine   40
their insolence with a sharp hand; but showe
to love, or like the mushrompes then will growe
up in a night, and be soe puft with pride
as he must be a gentleman and ride.[19]

Soe clawe[20] these kearne, and feede them at the table
yet will they to the woods when they are able.
Art cannot chaunge their kinde nor shun their shiftes,[21]
nor are they wonn with favour or with guiftes;
ravninge of wolves and bitinge of madd dogges
is sooner left than kearne leave woode and bogges;   50
as one[22] came latelie from the Flemish warres,
sparcklinge with silver as the night with starres;
but marke, within this yere, and you shall see
a lowsy mantell will his wardroabe bee,
and all the discipline that there he learnd,
[in] the next rebellion, you shall see it kearnd.[23]
Soe are these kearne like nettells too, and whie?
they lightly toucht will stinge, hard crusht will dye.
Then lett them still runn wild or curbe them soe[24]
as want of meanes may keepe their proud minde lowe.   60
The middle way which ever yet wee chose
nor getts us freinds nor takes away our foes.

Under what plannetts Constellacion
are kerne then, under Mercurie or none?[25]
Marchants of mischeife that doe live by lies
and gett by purchase what another bies;
like mercurie take never soe much paine
to kill it, time will make it quick againe.[26]

---

19. *Marginal note*: 'Whelpes of a hayre.' i.e. but if you show [them] any love, they will grow like mushrooms in the night and be so puffed up with pride that they are no longer good as servants but must ride horses like gentlemen . . .
20. flatter, soothe.
21. avoid their trickery.
22. i.e. as an example, one of them came back recently from the wars in Flanders . . .
23. A classic complaint of the English planters about the native Irish: that any civility they learned in other places was soon lost when they returned to Ireland.
24. i.e. crush them so that . . .
25. Those born in the astrological sign of the planet Mercury were said to be mercurial, volatile, undependable, always on the move.
26. *Marginal note*: 'Kearne like quick silver.' i.e. even if you think you have, after a great effort, destroyed mercury, it starts to move again after a while . . .

So to subdue the kearne doe you the best,
they wilbe rebells yf you give them rest.   70
But for that kearne be of a large extent,[27]
see by that name what vermine here are ment;
Bard, Rimer, Harper with tale, rime and songe
incite the rest, like boutefeux,[28] to wronge;
Horsboy and Carroghe,[29] Bastard and the younger brother
to hell and shame they prostitute their mother
whoe gives them all to Idlenes to nourse
that makes them such as Circe could not worse.[30]
These were the great lordes followers followinge still
like furies[31] for to execute their will.   80
But as the Jesuites doe all fryers excell,
soe are the sword kearne vicars here of hell.
They pray but for a prey and for their creede:[32]
the greater theefe (say they) the better speed,
and keepe but one commandement for ten:
they serve their Lord and feare nor God nor man.
Wherin the Jesuites and the kearne accord
both as a God adore their supreame Lord[33] ....

Whie should not kearne then still delight in blud
when we doe guild their sinne with seeminge good?[34]   90
Mac, fitz and O[35] 'in action' are we say,
when bare tayld rogues in woodes the rebells play.
Ah, shall we match Cales action Mars his fame
with base confution and a Tyrons his name?[36]
Noe, let us at the last be wise and learne
for peace and warr, how priestes instruct the kearne.
And by the fruit yf every tree be knowen,

---

27. *Marginal note*: 'The xii plagues of Ireland.' i.e. the twelve plagues of twelve different kinds of kerne ...
28. firebrands, those who cause trouble.
29. Ir. *carruage*, itinerant, professional gamblers. See Alan Fletcher, *Drama, Performance and Polity in Pre-Cromwellian Ireland* (Cork, 2000), pp. 53–7.
30. Circe turned the sailors of the *Argonaut* into pigs.
31. In the classical world, the Furies were female spirits of justice and retribution.
32. i.e. those who believe as they do. But the word might be 'dreede' = suffering.
33. i.e. the Pope. *Marginal note*: 'The accord and difference betwixt Jesuits and kearne.'
34. *Marginal note*: 'Connivence hurtfull.'
35. Mountjoy also used this phrase to mean the Irish chieftains and their followers in general. See Fynes Moryson, *An Itinerary* ... (London, 1617), II, ii, 138.
36. 'Cales' is obscure: but the lines clearly mean, in general terms: Should we equate the action of brave heroes with those of rebels like Tyrone?

See what religion they may call their owne.[37]
As[39] some discourse uppon that sacred theame
which hong together like a sickmans dreame,   100
one, wiser then the rest, askt if they knew
which was the best religion, old or new?
'The old by odds, whoe makes a doubt' quoth one,
'our Catholike without Comparison.
For wee spoyle, rob, ravine, rape and kill,
we pay the priest his due and doe soe still,
when they that of the Queene's religion be
are hangd if they but thinke to doe as we.'[39]
Ah blessed Queene's Religion to thee came
by aunciente true descent allwayes the same;[40]   110
but kearne must have a thinge like to it call
religion for cloake their shame with all,
and be a fuke[41] to paint rebellions face
which els would be in Catholike disgrace.
Come Drunckards come, singe me an 'Io' pæan,[42]
for your Tirone[43] whoe was a holie man
the champion of Religion stout and stronge;
and yf the pope would put him in the thronge
of Saintes of the lower house, his preest blest life
would match St Clements Jesuited knife.[44]   120
And then might Drunckards to their owne saint pray
as well as murderers on their holie day.
A brave religion which the Jesuites teach
above the commune Catholike dull reach[45] . . . .

---

37. *Marginal note*: 'The kearnes Religion.'
38. Read: For example, at . . .
39. A reiterated complaint of protestants at this time was that, while they were ruled by their consciences and dealt directly with God in matters of good and evil, catholics could confess their wrongs to priests, receive absolution and then commit the same crimes again with impunity.
40. Parr asserts the continuity and purity of 'the Queen's religion', i.e. Queen Elizabeth's protestantism.
41. a lock of hair hanging over the face. The lines mean: Kearn must have something like it which he calls religion, with which he cloaks his shame and behind which (as if it were a lock of hair) he hides when he is in rebellion – since rebellion would, otherwise, be a disgrace to a catholic.
42. i.e. a song of celebration.
43. Hugh O'Neill, Earl of Tyrone, the most famous Irish leader of the Elizabethan period.
44. St Clement (*d*. 100), a martyr whose bones were miraculously recovered many centuries after his death. The link with the Jesuits is obscure.
45. *Marginal note*: 'Jesuits.'

All Lawes fitt not all natures:[46] yf to steale
in Sparta had bene death, that Communeweal
had endinge soone. Yf sodomy were theft,
few Cardinalls in Rome had now bene left.
Yf Drunckards should be censarde, where were then
the Moscovites and some too better men?   130
Nor any nation more addicte can be
to any vice than kearne to perjurie.[47]
Lawes must be fitlie[48] by discreations line,
as natives and their natures doe incline;
though well I knowe to innovate the lawes
publike and private mischeefe with it drawes,
Yet were it good to add some new decrees
that we were not the flies and they the bees;
with strength of oathes they breake through our trialls
when we are caught fast in our just denialls.   140
What was it then that governd kearne before
they had our Law? The Brehouns word noe more;
whoe first was sure to his lord the best,
the next share to himselfe, they had the rest.
This Brehoun Lawe like to the Lesbian square[49]
doth bowe and bend as lords and kamores[50] are.
They have noe courtes to pleade, nor bookes to learne,
the art to judg or cases to discerne.
How comes [it] then? by inspiration? No!
Extraduce[51] as kinde and kindred goe;   150
for of the Brehoune sept all Brehouns make[52]
that have a tonge to talk or hands to take.
As law, soe phisick and soe ryminge flowe
from sire to sonne;[53] but preesthoode doth not soe,

46. *Marginal note*: 'Lawes fitted to the people make the people obedient to the Lawes.'
   Settlers like Parr were constantly agitating for tougher laws to protect their property and
   rights.
47. Another constant complaint of the English settlers was that the native Irish frequently
   perjured themselves in English-style courts, bringing about judgments against the
   planters. The planters were also contemptuous of the traditional Irish Brehon laws,
   handed down orally from generation to generation.
48. fitly, i.e. laws much be discretely and appropriately framed . . .
49. A flexible ruler for measuring curved mouldings.
50. peers, perhaps Ir. *chomh mór* = peer.
51. = extrajuce, outside the law. The phrase seems to mean that anyone who was not a
   member of the Brehon septs is outside the world of the law.
52. The right and skill of the Brehon lawgiver were handed down from father to son.
53. In ancient Irish society, the positions of physician and poet were also handed down from
   father to son.

for whoe of all is like to prove a knave,
must goe beyond seas and his crowne there shave,[54]
and yf a little learninge there he find
he's English fine in tonge, French fine in minde.
For cominge back he is no better found,
rather by educacion more unsounde.   160
Of a poore preest he growes a runninge mate
and talkes not of the church but of the state;
and yf he preach his text, hath noe more partes
then raylinge on the best to make false heartes,[55]
and tells his auditores som lies unknowen
when they can tell him greater of their owne;
and soe the preest and kerne doe well agree
in oathes and lies the bulke of popery,
from whence as a most damned progenie
comes that daringe mounster perjury.   170
They care noe more to straine an oath or oathes
than drinke their milke unstraind or through foule clothes . . .

Go now and brag and tell the king and state
while false tonges in their ordinaries[56] prate,
that there are made plantacions to subsist,
whoe doubts of soe long as rebells list.[57]

Go brag I say, and tell of men and armes
when we yet lie (yf not served by charmes)
open to all attempts. Did Viner live,
you may devine what lesson he would give![58]   180
'Dwell not in cabbins in the woods' saith [he],
'for woods and bogs kearnes sanctuaries bee;
nor make your porter to secure your roome,
a bush of thornes which made my bedd my toome.[59]

54. i.e. be tonsured, as a novice in a religious house.
55. i.e. has no more skills than to rail against the best (among his flock), trying to turn them into traitors . . .
56. common eating-houses.
57. *Marginal note*: 'Too great security proves always Daungerous.' The implication of this passage is that, though people in London talk confidently about the new plantations in Ireland, these plantations will exist only as long as the rebels want them to.
58. *Two marginal notes*: 'Viners lesson' and 'Viner a gentleman murthered in a poore cabbin.'
59. The implication is that Viner had stuffed gorse bushes against the door of his bedroom as an (unsuccessful) protection against intruders.

No, such plantation doe more hurt than good
makinge a bootie for a Robin hood.
As late two whelpes that suckt the wolfe their mother
did cutt my throate from one eare to the other!' . . .

Untill you plant religion in the lande,[60]
Iniquity will have the upper hand,   190
and that which hath bene ever wilbe still;
by force or fraud the kearne have their will.
For when as peace did joyne all ells in on[e][61]
Rebellion here durst shew hir face allone[62]
and that shee did but shew that and away
whoe but gives God the glory of the day;
for when they were in armes resolvd to fight
a bullett like to David's stone flew right
and slew their champion which affrighted soe
as all were conquered by his overthrowe.   200
But since were traind kearne to the peece and pike[63]
Dutie must teach them on which side to strike.
Dutie must be by inward Conscience taught
and conscience by religion must be wrought.
Religion must be squared by the word
and that must be maintayned by the sword.
Then lett religion be the king's prime care,
Since kings are Gods, whoe hinder can or dare.[64]
Is not the septer in the Lions hand?
How can the wolfe the lion then withstand?   210
Then let the Lyon both in armes and hart
A God in God's cause take Religion's part . . .

I speake, not I, of malice, spite or hate,
but longe to see Truth triumph in this state;

60. *Marginal note*: 'Religion the ground of all true vertue.'
61. An ell was a measure of length which varied from country to country, so this phrase seems to mean that peace had reduced the differences between peoples.
62. *Marginal note*: 'Odohartys rebellion.' The lines refer to the rebellion of Sir Cahir O'Doherty in February 1608. The meaning of the lines is: And who does not give glory to God for the fact that rebellion just showed her face and went away? For when they were in arms . . .
63. i.e. but since that time, kerne have been trained to use the gun ('the piece') and the pike – new and more powerful weapons than those traditionally carried by the Irish.
64. i.e. who can, or dare, hinder them?

and soe I end, but never cease to pray
that in the sunshine of this Halcion day,[65]
wherof Heavne graunt wee never see the night
nor any comett, or eclipsinge light,
our Salomon[66] with his unbluddy hand
may build Jehovas temple in this Land   220
where Truth and Peace may kiss each other long
whom Hell nor Rome[67] with kearne or priest may wrong,
And for our church I pray and ever shall.
God mend hir first that shee may mend us all.

---

65. halcyon day, day of peace and quiet.
66. Solomon; the lines mean: our king, his hands guiltless of blood, may build the church of
    God in this land.
67. i.e. neither Hell nor Rome . . .

ANONYMOUS
(1622)

In September 1621, a large numbers of starlings gathered near the city of Cork; the birds proceeded to attack each another, and thousands of them fell dead to the ground. The event gave rise to a ballad which circulated widely. Eight months later, much of Cork city was ravaged by fires started by lightning strikes during a storm. It was widely believed that the two natural events were somehow linked and clearly the most satisfactory explanation for a double visitation of such disaster must be the wickedness of the inhabitants of Cork. The full title of the ballad which follows is: *The Lamentable Burning of the City of Corke (in the province of Munster in Ireland) by Lightning: which Happened the Last of May, 1622. After a prodigious Battell of the Stares*[1] *which Fought most strangely over and neere that Citty, the 12. and 14. of May 1621.*[2]

The Lamentable Burning of the City of Corke . . .

Who please to heare such newes as are most true,
Such newes to make a Christians hart to rue:
Such Newes as may make stoutest hearts to shake,
And Sinners justly to tremble and to quake.

Reade this, and they shall have just cause to feare,
Gods heavy hand on sinne reported heere:
Twas lately heard that Birds all of a feather,
Did strangely meete, and strangely fought together

At Corke in Ireland, where with might and maine,
They fought together till score of them were slaine: 10
Their Fight began and ended with such hate,
Some strange event it did Prognosticate.

What was presag'd fell out this last of May
Which was at Corke a [*illegible*] dismall day:
This last of May the Morning was most faire,
Towards iij.[3] a clocke, Cloudes gathered in the Ayre

Which Cloudes obscur'd, and darkened so the light,
That Midday almost was as darke as Night:
Whilest at such darknes Cittizens did wonder,
Forthwith they heard a dreadfull clap of Thunder.   20

1. starlings.
2. The ballad on the starlings gives the date of their battle as 8 September 1621.
3. three.

148

And with the Thunder, presently there came
Such Lightning forth the Clouds did seeme to flame:
But heere observe, this Citty towards the East,
Stands high, but falleth lowe towards the West.

As at the East the Stares began their Fight,
And there fell downe the Birds first, kild outright:
So at the East began the Fire to flame,
Those at the West did soone beholde the same.

And towards the East, to see and helpe they ranne,
Before halfe way, a wofull Cry began: 30
Behinde them, seeing the West end was on Fire,
They so recall'd, began for to retire.

As from the East, towards the West they turne,
They saw the middest of the Citty burne:
So at an instant all was on a flame,
There was no meanes to helpe to quench the same.

Although great store of Water was in place,
Water could not helpe there in such a case:
For why? that Fire which from the Skyes doth fall,
Is not with Water to be quencht at all.   40

Now were the Cittizens overwhelm'd with woe,
For no man knew, which way to runne or goe:
For in the City no man could abide,
The Fire raged so on every side.

Some were enclosed with Fire, they for their safety
Fled to the Churches, which were in the Citty:
Some to an Iland, and the Fields hard by,
To save their lives, with grieved hearts did flye.

Who was not then tormented in his minde,
To flye and leave all that he had behinde?   50
When that the Husband, for to save his life,
Might not make stay to bring away his Wife,

149

Or save his Children: in like case the Mother,
Fled from her Children, Sister fled from Brother:
All were amazed in this wofull Day,
Not knowing where to flye nor where to stay:

Nor where to seeke or after Friends enquire,
They knew not who was sav'd, who burnt by Fire:
A dolefull thing it was men might not tarry,
Out of the flames, their dearest Friends to carry.   60

The Second part

O That this wofull chance of *Corke* might rent
The hearts of men and cause them to repent
Their wicked lives for to escape the Rod,
Which they have cause to feare, will fall from God.

Corke to all Citties, may example bee,
To know they are not from Gods Justice free:
For being Sinners they may feare the like,
As fell to *Corke*, God in his wrath will strike.

But they will say, God's mercifull, 'tis true,
But in this case, let them give God his due: 70
Let them not so unto his mercy trust,
But let them know that God is also Just.

God's mercifull to Sinners which repent,
His Justice is towards lingring sinners bent:
Who will take holde of mercy and of Grace,
Let them repent whilest they have time and space.

Repentance only pacifies Gods Ire,
Preserves from sodaine,[4] and Eternall Fire:
This word Repentance, is a wicked thing,
To wicked Livers, 'tis a Serpents sting.   80

4. sudden.

Why should Repentance be so bitter, when
Tis the onely salve to Cure sinfull men?
And furthermore when as we are most sure,
That dye we must, we cannot long endure.

When we are sure, we from this world must goe,
But by what kinde of Death, we do not know:
No more than *Corke* did when that God did powre[5]
The Fire upon them in a dreadfull houre.

Why should not we be well provided then,
Against a certaine Death, but know not when: 90
Nor by what kinde of death, Death will us take,
Then let Repentance our attonement make.

If men Repentance in this life doe stay,
Let them consider of the Judgement day:
When God to Sinners, shall say in his Ire:
Goe hence ye Cursed to Eternall Fire.

But who in Life did faithfully Repent,
When they shall come to appeare at that Judgement
The Judge will say: *Goe Children of all Blisse,*
Enter the Kingdome, for you prepared is.   100

The God of Heaven graunt, that all Sinners take,
That course which may them blessed creatures make,
That come yee Blessed, with a joyfull eare,
They from the Judge at that maine[6] day may heare.

5. pour.
6. great.

EDWARD BLETSO
(*fl*.**1622**)

Edward Bletso seems to have been a member of the English family which later took the name St. John, and may have been a soldier in Ireland. He appears to have developed close links with settlers and native Irish in the north of Ireland and another poem by him, 'The Complaint of Gullo mac Shaneboy August 13 1622', contains several words in Irish. The Owen O'Hara commemorated in this strange, learned little poem was the governor of Carrickfergus, and of Scottish descent. He was apparently killed on 10 August 1622 by a runaway horse during races on the strand there. This may well be the earliest reference, in English verse, to horseracing in Ireland.

Dialogus inter Viatorem & Heremitam
in obitum Armigeri validissimi Owen O'Hara[1] August 10 1622

Her: Telle mee now, thou pilgrime poore,
    Wel I know that thou hast seene
    Many lands thou hast gon ôre
    True experience for to win;
    What dost thou esteeme most blessed
    In this terrene[2] universe?
    For few rightly have expressed
    What is blessed, what adverse.

Viat: Holy father, though my learning
    Unsufficient is to answere,   10
    Yet in my corrupt discerninge
    You are blessed by my censure.
    Above the primum mobile,[3]
    Thou whordest[4] thy wealth celestiall,
    And despist base trash ignoble,
    Vile, inconstant & terrestiall.
    Tis not wealth nor worldly glory,
    Bewty, strength, or wit to know
    All earths pride is transitory
    Fayre in sight but is not soe.   20

---

1. A dialogue between a traveller and a hermit on the death of the worthy knight, Owen O'Hara.
2. earthly.
3. i.e. in heaven. The *primum mobile* was the outermost sphere in the Ptolemaic system of astronomy, supposed to revolve around the (static) earth once every twenty-four hours.
4. i.e. hoardest.

Ah I know & greive to tell
Of *Owen Oharas* fall;
Mutually wee both lov'd well
Each to other above all.
Cahall his sire[5] noe vice defiles
famous both for Strength & bounty;
Doole oge[6] of the Scottish iles
His grandsire so stord with plenty
Yet on Carrickfergus strande
a furious horse at a race   30
While hee unadvised did stande
Slew him, mauger vertues grace.[7]

Her: Since the world doth nought delight thee,
              Learne with mee therto to dy;
              Let its ficklenesse incite thee.

Viat: So I shall, farewell vanity.

---

5. father or, perhaps, lord.
6. young Dougal.
7. despite the fact that he was graced with virtue.

THOMAS PESTELL
(*c*.1584–**1624**(?)–*c*.1659)

Thomas Pestell, a poet and clergyman who became chaplain to the third Earl of Essex, was also connected with the Beaumont family of Cole-Orton in Leicestershire. In 1622, Lord Beaumont, who was a kinsman of the Duke of Buckingham, went to Ireland to arrange a match between the son of his heir, Sir Thomas Beaumont, and Lady Katherine Boyle (1614–91), fifth daughter of Richard Boyle, first Earl of Cork. The match was agreed and, in 1624, the young Katherine Boyle was sent over from Lismore Castle to Leicestershire to be brought up with Lord Beaumont's family at Cole-Orton. Here she must have encountered Thomas Pestell, who was probably chaplain to Lord Beaumont at the time, and Pestell must have presented the little girl with a Bible and the verses which follow.

Lord Beaumont died soon after Katherine Boyle arrived at Cole-Orton, and the wedding between her and Sapcote Beaumont was eventually called off.[1] Instead, she married Arthur Jones, later Lord Ranelagh and, as Lady Ranelagh, she became one of the most celebrated intellectuals of her day, noted for her devotion to religion and learning.

Verses on a bible presented to the Lady K[atherine] C[ork]

> This world is gods large booke wherin we learne
> Him in his glasse of wonders to discerne;
> But since the print was darke and we synnblind,
> His word became the Mirrhour of his mind,
> And as the eternall father on the sonne
> His forme engrav'd, before all worlds begun,
> So what he is, what god in him, to us
> The spirit of both, does in this booke discusse.
> Cleare Spring of wisedome! Truths eternall mine!
> The whole a Temple, & each leafe a shrine;   10
> And as on clouds, on mountains, and on streams,
> The sunne letts beautie fall in golden beams
> But with his owne pure light the starrs inspires
> And through their bodies thrusts his living fires,
> So other holy books can but reflect
> Those rays which here are native & direct,
> Which apt to dazle & confound the wise
> Are yet a gentle light to childrens eyes.
> And you, bright mayd (whose name if I rehearse[2]
> I shall a Rubricke[3] make and not a verse,   20

---

1. For the details, see Nicholas Canny, *The Upstart Earl: A Study of the Social and Mental World of Richard Boyle, first Earl of Cork, 1566–1643* (Cambridge, 1982), pp. 60–1.
2. utter.
3. A 'red-letter' entry of an important saint's name in a church calendar.

And were such gold found in Italian mines
They would have twentie new St Katherines),[4]
As litle ones in gardens take delight,
Here gather fruicts for taste, & flow'rs for sight.
The flow'r of Jesse,[5] that fresh and lasting rose
The fruict of knowledge, and of life here grows.
On babes as tender Virgins love to looke,
Behold that blessed babe within this booke;
Pure, faire & deckt in roabs of white & redd,
A crowne of radiant starrs about his head.   30
If you be sicke, if head or heart shall ake,
To Jhesus name turne, & the paine will slake.
Read it[6] when first you rise &, gone to bedd,[7]
Under your pillow let it bear your head.
All books in one, all learning lies in this;
This your first ABC, and best Primer[8] is
Whence, having throughly learnt the Christcrosse row,[9]
You may with comfort to Our Father goe,
Who will you to that highest lesson bring
Which Seraphins[10] instruct his saincts to sing.   40

---

4. i.e. if such a good person were found in Italy, she would be made a saint twenty times over. Two of the three saints named Catherine in the church calendar are from Italy, from Genoa and from Siena.
5. Jesus was said to be the flower which grew on the stem of Jesse (see Isaiah 11. 1), i.e. he was a descendant of Jesse.
6. i.e. this bible.
7. i.e. when you have gone . . .
8. an elementary school-book for teaching children to read.
9. the alphabet, so called because the figure of the cross was prefixed to it in horn-books. [A horn-book was a leaf of paper on which was written material which children had to learn at school – the letters of the alphabet or the Lord's Prayer, for instance. The paper was protected by a thin sheet of horn and the whole was mounted on a tablet of wood with a handle.]
10. The highest class of the angels.

RICHARD BELLINGS
(*c*.1598–**1624**–1677)

Richard Bellings, one of the most prominent catholic lawyers of seventeenth-century Ireland, was born into a well-established family which owned estates in counties Wicklow and Kildare.[1] He went to London as a young man to be educated at Lincoln's Inn and, while there, undertook the same task as Gervase Markham – he wrote a sixth book to continue the unfinished story of Sir Philip Sidney's *The Countess of Pembroke's Arcadia*. This substantial prose text was published in Dublin in 1624 and appeared as part of the *Arcadia* in editions published in the late 1620s. Bellings later played an central role in Irish political life in the 1640s becoming secretary to the confederate supreme council. He wrote a detailed history of the period which remained in manuscript until edited by Sir John Gilbert and published as *A History of the Irish Confederation and the War in Ireland*, 7 vols (Dublin, 1882–91). This work is now recognised as one of the most valuable accounts of mid-seventeenth-century Ireland.

As well as writing history and fiction – and large amounts of official correspondence – Bellings wrote poetry throughout his life. The most substantial collection of his verse is in the 1624 Dublin printing of his sixth book to the *Arcadia*, where there are not only several pages of eclogues in the main text but also an appendix which includes love poems and occasional verse. In addition to the 'Description of a Tempest' and 'Directions to a Painter to draw his Mistris' printed below, this appendix includes several poems on a mistress whom Bellings describes as his 'neere kinswoman' and a poem 'On the beauteous black Ophelia'.

The first poem below comes from the eclogues, or pastoral dialogues, which bring Bellings's sixth book of the *Arcadia* to an end. Sidney had ended each book of the original *Arcadia* with an eclogue and, in this as in everything, Bellings strove to copy the original. The *Arcadia*, as a whole, was seen as a manual for courtly conduct, and the characters provided examples of honourable or dishonourable behaviour. As Bellings's sixth book comes to an end, a character called Agelastus – who is described as a 'thinking man' who maintains a 'religious sorrow' and mourns 'the vanitie of greatnesse' – 'disburthens his mind' on the subjects of fate and honour. These subjects were to be of vital importance to Richard Bellings and those like him who lived through the turmoils of the 1640s.[2]

from: Eclogue to A Sixth Booke to the Countesse of Pembrokes Arcadia

[Agelastus's reflections on fate and honour]

Nor fate, nor fortune, whose inforcing power
Man still complaines, upon his state, to lower,

1. See Raymond Gillespie, 'The Social Thought of Richard Bellings', in *Kingdoms in Crisis: Ireland in the 1640s*, ed. Micheál Ó Siochrú (Dublin, 2001), pp. 212–28; the family landholdings are detailed on pp. 217–20.
2. See Gillespie *passim*.

Do worke these changes:[3] man himselfe's the cause.
They be but wheeles that keep their movers lawes.[4]
Yet alway, when he sees his fault too late,
He turnes it over[5] upon chance or fate.
Each man is borne a King: his passions be
The practise of his soveraignetie:[6]
Who though they stil their soveraign's good pretend
Conspire his ruine for their private end.   10
The love of skin-thick beautie drawes his eye
To yeeld to love, his reason's Majestie.
His feare throwes Bugbeares in his way, his state
Is still infested by revengefull hate.
His idle griefe, for what he might prevent,
Or might not, doth usurp his government.
Thus he whom God ordain'd a King to be,
Obeyes his subjects,[7] and is never free.
Besides, whose state's so firme, into whose way
The world flings not his joyes injurious stay?[8]   20
The surges of the deepe, whose jawes devoure
The Merchants far-fetcht hopes, the skies that poure
A second deluge on the plow-man's corne
When now his fields are readie to be shorne;
The souldiers long remat,[9] the doubtfull chance
Of bloudie warre, the new-found ordinance,[10]
The Citie hornes,[11] the Courts brave flatterie,
Doe force content to dwell with poverty.

---

3. i.e. it is not fate or fortune, (whose power man – because of his high rank – grumbles should be less than it is) which bring about these changes . . .
4. their creator's laws.
5. blames.
6. i.e. his passions are the place where he must practise sovereignty – in controlling them.
7. with the double meaning of his passions (which should be subject to him) and of his people.
8. i.e. the harmful end (stay) of his joys. The reference is to the actions of fate.
9. This might be a mistake for 'remit', i.e. the state of being under the control of someone or something – in this case, perhaps, the new-found 'ordinance' or disposition of soldiers in battle; but the lines are obscure.
10. either (as suggested in the previous note) the disposition of soldiers in battle, or a decree or command.
11. This word is hard to decipher: it seems to be 'hornes' i.e. horns. The horn was blown three times at the town centre to announce the 'horning' of someone – i.e. that he was an outlaw or criminal – usually because he had refused to obey a royal summons to pay a debt. If the word is 'horns' and this interpretation is correct, the line (like the rest of the sentence) refers to the loss of money.

Honor, thou spongie Idoll of mans minde,
That sok'st[12] content away, thou hast confinde   30
Ambitious man, and not his destinie,
Within the bounds of forme and ceremonie.
Oh happie life of shepheards, whose content
Rests in a soule that's free and innocent:
They stay their lodging[13] and remove their roofe,
Not for their owne, but for their flocks behoofe;
While some[14] (to fill the blanks of their meane story)
Do travell[15] in their cares to gaine vaine glory.
They[16] never leave the plaines, unlesse some time
To looke about them, they the mountaines clime,   40
But dwell not there; for even this change doth show
What choyser sweets[17] they doe enjoy below.
Here the rough windes do buzze about their eares,
The rackie steepnesse adds unto their feares:
Here they are readie to be torne assunder,
By malice's hatefull blasts, and envie's thunder.[18]
From hence they may descend; but greatnesse stay,
If you[19] come downe, it must be th'other way:[20]
For 'tis a bliss in which your honour shares,
That though you would, you cannot leave your cares.   50

The Description of a Tempest[1]

Bound for my countrey[2] from the Cambrian[3] shore,
I cut the deepe;[4] the Mariners implore,

---

12. soakest.
13. i.e. they stop building their own lodging place, and even remove the roof from it so that their sheep can use it . . .
14. i.e. others.
15. = travail, labour.
16. i.e. the shepherds.
17. more attractive delights.
18. These shepherds exist only within the literary convention of the pastoral romance: it is courtiers in high places who are torn asunder by malice and envy.
19. i.e. the princes, to whom Agelastus is speaking.
20. The implication seems to be that princes can only descend from their heights of greatness when they die.

---

1. This is one of eight poems by Bellings which make up an appendix to the 1624 Dublin printing of his sixth book to the *Arcadia*. They are introduced as follows: 'These following verses at severall times came to the hands of the right worsh. Sir R.C. who being the Authors deere friend, & therfore thinking them too good to perish, hath caus'd them here to be annexed to his booke.' (sig. O3r.)
2. Ireland.
3. Welsh.
4. i.e. I pass through the sea.

With whistling prayer, the winde growne too milde,
To hasten to beget their sayles with childe.[5]
The humble Sea, as of our ship afraid,
Pale, breathlesse, prostrate at our feet, is laid.
The morne, scarse out of bed, did blush to see
Her rude beholders so unmannerly.[6]
She scarse had blusht, when she began to hide
Her rosie cheekes, like to a tender Bride.   10
To sute Aurora,[7] all the heavens put on
A mournfull vayle of black, as shee had done,
And gave the garments to the Sea they wore,
Wherewith it growes more blew[8] now than before.
This stage being set, the lightnings tapers were,[9]
The drumms such thunder as afright each ear.
Upon this summons great King *Eolus*,[10]
Attended on by *Nothus* and *Zephirus*,[11]
Enters, and where the King his steps doth place,
The waves do swell, trod with so proud a grace.   20
He was to speake, but opening of his mouth,
The boisterous winde did blow so hard at South,
I could not heare, but as the rest told me,
He spoke the prologue for a tragedie.
Behold huge mountaines in the watry maine,
That lately was a smooth and liquid plaine,
Ore which our Sea-drunke Barque doth reeling ride.
She must obey, but knowes not to which tyde;
For still she plowes that rugged mutinous place,
All skillful Pilots call the breaking race.[12]   30
A while ambition bare her up so hie,
Her proud discoloured flagg doth touch the skie;
But when the winds these waves doe beare away,[13]
She hangs in ayre, and makes a little stay:
But downe againe from such presumptuous height
Shee's headlong borne by her attractive weight[14]

5. i.e. the sailors are 'whistling for the wind'.
6. i.e. the morning blushed to see the sailors behaving in such an unruly fashion.
7. = suit, harmonize with, fit in with (the mood of) Aurora, the dawn.
8. i.e. blue. Blue lighting could be used in the theatre to suggest a fearsome environment.
9. Before the advent of electricity, stages were lit with tapers.
10. god of the winds in classical mythology.
11. the south wind (*recte* 'Notus') and the west wind.
12. a strong, rushing current of water which, in this case, is topped by breaking waves.
13. move away.
14. i.e. drawn down by the force of gravity.

Into the hollow of a gaping grave,
Intomb'd of each side with a stately wave.
Downe poure these billows from their height of pride:
Our Barque receives them in at every side.   40
But when they finde no place where to remaine,
The scuddle holes[15] do let them out againe.
At length, as Castles where no force can finde
A conquest, by assault are undermin'd,
So in our Barque, whose walls no waves could breake,
We do discover a most trayterous leake.
To this, though much our hopes do now decline,
We do oppose the Pump,[16] our countermine:[17]
That midway breakes,[18] whereat our Master cryes
All hope is past, the Seas must close our eyes;   50
And to augment death's hideous show the more,
We in the poope[19] can scarse discerne the prore;[20]
Such ugly mists had overcast the ayre,
That heaven, I thought, had meant we should despayre.
But in the last act of this Tragedie,
Behold, our great God's all-discerning eye
Caused in an instant these thick mists disband;
The winds are calm'd, and we at Skerries land.

Dread ruler of the floods, whose powerful will
Each thing that hath a being must fulfill,   60
Whose hand markes forth the end of each man's dayes,
And steers our humane[21] ship in unknown wayes;
To thee, great guide, the incense I present:
Thou gav'st me time to live, and to repent.

---

15. scuppers.
16. i.e. although our hopes are dashed, we use the ship's pump to counter the effect of the leak.
17. i.e. our way of outwitting the enemy. A countermine was a subterranean passage constructed by the defenders of a fortress under attack to intercept a mine made by the besiegers.
18. i.e. halfway through the operation of pumping the ship, the pump itself breaks.
19. the high deck at the stern of the ship.
20. = prow.
21. human.

Directions to a Painter to draw his Mistris[1]

Poet: Welcome *Apelles*:[2] may a faithfull eye,
A steadie hand and painfull industry
Crowne thy endevours. Here my Mistris stands;
Draw such a face, such hayre, such eyes, such hands.
The pencil's ready, and the Painter's set;
The table's plac't must beare her counterfeit.[3]

He views her face, and with that look there sinkes
A powerful charme, as who of Lethes drinks,
He stupid stands,[4] forgetfull of his Art,
While wonder carves her figure in his heart.   10
At length reviv'd, he weanes his charmed sight,[5]
And then all things seeme overcast with night.
His trembling hand an ill form'd line indents,[6]
Meander-like, erring in thousand bents:[7]
For now his eye, though that her face be neere,
Powers[8] in the *Species*[9] to his heart, not heere.
Asking at length how such a shivering cold
So soone withdrew his bloud, the cause he told,
And did entreat she might retire from thence,
Whose aspect dimm'd his sight and bound his sence.[10]   20
Shee's gone: he then desires my tongue should bee
The glasse,[11] wherein my Mistris he might see.
I doe obey, willing to beare a part[12]
In her description, with the Painter's Art.

1. The description of a mistress in the form of instructions to a painter was a common trope of seventeenth-century verse. The conceits used by Bellings in this poem – particularly between lines 25 and 74 – suggest that he may have been influenced by the love poetry of John Donne, which was circulating in manuscript in London during Bellings's time at Lincoln's Inn.
2. A celebrated painter who lived in the age of Alexander the Great.
3. i.e. the board on which her likeness is to be painted is in place.
4. i.e. he stands deprived of reason, like someone who has drunk the waters of Lethe. Those who drank the waters of Lethe (one of the rivers of hell, according to ancient mythology) forgot the past.
5. i.e. he forces his enchanted eyes away from the sight . . .
6. draws (making an indentation on the board or canvas).
7. i.e. drawing a thousand false curves, like the river Meander in Phrygia (the Greek name for a country in Asia Minor).
8. = pours.
9. i.e. the idea – a term from Platonic philosophy.
10. i.e. the sight of whom dimmed his sight and constricted his perceptions.
11. mirror.
12. to play a part.

Draw first an Orbe, a perfect Spheare-like round,
With amber lockes disheveld, bravely crownd:[13]
Let Ivorie and never-melting snow,
Both soft and sleek, upon her forehead grow.
Draw then *Favonious*[14] sweetly breathing heere,
And softly bounding from my Mistris leere.[15]   30
Let him beare back, when thence he smoothly purles,
Her waving tresses in the golden curls.[16]
Oh give him leave a while to kisse her hayre,
To binde himself, then loose the captive ayre:
But when, constraind, he needs from thence must go,
Paint him unwilling, for I know he's so.
Draw here bright *Phoebus*[17] in his mid-day Coach,
And let his rayes my Mistris eyes approach;
Then, like the Ocean 'gainst a high swolen streame,
A while let them encounter beame to beame.   40
At length, draw him[18] eclipsd, to end these warres,
With greater light, as he doth smaler starres.[19]
Then draw her nose, whose alabaster white
May joyne, in all eyes, wonder with delight.
Here place the ayre, still wayting to succeed
His fellow servant,[20] who, too, largely feed
For his attendance,[21] passe her pretty pores,[22]
Their sweetly breathing ever-open dores,
And, save the inward treasure of her heart,
Stor'd with her thoughts, all goodnesse chiefest part.[23]   50
When hee's[24] compeld from thence to take his flight,
O let him often stay, to bless his sight,

13. i.e. with hair.
14. the name of one of the winds.
15. cheek.
16. i.e. let him support the waving tresses of her golden hair as he (the breath of wind) smoothly curls himself away.
17. the sun (who crosses the sky in his chariot every day, according to classical mythology).
18. i.e. the sun.
19. Donne uses a similar image in 'The Sun Rising' line 15.
20. i.e. the air (touching the mistress's face) which is waiting to be inhaled by her and to replace the air which she will breathe out. In scholastic metaphysics, air was considered the most pure of the elements and some thinkers considered that it acquired the purity of the person who breathed it. See Donne's 'Air and Angels', line 14.
21. The meaning of this line is obscure, but it seems to be that the air inhaled by the mistress is also ('too') richly rewarded ('largely feed') for its 'attendance' on the mistress.
22. i.e. passes through her pretty nostrils ('pores').
23. i.e. the doors to the mistress's lungs (her nostrils) are – except for the inward treasure of her heart which is stored with her thoughts – the chief part of all goodness.
24. i.e. when 'the ayre' (of line 45) is . . .

From self-swolne mountaines of encreasing ayre,
With the best prospect of so sweet a fayre.
But when these liquid hills,[25] striving to stay,
Oreturnd with pride of greatnesse, breake away,
Then let him vanish, and unseene remaine
As now despayring to returne againe.
Draw next her cheeks, and let a crimson redd
(Not strictly bounded, nor too largely spredd)   60
Be heere enthron'd: draw then her pure white skin,
The veyle transparant of the bloud within.
From these two founts[26] convey[27] (but underground)
The rosie dye, which in her lips is found.
Now paint them shut, that so their mutual kisse
May be the modell of a peacefull bliss.
Now let her speake, then let the gentle winde
Close up his lips, to hear my Mistris minde.
Nay, this *Favonious* must observe I know,
His ears being charm'd, he must forget to blow.   70
Shape here a figure to perclose[28] the face,
Not meerely round nor pointed, both disgrace
Her perfect feature: but Ile bring her in;
Though I want words, you may expresse[29] her chin.

Painter: O stay, you'r better to dispence with some
Than cause me leave a blank for what's to come.

Poet: Then draw, but what? alas a shadowing night
Now stops the current of mine eyes delight.
Her Band,[30] her Gown, be envious vayles[31] that hide
Her stately neck, her round and slender side;   80
Yet now awhile againe that cloud remove,
And draw her hand, the adamant[32] of love.
Here meare[33] the soft and alabaster plaines,
With the neat windings of her azure vaines;

25. i.e. of exhaled air – a witty, metaphysical conceit similar to those for which Donne is
   renowned.
26. fountains, springs; i.e. her cheeks.
27. = 1) picture (addressed to the painter) and 2) transport (i.e. the movement of blood below
   the skin).
28. a shape to unite . . .
29. portray, represent.
30. a neckband or other encircling feature of her clothes.
31. enviable (not 'envious' in the modern sense) veils.
32. loadstone, centre of attraction.
33. = mere, to mark out or delineate the boundaries of . . .

And cause them first from forth five Rocks of snow,[34]
As from their springs, in manie streames to flow.
And let them still encrease, as swolne with pride
Nature had made them through such fields to glide.
Now, Painter, you may draw her outside down:
Your Art (without my helpe) can paint a gowne.   90
O draw it not so long, 'twill hide her foot,
These graces sweet support, and graceful root.
Paint not a spangled rose, to show the In[35]
Where such a neate, fine guest is lodg'd within.
Now all is done, but Painter you must censure[36]
If this come near my Mistris portraiture.

Painter: Yes sir, this colour, and this forme of face
Resemble somewhat; but the life of grace,
Life's active motion in her rowling eye,
Her humble state, and courteous majestie,   100
What art can paint, or what mellifluous tongue
Can fit the subject with a worthy song?

Then to conclude, good sir, I must confesse,
Your tongue did little, and my hand did less.

---

34. i.e. her fingers.
35. = inn. The line seems to mean: do not paint a beautifully decorated rose (i.e. the symbol
of feminine beauty decorated with gold spangles) to act as if it were an inn-sign to show
the inn . . .
36. give a judgement.

W. MARTIN
(*fl*.**1624**)

This entertaining short poem is one of five prefixed to the 1624 Dublin printing of Richard Bellings's sixth book to Sir Philip Sidney's *Arcadia*. The author was probably a member of the prominent catholic family of the Martins of Galway – perhaps a brother of the well-known lawyer Richard Martin, who had known Bellings in London where both men attended Inns of Court in the early 1620s.

The poem gives a glimpse of the social and cultural world of the young Irish catholic élite of the time – men trained in the humanist mould, many of them lawyers, who would later come to prominence in the Confederacy of the 1640s.

To his Approved Friend the Author[1]

I read thy booke on[e] night late, and did feare
Still as I read, I saw appearing there
Sir Philip Sidney's ghost; yet look't about
And nothing could espie might breed that doubt
But thy sweet, harmlesse Booke; so like in all
Was matter, phrase, and language which did fall
From thy chaste pen, that surely both being gone,[2]
Next age will write your characters in one.
And doe I envie this? Yes, sure I do,
So farre as to have had the glorie too   10
T'have finisht such a worke. But since 'twas left
For thee alone, tell me (of faith bereft)
Where you two spoke together, and I vow
To keep it from the world, as I doe now
Not knowing it; that so, before to morrow,
I might in honour of thy worke, but borrow
Some little portion of his sacred Muse,
That might to me like[3] flames and spirit infuse;
For none but such, can reach that height of glory
Which thou hast got by this immortal story.   20

1. Richard Bellings.
2. i.e. when both Sidney and Bellings are dead.
3. i.e. similar.

LADY ANN SOUTHWELL
(1571–**1626(?)**–1636)

Lady Ann Southwell (née Harris) and her first husband Thomas Southwell came to Ireland early in the seventeenth century as planters. They lived for many years at Poulnelong Castle in County Cork and developed a wide circle of friends and acquaintants. Her common-place book, which is now in the Folger Shakespeare Library in Washington DC, contains copies of letters or poems to the lord deputy, Lord Falkland, to the Earl of Castlehaven and to the Bishop of Limerick, among others. Lady Southwell's verse-letter to the bishop is an ambitious and complex poem which shows her to have been a highly intelligent woman with a grasp of contemporary intellectual debate and a remarkable understanding of neo-Platonism. The same lively intellect appears in the ambitious (and ambiguous) mock-elegy below, in which Lady Southwell shows a metaphysical delight in wordplay and a fascination with complex ideas. The Countess of Londonderry, whose soul is the subject of the poem, had been a maid of honour to Queen Elizabeth in her youth. When Lady Londonderry really died in 1627, Lady Southwell wrote 'An Epitaph' on her and referred to this poem as recently written, so it can probably be dated about 1626.

An Elegie written by the Lady A: S: to the Countesse of London Derrye
supposeinge hir to be dead by hir[1] longe silence

Since thou, fayre soule, art warbleinge[2] to a spheare
from whose resultances theise quickned weere,
since thou hast layd that downy Couch[3] aside
of Lillyes, Violletts, and roseall[4] pride,
and lockt in marble chests that Tapestrye
that did adorne the worlds Epitome[5]
soe safe that Doubt it selfe can never thinke
fortune or fate hath power to make a chinke;[6]
since thou, for state, hath raisd thy state soe farr,[7]

1. her.
2. A term from falconry meaning to cross the wings together over the back. Neo-Platonism asserts the high origins of the human soul and concerns itself with ways in which that soul may return to its eternal home. In this case, the soul of the countess is imagined as rising, physically, through the skies. The first two lines could be paraphrased: Since you, fair soul, are winging your way to the heavens, from the debris of which this world was created . . .
3. i.e. the body.
4. roseate, rose-coloured.
5. the representation of the world. (here) = the body (now in a marble tomb).
6. This seems to mean that not even a person full of doubt could imagine that either fortune or fate could crack open the coffin in which lie the earthly remains of the countess.
7. 'state' can mean the mode of existence of a spiritual being: the line is thus a play on words, and the couplet means, roughly, 'since you, to become a spirit, have raised yourself so far that you have risen above the circular vault of the skies to the great heaven' . . .

to a large heaven from a vaute[8] circular,   10
because the thronginge virtues in thy brest
could not have roome enough in such a chest,
what need hast thou theise blotted Lines should tell;
soules must againe take rise, from whence they fell,
from Paradice, and that this earths Darke wombe
is but a wardrobe till the day of Do[o]me
to keepe those wormes, that on hir[9] bosomes bredd,
till tyme, and death, bee both extermined?
Yet in thy passage, fayre soule, let me know
what things thou saw'st in riseinge from below: 20
Whether that Cynthia, regent of the flood,[10]
will[11] in hir Orbe admitt of mortall brood?
Whether the 12 Signes serve the Sun for state,
or elce confine him to the Zodiaque,
and force him retrograde to bee the nurse
(whoe circularly glides his oblique course)
of Alma Mater,[12] or unfreeze the wombe
of Madam Tellus[13] – wch elce Proves a tombe?[14]
Whether the starrs be Knobbs uppon the spheres?
Or shredds compos'd of Phœbus goulden hayres?   30
Or whether th'Ayre be as a cloudy sive?
The starrs be holes through wch the good soules drive?
Whether that Saturne that the 6 out topps[15]
sitt ever eatinge of the bratts of Opps,[16]

---

8. vault.
9. i.e. the earth is but a clothing ('wardrobe') for the soul to support those worms (i.e. humans) that breed on the bosom (of the earth) until death and the end of time.
10. The passage which follows assumes a knowledge of the Ptolemaic system of the universe in which a series of concentric spheres, punctured by the holes of different sizes through which shone sun, moon, planets and stars, were constantly moving, each in its own way, around the earth. As the countess's soul passes through the spheres on its way to the distant heavens, it gets a chance to see what happens on each level. The first level encountered is that of Cynthia, the moon, who, personified as a goddess, controls the tides (the flood). The question is, are there men on the moon or, at least, on the moon's sphere?
11. MS reads 'wth'.
12. The ancient Romans gave this name, 'the white mother', to the nurturing goddesses, particularly Ceres. Here it is applied to a sign of the zodiac through which the sun has to pass on an oblique course so that, like a nurse, he can give life to the earth.
13. goddess of the earth. Some of the symbolism of the signs of the zodiac is linked to the seasons of the year, the ploughing of the land being associated with Taurus, the bull.
14. i.e. the earth would be a tomb if it were not warmed by the sun and if the seasons did not pass.
15. At the time this poem was written, it was thought that there were six planets of which Saturn was the most distant from earth.
16. The god Saturn was in the habit of devouring the children born to him by his wife Ops, though she did manage, according to some legends, to save some of her children, including Jupiter, Neptune and Pluto, from their father.

whose jealousye is like a Sea of Gall[17]
unto his owne Proves Periodicall?[18]
But as a glideinge star whoe falls to earth
or lovers thoughts, soe soules ascend theyr birth,
wch makes mee thinke, that thyne had noe one notion
of those true elements, by whose true motion   40
all things have life, and death;[19] but if thyne eyne
should fix a while uppon the Christalline,[20]
thy hungrye eye, that never could before,
see, but by fayth, and faythfully adore,
should stay, to marke the threefould Hierarchye,[21]
differinge in state, not in fælicitye,
how they in Order, 'bout Jehova move,
in severall Offices, but wth one love,
and, from his hand, doe hand in hand come downe,
till the last hand doe heads of mortalls crowne.   50
Fayne would I know from some that have beene there
what state or shape cælestiall bodyes beare?[22]
For Man, to heaven, hath throwne a waxen ball,
in wch hee thinks h'hath gott true formes of all,
and, from the forge howse of his fantasie,
hee creates new, and spins out destinye.
And thus, theise prowd wormes, wrapt in lothsome rags,
shutt heavens Idea upp, in letherne baggs.[23]
Now since in heaven are many Ladyes more,
that blinde devotion busyely implore,   60
Good Lady, freind, or rather lovely Dame,
if yow[24] be gone from out this clayie frame,
tell what yow know, whether th' Saynts adoration
will stoope to thinke on dusty procreation.

17. See Job 16. 13.
18. The reference is to the regular movements of the planet Saturn.
19. Like her contemporary John Donne, Ann Southwell was fascinated by the paradoxes
    inherent in a world where the facts and definitions of the new science came up against
    the poetic and symbolic ideas of the old world-view.
20. i.e. upon the highest level of the heavens where, according to Ptolemy, a crystal sphere
    existed between the *primum mobile* and the firmament.
21. According to Dionysius the Areopagite, there are three divisions of angels, each one
    comprising three orders. Angels live in the highest levels of heaven, around Jehovah: but
    they also descend to earth to perform tasks such as crowning kings (line 50).
22. Another key question of the age: what type of bodies will the righteous have in heaven?
23. A wax ball would take an image imprinted on it: so these lines could be paraphrased: man
    has created a heaven out of his own fantasies and, 'prowd worme' that he is, has shut up
    what he knows of the perfections of heaven ('Heavens idea') in leathern bags, i.e. books.
24. you.

And if they will not, they are fooles (perdye)
that pray to them, and robb the Trinitye;[25]
The Angells joy in o[u]r good conversation,
yet see us not, but by reverberation,[26]
And if they could, yow[27] s[ain]ts as cleere eies have,
if downe yow looke to earth, then to the grave,   70
tis but a Landkipp,[28] more, to looke to Hell;
in viewinge it, what strange thinges may yow tell?
From out that Sulphrous and bitumeous lake,
Where Pluto doth his Tilt and Tournay[29] make,
Where the Elizium and theyr Purgatorye[30]
stande, like two suburbs, by a Promontarye,
Poets and Popleings are æquippollent,[31]
both makers are, of Gods, of like descent;
Poets makes blinde Gods, whoe with willowes beates them,[32]
Popelings makes Hoasts of Gods, & ever eates them.[33]   80
But let them both, Poets & Popleings, passe;
whoe deales too much with eyther, is an Asse.
Charon conduct them, as they have devised.[34]
The Fall of Angells, must not bee disguised;[35]
As 'tis not tirrany but loveinge pittye
that Kings build prisons in a populous Cittye,
soe the next way to fright us back to good
is to discusse the Paynes of Stigian[36] flood.
In Eve's distained[37] nature, wee are base,
And whipps perswade us more than love or grace,   90

---

25. Criticism of adherents of the Roman catholic church who pray to saints and so 'robb the Trinitye' (i.e. God himself) of prayers. perdye = pardie = By God!
26. reflection. Whether angels, saints and departed souls had senses as we understand them were hotly debated questions.
27. i.e. you saints have such vision that . . .
28. landscape.
29. Pluto was god of the underworld: Southwell imagines him organising chivalric contests.
30. Elysium was the abode of the blessed departed in Greek mythology: purgatory was the place where souls were purged of their sins before entering heaven, according to the catholic church. Since belief in purgatory was specifically condemned by the protestant churches, the protestant Southwell describes it as 'their' purgatory.
31. equally powerful. Popelings = little popes, presumably catholic priests.
32. This line is obscure.
33. A reference to transubstantiation; again, Southwell shows her disapproval of the beliefs of the Roman church.
34. i.e. let Charon (the aged ferryman who, in Greek mythology, carries the shades of the dead across the river Styx in the lower world) take them as they have planned.
35. i.e. we must not pretend we are without sin.
36. of the river Styx. The pains are the pains of hell.
37. dishonoured.

Soe that if heaven should take away this rodd,
God would hate us, and wee should not love God.
For as afliction, in a full fedd state,
like vinegar in sawces, doe awake
dull Appetites and makes men feed the better,
soe when a Lythargye[38] o[u]r braynes doth fetter,
the onely way to rouse againe o[u]r witts
is when the Surgions cheifest toole is whips.[39]
Brasse hath a couseninge[40] face and lookes like gould
but where the touchstone comes it cannot hold.[41]   100
That Sonne of ours, doth best deserve our rent[42]
that doth wth Patience beare o[u]r chastisement.
Each Titmouse can salute the lusty Springe,
and weare it out wth joyllye revellinge,
but yo[u]r pure-white and vestall[43] clothed swan
sings at hir death, and never sings but then;[44]
O noble minded bird, I envy thee,
for thou hast stolne this high borne note from mee!
But as the Prophett[45] at his M[aste]rs feete,
when hee ascended up the Welkin fleete,[46]   110
Watcht for his cloake, soe every bird & beast
When princely Adam tumbled from the nest,
catcht, from his knoweinge sowle, some qualitie,
and humbly kept it, to reedifye
theyr Quondam kinge;[47] and now, man goes to schoole
to every Pismire[48] that proclaymes him foole.[49]

---

38. depression, sense of apathy.
39. A reference to a not uncommon treatment for lethargy or depression.
40. = cozening, cheating, deceiving.
41. Henry VIII had ordered the systematic adulteration of gold coins with brass: a touchstone (a piece of fine-grained jasper stone) would show the difference between true coins and base ones since it produced a streak of one colour when rubbed with pure gold and a streak of a different colour when rubbed with gold mixed with brass.
42. payment. The couplet implies that Jesus ('That Sonne of ours') is no fraud.
43. like a virgin.
44. The swan was said to sing only once – at the moment of death. The lines mean that ordinary creatures (mice) can rejoice as much as they like, but the white, virgin soul of the countess, like the swan, can communicate only at the time of her death.
45. Elisha, who took up mantle of Elijah, who had been received into heaven in a whirlwind. II Kings 2. 11.
46. the shifting sky.
47. re-edify = restore; quondam = former. Before the Fall, Adam had been king of the beasts. Genesis 1. 19.
48. ant.
49. i.e. man is now less wise than even an ant.

But stay my wandringe thoughts! alas where wade I
In speakeinge to a dead, a sencelesse[50] Lady?
Yow Incke and paper, be hir passeinge bell,
The Sexton to hir knell,[51] be Anne Southwell.   120

---

50. i.e. who is now incapable of sensation.
51. i.e. I, Ann Southwell, will act as the sexton who produces the sound of the passing bell (this poem) for the countess.

ANONYMOUS
(1625)

Sir Arthur Chichester (1563–1625) was born in Devon. His military career included service against the Spanish Armada in 1588, a spell in the West Indies with Sir Francis Drake and service on the Continent before he arrived in Ireland in 1599 as governor of Carrickfergus. Once in Ireland, Chichester showed himself a brilliant but ruthless commander and, in addition, soon made himself one of the largest landowners and planters in Ulster, with an estate of 30,000 acres, much of it land previously controlled by Hugh O'Neill, the Earl of Tyrone. In 1605 he became lord deputy and, for the eleven years of his appointment, he attempted to anglicise Ireland and to reduce the power and influence of the catholic church. From the English point of view, Chichester was a highly effective lord deputy, but from another perspective, he can be seen as a protestant fanatic and a ruthless land-grabber. Though he succeeded in introducing English rule and law into most of Ireland, Chichester's vigorous attempts to extirpate the catholic church and destroy its hierarchy were a failure. He was elevated to the peerage as Lord Chichester of Belfast in 1613 and died in 1625. The text below is on the magnificent Chichester family monument in St Nicholas's Church, Carrickfergus.

Sacred to God + aeternall memore Sr. Arthure Chichester Knight, Baron of Belfast ...

Fatum mortis, a Domino injunctum est.[1]
If that desire or chanche thee[2] hither lead,
Upon this marble monument to tread,
Let admiracion, thy best thoughtes still feed,
While weeping thou, this epitaph doest reade:
& let distilling teares, thy commaes[3] be,
As tribute due, unto this elegie.

Epitaphe

Within this bedd of death, a viceroy lyes,
Whose fame shall ever live, vertue nere dyes:
Nor he did vertue, & religeon norishe,[4]   10
& made this land, late rude,[5] with peace to florish.
The wildest rebell he be[6] power did tame
& by true justice gaynd an honord name:

1. The destiny of death is imposed by the Lord.
2. i.e. the visitor to the church.
3. commas, pauses; i.e. let your tears make you pause (?)
4. i.e. nor did he only nourish virtue and religion: he also made this land ...
5. violent, turbulent.
6. by.

Then now, though hee in heaven with angells be
Let us on earth, still love his memorie.

By him interd his noble ladye is,[7]
Whoe pertake with him, in heavenly blisse;
For while the earth unto them was a seate,
Unmacht they were, being both good & great.

With them doth rest, theire one & only sonne, 20
Whose life was short, & soe his glasse soone run;[8]
The heavens, not earth, was his allotted right,
For which he badd the world soe soone goodnight.

Intombd by them, here allsoe doth remayn,
His worthy brother, by base rebells slayn:[9]
As he in martiall, & brave warrelike feight,[10]
Opposde theire eurie,[11] in his cuntreys right.

& in memorill of theire endles praise,
This monument is left to after dayes.

7. Lettice or Letitia, daughter of Sir John Perrot.
8. See, p. 134, the poem by Sir John Davies on the death of the infant son of Sir Arthur and Lady Chichester.
9. Sir John Chichester, killed in a skirmish with the forces of Sir James MacDonnell in 1597.
10. fight.
11. eure, an obsolete word meaning 'destiny'.

ALEXANDER SPICER
(*fl*.**1625**)

Alexander Spicer seems to have been a clergyman based in the north of Ireland. Though his only other recorded publications were the enlargement of a work called *David's Petition* and a sermon he preached at Coleraine in 1617, it is hard to believe that this ambitious elegy (of which only a selection appears below) was his only verse. The poem made three appearances in print in the seventeenth century. The first was at the time of the death of Lord Chichester of Belfast in 1625, the occasion for which it was written. Its second appearance (most inappropriately and with its text partly amended) was as an elegy on the death of Sir Simon Harcourt in 1642. The third printing was dated 1643 – a year described as 'the yeare of mourning' on the title-page; on this occasion, Chichester was returned to his rightful place as its subject, and the original text was restored.

This disarmingly hyperbolic eulogy of the controversial lord deputy presents a view of him which would only have been recognisable to his most ardent supporters; to others, he was a man responsible for brutal repression and for the slaughter of hundreds during his time in Ireland.

from: An Elegie on the much lamented death of the Right Honourable Sir Arthur Chichester, Knight,

Lo. Baron of Belfast, Lo. high Treasurer of Ireland, one of the Lords of his Majesties most Honourable Privie Counsell, and of the Counsell of War . . .

> Dead? and before we heard him sicke, incline
> To draw his breath towards that utmost line
> Which leads to earth? this moves me to enquire,
> Why noble *Belfast* should so soone expire.[1]
> 'Twas thus: death knew that such a gallant pray
> Could not be had unles 'twere snatcht away,
> And therefore strucke him in a deadly hower,
> Beyond recovorie by Physitians power.
> But we are bound to fame which keeps alive
> This Noble-man, whom death would not reprive . . .   10
>
> From *Chichesters* discent he tooke his name,
> And in exchange of it, return'd such fame
> By his brave deeds, as to that race shall be
> A radiant splendor for eternitie:[2]
> For fame shall write this Adage: *Let it last*
> *Like the sweet memorie of my Lord* Belfast.

---

1. Chichester had been relieved of the lord deputyship of Ireland in 1616, and it was not clear whether his last years were ones of honourable retirement or of disgrace.
2. Chichester was the younger son of a family of minor Devon gentry.

When once the time of childhood did begin
To step aside, that youth might enter in,
He went to *Oxford*, that the liberall Arts
Might be ennamel to his native parts.[3]   20
Faire education with good parentage
Made all his vertues walke in equipage,[4]
That they who knew him young, presag'd his scope
Was ever bending to that Cape of Hope
Where Honour rides;[5] For after he had seene
The *Muses*, he return'd to serve his Queene
With armes of valour; the report of them
May be a *Chronicle*: for so large a theame
Requires a booke in *Folio*, not one leafe,
To shew the homage due to *Josephs Sheafe*.[6]   30
All bow'd to his, and no worth finds extent
Beyond the bounds of his, whom I lament.
Grave, brave, sure, pure; and like a heavenly star,
In peace, war, speech, and life, was *Chichester*.
Renowned Lord, whose noble acts yeeld matter
For me to praise, and yet abhor to flatter.
Besides the severall voyages which he made
Against the Spanish foe, which would invade
Our Brittish coast, the civill warres of France
Drew forth our English *Scipio*[7] to advance   40
His colours there, which he displaid, and wonne
Honourable knighthood, when the fight was done.

---

3. Chichester matriculated at Exeter College Oxford in 1583. Enamel was highly regarded in the Renaissance and 'to enamel' meant 'to adorn magnificently' or 'to impart an additional splendour to'.
4. ceremonious display.
5. An extended footnote at this point reads: 'He was a Captaine of the ship called the Victorie, under the command of the Lo. *Sheffield*, employed against the Spanish Invasion *Anno* 1587, & 88. Afterwards he was Captaine and Commander in the Portogal voyage of 200 foot, in the Regiment of the Generall sir *Fra. Drake*, 88 and 89. He went with sir *Fra. Drake* to the West Indies, where he was Captain of a Companie of foot, and Lieutenant Colonell of a Regiment. And in Porterico he set fire to the Admirall of the Spanish Frigats, 95 & 96. After their return from that voyage, he was employed in France, being Captain and Lieutenant Colonel of a regiment with Sir *Th. Baskervile*, 96. After his returne out of France, he was employed into Ireland with the Earle of Essex, &c.' Not all the details here are confirmed by modern research.
6. A reference to the dream Joseph recounts to his brothers in Genesis 37. 7; 'For, behold, we were binding sheaves in the field, and, lo, my sheaf arose, and also stood upright; and behold, your sheaves stood round about, and made obeisance to my sheaf.' Joseph's brothers subsequently sold him to a passing Ishmaelite.
7. one of the greatest generals of the ancient Roman empire.

Henrie the 4. of France in gracefull manner,
Upon desert confer'd this warlike honour,[8]
And fame imprints this Character on his shield,
Knighted by *Burbon*, in the open field.
Desert neglected, droopes; encourag'd beares
Its motions well, as the well ordered Spheares.
Our minds prove then, best active, when we know
Our plants are set where they are like to grow.   50
The home-bred flames of France extinct, our owne
Portend a hot combustion by *Tyrone*,[9]
A Traitor, who like a Tyger gnawes
The wombe which bare him, with his bloudy pawes.
The Queene bestow'd some favours, and he thought
Had she done more, s'had done but what she ought.
Through the perspective of his fantasie,
He dream'd he saw his vertues grow so hie
That part of *Ulster*, for the great *Oneale*
Was not so fit as was a common-weale;[10]   60
So, by ambitious projects, look't for gales
Which might fill full, and yet not rent[11] his sailes.
Among the valiant chieftaines which were sent
To stop the current of his proud intent
Came *Chichester*, whose acts did carrie sense
And weight of honour with experience.
His colours flew with such auspitious fate
As if that faire *Bellona*[12] there had sate
With wreathes of gold to make a crowne for him,
Who harboured prowes in each manfull limbe,   70
And made him after his victorious triall,
The Sergeant Major of the armie royall.[13]

---

8. Chichester was knighted by Henry IV (1553–1610) king of France and head of the younger branch of the Bourbons, after the siege of Amiens in 1597. Lines 47–50 are lines of general reflection.
9. Hugh O'Neill, Earl of Tyrone (1550–1616).
10. The Treaty of Mellifont of 1603 allowed Tyrone to return to his traditional land in Ulster. He had earlier shown that he considered himself an appropriate ruler of Ireland as a whole, and this jibe shows that he was thought to harbour the same aspirations after 1603.
11. split.
12. The Roman goddess of war.
13. The Earl of Essex had appointed Chichester sergeant-major-general of the English army in Ireland in 1599.

The Lord *Mountjoy*,[14] Lord deputie of that realme,
Who sate as Pilot in that dangerous healme,
Wrote to the Lords in England his opinion,
Touching the safetie of that sicke dominion.
Because experience taught him oft to learne
That boggs and fastness made the Irish kerne
To nestle in the North, he did propound
That some one man whose judgement was profound   80
And valour matchles, might have forces readie
To curbe the rebells at the first, if headie
Attempts should move them to an insurrection,
Or draw them (as they speake) to go in action:
For this imployment (so records affirme,
And Il'e deliver it in it's proper terme)[15]
Sir *Arthur Chichester is the fittest man*,
(Saies he) *in England or in Ireland*. Can
Fame be more copious in her bountie than
To praise his worth above a world of men?   90
That campe had many worthies who survive
And live to see their reputation thrive.
Yet all with famous Mountjoy doe agree
To write in that of *Chichester*, *this is he*:
But now they write *he was*, from whence abound
Our flouds of griefe like Spring-tides to surround,
Tyrone himselfe, whose lewd affections stood
To crosse, with malice, the increase of good,
Who lay in wait with unappeased spleene,
In secret ambushments, to wrecke his teene[16]   100
On carefull *Chichester*, did protest, so many
Parts of a Souldier were in him, that any,
Who leade in warlike marches, could not be
More just, more valiant, nor more wise then he.
Those flames of good desert must sparkle hie,
Whose brightnes is approv'd by enmitie . . .

He lov'd both Arts and Armes: just such another
As *Pembrokes* Uncle, or as *Leicesters* Brother.[17]

14. Charles Blount, Earl of Devonshire and Baron Mountjoy (1563–1606); Mountjoy did, as the poet asserts, recommend Chichester for the position of lord deputy.
15. i.e. I'll put it down here in the actual words.
16. to wreak his teen; i.e. to do him injury or damage.
17. i.e. Sir Henry Sidney (whose daughter, Mary, married the second Earl of Pembroke) or his son, Sir Philip Sidney, brother to the first Earl of Leicester.

177

A *Sydney*, a *Chichester*, and that's as much,
As to write in plaine English, a *None such*:[18]   110
For in good sooth, never before or since
Could a Vice-roy doe more honour to his Prince.
The people praid, *Lord if it be thy will*,
Let this Lord be Lord Deputy with us still.
I seeke not to detract, *Boetius*[19] saies,
Good is diffusive and hath ample praise,
To give this man his due, and yet retaine
Good store for others, when it gives againe.
One writes, the Deputies of that Kingdome are
Like Aple-trees, and if their fruit be faire,   120
The Cudgels then must flye:[20] 'Twas so with him,
For some Informers, whose aspect was dimme,
Who see no right, nor can discerne religion,
Unlesse i'th habite of their superstition,
Tax him of much injustice, by a rabble
Of false suggestions at the Councell table.[21]
But Royal *Salomon* did observe the cause,
And found 'twas not his Deputy, but his Lawes
Were call'd in question: therefore daign'd to give,
Words which might make a dying man to live.   130
This man is cleere, upon examination,
I finde that all's an unjust accusation,
With other Princely speeches which transcend,
Nor can they, as they ought, by me be pen'd:
When *innocence*, his truest *advocate*,
Made replication[22] to the Plaintiffes hate,
And that the Agents for their false report,
Should undergoe the Censure of that Court;
His meeknesse followed and besought the King
To pardon his accusers, who did bring   140

18. a person without equal.
19. This seems to be a reference to one of the most widely respected books of the late Renaissance and early modern periods, *De Consolatione Philosophiae* by the Roman philosopher Boethius (*c.* 480–524).
20. Apple trees were struck with cudgels to dislodge their fruit at harvest time. 'Whose aspect was dimme' (l. 122) means 'whose ability to see clearly was poor'.
21. In 1613, the Old English catholics declared themselves outraged at Chichester's behaviour and went to London to complain about him to James I. After some delay, Chichester himself was also summoned to London. But when the king gave his judgement in the case, on 20 April 1614, he supported Chichester fully and dismissed the allegations of the catholic delegates. 'Royal *Salomon*' = James I.
22. reply.

Their owne disgrace, not his; a rare example,
In these malitious times, inimitable.
They sought his ruine, he their good: we see
The lesson kept, Christ taught him, *learne of mee* . . .

One night, not long since, in the skie was showne,
A *Star* depending on[23] the forked *Moone*:
But now the *Moone* waites on the glorious *Starre*,
Whose brightnes doth surpasse the Moon-shine far.
Honour and Life, like to the *Moone*, have waines;[24]
Christ is the morning starre: in piercing paines   150
Of death, this Lord disdain'd the *Moones* respect,
For the felicity of the *Starres* elect:[25]
He did confesse, that like Divine S. *Paul*,
Christ was his gaine, his hope, his life, his all.[26]
His Tongue was tipt with golden sentences,
Which recollect the Soule,[27] when her offences
Have made her thoughts unsteaddy, that shee stands
Giddy, like the foundation on the sands,
Untill that Word of God afford a light,
To put the Soul in a more hopefull plight.   160
The goodly structures which were framed by
The curious platformes of his industry
In earthly things, he did conclude were winde,
And subject to corruption: that his minde,
Empty of her own good, might mount up higher,
Whither a Christian ought for to aspire.
The Angels were on wing, to beare away
His soule, and yet he argues, their delay
To be o're long, lamenting his aboad
Was yet on earth, divided from his God.   170
Each faculty of his soule striv'd which should be
Best learned in the schoole of piety.
Zeale mov'd as lively in those christian straines,
As blood enclosed in the narrow veines.

23. hanging down from, dependent on. In the next lines, the natural order is overturned and the moon is seen to be in attendance on the star (the recently deceased Chichester), which has become brighter than the moon itself.
24. wanes, periods when they grow less.
25. Since Christ is the morning star and the other stars are blessed souls in heaven, the dying Chichester ('this Lord') considered the moon less worthy of honour than the stars.
26. Philippians 1. 20–1.
27. i.e. which bring the soul back to a state of composure.

To see him dye was dolour: thus to dye,
Ravish'd the Mourners with alacrity,
Because they saw he went, a glorious Guest
At Supper-time, unto the *Mariage feast*.
Thus he expir'd; nor could a humane Creature,
With more content discharge a debt to Nature.   180
England laments: and where his body goes,
That Land is drowned with a Sea of woes.
Would I might live here[28] still, the Irish Shores,
Will be as gloomy as the tawny Moores:
Their blacke-dide countenance will misinforme
The skillfull Pilot: and as in a storme,
Confusion will succeed; for beds of sand,
Will move the waves to drive them toward land,
That they may vie their multitudes with *All*,
Who shed a teare at his sad Funerall.[29]   190
Tis well *Knockfergus*[30] stands upon a rocke,
For otherwise the fierce impetuous shocke
Of dismall outcries when the Corpes comes thither,
Will make the Fort and Wall and houses shiver,
Or crumble into dust, like *Jericho*,
When *Josuahs Rams hornes* were observ'd to blow.[31]
Yea the whole Realme will make a dolefull cry,
To make an Earth-quake for his *Elegie*.
The swift wind will be reasty,[32] as afraid
To waft the noise, lest all the land be made   200
Subject to ruine, in astonishment,
With much bewailing this dire accident.
Joy-mount can be no mount of joy,[33] but moane,
Like to the Turtle[34] when her mate is gone.

---

28. i.e. (presumably) in England (see l. 39). The next line assrts that the shores of Ireland will be as dark as the face of a black African. (In the seventeenth century, 'Moors' were still thought to be black-skinned).
29. The most absurd of the hyperboles of the poem.
30. Carrickfergus, Co. Antrim, where Chichester was buried.
31. In one of the most famous stories of the Old Testament, Joshua, leader of the children of Israel who were besieging the city of Jericho, instructed the people to shout loudly after the priests had marched round the city walls seven times blowing trumpets made of rams' horns. The city walls duly fell down. See Joshua 6.
32. = restive, still.
33. Joymount was the name of Chichester's magnificent mansion in Carrickfergus. He had named it, reputedly, as a compliment to Lord Mountjoy, his patron.
34. the turtle dove.

The Drums and Fifes, clad in their mourning suite,
Will sound, as if his death had made them mute.[35]
The aire will be all blacke, and like a Fuller,[36]
Dye the light Banners in a sable colour.
The buriall must be wet, sith[37] no eye's dry,
I'th swelling deluge of this misery.   210

Among the presse,[38] my *Muse* desireth roome,
To speake one word to him, who makes the Tombe:
Be sure to cut his Eare *indifferent*;[39] and
A golden Pen in his laborious hand.
Shew forth his eyes with such resplendent light,
As one who still retaines his wonted sight.
As for his Robes of Parliament, let them be
Put on with such advice,[40] that we may see
His Sword, and know a Souldier: on his Armes
Write this: *The Bucklers to defend from harmes*   220
His Prince and Countrey. And beneath his head
A Pillow, as if he were gone to bed.
Thou maist limme[41] Honour, speaking; *This is he*
Whose brave exploits hath thus deserved me.
Let it not be as if he sought for her,
For that will wrong the King, who did prefer[42]
His Deputy, of himselfe, and gave th'impresse,[43]
Ile honour him, who sought for nothing lesse.
Make his Tombe wide and high, to imitate
The copious circle of his ample fate.   230
If in thy fabricke thou dost want a stone,
Sith griefe hath made me *Niobe*,[44] Ile be one.

---

35. i.e. the drums will be muffled.
36. One who shrinks and thickens woollen fabric. The lines mean that the air will be so black (in mourning) that it will dye the light-coloured banners black.
37. since.
38. the crowd at the funeral.
39. i.e. the one making the effigy of Chichester is to show, in the way his ear is carved, that he listened to both sides of a cause. Whoever actually carved the representation of Lord Chichester on his memorial in Carrickfergus Church paid no attention to the advice in the next few lines.
40. i.e. in such a way.
41. portray.
42. promote.
43. motto, sentence accompanying an emblem in heraldry.
44. In Greek mythology, Niobe was so grief-stricken at the death of her children that she turned into a stone.

I wish this happiness to his Heire; *Inherit*
Like to Elisha, this Eliahs spirit:[45]
For that's a stately impe[46] of Fame, by which
More honour is, than is by being rich.
Lord, What is man? when such a man as he,
Whose parts excelled in the high'st degree,
Dies by a *Plurisie*, a corrupted tumour,
Proceeding from a bad unhealthfull humour.[47]   240
How ought we then, who are but Atoms small,
And in respect of him, are not at all,
To know our bodies but an house of earth,
And thinke on God before the soule goes forth?
His last to me was this; *Much thankes, Good night.*
May my best service study to requite[48]
His noble complement: For it I returne,
Millions of teares on his bewailed Urne.
And sith the bed he sleepes on is his Biere,
Ile bid *Good night*, and draw the Curtaines here.   250

45. The spirit of Elijah doth rest on Elisha. II Kings 2. 11.
46. scion, offspring.
47. The reference is to the medieval theory of the humours – that illness was a result of imbalance in one or more of the four humours (phlegm, blood, choler or black bile); such a theory gave a coherent explanation for an inflammation such as pleurisy.
48. repay.

ANONYMOUS
(1626)

The first quarter of the seventeenth century was a time of uncertainty and tension in Ireland as the catholic Old English – still a powerful political force – struggled to prevent the Irish government, with its protestant and New English sympathies, from eroding their rights and appropriating their land for plantation. The English government needed the support of the Old English, not only to provide funds to pay for its army in Ireland but also because it was generally accepted that if Spain were to invade England, it would do so through Ireland: thus it was vital to strengthen the loyalty of the Old English in Ireland to the English crown. Concessions had to be made to them and, in 1626, Charles I sent a list of proposals to the lords of Ireland asking for support for an enlarged army in exchange for the easing of religious tests; the lord deputy, Henry Cary, Lord Falkland, invited the lords to come to Dublin Castle to discuss the king's offer.

The song which follows appeared, presumably on the streets of Dublin, as plans for the assembly were being prepared. The text is full of ironies, the most potent of which is that the poet places the assembly not in Dublin Castle – the symbol of alien rule in Ireland, where it did, in fact take place in November 1626 – but at the Hill of Tara in County Meath, the traditional centre of Ireland, home of the high kings, and the place where legislative assemblies met in pre-conquest Ireland.

Mount Taraghs Triumph 5 July 1626

To the tune of the *Careere*

King *Charles* be thou blest, with peace and with rest;
    who caus'd this assembly hither.
Welcome yee *Peeres*, yee *Earles* of our Shires
    yee *Viscounts*, and *Barons* together.
Taragh the Mount, his joyes doth account,
    being grac'd with your gratefull presence.
Nobles then all, at *Falkland*[1] his call,
    to *Charles* see you now give your obeysance.

Knights of great merits, generous of spirits,
    to *Taragh* ye'are welcome this day: 10
Esquiers, and gentrie, the force of our Countrie,
    to march on in battle array:
Spirits of great worth, from the South to the North,
    whose hearts doe to honor aspire,
To stand with renowne, for *Charles* and his crowne,
    is your onely delight, and desire.

---

1. Henry Cary, Viscount Falkland (*d.* 1633), lord deputy of Ireland 1622–9.

The Squadrons appeere, the Troupes they Careere,
    from the foote of the Hill, to the top:
With force (like a flood, being mainely[2] withstood)
    their courage indureth no stop.   20
King *Charles* to thy Troupes, the hill of *Taragh* stoupes
    that long a Royall Mansion hath beene:
With Ecchoes in the skies, it shouts and it cries,
    long life to King *Charles* and his *Queene*.

What can your foes expect but your blowes,
    and the force of your conquering hands?
If they be bent to take their event,
    to approach to your shears, or your sands;[3]
Backe you will send them, or altogether end them:
    for the heavens and your right will uphold you: 30
Captaines why then, come marshall your men,
    as if *Mars*, or King *Charles* did behold you.

Falkland behold, this Armie most bold,
    most constant, and loyall of hearts;
To make up their Fortes, or to maintaine their Portes,
    prepar'd to performe their parts;
With hearts they doe show such homage as they owe,
    and straight at a call doe attend:
King *Charles* his Pavillion against an arm'd Million
    of foes, they will stoutly defend.   40

The *Median-soyle*,[4] unpatient of the foyle,[5]
    is the heart of our native land
Mount *Taragh* of fame, is the heart of the same,
    whereon this Royall armie doth stand.
That heart, of her heart, with every other part,
    faire *Ireland* presents to her King,
With Trumpets and Drums (not fearing foe that comes)
    King *Charles* his triumph let us sing.

Yee *Gentlemen*, and *Squiers*, yee *Knights* of the Shires,
    your service with courage maintaine: 50

2. with vigour.
3. obscure.
4. land in the middle. The Hill of Tara is said, inaccurately, to be in the geographic centre of Ireland.
5. foil, weapon(s).

In everie degree let noble *Falkland* see
   that your hearts, with your *Prince* doe remaine:
Then will be relate unto the King and State,
   that *Ireland* breeds subjects most loyall,
Yee *Barons*, *Viscounts*, *Earles*, give thanks to King *Charles*,
   who caus'd this assembly most royall.

GOD SAVE THE KING

FRANCIS QUARLES
(1592-**1629**-1644)

Francis Quarles, best known for his frequently reprinted *Emblems*, was born in Essex. He secured some powerful patrons and published a number of translations and meditations in London before being appointed private secretary to James Ussher, Archbishop of Armagh. Quarles moved to Dublin to live in Ussher's household in 1626 and the preface to *Argalus and Parthenia*, a poetic romance based on a story from Sir Philip Sidney's *Arcadia*, is dated March 1628 and written from Dublin. It is quite possible that one of the people Quarles met in Dublin was Richard Bellings, whose *A Sixth Booke to the Countesse of Pembrokes Arcadia* had been published in Dublin in 1624.[1] In the extract below, Parthenia's planned marriage to Argalus is thwarted by the villain Demagoras.

from: Argalus and Parthenia

Sayle gentle *Pinace*:[2] Now the heavens are cleare,
The winds blow faire. Behold the harbour's neere.
Trydented[3] *Neptune* hath forgot to frowne;
The rocks are past; The storme is overblowne;
Up wetherbeaten voyagers, and rouze yee,
Forsake your loathed *Cabbins*; up, and louze[4] ye
Upon the open decks, and smell the land;
Cheare up; the welcome shoare is nigh at hand:
Sayle gentle *Pinace*, with a prosperous gale,
To th'Isle of *peace*: Saile gentle *Pinace*, saile;   10
Fortune conduct thee; Let thy keele divide
The silver streames, that thou mayst safely slide
Into the bosome of thy quiet *Key*,
And quite thee fairely of[5] th'injurious *Sea*.
Great Seaborne Queene,[6] *thy birthright gives thee power*
T'assist poore suppliants; grant one happy houre.
O, let these wounded lovers be possest,
At length, of their so long desired rest.[7]

1. As David Freeman notes (p. 39, n. 4 and p. 215) in his edition of this text (Folger Books, 1986), there is a detail in Quarles's text which may well have come from Bellings's sixth book of the *Arcadia*.
2. a small, two-masted sailing boat.
3. three-toothed. Neptune, god of the sea, was traditionally portrayed holding a trident or spear with three points, such as was used to spear tunny.
4. i.e. clean the lice from your clothes.
5. free yourself completely from . . .
6. i.e. Venus.
7. These four lines constitute a prayer, probably addressed to Aphrodite, goddess of love and of the sea, on behalf of Argalus and Parthenia.

Now, now the joyfull mariage *day* drawes on;
The *Bride* is busie, and the *Bridegroome*'s gone   20
To call his fellow Princes to the feast;
The *Girland*'s made;[8] The bridall *chamber*'s drest;
The *Muses* have consulted with the *Graces*[9]
To crowne the day, and honour their embraces
With shadow'd *Epithalmes*:[10] Their warbling tongues
Are perfect in their new made *Lyrick* songs;
Hymen[11] begins to grumble at delay,
And *Bacchus* laughs to think upon the day;
The virgin tapors,[12] and what other rights
Doe appertaine to *Nuptial* delights,   30
Are all prepar'd, whereby may be exprest
The joyfull triumph of this mariage feast.
But stay! who lends me now an yron pen,
T'engrave within the marble hearts of men
A tragick sceane; which whosoe're shall reade,
His eyes may spare to weepe, and learne to bleed
Carnation teares:[13] If time shall not allow
His death prevented eyes to weepe enow,[14]
Then let his dying language recommend
What's left to his posterity to end.   40
Thou saddest of all Muses,[15] *come; afford*
Thy studious helpe, that each confounding word
May rend a heart (at least;) that every line
May pickle up a kingdome in the brine
Of their owne teares: O teach me to extract
The spirit of griefe, whose vertue may distract
Those brests, which sorrow knowes not how to kill,[16]
Inspier, ô inspire my melting Quill,
And, like sad Niobé, *let every one*
That cannot melt, be turn'd into a stone:[17]   50

---

8. As Freeman notes, this refers to the nuptial garland, a symbol of concord.
9. The three Graces, daughters of Zeus, were, like the Muses, devoted to music and dancing.
10. epithalamia, wedding songs.
11. The goddess of marriage.
12. tapers, wax candles.
13. i.e. tears of blood.
14. enough.
15. Probably a call to Melpomene, muse of tragedy.
16. i.e. teach me to distill the very essence of sorrow which may distract even those whose hearts can not be killed by sorrow . . .
17. In Greek mythology, Niobe was so sticken with grief that she was turned into a block of marble.

Teach me to paint an oft-repeated sigh
So to the life, that whosoe're be nigh
May heare it breathe, and learne to doe the like
By imitation, till true passion strike
Their bleeding hearts: Let such as shall rehearse
This story, houle like Irish *at a Herse.*[18]

Th'event still crownes the act: Let no man say,
Before the evening's come, Tis a faire day:
For when the *Kalends*[19] of this bridall feast
Were entred in, and every longing brest   60
Waxt great with expectation, and all eyes
(Prepar'd for entertaining novelties)
Were growne impatient now, to be suffis'd[20]
With that, which *Art* and *Honour* had devis'd
T'adorne the times withall, and to display
Their bounty, and the glory of that day,
The rare *Parthenia* taking sweet occasion
To blesse her busie thoughts, with contemplation
Of absent *Argalus*, whose too long stay
Made minutes seeme as dayes, and every day   70
A measur'd age, into her secret bower
Betooke her weary steps, where every houre
Her greedy eares expect to heare the summe
Of all her hopes, that *Argalus* is come.
She hopes, she feares at once; and still she muses
What makes him stay so long; she chides, excuses;
She questions, answers; and she makes reply,
And talkes, as if her *Argalus* were by;
Why com'st thou not? Can *Argalus* forget
His languishing *Parthenia*? what, not yet?   80
But as she spake that word, she heard a noise,
Which seem'd as if it were the whispering voice
Of close conspiracy: she began to feare
She knew not what, till her deceived eare,
Instructed by her hopes, had singled out
The voice of *Argalus* from all the rout,
Whose steps (as she supposed) did prepare
By stealth to sieze upon her unaware.

18. funeral; a reference to the presence of professional mourners at Irish funerals.
19. month or season. The use of the Latin word 'Calends' for the first day of any month was still current in the seventeenth century.
20. satisfied.

She gave advantage to the thriving plot,
Hearing the noyse, as if she heard it not.   90
Like as young Doves, which ne're had yet forsaken
The warme protection of their nests, or taken
Upon themselves a selfe-providing care,
To shift for food, but with paternall fare
Grow fat and plump, think every noise they heare,
Their full cropt parents are at hand, to cheare
Their craving stomacks, whilst th'impartiall fist
Of the false Cater,[21] rifling where it list
In every hole, surprises them, and sheds
Their guiltlesse blood, and parts their gasping heads   100
From their vaine struggling bodies; so; even so
Our poore deceiv'd *Parthenia*, (that did owe
Too much to her owne hopes) the whilst[22] her eyes
Were set, to welcome the unvalued[23] prize
Of all her joyes, her dearest *Argalus*,
Stept in *Demagoras*, and salutes her thus:
Base Trull; Demagoras *comes to let thee see,*
How much he scornes thy painted face and thee;
Foule Sorceresse! Could thy prosperous actions think
To scape revenge, because the gods did wink   110
At thy designes? Think'st thou thy mothers blood
Cryes in a language, not to be understood?
Hadst thou no closer stratagem, *to further*
Thy pamper'd lust, but by the salvage murther
Of thine owne aged parent, whose sad death
Must give a freedome to the whisp'ring breath
Of thy enjoy'd adult'rer? *who (they say)*
Will cloake thy whoredome, with a mariage day;
Nay struggle not; here's none that can reprieve
Such pounded[24] *beasts; It is in vaine to strive*   120
Or roare for helpe: why do'st not rather weepe,
That I may laugh? Perchance, if thou wilt creepe
Upon thy wanton belly, and confesse
Thy selfe a true repentant murtheresse,
My sinfull Page *may play the foole, and gather*
Thy early fruit into his barne, and father

---

21. caterer, i.e. a man or boy out searching for food – in this case, young pigeons.
22. while.
23. impossible to value – because so precious.
24. impounded, caught.

Thy new-got Cyprian *bastard*,[25] *if that he*
Be halfe so wise, that got it, but to flee.
Hah! dost thou weepe? or doe false mists but mocke
Abused eyes? From so obdure[26] *a rock*   130
Can water flow? weeping will make thee faire;
Weepe till thy mariage day; that who repaire
To grace thy feast, may fall a weeping too,
And, in a mirrour, see what teares can doe.
Vile strumpet! did thy flattering thoughts e're wrong
Thy judgement so; to thinke, Demagoras *tongue*
Could so defile his honour as to sue
For serious love? So base a thing as you
(Me thinks) should rather fixe your wanton eyes
Upon some easie groome, that hopes to rise   140
Into his masters favour, for your sake;
I,[27] *this had beene preferment, like to make*
A hopefull fortune: thou presumptuous trash!
What was my courtship? but the minuts dash
Of youthfull passion, to allay the dust
Of my desires, and exuberous[28] *lust?*
I scorne thee to the soule, and here I stand
Bound for revenge, whereto I set my hand.
With that, he grip'd her rudely by the faire
And bounteous treasure of her *Nymph-like* hayre;   150
And, by it, dragd her on the dusty floore:
He stopt her mouth, for feare she should implore
An aid from heaven, she swounding[29] in the place,
His salvage[30] hands besmear'd her livelesse face
With horrid poyson; thinking she was dead,
He left her breathlesse, and away he fled.
Come, come ye Furies, *you malignant spirits,*
Infernall Harpies, *or what, else, inherits*
The land of darknesse; you, that still converse
With damned soules; you, you that can rehearse   160
The horrid facts of villains, and can tell
How every hell-hound lookes, that roares in hell;

---

25. Argalus was from Cyprus, 'From th'ancient stocke of the great *Cyprian* Kings' (I, 712).
26. obdurate.
27. Aye.
28. exuberant.
29. fainting.
30. savage.

Survey them all; and, then, informe my pen,
To draw in one, the monster of all men;
Teach me to limme[31] a villaine, and to paint
With dextrous art, the basest Sycophant,
That e're the mouth of insolent disdaine
Vouchsaf'd to spit upon; the putrid blaine[32]
Of all diseased humours, fit for none
But dogs to lift their hasty legs upon: 170
So cleare mens eyes, that whosoe're shall see
The type of basenesse, may cry, This is Hee;
Let his reproach be a perpetuall blot
In Honours booke: Let his remembrance rot
In all good mindes: Let none but villaines call
His bugbeare name to memory, wherewithall
To fright their bauling bastards: Let no spell
Be found more potent, to prevaile in hell,
Than the nine letters of his charme-like name;
Which, let our bashfull Chriscrosse row[33] disclaime   180
To the worlds end, not worthy to be set
In any but the Jewish Alphabet[34] . . .

Like to the Damaske Rose[1]

Hos ego versiculos[2]

Like to the damaske Rose you see,
Or like the blossome on the tree,
Or like the daintie flowre of May,
Or like the Morning to the day,

31. draw, engrave, limn.
32. blister.
33. The Latin (English) alphabet, as set out in a school-book, with a cross at the head of it.
34. Properly, this is a reference to the alphabet of the Aramaic language which developed into that of Hebrew. Here it is probably being used much more loosely to refer to the use of Hebrew script for the names of God and Satan, and for the representation of arcane words used in spells and charms, sometimes seen in seventeenth-century emblem books and engravings.

1. This much-anthologised poem, which was appended to *Argalus and Parthenia*, may have been written in Dublin in 1626 or 1627. See J.W. Hebel and H.H. Hudson, *Poetry of the English Renaissance 1509–1660* (New York, 1929), pp. 1022–3, and Freeman, p. 222. A 'damaske' rose is a variety of pink rose thought originally to have come from Damascus.
2. This is the first half of a line from Virgil: *Hos ego versiculos: tulit alter honores*, 'I made these little verses: another took the honour.' In putting this verse here, Quarles is asserting his authorship of the poem, stanzas from which had appeared in an anthology printed in London in 1628. As was the case with most seventeenth-century verse, the poem had probably been circulating in manuscript.

Or like the Sunne, or like the shade,
Or like the Gourd which Jonas had,[3]
Even such is man whose thred is spunne,
Drawne out and cut, and so is done.

The Rose withers, the blossome blasteth,[4]
The flowre fades, the morning hasteth;   10
The Sunne sets; the shadow flies,
The Gourd consumes, and man he dies.

Like to the blaze of fond delight;
Or like a morning cleare and bright;
Or like a frost, or like a showre,
Or like the pride of *Babels* Towre,[5]
Or like the houre that guides the time,
Or like to beauty in her prime;
Even such is man, whose glorie lends
His life a blaze or two, and ends.   20

Delights vanish; the morne o're casteth,
The frost breakes, the shower hasteth,
The Tower fals, the houre spends,
The beauty fades, and mans life ends.

3. Though God provided a large gourd to shade the prophet Jonah from the sun, He also
   prepared a worm which 'smote the gourd [so] that it withered'. Jonah 4. 6.
4. withers.
5. Genesis 11 tells how the people of the earth, who at this early stage after the creation, all
   spoke a single language, built a city and a tower, the top of which was intended to reach
   to heaven. The tower and the city were called Babel. Because of the pride of the people,
   God scattered them and confounded their language. The people never finished the tower
   and they never again spoke a single language.

DUDLEY BOSWELL
(*c*.1608–**1630**–1650)

This poem was written after the death of Catherine Boyle, wife of the great Earl of Cork. Once he arrived in Ireland in the late 1580s, Richard Boyle (1566–1643) rose rapidly from being a penniless planter until he was not only the largest landowner in Munster but also (from 1620) Earl of Cork. As the ruthlessness of his early years in Ireland gave way to astuteness in his later years, Boyle established himself and his family so firmly in the political and social life of Ireland that they seemed only slightly less important than old-established families such as those of the dukes of Ormond and Kildare. One of the institutions to which Boyle paid attention was Trinity College Dublin, and about a year after the death of his second wife, Lady Catherine, the fellows and scholars of the university published a remarkable volume of poetic tributes to her, *Musarum Lachrymæ* (Dublin, 1630). The verses are in Latin, Hebrew, Greek and English. Dudley Boswell, author of the unusual poem which follows, was a fellow of the college. He had entered Trinity as a scholar in 1623 and later had a career as a Church of Ireland clergyman, holding several livings in Dublin. Boswell clearly thought of himself as a wit – in the sense in which Donne and Herbert were wits; he pursued paradoxes and delighted in wordplay, even where this might make his theology a little suspect.

A Theologicall description of the divine rapture and extasie that the blessed soule of this Countesse was in at it's separation from the body

> But is it sure? what, is it possible
> My soule enjoyes these joyes unspeakable?
> Am I in heaven? is't certaine that I rise
> By death to life, from earth to Paradise?
> It cannot be, Angels nor Saints above[1]
> Halfe of those joyes possesse that my soule move.
> Surely I dreame, it's my phantasticke braine
> Doth frame these figments, these chimera's[2] feigne.
> O pleasant dreame: if this a dreame can be,
> Would I could dreame thus in eternitie.   10
> If I such Pleasures in my sleepe can take,
> Would I could always sleepe and never wake.
> And never wake: O happie then were I
> Thus still to dreame, still sleepe, still live, still die.
> Still live, still dye: a thing that cannot be;
> Yes if I always dreame I live, I die,

---

1. i.e. neither angels nor saints above possess half . . .
2. a wild fancy.

As now I doe, methinkes no life I have,
And yet a better life I cannot crave.
But doe I dreame? can unto mortals flow
From dreames a moy'tie³ of these joyes I know.   20
No sure, I wake, for farre above the skye
On Angels wings I in a moment flye.
O glorious sight: looke, for behold I see
Christ and his Saints are come to wel-come me.
All haile unto the King of earth and heaven,
Of all the blessed Angels, Saints and men.
Hosanna unto *Davids* royall sonne
For all the favours he to me hath done.
All praise to God that dwelleth up on high.
My soule thy mercies still will magnifie.   30
All halleluiah, glory, honour, power,
Unto the Lord, my God, my Saviour,
Unto the Lambe my spouse, my Jesus Christ,
To my Messias Prophet, King and Priest.
Praise him with me, ye Angels, Saints and men
Both now and ever more, amen, amen.

---

3. moiety, half.

GEORGE BRADY
(*fl*.**1630**)

Like Dudley Boswell, George Brady was a contributor to *Musarum Lachrymæ*, the volume
of poems produced by the scholars and fellows of Trinity College Dublin on the death of the
Countess of Cork. Though he is described in that volume as Master of Arts, Brady's name
does not appear in the records of the college. His poem was clearly designed to flatter the
Earl of Cork by parading before the reader the names of the family's distinguished forebears,
and reminding him of the power and wealth of those into whose families the earl was busily
marrying his many sons and daughters. Since the earl himself came from a humble
background and had, in effect, no family to boast of, the ancestors paraded here are, in many
cases, those of his well-born second wife, Catherine Fenton, in whose memory the volume
had been produced. The earl must have been delighted with this poem, which fitted perfectly
his project of establishing the importance and respectability of himself and his family by a
series of noble alliances.

from: An Elegie upon the death of the right noble, and vertuous Lady, the La: *Katherine* Countesse of Corke

To thee deare soule I consecrate my verse
Not to adorne, but blot thy sacred herse
With teares of sorrow; for whil'st other men
Extoll thy worth, I wish some angells pen
Might write what my sad soule cannot expresse;
The more griefe strives, it still performes the lesse;
And when it thinkes on thy eternall sleepe,
Growes dumbe, and sighes to teach the world to weepe.

   Thou perfect embleme of th'uncertaine state
Of this vaine world; in thee the lawes of fate   10
Truely appeare; for though the glorious rayes
Of glittring honour, wealth and peacefull dayes
Dazle the pur-blind[1] sense of wretched man,
Whose earth composed substance never can
Aspire to heav'nly thoughts, or once forsee
The fearefull period of prosperitie,
Yet all from thee may Learne their *Christ-crosse row*,[2]
And spell out that[3] their wisedome could not know,

---

1. stupid.
2. alphabet (so called because a cross was placed at the beginning of it in school-books).
3. what.

And teach this lesson to secured breath:
Nothing can stopp th'insatiate jawes of death.   20

   If honour could or aw'd authoritie,
If pow'rfull wealth, religious pietie,
If vertues fairest selfe with all her traine
Of heav'nly issue free from spot or staine,
Or all that styles man happie in this life,
Or can adorne a noble loyall wife,
Could worke this feate;[4] soe soone thou hadst not fled,
Nor thou dead-living left us living dead.
For all these things thou didst at full possesse,
And heav'ns high hand thy auncestors did blesse   30
With all that might the name of blessing gaine.
And thou that sprung'st up from that noble straine,
And did'st to such a pitch of vertue mount,
Art the briefe totall of their large account.

   What should I heere thy famous Grand-sire cite
Thrice learned *Doctor Weston*?[5] whose cleare light
Of law, and conscience shin'd so bright (the while
That noble Sydney[6] rul'd this auncient Ile)
That he was made Lord Chanc'llor of this land,
And weigh'd proceedings with so equall hand   40
And conscionable poize, that 'mongst the rest
This kingdomes annalls rank't him with the best
For learning, law and vertue. This was he
Who 'midst a world of honours did fore-see,
That needlesse merchandize would soone o'resway
His soules faire ship: and rather would give way
To throw o'reboord his trafficke than endure
Danger of ship-wracke: and to make sure
(Whils'st some ambitious worldlings with full s[c]ent
Pursu'd their fortunes) he with pure intent,   50
Made suite unto his Prince to be relea'st
From part of his great honours, yet not cea'st
From vertuous actes: to whom his Prince replyes
(Viewing his lowe desires with gracious eyes)

4. i.e. stop the insatiate jaws of death.
5. Lady Cork's grandfather had been Dr Robert Weston, lord chancellor of Ireland 1567–73.
6. Sir Henry Sidney, lord deputy for three terms between 1565 and 1578.

'*Weston* I've oft beene su'de to, to augment
Office and honours since my government,
But ne're beheld petition to aspire
To th'umble height of true contents desire
Untill I read thy suite.' Or what should I
Upon thy honour'd fathers worth relye   60
Sir *Geffrey Fenton*?[7] whose approved witt,
Deepe judgment, loyall heart, made him most fitt
To be state secretarie of this Realme,
And privie Counsellor, To whose cleare streame
Of honour'd worth those sacred springs doe runne,
Which in thy mothers breast were first begunne;[8]
Whose heav'nly lustre, and bright shining rayes
Of vertue, makes her wonder of her dayes
And mirrour of her sex, where all may spie
The least spot of their soules deformity.   70
Her Charitie full of religious fire
The best of men extoll, the worst admire.
And thou that issu'dst from so faire a spring,
How could'st thou but faire fruits of vertue bring?
Each drop of blood she gave thy veines to fill,
Some vertue did into thy soule distill.

But would thine owne worth put death to a stand,
Or have the pow'r to smooth his rugged hand,
T'a wise, rich, noble Earle thou wast a mate,
Whose wisedome now sits at the helme of state   80
To guide the ship of justice through the seas
Of this corrupted age;[9] which now at ease
Sailes ev'n and faire unto her heavenly port.
No golden fisted Syrens[10] dare resort
Unto her hallowed seate; No greatnes can
Oppresse the poore distressed wronged man.

---

7. Lady Cork's father, Sir Geoffrey Fenton (1539?–1608), translator and government official, who served as chief secretary in Ireland and a member of the privy council for the last twenty years of the sixteenth century.
8. Lady Cork's mother had been Alice Weston, daughter of the lord chancellor.
9. At the time of this poem, Lord Cork was one of the lords justices of Ireland.
10. The sirens of Greek mythology were half-woman, half-bird; their enticing song attracted sailors, whose ships were driven onto the rocks. A wise captain (like Odysseus or the Earl of Cork) knew how to outwit sirens, mythological or real.

And to thy hearts content didst live to see
The pawnes of love betwixt thy Lord and thee,
The hopefull issue of thy loyall bed
Like clustred grapes did round about thee spread   90
With sweet love and imbracements to entwine
Thee, as their happie, faire, and fruitfull vine.

Five sonnes, whereof two Viscounts, heav'n did lend,
A third a Baron; nor did there intend
To set a limit to thy happinesse
But with eight daughters, did thy bosome blesse.

Thus did'st thou live his true contented wife;
And the sweete blessings of thy happie life
Did'st from faire honours spring to amply drawe,
That three brave Lords became thy sonnes in lawe,   100
Earle *Barrimore* that auncient honour'd Peere,
With noble *Digbie*; and the hopefull Heire
Of great Lord Goring; as a pledge assign'd
Of other summes of honour yet behinde,
Which Heav'ns out-stretched hand meanes to bestowe,
That honour still may with thy vertue growe,
And her blest seed in they faire bosome nourish,
That fruitfull vertue after death may flourish.[11]

For 'tis prepar'd with sacred nuptiall rite,
Three more of thy faire Daughters to unite   110
To three, whose worth and well deserved fame
May still eternize[12] thy thrice honour'd name;
Renown'd *Kildare* prime Earle of this our Ile,
Whose auncient race, and still continued stile
Of honour, vertue, valour (from the time
His Auncestours bare sway within this Clime)
Filling the writings, mouthes, and hearts of men,
Commaund a silence to my worthlesse pen;[13]
Next Viscount *Ranaloghes* right noble Heire,
Whose Grandsire erst these honour'd titles bare,   120

11. Lord Cork was ruthless in forcing advantageous alliances on his children. The three
    eldest daughters were all married to noblemen, Alice to Lord Barrymore, Sarah to
    Robert Lord Digby, nephew to the Earl of Bristol, and Lettice to Lord Goring.
12. make everlasting.
13. Of the Earl of Cork's three next daughters, Joan married the Earl of Kildare, Catherine
    married Viscount Ranelagh and Dorothy married Arthur Loftus of Rathfarnham.

Dublin's Archbishop, and of all this Land
Lord Chauncellour, who rul'd with great command.[14]
The third is to be joyn'd in *Hymens* rite
Unto the issue of that noble Knight
Sir Adam Loftus counsellor of state
His worthy heyre: whose great grandfather sate
In that same chayre of double government,[15]
And sway'd his double charge with such contente,
That with a full applause he did inherit
That double honour, by a double merit   130
Of well-squar'd justice, and true Pietie,
Whereon the life of Church and weale relye . . .

   By these united blessings all may see
Honour, wealth, worth, Justice, Integritie,
And all that can compose a happie state,
In thy faire blood to be incorporate.

   And to augment thy store and make compleate
Thy sweet content, heav'n made thy heart the seate
Of lineall vertue, from thy Grand-sires sprung,
Where, (thy owne graces being mixt among)   140
That which from them but droppingly distill'd
Grew to a sea, and that rich vessell fill'd.
But O, these streames of joy bee'ng joyn'd in one,
Heav'n call'd, death strucke, and thou alas art gone.

   O death that nothing but privation art,
Yet shak'st the courage of the stoutest heart,
Thou sterne destroyer of all flesh and blood,
Thou awe of bad men, comfort of the good,
Natures grimme Sergeant, messenger of *Jove*
That summon'st all to his high Court above,   150
How cruell was thy barbarous intent,
To robbe the world of this rich ornament?

   Could not thy curious searching eye find out
Some painted peece of clay that trip't about

---

14. Lord Ranelagh's grandfather had been Thomas Jones, Archbishop of Dublin and lord chancellor from 1605 to 1619.
15. Adam Loftus had also held the two posts of Archbishop of Dublin and lord chancellor.

With outward borrowed glory to amaze
The eyes of fooles that vainly stand at gaze
And idolize weake flesh? this prize might well
Adorne thy poore rich melancholy cell.
But thou must grow ambitious in thy choyce,
And snatch her in whom heav'n and earth rejoyce;   160

    Shee that might boast her glory was her owne,
Be'ing lock'd up in her breast, not outward showne,
Where heaven's hand kept it from the world's vaine eye
Wrapt in a veile of humble modestie.
Thy conquest in an empty Caske doth lye;
The jewels plac'd in heav'ns rich treasurie;
For her refined soule more pure than gold,
Brookes not[16] the prison of base earthy mould.

    But how doth greife transport my wandring minde?
In thee, sweet death, faire attributes I finde;   170
Thou are a peacefull Port after the storme
Of this world's troubled sea, and though thy forme
Seeme uglie to a sinfull sensuall man,
Thou art heav'ns doore, and that judiciall fan
That winnowes all the deeds of mortall breath,
For no man's truely happy but in death.
This did that blessed soule long time fore-see
And shun'd thee not, but dayly look'd for thee.
Through thy transparant *Carcasse* she did spye
A doore that led to immortality.   180
So thou that worldly men with feare do'st vexe,
At last art conquer'd by the weaker sexe.

    Her rent to Nature's pay'd, and all's made even,
For she hath payd her chief-rent[17] unto heaven,
Where, with cælestiall angells she doth sing
Sweet hymnes in honour of her heav'nly king.
      Sing on sweet soule in blest eternity,
      While we with sighes, sobbes, teares, keep time to thee.

16. does not enjoy.
17. quit-rent: a small rent paid by a tenant in lieu of services which might be required of him.

200

EPITAPH

The Curious Cabinet of heav'ns rich treasure,
Chast[18] vertue, honour, worth, by death's sad seisure   190
Heere freed from worldly cares, doth sweetly rest,
Earth holds her grosser part, but heav'n her best.

18. chaste.

JOHN SHANK (?)
(*fl*.**1630s**)

Historians of the theatre have connected this strange song, which occurs in various manuscript and printed miscellanies of the seventeenth century, with John Shank (*d*. 1636), a comedian who specialised in song-and-dance turns,[1] and have described it as the earliest known Irish 'character' song or popular theatrical presentation of an Irishman. The text is always garbled and sometimes unintelligible and it seems likely that it was taken down at dictation by people who either did not hear it properly or who did not understand it, and also that the text was modified in performance. The version which follows was collected by the Oxford antiquary and librarian Thomas Hearne (1678–1735). The song has no title in the Hearne manuscript but elsewhere is given various titles, including 'The Irish Footman's *O hone*', 'Shanks's Song' and 'The Irish Exile's *O hone*'. The influence of the Irish language can seen in the use of assonance, rather than full rhyme, at various places in the verse, and the metre itself is a version of an Irish *amhrán* metre rather than anything used in English-language songs. The piece was probably sung to a traditional Irish air, perhaps in the street.

[The Irish Exile's Song]

I. Now Christ my save, poore Irish knave, *a hone*, *a hone*,[2]
    Round aboute, the towne throughout, is poor Shone[3] gone,
    Master to find, loving and kind, but Shone to his mind, ne'er the
        near,
    Shone can find none here, which makes [him] cry for feare,
        a hone, *a hone*.
    Shone being poor, his feate[4] being sore, for which he'le noe more
    Trott about, to find a master out; fait,[5] he'le rather goe without,
        a hone, a hone.

II. For Ladyes sake,[6] some pitty take, *a hone*, *a hone*,
    I servd, alas, where was no Masse, no fait none;
    Oft was I beat, cause I do not eat, on Friday beafe and meate,
    Twise a day; and when I went to pray, take holy beades away,
        a hone, a hone.   10

---

1. See J.P. Collier, *History of English Dramatic Poetry* (London, 1879), III, 483; W.J. Lawrence, *The Lady of the House* (Dublin), Christmas 1923; and J.O. Bartley, *Teague, Shenkin and Sawney: An Historical Survey of the Earliest Irish, Welsh and Scottish Characters in English Plays* (Cork, 1954), pp. 23–6.
2. alas, alas; Ir. *ochón*.
3. = Seón, an alternative form of the name Seán.
4. feet: for an analysis of Hiberno-English pronunciation at this time, see Alan Bliss, *Spoken English in Ireland 1600–1740* (Dublin 1979).
5. faith. See note 4.
6. 'For [Our] Lady's sake' perhaps?

Make Church to goe, whither will or no; Ile dye or Ile doe so,
  Grace a Christ;[7]
Ile love a Popish priest, poore Catholick thou seest, *a hone, a hone*.

III. I was so curst, that I was forct, *a hone, a hone*,
  To go barefoot, with stripes to boot, noe shoes none;
  None English could [I] speake, my mind for to break,
  And many laught to heare the moan I made,
  And I like a tyard jade[8] that had noe work, noe trade, cry *a hone*,
  Instead o breakefast, I was fain to run apace,[9]
  And get no stomak to my hungry throate,
  And when for friends I sought, they cal[led] me all to nought,
    a hone, a hone.   20

IV. Good honest Shone, make no more moan fo[r] thy master lost.[10]
  I doe intend, something to spend, on Catholiks thus crost,
  Take this small gift, with it make a shift, and be thou not bereft
  Of thy mind; although he was unkind, to leave thee thus behind,
    to cry *a hone*.
  Take thee some beare and eat good cheer, nothing for thee too dear;
  So, adue, be constant still and true, thy country do not rue,
    nor cry *a hone*.

V. Good shentlemen,[11] yf [ye] doth intend to help poore Shone
    at's neede,
  Mine patrone heare hath given me beare, and meate whereon
    to feed;
  Yea and money too, and soe I hope that you, will do as he did,
  For my relif; to ease my paine and greife, Ile eat no
    powderd beef,[12] whate'er ensue,   30
  But keepe my fast, as I did in time past, and all my vowes and
    prayers Ile renew,
  Cause freinds I find but few, poor Shone will still prove true,
    and so adue.

---

7. Thanks be to Christ.
8. tired jade, an exhausted old horse.
9. Presumably as a footman, carrying a sedan chair. 'I was fain' seems to signify 'I had to',
   an unrecorded meaning of a phrase that normally indicates that one is pleased to do
   something. (The other possibility, that the phrase is linked to the obsolete dialect
   expression 'fains I' meaning 'I do not want to . . .' does not seem correct.)
10. This stanza is spoken by a gentleman who intends to give Shone money.
11. Shone addresses a new set of potential sponsors.
12. spiced or cured beef.

MICHAEL KEARNEY
(*fl*.1635)

Michael Kearney, a member of a well-connected family from County Tipperary, was the first to translate Geoffrey Keating's great history of the peoples of Ireland, *Foras Feasa ar Éirinn*, into English.[1] He probably made the translation – as he did a number of others – for Archbishop Ussher, who, like Sir James Ware, needed access to materials in Irish for his research into early Irish history.[2] Though Kearney translated the bulk of *Foras Feasa* into prose, he decided to render the verse quoted by Keating into English verse. Since Keating habitually quoted verse from his source manuscripts to add colour to his text,[3] the Kearney translation (RIA MS. 24 G 16) is sprinkled with small snatches of English verse carrying pointed comments on ancient Irish kings and their doings. The verse selected below came from a variety of sources including, according to Keating, the Psalter of Cashel and the Book of Armagh; there is also a selection from a chronological or topographical poem written by Seán Ó Dúbhagáin in the 1370s retelling the history of the kings of Cashel over the previous thousand years.

For Kearney, as for others brought up in the world of the Irish-speaking Old English, verse was the proper medium for the tales of the heroic past. When Kearney translated into English verse, therefore, he was trying to emulate in English the effect of the Irish text rather than to write elegant English verse according to the conventions of English prosody. He was aware of this, and used the terms 'poeticized' or 'Englished' to introduce his verse translations. Kearney usually sought end-rhymes for his verses, but his understanding of the rhythms of spoken English was different from that of a native English-speaker so that some of his verses sound ungraceful and, in places, rough, particularly when he makes use of the long seven-stressed 'fourteener', a metre common in Tudor times but very old-fashioned by the 1630s. The real interest of these texts lies in the glimpse they afford of interaction, in verse, between the two dominant cultures of seventeenth-century Ireland. For details of the persons and places mentioned in these extracts, see *The History of Ireland* by Geoffrey Keating, ed. and trans. by Patrick S. Dinneen, 4 vols (London, Irish Texts Society, 1902–14), II, 103, 105, 133, 169, 236, 334, 343; III, 217; I, 125.

Passages in English verse from translation of Geoffrey Keating's *Foras Feasa ar Éirinn*

I. Two brothers, kings of Ireland, Eibhear and Eireamhon, draw lots to determine who will keep the best poet of the day in his household, and who the best harper

The brothers yield the harper and rhymer to divide
Between them two, that difference for to decide.

---

1. Kearney's translation appeared within three years of the completion of Keating's history. For biographical details of Michael Kearney, see Donald Jackson, 'Michael Kearney of Ballylosky: Irish Scribe and Butler Servant', *Journal of the Butler Society*, vol. 2, no. 1 (1980–1), pp. 84–5.
2. See P. Walsh, 'The Book of Lecan in Ormond', *Irish Book Lover*, vol. 26 (1938), p. 62. For an assessment of Kearney's importance as a translator in mid-seventeenth century Ireland, see Bernadette Cunningham, *The World of Geoffrey Keating: History, Myth and Religion in Seventeenth-Century Ireland* (Dublin, 2000), pp. 183–7.
3. On medleys of verse and prose (common in Irish), see Alan Harrison, *The Irish Trickster* (Sheffield, 1989), p. 57 and references.

The harper fell to him that over the South of Ireland raigned,
    Where sithence[4] in Musicke the true cadence remained.
And the ruler of the North the poet by lott obtained,
    And preheminence in rhimeing the Northerne sithence maintained.

II. The causes of the dispute between Eibhear and Eireamhon

Herber and Hermon all Ireland parte
    And therein for a yeare both quietly sate.
Till then their wives with pride being puffed,
    from settlement that just division brake.
For Herbers wife with pride did vowe
    That she Drome Classaigh must onely hold,
Drome Behach and Drome Fynyn sure,
    Or never rest one night in Ireland bolde.
The brothers thus by women edg'd, to hatred, spoyle and rue
At Geisille fought, and Hermon there his brother Heber slue.   10

III. The nature of the assembly at Tara

For making acts and wholesome lawes, each third yeare at Tharragh sate
In parliament still the Irish Kinges, and all their princely Mates;
By common voyce decreed there was what place each one should hold;
From high to low, none durst oppose that edict once being told.
Their generall hoast to joyne in love three dayes before all Saincts,
And after it three other dayes, in feasting still they spent.
In all that tyme no rapine was, nor bloudshedd once attempted,
And murmuring tongues there had noe use, to peace all friendly assented.
If any did offend those wayes or once his sword but drawe,
He death did owe, noe ransome else did purge those crimes by lawe.   10

IV. How the men of Ireland regarded foreigners

From different stocks though they have moved, a likeness doth remayne
Between the Neills and ancient Scotts, which firmly they retaine.
The Mounstermen, of Saxons loved, and favored still they were,
As Spaniards did to the Northerne folkes a friendly likeing beare.

4. ever since.

The Brittaines still with deare respects, the Conatians[5] did demeane,
And Leinstermen like firme good will, to the French did well ordaine.

V. Lines on King Cairbe Chinn Chait

Hard Cairbre gained all Ireland large,
from South to North to beare his charge;
The Eares of a Catt his uggly head ill bore;
and of Catt-like pile,[6] his eares did yield full store.

VI. King Cormac's grinding maid

King Cormac captured Ciarnait, the beautiful daughter of the king of the Picts, and took her as his concubine; when his wife heard of this, she humiliated the girl by forcing her to grind large quantities of corn each day. However, the king made the girl pregnant and, as she came near the time of delivery, she found she could no longer grind the corn as before. When she told this to the king, he sent overseas for a miller to help her: since that day, there have been mills in Ireland.

Kiarnath Cormacks grindinge Maide, with a Querne[7] a 100 did dayly
feed,
Nyne pecks[8] to grinde each day her taske, did farr her Sex exceed.
Her finding alone, her body he used, and with child he then her left,
Which burthen her strength soe weakly wrought, that to grinde small
force shee kept;
Whose wants to help at her humble Suite, from beyond the Seaes a
Miller.
Cormacke fetches one, her with a myll to ayde, who of mills was here
first builder.

VII. The proper household for an Irish high king

The Regnall messe[9] these persons make, whose names I here rehearse,
For a King, a Sage as his Mate all times, they tenn in number raise.[10]

---

5. the people of Connacht.
6. i.e. fur.
7. a small mill for grinding corn, the upper stone of which was turned by hand.
8. a fourth part of a bushel – generally used to mean 'a lot'.
9. royal entourage, the people in a king's household.
10. i.e. the number of persons in a king's household (line 1) amounts to ten; I will repeat their names here . . .

A Judge to rule his subjects right, a poet his acts to guyde
With praise or blame as men deserve, their acts to free from pride.
A Magitian skilled his wayes to leade, for life and old oblations,
A Chronicler knowing descents to keep, and pedegrees from violation.
A Harper sweet with musicall tunes, his heart and mynde to please,
A Phisitian at hand the sick to heale, and hurts to cure with ease.
Three wayting men to these adjoyned, to make the messe[11] upright,
Or else the King at Tharragh place shall misse and wynn despight;[12]   10
Being foyled in warr, or in peace betrayed, noe ransome doth he meritt
That from his Court these ten refraine, ympairing much his credditt.[13]

VIII. The incantation of the devilish minstrels[14]

At the behest of his queen, King Donnchadh of Meath had a ditch (a defensive mound) raised around the church and churchyard of Seirkieran. As the workmen were building this ditch, the body of Donnchadh, king of Osruighe (father of the queen), was brought for burial in the churchyard. As soon as darkness came that evening, Kearney's translation tells us, 'nyne spiritts with blacke lockes of haire came upon his Tombe, and began there to sing like idle Minstrells; they were terrible to bee looked upon, as haveinge their eyes and teeth whiter than snow, and every other member of theirs blacker than smiths coales'. The spirits continued to haunt the graveyard and transferred their attention to the grave of King Donnchadh himself, after his death, much to the alarm of the priests, who knew him to have been a pious man. But an angel told them that the nine fiends were devilish clergy who had come to Ireland out of hell. To get rid of the fiends, the priests should say mass at the king's graveside and sprinkle holy water upon the grave. As soon as this was done, the spirits turned into blackbirds and disappeared into the air. This is the song which the devilish minstrels sang each night.

Great Donochoe McKealla, his family maine
    Were of hunters whooping & of soldiers a great Traine.
Fields filled with forces, for martiall frayes.
    Houses puffed with drinkers to exhaust it alwayes.
White maidens lovely, and givers freely giveinge,
    Grave Patrons maintenance to Misers extendinge;
Clearkes sweetely singing, and waiters on him attending,
    Idlers drowsily slumbering in the Suns bright shineinge.
Harpers and minstrells good musick resoundinge,
    Warriours wearyed sinewes with wholesome bathes annoyntinge, 10

11. (in this case) the eating or feasting.
12. i.e. or else the king will not be respected at Tara (i.e. among his equals).
13. i.e. the king who does not have these ten in his court does not merit a ransom, should he be defeated in battle or betrayed in peace; his reputation is damaged.
14. See Alan Harrison, 'Séanadh Saighre', *Éigse*, vol. 20 (1984), pp. 144–6. For a modern translation, see Harrison, *Trickster*, pp. 107–8.

Poets rhymeinge rightly, still good orders keepeing
    With Raighne Ruithaibh kept their constant meeteinge.

Doddar Doddane,[15] king Raighnes son, yow are changed;
    Great pleasures fade, your fathers games are daunted.
These blasted joyes which hee held fast
    Makeinge his life joyfull, dyed with him at last.
Baptaise, Baptaine,[16] with his life farewell;
    The place is the better where hee doth dwell.

IX. How Corc, son of Lughaidh, captured Cashel and celebrated his
success[17]

    But Corcke his sonn, a valourous branch,
        Did Casshel first entrance yield;
    By foggs concealed, till at last by chance,
        Two swyne-heards found that field.

    One Durdaire called, the king of Muskry served,
        And the other Kiolarne, from Eile kinge;
    These Swyne keepers two, there fatting their hoggs,
        To our view this place did bringe.

    To these two at first Druim Ffiodhbhuidhe was
        Discovered, which Corcke did much affect;   10
    That soyle from faults more clearly being,
        His mind did it respect.

    And for Joy to gain that eminent place,
        Corcke's nutrix[18] largely feasted;
    And freely spent fatt porkes amaine,[19]
        Casshel's forts to frame well seated.

15. 'Dod dor dod dan' in the manuscript. This is not, as has been thought, a meaningless jingle but, according to Harrison ('Séanadh Saighre', p. 146) an archaic verbal form meaning 'You will get'. Harrison translates the line: 'You will get your poem, O son of Raighne.'

16. Another unusual verbal form meaning 'baptised with the baptism'. Harrison translates: 'His soul is baptized with (the true) baptism.'

17. Though Keating only included in his text the first two stanzas of this long poem by Seán Ó Dúbhagáin, Kearney copied out about eighty stanzas of the poem in Irish at the appropriate point in his translation, and rendered them all into English.

18. nurse or foster-mother (Latin).

19. vehemently, without delay.

Raithlionn the Daughter of Datho the stronge,
    Was Corcke Chaisshill's foster mother called;
Three hundred beefes and hoggs as many,
    Her cauldron to that feast well boyled.   20

And that furnace thrice with meate shee filled,
    That feast to fitt with credditt;
Of Shannayne the Lord of his Traine to please,
    Ffrench wynes did raise her merritt.

ANONYMOUS
(*c*.1636)

The setting for this very early hunting song is the countryside of Fingal, north of Dublin, and the location for the meet of huntsmen and hounds is Howth Castle, the seat of the St Lawrence family, Lords of Howth. Since those named in the first stanza were active in the 1630s, the song, in its earliest form, dates from that period. The earliest written text, however, is scribal copy of the mid-eighteenth century, which is clearly corrupt. Since the song had been sung for a hundred years before it was captured on paper, it is not surprising that its metrical pattern had become muddled and some of its words garbled. The text has been lightly edited for this printing. Though the song is in English, the influence of the Irish language can be seen in the use of assonance rather than end-rhyme in places. Some words are also spelled to indicate Hiberno-English pronunciation. See Alan Bliss, *Spoken English in Ireland 1600–1740* (Dublin, 1979).

Ye merry Boyes all that live in Fingaule

Ye merry Boyes all that live in Fingaule
I will tell you a Tale, how a Hare catch't a fall.
There was Michael St. Lawrence and Patrick Aspoor,
Robbin Hod-goor, and Jacky Radmoor.
With Robbin Hilliard (with his gay little Grey)
And Stephen Ash-pole, a gay merry Boy.

They met on a Day in St. Lawrences[1] Hall,
Where he gave 'em hot waters, good meat, and strong Ale.
And one ting more may be said for his fame,
For his Sport he ventur'd his Ey and his Arm.   10

There was St. Lawrence's Scutty,[2] and her Daughter Betty,
Short cropt curryd Iron, and Merry-hunting Don,
Ho[d]goiers Hector's a Gay Gray-hound,
Hee'l take three Yards at every Bound,
And tho' he had a blemish upon one Eye,
It was hard for all that to give him the go-by.[3]

They went over the Ditches with their Dogs and Bitches,
They spar'd not to beat Bear,[4] Barley and wheat.

---

1. *Marginal note*: 'The Ld. of Hoths.' The head of the family in the 1630s was Nicholas St Lawrence, 23rd Lord Howth.
2. These are names of hunting dogs.
3. not to include him. s.v. 'go' II, 2, (a) (Joseph Wright, *English Dialect Dictionary* (Oxford, 1898)).
4. barley. to beat = moving noisily through the fields to scare out game.

Last out of some Bryars, they got their Desires,
There started a Hare, that runned most rare   20
Which set 'em a barking with all their train,
Till the merry light Hare was very ny Slain.

But in a fine Mead, she being almost spent,
She made her last Will, ay[5] and Testament;[6]
Cropt Curr, with thee, says she, I will not stay,
Nor with true running Cutty, that show'd such fair play,
But to thee, brave Hector, I yeild up my Leef;
And so Hector bore her and ended the Streef.[7]

Then Hodgier came in to bear up the Hare
His Breeches fell down, and his Ars it was bare,   30
But Patrick Ash pole he spoke a bold word,
He woud go to Baldoyle[8] to see what the Town coud afford.

And when the Boys came to the gay Town,
They got salt pork and Yellow Ba-coon,[9]
Which they then just cut down from the smoke.
And Patrick Ash pole play'd a very good Cook,
He slash'd it, and wash'd it, and I[10] know not what,
Meat[11] not one bit he left on't but 'twas all he Eat.

The Drink it was good and so was the Bread,
They took off their Liquors till they were all Red,[12]   40
And when they had done they sang the Hares Knell,
And if I had more,[13] faith more I wou'd tell.

---

5. MS reads "EE".
6. The belief that a hare makes a will as it dies and gives permission to a particular dog to kill it is of ancient origin.
7. strife.
8. MS. reads: "Baldoit". Baldoyle is a town in Fingal, not far from Howth.
9. For the significance of this stress on the first syllable, see Bliss pp. 194–8. Richard Stanihurst had noted in 1577 that in Wexford (where the pronunciation of English was very similar to that of Fingal), "most commonly in wordes of two sillables, they give the last the accent". (Raphaell Holinshed, *The Firste Volume of the Chronicles of England, Scotlande, and Irelande* (London, 1577), f.31r, col. 1).
10. MS reads "EE".
11. Conjectural reading: MS reads "Mut", but the word could well be "But".
12. i.e. red in the face. took off = drank eagerly.
13. i.e. (presumably) more liquor.

JAMES SHIRLEY
(1596-**1638**-1666)

When James Shirley, the famous London playwright, came to Dublin in 1636, he was leaving a city where the plague had forced the theatres to close, and coming to one where he could reasonably hope to develop his career. His friend John Ogilby (soon to be appointed Master of the Revels by the new lord deputy, Sir Thomas Wentworth (1593–1641) had moved to Dublin,[1] and a new theatre – the first public theatre in Ireland – was being, or had just been, built in Werburgh Street.[2] Shirley wrote three plays for the new theatre during his time in Dublin, as well as several prologues for plays by others. Not everything went as Shirley had expected, however. Though his plays were successful, life in Ireland became difficult, and audiences were smaller than he had hoped – as his comments in the three prologues which follow demonstrate clearly. Shirley returned to London in 1640, not long before the Werburgh Street theatre itself was closed and its company of actors and hangers-on were dispersed as a result of the rising of 1641.

A Prologue to *The Irish Gent.*[3]

It is our wonder, that this fair Island, where
The aire is held so temperate (if there
Be faith in old Geographers, who dare
With the most happy, boldly this compare)
That to the noble seeds of Art and Wit,
Honour'd else-where, it is not naturall yet.[4]
We know at first, what black and generall curse
Fell on the earth; but shall this Isle be worse?
While others are repair'd, and grow refin'd
By Arts, shall this onely to weeds be kinde?   10

1. Ogilby had arrived in Dublin as part of the entourage of the lord deputy, Sir Thomas Wentworth, in 1633. He was appointed Master of the Revels on 28 February 1638.
2. See Alan Fletcher, *Drama, Performance and Polity in pre-Cromwellian Ireland* (Cork, 2000), pp. 261–77) for the best modern account of the Werburgh Street theatre and its playwrights. Fletcher discusses the probable date of the opening of the theatre on pp. 261–4.
3. There are two ways of interpreting this title. It is possible that the prologue was for a play called *The Irish Gentleman*; there is no record of such a play but Shirley might have adapted and temporarily retitled his play *The Gentleman of Venice* for a Dublin performance; as Fletcher notes (p. 444, n. 59), that play was probably performed in Dublin. Alternatively, as Shirley's nineteenth-century editors, William Gifford and Alexander Dyce, thought, the poem might be addressed to the Irish *Gentry* – in which case it may have been intended to be spoken before the Werburgh Street playhouse performance of *The Royal Master*. See *The Dramatic Works and Poems of James Shirley*, ed. William Gifford and Alexander Dyce, 6 vols. (London, 1833, reprinted New York, 1966), IV, 102.
4. i.e. the people of Ireland do not yet have any feeling for art and wit.

Let it not prove a storie of your time,
And told abroad to staine this promising Clime,
That wit, and soule-enriching Poesie,
Transported hither must like Serpents dye,
Unkinde to both alike, shall the faire Traine
Of Virgin Muses onely here be slaine?
Forbid it *Phœbus*,[5] that this aire should still
Like things of venome all thy Prophets kill:
Disperse thy beames through these cold killing parts,
And make it fruitfull in thy owne great Arts.   20
Oh doe not bury all your Braine in Glebes,[6]
But tune your Harps to build the walls of *Thebes*;
With harmony new Towers frame, to be
Dwellings for you, and your posterity.
But truce Poetick rage, and let not what
Concernes the Countrey, fall upon a spot
Of it, a few here met to see a Play:
All these are innocent; the better they
To tell this fault abroad, that there may be
Some repaire done to injur'd Poesie.   30
Then we may grow, and this place by your raies,
Cherish'd, may turne into a Grove of Bayes.[7]

A Prologue to another of Master Fletcher's Playes there[1]

Are there no more?[2] and can this Muses sphere
At such a time as this, so thinne appeare?
We did expect a Session, and a Traine[3]
So large, to make the Benches crack againe.
There was no Summons sure: yes, I did see
The Writs abroad, and men with halfe an eye

---

5. i.e. Phœbus Apollo, god of (among other things) the arts, music and poetry.
6. i.e. in the clergy.
7. laurel trees. Sprays of laurel, woven into a wreath, were signs of honour for a conqueror or a poet in classical times. 'your' in the previous line may refer to the audience listening to the prologue – or back to Phœbus (line 17).

---

1. i.e. in Dublin. The play was one by John Fletcher (1579–1625). For a consideration of which one it might have been, see A. H. Stevenson, 'Shirley's Publishers: The Partnership of Crooke and Cooke', *The Library*, 4th series, vol. 25 (1944–5), pp. 140–61, pp. 150–1).
2. members of the audience.
3. session = a gathering; traine = train = a group of people travelling together.

Might read on every Post, this day would sit
Phœbus himself, and the whole Court of Wit.
There is a fault, O give me leave to say,
You are not kinde, not to your selves, this day;　　　　　10
When for the pleasure of your eare would come
Fletchers deare shade, to make *Elsium*
Here, where each soul those learned groves might see,
And all the sweets are fam'd in Poesie.

Were there a Pageant now on foot, or some
Strange Monster from Peru, or Affrick come,
Men would throng to it; any Drum will bring
(That beats[4] a bloodlesse prize, or Cudgelling)
Spectators hither; nay, the Beares invite
Audience, and Bag-pipes can doe more than wit.　　　　　20
'Tis pittie, but awake, brave soules awake,
Throw off these heavy Chains for your owne sake:
Oh doe not grieve the Ghost of him, whose pen
Had once the vertue to make Statues men,
And men turn Statues, lesse could not befit
Their justice, and the wonder of his wit.
Stoop, when you touch the Laurels of dead,
Be wise, and Crowne agen the Poets head.

A Prologue to a Play there; call'd *No Wit to a Womans* [1]

We are sorrie Gentlemen, that with all our paines
To invite you hither, the wide house containes
No more. Call you this terme?[2] if the Courts were
So thin, I thinke 'twould make your Lawyers sweare,
And curse mens Charitie, in whose want, they thrive,
Whilst we by it, woe to be kept alive.
Ile tell you what a Poet sayes, two yeare
He has liv'd in *Dublin*, yet he knowes not where

---

4. i.e. beats to announce . . .

1. i.e. in Dublin. The play was *No Wit, No Help like a Woman's*, by Thomas Middleton.
   Shirley published an adaptation of this play in London in 1657 and it is this adaptation
   which, according to Fletcher, was performed in Dublin (Fletcher p. 443, n. 58.)
2. i.e. the season when plays were performed – linked to the idea of the law 'term' when
   courts are in session.

To finde the City:[3] he observ'd each gate,
It could not run through them, they are too strait:[4]   10
When he did live in *England*, he heard say,
That here[5] were men lov'd wit, and a good Play;
That here were Gentlemen, and Lords; a few
Were bold to say, there were some Ladies to:
This he beleev'd, and though they are not found
Above, who knowes what may be under ground:
But they doe not appeare, and missing these,
He sayes he'll not beleeve your Chronicles
Hereafter, nor the Maps, since all this while,
Dublin's invisible, and not *Brasile*.[6]   20
And all that men can talke hee'll thinke to be
A fiction now above all Poetrie:
But stay, you think hee's angry, no, he praid
Me tell you,[7] he recants what he has said,
Hee's pleas'd, so you shall be, yes, and confesse
We have a way 'bove wit of man to please;
For though we should despaire to purchase it
By art of man, this is a womans wit.

---

3. i.e. the people who make up the city.
4. narrow. The line seems to imply that the people cannot have left the city since the city
   gates, which the poet (i.e. Shirley) has examined, are not wide enough for them all to get
   out. (The problem is that the people are not in the theatre.)
5. i.e. in Dublin.
6. Hy Brasil, the mythical land said to lie off the west coast of Ireland, but not on any map.
7. The prologue is spoken by an actor.

ANDREW COOPER
(*fl*.**1638**–1660)

Andrew Cooper, an English royalist news reporter and poet, is best known for *Stratologia or The History of the English Civil Warrs, in English verse . . . by an Eye-witnesse of many of them* (London, 1660); earlier, he had written a detailed and accurate account of events in and around the royalist camp at York in 1642. Though nothing is known of Cooper's life, he must (on the evidence of the poem below) have spent part of the 1630s in Dublin.

The poem which follows is one of ten commendatory verses which prefix the Dublin and London 1638 printing of James Shirley's play *The Royal Master*, a play about political and sexual intrigue in the court of Naples, which had been acted before Lord Deputy Wentworth both in Dublin Castle and in the new theatre in Werburgh Street.[1] The authors of the commendatory verses included prominent members of the circle surrounding Wentworth, among them John Ogilby (the manager of the theatre), William Smith (two of whose poems appear elsewhere in this anthology, see pp. 273–5), and Richard Bellings, soon to be secretary to the supreme council of the Irish Confederation. Authors of other verses printed before the play included James Mervyn, Francis Butler and W. Markham. Some, if not all, of these authors were catholics and all were royalists. Cooper's poem is the only text in this anthology which acknowledges the existence of a national poetic tradition in seventeenth-century Ireland.

Upon Mr James Shirley his comedy, called *The Royal Master*

> When Spenser reign'd sole Prince of Poets here,
> As by his Fairy Queen doth well appear,
> There was not one so blind, so bold a bard,
> So ignorantly proud or foolish-hard
> To encounter[2] his sweet Muse, for Phœbus vow'd
> A sharp revenge on him should be so proud;
> And when my Shirley from the Albion shore[3]
> Comes laden with the Muses, all their store
> Transfers to Dublin, full Parnassus brings,
> And all the riches of Castalian springs,[4]   10
> Shall we not welcome him with our just votes?[5]
> And shall we do't with harsh and envious notes?

1. See Alan J. Fletcher, *Drama, Performance and Polity in Pre-Cromwellian Ireland* (Cork, 2000), pp. 265–77, particularly pp. 272–3.
2. to meet as an adversary, to confront. Phœbus = (here) Apollo, god of the arts.
3. England, from which Shirley came to Ireland in November 1636.
4. waters of a fountain on Mount Parnassus; those who drank them were granted poetic gifts.
5. i.e. our appropriate declarations of support – presumably a reference to the commendatory poems printed before *The Royal Master*. 'notes' in the next line = songs, again referring to the verses.

No, no, Thalia![6] Envy shall not sit
So high above our judgment, and our wit
As not to give just merit his due praise,
And crown thy Poet with deserved bays.[7]
   Shirley, stand forth, and put thy laurel on,
Phœbus' next heir, now Ben[8] is dead and gone,
Truly legitimate; Ireland is so just
To say, you rise the Phœnix of his dust;   20
And since thy ROYAL MASTER won so much
On each Judicious,[9] and hath stood the touch,[10]
Tis fit he should be more than private, when
He wears two crowns, their votes, and thy smooth pen.[11]

6. the muse of comedy.
7. The wreath of bay leaves (or of 'laurel' as in the next line) was the mark of honour for a poet.
8. Ben Jonson (1573?–1637), whose plays were favourites on the London stage, and who had died only a few months before this poem was written. Phœbus = Apollo, the god of the arts.
9. judgement. The reference is twofold: in the play, the King of Naples pardons all wrong-doers except the arch-villain, Montalto who, as he is banished, bestows on the king the epithet 'the Royal Master'; secondly, in Shirley's epilogue to the play, 'spoken to the Lord Deputy on New-Year's-Day, at night', the phrase 'Royal Master' is used to refer to Charles I in the couplet: 'Till for your ROYAL MASTER, and this isle, / Your deeds have fill'd a chronicle!'
10. This half-line seems to refer to applause for the play.
11. This complicated couplet can be paraphrased as follows: it is appropriate that he (the 'Royal Master' of the play) should be a person who holds public office since he has been crowned twice, once with the praise of the audience at the play and once by your (i.e. Shirley's) eloquent writing.

ANONYMOUS
(1641)

Though it has been asserted that Bishop John Atherton (1598–1640) was innocent of the crimes for which he was executed, and had been unjustly arraigned because of some irregularity over the payment of tithes, historians now accept that he was probably guilty as charged. His case attracted a lot of attention, and he was executed before an immense crowd in Dublin in December 1640. The poem which follows, which was printed in London, is a crude attempt to exploit the lurid nature of the bishop's crimes, but it does include vivid (if fanciful) vignettes of life in mid-seventeenth-century provincial Ireland.

The full title of the text is as follows: 'The Life and Death of *John Atherton*, Lord Bishop of Waterford and Lysmore within the Kingdome of *Ireland*, borne neare Bridgwater in *Somersetshire*. Who for Incest, Buggery, and many other enormous crimes, after having lived a vicious life, dyed a shamefull death, and was on the fifth of December last past, hanged on the Gallows Greene at Dublin, and his man *John Childe* being his Proctor,[1] with whom he had committed the buggery, was hangd in March following at Bandon Bridges, condemned thereunto at the Assises holden at Corke.'

The Life and Death of John Atherton . . .

Confusion, give my thoughts once leave to be
Exempted from thy lawlesse Tyranny:
If[2] for the space of but one poore halfe houre,
O give me leave to sit in quiets Bower,
That I with patience may delineate,
In lines of life this Prelates sordid state;
Who first in England did his life receive,
His education Oxford did him give,
Thence to a Benefice preferd he was
In which he vitiously[3] his time did passe,   10
And although married to a handsome wife,
Blest with sweet children, th'only joy of life,
Yet so farre basenesse did in him prevaile,
That unto Lust he himselfe set to saile;[4]
Defloured Virgins, Marriage beds defilde,
With many other vitious crimes too vilde[5]

---

1. An agent appointed by a clergyman to collect tithes for him.
2. if only.
3. viciously.
4. Atherton was born in Somerset and educated at Oxford before becoming incumbent of the parish of Huish Comb Flower, also in Somerset. He did have a wife and children, to whom he addressed 'penitent and pious letters' just before his death, according to the *Dictionary of National Biography*.
5. vile.

To be conceivd; beyond all measure proud,
Impudence and ambition did him shroud.
Amongst his flock he sew'd seditious strife,
Set friend 'gainst friend, husband against wife,   20
So that 'mongst many he did live alone,
And loving none, beloved was of none.
Lastly through pride, high fare, and lustfull life,
Incest committed with the Sister of his wife,
For which he sued his pardon, and then fled
To Ireland, where a worser life he led.
There through insinuation did obtaine,
The Parsonage of S. *John*, became Chaplaine
Unto that honored Lord and worthy Peere,
Lord Chancellor there, Lord Viscount *Loftus* here,[6]   30
By whose assistance he did eke require,
To be Sub-deane of Christ-church, one step higher,
Whose goodnesse for to guerdon[7] he did prove,
A Judas, and betrayd him for his love,
Brought him into disgrace with that great Sir,
Who brookt no Rivall nor Competitor,
Straffords sterne Earle;[8] a man[9] of eminent hight,
Knowledge, and wit, had it beene governd right.
Courage and resolution to those high
Imployments he had given him, but why   40
Should he his merits banish and so dye,
Imping his wings[10] with false felicity?
Winning on him,[11] by him he was preferd
Unto the Bishoprick of Waterford,
And of Lysmore,[12] where he did five yeares Lord it
In such sort, as all good men much abhord it.[13]
But in the Interim marke what did befall;
If so he had had any grace at all,

6. i.e. in England where this poem was published. Atherton was indeed prebendary of St
   John's in Dublin. The Lord Chancellor, Sir Adam Loftus, became Viscount Ely in May
   1622.
7. reward.
8. Thomas Wentworth, Viscount Wentworth and Earl of Strafford, who was lord deputy
   and lord lieutenant of Ireland from 1633 until his execution in 1641.
9. i.e. Atherton.
10. to imp means to graft feathers to a damaged wing.
11. i.e. ingratiating himself with Strafford – or perhaps with Lord Ely.
12. Lismore.
13. Atherton had been made chancellor of Christ Church, Dublin, in 1635, and was
    consecrated Bishop of Waterford and Lismore in 1636.

At which he aimd, but not the grace of God,
But at such Grace as had our Graceles Laud,[14]   50
He surely warned was to mend his life,
By his owne Sister Master Leakies wife,
Which, Master Leakies Mother being dead,
And in her life-time conscious how he led
His lustfull life, her Ghoast in gastfull wise[15]
Did oft appeare before her Sisters eyes;
But she, feare-strucken, durst not speake unto it,
Till oft appearing, forced her to doe it:
Then thus she spake: Mother in Law what cause
You from your rest, to my unrest thus drawes?   60
Who answered: daughter tis the wicked life
Your Brother leads, warne him to mend his life;
If not, then plainely tell him tis decreed,
He shall be hangd, bid him repent with speede:
Then shall my restlesse spirit be at rest,
And not till then; Thus vanisht. She addrest
Herselfe for travaile;[16] Into Ireland went
With this sad message unto him was sent:
Which how he took to heart may plaine appeare
By the slight answer he returned her.   70
What must be, shal be: If I must, I must dye;
Marriage, and hanging, come by destiny.
Thus scoft her counsell, sent her back, and when
Shee was returnd, he grew far viler than
He was before, if Viler man may be;
For one bad Act before, committed three.
Here, Lord-like Prelates, two things I propound:
Or leave your Seas, or in them your vice Dround.[17]
If ye will Bishops be, be such as was
That Godly Timothy,[18] make him your glasse;   80
Shun avarice, shun extortion, shun vaine pride,
Shun hate, dissimulation; let your Guide
Be godlinesse. Shun Lust, Shun Buggary,
Shun Incest, Rape, and shun Adultery.

14. A reference to the doctrine of 'Sacramental grace' espoused by Archbishop William
    Laud (1573–1645),
15. terrifying manner.
16. travel.
17. smother or submerge. i.e. either stop being bishops (leave your sees) or smother your vice.
18. Timothy, one of the first generation of Christians, is traditionally represented as Bishop
    of Ephesus.

Be practizers of every honest thing,
Be meeke like Christ, your Bishop, Lord and King;
So may you live belov'd, and dye to life,
Not by the Axe or by the hangmans knife,
A halter as this Bishop here hath done,
When being hangd your selves doe scarce bemone: 90
And Proctors, be ye warnd by John Childs fall,
Lest that his fate betide unto you all.
Lust, Avarice, Extortion of Fees
Caus'd him at Bandon[19] bridge his life to leese.
Y'are alike guilty: let not the same thing
Draw you like him to Heaven in a string.[20]
Now to the Bishop we returne agen,
With whose loath'd Crimes I loath to fowle my pen,
A strict Lyst being taken of each whore
He was knowne to use, amounts to sixtie fower.   100
Nor was it out of frailty he did sin
In this vile sort, That might excus'd have bin.
For when that nature faild all these to please,
To provoke Lust he used Cantharides,[21]
Nor did this Bravo,[22] as some Lechers use
When they have acted sinne, seeke to excuse
The same by mincing or a flat deniall;
He scornd such baseness, let him make a triall
Of any neighbours wife, as oft he did,
He would not have his dealing to be hid.   110
He'd rather justifie the act for good,
As thus,[23] twas done, to purifie the blood.
Or if a barren wombe he chanc'd to prove,[24]
Twas cause he did not the Stone Collick[25] love.
Some women he did doe in Charitie,
And some because they us'd good Cookery,

---

19. the text reads 'London' – a mistake for Bandon: see the title of the poem.
20. 'to go to heaven in a string' (meaning to be hanged) was used of Jesuits executed in the reign of Queen Elizabeth.
21. Spanish fly: an insect which, when crushed and taken in a potion, was esteemed as an aphrodisiac.
22. daring villain.
23. i.e. as, for example, . . .
24. i.e. if he chanced to make a woman who was previously barren conceive . . .
25. This unrecorded phrase seems to mean a pain in the testicles caused by lack of sexual activity. See Eric Partridge, *Shakespeare's Bawdy* (London, 1968), p. 192.

Knew how to please his pallat as his bed,
So that at once his Corpes[26] and Lust he fed.
Thus many salves he had for many sores,
But still the cure was wrought by the art of his whores.   120
If not, t'advance his Lust this Lustfull Elfe[27]
Had tricks enough whereby to helpe himselfe.
A man well knowne in Waterford had neede
To borrow a hundred pounds; in hope to speed,[28]
Unto this Reverend Lord he did addresse
Himselfe, and his sute, which thus he did expresse:
My Lord, I oft have tasted of your favour
And promises to doe me good, which rather
Induceth me unto this bould request.
Your Lordship wil be pleas'd to make me blest   130
With the Loane of 100 pound which Ile repay
Within a month or else on any day
Your Lordship shall appoint. This courteous Lord
Answer'd, Sir you shall have it on your word,
And more to doe you good; but let your wife
Be present, least there should be any strife,
If you should faile for to repay the same,
Or I for breach of payment should make claime.
He grants, and goes; shee comes, the mony's ready;
So is my Lord; And the poore Cuckold's needy.   140
Sir, saith my Lord, though't be an intire summe,
It is odd mony that to me is come.
Amongst it all, ther's but one piece of gould,
That with the rest not easie to be tould.
Goe draw it out within my study dore;
Ile trust you there, but will not many more.
But cause your credits crackt, Ile keep the Key,
The dore being lockt; mean while your wife shal stay
And talke with me: tis granted. In his seat
The Bishop mounts, and does the well knowne feat.   150
Another, when his Lordships watch digrest,[29]
As he himselfe did alwayes, to a feast
He invites himselfe: which ended, he requests
The Goodman of the house (there being no Guests

26. body.
27. mischievous fellow.
28. i.e. to get the money quickly.
29. digressed, needed to be adjusted to the correct time – with a pun on the bishops 'digressing' from the right path in the next line.

To spoyle his sport) That he would set his watch
At his Sunne Dyall, at which he doth catch,[30]
Proud of such favour, goes without deniall;
Meane while another's set by his wives noone dyall.[31]
These are but tricks of youth; now arme your eares
With patience, for to heare of pallid[32] feares: 160
Suppose a Devill from th'infernall Pit,
More Monsterlike, then ere was Devill yet,
Contrary to course, taking a male fiend
To Sodomize with him, such was the mind
Of this Lord Bishop; he did take a Childe
By name, not yeares, acting a sinne so vilde,
As is forenam'd; this Childe a Proctor too,
Nor him alone, but his Parrator[33] he must doe;
These and a Thousand like these he hath done
Besides endeavouring to eclipse the Sunne   170
Of this our Skie, by making Charles waine[34] draw
Sublunary, by subverting the Law
Fundamentall, and putting in the place,
Commission high, Popes Canons, Great Lauds Grace.
For the subverting of such Devillish plots,
From staining of our Kingdome with such blots,
For th'happy raigne of our most Sacred King,
And those that from that Royall Stocke doe spring,
For Parliament, and health of Martiall men,
All Loyall Subjects cry with me, *Amen.*   180

30. i.e. the Goodman agrees.
31. i.e. meanwhile, another watch is set by his wife's noon dial. For the sexual connotations of a clock or watch dial seen when the hands show twelve o'clock, see Partridge, *Shakespeare's Bawdy*, p. 93.
32. that make one go pale.
33. Someone who repeats something learned by rote (*OED*).
34. 'Charles's Wain', the name given to the seven bright stars of the Great Bear, grew to mean the heavens in general or the established order, particularly during the reigns of Charles I and II. Here the poet asserts that Atherton has attempted to subvert the established order by using high church ritual, borrowed from the catholic church or from the liturgical practices of Archbishop Laud. (cf. line 50 above).

PART III

1641–1660
From the Rising
to the Restoration

ANONYMOUS POLITICAL POEMS FROM THE **1640s**

The rising that began on 23 October 1641 marked the beginning of nearly twenty years of ruinous war for Ireland. Armies supporting various factions moved around the country skirmishing, looting and burning as they went; allegiances shifted, agreements were made and broken, old scores settled and new enmities created.

A surprising amount of verse has survived from this troubled period, thanks to the work of two contemporary collectors, a London bookseller named George Thomason, who saved a copy of everything which appeared in print in London in the 1640s and 1650s, and George Lane, secretary to the first Duke of Ormond, who kept all the verse that came into the Ormond office from the early 1640s until the duke's death in 1688. Thomason's collection of printed materials is now in the British Library and the Ormond collection of manuscript verse is in the Beinecke Library at Yale University. Since Ormond played a key role in Ireland in the 1640s, sometimes as lord lieutenant, sometimes as leader of the royalist forces, the verse sent to him gives a fascinating indication of how the events of the decade were seen by some of those living through them in Ireland, while the Thomason collection shows how events in Ireland were viewed from England. The anonymous poems below come from both collections.

Verse prophesy about the Irish (1641)[1]

> Their dayes a number small shall make,
> Another shall their Country take;
> Their Children Vagabonds shall be,
> Walk up and down most wretchedly;
> God shall them put to endlesse shame,
> And quite cut off their hateful name.

Verse written by the Irish Confederates (1642)[1]

> Most gracious Soveraigne, grant that we may have
> Our ancient Land and Faith: 'tis all we crave.

---

1. Almanacs were popular in Ireland throughout the seventeenth century, and the first two poems in this section are from London-printed almanacs designed for use in Ireland. This verse comes from *A Bloody Irish Almanack* (London, 1641).

---

1. Another London printing was *Bellum Hybernicale: or, IRELAND'S WARRE Astrologically demonstrated, from the late Celestiall-congresse* (1647) by George Watson, a well-known soldier turned astrologer. In the course of that work, Watson wrote: 'I remember a few verses that were written (by somebody) *Anno* 1641. They resemble the forme of a Petition, directed to his Majesty, by the confederate *Catholiques* of *Ireland*: they are pretty ones, and therefore I will here give you them, as I had them from a friend' (p. 28). Watson was mistaken about the year, since the confederates did not assemble until 1642; however, the verse encapsulates neatly the catholic Irish confederates' political demands to Charles I soon after the formation of the Confederacy, stressing loyalty to Charles as king and hatred of the protestant English parliament, which was clipping his wings.

Your *English*, and your *Scots*, (not so content)
Claime all that's Yours, by *Act* of *Parliament*.
Their Tyrannie we hate: confesse your right:
'Tis not 'gainst you, 'tis against them we fight.
Whilst you were *King*, we were your *Subjects*: scorne,
To be their *Slaves*: we're *Fellow-Subjects* borne.
    Heavens blesse your *Majestie*, encrease your Powers:
    You being your *Selfe* againe, we still are Yours.   10

An Elegie uppon the much lamented death of that famous & late Renowned knt & Colonell Sir Charles Coote (1642)[1]

What ailes thee, Sol,[2] that muffles up and shrowdes
Thy face within a mourning scarfe of clowds?
What makes thee, Neptune, in a fury roame
Wth wrinkled browes, & at the mouth to foame?
And why did Æolus breath[e] soe big a blast
& sigh soe deepe, as if it were his last?
All is not well, I feare, these signes portend
Some generalls fall, or great Commanders end.
Tell it, O Tongue, for it can never passe
in Sylence longe; then thus it is, alas: 10
Bellona's darlinge,[3] pearle of men at Armes,
Dublin's great protector from intestine harmes,
World's wonder, Coote, in chaesinge of the foe
(Who can but weepe) receaved a fatal blowe –
Yet still pursues the chase; chardge on, he Cries,
Chardge on (my harts); this haveing said, he dies.
About the tyme great Charles[4] fell dead a sleepe
blushing Aurora[5] did begin to peepe

---

1. Sir Charles Coote (*d*. 1642) was born in Devonshire. He came to Ireland with Mountjoy in 1600 and stayed to become, eventually, a substantial landowner, a famous military commander, vice-president of Connacht and the governor of the city of Dublin. He was noted for the savage treatment of Irish forces he defeated and was the model for the villain of Henry Burkhead's fascinating five-act verse tragi-comedy, *A Tragedy of Cola's Furie, or Lirenda's Miserie* (Kilkenny, 1646). Coote was shot dead during a skirmish for possession of the town of Trim on 7 May 1642. He had served under the command of the Earl of Ormond at the battle of Kilrush a few weeks before his death, which is probably why this poem was sent to Ormond.
2. Sol stands for the sun, Neptune the sea and Æolus the wind.
3. Bellona was the Roman goddess of war.
4. i.e. Coote.
5. Dawn. Coote was killed at the break of day.

Who, seeing this, to vent her sorrow, seeks –
While drib-like teares run tricklinge downe her cheekes   20
Uppon the pearled grasse. Who then would blame
Sad night for hanging heavens star-spangled frame
wth mourning cloth of darkness when that bright
& Mars-like⁶ Coote did vanish out of sight?
But what means all this noise? Mee thinks I heere
a sett of Mars musitians drawinge neere!
Hark how the Canons roare for greefe and sadnes!
The musketts' spoaky throats spitt fier⁷ for madnes,
The trumpett that when ever Charles did goe
did nothing but a shrill tantara blow   30
Now changeth note, & like a passinge Bell
in Mournfull manner, rings greate Charles his knell.
The ratlinge drum whose sound of late was feard
is well nigh speecheless & can scarce be heard
And, as if it feare some vile disgrace,
Mufles a mourninge cloak about his face.
The heavy-headed pike hangs downe its head,⁸
& all because their darling Coote is dead.
Shall all things thus a dolefull consort make
& shall the muses not a jott partake   40
Therein? O heavens forbid it! Nay, when ere
thy precious name (deere Coote) sounds in our eare,
Wee cannott but discharge with matchlee⁹ Cryes
a brase¹⁰ of liquidd bullitts from our Eyes
wch graze uppon our cheekes untill at last
for very greefe, these bullitts melt and roast.
And yet me thinks amid this mournefull noise
I hear great Charles his harte-reviving voice;
And thus he spake: What meane yow thus to moane
(my sad survivers) for the death of one?   50
I had command indeed to brave your Coaste,
to doe some service for the Lord of Hoste,
Who therefore sent a Charriot of fire
Wherein my shott-free spirritt might aspire,

---

6. Mars was the classical god of war.
7. fire.
8. Drums were wrapped in black cloth to muffle their sound for military funerals; weapons
   such as pikes were carried in reverse.
9. = matchless.
10. brace.

Elijah-like, to heaven,[11] yet must not enter
that heavenly Cittie till I did adventure
To scale the Wales.[12] Then in a brave bravadoe,
the walls of Heaven I mounted by sealado
on Jacob's ladder.[13] Christ whose divine nature
reacht heaven, whose human, toucht this earth's theatre   60
Thus mounted upp. Then in tryumphant manner
on heavens high walls, I did erect my banner,
Wherein Christs Crosse was to the life[14] displaied
Whereon by faith done, fast hould I laied.
Then to the generall of that Army roiall
of conquering martires that were ever Loiall,
I did present my selfe, & kneelinge downe,
was there invested[15] with an endles Crowne.
Then said the Lord of hosts, my faithfull sonn
& servant Charles, for thy good service don,   70
In honnor of my name, I will enhaunce[16]
thy name for ever, & my Charles advaunce
To Life and Honnor of a Tryumph too
(Whose gapinge wound with open mouth doth woo,
And stiffly plead, in its dumb oratory)
that Charles my servant may tryumph in glory.
A Triumph thou shalt have (ride on) my son
ride on in tryumph, thou the feeld hast won.
Then as wee ride, a quire of Angells sings
an Io Pean[17] to the kinge of kings.   80

His Epitaph
England's honour, Scotland's wonder,
Ireland's terror, here lieth under.

---

11. The prophet Elijah was taken up to heaven in a chariot of fire. II Kings 2. 11.
12. = walls.
13. The patriarch Jacob had a vision of a ladder stretching from earth to heaven in Genesis
    28. 12. The association of ladders with Jacob was so strong that any ladder could be
    referred to as a 'Jacob'; here a 'sealado' or ladder for climbing up the side of a ship is
    linked back to Jacob and the ladder to heaven.
14. life-size.
15. i.e. crowned in a formal way.
16. enhance, raise up.
17. a song of joy.

Anagram on Charles Coote (the younger) (1646?)[1]

CHARLES COOTE

anagram

ART HELS COOKE

Since thou into Rebellion fell,
Thou hast drest many [a] Dish for hell,
And to it dayly dost present[2]
From Hell's Caterer (Parliament),
Wch to the Province['s] charge and cost
Has made thee ruler of the Rost.[3]
Thou many a simple Swain hast tooke
From simpler plow, most simple hooke,[4]
Whose share now swords, whose crooke does show
A Putter to, and putter fro,[5]   10
And, thus taught thy rebellious trade,
Theire kings and neighbours rights invade.
And by thy Shebas[6] curst bewitching
Those scullions to the Devills kitching[7]

---

1. The Charles Coote of this anagram, who became the first Earl of Mountrath (*d.* 1661), was the son of the Charles Coote eulogised in the previous poem. A brutal but efficient military commander like his father, this Charles Coote transferred allegiance from the royalist side to the parliamentary side in 1643 and then back to the royalist side to support the incoming Charles II in 1659. This anagram was written sometime after 1645, by which time Coote had changed from being a brother officer of Ormond to being one of his opponents – a 'rebel'.
    Anagrams were popular throughout the seventeenth century, though their intellectual ingenuity sometimes militates against their effectiveness as poetry. Letters were deemed interchangeable at the whim of the poet, and a marginal note in this manuscript asserts that 'K & C, Z & S, Y & I are convertible letters and of the same force in Anagrams'. In this anagram, exhaustive play is made on culinary terms which sound similar to, or have double meanings with, military ones.
2. offer or place the food.
3. i.e. the roast (a punning play on the word 'roost'). The province is Connacht, of which Coote became lord president in 1645.
4. reaping hook.
5. This line is obscure; seventeenth-century meanings of the verb 'to put to' include 'to press hard', those of 'to put from' include 'to exert', and those of 'to put' (by itself) include 'to push into action, to incite'. The line probably means that the swains' reaping hooks and sickles have been turned into weapons which they use indiscriminately all around them as they invade their neighbours' rights. A 'put' could also mean a rustic.
6. A marginal MS. note at this point reads: 'revileing rayning Ministers'. This reference is obscure but may, in some way, refer to Coote's transferring his loyalty to the parliamentary side.
7. kitchen.

Who Christ did at the Altar eat,
Are now to Satan Guess and meat.[8]
Some thousands by thy conduct fell,
Food first for powder, then for Hell.
Thou thousands more provided hast
And wilt serve up thy selfe at last.   20
It can become a Cooke no less
Than to be th' Reave of his last mess.[9]
   Then make what hast[e] thou canst, I prethee,
   And much [good] doe the Divill wi'thee.
      Now I see plaine the proverb's not mistooke
      God sendeth meat, the Divill sends a Cooke.[10]

from: On the breach of the Peace (1646)[1]

1. You Irish which doe boast and say
'tis for the King you fight and pray,
tell me now, I you crave,
wherefore doe you a Peace deny
when he Commands and grants mercy,
unless your wills you have?

2. Now you discover[2] what you are,
and for what Cause you raysd this war;
not for the king's Renowne,
but to advance the Pope againe,   10
to be Supreme and into Spayne
for to translate his Crowne.

3. Unless the Churches you may have,
to use your Mass, and Altars brave,

---

8. MS. reads 'Sathan'. The line is obscure, but seems to mean: those scullions to the devil's kitchen who received communion are now both the guests of Satan and food for his table.
9. = reeve, an overseer or steward. mess = a meal or a group of people eating a meal together.
10. A proverb first recorded in Andrew Boorde's *Dyetary* (London, 1542).

---

1. During the spring and summer of 1646, Ormond and the confederates agreed terms for a peace. In August and September, however, official clerical disapproval of the peace was shown when the legatine synod at Waterford excommunicated all catholics who accepted it. This poem, which highlights the complexities of the situation at this time, is written from the point of view of a protestant, resentful of the rejection of the peace by the militant, clerical party of the confederates.
2. reveal.

loaded with Pictures vayne,
you will both grace and peace deny
and in Rebellion justifie
your Actions once again.

4. But Woods and Groves are fitter far
for Baalls Priests,[3] than Temples are,   20
or else a Barne or Stable,
to Mumble out your Latine masse
which you much like to Balams Asse[4]
to understand are able.

5. Cessations[5] to continue still,
I do believe it is your will,
for you are gayners by it:
and in the mean tyme, you doe leese
good Subjects lands, their corne, & sheepe,
sure you cannot deny it.   30

6. But O there is another fetch,[6]
doth almost goe beyond my reach;
yor Cleargy will mantayne
this holy war; and they have sent
Bealing o're for that intent
to the Pope & king of Spayne.[7]

7. They hope ere long he wil bring 'ore[8]
ten thousand men & money store,
& then goes to the pot
both Puritan, and Protestant,   40
Brittish, Dutch & they doe vant[9]
they will expulse the Scot.

---

3. Baal, one of the false gods of the Old Testament, was worshipped in woods and groves.
   I Kings 18. 19.
4. Balaam's ass was famous because she could see the angel of the Lord when her master
   could not. (Numbers 22. 25).
5. cessations in hostilities.
6. trick.
7. Richard Bellings (*c.* 1598–1677), writer, historian, poet and politician, was appointed
   secretary to the supreme council of the Irish Confederation in 1642. He was sent to the
   Continent in 1644–5 to seek support for the confederate cause. He had earlier written a
   supplementary book to Sidney's *Arcadia* and later wrote an important history of the Irish
   Confederacy. Some of his verse in included in this anthology, see pp. 156–64.
8. = o'er, over.
9. = vaunt, boast.

8. Duncannon it hath made them bold,[10]
they thinke now there is ne'er a hold
that can their force withstand.
Poore Inshequin,[11] with all his men,
they make no more to vanquish them
than they were in their hand.

9. Thus doe they brag what they would doe,
they will have Cork and Youghall too,[12]   50
when Munster they had got;
then into Connaght would they gang,
the Cootes, and Ormsbyes, thence to bang;
at length turne out the Scot.[13]

10. Thus these brave Rebbells swear and stare
and doe build Castles in the ayre,
thinking that's all theire own;
but I believe, ere they doe part,
the Scots will vex them to the hart,
and make them cry *oh hone*.[14]   60

11. That they thus mischeefe did begin,
in perpetrating such a Sin,
that doth God much offend
in fayth; and they were much to blame;
the Divill, owing them a Shame,
will pay them in the end.

12. But I hope they must reckon againe,
for all their forces out of Spaine,
whereof they so much boast.
For if one another's part wee take   70
wee have force enough to make
them reckon with theire past.

10. The fort at Duncannon, County Wexford, was besieged and captured by the confederates in 1645.
11. Murrough O'Brien, Lord Inchiquin (1614–74), was at this time (i.e. after 17 July 1644 when he abandoned the royalist cause and started supporting the parliamentary side) a parliamentary commander in Munster. Parliament appointed him lord president of Munster in January 1645.
12. The confederates had abandoned the siege of Youghal, County Cork, in September 1645.
13. i.e. to defeat the parliamentary forces (under Coote and Ormsby) in Connacht and to turn out the army of Scots covenanters (which, under Robert Monro, had been harassing Ulster for years).
14. alas; Ir. *ochón*.

13. Thus these brave Rebbells hope to be
among themselves a Nation free
in state and in Religion.
They doe but purpose, like to men;
but God will sure dispose of them,
unto their own confusion . . .

21. And now divisions they have bred
between Protestant and Roundhead,[15]   80
they doe on parties fall;
and in pretence that for the King,
the Roundheads into awe they'll bring,
they hope to conquer all . . .

50. As for the Irish, though they boast
of all their powerful Munster host,
that holds[16] with ease doth take,
observe the end, and you shall find
all things are yet not to their mind,
for they shall shortly quake.   90

51. For if that prophesyes be true
the Scots this kingdom shall subdue,
and make the Irish slaves;
then will they these their deeds repent,
and have just cause for to lament
over the English graves.

from: A New Ballad called a Review of the Rebellion (1647)
[Stanza on the Irish][1]

What Christian heart next doth not ake[2]
To see the poore Irish laid at th' Stake?

---

15. Those who supported the English parliamentary side in the Civil Wars were known as
   'Roundheads' because they wore their hair close cut.
16. strongholds.

---

1. This stanza is unusual in its expression of sympathy for those caught up in the Irish wars
   of the 1640s; it comes from *A New Ballad called a Review of the Rebellion* in three parts,
   a long royalist poem printed in London in 1647.
2. ache.

For their lives and lands, the Ordinance saith
May be bought for summs on the publick faith.[3]
    And now some men are so wise
    To think them lawfull prize
Because they're voted Rebells by our State.
    But were it not a Sinne?
    Yet they divide the skinne
Of the Beare among them e're they have't . . .   10

Anagram on Michael Jones, Governor of Dublin (1648?)[1]

Michael Jones

anagram

I am hels coine

And sayst thou so? then give the Devil's due:
Pay'm his owne Coine: pox on't, for shame be true
Amongst your selves: Hee's master of the Mint;
Here's his stamp too, why see, the Devill's in't.
Will you refuse[2] and stay till you be sent,
Or till the Divill's Bullion (Parliament)
Be minted all,[3] and goe in a grosse[4] Summe?
That shall be done (Divill), they come, they come.
    If you nor give yourselves, nor wee you send[5]
    Faith, 'tis all one, hee'l fetch you in the end.   10

---

3. Irish land was promised to those assisting the parliamentary cause under the Adventurers' Act of 1642, though, of course, that land still had to be wrested from its owners before it could be reallocated and/or sold; thus, those who bought Irish land under the act had to have 'faith' that they would eventually get possession of it.

---

1. Michael Jones (*d.* 1649) was son of the bishop of Killaloe and a strong protestant. Early in his career, he was a supporter of the Irish royalists, but he later moved to the parliamentary side and became one of the most effective commanders of English parliamentary forces in Ireland. Jones was governor of Dublin for the parliamentarians from 1647 to 1649, and in August 1649 inflicted a crushing defeat on Ormond's forces at the battle of Rathmines, near Dublin. He was appointed second-in-command to Cromwell, but died of a fever late in 1649. Not surprisingly, since it was sent to Ormond, this anagram, which plays on the notion of coinage and the value of money, is virulently antagonistic to Jones.

2. i.e. refuse to go to hell.

3. i.e. all be impressed with the sign of the devil – like you (Jones) are.

4. 1) the financial term = whole; 2) repulsive.

5. i.e. if either you don't hand yourselves over (to the devil) or we don't send you to him . . .

CORNELIUS MAHONY (?)
(*fl*.**1642**–1646)

This strange poem has only survived because it was, as the title page of the tract in which it appeared described it, 'A true copy of most wicked verses written in forme of a Ballad defying the English, being found in a Rebels pocket . . . ' The peculiarities of the text seem to confirm this story and though one might expect such a document to be in Irish rather than English, it is clear that whoever wrote it was a native speaker of Irish, not fully at ease with the English language. Examples of some of the poet's misunderstandings of the nuances of English are highlighted in the notes to the poem below.

The text itself shows signs of hasty composition and printing in the London printing house from which it was issued as an addendum to a newsletter; in addition, parts of it have become thoroughly garbled in the process of transmission, so that the resulting text is ambiguous in some places and unintelligible in others. The notes below should be seen as no more than an attempt to clarify a text which, in some respects, defies clarification. The poem is important, however, as a rare example of verse from mid-seventeenth-century Ireland which attacks the English in their own language – or at least in a variation of it.

The military and political events referred to in the poem show that it was written by someone familiar with the skirmishes which took place between crown and rebel forces in the countryside to the west of the city of Cork in February 1642. The forces of Sir William St Leger, lord president of Munster, aided by those raised by Lord Barrymore and Lord Kinalmeasky, son of the Earl of Cork (see lines 67–9), were defeated in a skirmish with rebel forces at Kilmallock, County Cork, early in February, after which St Leger withdrew to the area around Cork city (see lines 35–6). St Leger, Barrymore and Kinalmeasky all died later in 1642. The printed text of the poem is signed 'Cornelius Mahony'. Connor or Cornelius Mahony or O'Mahony was born near Muskery in County Cork early in the seventeenth century. He trained for the priesthood on the Continent and was ordained into the Jesuit order, eventually settling in Portugal, where he became professor of theology at Evora. Mahony is best remembered for *Disputatio Apologetica et Manifesta de jure Regni Hiberniae Adversus Hereticos* (Frankfurt [i.e. Lisbon], 1645). This bitter attack on the English for their occupation of Ireland urged Irish catholics to exterminate all protestants – a sentiment too extreme for most Irish catholics; Mahony's book was ordered to be burned by the common hangman in Kilkenny. Little is known of Mahony's early life, although he is said to have been in Galway in the early 1640s.

The poem is far milder than Mahony's Latin tract – see the last two lines in particular – and it is possible that it was written by another hand and circulated as if it were his. If Mahony did write it, however, he was almost certainly in Ireland in the early months of 1642, since the poem shows a good knowledge of events in Munster. Whatever its true origins, the poem is of considerable interest.

A kind of a Ballad,

briefly expressing the pride of Englishmen in this kingdom: an example to all men to be content with whatsoever they have; with their speech in the beginning of these Warres.

To the Tune of *Ha, for my pride I must perish*.

The mother of your evils your souls will receive;[1]
Hither[2] you came, surely us poore to deceive;
But such a good token[3] to you we will send
That soonly[4] will teach you your lives to amend.
Your Godfars and Gamers, you rich that are most,
Your wives and children shall pay fore the rost.[5]
Our anger weel write in blood of your men,
And bravely weel tune it in cries of women.
Your faith you have sold for pottage[6] and bread.
In chest[7] your sermons and songs you have read,   10
Your deeds in despaire: I need not to tell
The portent of your downfall, you know it full well.
Our souldiers and male men[8] are valiant and stout,
Our women and female are faire and devout,
Our riches were Heaven, and you were the God,
And so we permitted, until you were sod[9]
From Ireland to England, but what to doe there?[10]
Your pride and presumption not kept anywhere;

1. This line reads like an Irish curse, except that the future tense rather than the subjunctive is used. The phrase 'mother of your evils' – awkward in English – reflects the Irish *máthair an oilc* = the mother of evil = the source of something bad; the poet has translated the word *máthair* as 'mother' when he should have used its other meaning, 'source'. The line addresses the English settlers in Ireland and threatens that the source of their evils, i.e. the catholic church, will shortly receive their souls.
2. i.e. to Ireland.
3. present, sign.
4. A misunderstanding; the poet does not understand that because 'soon' is an adverb and not an adjective, it does not need the suffix *–ly* to turn it into an adverb.
5. These lines seem to mean: You who are richest, your grandfathers and grandmothers, your wives and your children shall pay by being burned out of their homes.
6. food, porridge, oatmeal i.e. you have sold your faith for food.
7. This word is hard to read in the text and could be 'chere' i.e. cheer, a mood of gladness. If 'chest' is the correct reading, it could = strife, contention.
8. Ir. *fearga* has two meanings in English: 1) male; 2) manly, brave. The poet has selected the wrong one.
9. to sod = to throw sods of turf at a person or thing; here = thrown out.
10. This couplet seems to mean: You thought our riches (i.e. Ireland) were heaven, and that you were the gods – and we permitted this until you were thrown out (from Ireland to England).

From England your succour I hardly beleeve,
Will come, long longed, such rogues to relieve;　　　　　20
Your King you have banished, and despised the Crowne,
But surely beleeve me, your pride weel pull down.
Linckt in your Saddles,[11] a Horse you ride,
The sight of us Irish you dare not abide.

Away good man, good masters away,
On yonder green Hill are a hundred this day.[12]
I vow and protest, good Gossip,[13] tis well,
To old Master *Langthon*[14] this wonder weel tell.
And stumbling and stambling away they do trot,
Their wives being weake to hang the black pot.[15]　　　　　30
The day you shall curse when first you begun,
And say with your selves our race we must run.[16]
With Gentlemens murder our minds were content,
But fainting in heart, we lately repent.[17]

In *Corke* my Lord President[18] shunneth the field,
His souldiers in treason[19] from harme to shield.
Of English bastards in *Bandon* a crew,
In prison enclosed for death is their due,[20]
In Warlike affaires mongst all the rest,
William Hull[21] Crookbackd accounted the best.　　　　　40

11. This seems to mean: As you ride a horse, you are linked to it in your saddle. (Irish horsemen commonly rode bareback or with saddles made of straw, which made it easy for them to leap off their horses: English leather saddles and metal stirrups connected an Englishman more firmly to his horse.)
12. This seems to mean that a hundred settlers have been assembled on a green hill after they have been turned out of their houses.
13. friend.
14. Thomas Lancton was the author of three letters from Dublin printed in London in 1642, each of which purported to bring good or true news from Ireland, i.e. news of victory over the 'rebels'.
15. 'The black pot' is probably the cooking pot hung over an open fire. Perhaps the implication is that the settlers' wives were not tough enough for life out of doors, or for cooking over open fires.
16. This couplet probably means: You will curse the day you started this project (in Ireland), and say to yourselves, 'we must get out of Ireland' (unless, perhaps, the second line means: 'we must stay and finish the race we have begun').
17. i.e. we were content to murder gentlemen (at the beginning of the rebellion), but now we have lost heart for this and repent – which is why you are not to be killed.
18. Sir William St Leger (1627–42). See headnote.
19. Anyone on St Leger's side was, from the point of view of this writer, 'in treason'.
20. Bandon was a protestant town; since the countryside around the town was controlled by rebel forces at this time, Bandon was, in a sense, besieged.
21. unidentified.

The chiefe to instruct to march with a rope
In order of hanging, grant Jesu that scope.[22]

Long time by mis-fortune we were your poore slaves,
You dancing in Courts, we mourning in Caves,
In some of our Lands, of our buildings of all,
When we should ourselves, you Lords we did call;
But being too much over-mastered by pride
At you and your folly we scoffe and deride.
For when the beginning of the Rebels began
From one to another they[23] oftentimes ran.   50
Prethee our Dermon[24] come hither I say,
And tell me from market what heard you this day,
In troth good master of help is no way,[25]
But that we must perish and wholly decay.
Why for 't our Dermon, you make me to fret,
My limbs are trembling; on feare they are set.
In *Bandon* proclaimed[26] and fully set forth,
That many Rebels keep campes in the North.
These newes amend them when first he did blaze
That they were undone and in a bad case,[27]   60
Through feare and dispaire in Cities they heape,[28]
The fruit of their mischiefes by dying to reape.

Good wife, take some Bacon and bread, do not want,
I rather should perish than that should be scant.
Their Cows and their Oxen we took for the rent,
And they with the pox[29] for the Divell are sent.

---

22. These lines seem to mean: He will be the first we order to march to the place of his hanging, carrying the rope – may Jesus grant us that.
23. i.e. the English settlers.
24. A variation of Dermot, a typical first name for an Irishman, in this case servant to one of the settlers.
25. This is a word-for-word translation of a sentence in Irish: *I bhfírinne a mháistir mhaith de chabhair níl aon tslí.* The line parodies the speech of an Irishman attempting to address his master in English by merely translating individual words into the new language.
26. i.e. the news of the rebellion has been proclaimed.
27. i.e. the first news – that the English were all ruined – was later amended.
28. i.e. they crowd to the cities.
29. A common expletive phrase. pox = venereal disease.

240

Weel hunt *William Sintleger*[30] like a broune Fox,
And you *Lewis Boyle*[31] goe shrub with a pox,
My Lord of *Barrimore*[32] go charge to the Beefe;
In faith by your Kinsmen an arrant greate thiefe.   70
By riches ill gotten preferment they gained
They like to be killed by them disdained.
Your Statutes not setled on any sure ground
Your wealth did augment, and others confound.[33]
Your fashions[34] are handsome, compleat I confesse,
But all being curious, your fayth did oppresse.[35]
But whether to kill them tis doubtful to say,
Or else to ship them and send them away.[36]

30. Sir William St Leger. See headnote. He was renowned for brutality and savagery to those
   he deemed rebels.
31. Lewis Boyle, Viscount Kinalmeasky (1619–42), son of the first Earl of Cork, killed at
   the battle of Liscarroll in September 1642. 'Go shrub with a pox' is unrecorded in this
   form but seems to be a contemptuous phrase of dismissal; a modern equivalent might be
   'Go scratch yourself, and to hell with you!'
32. David Fitz-David Barry, first Earl of Barrymore (1605–42), a landowner who raised
   troops to assist St Leger. 'To charge to the beef' meant to set up a hue and cry.
33. A reference to English law being applied to Irish land rights.
34. i.e. the way you do things.
35. This couplet seems unintelligible, but it might mean: The way you do things is
   handsome and complete, I confess, but you are all strange and your faith crushes you.
36. The idea that shipping Englishmen out of the country might be more appropriate than
   killing them goes counter to the bloodthirsty view of what should be done to protestants
   in Mahony's Latin tract of 1645.

241

GEORGE WEB
(*fl*.1636–1641, pub. **1643**)

Despite the unsettled times, the two great Renaissance scholars of Dublin, Sir James Ware and Archbishop Ussher, were editing and producing works on Irish history and antiquities throughout the 1620s, 1630s and 1640s. The first two volumes of Ware's biographical accounts of the bishops of Ireland were published in Dublin in 1626 and 1628, and their appearance inspired George Web, an Englishman who was Bishop of Limerick from 1634 until he was killed during the rebellion of 1641, to send the author the following verses.

On the Renovation of the Bishops of Ireland,
happily effected by the Piety and Ingenuity of the most Learned Sir James Ware,
Knight

Kind Muses now at length adieu,
Thus far's enough to trouble you;
A Mitred Muse can't wish to dye,
Pardon the Word, more Heavenly,
Than praising, Sir, your worthy Deeds,
Who Crowns so many Mitred Heads.
Whilst you the Bishops Lives restore,
(Too long opprest with Night before)
You take the most ingenious Course,
Learn'd *Ware*, thus to illustrate yours.   10
Believe me, Sir, more worthily
You can't oblige Posterity.
'Writers long Lives to others give,
By which Themselves do mean to live.'
Thus you the Bishops Years renew,
And Bishops Years you number too;
When yours are gone, inherit ours:
Which far surpassing Earthly Powers,
May vye with long Eternity;
Learn'd Men make Gods thus easily.   20

G. Limerick

ANONYMOUS
(*c*.**1643**)

This poem occurs in several manuscript and printed miscellanies of the seventeenth century, under various titles and with varying degrees of textual clarity. The best text, which is used below, is that of a printing of 1654, but the most colourful title is given to the piece in a printing of the 1690s where it is introduced as: *A Banter made upon an Irish Sheriff, on the Account of an Entertainment he gave to two gentlemen belonging to the Life Guard of Ireland, when the Duke of O. was Lord Lieutenant there, viz. about the Year 1643, called, 'The Irish Entertainment'*. The officers in the poem have been instructed to carry a message from Ormond to the high sheriff of Waterford, John, fifth Lord Power (*b*. 1596): Lord Power's peculiar behaviour in the poem may be linked to the fact that he was excused from transplantation under Oliver Cromwell on the grounds that he was then (in 1654) – and had been for the previous twenty years – bereft of reason. The poem may have been popular because it gave an English audience a glimpse into the exotic world of a substantial native Irish household just before such a way of life disappeared for ever.

An Account of an Irish Quarter[1]

From *Carrick*,[2] where noble *Ormond* met
Kilkenny's Supreme Councellors to treat
For *Ireland*'s peace, after I had let fly
At the lean half-boil'd fresh-beef Ordinary,[3]
All my own shillings, (and the Truth to tell 'ee,)
One more I borrow'd of my friend *Jack Belly*;[4]
'Twas time, I thought, to make a quick departure
With my Comrade, *Ned Griffith*, to free Quarter;
So calling *Ned*, said I, He that long tarries
In this Town, will not find it like *Beau-Maryes*,[5]   10
Where, when we wanted 12d, we cou'd dine,
Like Dukes, and only cry, *Peg* this makes nine:
Here's no kind Tap-wife, nor confiding Cook,
Will let you eat and drink and smoak by th' book;[6]
A just man, (should we grant you of that sort,)
Can't live by Faith here, tho' there's Scripture for't;

1. i.e. a place where soldiers were lodged.
2. Ormond met the leaders of the Irish Confederation at Carrick on Suir, County Tipperary, during the negotiations which led to the peace treaty of 1646.
3. An 'ordinary' was a common eating-house.
4. '*Bellew*' in most texts though the rhyme shows that the name was pronounced as spelt here.
5. '*Beau-Morris*' in most texts. Beaumaris, a fort in Anglesey, north Wales.
6. 'i.e. on credit.

But when your pocket's empty, faith, Sir, you
Must look your belly shou'd be ev'n so too.
To th' Country then, where we'l our Genius pamper
With Mustard and fat Bief, Mutton and Sampyer,[7]   20
And yet no Traveller shall after a feast
Make us repent the fouling of the reste:[8]
And reasons there are many, to persuade one,
That by our Landlord we shall be much made on;
For my Lord President[9] hath wrote a Letter,
That he should treat us like our selves, or better;
And then, for certain, he's a man of Bounty;
For hark, *Ned*, he's High-Sheriff of the County;
Besides, he's of the *Poors*, and so must be,
By consequence of our own family:[10]   30
They say, that he keeps dogs too, and will course
The Hare most fiercely, but the Fox far worse.
And faith, *Ned*, thou'rt a lad whom any right
Good fellow will bid welcom at first sight:
Thy countenance so rosie, straight inveagles,
And (to say Truth) we both are pretty Beagles.

This pleased *Ned* well, and straight we got two able
Horses out of my Lord Lieutenant's stable,
And to *Colefine*[11] 'twixt dinner time and supper,
We march't with our Port mantles at our crupper.[12]   40

Where when we came, we certain structures saw
All Perriwiggd with rushes, or with straw:[13]
So even and like, *Ned* swore by his Creator,
Some Leveller had been the Fabricator:[14]
So that to us was not distinguishable
Which was the Mansion, which the Barn or Stable.

---

7. 'i.e. samphire, a pickle made of the leaves of the samphire plant, often served with meat.
8. 'to foul a plate' with someone meant to have a meal (and so dirty the plates) with them. The line means: '. . . make us sorry we dirtied all the plates' i.e. ate all the food.
9. The Marquis (later the Duke) of Ormond.
10. The name Power was usually pronounced 'Poor'. The family is now known as De La Poer.
11. '*Coolfin*' in another text.
12. A crupper is a leather strap buckled to the back of the saddle of a horse: in this case the soldiers' portmanteaus, or carrying bags, were strapped to it.
13. i.e. thatched so that they looked like wigs.
14. The Levellers were extreme republicans, active in the 1640s. The exact significance of this line is unclear.

Ned, he alights, and leads (God bless us all)
His horse into his Worship's very Hall,
And looking round about, cries in great Anger,
Zownds,[15] here's a Stable has no Rack nor Manger.   50
Peace, *Ned*, (quoth I,) prethe be not so hasty,
This room's no stable, though it be as nasty;
I see a Harp and chimney too, and dare
Say, there was fire in't before the war;
So this is no place for your horse, you see,
'Tis then for very Beasts I'm sure (quoth he;)
I wish'd him be advised,[16] what he spake there;
For should such words come to the Sheriff's ear,
'Twas Gold to Silver that he wou'd be at us,
'Ere we were ware, with 's *Posse Comitatus*.[17]   60
Out *Ned* went laughing; I, (as is my Fashion,)
Fell straight into this serious contemplation:
If the High-Sheriff such mean dwelling have,
O hone! O hone! What has his Under Knave?

But searching further, one whose unsoald Shooes,
Like fetters hung about his feet, came to us;
And for our horses said he'd shew a room;
I ask'd him, if he were the Sheriff's Groom?
No, Sir, quoth he, I'm his first-born; but can,
For need, supply the office of his man.   70
I cry'd him mercy, wish'd him not be crost;
Off went my hat, and off went his almost.
He bade us go to th'house; and so we took
Our way to the place *Ned* and his horse mistook:
And after we a little there had wander'd,
In came the man who prov'd to be our Landlord;
Who for his face and garb, might pret'ly well
Pass English muster for Head Constable.
I with fit ceremony tow'rds him went,
And gave him th'Letter, from th' Lord President: 80
He took't and read it; and, for ought I know,
We welcom were; but he ne're told us so.

---

15. = God's Wounds! – a common oath.
16. careful.
17. i.e. it would be a sure bet (an apparently unrecorded saying) that, before we were aware of it ('ware), he would be after us with his men. A 'Posse Comitatus' was the body of men a sheriff could raise to quell a riot or disturbance.

Opening his mouth at length, he ask'd us, how
Corn sold beyond sea? and if men did plow?
When, and for what occasion, we came o'er?
And if we ever had been there before?
I answer'd so as pleas'd him well, I think,
For straight he bade the Butler fill some drink;
But seeing him in's half-pint dish of wood,
Sip like a maid, thought I, this man's no good   90
Companion, or else his drink's but small;[18]
Both which did prove too true: And this was all
My comfort now, I hop'd to find good fare:
And then for table-tipple, 'twas most rare.[19]

And now for supper, the round board being spread,
The Van,[20] a dish of coddled Onions led;
I' th' Body lay a salted tail of Sammon:
And in the Rear, some rank Potatoes came in.
To comfort *Ned*, said I, a short repast
Must serve this *Wednesday* Night, 'cause 'tis a Fast: 100
But Master Sheriff the next meal wil mend it
To our content. Quoth *Ned*, I pray God send it!
We sate, and soon had made of it I trow,[21]
A clean board, if his napkins had been so:
But opening one of them, I tell ye Truth,
My stomach was got full before my mouth.
Some house-wifes wou'd give groats[22] a-peece for these,
To have the washing of them, for the Grease.
At length it came into my fancy, that
They might be Reliques oyl'd with holy fat;   110
And that th' Apostles, when the Pascal Lamb[23]
Was eaten, wip'd their Fingers on the same.
My Landlord fed well, and seeing us to eat
Nothing, he bid us welcome to his meat;
And having done, he cross'd himself all o'er;
His Supper had done so for us before.[24]

18. of low alcoholic strength, light or weak.
19. i.e. the poet hoped to get good drink with his meal.
20. The first part of an army going into battle.
21. I suppose.
22. A groat was a coin worth fourpence.
23. The lamb sacrificed and eaten at the Jewish passover – here a reference to the Last Supper taken by Jesus and his Apostles; see Matthew 26. 20.
24. A double meaning of the word 'cross'; in the second line, it means the soldiers had been put into a bad temper by the food.

When bed time came, he bade one with a light,
Conduct us where we were to lodge that night:
He had himself gone with us, (I dare say,)
But that his Chamber did not lie that Way.   120
So to a Room we came; of which 'tis all
I'll say, 'twas correspondent[25] to the Hall.

Quoth *Ned*, I'll not unsheath, though I am drowsie,
These sheets were us'd before, and may be lowsie.
What then, said I; dost not thou know, thou Noddy,
Fresh Linnen is unwholesome for the body:
And lice are here no more an Infamy,
Than red Hair: th' are the Nation's lechery.
So down we lay, to Sleep full well inclin'd;
But through the gaping wall came such a wind,   130
That from my head my night-cap (this is true)
To th' farther side of all the room it blew:
And had there been in my fantastick pate,[26]
As many Windmills as I saw of late
Near *Wexford*, 'twould have whirl'd them all about:
And from my nose e're since (like a still snout)[27]
Such distillations fall, you'd ghesse by this,
My head were what the Prophet wished his.[28]
Now 'cause we could not sleep, we fell to pray,
More than we us'd, but 'twas for nought but day.   140
By th' Lord, quoth *Ned*, the Sun, if he shou'd sup,
And lodge like us, at midnight wou'd get up:
And I shou'd tumble less, and sleep more, had I,
Instead of thee, (dear Tom,) some handsome *Lady*.

But there's no night so long, but hath its morn,
And so had this; which, if we had been born
Stark blind, we had not been so glad to see:
No alarm'd Souldier cou'd be more quick than we,
Leap from his bed, and sooner dress himself,
So down went we, and play'd till hour the twelfth;   150

25. equal.
26. head.
27. The nozzle at the end of the tube in a pot still.
28. *Original note*: 'Fountain of Tears'. Jeremiah 9. 1. 'O that my head were waters and mine eyes a fountain of tears.'

Then was the table cover'd, but the same
Linnen I saw; for fish and flesh meals came;
Dishes as formally were brought in, odd;
Pork, Pork, and Pork, two boiled, and one sodd.[29]
I'll hang for 't, but he thought us *Scots* or *Jewes*,
And brought 's meat not to eat, but to refuse.[30]
But we fell on, with all our main and might,
Urged by two reasons to 't, hunger and spight:
His napkins fatness, leanness of his meat,
Nor want of salt, could hinder us to eat,   160
Nor henceforth shall; his *Eves* and *Embers* too[31]
Shall save him nought at all, at one meal we'll eat two,
Devouring swine's flesh so, that he shall dress
Some better meat, in hopes we will eat less;
And so live, and endure, till we shall be
Released next Gen'ral Delivery.[32]

Mean time, if any man think, I have told
More than the truth, let him come and behold:
And finding things not thus, I shall desire,
He'l call me (what I wou'd I were) a Liar.   170

And let that man that shall dislike my Rhymes,
Know, that I have made better twenty times.
Nor was my Muse in fault now, but the Liquor,
Had this been stronger, that had been much quicker.
Who drinks the like, I'll hold my ink and pen on't,
He'l write as bad;

                God bless my Lord Lieutenant.

---

29. boiled, often twice.
30. Orthodox Jews do not eat pork for religious reasons – but the reference to the Scots is obscure.
31. Less meat than usual was served on Eves (the evenings before days of feasting) and on Ember Days, three days of fasting which were observed four times a year in the church calendar.
32. This probably means 'discharged when next the army is reduced in size'.

ANONYMOUS
(1644)

This poem, which was printed in London, was the work of an English protestant planter who had settled in Ireland but who had retreated to England after his Irish property had been plundered during the troubles following the rising of 1641. It is in two parts, a short 'Complaint', which sets out the circumstances of the attacks on the poet and his property, and a long poem which contains extended poetic descriptions of animals found in seventeenth-century Ireland, domestic and wild, as well as accounts of typical human occupations. Creatures described include farm animals, snails, frogs, toads, pigeons, owls and parrots, and the human trades include soldier, lawyer and divine. The text provides interesting details about the state of ordinary life in Ireland in the 1640s, and the poem ends with an account of death. The 'Complaint' is printed below.

from: A Looking-Glasse of the World, or, the Plundered Man in Ireland:

His Voyage, his Observation of the Beasts of the Field, of the Fishes of the Sea, of the Fowles of the Aire, of the Severall Professions of Men &c.

Who can that hears or sees but bear a part
To help to bewaile our grievous smart?
Being lately blessed with perfect health,
And also endued with store of wealth,
Nothing afraid our happie state
Should change by any untimely fate:
Our people from the fields come runne,
To bring us news we were undone.
The countrey up against us rises,
Making our goods theire lawfull prize.   10
Often we trotted from Market to Faire,
And for good beast no money we spare,
To adde to our flood,[1] our herd, our flock,
That now we were come into a brave stock;[2]
Each year great droves[3] we could well affoard,
Of fatted good Beeves to send a ship-board.
First went[4] our fat, and after our leane,
Next at our Selves they draw their Skeene;[5]

1. flood (probably) = flote, a herd of cattle.
2. i.e. we had built up a fine herd of livestock.
3. Herds of cattle driven to the port for export by the drover.
4. i.e. the first victims of the rebels were our fat cattle . . . The line carries echoes of Jacob's dream of the fat and lean cattle in Genesis 41.
5. Ir. *scian*, dagger, long knife.

Our Market being spoiled thus on the Land,
And troubles increase as thick as the sand,   20
Some[6] catcheth the pickax for the hard ground,
Some shovle and spade to make the trench round;
Some constrained to carry the barrow,
While others the house top watch with the sparrow.
To tell all our Grief I mean not here,
Fearing lest some should let fall a teare;
Yet to think upon our settled place,
Whence we were thrust with foul disgrace,
This makes our heart with sorrow spring,
That have heard their mocks and libels sing;   30
But give such leave in height of their pride
Unto their own ruine fast to ride.
And all that doth against Gods Truth stand,
May fall as ship wrackt on the sand.
God end these troubles, and send peace,
That our estates and friends may increase;
Happily to live, comfortably to die,
On the wings of Faith to God to flie.

6. i.e. some of the English settlers.

PAYNE FISHER
(1616–**1645**–1693)

Payne Fisher was born in Dorset and educated at both Oxford and Cambridge. Though he enlisted in the army raised by Charles I to fight against the Scots, Fisher changed sides and abandoned the royalists after the king's forces were defeated at Marston Moor in July 1644. When he came to Ireland in July 1645, it was as commanding officer of a small force of troops apparently attached to the Scottish covenanter army led by General Robert Monro. After his adventures in Ireland, Fisher settled in London where he became a successful poet and was appointed poet laureate to Cromwell. His large output includes much verse in Latin and many panegyric poems. At the Restoration, Fisher changed sides again and he is said to have ended his days in poverty.

The three light-hearted verse letters which follow were written when Fisher was a lively young officer serving in Ireland. They were addressed to various military friends and provide unusual details of the daily life of the forces campaigning in Ireland in the 1640s; the first poem gives a vivid description of the effects which a rough, overnight voyage on Lough Neagh had on a troop of seasoned soldiers, the second details ordinary military life in the north of Ireland, and the third suggests the horrors of an Irish siege.

On a dangerous Voyage twixt Mazarine and Montjoy[1]

To my hono[re]d Freind Ma[jor] G. L.[2]

Wee had now weighed up our Anchors and hoist sayles,
Whiles Heavens serener breath in whisp'ring gales
Sighed forth our Farwell and, loath to dismisse
Such Freinds, did court us with a parting Kisse.

But oh! this Truce turn'd Tragicall, and Heat
Which we presum'd a Fortune, proved our Fate.
For now the windes gan mutine,[3] and grow wild
Oth' sudden, which before seem'd reconciled.
The wrinckled Ocean gan to loure[4] and shewe
Hir[5] supercilious anger in hir browe.   10
The Billowes playd at Bandy,[6] and toss't our Barke
Above the clouds, which mounted like a Larke.
The Surges dasht the Heavens as thoe they ment
To wash the face o'th' cloudy Firmament,

1. Two small harbours on the shores of Lough Neagh, the largest lake in Ireland.
2. unidentified.
3. mutiny.
4. lour, look dark and threatening (normally only used of gathering storm clouds).
5. her.
6. Bandy was a way of playing tennis which is no longer known or practised.

251

And make't more cleare; and truely it made us stare
To see the Water mingle with the Aire.

Old Fry that carried a Tempest in his looks,[7] now grew
Madd, and more blustring than those Windes that blew.
You'd think the Boatmen wilde to heare 'um hoope;
This haules out Larboard, t'other flancks the Poope:[8]   20
That, ha[u]les the Bowling[9] which was scarce made fast
Before a counter-gust ore'whelmd both Mast
And Maine-Yard both;[10] not leaveing us scarce sheet[11]
Enoughe to wipe those teares wee shed to see'it.
Both Card and Compasse faild.[12] The Pilot now
Could doe noe more than hee that holds the ploughe.
The Master was in his dumpes: the Seamen stood
Like senselesse stones, or statues made of wood.
Our Rudder too (the Bridle of our Shipp)
Quite broak in twaine lay tumbled in the Deepe.   30
Soe that the Vessell did at Randon[13] run
Threatning hir owne and our destruction.

Thus Fate and Feare beseiged us round about,
That Hope could not get in nor danger out.
Wee cry'ed for succors and lookt every way,
But still the more wee lookt, the lesse wee sawe.
Oft we Implored the windes: but they such noise
And murmuring made, they would not heare our voice.
Oft wee Invokd the Nimphes,[14] but they, poore Elves,
In this sad Pickle could scarce healp them selves.   40
Often wee takt[15] about but found how Crosse
The Current, and how vaine our labour was.

7. MS. reads 'loaks'. Old Fry must be someone known to the poet and the recipient of the poem.
8. Larboard was the name given to the left side of a ship, the side opposite from starboard – now known as 'port'. When the stern of a ship is higher than the rest of her because there are cabins there, that area is known as the poop. The poet implies that the crew did not know what they are doing, one placing the ship so that its larboard side was broadside to the gale, another turning the ship so that the wind was at her stern.
9. = bowline, a rope designed to keep the sail steady.
10. The main yard is the spar, attached to the main mast, which supports the main sail.
11. sail.
12. A card was a circular piece of stiff board on which were marked the 32 points of the compass.
13. = random.
14. The goddesses of the ocean or (in this case) the lough.
15. tacked.

Payne Fisher

Wee fathomed[16] oft but saw no ground was neere,
Noe ground[17] wee saw, alas, but of dispayre.

And now within us did a storme arise
More feirce; whiles from the floudgate of our eyes
The fluent teares fell downe, like showers of Raine,
Striveing to mix their Water with the Maine.[18]
Our Teares did swell the Tide! Our Sighes each sayle,
Our cryes might cleave the clouds, yet could not quell   50
The roaring Sea which, car[e]lesse of our moane,
Drowned all cryes and clamors in hir owne.

At length, nights sable Curtaines being undrawne,
The Infant-day appeared in hir first dawne.
The clouds with it began to looke more cleare,
The Sea more calme. Wee now arose to cheere
Our fainting spirits, and to each other speake
A generall joy. Some crept from of[f] the deck,
Some from the Plancks; and all like wormes at last
Crawld from their Crooked Holes, the Storme being past.   60
The Weather-beate[n] Souldiers who the night did supp
Were all growne Mawe-sick,[19] and did cast it up.
Those Bannick-eating[20] Blew-capps[21] too that deale
In noe other Dialect, then Haver-Meale[22]
Did now disgorge their geere[23] up: with which motion
And workeing of the Waves lookt like a Potion.[24]
One spawld,[25] another purged[26] and being inclined
To a loose disease was troubled with the wind.

And truely the wind did trouble most, and there
Was scarce one 'mong us all, but had his share.   70

16. took soundings of the depth of the water with a fathom-line.
17. reason, basis (echo, with a double meaning from the previous line).
18. the sea – here the water of the lough.
19. sick in the stomach.
20. Bannock was a cake made of oatmeal or barley mixed with water and cooked on a griddle.
21. The Scots traditionally wore blue caps or bonnets.
22. haver-meal= oatmeal; dialect (here) = local food; oatmeal is the typical, traditional food of the Scots.
23. (here) = the contents of their stomachs.
24. A dose of liquid medicine.
25. To spall = to sprawl, stagger or stumble.
26. emptied his bowels.

Some, voyd of sense, grew giddy; these forgott
Themselves, and took the Bark for Charon's Boat.[27]
Another was soe smear'd with pitch, you might
Had you not knowne him, sweare hee had beene a sprite.[28]
Some sprawling on the Decks were trodden on,
And soe dissfigurd that they scarce were knowne.
Some broak their shancks, some noses, and but few
But either had his head broak or his browe.
In fine, all finely handled were, and such
As seemd to have the least harme, had too much.   80

Thus Sir, you see how all night long wee weare
Turmoild, and tosst betweene hope and dispayre:
Till pittying Neptune[29] with his Trident did
Calme and controule those blustr'ing winds, which chid,[30]
Retired back to their cavernes, and noe more
Did dare molest us, till wee came a shoare.

Newes from Lough-Bagge[1]

alias the Church-Iland, upon the first discovery and fortifying of it

To my Honord Freind Serjant Major ffalk. Fll:[2]

Sr, I have read your lines: whose cheife
Heads[3] thus I answer by a Breife.[4]
Last week from Toome[5] wee did put of[f]
And, hois[t]ing sayles, ranged round the Lough
Æneas-like there, up and downe
Seeking some Plantation.[6]

---

27. i.e. the boat which conveyed souls of the departed to Hades, in classical mythology.
28. spirit.
29. God of the seas.
30. once they had been reprimanded . . .

---

1. Lough Beg, near the town of Bellaghy. The lough straddles the border between Counties Londonderry and Antrim.
2. unidentified.
3. points.
4. 1) a letter; 2) a short one.
5. Toome or Toomebridge is a town on the river Bann, between Lough Neagh and Lough Beg.
6. i.e. some place to set up camp. Æneas was often cited as the archetypal wanderer.

At last about[7] Bellahy a mile
Or more, we spyed a little Ile:
More by chance, sure, twas than by
Our Cunning in Cosmography.[8]   10

This little Ile, well veiwd and scand,
To us appear'd some new-found-land
And glad wee were, since twas our happ[9]
To finde what was not in the Mappe.
Arriveing heere, wee could not lesse
Than think wee weare in a Wildernesse;
Soe dismall 'twas, wee durst engage
Our lives 'thad beene some Hermitage,
And much it did perplexe our witts
To think wee should turne Anchorits.   20

In this sad Desart all alone
Stands an old Church quite overgrowne
With age and Ivie, of little use,
Unlesse it were for some Recluse.

To this sad Church my men I led,
And lodged the liveing mong the Dead;
Those that dwelt heere in this place, thus
Demolisht, sure kept open house.
The Roofe soe rent was and had beene
Soe hospitious[10] to all Comers-Inn   30
That Crowes and Screech-Owles every where
Dwelt and had Free Quarter[11] heere.
But since wee came, wee had none of this;
Wee have alterd quite th'whole Ædifice,
And whatsoever was enorme[12]
Before, wee have now made uniforme.
Those Birds and Crowes wee have disposesst
And given them their Quietus est.[13]

---

7. i.e. near Bellaghy, about a mile or so from it.
8. i.e. our skill in map-reading.
9. good fortune.
10. hospitable.
11. lodging.
12. abnormal.
13. The Latin means, literally, 'it is at rest'. The word 'quietus' meant a discharge from a duty or from life, so the line implies that the soldiers killed the birds – they gave them their discharge from life.

The rainy Roofe wee have dawbt up quite
'Tis now more lasting, thoe lesse light.   40
The whole Church wee have overspread
With shingle-boards in stead of lead;
Nor was it truely fitt or fayre
Wee should stand covered and it stand Bare.[14]

Thus like good Tenants wee have cured most
Of these Decayes at our owne cost,
And thoe wee noe Church wardens are,
Wee have put the kirke[15] in good Repayre.

Without[16] wee keepe a Gaurd; within,
The Chancells made our Magazine[17]   50
Soe that our Church thus armd may vaunt[18]
Shees truely now made Militant.[19]
With workes[20] wee have invirond round
And turnd our Churchyard to a Pound.[21]
Forts gaurd us on all sides soe that,
Thoe wee donte supererrogat[22]
Or stand prescisely on Popish quirks,
Yet heere wee are saved by our Works.[23]

Our little Navie in the Bay
At Anchor rides, ranged in Array.   60
Half-Moones and Brestworks[24] doe insconce
Our minor Skiffes, made for the Nonce,[25]

14. covered = with one's hat on; (here) bare = without a hat. i.e. that we should have our hats on (when it is normal to remove one's hat in a church) and it should be without a hat.
15. church (Scots). Fisher's men were from Scotland, and his poems contain several Scots words.
16. Outside.
17. store for guns and ammunition.
18. boast.
19. The phrase 'The Church Militant' means the church on earth at war with the powers of evil.
20. earthworks, small fortifications.
21. enclosure.
22. To supererogate is to do more than is required.
23. A joke: one of the points of dispute between catholics and protestants was whether salvation depended on faith or on good works. The poet plays on double meanings: 1) we are saved from damnation by our (good) works; and 2) we are saved from attack by our fortifications (see l. 53).
24. types of fortification; insconce = ensconce = to shelter behind a fortification.
25. for this particular purpose.

And thoe our Fleet have noe stone-wharfe
Yet 'tis secured by a Counterscarfe.[26]
As for the Rebells, they keepe of[f]
And seldome come within the Loughe.
Yet now and then wee at distance see
A Kearne stalking Cap-a-pe.[27]
About Bellahy lurke a Crew
Of Cannibals that lie Perdue.[28]   70
These seldome range[29] but closely keepe
Themselves like Woolves that watch for sheepe.
Wee see them likely every morning
And haveing seene them, give them warning.
Now, and then, wee send them such
Toakens[30] as they dare not touch
Wrapt in Fire, and smoak enough
To purge them worse than Sneezing-Stuffe.

Last night wee tooke upon the Loughe
A Callio[31] in a chicken-troughe   80
Which in hir Tree[32] did sliely steale
Just like a Witch in a Wall-nutshell.[33]
I've seene as large [a] Coffin sould
For a Child of six yeares old,
As was Hir Cott,[34] which to our Sayle[35]
Shewd like a Whiteing to a Whale.

Noe other Newes hath happned since
My commeing heere of Consequence;
In haste thus much, to let you knowe
Our Safetyes onely[36] and how wee doe.   90
Sr, were I not soe buisy aboard
The Barke, I had sent you exacter word.

26. Another earthwork fortification. The joke is that these terms normally apply to major
engineering works.
27. cap-a-pie = armed from head to toe. The phrase comes from Old French.
28. hidden; cannibals = the uncivilized native Irish.
29. go out into the countryside.
30. presents; i.e. the soldiers fire mortars at the Irish.
31. cailleagh, old woman. Ir. *cailleach*.
32. i.e. her dugout canoe or cot.
33. Witches were said to travel in walnut-shells.
34. her little boat.
35. sailboat.
36. i.e. just to let you know we are safe.

If therfore what I've writt, in matter
Or Forme bee weake, 'twas writt by water:
Now let it serve; when I send ore
John Hodges Boat, Ile tell you more.

Yours sincerely devoted to honor and serve you,
P ff.[37]

A March

To my deare Freind and Capt: F: G:[1]

The word was given, and soone wee had
Orders to draw from our Parrade,[2]
Each Leader marching in the Head
Of his owne men imbodyed.
The Souldiers after them gan dance
To th' tune o' th' Drumme, and both advance
Themselves and armes; who now did feele
Old courage in new jumps[3] of steele,
Nor could these Iron-sides[4] valour lack
Half steele and metall to the Back.   10

The Switzers and Walloones[5] began
The Day and marched in the van;[6]
A pretious Tribe; and those that knew
Them as well as I, would say soe too.
Grim were their lookes; noe outlandish Beares
Was halfe soe gastly or grimm as theirs.
Their face was fearfull[7] and their eyes

---

37. Payne Fisher. Later in life, Fisher signed his poems 'Fitzpaganus Fisher' or 'Paganus Piscator', and he entitled a collection of his verse *Piscatoris Poemata* (1656).

1. unidentified.
2. to move from our parade-ground.
3. coats. A 'jump' was a kind of short coat worn by men in the seventeenth century. In this case, the jumps were made of steel, so the garments were both breast- and back-plates.
4. Puritan warriors. The name 'Ironside' was first applied to Cromwell by Prince Rupert at the Battle of Marston Moor, but was soon transferred to Cromwell's soldiers, and was later used of any soldiers on the parliamentary side.
5. Swiss Guards and French-speaking Belgians.
6. front.
7. sufficient to instil fear.

Like Saucers were o' th' largest size.
Their Basket-hilted[8] Beards orespread
And grew like Ivie about their Head   20
That by their Bristles you might divine
Each Switzer was some Porcupine.

A Gallimaufry Hodge-Podge kind
Of Butterboxes[9] came behind
And followed them, Inferior
Noe whit to those that went before.
These were chippes o' th' selfesame Loggs,
Unhewne, mishapen Hogmagoggs,[10]
Bigg were their Bulkes, yet were their Hose
And Bucram Sloppes[11] more bigg than those.   30
Each one of these same Yonkers[12] bore
A knapsack that might serve a store,[13]
And for their armes, each one at once
More tackling[14] carried than a Sconce,
As thoe each single man had beene
A marching Camp, or Magazine.

Well, let 'um passe; it was our chance
And fortune next to lead the dance.
Wee brought all up, and after their
Example, marched in the Reare.   40
But hold! I had allmost forgatt
To tell you of the Rabble that
Came i' th' Fagg-end[15] of all, and these
Were Suttlers,[16] Bawds, and Laundresses,

8. A basket-hilt was the hilt of a sword which was shaped like a basket; the beards look like large sword hilts.
9. 'Butterbox' was a nickname for a Dutchman. The phrase means a ridiculous, clumsy muddle of Dutchmen.
10. Gog and Magog, gigantic effigies of two enormous, primitive figures, have been on show in London since the time of Henry V.
11. bucram = buckram, coarse linen; slops = loose, baggy trousers; hose = leggings or breeches.
12. younker = young gentleman.
13. i.e. as a place to store supplies.
14. arms, equipment. A sconce was a small, protective earthwork, here applied figuratively. A paraphrase of the lines might be: 'each man carried more equipment than you would need for a protective earthwork, so every man was like a whole camp or an arms supply on the move.'
15. the extreme end.
16. sutlers = those following an army selling supplies to the soldiers.

Following us like Spies aloof
With Bagge and Baggage and such stuffe.
These Gipsie-Jades[17] the whole day in
The Raine had marcht through thick and thin
All dagled[18] ore from Face to Feet
What with Raine and their owne Sweat   50
That hard it was to umpier[19] whether
Which was most Foule, they or the Weather.

Each one of these lookt like the Son
Or sister of an Amazon;[20]
In their Caparisons[21] each shee
Being bravely armed Cap-a-pe.[22]
Some bore th' Half-Pike and some the Spitt,
A weapon of more use than it;
For in what Quarters or what coast
Soe ere wee rome, these Rule the Roast.[23]   60
Others to approve their Metalls[24]
Were crownd with Cauldrons, and huge Kettells
As swarthy as their Face, and 'twas
A question too which was best Brasse.[25]

Thus with our Traine, at length wee come
And lodge our Armie fore the Towne,
Sending Items and Alarums
Unto the Burgers now in Armes
Who of our commeing notice had,
And shott as if they had beene madd,   70
And answering in as highe a straine,
Payd us back in our owne Coine.

Unable longer to endure
Such Peales,[26] wee now gan to Immure

---

17. cunning hussies – not necessarily members of the wandering, Romany race.
18. bedraggled.
19. umpire, judge.
20. The Amazons were a legendary race of fierce female warriors.
21. dress, ornamentation, trappings.
22. from head to toe.
23. 1) roost; 2) roast (for which the spit was essential).
24. i.e. to demonstrate how brave they were (metal *cf.* mettle)
25. most impudent.
26. discharges of guns.

Our selves with Workes, and soone wee layd
The Pike aside to use the spade.
Each Souldier thus assigned his Ground,
The Walls were soone invirond round,
The line being finisht in a Trice
Before you could scarce say whats this.   80

The Towne, againe awaket with Feare
And vext to see such Doeings heere,
Strait in massy Peeces[27] sent
Toakens of their Discontent,
Which greater Gunns Repoarting louder
Did their Errands with a Pouder.[28]
Their Musqueteers gave fire, as thoe
They would kill thousands with a Blowe.
Their Bullets did like Hailestones flie
Among us, and soe thick did lie   90
That our Pioneers[29] instead
Of golden mines digd mines of lead.
Thus still they shot, still wee defyed
Them for Hottshotts,[30] being fortifyed
And gaurding with strong workes about
Both safety in, and danger out.

Day and night both Horse and Foot
In their Armes stood stiffely too 't;
Each man did heere his station know
And where to finde his Freind from 's Foe.   100
Some walk the Round, some lie Perdue,[31]
All know their Compasse and their Cue.
Some sleepe whiles others, halfe afeard
Of Foes without, stand on their Gaurd.
Some i' th' morning soone were shott
And 'ere they were dresst, went to the Pott.
Others, 'ere they had time to have sed
Their Prayers, were knockt i' th' Head.

---

27. massy = heavy; peeces = pieces = large artillery; i.e. the large guns from inside the town
    fired mortars at the besiegers.
28. gunpowder.
29. the soldiers who constructed earthworks, fortifications and latrines. (A 'gold-digger'
    was a slang term for one who emptied latrines; see l. 92).
30. = potshots, i.e. shots taken at anyone one sees.
31. hidden.

Few there were but had some harme,
This lost a legge, that lost an arme,   110
This misst an hand, another by
A worse disaster, losst an Eye.
Most had their Markes, and those alone
Came bravest of[f] that nere went on.[32]

Postscript

Thus much from th' Camp, and one that scarce
Dares owne Minerva now for Mars.[33]
I have left the muses now since then
I changed the practise[34] of my Pen;
My Sword's i' th' Place, Sir, and you know it:
I'me a better Pikeman than a Poet.   120

---

[32]. i.e. those who never went into battle fared best.
[33]. In classical mythology, Minerva was goddess of the liberal arts, while Mars was god of war. To own (here) means to take as one's own property.
[34]. use.

ANONYMOUS
(1646)

Inscription on a monument in the church at Gowran, County Kilkenny

Here lieth the bodies of Mr. James Keally, sometime of the towne of Gawran, Gentleman, who died Ano Dni 16[ ] and of Mrs. Ellen Nashe his first wife who died the 30 day of the moneth of July Ano Dmi 1640 and of Mrs Mary White his second wife who died the [ ] day of the moneth of [ ] Ano Dmi 16[ ]. He erected this monument for himselfe, his wifves and children in the moneth of December Ano Dmi 1646.

Both wifves at once alive he could not have:
Both to injoy at once he made this grave.

JOHN BOOKER
(1603–**1646**–1667)

John Booker, one of the most successful London astrologers of the mid-seventeenth century, published almanacs every year from 1631 until the 1660s. One of the best known was his *Bloody Irish Almanack* of 1646 which prophesied a different future for Ireland and the Irish from that they had been promised in an almanac recently printed in Waterford. On the page facing the lively frontispiece appeared this verse 'The Explanation of the Frontispeece'.

The Explanation of the Frontispeece
of
A BLOODY IRISH ALMANACK, or, Rebellious and Bloody
IRELAND, Discovered in some Notes Extracted out of an
ALMANACK, Printed at *Waterford* in IRELAND for this Yeare 1646.
Whereunto are annexed some Astrologicall Observations upon a
Conjunction of the two *Malignant* Planets SATURNE and MARS in the
midle of the Signe TAURUS the *Horroscope* of IRELAND, Upon
Friday the 12 of *June* this Yeare 1646, with memorable *Prædictions* and
Occurences therein.
By JOHN BOOKER.

Marke and behold, yee bloudy *Irish* Nation,
This Heavenly Figure,[1] where my contemplation
Hath beene implyoyed. Your horrid deedes, mee thought,
Would into question in short time be brought.
Bloud cries for Bloud: mee thinks I feare each houre
God will his vengeance on that Island powre.
See Meger,[2] Palefac'd, *Saturne*, Furious *Mars*,
In *Taurus*, *Ireland*'s Signe, most dismall Starres
By God appointed, for to doe his will.
Fire, Famine, Sword, the Plague: of bloud their fill   10
Shall be their portion: *Phalaris* did frame
A brazen Bull, But when the burning flame
Had heate the Engine, He himselfe first felt
The cruell torments, which he would have dealt
To others.[3] *Irelands* case is farre more worse:
The children yet unborne that folke will curse.

1. i.e. the engraved frontispiece to the book.
2. meagre.
3. Phalaris, a notorious tyrant of the ancient world, used to roast his enemies alive in a hollow brazen bull. His own subjects rebelled against him and roasted him in his own brazen bull.

Through *Spain* and *France*, The *Pope*, that man of sin,
With his adherents, you to ayde begin,
And bring you succour; Vengeance cries aloud,
Tis heap'd as raine into a fearefull cloud;   20
Unlesse that God restraine Heavens menaceing,
This sad position will your ruine bring.

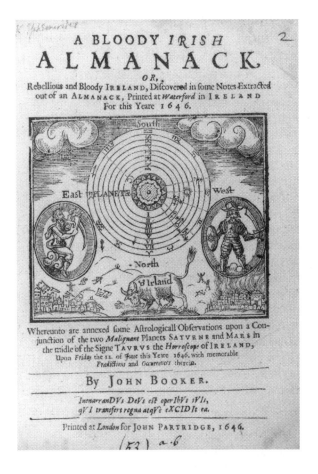

JOHN WATSON
(*fl*.**1646**)

The Ormond manuscript contains a number of simple praise poems addressed to Ormond by writers whose names are otherwise unremembered. This ingenious (and ingenuous) piece was probably sent to Ormond in 1646. The poet takes some liberties with letter equivalents in his anagram.

To the excellent and most noble Lord, the Lord Marquis of Ormond, James Butler

A double ⎰ Maj best rule / for / Bj me al's true ⎱ Anagram

My lord, I found a pretious Cabinet,[1]
whose gallant matter[2] was most richlie set
with Nature's beautie: my insatiate Eie
moved my greedy minde farther to trie
what sacred treasure this Caske might Containe.
The firme Lock did our Common Art disdaine.
At last, I got a Cabalisticke keie,
which, 'mongst the curious springs, did find the waie.
I checkt my rash desire, and in my griefe,
compar'd my selfe to the Cœlestial theife,[3]   10
for, there, I saw sparkes of that heavenlie fire,
which man doth with immortal heat inspire.
Aptitude and Election to Command,
all loialtie to soveraigne power, and,
an intimation of reducing those
to true subjection who, from freinds, fell foes;
so that he *best maie rule bie whom al's true*.
I blame my bold hands, and, with honor due,
enshrine againe the auspicious præsage:[4]
musing, what needfull, what impetuous age   20

---

1. an ornamental casket with (in this case) locked drawers.
2. Here 'matter' seems to mean surface.
3. In classical mythology, Prometheus stole fire from heaven and brought it down to earth.
4. presage, prediction.

should thus high hope produce; your glorious name,
Most noble Lord, I spide stamp'te on the frame.[5]
    Trembling I came, and in a lowlie greet,[6]
    Prostrate it, and my selfe, before your feet.
          John Watson

5. of the cabinet.
6. greeting.

SIR EDMUND BUTLER
(*fl*.**1648**)

This poem probably dates from 1648 when Charles I was in prison and Irish catholics (temporarily at peace) could still imagine themselves strong enough to send him assistance. There were at least two men named Sir Edmund Butler active in Ireland at this time who might have sent the poem to Ormond: one was the eldest son of Viscount Mountgarret,[1] and the other the son of a catholic landowner from Clogrennah, County Carlow and a distant relative of Ormond. The second Sir Edmund Butler had been trained as a lawyer in London (see Jane Ohlmeyer, 'Irish Recusant Lawyers during the Reign of Charles I' in *Kingdoms in Crisis: Ireland in the 1640s*, ed. Micheál Ó Siochrú (Dublin, 2001), pp. 63–89, p. 73). He became governor of Wexford.

Arise, distracted land

Arise, distracted land, rowse thee and bring
Timely assistance to thy captive kinge.
Ormond att length prevayled, tyme onely can
Reveale the Judgmnt of the Prudent man.
Hadst not thou left us first and then againe
Found safety in a shallop through the Mayne,[2]
Ireland had sunke; the people had not fedd,
Wanting an apt hand to dispense the bread.
Through thee (the darling of the Nation) flye
Those beamelings from imprisoned Majesttye   10
Which doe inlighten [us]; these doe increase
His bountye, and thy meritte, in our Peace.
Expend our substance, sacrifice our Bloode;
By such a comment 'twil be understoode.

The Irish Nation while their Kings deprest,
Disclaymes[3] in Interest and disdains to rest.

---

1. This Edmund Butler succeeded his father as fourth Viscount Mountgarret in 1642; he died in 1679.
2. A shallop was a large, heavy sea-going boat, a sloop. Ormond had been relieved of the post of lord lieutenant and had left Ireland in 1647. While returning to Ireland from France in the summer of the next year, he was shipwrecked near Le Havre and, presumably, completed his journey in a shallop. The poet asserts that Ireland was saved because Ormond had left and returned.
3. = declaims, i.e. cries out its concern.

ANONYMOUS
(1648)

Sir John Clotworthy, later first Lord Massareene (*d*.1665), a strong protestant, was a substantial landowner in County Antrim. He played an important part in the English parliament in the 1640s, forcefully representing the interests of protestant Ireland. He was impeached in 1647, accused, among other things, of embezzling supplies granted to Ireland by parliament. The complicated manoeuvrings of English politics at the time brought Clotworthy back into parliament between June and December 1648, during which period the following poem was addressed to him. The anonymous author clearly hoped that Clotworthy would once again assist protestant Ireland, and that the descriptions of the devastation visible throughout the island would help his case. However, though the poem applies to Ireland and is written with style and energy, the text is disappointingly short on detail and the poem reads more like a lobbying document than an eye-witness account.

from: *Hyberniæ Lachrymæ* [1]
or, a sad contemplation on the bleeding condition of Ireland
To the Honourable and excellently well accomplish [*sic*] Sir *John Clotworthy*
Knight, and Collonel.

> . . . Up sad *Melpomone*,[2] up and condole
> The Ruines of a Realme; attire thy soule
> In sorrowes dresse: O let thy fountaines rise
> And overflow the floodgates of thine eyes:
> Fill up thy sanguine[3] Cisternes to the brim,
> Spread forth thy expanded armes, and strive to swim
> In thine owne teares, that so thou may'st make knowne
> The griefe of others fully as thine owne.
> Oh! heere's a Theame indeed, if Mortals could
> Not now lament, the Rocks and Mountaines would: 10
> The melting Heavens whose influences steepe
> The stubborne stone,[4] would teach us how to weepe;
> The Blood-imbrued[5] Earth doth blush to see
> Such horrid Massakers, and shall not we?
> Sure should we not, we had lesse sense then those
> Hard hearts who were first Authors of these woes.

1. Ireland's tears.
2. the classical muse of tragedy.
3. blood-red.
4. 'Influence' is here used in its original meaning, i.e. the supposed flowing from the stars of an ethereal fluid which affected – and was affected by – human behaviour. steepe = saturate, soak.
5. impregnated.

Disastrous State! How beautifull, how faire
Thy Buildings, and how foule thy Vices were!
How were thy glorious blossomes turn'd to dust,
And blasted with the lightning of thy lust!   20
Brim'd with excesse, how did thy cups o'reflow
Faster than all thy trickling teares doe now!
How did thy crimes eclipse thee (and crying loud
For vengeance) masque thy forehead in a cloud!
Thy greatnesse but encreas'd thy fall, and that
Which was thy glory, usher'd on thy fate;
Thy wealth and plenty have but centuplyd[6]
Thy greater plagues, and made the wound more wide,
And what should most revive thee, and restore
Thine health, hath serv'd t'exulcerate[7] the sore.   30
Thy stately Forrests, which did once invite
The eye t'a feast of wonder and delight,
Prov'd but thy Funerall Faggots to consume
Thy glory, and t'exaggerate thy doome,
Whilst all thy blazing Territories have
But Torches been, to light thee to thy Grave.

And shall she perish, and we languish thus?
And is there none t'helpe her, or succour us?
Shall she pine thus unpiti'd? shall her griefe
Thus dayly finde a voyce, but no reliefe?   40
O happy *England*! which wilt scarce confesse,
(Lull'd within a lethargy) this happinesse;
Thy troubles were but triviall, and thy feares
But meerely Fantasies compar'd with hers.
'Tis she, 'tis she hath sufferd, and drunk up
Those dreggs whereof thou hast only kis'd the cup:
Those puny plagues which partially have met
In thee, have been so ample, so compleat,
And numerous in her, that nothing more
Could once be heap'd or added to the score.   50
But ah! complaints are shaddowes, and too briefe
T'expresse or show the substance of thy griefe:
And such whose fancy strives to utter it,
Shew not so much their sorrow as their wit:

6. multiplied by a hundred.
7. to aggravate.

Thou that wert once great Britaines chiefest glory,
Art now become a gazing stock, a story
Exil'd from humane helps and heavenly smiles,
O'rewhelmed and sepulchred in thine owne spoyles.
How doth black fate inviron[8] thee about,
That hope cannot get in nor horrour out?   60
Famine, thou sister of the sword and son
Of Death, how many worlds hast thou undone?
How dost thou tyrannize, and keep thy Leets[9]
And constant stations in her open streets?
Oh! how the palefac'd sucklings roare for food,
And from their milklesse mothers breast draw blood.
They cryd for bread that had scarce breath to cry,
And wanting meanes to live, found meanes to dye.
The Father gasps his last, and to his Heire
Bequeathes his pined[10] corps, the Nurses teare[11]   70
And quarter out their Infants, whilst they feast
Upon the one halfe, and preserve the rest:[12]
O cruel Famine! which compells the Mother
To kill one starved child to feed another.

    Thus is thy glory vanisht in a trice,
And all thy pomp lies buri'd in Abysse:
Thy joys are turned to sorrows, backt with teares,
Whilst thou, poore thou, li'st pickled up in teares:
Yet be thou ne're dismayd with boundlesse sorrow
These Nights of griefe may find a joyfull Morrow.   80
Cleare then thy clouded countenance, and calme
Thy discomposed looks; Heaven, Heaven hath Balme
As well as thunder-bolts, and be thou sure
Thou canst not bleed so fast as he[13] can cure.
'Tis he, 'tis he can heale thee, and crush those
That have insulted in[14] thine overthrowes.

---

8. environ, encircle.
9. = court leets, local courts held before a landlord or his steward.
10. starved.
11. = tear apart.
12. This is one of the last appearances of the old myth that cannibalism was practised in Ireland – a myth which had been circulating since classical times.
13. i.e. (presumably) God.
14. = exulted in (?).

And thou proud Prelate[15] (whose ambitiousnesse
A triple Diadem can scarce depresse;
Prostrate at whose proud footsteps, Legions lye,
And fall as low as Hell to keep thee high)   90
Shalt one day be subjected too, with all
Those Complices tryumphant in thy fall.[16]
Sad Realme! A day there is when Heavens decree
Shall call them to account as well as thee;
And the time will come (if Souldiers may divine)
To worke their ruine that have thus wrought thine.

---

15. A reference to Giovanni Battista Rinuccini (*c.* 1592–1653), papal nuncio to the confederate catholics of Ireland 1645–9, famous for his refusal to accept the peace concluded between Ormond and the confederates in 1646. To his enemies, Rinuccini symbolised the dangers of unlimited power in ecclesiastical matters, particularly when such power could influence political or military matters. The triple diadem was the crown worn by the Pope.
16. The poet looks forward to the day when bishops and their accomplices will be defeated and episcopacy will no longer exist in Ireland.

WILLIAM SMITH
(*fl.*1649–55)

William Smith or Smyth, a staunch catholic, probably came to Ireland from the south-west of England in about 1630. He was attached to the Butler family and acted for them in many capacities, as secretary, printer and attorney. He was also the author of twenty-two lines of commendatory verse printed with Henry Burkhead's tragi-comedy, *The Tragedy of Cola's Furie*, printed in Kilkenny in 1646.[1] William Carrigan states that Smith was 'brought over to this country by James, afterwards first Duke of Ormond, whom he served in the capacity of secretary. He became tenant of Damma, part of the freehold estate of the house of Ormond, and here his family resided for some generations . . .'[2] Towards the end of his life Smith wrote – it is probably acceptable to assume that he wrote it himself – the verse which appears on his gravestone in the church of St Mickle at Damagh, and which is printed here as the second of his poems.

The first poem, which comes from the Ormond collection at Yale University, seems to date from after the execution of Charles I in 1649. It is rallying cry urging the royalist catholics of Ireland to reclaim their churches and defend their faith. Now that the English Roundheads had disposed of the king, Ireland would clearly have to defend herself against them. But, as Smith noted, Ireland had powerful friends in Europe. For William Smith, as for many of his countrymen, the fight in which he was engaged was essentially one about religion.

To Ireland

Hayle sacred Island! whom noe Threat nor Art
Could tempt to falter in the Passive part:
Now be as Active, let no Powr nor frown
Yoke thy enfranchisd thoughts, or pull them down.
Have not thy Altars, where the spottless price
Of Man's Redemption, the true Sacrifice
Was Dayly offerd, layen too long recluse,
Or, being employed, servd to a different use?
Thy sumptuos pyles, built for Relligious vowes
Are the secure retreat of dawes[3] and Doves;   10
The Owls, the batts, the direfull birds of night
Have beene preserved before the Sonnes of light.

---

1. See Patricia Coughlan, '"The Modell of its Sad Afflications": Henry Burkhead's *Tragedy of Cola's Furie*', in Micheál Ó Siochrú (ed.), *Kingdoms in Crisis: Ireland in the 1640s* (Dublin, 2001), pp. 192–211, 194.
2. William Carrigan, *The History and Antiquities of the Diocese of Ossory*, 5 vols. (Dublin, 1905), III, 444.
3. jackdaws.

Amongst all Realmes, it was thy speciall fate
To have thy sons made illigitimate:[4]
On whom nor place nor profitt did descend
Whom neither Judge nor Justice did befriend;
But walloing in those ill gott spoiles of thyne,
Others layd up,[5] whiles thou didst digg the myne.

This thou has seene and sufferd: yet the sense
Of all those Evills, could find a Patience   20
Untill some Head borne Round in Gyddynesse
Of private Spirits durst soe farre transgresse
As to dismantle Englands crowne, and wring
The sapp of Honor from soe good a King.[6]
Then did the Object of thy sense direct
Thy stupid mind: thou feltst the disrespect
Done unto God by this: thence came the Byrth
Of thy fayre thoughts: For Kings are Gods on earth.

On, sprightly hearts, you whom the French, the Dutch,
The Pole, the Spaniard, court and love so much.   30
Let not these blush in your behalfe: mayntayne
That spring of honour, which no warre could drayne.
He's throughly armd, who to the field can bring
Th'interests of his Fayth, countrie, and king.

Inscription on monument in St Mickle's Church, Damagh, County Kilkenny

D. O. M.[1]

Heere lyeth the Body of William Smyth of Damag[h] Esq., some time
Secretarie to James Earle of Ormond and Ossorie

Long after all was made, I made, was marr'd
By error of my parents ere I err'd.
For to the world I came (through theyre ofence)
A sinnfull creature in myn innocence.[2]

---

4. i.e. unable to inherit – probably a reference to the imposition of English law.
5. i.e. others lined their own pockets while you kept on working.
6. i.e. Charles I.

---

1. *Deo optimo maximo* (Late Latin): To God, the best and the greatest.
2. The first four lines refer to the doctrine of original sin – that all humans are sinners at birth because of the original sin of Eve and Adam.

Through al my life, sinnes burthens on me lay;
Yet the dere Lamb of God took them awaye.
Reader, each frend (at least), remember mee
And doe as I (in life) thus did for thee.

Lord helpe all those which have helpen mee
Or prayed for mee, or showed to mee anye deed of pittye.   10

In Domino obdormivit 24 die mensis Apri: Anno Salutis 1655.[3]

---

3. He fell asleep in the Lord on the 24th day in the month of April in the year of salvation
1655.

ANONYMOUS
(1649)

By the middle of 1649, though Cromwell and his armies had decisively defeated royalist forces throughout England, Ormond and the forces loyal to the young King Charles II – as Ormond had proclaimed Charles Stuart to be after the execution of his father – were still powerful in Ireland. (The severe defeat inflicted on Ormond by Michael Jones at Rathmines was not to take place until 2 August.) As Cromwell set out with his army to try to subdue Ireland, the author of the lively, ironic verses which follow hoped – or pretended he hoped – that Ireland might prove for Cromwell, as it had for so many other English generals before him, the land where he would meet an inglorious end.

The Loyall Subjects Jubilee,

or, *Cromwels* Farewell to *England*, being a Poem on his advancing to *Ireland*,
July the 11. 1649.

'Tis high contempt not for to Fast and pray,
And hold as blest Saint *Cromwels* Holy day;
The Devils a Saint, if he deserves to be
One for his Machivillian Treacherie.
Insatiate Monster, that does swallow downe
At once a Kingdome and a glorious crowne,
Whose splendor dazled Mortalls while it stood
On *Charles* his head, but dim'd since dipt in blood.
May every stone that did adorne it round,
As witnesses against thee once be found,   10
And weigh thee down to Hell, thou horrid fel lion,
To have reward for this thy grand Rebellion.
But first thy progresse into Ireland take,
And see what preparations they will make,
(To entertaine thee) for that end a day
Weel set apart, and for thee this we'l pray;
Come yee grim Furies of the *Stigian Lake*,[1]
With hideous cryes, and make the welking[2] shake,
Rouze *Charon*[3] up, winds, Seas, and all implore,
To waft this Rebell to the *Irish* shore,   20

1. The Furies, female spirits of justice and vengeance in classical mythology, were often represented as living in the underworld, where the river Styx wound seven times around the kingdom of the dead. Stygian = of Styx.
2. the sky, the heavens.
3. The ferryman who, in classical mythology, took the souls of the dead across the Styx into the kingdom of the dead.

Where such a Feast prepar'd for him shall be,
The like at *Grocers-Hall* he ne're did see:[4]
Ormond chief Cook will be, to please his pallet,[5]
And send a fiery Bullet for a Sallet,[6]
Which shall such terrour to his Saintship bring,
And make him cry, would he had spar'd our King.
The blood methinks doth startle in his face,
That he no rest can take in any place.
His *Exits* come, *Ireland* the Stage must be
Where he must act his latest[7] Tragedie,   30
Where he his life shall spend in discontent,
And bid farewell to *Englands* Parliament.
May thy horses founder, thy Souldiers weary grow,
Upon their march they can no further goe;
Or if march on, upon the *Irish* sight,[8]
Take to their heeles, and finely give thee flight.
And may this noise of their most eager running,
Still make thee think that *Charles* the II[9] comming
To claime his due with a victorious hand,
And purge all Rebels from his *English* Land.   40
May the day look black, and soon convert to night,
Onely thy ruby Nose to give thee light;[10]
And that thou mayst to shipping safely get,[11]
Hell for thy life-guard shall the Furies set,
Charon thy Ferry-man shall be, and once being ore,
Mayst thou nere come to vex the *English* shore.

---

4. The formal headquarters of the London livery company of the Worshipful Company of
   Grocers, where visiting dignitaries might be entertained at a lavish feast.
5. palate.
6. salad.
7. last.
8. i.e. upon sight of the Irish army.
9. As noted above, Ormond had declared Charles II king of Ireland after the execution of
   Charles I. The poet supposes that, if Charles did land in Ireland and reclaim it, he would
   use it as a base from which to regain England.
10. Cromwell is said to have had a large, red nose.
11. i.e. so that you can safely get to the place where a ship awaits you . . .

GEORGE WITHER
(1588–**1649**–1667)

After his probable visit to Ireland as a young man (see pp. 135–8, poem for 1610), George Wither spent a long and active life in London, becoming author of nearly one hundred separately published poems. He also took part in the Civil Wars, and served as a major in the parliamentary army. The poem which follows – staunchly Puritan in tone, like much of Wither's later verse – commemorates the battle of Rathmines, and is included here as an example of the prevailing view in parliamentary circles in England that the war in Ireland was a holy war, and that any successes were directly attributable to the power of God. After the restoration of Charles II, Wither was stripped of his various offices and, for a while, imprisoned.

from: Carmen Eucharisticon:[1] a private Thank-Oblation, exhibited to the Glory of the Lord of Hosts,

for the timely and wonderfull Deliverance, vouchsafed to this Nation, in the routing of a numerous Army of Irish Rebells before *Dublin*, by the Sword of his valiant Servant, Michael Jones, Lieutenant-Generall for the Parliament of England.

> *Publicke Duties* being done,
> By my self, Ile now alone,
> Consummate a *Private-one*.
>   Therefore, O my Soul! awake,
> And let both, with heart and tongue,
> Such a *Song of Praise* be sung,
> That, thereby, both old and young,
>   Of God's mercies heed may take.
>
> For such *Trophies* (though now waved)
> *Moses*, *Deborah*, and *David*,   10
> When they from their foes were saved,
>   Did, with good appearance, raise;[2]
> And (though other *Thank-Oblations*
> Perish'd, with their Generations)
> God is yet, throughout all Nations,
>   Honor'd by their Songs of Praise.

---

1. A song of thanksgiving – translated as 'Thank-oblation' or solemn offering of thanks.
2. i.e. when the heroes of the Old Testament (Moses, Deborah and David) were saved from their foes, they would give appropriate thanks to God (raise such Trophies), though such things are not done now (waved = waived).

We, to thee, O Lord! have praid,
Thanks returned, sung, and said,
And our common-duty paid,
    As we could perform the same: 20
That, which we have seen, and heard,
Of thy mercifull regard,
Hath been openly declar'd,
To the glory of thy Name.

But, O God! we may as well
Close the *Seas* up in a *shell*,
As inabled be to tell
    Thy *Compassions* large extent;
Or to make full illustration
Of the favours to this *Nation*,[3]   30
In our frequent preservation
 From the furious *Foes* intent.

For, that *single mercy*, Lord,
Which this Day we do record,
Many *mercies* doth afford,
    More than all men can perceive.
That *Deliverance* made way
For another *joyfull-day*,
And that, peradventure, may
    Bring to passe, what we would have.[4]   40

With vain *Moab* did conspire
Ammon, *Amalek*, and *Tyre*,
Threatning, like consuming fire,
    To destroy thy *chosen Flock*;
And, in hope, their will to do,
They have hired *Balaam* too,
With *false Prophets* many moe,[5]
    To advance a *stumbling-block*.[6]

---

3. i.e. the English.
4. Perhaps a reference to the fact that Cromwell and his army had just landed in Ireland.
5. more.
6. Psalm 83 lists the enemies of the children of Israel and includes Moab, Ammon, Amalek and the people of Tyre (verses 6–7). The prophet Balaam was hired by Balak, king of the Moabites, to curse the children of Israel – which he refused to do (Numbers 23. 25.)

Of their vaine presumings proud,
They did Thunder from a cloud,   50
Did begin to roar aloud
    In deluded peoples ears;
And their empty vanities,
Blushlesse brags, and shamelesse lies,
Fill'd the hearts of men unwise,
    With false hopes, and causeless fears,

The fool'd *Welsh*, the faithlesse *Scot*,
And our *English* mis-begot,
Joyning in an *Irish plot*,
    Sought to root us from the *Land*:[7]   60
They with *Sulphur*, *Sword*, and *Flame*,
Round about our *dwellings* came,
And had brought us all to shame,
    Had not God stretch'd forth his hand.

But he thereof notice took;
And, as *Sisera*, he strook,
With his Host, by *Kishon-brook*:
    So, he smote them in their pride:
And, the same successe they had
Which befell to *Benadad*,   70
When the like account he made,
    That the *spoile* he should divide.[8]

For whilst *Ormond* and while *Taaff*
In their Tents did game and quaff,
(At our sad condition laugh)
    And of *Captives* predispos'd;[9]
Then, that *Arm* which they despis'd
Suddenly their *Camp* surpriz'd,
And the snares which they devis'd
    For our feet, their owne inclos'd.   80

---

7. i.e. Ireland.
8. 'Do unto them as unto the Midianites: as to Sisera, as to Jabin, at the brook of Kison'
    Psalm 83. 9; (the prophets of Baal were all slaughtered by the brook Kishon: see I Kings
    18. 40). For the complicated story of Ben-hadad and the king of Israel, see I Kings 20.
9. i.e. Ormond and Taaffe (who were besieging Dublin) thought that the parliamentary
    soldiers would become their captives.

Mich'el[10] and his *Angells* there
Threw their *Dragon-Cavaliere*[11]
With his *Angells*, from our *Sphere*,[12]
 In confusion, to their owne;
Where, unable to repent,
They despairingly lament,
And blaspheme with discontent,
    Him, that hath such *mercy* showne.

For, though (blinded in their sin)
Outwardly they jeer and grin;   90
Hellish horrors lurk within,
    Filling their faint hearts with fears:
Their *chief refuge* is a *lie*,
And, which way soe're they fly,
Guilt pursues them with a cry,
    Which the God of Justice hears.

Their accusing *conscience* feels
Vengeance following them at heels,
And her dreadful Chariet wheels
    Threatning, what to them is due: 100
Yet, infernall indignation
Stirs them up to vindication,
Height'ned by a desperation
    Of those ends, which they pursue.

And that make them take the field
(Trusting in their sword and shield)
When their conscience bid them yeeld:
    But, they soon did back retire,
And to fly away began,
As when the *Philistines* ran,   110
From the sword of Jonathan
    And, but one sleight armed *Squire*.[13]

10. The archangel Michael – and the general Michael Jones.
11. i.e. their horsemen who could destroy dragons (punning also on the word 'cavalier' –
    supporter of the royalist side in the Civil Wars – as opposed to 'roundhead' – a supporter
    of parliament).
12. 1) the heavenly sphere of the archangel; 2) the earthly sphere of 'our' world (camp) and
    'theirs'.
13. The Philistines 'fell before' Jonathan, son of Saul, and the young man who carried his
    armour (I Samuel 14. 13).

Never was there such a day
Seen till then at *Ballacleagh*,[14]
Since the *Liffy*[15] wash'd her Kea,
   And, there, first, the *Sea Nimphs*[16] met:
For, God's arm, did there, and then,
Give us *Limster*[17] back agen,
When it was nigh lost; and, then,
   Hope, was with *despairs* beset.   120

Yet, as if that daies successe
Had too little been, unlesse
He consider'd our distresse,
   In our *London-Derry* friends;
Or, lest els, blind *ignorance*
Might judge that an act of *chance*,
He, our free *deliverance*,
   Into *Ulster*, too, extends,[18]

And, by that redoubled blow,
Gave another overthrow;   130
For *Designements*[19] one or two,
   By that means dissolved be,
Which hath so inraged them,
That they raile, revile, blaspheme,
And their own beleefe condemn,
   For believing what they see.

Oh! what pen, or tongue is there
Fully able to declare,
What, to us, God's *Mercies* were
   Since our *Champion* he hath been?   140
Nay, who can half that recite,
Which for us in open sight,
He hath done since *Nasby-Fight*,[20]
   Where he, first, was plainly seen?

---

14. *Marginal note*: 'Dublin'; surprisingly, Wither uses an anglicization of the Irish name, Baile Átha Cliath.
15. *Marginal note*: 'The River'. kea = quay.
16. *Marginal note*: 'The Sea Water'.
17. Leinster.
18. The siege of a parliamentary force in the city of Derry had been raised on 8 August.
19. crafty schemes.
20. The battle of Naseby (14 June 1645), where the forces of Charles I were decisively defeated by the New Model Army of the parliamentarians.

He hath magnifi'd his *worth*
In most glorious marchings forth,
From the *South*, unto the *North*,
   And, through all our *British-Coasts*;
England, Scotland, Ireland, Wales,
Towns, and *Fields*, and *Hills*, and *Dales*,   150
Sea, and *Land*, him, justly calls,
   The Victorious Lord of Hoasts . . .

ANONYMOUS
(1649)

The poem which follows was, at least in part, intended to provide news for readers in London who could learn, from the list in the middle of the piece, the scale of the defeat suffered by the Irish royalist army at the battle of Rathmines. The format of a verse dialogue between two ordinary soldiers gives the poem an unusual perspective on the events of war, and the language of their 'chat' is forthright and unstilted. The event which the poem commemorates was a turning point in the fortunes of Ormond and the royalist army besieging Dublin; on 2 August 1649, they were surprised by a small force of parliamentary soldiers under Michael Jones, and suffered huge losses.

Ormondes Breakfast,[1]

or A True Relation of the Salley and Skirmish Performed by Collonel *Michael Jones* and his Party, against the Marques of *Ormonde*, and his Forces encamped before *Dublin* the second of *August* 1649

In a Dialogue between a *Chevalier* and a *Roundhead*

To the Reader

> Reader, This is but private Soldiers chat,
> As rough, as is his Amunition Hat:
> Do thou but only looke for Truth & Sence,
> For hee knowes neither wit, nor Eloquence.
> That Break-fast here for sixpence thou hast found[2]
> Which cost James Butler[3] forty thousand pound:
> I hope thou wilt digest it well: if not,
> Alls one to mee, Sith I am payd the shot.[4]

Roundhead:	Stand, what art thou? The word![5] Think not to fly
	Beyond my sharpe revenge? for thou shalt dye 10
	Unlesse thou dost in time for mercy cry.
Chevalier:	O stay thy hand, bold Roundhead; tis thy day
	Bravely to fight, and ours to runne away;
	The man halfe dead before, thy vallor will not slay.[6]

---

1. For the spelling of the name Ormond(e) in the seventeenth century, see the Note on the Texts, p. 33.
2. The purchase price of the pamphlet.
3. i.e. the Marquis of Ormond.
4. the shot = the bill; the line means 'It doesn't matter to me since I have been paid' [for writing the poem].
5. The Roundhead sentry challenges the cavalier to give the pass-word.
6. i.e. you are too honourable to kill a man who is already half-dead.

Roundhead:	Rest thee: for I perceive the feare of death
	Hath made thee runne till thou art out of breath.
	By this time, I beleeve the worke is done;
	The day is ours, and wee the field have wonne.
	Wherefore sit downe, refresh thy tyred sence,
	Then tell mee who thou art, thy name, and whence. 20
Chevalier:	My name is Royallist, of Parents good,
	My fortunes much Inferiour to my blood;
	Yet was I never wretched untill now
	That feare, and not thy force, hath made mee bow:
	Yet he deserveth justly, to be shent[7]
	Which takes a Coward for its President;
	Hell take those Leaders which lead men astray;
	Soe shall that man be damn'd which first this day
	Did turne his backe: and basely runne away.
Roundhead:	O strange! Is this the first fruits of that breath 30
	Which mercy hath soe late repriv'd from death –
	To curse, and yet which is a greater evill,
	To give thy wise Commanders to the Divell?
	'Twere better at this Instant thou shouldst dye
	Than live; unlesse thou live in Charity.
Chevalier:	Call you them wise Commanders? Surely they
	Had soe much wit, wisely to runne away;
	But els, though you are pleas'd to taerm them wise,
	I doe not know where their discretion lyes.
	Base dull security was never yet, 40
	As I conceive, signe of a Souldiers wit.
	They might have thought, if they had bin soe wise,
	That you would make a Salley, and Surprise
	Our carelesse Campe, for they knew long before
	That you had done as much as that, or more.
Roundhead:	You meane at *Dungans-hill*:[8] my selfe was there
	When they[9] were kild, and tane,[10] in their owne snare.
	That Bogge which they did fly to then for aide,
	Them to the fury of our Swords betray'd.
	The wood all shelter unto them deny'd 50
	As though it loath'd their Cowardize to hide.

7. disgraced.
8. The Irish confederate forces had suffered a catastrophic defeat at the hands of the parliamentary forces at Dungan's Hill, County Meath, in August 1647.
9. i.e. the confederate forces.
10. taken.

When Heaven commands, all Creatures must obey;
None can Protect when he commands to slay.
But to the present busines, what dee[11] thinke
Of this dayes worke? Had you good store of Chink[12]
Within your Campe? For surely such an Host
Was not maintained with a little cost,
And every day fed both with boyld and Rost.

Chevalier: The Officers had Cash; our stock was small,
For, Sir, you know tis soe in Armies all,   60
Which made this Phrase: *The weakest goes to th' wall*.
But see the judgment now, in this defeat,
On Officers which did their Souldiers cheat.
Though they have Coseen'd[13] many, when they fall
One Single man doth strip them out of all.[14]

Roundhead: What number was your Army, horse and foot,
That thus you runne and stood no better too't?

Chevalier: Sir, I conceive the number of our Force
Was seaven thousand Foot, three thousand Horse:
Our Vassayles,[15] if you reckon Knave & Whore,   70
Did make the number halfe as many more;
These latter did our Campe more hurt than good
In daily eating up the Souldiers food.
For say all what they will, your Leager Queane[16]
Makes two Shirts fowle, for one which she makes cleane.

Roundhead: Where is your Viceroy now, that man which claimes
Soe many tytles, and soe many names
That Schoolboyes, should he reigne another yeare
Would raile at him, for making Paper deare?[17]
This day hath added something to his store   80
For it hath grac't him with one title more.[18]

Chevalier: I cannot tell which way the *Marques* went,
Or whether you might find him by the sent;[19]

---

11. do you.
12. ready cash.
13. cozened, duped.
14. deprive them of everything.
15. servants, camp-followers.
16. = leaguer quean, a female who follows an army, in this case a washerwoman.
17. i.e. Ormond. The line means that Ormond's many titles would take up so much paper if written out that there would be a shortage of paper – which would therefore sell at a higher price.
18. i.e. that of coward.
19. scent, smell.

> But this I know, it ill became his Grace
> To bring his Masters Army[20] to this Place,
> And then to goe to Cards, with the Lord *Taaffe*[21]
> Before he saw his Squadrons lodged safe;
> Or, while he sporting was at *Venus* game,[22]
> Thus to be routed both with losse and shame.

Roundhead: Indeed his Lordship dealt not wisely there; 90
> But hee'l recruite againe,[23] you need not feare.
> Mean while I pray peruse this following List:
> Tis *Billa vera*,[24] my *Antagonist*.
> Then tell me what you thinke of this days rout –
> Allthough your name's Ingeniously left out.
> Was it not bravely followed, bravely runne?
> Was it not bravely lost, and bravely wonne?

Prisnors taken the second of August 1649

Feild Officers	Sir *George Bingam* Baronet.
Earl of *Fingall*	39 Cap. 52 Lieutenants.
Colonell *Richard Butler*	40 Ensignes. 6 Cornets.
Brother to the Lord of *Ormonde*	8 Quartermasters.
Col. *Christopher Plunket*	8 Troopers. 9 Gentlem.
Michaell Searle Agitant	*Robert Hambleton* Minister.
Generall & Lieut Colonell	
Lieut. Coll.	John Bellew, Lieutenant of the Ordnance.
Aleworth	Cleark of the Store. 10 Servants.
Stanley	6 Gunners. 6 Trumpets. 6 Chyrurgions.[25]
Fortescue	10 belonging to the Artiliry. 69 Serjants.
Taaffe	56 Corporalls. 20 Drums.[26] 59 Fewsees,[27] and Gerrald their Lieutenant.

20. i.e. the army of the recently proclaimed king, Charles II.
21. Theobald Taaffe, Viscount Taaffe and (after 1660) Earl of Carlingford (*d*. 1677), commander of the forces of the catholic confederation 1644–7 and, at this time, Ormond's second-in-command in the royalist forces.
22. i.e. with a woman.
23. reinforce the army with fresh troops.
24. i.e. a true list.
25. surgeons.
26. drummers.
27. fusees, men in charge of the fuses for shells, assistant gunners.

Majors
Roger Garland   2100 Private Suildiers taken,
Oliver Fits Simonds   3500 & odd slaine, amongst
Cummis   which were severall Officers,
Kildare   and men of great Note.
Henry Littell
Charles Norwood   5 Peeces.[28] a Morter Peece and
Fleetwood   a great Peece.

                                         200 Oxen, and all their Armes,
                                         Ammunition, Tents, Waggons,
                                         Bagge and Baggage.

                        Thus God hath caused us to sing *Victoria*,
                        And wee will answer: *Soli Deo Gloria.*[29]
Chevalier: If this be true which here I finde exprest,   100
                        Ile sigh the Preface, and weep out the rest.
                        If there be kill'd and took which you have reckon'd,
                        Alas, what wilt thou doe, poore *Charles* the Second!
                        My heart doth bleed for thee, and thy faire traine
                        Of Englishmen, should this[30] be tooke, and slaine;
                        Those men which never could have lost the day
                        Had not the *Irish* basely runne away;[31]
                        Those hatefull Cowards which did never stand
                        Gainst equall Force either by Sea, or land,
                        For which if Heaven or Hell have not a worse,   110
                        Yet may they not scape my deserved Curse.
                        That when a Drum or Trumpet they shall heare,
                        They may runne frantique, or starke mad for feare,
                        And in that frantique humor, kill each other,
                        The Sonne his Sire,[32] Wife, Sister, Childe, and Mother,
                        And after may the wretched senceles Elfe
                        Draw forth his hated skeyne,[33] and kill himselfe,
                        That soe not one of all the Family
                        May raise the Hubbub or that Heathen cry[34]
                        Whereby their Neighbours, to their help they draw,   120
                        But may the Wolfe intombe them in his Maw.[35]

28. pieces of artillery, guns.
29. Glory to God alone.
30. i.e. those of this list.
31. Irish soldiers were regularly (and unjustly) accused of running away during battles.
32. father.
33. skene, dagger, knife, Ir. *scian*.
34. Probably a reference to keening.
35. stomach.

Roundhead:	If thou art as thou sayest a *Chevalier*
	Thou dost quite derogate from *Common Prayer*.[36]
	Of all the *Sects*, this is the strangest way
	That ere I heard or[37] man or woman pray.
	Either pray better, or pray not at all!
	He prayes ill, that prayes for his brothers fall.
Chevalier:	Ther's many a Gallant man is fallen this day
	Which I could wish had scap't with life away;
	Our men of vallour which stood bravely too't 130
	Were knoct i'th head; they scorned to face about.
	O *Inchiquine*[38] hadst thou been on the plaine,
	Soe many of thy men had not been slaine.
	Thou wouldst have charg'd them, Maugre[39] all the Force
	Of their mad foot and desperate fighting Horse.
	Thou wouldst this day, have put the Roundheads toot[40]
	And beat them, both on Horseback and Foot.
Roundhead:	Had *Inchequine* bin there, you must confesse,
	Yet was th'Almighties power no whit the lesse.
	'Twas He which lead us forth, and brought us in: 140
	'Twas He which made you lose, and made us win.
	We were the instrument, but it was Hee
	Which did the worke – to whom all praises be.

---

36. Royalists would be expected to support the Anglican church and its Book of Common Prayer.
37. either.
38. Murrough O'Brien, Baron Inchiquin (1614–74), an important military commander in Ireland throughout the 1640s; at this time, Inchiquin was on the royalist side, but he was not at the battle of Rathmines.
39. despite.
40. to it.

EDWARD CALVER
(*fl*.**1649**)

Edward Calver was an Englishman, probably from Wilbie in Suffolk. He was a supporter of
the parliamentary side in the English Civil War, and published various poems on the state of
England in the 1640s. The following poem may be seen in the context not only of Irish
politics but of the struggle between various denominations of protestantism in England after
the execution of Charles I. It seems possible, even likely, that this poem was commissioned
by bishops of the Church of Ireland when they heard that the parliamentary forces were
about to set sail for Ireland. The fawning and obsequious tone of much of the piece reflects
the dire position in which the leaders of the church found themselves, caught between the
catholic confederates, who had usurped the church's rights and revenues, and a puritan
relieving army supplied by a puritan English parliament. The Church of Ireland needed to do
all it could to trumpet its gratitude for past help from protestant England, and its confident
hope of more to come.

    Zions Thankfull Ecchoes is, thus, a poem carefully crafted to impress on the English
parliament and the incoming forces the need to move rapidly for the restoration of Ireland to
the English protestant fold, and the restoration of the Church of Ireland to its position as the
church of the Irish state. The poem is in four parts: in the first, the Church of Ireland
addresses her elder sister, the Church of England, stressing the divine nature of the bond
between them; the 'Parliament of England' is addressed in the second part of the poem, and
Lord Fairfax, at this time expected to be the commander of the force coming to Ireland, in
the third. In the fourth part, the Church of Ireland (pragmatically) addresses herself to 'The
English Commanders and Souldiers assigned for the reliefe of Ireland'; since these would be
the men dividing the spoils after the anticipated victories over the native Irish, it was
important to tell them what tempting spoils were to be had in Ireland, and also to remind
them that the Church of Ireland was the church which had a legal right to establishment.
Those familiar with the puritan rhetoric of the time could be expected to respond positively
to reiterated references to Ireland as 'Zion' and to the use of biblical parallels.

from: Zions Thankfull Ecchoes from the Clifts[1] of Ireland,

or the little Church of Christ in Ireland, warbling out her humble and gratefull
addresses to her Elder Sister in England: And in particular, to the Parliament, to
his Excellency, and to his Army, or that part assigned to her assistance, now in
her low, yet hopefull Condition

The Messengers Humble Presentation

      Renowned Christians, what I heere present,
      As from a persecuted Sister sent
      By my rude[2] hand, to your judicious eye,
      Please to accept, and graciously survey:

1. clefts, fissures, divisions.
2. simple.

'Tis neither hyperbolicall, nor newes
From either Turkes, Antipodes,[3] or Jewes;
But Ecchoes sounding, what you ought to know,
The state of *Zion* in a land you owe:[4]
    Her sighs, her suits, & in the same made known
Her thankful spirit for your kindnes shown,   10
And hopes of comfort by you late assign'd,
And blest assistance to relieve her minde.
    As in this humble tender[5] you may view
In her owne language; Characters full true
Which *I* her servant, though the most unmeet,[6]
Am thus injoyn'd[7] to offer at your feet,
Which Heavens make powerfull in your hearts; so be't.

EDWARD CALVER

Part I: To her Elder Sister in England

Oh, thou my English eldest sister deare,
Who hast tooke notice of my troubles heere
These times of sorrow, and hast had a heart
To yeeld me succour, (which thou hast in part,)
But wanted power to make thy purpose knowne,
By reason of distractions of thine owne;
    Thou hast againe recal'd my cares to minde,
And such assistance to my ayd assignde,
That, if that malice doe not it prevent,
I may be happy in your blest content.   10
    But thou that hast this blessed helpe assignd
Wilt not, I see, by a contrary winde
Be beaten off thy purpose, when I see
The windes againe doe with thy will agree.
    No, no, deare sister, thou hast more respect
Unto my case than to my cares neglect;

---

3. people living in the southern hemisphere.
4. own, possess. 'Echo' poems – in which the end of one line was repeated at the beginning of the next so that an effect of an echo was created – were popular throughout the seventeenth century (see p. 445, for example).
5. offering (i.e. the poem).
6. unworthy.
7. enjoined, instructed; the word supports the supposition that the poem was commissioned.

Thou wilt not so our sister-hood betray,
Nor doth thy safety stand with my decay.
   Our heavenly Father, in his tender care,
Doth to his children like[1] affection beare,   20
And hath us ti'd by his most sacred Lawes;
We one should venture in anothers cause.
But I have sin'd, tis true, but I repent,
And teares have vertue to dissolve a flint,
But teares distild from tender childrens eyes,
They stir the fountaine where compassion lies.
God such affection to his children beares,
That, out of question, he bewayles their teares;
And in his time, will also still[2] their cries,
And grant their suits, and wipe their watery eyes.   30
   But in his wisedome, he for us thinks meet,
We should have heere much bitter with our sweet:
His grapes must be the most exactly prest,
His wheat must be with greatest labour drest:
His Dove must live where Ravens and Vultures flie:
His Lambs must feed where Wolves in covert lie:
His Lillies must among the thistles grow:
His Rose of Sharon, with the briers blow:[3]
Ishmael and Isaac must be kept alive,
Esau and Jacob must together strive.   40
   And therefore is it policy divine,
That Isaac should with Israel combine
And be united in a mutual band,
Who have such potent forces to withstand?[4]
   Besides, our concord and our mutuall care,
They are the garments we are bound to weare
By Heavens injunction, that we may thereby
Appeare we doe belong to the most High,
Whose children heere are clad in peace and love,
To make them fit to swell with him above,   50
Where faith, and hope, and patience shall surcease,[5]
But love and peace and unity increase.

---

1. similar, i.e. the churches are equals.
2. quieten, calm down.
3. blow = bloom. The Rose of Sharon, a flower of great beauty. Song of Solomon 2. 1.
4. The biblical images and names in the preceding twelve lines are intended to encourage the reader to see Ireland as the new Zion.
5. come to an end.

Faith, hope and patience are our weapons heere,
But Love the spirit that gives life and cheere,
And we shall fayle in all our other parts
Unlesse that sacred fire enflame our hearts.
　　But wherefore, Sister, should I goe about
To bring thy love and care of me in doubt?
When as I see thy love is so divine
Thou canst not from that principall decline.　　　　　60

from Part II: *To the Parliament of England*

And you, whom God, who passeth all selectors,
Hath made his choice of to be our protectors,
To labour to defend us by your Lawes,
Who have besides, some interest in our cause,
I blesse thee, Heavens, that you have heard our cries
Which have been earnest with you for supplies,
And out of sacred, sympathizing care
Have tooke in hand our low estate to rear,[1]
And still are acting, and in counsell sit
To adde more comfort to our causes yet,　　　　　10
Like brave and Christian Senators in trust
That feare no danger in a cause so just.
Most brave resolve, ride on and prosper still,
And what you have so well begun, fulfill.
No doubt but God who set you such a hard
And tedious taske, hath set out your reward,
And will bestow it on you, if not heere,
Yet when it shall to all the world appeare . . .

. . . I need not question that you will be just
And wise, and watchfull in your charge in trust,　　　　　20
Not onely in relation to that hand
That made you great, and put you in command,
But also in a serious respect;
So many eyes upon youre acts reflect,
That almost all the Christians of this age
Are gazers on the Actions of your stage.

1. raise up.

And lastly, in regard unto the cry
My elder sister, in your armes, and I
Within your trust, upon our knees do make,
That you will not our case in hand forsake,   30
But speed and prosecute it in that kinde
And blessed manner that you have design'd,
And that division, that same bane of Peace
And foe to Vertue, do not make you cease
That work you have begun, and so far wrought
Untill it be unto perfection brought.

from Part III: *To His Excellency the Lord FAIRFAX*[1]

Most Noble Champion, England's chief Commander,
Who in the tedious dangerous *Meander*
Of Englands winding, waving, desperate waies,
In wars intestine,[2] have got through with praise;
And brought those swelling, raging, roaring Seas,
Through Gods assistance to a calme and peace.
    For which your Kingdome, and therein my sister,
That through your labours, God hath late so blest her,
Are bound to write your name in gold so pure,
That time nor envy,[3] may the same obscure,   10
But after ages may so happy be,
To read your worth, as we are blest to see.
    And now you have those craggy mountains past,
And gain'd a valley, well secur'd at last,
Whiles friends at home are singing your deserts,
Your care is how to succour other partes . . .

    I long indeed have sighed for relief,
And fill'd the aire with ecchoes of my grief,
In hope the winds would on my woes so smile
To beare the sense thereof into your Isle.   20
    But long I look'd for what I long'd to heare,
A sweet return of what the windes should beare,

1. Thomas Fairfax, third baron Fairfax (1612–71), commander-in-chief of the parlia-
   mentary forces and the man expected to lead the army coming to Ireland in 1649. In fact,
   Cromwell himself assumed that command.
2. i.e. the Civil Wars.
3. i.e. neither time nor envy.

A happy answer of my heavy cry,
Before my wofull wants could have supply.
　But now I see, and to my comfort finde,
The cause my suits have been so long declin'd
Was not for want of pity in the rest,
Nor want of courage in your noble breast,
But want of opportunity to send
Such ayd and comfort as you did intend . . .　　　　　30

　Proceed and prosper then, as you have done;
Here is another conquest to be won,
Which heaven, I hope, which have the same in birth,[4]
Will adde unto the Trophies of your worth . . .

　Now in assurance of the same, I stand
Attending on Gods pleasure in your hand,
And in submission to the same shall rest,
Presenting of my most intire request
Unto the heavens, that they your part may take,
And favour all that fight for ZION's sake.　　　　　40

from Part IV: *To the English Commanders and Souldiers assigned for
the reliefe of Ireland*

Welcome that will come, noble friends indeed,
That will vouchsafe a visit where is need:
The rich, tis true, have many friends, but such
As do want riches, do want friends as much.
　But with you, Worthies, it is otherwise.
You seem to grace what others do despise.
Oh, that I had but means unto my mind
To welcome you, and those that are behind,
That you might tast[e] my thankfulnesse, and they
Might heare thereof, and make no more delay!　　　　10
. . . But though my hand be empty, I am poor,
Yet there are riches plenty on my shoare:
Such as have ro[b]b'd me, they have riches left
They stole from me, to take which is no theft;

---

4. A reference to the doctrine of predestination – the belief that the outcome of events was
ordained in heaven before the world began – held by some puritans at this time.

And what is missing, tis but justice shown,
If they make restitution of their own.

    Besides this Island is a fruitfull field,
Or pleasant Garden which doth plenty y[i]eld:
The Sun, the Moon, the Stars consenting be,
The Elements do all therein agree.   20

    The fire is not predominating here,
But cold and heat do moderate appear:
The Ayre so rare an Antidote and pure
That nothing poysonous can the same indure.[1]
The water sweet, and pleasant streames abound,
Where foules and fishes are in plenty found.
The earth a Garden, from whose fatnesse springs
A blessed fullnesse of terrestriall things.

    Besides these strong inducements which invite
In the respect of profit, and delight,   30
You also have some int'rest here, 'tis known,
That you, in part, contend but for your own –
Your own by conquest – and should that be lost
Through want of care, which in atchieving, cost
Your noble and renowned fathers dear,
The price of blood, the work of many a year?

    Should that, I say, then, which bold fathers got
Be lost by children? Oh! it were a blot,
A scar, a shame, a scandall to your deeds,
That England's Cedars should become such reeds,   40
The off-spring of such active, valiant, strong,
And conquering hands, should put up such a wrong,
Besides the losse – which is so great, that sure,
True English hearts will not the same indure.
They will not have it in records to find,
That English spirits can be so declin'd . . .

    Gods case is your case, as his instruments;
And he in his especiall providence
Hath call'd you hither, as it doth appeare,
To fight the battels of Jehova here.   50
    His holy word, his worship, truth, and name,
With all sincere Professors of the same,

1. A reference to the fact that no poisonous reptiles exist in Ireland.

Have here a long time persecuted bin
By Antichrist,[2] that active man of sin,
And his adherents, who have here of late
Prevail'd, insulted, seem'd predominate.
   But now I hope the heavy sighes and grones,
And cryes and teares of Gods afflicted ones,
Together with the jealousie and care,
He doth unto his word, and worship beare,   60
Hath wrought upon his clemency so far,
That he intends to be at open war
Against his, and my enemies, and yours,
And will reprove them, and confound their powers . . .

   He now I hope will, in his tender love,
His power and wisedome in this Land improve,
In once more sowing it with holy seed,
His sacred truths, and the most saving Creed;
His worship, Sabbaths, Sacraments and Saints,
In purest sense, and without sad restraints;   70
And make this Kingdome (which hath been a cage
Of unclean spirits, and a very stage
For Antichrist to Act upon at pleasure,
Too many years, and in too great a measure)
To become now an holy Land, excelling
In vertue, truth, and righteousnesse: a dwelling
For God himselfe, in holinesse and grace,
An earthly ZION for his Saints, a place
Where I in peace may henceforth sit and sing
The holy praises of my heav'nly King . . .   80

   Proceed, proceed then, doubt not of successe;
Your case in question promiseth no lesse;
God will not faile you, nor your spirits yield,
Which are by God and Conscience clear up held.
   As for supplyes, you need not fear delay;
As for reward, Gods is the only pay;
His service with the best supplyes abound;
His Souldiers with the richest Garlands crown'd.
   And as for men, I dare presume so far,

---

2. Seventeenth-century protestants often referred to the Pope as 'Antichrist'.

That, where their purses to your former war   90
Were oft forc'd ope, they to reliefe of me,
Now out of zeal and pity will be free;
Their purses, hands, and hearts to this designe
Will freely ope, and joyfully incline:
In which so fully is to be discern'd
Both their owne safety, and Gods cause concern'd.[3]

  Besides, what here you, by your valour shown,
Shall conquer, shall in part become your own;
You shall not beat the ayre, or the winde,
But booty pray and pay, are yours assign'd,   100
That with the greater courage you maintain
This enterprize, the more shall be your gain.
Do then, oh do then your brave hearts expresse,
As to your honour, you declare no lesse,
And stop the mouth of malice, and compell
Meer envy on your actions to speak well.

  Whiles I, and all the Saints on earth shall pray
That you may prosper, and our foes decay:
That ZIONS side may have the upper hand,
And Romes impostures be expel'd this Land.   110

3. This might seem an unduly optimistic view of the likely generosity of adherents of the
   Church of Ireland to the soldiers and adventurers of the parliamentary force.

THOMAS COBBES
(*fl.***1650**)

In the long prose dedication to the marquis of Ormond which accompanied the following poem, Thomas Cobbes reveals that he had received his early education from the same man who had taught Ormond in the early 1620s, Roger Conyers of Finchley, a village north of London. It seems likely, since Ormond's Finchley tutor was a catholic, that Cobbes was born into a recusant family in England, and he may well have been the son of the Jacobean dramatist and translator James Cobbes, who was active between 1619 and 1623.[1] Thomas Cobbes then travelled extensively in England, Scotland, France 'and other kingedomes, States and Republiques' and was probably ordained a catholic priest. He refers to friends with whom he had discussed the deplorable state of Ireland as being now 'heere and there dwelling in this Province': the use of the word 'province' suggests that he was an order priest, and he may well have been a Jesuit. He came to Ireland from France at Whitsuntide in 1649 and lived in a city (Kilkenny?) in what he called 'voluntary exile'.

Cobbes was a fanatical, catholic royalist and the purpose of his poem was to inspire any Irishman who read it to fight to the death against the Cromwellians. Although his rather heavyweight couplets can tire the ear, Cobbes emerges from this long poem as a lively and inventive poet, and his ringing exhortation to the people of Ireland not to allow themselves to be crushed by the 'rabble of rebellious racailles'[2] in Cromwell's Irish army is one of the most colourful rallying cries of seventeenth-century Ireland.

The poem was presented to Ormond after the siege of Waterford (December 1649) and before his term as (royalist) lord lieutenant of Ireland came to an end in December 1650. In its hard-line determination to fight protestants and Cromwellians to the death, it reflects the position often associated with Cardinal Rinuccini, the papal legate to the Confederacy, and some of those close to him.

A Poeme uppon Cromuell and his Archtrayterous Rabble of Rebellious Racailles, and Englandes Jaolebirdes,

levelled and arraunged nowe togither with a compendious runninge over of Greate Britaines present deplorable state, and a more ample description of Irelandes auncient, late, more moderne, and nowe imminent condition, if the Inhabitaunts thereof (as beneath exhorted) doe not unanimously and seriously addresse themselves to defende their auncient religion, theire kinge, theire countrey, the pristine Rights, lawes and customes of their countrey, their wives, their cheildren and their owne Landes and Personall Estates

Who coulde imagine that furious cutthroat Cromwell,
Shoulde on his barrells' heades[3] sounde out the drumme well?

---

1. See Robert M. Schuler, 'James Cobbes, Jacobean Dramatist and Translator', *Papers of the Bibliographical Society of America*, vol. 72 (1972), p. 68.
2. rakehells, scoundrels, rascals.
3. *Marginal note*: 'As being a Brewer not many years since'. The rumour that Cromwell was the son of a brewer was widespread, and was often used by his enemies. The idea is that Cromwell uses barrels as drums.

Or that from brewinge or from the Drayman's Carte
Soe mischeivous a stickler should up starte?
That hopps and Malte, ill buoil'd, and mash'd togither
Should Rogues transport, the Devill knows not whither?
That impious Oliver and his abortive sonne,
Whome heaven must needes renounce, damn'd Iretonne,[4]
Should sett on fire three kingdomes, murder the king
And o'er them dayly loude Alarms ringe?   10
Make them all streame from every springe, or floode,
True loyal subjects, pure and guilltelesse bloode?
Renverse[5] olde Sacred Rites, quite topside turvey,
Infect sounde Churchmen with confoundinge scurvey?
Defile, seduce, pollute their leaprous soules,
Their braines inebriate, with envenomed boules[6]
Of most pestiferous blasphemies? heresyes
Which make earth tremble, and overcloude the skyes?
The hell-hounde Mahomett, hardely could invente
Such leude Impostures as these fiendes have sente,   20
T'intoxicate our Monarchyes, to surrounde us
With more than Egipte plagues[7] for to confounde us!
Damn'd Antichrist[8] his parents, the grimme devills
Can scarcely heape on us more dismall evills
Than these two Miscreants, with their hell-hatch'd bande,
Have pour'd uppon our heades by sea and lande.
Their piquerons[9] and Pyratts have contested
Against our safetyes, all our coasts infested
With rapines, massacres, dyed the foaminge waters
With sanguine tinctures of our bloode and slaughters,   30
Pillag'd our Lands from ships, our houses plunder'd,
O'er hills and valleyes martial clangours thunder'd,
Empeached our lawful trafficke, commerce embarr'd,
With fire and sworde against us and ours have warr'd;

4. Henry Ireton (1611–51), Cromwell's son-in-law and his second-in-command in Ireland.
5. reverse.
6. meaning uncertain: probably = boils.
7. i.e. the plagues which afflicted the children of Israel in Egypt, Exodus 7–14.
8. *Marginal note*: 'Most divines doe probably conjecture, that the father of Antichrist shall be the devill that shall begett him of a common strumpett.'
9. picaroons, rogues.

Grosse[10] women frighted in their naked bedds,
Ravishd, from spottlesse virgins, maidenheads;
Deflour'd wives, widows, matrons, doe defye
To suffer in that sexe, due modesty.
Many, their fellow subjects, have they slaine,
Cryinge for quarter,[11] though too much in vaine.   40
Some they have tortur'd, others have they cast
Into th'Ocean, or hang'd on th'mast.
Our lande they've robb'd, and turn'd churches to stables
Or in them preached horrid lyes and fables.
Assasind[12] Priests, and Prelats, Jesuites, Fryers,
And who[13] but thwarted their most base desires.
They've ransacd their owne Ministers, slaine Divines
That scorn'd to plott with them in dam'nd Designes,
Spar'd neither age nor sex nor any sect
They coulde not poyson or at least infect   50
With impious doctrines: they have raised seditions
And puffd men upp, with Lucifer's ambitions.
Their true and lawfull Soveraigne they have smote,
For which, alive may they and theyrs rotte.
All royal bloode they have aimed to raze out,
That none may sway us but a sottish route
Of base Mechanicks;[14] butcheringe, brewinge knaves
Have mark'd us out for shambles,[15] or for slaves.
Nobles are levell'd, brave heroick heartes
Must stoope in homage to the Brewers' Cartes.   60
Two rebel rascals, Cromwell and Iretunne
Ore three faire kingdomes have their raignes begunne.

Oh Englande, Scottlande, Wales! What a Crewe
Of hedge borne[16] vagabondes nowe force you to sue
Your starre crosst fortunes: when no right, no lawe
But Tiranny, your lives and states must awe.[17]

---

10. independent, i.e. living outside a settlement.
11. exemption from being immediately put to death when defeated in battle.
12. assassinated.
13. i.e. anyone who.
14. people involved in manual labour, of low birth.
15. the slaughterhouse, i.e. the drunken rout of soldiers will kill us like animals or will enslave us.
16. i.e. born in the open air, of homeless parents.
17. i.e. when it is not right or law but tyranny which holds your lives and estates in awe (that is, controls them and you through the influence of fear).

Some thousands of Watt Tylers and Jacke Strawes[18]
Doe Coope you upp in Cages, like jack dawes;
Some Broakers, Bottchers, Slaves of clouting trades[19]
Doe Curbe you more than millions of Jack Cades.[20]   70
This John a Stiles, that rogue John an Oates[21]
Sittes, when he lists,[22] upon your skirts and cloakes.
Every Dunghill rascall vaunts and Domineers
As are their villains,[23] heretofore greate Peers.
And thou, deere Irelande, sole Relict[24] of the three
Faire Puissaunt Monarchyes, that continues free
From slavish thralldome, rouse thyself to meete
Those that attempte to tread thine[25] under feete.
Encounter them with courage that woulde bringe
Thy lovd inhabitants to slaughter with thy kinge,   80
That woulde plowe up and bury in iniquity
Both roote and braunch of venerable antiquity,
That would prophane your temples, drive your nation,
Precipitate, unto dismall desolation,
Make your Religion, shadowes; phantomes vaine
And franticke Whimseyes of each maddcappe braine
Woulde drive you to forget, what eare's Catholicke[26]
Yea, and what's sacred Christian, Apostolicke.
More, soe they startle at's revengeful rodd[27]
They would extinguish th'memory of your God,   90

---

18. *Marginal note*: 'Watt Tyler & Jacke Strawe two Rebell Rogues, stirred upp ye very Scumme of all Kentes and Essexes Mechanicks against kinge Richard the seconde.' Watt Tyler and Jack Straw were the leaders of the Peasants' Revolt of 1381 which threatened the young Richard II and led to widespread disturbances in the south-east of England and in London. The point of the reference is that Tyler and Straw, like those they led, were mere peasants.
19. pedlars, cobblers, rascals who do rough jobs.
20. *Marginal note*: 'Jack Cade a Rebellious Mechanicke against King Henry ye sixt who termed himself Mortimer.' Like Watt Tyler and Jack Straw, Jack Cade led a rising of peasants against the authority of the king – this time in 1450 and against Henry VI.
21. The names 'John a Stiles' and 'John a Nokes' were used to represent fictitious persons in stating cases of law. The terms are used by Samuel Butler in *Hudibras* (London, 1663), Part III, canto 3, l. 715.
22. wants to.
23. villeins, peasants or small tenants, i.e. every rascal boasts that those who were once great lords are now his inferiors.
24. the only one that is left.
25. i.e. your 'Faire Puissaunt Monarchy'.
26. i.e. what is always catholic.
27. move rapidly, rush. The lines mean: Moreover, they move so rapidly with the rod of their vengeance that they would extinguish the memory of your God . . .

And make you grounde your soule saving beliefe
On cursed Cromwell, or such other theife,
Whom hell doth gape for, strettchinge forth vast vaults
To swallowe upp, with his most devilish faults.
In breife, they woulde extirpate all that's deare
Or near unto you, under this orbe or sphere.[28]

Advaunce thy selfe[29] then, and addresse complaints
Unto the thousands of most glorious Saints
That heeretofore possessed thee,[30] in times past;
For brightest vertues, thou illustrious wast: 100
Millions of godly men, thy Countyes nourishd:
In thee religion, zeale and learninge flourishd.
Thine Inhabitaunts weare valiaunt, and durst wade
Through their owne bloodes, their foes for to invade:
Confronte maine[31] daungers, purchase life, and breath,
In spight of fury and orewhellminge death:
Looke backe on thy progenitours, thou shalt see
By dinte of sworde, they gained prosperity;
They scornd to leave their Generalls in the lurch
And to deserte their auncient mother church[32]   110
Or to forsake their Lords and Magistrates
Their lives amongst them gaginge and estates.[33]
They gave no cause for men turned wolves to prate
They purchase peace from them at any rate;
They quelled such sycophants as basely shoulde delude
Or aime, t'enslave their waveringe multitude.
In fine,[34] Cromwellian syrens[35] they detested,
That with infernall fraudes, their freinds infested.
Fly such Impostours! Still doe lurking lye
Soule killing Adders in hypocrisy.   120
Never beleeve, when Foxes on you grinne,
They have no trappe abroad, to catch you in;

28. i.e. in the world.
29. i.e. Ireland, and those who fight for her.
30. i.e. lived in Ireland.
31. mighty.
32. *Marginal note*: 'or deerest mother church'.
33. gage = engage, pledge; i.e. pledging their lives and estates to them (their lords and governors).
34. In short.
35. anyone who deceives (so called from the Siren maidens of classical mythology).

Or, thousand Times, what faith they once betraide,
For to betray the same rogues prove affraide.
The Rankest poysons, which will your bodyes cast
Into a leaprousy, may be sweete in tast[e];
That tirant to captive you,[36] most doth seeke
Will lure you first by wayes both milde and meeke.
But when hee hath griped you fast, between his pawes
Heele drage you soone to death, amiddst his jawes.   130
I dreade a Sinon[37] and a horse of Troy,
When theise damnd villaines fawne, will you destroy.
Crimes, when they hattchd, woulde make earths centre tremble;
Then, did they most both flatter and dissemble.
Shake not your fetters off soe much, in vaine
To clogge yourselves with heavier farre againe.[38]
Lett not your neickes for yoakes bee made soe fitte,
That them unto meere slaves you will submitte.
Your oathes redoubled, scorne once to revoke,
And God and's Angells unto wrath provoke.   140
Your sacred temples with much toyle, more bloode
Extorted, that you may bee counted good,
By base scurrill[39] Mechanicks, passe away not,
And unto Cromwells prophane rites betray not.
Whilst an insultinge Brewer shall pollute
Your holy mysteries, will you stande all mute?
More, where th'immaculate lambe to pious hearts
Soule savinge foode assidually[40] impartes,
Shall Canniballs bee fedd? Shall reavenous hounds
Devoure what you have purchast with your wounds?   150
Shall this newe uppstarte, Independent rabble
Converte your tubbs[41] to pullpitts and there babble?
Why in a moment will you fouly yeilde
More then you gaind by your octenniall fielde.[42]

36. i.e. that tyrant who most seeks to capture you . . .
37. The traitor who duped the Trojans into allowing the wooden horse to be brought into Troy.
38. i.e. do not shake off your fetters so much, simply to burden yourself with far heavier ones again.
39. = scurrilous.
40. constantly.
41. pulpits. Normally, the word 'tub' referred to pulpits in nonconformist meeting-houses and the word 'pulpit' to the pulpit in episcopalian or catholic churches; here the meaning is the exact opposite.
42. *Marginal note*: 'eight yeares warre heere'.

Why have you wasted your zealous ire and breath,
And why, soe stoutly have defyed death?
Wast but your frenzy?[43] Who woulde even thinke
Your Fervour shoulde soe soone decaye or shrinke?
Woulde one beleeve such flames should turn to frost,
And ardent zeale bee, in an instant, lost?   160

Oh call to minde that you of late yeares, but few,
Yea, an unarmed and confused crewe,
A weake, poor people, many meerly rude,[44]
At best, a too much curbed multitude,
Not skill'd in armes and half scarcely arm'd,
With pristine bad successes,[45] quell'd and charm'd
By rigid laws and magistrates kept under,
Divid'd 'twixt yourselves, dispersed asunder,
Invaded by England's champions, who o'er land
And sea, both farre and neare did beare commande,   170
A populous, valiant, rich, and puissant state,
Whose strength in shippinge did them animate
To great and high achievements, yet, durst ye
Advance and them assaile couragiously,
And though in all unequal but your cause,
You wring'd yourselves out of the griping pawes
Of Britain's rebels, and would ne'er consent
For to submit unto their parliament,
Most traiterous, most seditious, in all thinges,
Confrontinge both your lawes and lawfull kinges;[46]   180
And which conspired, under gaudy cloakes
Of equity, to burthen you with yoakes
Of slavery: make you greive, and lowre
Captivd, to worse than Turkes insulting power.[47]
And then did Limrick's well fortified castle
Against your batteryes much contest and wrastle;
The puissant towne too, of faire Galloway
Refusd your martiall squadrons to obay.[48]

---

43. i.e. Were you just mad?
44. uneducated.
45. *Marginal note*: 'viz in Queene Elizabeth's rayne'. i.e. despite former failures (in Queen Elizabeth's reign).
46. This very long sentence reminds the Irish that they had, during the height of the Confederacy of the 1640s, successfully defied the power of the English state and the treacherous English parliament.
47. i.e. to an insulting power worse than that of the Turks.
48. The siege of Limerick was raised in 1642, that of Galway in 1643.

Duncanons bullwarke, of mighty power and strength
Scarce forced was to stoope t'assaults at length,   190
For it beinge sited on a lofty rocke
Retorted every furious storme or shocke.[49]
What shall I say of Waterforde? Soe stronge
By sea and lande that it continued longe
A Checke to your designes; its situation
Contemn'd fierce stratagemmes from your daringe nation.[50]
It prov'd a threateninge rocke, which doth detaine
Three Rivers as though fetterd in one chaine,
Rivers which you, alas, weare noe wayes able
With shipps or boates to make navigable.[51]   200
The very Ocean seemd from you embarrd.
Yet, 'gainst those mischieves,[52] have you stoutly warrd
And rather chose to pine away or starve
Than from your sacred league[53] decline, or swarve.

But now (most infamous!) abandninge true freindes
You dare enslave yourselves to bloody fiendes.[54]
After y'have plowd through rockes and boisterous seas,
You needes will yeilde to Hellhounds[55] for your ease.
After Castles stormd, by your undaunted powers
With bullwarks, rampires,[56] cittyes, townes and towers,   210
After Scotch legions, in Bemberbs champaigne plaine
Neere Bannon's streaming floods, by prowesse slaine,[57]
After Ormonds Marquis's love and charity
Drewe him from's wife and incolumity[58]
To fronte maine daungers both by sea and lande
For to afforde you his assistinge hande,

49. The fort at Duncannon, County Wexford, fell to the parliamentary forces in March 1645.
   The fort was significant because it commanded the waters of Waterford harbour.
50. i.e. Its situation made it impossible for your daring nation's stratagems to be successful.
51. Cromwell besieged Waterford on 24 November 1649 and captured it eight days later.
   The poet seems to be referring to Waterford after its capture by the Cromwellians.
52. = mischiefs, misfortunes.
53. *Marginal note*: 'as by them esteemed'. The reference is to the oaths of association drawn
   up by the confederate catholics of Ireland at Kilkenny in 1642. swarve = swerve, deviate.
54. During the confusions of 1650, many catholics – particularly those threatened by the
   parliamentary forces – were keen to surrender to the Cromwellians.
55. *Marginal note*: '(viz: Cromwell and his consorts)'.
56. = ramparts.
57. A reference to the defeat of the Scottish army under General Munro by Owen Roe
   O'Neill in June 1646 at Benburb, County Tyrone. champaigne = a field of military
   operations.
58. freedom from danger, safety. *Marginal note*: 'to witte in Fraunce'.

After that hee hath firmly you united
And to your wonted happyness you invited,
After unto your selves, and to your kinge
Hee hath conjoind you, and in every thinge   220
Would cherysh you, that doe desire rather
To embrace your worst of foes, than such a Father;
Howe vigilant heere hee proves. Howe hee doth toyle
You to enrich, and your much wasted soyle!
Noe cost by him is spard, noe care nor paine
That you unto yourselves he might regaine.
And what transports mee from my selfe to rage
After that hee, on's life, your tutelage
Hath so assumd, as that he dayly runnes
To threateninge daungers, of picques,[59] swords, and gunnes,   230
Yet, at the name of Cromwell, as men crazd,
You quake, you quiver, and are starke amazd.
What stupidd Feares, what fonde, slavish terror
Hurryes your thoughts into so grosse an errour?
To turn vile Cravens[60] maketh you neare blush,
Nor into Cowardice, others headelonge push.
When of your high Commaunders, you have use
You damne all thought of any feare, or truce
With such infernall Caterpillars as do strive
Through your confusions to growe greate and thrive.   240
At first, you made th'worlde emulous,[61] to endeavour
Like you, 'gainst enemyes resolute to persever.
Nowe, since you faulter, thats perplexd with griefe
To your aery valours, eare[62] it gave beliefe.
This Waveringes hainous, and th' authours of such crime
Shall be recorded impious t'after time.
My tongue disclaimd soe base, so light a fact
And still denide your nation might it act.
But what's so odious, that deny it can,
May bee committed by unconstant man?[63]   250

---

59. pikes.
60. *Marginal note*: 'cowardes'.
61. covetous, wanting to emulate you.
62. e'er, before. i.e. Now, since you falter, that wish of others to emulate you is troubled with grief, even before it was able to believe in your brave, heavenly deeds.
63. This couplet seems to mean: But who can deny that what is as odious as this can be committed by men who are not steadfast?

Sure, hell ore heaven must obduct[64] thicke cloudes
And all orewhellme, with nights darkest shroudes:
Christ's choisest prelates must his Church defye,
And tumble headlonge to Apostasye;[65]
Your shepheardes must to wolves your flockes betray,
And leave their sheepefoldes unto them to sway,
When of meere reprobates, Epicures, sensuall logges,
Or faithlesse harlotts, worse than mungrell dogges,
You will crave quarter, or, assered[66] accept
From rascalls out of Gaoles, and dungehills crept.   260
Ambition[67] to bee happy, labour, toile farre more
To save your countrey than its fall deplore.
Confounde theise renegates, fight valiauntly, pellmell;[68]
Damne treatyes with them, to the pitts of hell.
Reject terrestriall pleasures, never joye,
But when theise rebells you can most annoye.
Dreade not their cruellties, and neare lett their baites[69]
Transfixe your breasts with forg'd and fonde deceites.
Beware that cowardice or some more stupidd fate
Chase not your church into a gaspinge state,   270
Make forraigne warriors prattle that in vaine
You've seen so many in your quarrells slaine,
That you unsheath'd your swordes theise eight yeares past
Only to hacke them and your freinds to wast,[70]
And what you have atchiev'd by long delay
Shoulde in a trice be swept and borne away.

Infernall furyes have bewitch'd your lande
By an enchaunted draught from Cromwell's hande.
Here's viperous heresyes, and his weapons there
Have you concluded, that you scarce know where   280
To shewe your faces, but still flyinge dreade
Lest both at once shoulde seise and strike you deade.

---

64. cover (to obduce = to cover or envelop).
65. apostasy. In the confusion of 1650, when the catholic bishops had excommunicated
   those who supported Ormond, it was far from clear what was apostasy and what was the
   word of the true church.
66. liberty. 'assertion' = the act of setting a slave or other captive free.
67. strive.
68. recklessly, indiscriminately.
69. i.e. never let their temptations.
70. waste. i.e. to no purpose.

Disdaine the world of you should heare this tattle,
Or think you tremble at the noyse of battle.
Defye theise murmures; Worthyes dye or live,
And what man can not, God to you will give.
He will eternize[71] your heroicke names
And 'mongst bright Angels glorifie your fames.

71. immortalize.

POEMS FROM THE **1650s**
ANONYMOUS

This mildly indecent poem is found in the same manuscript as 'Ye merry Boyes all that live in Fingaule' of 1636 (British Library MS Sloane 900), and may be as early as that poem, p. 210. Its language, the Fingallian dialect of Hiberno-English, is notable for the survival of archaic linguistic forms, and for the fact that the stress in polysyllabic words is sometimes postponed to the final syllable.[1] Both characteristics are seen in the poem, with archaisms throughout the text and the rhyming words in lines 3, 9 and 12 exhibiting postponed stress.

The Fingallian Dance (*c*. 1650)

On a Day in the Spring,
As I went to Bolring[2]
   To view the jolly Daunciers,
They did trip it so high
(Be me shole!), I did spee[3]
   Six C——[4] abateing[5] Seav'n hairs.

But wondering on 'ame,[6]
Fat make 'em so tame,
   Fen de catch at their Plack-keet,[7]
The Maids of y-yore   10
Wou'd y-cree, and y-rore,[8]
   And y-make o foul Rac-keet.

1. For a full analysis of Fingallian, see Alan Bliss, *Spoken English in Ireland 1600–1740* (Dublin, 1979).
2. The bullring. Bull-fighting, like bear-baiting and cock-fighting, was widely practised in seventeenth-century Ireland.
3. i.e. by my soul, I did spy . . .
4. Cunts. The convention of veiling 'four-letter words' behind dashes or asterisks lasted from about 1700 – the manuscript from which this text comes is a mid-eighteenth century one – to modern times. It was generally thought that the writing or printing of such words was a criminal offence under English law, though this was never tested. The law was changed in 1959.
5. probably = abutting, bordering on.
6. them.
7. These two lines seem to mean: what made them so tractable when someone caught at their placket. (Properly, a placket is a slit at the top of a petticoat, but it is usually used to mean the female pudenda.)
8. y-cree (cry) and y-rore (roar) are survivals, in a debased form, of the *ge-* prefix used in some Old English past participles; y-yore (*y*– with an adverb) is a unique usage, possibly a burlesque comment on the sound of the other archaisms.

But fire take 'ame,[9]
They made me ashame,
   And when I went home to me weef[10]
And told her the Chaunce[11]
Of the Maids in the Daunce,
   'Peace thy prateing,' sayd shee, 'for dee[12] Leef!'

This is part of one of the poems presented to James Butler, Marquis of Ormond, soon after Oliver Cromwell was installed as Lord Protector (December 1653).

from: On the Protector (*c.* 1653)

What's a Protector? 'tis a stately thing
That Apes it in the Image of a King.
A tragique Actor, Cesar in the Clowne:
Here's a brass farthing stamped with a Crowne.
Aesop's Asse maskt with a lyons skin:[1]
An outside Saint lyn'd with a devill within:
An Eccho whence the Royall sound doth come,
Hees but a Barrells head unto a drume . . .

  . . . A counterfieted peece,[2] but one that showes
Charles[3] his Effigies with a Copper nose.   10
Fantastique shaddowe of ye Royall head,
The Brewer with the king's arms quartered.[4]
    In fine, hees one wee must Protector call,
    From whom the king of Kings protect us all.

9. i.e. But fire take them! – an expression equivalent to 'To hell with them!'
10. wife.
11. chance, i.e. told her what had happened.
12. thy. The wife's speech might be paraphrased: 'Oh keep quiet, for goodness' sake!'

1. In Sir Roger L'Estrange's 1694 collection of *Æsop's Fables*, the ass who puts on a lion's skin finds that the world is his own, and man and beast fly before him. But his voice and his ears betray him and, once he has been discovered, he is 'well cudgell'd for his pains'.
2. coin.
3. Charles I.
4. As in the earlier poem by Thomas Cobbes, see p. 299, these references are to the belief that Cromwell was the son of a brewer, and to the prominence of his nose.

Sympathy for the dispossessed and defeated people of Ireland lies behind this stanza from a long poem entitled *A Medley of the Nations*. Though an exaggerated Hiberno-English is used for the speaker's words, the effect is less to make the reader laugh at him than to show the desolation and misery of the Irish outcast.

from: A Medley of the Nations [The Irish] (1655)

O hone, O hone, poor Teg and Shone,[1]
  O hone may howl and cry,
St. Patrick help dy country-men,
  Or fait and trot we dye;
De English steal our hoart of Usquebagh,[2]
Dey put us to de Sword all in Dewguedagh:
Help us St. Patrick we ha no Saint at all but dee,
O let us cry no more, O hone, a cram, a cree![3]

---

1. A rough paraphrase of this text is as follows: Alas, alas, poor Teig and Shone (two names for Irishmen), alas we may howl and cry; St Patrick, help thy countrymen or, faith and truth, we die. The English steal our hoard of whiskey, they put us to the sword in Drogheda. Help us, St Patrick, we have no saint but thee! O let us cry no more, alas, my dear!
2. whiskey. Ir. *uisce beathadh*.
3. a cram, a cree = gra-ma-cree, darling; Ir. *grádh mo chroidhe*, love of my heart.

WILLIAM WHEELER
(*fl*.**1656**)

In this poem and the one that follows it, William Wheeler and William Wright engaged in a verse exchange unique in seventeenth-century Ireland. The poems come from a particularly complex moment in the history of Irish boroughs. Following Cromwell's conquest of Ireland, all Irish boroughs except those of Dublin, Belfast, Carrickfergus and Youghal were brought under military rule.[1] While this lasted, from 1649 until 1656, everything previously under the jurisdiction of the corporation, including the imposition of local taxation through rates, was controlled by the military authorities. In addition, as a means of ensuring that boroughs would be controlled by protestants in future, the Cromwellians forced catholics out of the walled towns. Many of them settled in suburbs just outside the city walls. Cork, which had been controlled by catholics before 1649, was a city where this displacement was of particular importance.[2]

Given that many catholics were living in the southern suburbs of Cork in 1656, William Wheeler's mock-heroic 'Complaint of the South Suburbs of Corke' can be seen as a veiled objection by them to the level of rates imposed by the authorities based in Cork city.[3] One of the grounds of the complaint, that their suburb was suffering economic decline, is not at all surprising, since the policy of expelling catholics from the towns had led directly to a decline in economic activity and a fall in rents in and around the towns.[4] At the end of Wheeler's bantering 'Complaint' is an excited appendix headed 'Corks Jopean' (probably 'Cork's Io Paen', i.e. Cork's song of joy) in which he anticipates the imminent restoration of civic rights to the city. Like others whose charters had been removed in 1649, the citizens of Cork had been petitioning the Dublin authorities for the return of their charter; a new one was issued on 27 April 1656.[5]

Little is known of William Wheeler except that he was made a freeman of the corporation of Cork in October 1656, and empanelled as a grand juror of the city in 1660. In the relevant documents, he is described as a 'gent'.[6]

To the Honorable Commissioners for Assesments,
The Complaint of the South Suburbs of Corke

COPERNICUS,[7] whose working brain found out
The Earths swift motion, how it whirls about,

1. T.C. Barnard, *Cromwellian Ireland: English Government and Reform in Ireland 1649–60*, 2nd ed. (Oxford, 2000), pp. 50–89.
2. See Mark McCarthy, 'Turning a World Upside Down: The Metamorphosis of Property, Settlement and Society in the City of Cork during the 1640s and 1650s', *Irish Geography*, vol. 33, no. 1 (2000), pp. 37–55 for a full assessment of the mid-seventeenth-century displacement of Cork catholics, and of its consequences.
3. The south suburbs were in the parish of St Finbarr's and St John's, the north suburbs in the parish of Shandon. See the map at McCarthy, p. 44.
4. Barnard, pp. 51–2.
5. Barnard, p. 63.
6. See Cork Freemen's Register 1656–1741 (Cork Public Museum) and the transcript of the Cork d'oyer hundred court book (Cork Archives Institute U/127). I am grateful to Toby Barnard for these references.
7. Nicolaus Copernicus (1473–1543).

And that great *Plato*, who broacht long agoe
Opinions strange, as many Men doe know,
How that ere forty thowsand yeares be come,
(Which Some conceit[8] he means the day of Doome)
Times wheele shall turne all States we now behold,
Making the old Man young, the young Man old;
And that such changes have bin heretofore,
Stories doe plainly tell us 'ore and 'ore;   10
How one, while that increases, this decayes,
Is truly manifested in our daies.
For not long since the *South-side* of this City,
Had Water, Wit, and Wealth good store: But pitie
It is to see in what a little space,
They all have left the people and the place;
For now the *North-side* hath engrost[9] that store,
Of Water, Wit, and Wealth we had before,
And to our greifs those Men that now enjoy them,
To wrong us and opresse us doe employ them.   20
For they have shipt our Wit and Wealth together,
'Tis said to *Hull*, or else I know not whether,[10]
And are resolv'd by Water to return us
In liew (mere druggs) base Stons and Lyme to burne us.[11]
The *Borian-side*[12] are still contriving plots,
(At which they are more cunning than the *Scots*,)
To beare all down before them that oppose,
What they resolve by over-voting those
Who labor for an equall right proportion,
In the applotment of the Contribution,[13]   30
As witnes may these twelve last Months made Rates,
Wherin they equall us, with their Estates,
When as in Wealth, and Trade, they us exceed,
As far as doth brave *Thames* the River *Tweede*.[14]
And *Haunce* the Gally-pot that thrives by stuff
Which to drench Horses is but good enough

8. imagine.
9. bought up.
10. whither. The Humberside port of Hull may be pronounced to sound like 'hell'.
11. Worthless stone could be crushed and mixed with lime to make mortar; but lime is
   powerfully caustic. The exact point of the joke is not possible to retrieve.
12. The north side – from Boreas, the north wind of classical mythology.
13. applotment = apportionment. Clearly, the rate had to be voted on at a meeting of the
   commissioners.
14. The river Tweed, in southern Scotland, is only navigable as far as the town of Berwick.

Must side to curry favour and comply,
To Vote, and Signe, what since he does deny.[15]
And *Robin* busy-body,[16] I Sir, no Sir,
Like *Jack* on both sides, sayes it must be so Sir.   40
I could say somthing of their late projection,[17]
Which they pretended for a Corporation,
Wherin there *Archimedes*[18] shew'd his skill,
Fooling the Towne, thereby his Purse to fill:
Who for one Sporting Journey to *Kilkenny*,
Had Twenty pounds Collected 'ery penny.
Their buildings and their Trading doe encrease,
And we, in both, grow dayly lesse and lesse.
Our houses, wanting Tennants, emptie stand,
Our Plow-men doe neglect to dresse the Land,   50
And those who heretofore could somthing pay,
And helpe to bear the burthen of the day,
Doe now want bread, and have not wher with all,
To feed their hungry Children when they call.
Their povertie is such I greive to tell,
Their household goods th'are forc'd to pawn or sell
To pay their Rates, for fear lest by distresse,
They should be taken, and then sold for lesse.
We often have complayn'd we are opprest,
And have endeavor'd, for to ha'it[19] redrest.   60
Redress we begg before it be too late;
When all is gon, 'tis vain to shut the Gate.
For those that should pay most, doe now pay least,
Just as the Doaling was at Scogans feast.[20]

---

15. Haunce, who is unidentified, had voted in favour of the rate struck; a gallipot = an apothecary, so called after a small pot of the same name used for ointments; stuff . . . to drench Horses = a medicine for horses; side = join (the other) side in a dispute; curry favour = to solicit favour by employing flattery.
16. unidentified. I = aye.
17. This seems to be a reference to some proposal for self-government for Cork and its surroundings, falling short of the restoration of the original charter and corporation. See Barnard, p. 62, for the situation in Youghal during the period of military government.
18. Archimedes (*c.* 297–212 BC), Greek mathematician and inventor. The man referred to here as 'their Archimedes' had, presumably, proposed something from which he would benefit.
19. have it.
20. to dole = to give out in small or niggardly quantities; 'Scogans feast' is a reference to a story in the well-known jest book, *The First and Best Part of Scoggin's Jests*, gathered by Andrew Boorde and first published in 1626.

ANAGRAM[21]
We mai well heal'ir

Heale hir right well, you may and so we trust,
You speedily will doe, for 'tis but just.
Proportion Town and Suburbs, each parts pay,
'Twill end all strife, for which I humbly pray.

WILLIAM WHEELER

CORKS JOPEAN

CORKE, leave thy floating mount[22] upon the Wings
The *Fletcher* is preparing: For he brings   70
The joyfull tidings of a Corporation,
Which will soone raise thee to thy former Station.
Thy CHARTER which so long has bin neglected,
Wants but the *fiat*,[23] shortly 'tis expected.
Choose a Wise Maior, grave Aldermen in Scarlets,
Make Ensignes to be borne in State by Varletts.[24]
Th'art light enough to mount, being meere bereft
Of all thy Trade, and Treasure, Scarce ought's left
But empty ruin'd houses, And a Crew
Of undon People, who these Times doe rue.   80
Yet hope, things may be brought to better order,
By your wise Town-Clarke, and a good Recorder.
Act like your selves, and purchase a *Laudamus*,[25]
Fit to be enter'd, by your Ignoramus.

WILLIAM WHEELER

---

21. In this (imperfect) anagram on William Wheeler's own name, the word 'her' appears as ''ir'.
22. The joke is obscure but may link a number of things: a bottle-cork floats, much of Cork city is on an island in the river Lee, and Cork city was about to receive its charter and arms back after military rule. 'Wings' are the feathers fitted to an arrow by a fletcher – and Fletcher is also a proper name.
23. The authorisation from the government for the issue of the charter by the Dublin court of chancery.
24. ensigns = banners, flags; varlet = 1) an attendant; 2) a rogue.
25. 'let us praise' (Latin). The reference seems to be to a praise poem such as that sung at the mayor's feast in Youghal early in the seventeenth century, as described in Thomas Scot's 'An Irish Banquet or the Mayors Feast of Youghall' earlier in this anthology, see p. 128.

WILLIAM WRIGHT
(*fl.* **1656**)

This witty response to William Wheeler's 'The Complaint', rejects the complaints of the inhabitants of the south suburbs of Cork as unnecessary, and mocks the passions which 'boyle thus in your brest' (line 70). Wright appeals for an end to any ill feeling between the citizens north and south of the river Lee, but also proposes a solution to the problem articulated by the citizens of the south suburb: they should stand for election as 'Raters' in which case they would be in charge of future assessments (line 72). Wright proves himself more than a match for Wheeler in wit with his clever concluding anagram and epigram. Nothing is known of William Wright.

A Preparative to a Pacification betwixt The *South*, and *North*, Suburbs of *Corke*

For Mr William Wheeler[1]

As Neighbours will, (though none doe them desire),
Quench kindling sparks before a House take fire,
So I, I hope, none will me for it blame,
Desire to quell a strife before it flame.
Copernicus, his brain (I think) was giddy,
Who said the Earth whirl'd round and Sun stood steedey,[2]
And *Plato* strange Opinions broacht long since;
'Tis hard to tell, who shall his words convince,
Or see him (gravely) teaching in his Chaire
His Schollers, after forty thousand yeare.   10
If he speak true, then we may thence infer
You then in *Court*[3] may keep a *Register*
Of pleasant sports and mery-trix[4] a many,
Which then (perhaps) may bring in many a penny
To *Friday* Market, where then may be sold
Private Commodities both Young and Old,
And by that means (perhaps) wealth may encrease.[5]
But fret not now, when most mens Trades decrease.

---

1. A point by point response to the previous poem. References clarified there are not repeated here.
2. Conjectural reading: could be 'steede' with the same meaning, 'steady' – a suitably droll rhyme.
3. Probably a reference to the court of d'oyer hundred, a body of assembled freemen.
4. 1) merry tricks; 2) meretrix, prostitute.
5. It is impossible to recover the point of this jibe which is presumably directed at William Wheeler.

You *Southern* men doe with the *North* contest
And say's by them you have bin much oprest.   20
Their over-rating you You doe Complaine,
And therefore you doe *Rate*⁶ at them againe.
Once Water, Wit and Wealth you plenty had,
(If you have lost all those, your case is sad),
Water (I thinke) doth with you still remaine
And keeps its course, you need not much Complaine.
As for your Wit, (you show) 'tis very fine,
And may encrease, if water'd well with *Wine*.
Nor yet have Wealth deserted all that place,
Some on your side doe *Crook*⁵³ it in a pace.   30
The *Northern* men have not engrost your Store;⁸
They keepe their Station, where they were before,
Nor all your Wit and Wealth have shipt to Hull.
Some builds new Houses, and your braines are full
And over-flowes, Jeering the *Borian* side,
And City too, or else you are bely'd.⁹
You need not fear those on the *Northern* strand,
For on your side a mighty Forte doth stand,¹⁰
And if you mean to build, you Lyme and Stone
Have at your Doores: but they (for Lyme) have none.   40
The Citizens you Jeere, and shew no Cause,
Slighting their *Charter*, Rites, and Ancient Lawes,
And then you bid them Choose a Maior that's wise;
If seriously, then you did well advise.
But then you Jeere their *Aldermen* with Scarlets
As making Ensignes, to be borne by *Varlets*.¹¹
You *Robin* busy-body, one man call,
Though he was busy for the good of all;
And some men say in that you were to blame,
And you, your *selfe*, fitter deserv'd that name.   50
You like a *Fencer* (with a Quarter-staff)¹²

---

6. rate = 1) berate, scold; 2) assess rates upon.
7. = 1) haul it in – as a shepherd pulls a sheep to him with his crooked staff; 2) the name of
    a wealthy citizen. A Thomas Crook is listed in Susan Hood (ed.), *Register of the Parish
    of Holy Trinity (Christ Church) Cork 1643–69* (Dublin, 1998), p. 65.
8. i.e. bought up all your store for resale.
9. belied. The meaning is: or else someone has been misrepresenting you.
10. Blackrock Castle, on the south bank of the Lee.
11. See note to lines 75–6 of the previous poem.
12. A fencer uses a light, rapier sword; a quarter-staff is a large, blunt weapon used by rough
    foot soldiers.

Doe lay about you; who can choose but laugh?
You (by comparison) doe bang[13] the *Scots*,
Then, (wheeling), mawl the *Dutch-mans* gally-pots.[14]
You with the *French* had strife, [as some relates
Though in Conjunction[15] (now) in these debates].
Then all the *Towns-men* you call Fools, and say
That twenty pounds they did collect, and pay
To *Archimedes*, who did shew his skill
To serve the Town – you say his purse to fill.   60
You of their mean Estates makes slight accompt,[16]
Bids *Corke* leave Floating, and take Wings and mount.
'Twas well for you that *Corke* did stand so neere,
Else you had not liv'd where you doe to Jeere.
More fit you should (with joy) Congratulate
Their welcome *Charter*, Liberties, and State.
Doubtlesse the difference (in so long a space)
You may descerne, betwixt the *Sword* and *Mace*.[17]
You were by Rates[18] wrong'd (you say), opprest,
Which caus'd your passions boyle thus in your brest.   70
Leave off to fret, and be no more thus vext,
But strive to be a Chosen *Rater*[19] next.
Then (doubtlesse) some will *Rate* at you as fast,
And Coole you with *Boreas* bitter blast.
What is the cause that so near aly'd
Should, o're the Water and the Walls, thus Chide?
Is not *Pythagorus* his Doctrin true?[20]
Are *Fryers-Soules*, crept into Bodies new?
Then that may be the cause of this debate,
For *Augustines*, *Franciscans*, much did hate   80
And the *Franciscans*, though they seemed poore,
Did scorn the *Augustines* as much, or more.
But they are gon, and here their strife doth Cease.
Let us be wise, and follow after Peace.

---

13. attack.
14. See note to line 36 of previous poem.
15. on the same side. The reference is obscure.
16. account.
17. i.e. between rule by military government and that by an elected corporation.
18. A misprint for 'Raters'.
19. One who carries out rates assessment.
20. The main doctrine formulated by Pythagoras was that the soul is immortal and that, at the point of death, it migrates to another living being. The next line asks whether the quarrelsome souls of friars, departed since the Reformation, have crept into the present-day citizens of Cork.

(You know) they both 'gainst us[21] did joyne of late,
Which ought to teach us to leave off debate.
For time to come, you may expect a mends;
I hope the *middle* will Compose[22] both ends,
Acting for Truth, for Peace, and for good Order,
Assisted by their *Town-Clarke* and *Recorder*,   90
And, in due time, may purchase a Laudamus,
Not to be Censur'd by each Ignoramus.

WILLIAM WHEELER his ANAGRAM,
We may well heal'ir

If *William Wheeler* ever hopes to heal her
He gentlier Languadge (I conceive) must deal her.

An ANAGRAM upon my Name, } *WILLIAM WRIGHT*,
An EPYGRAM upon the same. } *Will, Might, War.*

Will, Might, and War great troubles doe encrease,
  Yet Will, Might, War labours this time for Peace.
Will, Might, and War did late this Land infest,
  Now, Will, Might, War desireth Peace and Rest.

WILLIAM WRIGHT

---

21. i.e. against the protestants of Cork. The reference is to the fact that the 'rebel' forces of
    the 1640s had included friars and other catholic clergy.
22. settle the difference between.

FAITHFULL TEATE
(*fl.1658*)

Faithfull Teate was born in County Cavan and educated at Trinity College Dublin. He was ordained into the Church of Ireland and became rector of Ballyhaise, County Cavan. He is said to have suffered considerably during the 1641 rising when, according to the *Dictionary of National Biography*, 'his house was plundered and burnt, his wife and children cruelly treated, three of his children dying of the injuries.' This treatment was meted out to him because, apparently, Teate had passed information to the government on the movement of 'rebels'. He moved to England during the Commonwealth period and was 'preacher of the word at Sudbury in Suffolk' at the time he published his long, meditative poem *Ter Tria: or the Doctrine of the Three Sacred Persons, Father, Son, & Spirit* . . . Teate returned to Dublin after the Restoration.

Although Teate's verse was clearly influenced by the metaphysical poetry of George Herbert (1593–1633), *Ter Tria* is a poem of remarkable originality, freshness and wit. The main part of the work is a long poem on the Trinity which is divided into three sections, one concerning God the Father, one God the Son and one God the Holy Spirit; this is followed by poems on the three principal graces, Faith, Hope and Love, and on the three principal duties, Prayer, Hearing and Meditation. The whole is infused with the imagery and iconography of the Bible, and resonates with echoes of its language.

Ter Tria is, in many ways, a forgotten masterpiece, full of life and energy, reflecting (as well as the faith of its author) an infectious delight in wordplay and in metrical experimentation. Though it must have seemed old-fashioned even when it appeared, the poem was sufficiently popular to have been reprinted in 1669, and a German translation was printed in Leipzig in 1698.

from: *Ter Tria, or The Doctrine of the Three Sacred Persons, Father, Son, & Spirit,*

Principal Graces, Faith, Hope, and Love. Main Duties, Prayer, Hearing, and Meditation. Summarily digested for the pleasure and profit of the Pious and Ingenious Reader

'To the WITS of this AGE, Pretended or Real'
[a dedicatory poem to *Ter Tria*.][1]

You Candidates for Fame, who ne're could gain
The Name of WITS, till you darst be profane,
Nor get the knack on't, till the Witty Devil
Gave you a smartness of a Theme was evil,
Who by elated strains, taught you to raise
Some piece of clay, 'bove him who's above praise,

---

1. These lines, which are by John Chishull, the author of *Theological Treatises* (London, 1657), are prefixed to the second (1669) edition.

And having lost the God head in it's place,
By flattering lines to set some painted face:
Or with ingenious tartness to deride
The Scripture stile, and all that's good beside,   10
Let fall your wanton pens, and blush to see
Your selv's out-done by Sacred Poetry.
Let all wise-hearted savo'ring things Divine,
Come suck this TEAT that yields both Milk and Wine;
Loe depths where Elephants may swim, yet here
The weakest Lamb of Christ wades without fear.
And you, great Souls, who bathe in Contemplation,
Come, here's a prize, Wits worthy Recreation;
Myst'ries as sweet as deep, Pray read and try,
You'l be immerst in pleasure by and by.   20
If words or things will please, here they accord,
Each other their benign aspects afford;
Words fit for Matter, matter fit for Men,
Baxter or *Boyle*[2] may read and read again;
Who weighs the things, will say, TEAT did inherit
The subject of his lines, the Holy Spirit;
He that the Dress, (I mean) his Verse peruses,
Will say, that *Teat's Thrice Three*[3] surely were Muses,
So full of Wit and Grace, 'tis hard to say,
Whether the Head or Heart hath got the day;   30
A Heart so headed and a Head so hearted,
(Blest Concord) pitty they should e're be parted.
I'le wish that TEAT's and HERBERT's may inspire
Randals and *Davenants*[4] with Poetick fire;
May th' *Wits* be *Wise*, and *Faithful*, *Teat*, like thee,
To Consecrate their Pens to thy *Thrice Three*.

2. Chishull is recommending that *Ter Tria* be read by two notable clerical wits and writers of the day, Richard Baxter (1615–91), one of the best-known presbyterian (and later Anglican) divines of the seventeenth century, and Michael Boyle (1609?–1702), chaplain-general to the English army in Munster at the time of this poem and later Archbishop of Armagh.

3. Teate's volume is built around the notion of three times three: *Ter Tria* (which means 'three times three') itself has three parts, and is followed by three poems on the principal graces, and three poems on the main duties of a Christian.

4. i.e. modern poets and dramatists. 'Randall' was Thomas Randolph (1605–35), one of the brightest and most promising writers and wits of his day; the other reference is to Sir William D'Avenant (1606–68), a prolific and successful poet and dramatist who had been appointed poet laureate in 1638.

from: *Ter Tria* section one

FATHER

Thou that begin'st All things, begin my verse:
My words are wind:
Thy words are works;
Thou'lt lightness find
Where darkness lurks:
My Pen and Ink may me, not Thee, rehearse.

My Pen is but a feather's vanity,
Like me that write;
Yet shall this feather,
If thoul't indite,[1]   10
Help me fly thither
Where Angels wings make Pens beyond the sky.

Father, mine Inkes dark hue presents[2] mine heart.
Ink's not more dark,
Ink's not more black;
One beam, one sparke
Supply this lack.
Father of Lights, now shew thy perfect Art.

Lord teach me speak, and I'll not hold my peace,
Which if I should,   20
The stones would come;[3]
Though deaf, yet would
They not be dumb;
Break into praises, stonie heart, for these.

No man hath seen thee, Father, but He who
Did sometime come
(Thy Son it was)
Thy bosome from,
Thy Looking glass;
Hee's the wise Child that doth his Father know.   30

---

1. i.e. enable me to set this poem down in words.
2. i.e. brings my heart into your presence.
3. i.e. come alive and speak.

Who else sings thee, sings what he hath not seen:
                    My Verse hath feet,
                    And fain would run,
                    Thy praise to meet;
                    But lest the Sun
Should hurt weak sight, the Clouds do interveen.

            Then may I in thy Son thy self discover;
                    Sure Hee's the Mirrour
                    That shews thy face:
                    Prevent mine errour;   40
                    Christs flesh like glass
A brighter Glory, but unseen, doth cover.

            Since then I must be silent, or begin
                    To sing th' unseen,
                    Father of Mercies,
                    That set'st the screen,
                    Forgive my Verses;
O thou that vail'st[4] their subject, vail their sin.

            Father's a word my child learns first to mutter,
                    And thy child too,   50
                    Thy new born Babe
                    First thing't can do
                    Is to cry Ab;[5]
But both come last to know what first they utter.

            Thou art the Father of that Son that made
                    That womb on earth
                    That, without Father,
                    Did give him birth;
                    And might the rather
He bee'ng begot where He no Mother had.   60

            Then shall I call thee Father? Lord, thy Son
                    Was call'd no less
                    Before his birth;
                    Prophets confess

---

4. coverest with a veil or screen. vail = veil.
5. = Abba, the name Jesus used when addressing God: 'And he said, Abba, Father, all
things are possible unto thee.' Mark 14. 36.

He had on earth
His children, seed and generation.[6] . . .

. . . Yet thou'rt the Father still: Those sparkling things,[7]
Are Sons of God:
Those winged flames
That fly abroad,   70
(Thou know'st their names)
Made without Bodies, made all face and wings.

Faces they have, and eyes, and tongues, withall[8]
To see and sing:
But O their Grace!
A sixfold wing
To ev'ry face!
Wise, happy, humble, obediential.

Lend's wings, dear Dove;[9] we lag and lose our traffick,[10]
Poor short-leg'd Rhymes,   80
Verses on foot
Reach Seraphims,
They cannot do't,[11]
Lord, now if ever, make my Muse seraphick.

Or if I mayn't have wings, and so keep sight
Of these bright flames,
Shades of thy glory,
Yet tell's[12] their names,
And tell's their story;
And lend's a quil, dear Dove, and I'll go write.   90

Write Angels, Lord, 'tis done:[13] but who are they?
Servants, or sons?

---

6. i.e. the children of God existed before the birth of Christ.
7. i.e. angels.
8. in addition.
9. In Christian iconography, the Holy Spirit is often represented as a dove.
10. communication.
11. i.e. verses on foot (double meaning with metrical 'feet') cannot reach Seraphims (the highest order of the angels). seraphick (line 84) = seraphic, having the attributes of the seraphim.
12. tell us.
13. i.e. a short dialogue. 'Write the word "Angels".' 'Lord, 'tis done.'

Subjects or Kings?
Footstools or Thrones?
Inferiour things
Or Principalities? What shall I say?

Sometimes I hear thee call them Elohim;[14]
Yet they were made:
These plumed[15] things
Are but the shade   100
Of thy bright wings,
Before whose Sun-Shine, all these Stars are dim.

Sometimes't should seem that they but servants are;
Or Ministers
To wait upon
Salvations heirs,
And guard thy Throne:
Yet these stand cover'd where thy sons stand bare.[16]

Servants they are, and yet Dominions:
Each holds his Crown   110
By casting it
Most humbly down
Before thy feet.
Father, thy Throne's erected on the Thrones.

Thousands of thousands of the finite Gods
On ev'ry side,
I mean the Cherubs,
When thou dost ride,
Some serve for stirrups,
And some thou holdest in thy hands for rods.   120

Arch-Angels, Angels that six-winged Nation[17]
Stand trembling, Lord,
Prest to obey
Their Makers word;

14. One of the Hebrew names of God, or 'the gods'.
15. i.e. with wings.
16. i.e. yet these stand with their wings covering their heads while your sons stand bare-headed.
17. Angels were sometimes portrayed as having six wings.

And glad they may
By all their running but maintain their station.

These can't forget that early Funeral;[18]
These can't forget
Those morning Stars
That rose and set,   130
Whose inbred wars
Blew up themselves. But —— oh their fall!

Yet thou'rt the Father still: these Absoloms[19]
Their beeings had
And beauties, Lord,
But not their trade
Nor Traiters Sword
From Thee, from whom all good, and only comes.[20]

How came these then to fall? 't should seem that under
Their Angels wings   140
Each laid some evil
(Oh wretched things!)
And hatch't a Devil.
And so by sinning sing'd their wings. What wonder?

Thy fine white linnen, Lord, sin burnt to tinder.[21]
Satans thy creature,
But now doth want
First form and feature,
Oh miscreant!
Thou mad'st him bright, but sin turn'd all to sinder.[22]   150

Yet thou'rt the Father still; those Stars in view,
Lanterns hung out
In all men[s] sight
Thy Court about,
Those various lights
Father of Lights there dwelling, clearly shew.

---

18. A reference to the fall of Satan and the angels; see II Peter 2. 4; Jude 6; Revelations 20.
 1–2; and Isaiah 14. 12–15.
19. Absalom rebelled against his father, King David. II Samuel 14–18.
20. i.e. and only good comes – with the implication that God is the source of all good.
21. Tinder to catch a spark, and so make fire, was formerly made of partially charred linen.
22. cinder.

That golden Globe comes trundling from thine hand:
        Father, thou saist,
        Thou Sun of mine
        Run East and West   160
        Cease not to shine
Rounding my Bowling-green of Sea and Land.

That burnisht silver Ball's hurl'd forth by Thee:
        That Moon of thine
        That always ranges,
        Doth sit and shine,
        In constant changes,
Says plainly, He that changeth not made me.

The Pleiades,[23] cluster of six, call'd seven,
        The Signs twice six,   170
        The Errant Train,
        The Stars that fix
        The Northern Wain
And all the Constellations of the Heaven:

The great Orion with those bands of his:
        Stars Great and Least:
        The Milkie way,
        With All the Rest,
        Doth plainly say
That He whose breasts drop Lights their Father is.   180

Th' Archt Expanse, whose props who can descry?[24]
        That surging Roof,
        And Saphire cieling[25]
        Yeelds ample proof,
        To all mens feeling
It had its rise from Thee, O thou most high!

23. The Pleiades is a group of small stars in the constellation Taurus, commonly spoken of as containing seven stars, though only six are visible to the naked eye. Other references in this stanza and the following one are to stars, constellations and the signs of the zodiac. 'The Northern Wain' (line 173) refers to the seven bright stars in the constellation known as the Great Bear, often called 'Charles's Wain'.
24. catch sight of.
25. The references to the Ptolemaic universe.

Those stately Offices all on a row,[26]
Standing about
Thy spangled Court,
And yet without   190
For greater Port;
Thee Father of Heav'ns Family do show.

There stands thy minting house, thy Bulloign[27] brought
From 'ts place of birth;
Vapours, I mean,
From drossie earth
Are there made cleane:
And, as thou pleasest cast and coyn'd & wrought.

There stands thy Treasurie, that doth contain
Gems in great store   200
Of orient hue:
Who can count o're
Thy Pearls of dew?
Thy golden Lightnings? or thy silver Rain?

There stands thy Wardrobe. Lord, the purple shrouds
Which thou dost use,
And dapled skie,
Like Ermins, shews
Thy Majesty.
And when thou wilt thou wear'st the gold-fring'd clouds.   210

There stands thy stable-room. Sometimes thy mind's
To ride abroad;
That men below,
There is a God
Above may know,
Hearing the neighings of thy prancing winds.

There's thy distillatorie. Thence thou dost
Heav'ns drops distill
In such great store
Earth drinks its fill   220

---

26. This seems to be a reference to the planets which stand about God's spangled court but
stay outside it, so that they make a more impressive 'port' or train of attendants.
27. bullion. The stanza refers to the mist and fog.

Till 't need no more.
Then the cold ashes are cast forth in Frost.

There stands thy great Confectionary. There
Those heaps of Snow
Double-refin'd
Do clearly show,
And bring to mind
That they belong to th' Great Confectioner.

'Tis he that makes those Frost works. He that makes
Moist Drops, when cast   230
In's comfit mold[28]
Hail stones at last,
When they grow cold,
'Tis He that candies all the Icie flakes.

There stands thy Magazine.[29] Thou dost erect
Thy flaming forges,
And there prepare
Thy shafts and scourges,
Weapons of War
Which, when thou wilt, thy rebel foes correct.[30]   240

Storms, tempests, thunders, thunder-bolts, with these
Great and small shot,
Brimstone and fire,
Father, what not?
If thou require,
Dart thence to chastise those that thee displease.

Whole Egypt from thy storm of Hailshot runs.
His Heathen-Head,
That Royal slave,
Slunk under bed   250
When th' Heavens gave
But one round volley from thy greater guns.[31]

28. A mould for shaping sweets or sweetmeats.
29. A place for storing ammunition and artillery.
30. i.e. they correct those who rebel against you.
31. One of the plagues which Moses caused to smite the land of Egypt was a terrible hailstorm (Exodus 9. 23–5); Pharaoh sent for Moses and Aaron and entreated them to tell the Lord to send no more hail.

Thou'rt the Rains, Father. Frost thou'st gendred?[32]
What Prose or Verse
Can better shew
Thy tender Mercies
Than melting Dew?
This shews thine Heart, and hoary frost thine Head.

Th' Ancient of Days begat me, says the Snow.
The Lord of Hoasts   260
's my Fathers Name,
The Thunder boasts,
And Lightnings flame:
I carry Fathers Colours, says the Bow.

So thou'rt Father still: Lord, 'tis alledg'd
By th' feathered Hoasts,
That here and there
Th' Aerial Coasts
And Quarters bear,[33]
Under thy Wings they were both hatch'd and fledg'd.   270

That Bird of Paradise, Lord, thou must owe it.[34]
With chattering cryes,
Swallows and Cranes
Plead th' Only wise
Did hatch our Brains,
And He that made our season, made us know it.

'Twas God All-seeing made my piercing Eye,
Doth the Eagle say.
To th' God of Love
Our broods we lay,   280
Saith Stork and Dove:
If these be ours, sure we're thy progenie.

With early visits and salutes from Earth,
Up the Lark climbs,
As if it meant,
With Seraphims

32. engendered, created.
33. i.e. that sustain themselves [i.e. fly] here and there about the borders and other parts of
the air.
34. i.e. you must acknowledge that you made the bird of paradise.

Of high descent
By vieing notes and wings, prove equal birth.

The plumed Ostriches forget their young;
But thou their Father   290
With careful hand
Their Eggs dost gather
Laid in the sand,
Hatching to life, and hiding them from wrong.

The goodly Peacock with his Argus train,[35]
His Angel plumes,
His well-set border,
Strongly presumes[36]
To th' God of Order,
Unto whose pomp this splendour doth retain.[37]   300

The tumbling Deeps where all the waters gather
Roundly declare
That Name of his
Whose Counsels are
The Great Abyss;
Seas swell too big to own a meaner Father.

Surely the Ocean's thine, Lord is it not?
Thou bid'st it boyle,
But not boyle o're;
And't does recoile   310
Within the shore,
Thou dost both furnish, Lord, and salt the Pot . . .

. . . Under the covert of those raging Seas
Those armed Bands[38]
(Each joynted scale
Like Armour stands,
Or Coats of Male)
March here and there securely as they please.

35. The patterns on a peacock's tail or train resemble eyes and were sometimes likened to
    the eyes of Argus, a jealous husband who, in classical mythology, is said to have had one
    hundred eyes with which to watch his wife.
36. presupposes.
37. belong.
38. i.e. of fish.

Leviathan that moving Mount or Fort,
Who can deride   320
Storms battering,
Of Sons of pride
Thou call'st him King;
There tumbles he to make his Maker sport.

So thou'rt Father still. Ev'n Earth can cry
From Cliffs and Mountains,
Hills high and steep;
Springs, Mines, and Fountains
That run so deep,
How deep's thy wisdom, Lord? thy pow'r how high? . . .   330

This spacious House[39] thus built and furnisht so;
Come let's convey
Our Image just,
Did th' Father say,
To breathing dust:
Leaving our likeness to keep House below.[40]

Then was clay stamp'd, by Act of Parliament,[41]
With God's bright face:
A Creature Crown'd
With Life and Grace: 340
Heav'n born, Heav'n bound,
Of upright aspect, of Divine descent.

Father, thy footsteps we may find and gather
All other where,
But in this creature
Thy face shines clear,
Witness his feature;
Who reads mans face may quickly spell his Father.

Said I, one may? my God, I should have said
One might have done: 350

---

39. i.e. the world. This passage comes at the conclusion of descriptions of the natural world.
40. i.e. leaving man (who is made in the image of God) to look after the world.
41. i.e. by God, the supreme authority – since parliament was the supreme authority in England and Ireland when Teate wrote this poem. 'stamped' because the ruler's face was normally stamped on a coin.

But things fall cross:[42]
Flesh turns to stone,
Pure Gold to dross,
Silver degenerates to dirt and lead.

Said I, there is? I should have said there was:
My God! there was
Thy countenance
So in his face
That every glance
The shining Sun in brightness did surpass.   360

Father, this walking, talking Plant was Hee
Whom thou didst love
Whom thou didst prize
All Plants above.
Thy Paradise
Thou soon didst quit when thou hadst lost this Tree.[43]

From th' side whereof a female plant did spring,
A splendid pair?
Now as th' Earth begins
T'outshine the Air,   370
Where Heavens bright twins
(The Sun and Moon) their Light, as tribute, bring.

Woman to man's a gift of Gods own giving,
(That man alone
No more might be;
Yet as much one,
And one with thee)
A gift endorsed with Donors Name, the living.

This Royal consort to compleat mans joy,
Thou God of Union   380
Didst well provide
For chaste Communion
As his dear Bride,
Whom thou has crownd on Earth as thy Viceroy.

42. fall away from perfection.
43. This Tree = Adam. These lines mean that God himself left paradise once Adam had sinned.

So th' little world, with greatest work and skill,
    Was fram'd at last,
        And being the best
        Its grace was past
    To rule the rest.
Nothing's forbidden but its knowing ill . . .   390

from: *Ter Tria* section two

SON[1]

When Christ was gone, say they, we might have guest[2]
        What light 'twas brought
            So bright a day
    To darkest Scriptures; might have thought
        The *risen Sun* was in our way
Finding our hearts so *burn* within our breast.
    Then they return back to *Jerusalem*
        Brimfull of joy
            To feast
            The rest;[3]   10
        But they are coy
Till Christ himself stands in the midst of them.

    And 'tis so still. Whoever'd sent about
        To tell thy story,
            Hardness of hearts
    And unbelief blinds all thy glory:
        Lord, who believes? Lord, who converts?
    Till thy dear presence puts all out of doubt.
Their doors bee'ng shut, and hearts much more, that even
        My Lord to put   20
            All out
            Of doubt;
        (None else can do't)
This newes imparts in person to th' eleven.

---

1. The second part of *Ter Tria* consists of an extended verse paraphrase of the life of Christ.
The passage which follows comes towards the end of this section of the poem; two
disciples, who have been sharing a meal with an unknown guest at Emmaus, suddenly
perceive that he is the risen Christ. See Luke 24. 13–36.
2. guessed (with a pun on 'guest').
3. i.e. to tell the other disciples. See Luke 24 for the rest of the story told in these stanzas.

Yet oh how hard a thing is this believing?
A sprite appears
As they suppose;
The same that in their storms of fears
Walk't on the Seas when winds arose.
Phant'sies fools bolt,[4] how't hinders truths receiving.   30
Jesus salutes them with a Peace be to you
Once and agen:
'Tis I;
Sirs, why
Distrust you then?
Why do you let such thoughts arise, why do you?

Down doubtings; I'm got up: And ready have
(Sirs come and see
And feel, I pray)
A Tombe, dead unbelief, for thee   40
Dig'd in my side but t'ther day,[5]
And for your doubtings, in each hand, a grave.
If these suffice not, handle, feel my feet
There are two more.[6]
Doubt not,
I've got
All as before:
Rather than miss their faith, their sense he'll meet.

Then for the further feeding of their faith
He calls for food;   50
They give him fish
And Honey-Comb: but, oh! his blood
And body is a sweeter dish.
Then, breathing, take the Holy Ghost, he saith.
Now doth the frost-nipt tree of life recover:
Puts forth again
New springs,
And brings
Fruits that remain,
Spirit and Life, so prove's Deaths Winter's over.   60

4. i.e. fantasy fetters fools, how it stops them from receiving the truth.
5. i.e. I have ready for you to examine (Sirs, come and see and feel, I pray) a tomb dug in my side the other day – may unbelief be dead! . . .
6. i.e. two more wounds (like those described as a tomb and a grave above).

Thomas mean while bee'ng absent from the rest[7]
Freezing from th' fire,
(Like them that miss
Th' assemblies Christ is wont t'inspire
With sweet assurance, joy and bliss)[8]
Can't feed his faith with hear-say of a feast;
He must first hold a Coroners inquest;
Must see Christs ayles,
And must
First thrust   70
I'th' print o'th' nailes
His fingers, e're this faith enter his breast.

His faith must go on stilts, or not at all;
See with the eye,
Feel with the hand,
His faith must in his fingers lye,
His faith must in his feeling stand,
At th' bound from sorry sense he'll catch the ball.
Th' week after, he and they be'ng all together,
With blessed greeting   80
(Increase
of peace)
Christ Crowns their meeting.
Thomas, saith he, come reach thy finger hither.

As men are wont who've Children to be taught,
My Lord was fain
(Though ev'ry letter
In's hands and feet were printed plain)
With's finger teach him spell the better,
The Child to faith by fealing must be brought.   90
My Lord! and my God! (how this sight relieves me!)
Poor *Thomas* cries.
Christ saith:
Thy faith
May thank thine eyes;
Blessed is he who sees not, yet believes me.

---

7. For the story of doubting Thomas, see John 20. 24–9.
8. i.e. like those who do not come to church.

Disciples after this, a fishing go;[9]
But nothing's caught,
Throughout the night;
Till Jesus comes, and brings a draught;   100
Lord shew me so which side's the right,
When to catch souls thy Gospel net I throw.
Christ look't into their cup-board just before;
Children, have ye
Got meate
To eate?
Else come to me;
I've food and firing[10] for you on the shore.

Hence sinfull cares, infest my soul no longer,
Base diffidence;   110
Doubtings retreat;
Soul, mind thy Saviours providence;
Do thine own work, and he'll find meat,
Or give thee something's better if thou hunger.
Dinner bee'ng done, Christ speaks of working then;
And so should we;
Our whet[11]
Not let
Our food should be.
Shepherds[12] Christ feeds, to feed his sheep agen.   120

Shepherds who love to eat but not to seed
Are what they're not,
Not what they are;
(A Paradox, and Gordian knot,[13]
Which Christ will cut, and will not spare)
Shepheards in name, but rav'ning wolves indeed.[14]
Peter, dost love me more than these?[15] I'll prove thee.

9. See John 21. 1–14.
10. firewood.
11. whet = an appetiser or small drink. The line seems to mean: We should not let our whet be our food.
12. clergymen, ministers – like Teate himself. The line means: Christ provides spiritual food for his ministers so that they may pass the nourishment on to his sheep.
13. something of great difficulty. Gordius, a peasant chosen to be a king, tied his wagon to a beam with a knot so ingenious that no one could untie it. Alexander the Great, however, cut it with his sword.
14. cf. Milton's *Lycidas* lines 112–29.
15. For this story, see John 21. 15–18. prove = test.

Then feed and keep
My flock;
My stock   130
Of Lambs and Sheep.
All knowing Lord, saith he, thou know'st I love thee.

Peter, when thou wast young, then thou wast free
To come and go
As thou'dst a mind,
Girding thy self: 't shall not be so
When thou art old, others shall bind,
And gird, and carry thee. Man! follow me.
Peter replies, and what must this man do?[16]
What's that to thee?   140
Follow
Me thou.
How busie wee
Are to mind others works, our own not so . . .

Mean while Christ summons others from the dead
To evidence
His Resurrection:
From types, from texts, from faith, from sense,
Of proofs how full, how fair collection.
Shew'ng Christ is Risen as the Churches head.   150
Now, O devourer![17] where's thy victory?
Out of the grave
That old
Strong hold
And eating Cave
Comes meat and sweetness; which who tast[e]s can't die.

Ev'n Christ comes thence. And now in *Olivet*
Where he laid down
In part of pay
For th' purchase of his new bought crown,   160
His bloody sweat, ev'n there this day
To see's Inthronization, Saints are met:[18]

16. i.e. what must I do?
17. The poet is addressing death.
18. For the story of Christ's ascension from the mount of Olivet, see Acts 1. 4–12.

Wilt thou restore the kingdome, Lord, they cry,
To Isr'el yet?
For you
To know
Times is not fit:
I'll send my spirit! That's my Lord's reply.

O what an eager foolish thing is man!
Busie to know   170
What least concerns him!
But to take forth, alas! how slow
The lessons that my God would learn him.[19]
A sieve that lets go th' flower,[20] but holds the bran.
Melchisedeck[21] mean time, our Priest for ever,
With lift up hands
On his
All bliss
And grace commands;
Whom clouds receiving from their sight do sever . . .   180

from: Hope[1]

Drive on, my Muse, till thou'rt got through;
Let not Hope find thee in a slough;
Let that that drives the Farmers plough,
    Drive thine much more.
To th' Hope of *Isr'el* let me yet
In hope my running rhyme commit,
And humbly say, God prosper it;
    Or 'twill be poor.

Hope is a door, the Scripture saith:
And so is Christ, and so is Faith;   10
Who're out of these doors are in wrath
    And Condemnation.

---

19. i.e. but how slow, alas, to receive the lessons that my God would teach him.
20. flour.
21. A priest who served Abraham in the Old Testament, Melchizedek was revered as the archetypal priest-king; here he seems almost identified with the ascending Christ.

---

1. This is the second of three poems on the principal graces which follow *Ter Tria*.

Faith into Christ doth first advent're;
Christ into Hope allows me enter:
Hope makes my very Soul to center
   On Gods Salvation.

Hope is Faiths expectation;
Faith is the *Moses*, Hope's the stone
That Faith in Pray'r doth rest upon
   Till't overcome.   20
Faith doth upon Hopes tip toe stand
Stretching its neck to look for land
Beyond deaths gulf, and life beyond
   The day of doom.

Hope is next door to Heav'ns gate:
'Tis but a step from this to that;
Nay Hope doth Heaven antedate,
   And bring down hither.
Hope's th' antidote against despair;
Coffin of fear; and Couch of care;   30
Cradle of patience; Hope hath fair[2]
   Even in foul weather.

Hope is the mourner's Handkerchief;
Hope is the Balme of ev'ry grief.
Hope doth endorse the beggars brief[3]
   Ere it's collected.
In Hope I have, what yet I want:
Hope makes me full, while things are scant;
Hope doth consummate, what I can't
   Yet see effected.   40

Hope hath an harvest in the Spring;
In winter doth of Summer sing;
Feeds on the fruits whilst blossoming,
   Yet nips no bloom.
Hope brings me home when I'm abroad,
As soon as th' first step homeward's trod;
In Hope to thee, my God! my God!
   I come, I come.

2. is likely to succeed.
3. confirms the validity of the beggar's case.

Hope sends the Ship to Sea, and then
E're it returns, brings't home agen;
The port of all Seafaring men
    Is this *Good Hope*.
I am a Sea-man too. My Soul,
Though toss'd with doubts when weather's foul,
Doth like some Sea-sick Vessell roul;
    Yet Heav'n's its scope.[4]

Hope doth the Souldiers weapon wield;
By Hope the Souldiers Helmet's steel'd;
Hope gives him, e're he fights, the field;
    Hope holds his station.[5]
I am a Souldier too. My Sword,
Is that o'th' Spirit, th' two-edged word;
Now for an Helmet, give me, Lord,
    Th' hope of Salvation.

Hope lets the poor Apprentice free
First day he's bound. And why not me?
Thou hast Indentures[6] Lord by thee
    Wherein I'm tied.
Mount *Sinai*'s Covenants they bee;
Yet hope doth, Lord, Enfranchize mee
In *Sion*-hill, where all are free
    That do reside.

In hope the School-Boy doth commence
Master of Art, and fair science;
Yea, whilst i'th' lowest form, steps thence
    To th' Doctors Chair.
I'm a School Schollar too, my God!
But yesterday I felt thy rod;
Yet still with hope am girt and shod.
    Away, despair.

'Tis hope that doth the sower feed;
Who seems to cast away his seed,

50

60

70

80

4. purpose, object.
5. i.e. helps him stay in his position.
6. The contract by which an apprentice is bound to his master.

But doth preserve in very deed
 And mend his store.
I am a Seeds man too, my Lord!
And but for Hope thou would'st affoard
Thy blessing, when I sow thy word,
 I had forbore.[7]

I am a Seeds man; every teare
I sow in Hope, 'twill bring an eare   90
Fit for thy floor in time of yeare
 For thee to gather:
Were't not for Hope the heart, some say,
Would break; yet Hope led me one day
Weeping along the Milky way
 To thee, O Father!

I am a Seeds man casting bread
On th' waters[8] where it seems lye dead;
Yet Hope assures me't shall be fed,
 And then restored.   100
Hope doth the pris'ners bolts unlock:
His fetters doth in sunder knock:
Hope drives the Freeman's trade and stock.
 My dearest Lord!

I am a captive too. Sins chain
Doth hold and hamper, but in vain:
By Hope I'm saved, and set again
 At liberty.
I am a Tradesman too. Thou art
That God with whom I deal. My heart   110
Takes Heav'n to be the only Mart
 Thither trade I;

Exporting groans and broken pray'rs
That scarse can clamber up the stairs.
Importing rich and precious wares,
 Ev'n joy and peace.

7. not have done it.
8. Cast thy bread upon the waters: for thou shalt find it after many days. Ecclesiastes 11. 1.

Joy that exceeds all understanding,
O'th' Spirits sealing, Christ's own handing:
Peace that is of Gods commanding,
    And can't surcease.[9]   120

Hope makes the labourer to run
A race as 'twere with each dayes Sun
Paying his wages ere's work be done,
    And mine much more.
I daily dig and delve within
Stubbing at th' roots and stumps of sin,
And but for Hope one day to win
    I should give ore.

O come that long'd for day! come quickly!
This Hope defer'd makes my heart sickly.   130
Grace is a Rose, but sin is prickly
    And still adheres.
Amphibion like the Diver tries,
Whet sharp with Hope, t'anatomize
And geld the deeps:[10] his hop'd for prize[11]
    Forbids his fears.

I am a Diver too. Thy word
Doth richer rarities affoard:
A greater deep, and better stor'd
    With Pearls and Treasure;   140
Angels desire to dive into
These deeps; and so I daily do,
Whose Pearls are rich and Cordial too;
    Health, Wealth, and Pleasure.

'Tis Hope that makes the racer fleet,[12]
Bringing the wager to his feet.
Make haste, saith Hope, what? don't you see't?
    You've won, you've won.

9. come to an end.
10. Amphibion seems to be an invented name for a pearl diver. Seventeenth-century travellers' tales contained accounts of the feats of Sicilian and Greek pearl divers who were able to stay under water for so long that they seemed almost amphibious. whet = sharpened; anatomize = investigate closely; geld = take the value from.
11. i.e. pearls.
12. fast.

I am a racer too. My race
From sin to Glory is by Grace;   150
Hope sets Heav'ns Bliss before my face,
    And then I run.

I heard the witty world once say
The bird i'th' bush may fly away:
Take Heav'n who will, 'tis present pay
    For which we trade.
To Faith and Hope I told this story;
Their havings are but transitory,
Said Faith; said Hope, and I have Glory
    That cannot fade[13] . . .   160

---

13. i.e. 'Their havings (possessions) are but transitory,' said Faith; said Hope, 'And I have
    Glory that cannot fade.'

JOHN PERROT
(*fl*.**1659**–1671?)

There is some confusion about the origins of John Perrot, one of the best known of early Irish Quakers. It has been asserted (without hard evidence) that he was the son or grandson of Sir John Perrot, lord deputy of Ireland, who was, himself, probably a natural son of Henry VIII; but it is also claimed that he was a blacksmith from the north of England.[1] What is certain, however, is that Perrot was a convinced Quaker who is recorded working as a preacher in Limerick in 1655, and that he had a wife and children in Waterford.

Perrot was a colourful and eccentric figure whose many pamphlets show him to have been, for substantial periods of his life, unbalanced. As an active Quaker, he suffered many periods of imprisonment, in Kilkenny, Waterford, Limerick and Dublin in the mid-1650s, in England and on the Continent later. In 1656, Perrot set out on a mission to Rome to convert the Pope to Quakerism, as a result of which he was questioned by the Inquisition and imprisoned in 'The Rome-prison of Mad-men' for a period. He also spent time in the leper colony in Venice. Eventually Perrot was released and returned to England, from where he emigrated to the New World as a Quaker missionary to Barbados, Maryland and Virginia. He developed his own brand of Quakerism and was expelled by the main movement, which was at this time led by George Fox. He died in poverty in Jamaica in about 1671.

The text which follows comes from one of Perrot's long visionary poems. In this verse, as usual with Perrot, God is speaking to him directly. The poem was written in 1659, when its author was in Rome.

from: A Song for that Assembly[2]

> . . . Standing a little *still*, I heard, as read,
> A *Voice* ascending out of *Deeps* in dread.
> My *Int'rogations* quickly had an *end*,
> The Word *responsive*[3] did me *comprehend*;
> Things *sealed up* in Eternal *Decree*
> From *Ages past*, in great fear *compast me*;
> So dreadful was the *Word*, which oft did *make*
> Me in my motion *stagger*, *reel* and *quake*.
> Thus said the Lord, *Hear*, *Man*, and I'l *demand*,
> Who round the *swelling Seas* hath fixt *dry Land*?   10
> Who's he that maketh ev'ry *Fish's way*?
> And, who doth *bar* the *Night*, and *open Day*?

1. See Kenneth L. Carroll, 'John Perrot: Early Quaker Schismatic', *The Friends Historical Society Journal*, supplement no. 33 (1971). Peter Somerville-Large, *Irish Eccentrics*, second edition, Dublin, 1990) also gives a lively account of Perrot (pp. 56–72).
2. 'that Assembly' is 'The Congregation in the Valley of Megiddon' and the poem takes up seventeen pages of *A Sea of the Seed's Sufferings, Through which Runs a River of Rich Rejoycing . . . Written in the Year 1659, in Rome-Prison of Mad-Men, By the extream Suffering Servant of the Lord, John* (London, 1661).
3. i.e. the word of God, responding to the poet's questions.

Who hath created *Wonders* in the *Deep*?
And who feeds *Worms* which in her bottom *creep*?
Where's *he* who by his *Wisdoms* words or *wishes*,
That's able t'answer me among the *Fishes*?
The *Lempits spaun*,[4] what Man hath seen to *tell*?
And how gain'd she her Cov'ring of *a Shell*?
Who gave *her strength* fast to the *Rock to cleave*,
That no Fish *else* of *life* can her *bereave*?[5]   20
Can Man this *secret* unseal and unlock,
Whether another *substance* than the *Rock*
Doth she *feed on*? let him in *Wisdom* speak,
What *Instrument* hath she *the Rock* to *break*?
Who knows the *Spaun* which *Cockles* & *Musles* shed,
And what's the *substance* wherewith it is *fed*?
Who knows *the time* of their Natures *conception*,
And when's the *moment* brought unto *Perfection*?
Who leads the *Wrinckles*[6] over *Mountains* high
Of *craggy Rocks*, which in the *Oceans* lye?   30
Who built the *House* which she *bears* on her *back*,
Wherein she's hid, as in a *sealed* Sack?
Her *one Scale* opens and shuts; it's her *Door*,
Wherewith she seals *salt moysture* up in *store*,
That when the *Ebb* her Lodge to *Air* doth *give*,
Till *Flood* returns, she hath enough to *live*.[7]
Was it by *Art* of Wise *Princes* or *Kings*,
Or, who gave to the *flying Fish* her *wings*?
Which when pursu'd by other *Fishes* great,
That would her *Life destroy*, and *Body eat*,   40
Therewith in ev'ry *Chase*, *Life* to *defend*,
Doth out of *Natures* Element *ascend*?
Who gave the *Dolphin* her dear *tender Love*,
And made her *swiftest*, which in *Seas* do move?
Who made *two Fishes* Weapons for to *wear*,
Whereby they *swim*, dreadful with *Sword* and *Spear*;
Though being *little*, and in substance *small*,
Yet are a *Terrour* to the mighty *Whale*?

4. the spawn of the limpet.
5. deprive.
6. winkles, periwinkles.
7. i.e. when the retreating tide exposes her shell to the air, she has enough salt moisture (in her shell) to survive until the tide returns.

Who makes the *Oyster* gape with *ardent heat*
In *Summer-time*, as if she wanted *meat*?   50
And whilst yet thus her *shells* stand *open wide*,
Who taught the *Crab-fish* to draw near *her side*,
And with his *claw* a *Stone* therein to *put*,
Whereby to save *her life*, she cannot *shut*,
And thus is made the other *Fishes Bait*,
Which, for the same, takes time to *watch* and *wait*?
Who gave some Fishes *fins*, others *walking leggs*,
And makes some *spaun*, and others to *lay Eggs*?
Who hatches *Tortles Eggs* hid in the *Sand*,
And who sustains their *Life* by Sea and Land?   60
Who of a *Seed* hath made thee *flesh* and *bone*,
And whereof made I every *precious Stone*?
Of what's compos'd *Earth*, *Trees* and ev'ry *Plant*?
And which was *first*, *LIGHT*, or the *ADAMANT*?[8]
Who answers? What, can Man *reveal* to me
The *substance* whereof I compos'd the *Bee*?
Who knows his *Art* which makes the *Honey-comb*?
And, who made *Man* before a *Woman's Womb*?
What's the *Infusion*, who can it *resemble*,
Which at the *Cock's-Crow* makes the *Lyon tremble*?[9]   70
The same which fills the *Elephant* with *fear*,
When that a *Mouse* before him doth *appear*.
Who taught *Jack-halls*[10] to hunt the *Lyon's prey*,
And *Pilot-fish*, to lead the *Shark* her way?
One knows the *thing*, which to all flesh seems *strange*,
How that *Camelion* her self doth *change*
Into *all Colours*, perfect *White* excepted,
Which by the *Law* for *Man's meat* is rejected.[11]
I bend th' exalted *flames* of *Phœbus* low,[12]
Autumn[13] to usher *Winter's birth* of Snow,   80

8. Adamant is really the mineral corundum; but in the ancient and early modern worlds, the term was used to refer to some hard rock in the earth, perhaps diamond, with almost magical properties; or it might be a lodestone or magnet. Here it seems to mean the universe as a whole.
9. The lion is said to tremble when it hears a cock crow. The question is, what man-made potion or liquid can do this?
10. jackals.
11. The chameleon, a lizard-like creature which can change colour to suit its environment, is defined as 'unclean' and not to be eaten in Leviticus 11.
12. i.e. God also controls the sun and the seasons.
13. i.e. in the autumn.

Her *Travel*,[14] as a *Vest*, on Earth doth spread,
Wherein the Night-steps of *Wild-beasts* are read;
Which though the *girdings*[15] of the *Night* conceals,
Day dawned, printed *Lines* to Man *reveals*.
Though *Lions roar*, and *Wolves* do *howl* and *bark*,
Panther, with them I sent to *Noah's Ark*;
A *golden thrid*[16] I've given with *clear sight*,
To measure the *blind Bats* and *Screech-Owls* flight,
The *Moles* dark paths, a *Laborynth* obscure,
Yet *scrutal*[17] *Worm* doth comprehend it sure . . .   90

. . . Who answers me among the *Fowls of Heaven*,
Which in the *Ark* were *sav'd* by numbers seven?[18]
Since *Noah's* day, who all their encrease *took*,
And *registred* their *Numbers* in a *Book*?
Who *couples* them in *season*, as yoak't *even*?
I'l yet demand of *Man* concerning *seven*.
Who gave the *Wren* her *treble Voice* to sing,
Consorting[19] *Musick* with the *Timbrel*[20] *string*;
And in *much Joy*, sav'd from an *evil chance*,
Makes her *in Summer* in Vine branches *dance*?   100
The *Red-breast's* shril Notes singing on a *Rock*,
Sounds as a *Shepherd piping* to his *Flock*;
Who gave the *love* which she *bears* in her *breast*,
And *Innocency* for a seat of *rest*?
Who makes the *Thrush* in *Spring-time* to rejoyce,
And gifted her with a *loud chanting Voice*?
Who gave the *Hand* her *quavring Keys* to feel,[21]
And *guides* the same, which turns her *Cymbal-wheel*?[22]
Who[23] *Black-birds* whistle, which makes *Woods* to ring?
Sweet *Valleys* eccho whilst yet she doth *sing*,   110

14. travail, i.e. winter's action of giving 'birth' to the snow. The word also means the action of travelling.
15. the girdling. The line means that the wrapping of the night (i.e. darkness) conceals the movements of wild beasts at night.
16. an (imaginary) thread.
17. an apparently unrecorded word connected with scrutiny; so = scrutinising.
18. Perrot often ponders the significance of the sacred or magic numbers 1, 3 and 7.
19. playing music together.
20. A tambourine-like percussion instrument.
21. meaning uncertain. Perhaps a reference to a (human) hand imitating the bird's song on a keyboard(?)
22. Some kind of a percussion instrument with small cymbals in a circle; or, perhaps, a dulcimer.
23. i.e. who creates the blackbird's whistle?

In *Deserts*; who from under *shadows* mute
Raiseth her *Voice* to sing unto the *Lute*?
Who fills the *Nightingale* with *Harmony*,
Her Tune *transcending* all in *Air* that fly?
Who strain'd her *seven strings* unto perfect *tryal*?
Which makes *the Musick* on her well set *Vyal*;[24]
Who makes the *Lark* ascend with *out-stretcht wing*,
A Song of *Melody* on high *to sing*?
Who hath her *Organ* unto *sweet Notes* bound,
And *blows* the *Bellows* for her *Pipe* to sound?   120
And who hath given unto the *Turtle-Dove*
Her mind of *Chastity* and *pure Love*,
And made her of her *Mate*, so dear a *Lover*,
That chusing *ONE*, she'l never chuse *Another*? . . .

24. viol.

PART IV

1660–1685
The Reign of Charles II

THE CORPORATION OF BELFAST
(1660)

After the removal of Henry Cromwell from the position of lord lieutenant of Ireland in June 1659, a complex power struggle – similar to that in England – developed among the army officers in Ireland. Eventually, those supporting General George Monck (1608–70) emerged as the most influential. Monck, a gifted soldier who knew Ireland well and had served there in the 1640s on the royalist side, had been governor of Ulster during the difficult years 1647–9. After the collapse of the royalists, he had fought with the parliamentarians in England and Scotland and had risen to become commander-in-chief of the army. Following the death of Oliver Cromwell, Monck assumed a pivotal role in England and master-minded the manoeuvres which led to the dissolution of the Rump Parliament and the election of a new one. But he was also in negotiation with the exiled Charles II and it became clear to almost all observers, in Ireland as well as in England and Scotland, that it was just a matter of time before Charles II was restored to the throne, and that George Monck was the man who would bring this about.

Naturally, Irish protestants of all shades wanted to retain what they had gained during the Commonwealth and to be sure that the incoming king, as well as the man he had appointed to be his viceroy in Ireland,[1] knew of their loyalty to the Stuart cause. The corporation of Belfast therefore sent the following loyal poem to Monck some time in the spring of 1660, in the hope that its sentiments would not be forgotten during the next few challenging months. The poem refers specifically to Monck's demands that there should be a newly elected parliament in Westminster, highlights the loyal burghers' dislike of the old Rump Parliament, and unambiguously declares that Belfast was to be counted as a supporter of the incoming king.

Verses Sent to Generall Monck by the Corporation of Belfast

> Advance George Monck, & Monck St. George[2] shall be,
> England's Restorer to Its Liberty,
> Scotland's protector, Ireland's President,[3]
> Reduceing[4] to a ffree Parliament;
> And if thou dost intend the other thinge,
> Goe on, and all shall Crye, God save the Kinge.

> R ⎫   R doth rebellion Represent;
> V[5] ⎬   by V nought els but Villainyes is meant;
> M ⎬   M Murther signifyes, all men doe knowe;
> P ⎭   P Perjuryes in ffashion growe   10

> Thus R and V with M and P
> conjoyn'd make up our miserie.

---

1. In fact, Monck never took up the appointment.
2. St George is the patron saint of England.
3. i.e. lord lieutenant. Monck was formally appointed in June 1660 but replaced, on 25 July, by Lord Robartes.
4. bringing back, restoring.
5. The letters U and V were interchangeable in anagrams.

WILLIAM FULLER
(1608–**1661**–1675)

William Fuller was born in London, educated at Oxford and ordained into the Church of England. On the restoration, he was appointed dean of St Patrick's, Dublin, and it was in this capacity that he wrote the words of the following anthem. Fuller later became Bishop of Limerick, Ardfert and Aghadoe before being translated to Lincoln in 1667.

The occasion for which the anthem was written was the grandest ever seen in the Church of Ireland. To mark the triumphant restoration of the Church of Ireland to its position as the established church – after the troubles of the 1640s when catholicism had almost supplanted it and of the 1650s when it had almost been destroyed by presbyterianism – twelve bishops were consecrated in a single ceremony in St Patrick's Cathedral, Dublin, on 27 January 1661.

The ceremony caused a considerable stir; grand processions of the lords justices, the mayor and corporation 'in their scarlet robes', the 'General Convention' (a parliamentary assembly called shortly beforehand) led by their speaker, and large numbers of ecclesiastical and academic dignitaries – including the twelve bishops-to-be – passed through the streets of Dublin watched, reportedly, by an enormous crowd. The cathedral itself rang with the sounds of choirs, organs and bells. The whole event was described in detail in a newspaper called *The Kingdom's Intelligence* and in a pamphlet written by Dudley Loftus, at this time pro-vice-chancellor of the University of Dublin;[1] the anthem was sung just after the twelve bishops – including two archbishops – had been consecrated.

An antheme sung at the Consecration of the Arch bishops and Bishops of Ireland, on Sunday the 27 of January 1660[2] at St Patrick's in Dublin.

Treble	Now that the Lord hath re-advanc'd the Crown;
	Which Thirst of spoyle, and frantick zeal threw down:
Tenor	Now that the Lord the Miter has restor'd
	Which, with the Crown, lay in the dust abhorr'd:
Treble	Prayse him ye Kings,
Tenor	Prayse him ye Priests,
Chorus	Glory to Christ our High Priest, Highest King.

---

1. *The Proceedings Observed in order to, and in the Consecration of the Twelve Bishops, in St. Patrick's-church in Dublin* . . . (London, 1661). There is also a full description of the ceremony in William Monck Mason, *The History and Antiquities of the Collegiate and Cathedral Church of St. Patrick near Dublin* (Dublin, 1819), pp. 192–4.
2. Until 1752, the first day of the new year in England and Ireland was Lady Day, 25 March; thus the consecration service which contemporaries dated 27 January 1660 took place on what we call 27 January 1661. For a succinct explanation of the problems of dating documents from seventeenth-century Ireland, see *A New History of Ireland: Early Modern Period* (Oxford, 1976), p. xxxviii.

Treble	May Judah's Royal Scepter still shine clear![3]
Tenor	May Aaron's Holy Rod still Blossoms bear![4]
Treble & Tenor	Sceptre and Rod, Rule still and Guide our Land! 10
	And These whom God Anoints, feel no Rude Hand;
	May Love, Peace, Plenty, wait on Throne and Chair,[5]
	And may Both share in Blessings, as in Care.
Chorus	Angels look down, and Joy to see
	Like that above, a Monarchie.
	Angels look down, and Joy to see
	Like that above, an Hierarchie.

---

3. Judah, son of Jacob, was considered one of the fathers of the Jewish race and his name was often used to represent all Jews. When Jacob blessed Judah (Genesis 49. 8–12), he included the phrase: 'The sceptre shall not depart from Judah' (verse 12). Judah's name here represents the civil power.
4. During the troubles of the children of Israel in the wilderness, God told Moses to collect a rod from each of the twelve tribes of Israel. The rods were placed on the tabernacle and God promised he would show his favour to one tribe by causing its rod to bud and blossom. The rod which budded was that belonging to Aaron (Numbers 17). Since Aaron was a priest, his name represents ecclesiastical power.
5. i.e. the throne of the king and the chair of the bishop.

ANONYMOUS
(1662)

Though anonymous panegyric poems seldom rise above the predictably banal and often sink below the readable, they are sometimes useful indicators of cultural or social change. The appointment in February 1662 of James Butler, first Duke of Ormond, as lord lieutenant of Ireland ushered in a period of considerable cultural and social change in Dublin and throughout the island. Ormond was the premier nobleman of Ireland, cultured, wealthy and an experienced leader. He had been Charles I's lord lieutenant in the 1640s, and had come out of those turbulent times less hated and mistrusted than most men. He was an impeccable royalist and could be expected – provided his unpredictable royal master did not interfere with his plans – to bring to a ravaged island, and its capital, some order, some decency and some calm. He had spent the years of exile in France, close to Charles II, and while abroad he had learned, as Maurice Craig puts it, the importance of 'the centralised state and the ceremonial capital'.[1] Much was expected of Ormond and the following poem, though it does exhibit some of the typical leadenness of Restoration panegyric, gives an insight into what many people in Ireland must have felt when they heard of the appointment.

from: To his Grace James Duke of Ormond Lord Lieutenant of Ireland &c. upon his returne to this Kingdom and Government

> Now have our Seas resign'd unto the shore
> The welcom'st burthen they e'er hither bore.
> Tho' English monarchs have this voyage made,
> You come to rule where they came to invade.
> Your presence makes this long afflicted Isle
> See fortune once againe upon her smile,
> And feel the dawning of a better day
> Reviveing warmth through all her parts display . . .
>
> . . . Tho God first made ye Chaos, his cheif prayse
> Is what he did from thence – this order rayse.   10
> You find a Chaos here, but yet 'tis true
> The best work of Creation's left to you.
> The beauties of your person and your minde
> Assure us what wee in your worke shall finde.
> Your even temper just proportions shew
> In all affaires, your judgement will be soe . . .

---

1. Maurice Craig, *Dublin 1660–1860*, second ed. (Dublin, 1980), p. 4.

... Disloyal ways which ev'en Crownes did not spare
Nor that most sacred Head that did them wear,
Pursues your life wth such unwearyed hate
As seemed to sett it at an equall rate.[2]   20
Nor is the reason of that hate unknowne,
You're one of the best jewels of the Crowne;
Priz'd by your Prince, and worne more neer his Heart
Than is his George, thô pendant next that part.[3]

When Charles was Exile, of all [that] with him stood
The greatest name was Ormond, next the Blood;[4]
You followed all his steps with equall pace
And trod the windings of that dissy[5] maze.
Second in all his sufferings, you durst,
When danger did approach, be still the first.   30
A faith so tryed, most justly thus is grace't:
His second Crowne[6] is on your temples place't.
Their second Love the people pay to you
(The first they know to Majesty is due);
The Prince's favor and the peoples Love
At once your merit both reward and prove.

Amphions harpe made stones from ye rude heap
Into the beauty of faire Cittys leap:[7]
Orpheus made woods and rocks and beasts of prey
Forgett their wildnesse, and his voyce obey.[8]   40
Such miracles as these old poets feigne
To grace the Golden age of Saturnes reigne,
But whilst they truely are performed by you,
Our age more happy is, and glorious too.

Within our streets new buildings rise each day
And if wee aske the cause, 'tis you, they say;

2. A reference to the fact that Ormond had been pursued by the forces of the parliament.
3. From the collar of the Order of the Garter, of which order the sovereign is always the chief member, hangs 'The George', a gold medallion depicting St George encountering the dragon.
4. i.e. next to those of royal blood.
5. dizzy, confusing.
6. i.e. the position of the king's deputy in Ireland.
7. Amphion was a figure in Greek mythology who was said to have played the lyre so exquisitely that stones moved and built themselves into the walls of the city of Thebes.
8. Orpheus, son of Apollo, charmed all nature with the beauty of his playing on the lyre.

As if, like flowers, they started from their seat
At your approach, as at the vernall[9] heat.

Our woods and mountains, civilized by you,
What charmes are in your power will quickly shew.   50
Giveing Prosperity was Orpheus arte,
That made thick woods to open order parte,
That trimd the feilds, and from the rocky denn
Drew forth both beasts, and much more beastly men,
That Gardens drest, and Palaces did rayse,
And shall for you build Pyramids of prayse.

Of all our wishes, we have now the summe:
Great Ormond to the Government is come;
The single Items hee'll each day bestow,
And as our wants soe will his bounties grow;   60
For of supplies, 'tis He has all the springs,
The best Lieutenant to the best of kings.

9. vernal, of the spring.

ANONYMOUS
(*c*.**1663**)

One of the biggest difficulties facing the Duke of Ormond and the Restoration government in Ireland was land distribution. However the problem was viewed, there were far more claimants than there was land to satisfy them. The confederate catholics, who had never wavered in their loyalty to the king, had expected the restoration of the king to bring with it the restoration of their land. But there were also protestant army officers who had served the Commonwealth in Ireland and who had supported General Monck in calling for the restoration of the monarchy: these men, naturally enough, were equally determined to retain the lands they now possessed. A royal declaration on the matter was followed by the 1662 Act of Settlement which was interpreted by a 'court of claims' which allowed more catholics to regain land than many protestants thought was fair. The next legislation, the Act of Explanation of 1665, gave further hope to still dispossessed catholics that they would get some of their land back since it required protestant soldiers and adventurers to surrender one-third of theirs for redistribution.

The following poem in the Ormond papers dates from some time in the 1660s – probably from 1663 when the first court of claims was sitting – and reflects the optimism of a catholic claimant who had supported the royalist side in the 1640s.[1] He was probably less happy a few months after penning this vituperative little piece.

On the Act of Settlement

Stand, passers by, here's good newes come to towne,
The '48 are up, the '49 are downe.[2]
The floods are ceased; loe there appear the sands.
We've gott the jack, and nowe bowle for our lands.
Rubb and a good Cast is the gamster's creed;[3]
You'le say he winnes that winnes at Last indeed.
Behould the ffloods are ebd, our Land appears,
And Catholickes defy the Presbyters.[4]
They were the blades[5] that first did put theyr hands
Not on our Swords, but blood,[6] and next our lands.   10

---

1. A useful guide to the complicated subject of the Restoration land settlement in Ireland is L. J. Arnold, *The Restoration Land Settlement in County Dublin, 1660–1688* (Dublin, 1993).
2. Arnold's definition of 'forty-nine officers' (as the term was understood after the Restoration) is 'those Protestant officers who, having served the Royalist cause in Ireland until 5 June 1649, subsequently received no satisfaction for the arrears under the Cromwellian settlement'.
3. The image is from the game of bowls: a 'jack' is the small bowl at which the larger bowls are aimed: a 'rub' is an impediment which hinders or diverts a bowl from its proper course, and a 'cast' is the action of bowling the ball.
4. presbyterians, covenanters.
5. fellows – but with the echo of the other meaning of swords.
6. families.

But it hath pleased St Patrick and the fates
To gett our lands; Let them did own Estates[7]
Turne out your Pedlars[8] and your new upstarters
That sells your pinnes and inckles[9] without Charters.
Goe gett you packing, see that you make no stopp;
Take down yr signs lest we hang some what[10] upp;
And if the English doggs beginn to barke,
Weele stop theyr mouthes and arslickes without Corke.

7. Conjectural reading: unclear in manuscript.
8. The editors of the Historical Manuscripts Commission report on the Ormond manuscripts (*HMC 14th Report*, Appendix, part VII (London, 1895), p. 113) read this word as 'lev'lers': but it is clearly 'Pedlars'.
9. inkles, linen tapes.
10. something, i.e. the upstart pedlars.

KATHERINE PHILIPS
(1632–**1662**–1664)

Katherine Philips was born in London. Though her husband, a Welsh landowner named James Philips, supported the parliamentary side in the 1650s, Katherine Philips was a royalist. She became known in England and Wales during the 1650s as a wit and as a poet and, partly to assert claims which she had on land in Ireland, came to Dublin in 1662. She soon attached herself to the court, becoming friendly not only with the Duke and Duchess of Ormond but also with Roger Boyle, Lord Orrery (1621–79) and his countess, with Wentworth Dillon, Earl of Roscommon (1637–85) and his countess, and with some of the younger members of all these families. Within the court at Dublin Castle, Philips and her friends constituted a recognisable group, the members of which addressed each other by mock classical names: Lady Elizabeth Boyle was 'Celimena' for example, Lady Mary Cavendish 'Policrite', Lady Anne Boyle 'Valeria', Sir Edward Dering 'Silvander' and Katherine Philips 'Orinda' – known to her admirers, then and ever since, as 'the matchless Orinda'. Poems circulated within this group and were not intended for publication, but the members do not seem to have amended each other's verses in the way that was done in some earlier seventeenth-century coteries. However, since the Dublin court included active poets like Roscommon and active playwrights like the Earl of Orrery as well as Philips herself, there was much to circulate and to discuss. Dublin Castle suddenly became a centre of considerable literary activity.

Katherine Philips's most famous Dublin achievement was her translation of Corneille's tragedy, *La Mort de Pompée*. Soon after she had started work on this translation, a portion of it fell into the hands of Lord Orrery who encouraged her to finish it and, when the work was staged in the new theatre in Smock Alley, Orrery provided one hundred pounds towards the cost of the production.[1] Some of Philips's verse also found its way out of her circle and into the hands of the Dublin bookseller Samuel Dancer who, without permission, included three of her poems in his volume *Poems by Several Persons of Quality and Refined Wits* (Dublin, 1663). Katherine Philips became a well-known Dublin figure and may even have acted in the first performance of her translation of *Pompey*.

The poems below all date from Philips's time in Dublin, and have been chosen to illustrate both her ability to write intimate verse to close friends and her skill with more public poems. Although she was in Dublin for only twelve months (from June 1662 to June 1663), the accounts Philips left of the cultural life of Dublin in a series of letters she wrote to her London friend, Sir Charles Cotterell, as well as her own poems and her play, have ensured her an enduring place in the cultural history of seventeenth-century Ireland.[2]

To the Lady E[lizabeth] Boyl[3]

Ah, lovely Celimena! why
  Are you so full of charms,
That neither Sex can from them flie,
  Nor take against them arms?

---

1. For a fine reconstruction of the first night of *Pompey*, see Christopher Morash, *A History of Irish Theatre 1601–2000* (Cambridge, 2002), pp. 21–9.
2. *Letters from Orinda to Poliarchus* (London, 1705). The volume contains many detailed observations on literary activity in Dublin between June 1662 and June 1663.
3. One of the five daughters of Lord and Lady Orrery.

Others in time may gain a part,
But you at once snatch all the heart.

Dear Tyrant, why will you subdue
   Orinda's trivial heart,
Which can no triumph add to you,
   Not meriting your dart?   10
And sure you will not grant it one,
If not for my sake, for your own.

For it has been by tenderness
   Already so much bruis'd,
That at your Altars I may guess
   It will be but refus'd.
For never Deity did prize
A torn and maimed Sacrifice.

But oh! what madness can or dare
   Dispute this noble chain,[4]   20
Which 'tis a greater thing to wear,
   Than Empires to obtain?
To be your slave I more design,
Than to have all the world be mine.

Those glorious Fetters[5] will create
   A merit fit for them,
Repair the breaches made by Fate,
   And whom they own[6] redeem.
What thus ennobles and thus cures,
Can be no influence but yours.   30

Pardon th' Ambition of my aim,
   Who love you at that rate,
That story cannot boast a flame
   So lasting and so great.
I can be only kind and true,
But what else can be worthy you?

---

4. Presumably a gift from Lady Elizabeth Boyle – a necklace?
5. Presumably another gift – a set of bracelets?
6. claim as their own.

To the Lady Mary Butler at her marriage with the Lord Cavendish, October 1662[1]

At such a time as this, when all conclude
Nothing but unconcernment[2] can be rude,
The muses, Madam, will not be deny'd
To be the bride maides where you are the bride.
They know in what those wishes have design'd,
What bright opposers they are like to find,
Whose birth and beauty never will give way
To such obscure competitours as they.
But yet, as injur'd princes still do strive
To keep their title and the claime alive,   10
So they affirme they do but ask their due,
Having hereditary right in you.
And they againe would rather undergo
All that malicious ignorance could do,
When fortune all things sacred did oppresse,
Then in this brave ambition want successe.
Admit them, beauteous Madam, then to be
Attendants on this great solemnitie,
And every muse will in a charming straine
Your honour and their owne pretence maintaine.   20
    The first your high extraction shall proclaime,
And what endear'd your Auncestors to fame,
Who do not more excell another stemme,
Then your illustrious father hath done them;
Who fortune's stratagems hath so surpast,
As flattery can not reach, nor envy blast;
In whom vice-gerence[3] is a greater thing
Than any crowne, but that of England's King;
Whom foreigne princes do with envy see,
And would be subjects to be such as he.   30
Another shall your mother's glories raise,[4]
And much her beautie, more her vertue praise;

1. Lady Mary Butler, youngest daughter of the Duke and Duchess of Ormond, married William Cavendish, fourth Earl (and later first Duke) of Devonshire, in Kilkenny in October 1662. The marriage was the most glittering social event to take place during Orinda's time in Ireland.
2. lack of concern.
3. i.e. being a viceroy, the king's representative.
4. Before her marriage to Ormond (who was her cousin), the duchess had been Lady Elizabeth Preston, Baroness Dingwall, only daughter of Richard, Earl of Desmond.

Whose suffering in that noble way and cause,
More veneration than her greatnesse drawes,
And yet how justly is that greatnesse due,
Which she with so much ease can govern too!
Another shall of your great lover sing,[5]
And with his fame inspire some nobler string,
Whom Nature made so handsome and so brave,
And fortune such a lovely mistresse gave.   40
This shall relate how fervently he woo'd,
And that, how generously 'twas understood:
Shall tell the charmes which did his heart invade,
And then the merits which did yours persuade.
   But all the muses on you both shall treat,
   Who are as justly kind, as you are great,
   And by observing you, assure mankind
   That love and fortune are no longer blind.

To the Countess of Roscomon, *with a Copy of* Pompey[1]

Great *Pompey*'s Fame from Egypt made escape,
And flies to you for succour in this shape:
A shape, which, I assur'd him, would appear
Nor fit for you to see, nor him to wear.
Yet he says, Madam, he's resolv'd to come,
And run a hazard of a second doom:
But still he hopes to bribe you, by that trust;
You may be kind, but cannot be unjust;
Each of whose[2] favours will delight him more
Than all the Lawrels that his temples wore: 10
Yet if his Name and his misfortunes fail,
He thinks my intercession will prevail;

5. Lord Cavendish succeeded his father as Earl of Devonshire in 1684 and was created a
duke by William III in 1694. He was lord steward of William's household.

1. Katherine Philips, *Pompey: A Tragedy* (Dublin, 1663). The play, the original of which is
by Pierre Corneille (1606–84), is set in Ptolemy's Egypt before, during and after the
assassination of the noble Roman leader, Pompey the Great. Ptolemy sums up the
themes of the play in the first scene: 'That is unsafe, and this ignoble is; / I dread
injustice or unhappiness. / And angry fortune each way offers me / Either much danger
or much infamy.' Many of those who saw the performance in Dublin would have
recognised parallels between the dilemmas facing Ptolemy and those which they had
faced during the previous ten years.

2. i.e. your.

And whilst my Numbers[3] would relate his end,
Not like a Judge you'l listen, but a friend;
For how can either of us fear your frown,
Since he and I are both so much your own.

But when you wonder at my bold design,
Remember who did that high task enjoin;
Th'illustrious *Orrery,*[4] whose least command,
You would more wonder if I could withstand: 20
Of him I cannot which is hardest tell,
Or not to praise him, or to praise him well;
Who on that height from whence true glory came,
Does there possess and thence distribute fame;
Where all their Lyres the willing Muses bring,
To learn of him whatever they shall sing;
Since all must yield, whilst there are Books or Men,
The Universal Empire to his Pen;
Oh! had that powerfull genius but inspir'd
The feeble hand, whose service he requir'd,   30
It had your justice then, not mercy pray'd,
Had pleas'd you more, and better him obey'd.

The Irish greyhound[1]

Behold this Creature's Form and State,
Which Nature therfore did create;
That to the World might be express'd
That meen[2] there can be in a Beast;
And that we in this Shape may find
A Lyon of another kind;
For this Heroick beast does seem
In Majesty to Rivall him:

---

3. verses.
4. Lord Orrery had encouraged Philips to complete the translation and had paid for the '*Roman* and *Egyptian* Habits' for the performance.

---

1. The dog celebrated here was of the breed now known as an Irish wolfhound. As Philips's modern editor, Patrick Thomas, notes: 'It is probable the dog which is the subject of Orinda's poem belonged to [her friend] Lord Orrery' who was a connoisseur of Irish greyhounds. *The Collected Works of Katherine Philips, The Matchless Orinda* ed. Patrick Thomas, 3 vols (Stump Cross, 1990–3), I, 374.
2. mien, appearance.

And yet vouchsafes, to Man, to shew
Both service and submission too;   10
From whence we this distinction have,
That Beast is fierce, but this is brave.
This Dog hath so himself subdu'd,
That hunger can not make him rude,[3]
And his behaviour does confess
True Courage dwells with Gentleness.
With Stearnest Wolves he dares engage,
And acts on them successfull rage;
Yet too much courtesy may chance
To put him out of countenance.   20
But when in his opposers' blood,
Fortune hath made his vertue good;[4]
This Creature from an Act so brave
Grows not more sullen, but more grave;
Man's Guard would now be, not his sport,
Beleiving he hath ventur'd for't;
But yet no blood or shed or spent
Can ever make him insolent.
    Few Men of him to doe great things have learn'd,
    And when th'are done, to be so unconcern'd.   30

3. rough, violent.
4. i.e. when he has killed a wolf . . .

'PHILO-PHILIPPA'
(1663)

Shortly after the first performance of her play *Pompey*, Katherine Philips wrote to Sir Charles Cotterell: 'I have had many Letters and Copies of Verses sent me, some from Acquaintance, and some from Strangers, to compliment me upon POMPEY which, were I capable of Vanity, would even surfeit me with it; for they are so full of Flattery that I have not the Confidence to send them to you. One of them, who pretends to be a Woman, writes very well, but I cannot imagine who the Author is, nor by any Inquiry I can make, have hitherto been able to discover.'[1]

She was referring to the extraordinary, baffling poem that follows. Conventional expectations of what a woman living in Dublin in 1663 (and who thought of Ireland as her land – see line 79) would be likely to write to the author of *Pompey* – and, indeed, of the language she would be likely to use – are completely overturned by this ardent, radical, feminist verse epistle. What else, one wonders, did this remarkable woman write? Who was she? Where was she educated? In what environment could she have explored her ideas before presenting them in as confident a manner as she does here? Can we assume that other verse of this calibre and vigour was circulating in court circles in Dublin Castle in the early 1660s or is this piece unique in style and in content? Was 'Philo-Philippa' really a man? There are answers to none of these questions. What is certain, however, is that this piece survived only because it was included (surprisingly) in both the unauthorised 1664 edition of Katherine Philips's poems and the authorised one (edited by her friend Sir Charles Cotterell) in 1667.[2]

To the Excellent *Orinda*

Let the male Poets their male *Phœbus* chuse,
Thee I invoke, *Orinda,* for my Muse;
He could but force a Branch, *Daphne* her Tree
Most freely offers to her Sex and thee,
And says to Verse, so unconstrain'd as yours,
Her Laurel freely comes, your fame secures:
And men no longer shall with ravish'd Bays
Crown their forc'd Poems by as forc'd a praise.[3]
    Thou glory of our Sex, envy of men,
Who are both pleas'd and vex'd with thy bright Pen   10

---

1. [Katherine Philips] *Letters from Orinda to Poliarchus* (London, 1705), p. 124. 8 April 1663.
2. Both editions carry the title: *Poems by the deservedly admired Mrs Katherine Philips, The Matchless Orinda* . . . and the poem is found on sigs. c2r–d2r in both volumes.
3. The poem begins in a radical way by turning the normal invocation to the muses completely on its head. Daphne escaped the god Apollo (Phœbus), who was trying to rape ('force') her, by changing into a laurel tree. Apollo took a branch of the tree, which thereafter became the symbol for Apollo and for poetry. The contrast is between the female Daphne, who offers the gift of poetry freely to the woman poet, and Apollo (and other men), whose poems are forced on their readers and are the result of the rape of the muse.

Its lustre doth intice their eyes to gaze,
But mens sore eyes cannot endure its rays;
It dazles and surprises so with light,
To find a noon where they expected night:
A Woman Translate *Pompey!* which the fam'd
Corneille with such art and labour fram'd!
To whose close version the Wits club their sence,
And a new Lay poetick SMEC springs thence![4]
Yes, that bold work a Woman dares Translate,
Not to provoke, nor yet to fear mens hate.   20
Nature doth find that she hath err'd too long,
And now resolves to recompence that wrong:
Phœbus to *Cynthia*[5] must his beams resigne,
The rule of Day, and Wit's now Feminine.

    That Sex, which heretofore was not allow'd
To understand more than a beast, or crowd;
Of which Problems were made, whether or no
Women had Souls; but to be damn'd, if so;
Whose highest Contemplation could not pass,
In men's esteem, no higher than the Glass;   30
And all the painful labours of their Brain,
Was only how to Dress and Entertain:
Or, if they ventur'd to speak sense, the wise
Made that, and speaking Oxe, like Prodigies.[6]
From these thy more than masculine Pen hath rear'd
Our Sex; first to be prais'd, next to be feard.
And by the same Pen forc'd, men now confess,
To keep their greatness, was to make us less.

    Men know of how refin'd and rich a mould
Our Sex is fram'd, what Sun is in our Gold:[7]   40
They know in Lead no Diamonds are set,
And Jewels only fill the Cabinet.[8]
Our Spirits purer far than theirs, they see;

---

4. SMEC (or 'Smectymnuus') means a work written by several people. It was an invented
name used in a pamphlet published in 1641, the letters being the initial letters of the
names of some of the authors. The reference here is to a translation of Corneille's *La
Mort de Pompée* undertaken by several London wits and produced the year before
Katherine Philips's own translation.
5. i.e. the (male) sun must give supremacy to the (female) moon.
6. i.e. a woman speaking sense was deemed as extraordinary as a talking ox.
7. The sun was thought to create gold as it moved around the earth; again, the idea is that
men can see the true quality there is in women.
8. A jewel box or display case.

By which even Men from Men distinguish'd be:[9]
By which the Soul is judg'd, and does appear
Fit or unfit for action, as they are.

    When in an Organ various sounds do stroak,
Or grate the ear, as Birds sing, or Toads Croak;
The Breath, that voyces every Pipe, 's the same,
But the bad mettal doth the sound defame.[10]   50
So, if our Souls by sweeter Organs speak,
And theirs with harsh, false notes the air do break;
The Soul's the same, alike in both doth dwell,
'Tis from her instruments that we excel.[11]
Ask me not then, why jealous men debar
Our Sex from Books in Peace, from Arms in War;
It is because our Parts will soon demand
Tribunals[12] for our Persons, and Command.

    Shall it be our reproach, that we are weak,
And cannot fight, nor as the School-men[13] speak?   60
Even men themselves are neither strong nor wise,
If Limbs and Parts they do not exercise.

    Train'd up to arms, we *Amazons*[14] have been,
And *Spartan* Virgins strong as *Spartan* Men:[15]
Breed Women but as Men, and they are these;
Whilst *Sybarit* Men[16] are Women by their ease.
Why should not brave *Semiramis*[17] break a Lance,
And why should not soft *Ninyas*[18] curle and dance?
Ovid in vain Bodies with change did vex,
Changing her form of life, *Iphis* chang'd Sex.[19]   70

---

9. The idea that women's spirits were purer than those of men goes against the theology of the time.
10. i.e. the air that makes the organ pipe sound is the same, but the metal of which the organ pipe is made can distort the sound; 'metal' also means the character.
11. i.e. If our souls make a sweeter noise than theirs (and souls are the same for men and for women) then it must be because the 'metal' out of which the soul's instruments are made in us is superior to the 'metal' in men.
12. i.e. we demand to be heard in a court of justice.
13. teachers of logic, metaphysics and theology in medieval universities.
14. warrior women.
15. The young women of Sparta were expected to exercise and become as strong as the young men.
16. The inhabitants of Sybaris, a town in Italy, were famed for their effeminacy and love of luxury.
17. A queen of Assyria famed for her military prowess.
18. The son of Semiramis, a weak man.
19. Ovid tells the story of a girl called Iphis whose parents dressed her as a boy and betrothed her to a maiden. The goddess Isis transformed Iphis into a man just in time. *Metamorphoses*, 9, 666–797.

Nature to Females freely doth impart
That, which the Males usurp, a stout, bold heart.
Thus Hunters female Beasts fear to assail:
And female Hawks more mettal'd than the male:
Men ought not then Courage and Wit ingross,[20]
Whilst the Fox lives, the Lyon, or the Horse.
Much less ought men both to themselves confine,
Whilst Women, such as you, *Orinda*, shine.

    That noble friendship brought thee to our Coast,
We thank *Lucasia*,[21] and thy courage boast.   80
Death in each Wave could not *Orinda* fright,
Fearless she acts that friendship she did write:
Which manly Vertue to their Sex confin'd,
Thou rescuest to confirm our softer mind;
For there's requir'd (to do that Virtue right)
Courage, as much in Friendship as in Fight.
The dangers we despise, doth this truth prove,
Though boldly we not fight, we boldly love.

    Ingage us unto Books, *Sappho* comes forth,
Though not of *Hesiod*'s age, of *Hesiod*'s worth.[22]   90
If Souls no Sexes have, as 'tis confest,[23]
'Tis not the he or she makes Poems best:
Nor can men call these Verses Feminine,
Be the sense vigorous and Masculine.
'Tis true, *Apollo* sits as Judge of Wit,
But the nine Female learned Troop[24] are it:
Those Laws for which *Numa* did wise appear,
Wiser *Ægeria* whisper'd in his ear.[25]
The *Gracchi*'s Mother taught them Eloquence,[26]
From her Breasts courage flow'd, from her Brain sence;   100
And the grave Beards, who heard her speak in *Rome*,
Blush'd not to be instructed, but o'recome.

---

20. engross, monopolise.
21. The coterie name of Anne Owen, Philips's friend, with whom she had come to Ireland in June 1662.
22. Sappho is the women poet most admired by other women poets: she was born in *c.* 618 BC, about a century after the Greek poet Hesiod.
23. This was commonly taught in the sixteenth and seventeenth centuries.
24. The nine muses.
25. Numa was the second king of Rome; Ovid states (*Metamorphoses* 15, 482–551) that he was advised by a nymph named Ægeria who became his wife.
26. Cornelia, mother of 'the Gracchi' (Tiberius and Gaius) taught them everything they knew. Cornelia was also the name of an important character in the play *Pompey*.

Your speech, as hers, commands respect from all,
Your very Looks, as hers, Rhetorical:
Something of grandeur in your Verse men see,
That they rise up to it as Majesty.
The wise and noble *Orrery*'s regard,
Was much observ'd, when he your Poem heard:
All said, a fitter match was never seen,
Had *Pompey*'s widow been *Arsamnes* Queen.[27]   110
    Pompey, who greater than himself's become,
Now in your Poem, than before in *Rome*;
And much more lasting in the Poets Pen,
Great Princes live, than the proud Towers of Men.
He thanks false *Egypt* for its Treachery,[28]
Since that his Ruine is so sung by thee;
And so again would perish, if withall,
Orinda would but celebrate his Fall.
Thus pleasingly the Bee delights to die,
Foreseeing, he in Amber Tomb shall lie.[29]   120
If that all *Ægypt*, for to purge its crime,
Were built into one Pyramid o're him,
Pompey would lie less stately in that Herse,[30]
Than he doth now, *Orinda*, in thy Verse:
This makes *Cornelia* for her *Pompey* vow,
Her hand shall plant his Laurel on thy brow:
So equal in their merits were both found,
That the same Wreath Poets and Princes Crown'd:
And what on that great Captains Brow was dead,
She Joies to see re-flourish'd on thy head.   130
    In the French Rock[31] *Cornelia* first did shine,
But shin'd not like herself till she was thine:
Poems, like Gems, translated from the place
Where they first grew, receive another grace.
Drest by thy hand, and polish'd by thy Pen,
She glitters now a Star, but a Jewel then:

---

27. Pompey's widow was Cornelia. There is no character called Arsamnes in *Pompey* and the reference is impossible to clarify.
28. Pompey was murdered as he set foot in Egypt. The play contains a vivid account of the murder in Act II scene ii.
29. Amber is a fossilised resin used in jewellery. The fossilised remains of insects caught in the resin can sometimes be seen in amber.
30. mausoleum.
31. i.e. in Corneille's French text.

No flaw remains, no cloud, all now is light,
Transparent as the day, bright parts more bright.
Corneille, now made English, so doth thrive,
As Trees transplanted do much lustier live.   140
Thus Oar[32] digg'd forth, and by such hands as thine
Refin'd and stamp'd, is richer than the Mine.
Liquors from Vessel into Vessel pour'd,
Must lose some Spirits, which are scarce restor'd:
But the French wines, in their own Vessel rare,
Pour'd into ours, by thy hand, Spirits are;
So high in taste, and so delicious,
Before his own *Corneille* thine would chuse.
He finds himself inlightned here, where shade
Of dark expression his own words had made: 150
There what he would have said, he sees so writ,
As generously to just decorum fit.
When in more words than his you please to flow,
Like a spread Floud, inriching all below,
To the advantage of his well meant sence,
He gains by you another excellence.
To render word for word, at the old rate,
Is only but to Construe, not Translate:
In your own fancy free, to his sense true,
We read *Corneille*, and *Orinda* too: 160
And yet ye both are so the very same,
As when two Tapers join'd make one bright flame.
And sure the Copier's honour is not small,
When Artists doubt which is Original.
    But if your fetter'd Muse thus praised be,
What great things do you write when it is free?
When it is free to choose both sence and words,
Or any subject the vast World affords?
A gliding Sea of Chrystal doth best show
How smooth, clear, full and rich your Verse doth flow: 170
Your words are chosen, cull'd, not by chance writ,
To make the sence as Anagrams do hit.
Your rich becoming words on the sence wait,
As Maids of Honour on a Queen of State.
'Tis not White Satin makes a Verse more white,[33]

---

32. ore.
33. i.e. subject matter does not make the poem.

Or soft; Iron is both, write you on it.
Your Poems come forth cast, no File you need,
At one brave Heat both shap'd and polished.[34]
　　But why all these Encomiums of you,
Who either doubts, or will not take as due?　　　　　　　180
Renown how little you regard, or need,
Who like the Bee, on your own sweets doth feed?
　　There are, who like weak Fowl with shouts fall down.
Doz'd with an Army's Acclamation:[35]
Not able to indure applause, they fall,
Giddy with praise, their praises Funeral.
But you, *Orinda*, are so unconcern'd,
As if when you, another we commend.
Thus, as the Sun, you in your Course shine on,
Unmov'd with all our admiration:　　　　　　　　　　190
　　Flying above the praise you shun, we see
　　Wit is still higher by humility.

34. 'Philo-Philippa' speaks with such confidence about Philips's poems that it seems certain she had seen them. There are only two ways in which this would have been possible: in manuscript (which means that 'Philo-Philippa' was privy to the verse circulating in the group around Philips at Dublin Castle) or in Samuel Dancer's 1663 Dublin printing of three poems by Philips (though there is no indication in the volume that they are her work) in the unauthorised collection *Poems by Several Persons of Quality and Refined Wits* (Dublin, 1663). On balance, it seems more likely that 'Philo-Philippa' had seen the work in manuscript.

35. Divination by the behaviour of birds was practised in the Roman army: in this case, the story is of birds which, frightened by the shout of the soldiers, fell out of the sky.

WENTWORTH DILLON, EARL OF ROSCOMMON
(1637–**1663**–1685)

Wentworth Dillon was born in Dublin into an Old English family. His mother was a niece of Sir Thomas Wentworth, lord deputy in Ireland at the time of his birth, and the young poet was named after his uncle. He spent most of his youth in England and on the Continent, but returned to Ireland in 1660 to lay claim to his estates and his title. Roscommon and his young wife Lady Frances Boyle, one of the daughters of the Earl of Cork, became active in the court around the Duke of Ormond and he began to write verse, contributing a prologue for the first performance of Katherine Philips's *Pompey* and an epilogue to a tragedy about Alexander the Great. In both poems, Roscommon (who was an ardent royalist) was at pains to draw parallels between the heroic actions represented on the stage and those in the real world about him, stressing the almost superhuman nature of Charles II; he also asserted that Ireland was innocent of any disloyalty to the crown during the Commonwealth – a position which was certainly true of Roscommon's own family, but hardly accurate when applied to the country as a whole.

Roscommon spent about twelve years in Ireland, taking an active part in the House of Lords when it sat and gaining a reputation for fine oratory and deep gambling. He moved to London about 1682 and set up an informal academy in which he and his literary friends discussed the verse they were writing. It was at this time that he wrote his elegant and lucid *Essay on Translated Verse*, the poem for which he is now chiefly remembered.

Epilogue to *Alexander the Great* [1]
when acted at the Theatre in Dublin

You've seen tonight the Glory of the East,
The Man, who all the then known World possest,
That Kings in Chains did Son of *Ammon* [2] call,
And Kingdoms thought Divine, by Treason fall.
Him Fortune only favour'd for her Sport,
And when his Conduct wanted her Support,
His Empire, Courage, and his boasted Line,
Were all prov'd Mortal by a Slave's Design.

Great *Charles*, [3] whose Birth has promis'd milder Sway,
Whose awful Nod all Nations must obey,   10
Secur'd by higher Pow'rs, exalted stands
Above the reach of Sacrilegious Hands;

---

1. A play about Alexander of Macedon (356–323 BC), the greatest military commander of the ancient world.
2. A name for Alexander the Great. His father, Philip, had claimed descent from Hercules and therefore from Jupiter, king of the gods; Ammon was the name given to Jupiter in Libya.
3. i.e. Charles II.

Those Miracles that guard his Crowns,[4] declare
That Heav'n has form'd a Monarch worth their Care;
Born to advance the Loyal, and depose
His own, his Brother's,[5] and his Father's Foes.
Faction,6 that once made Diadems her Prey, ⎫
And stopt our Prince in his triumphant Way, ⎬
Fled like a Mist before this Radiant Day. ⎭
So when, in Heav'n, the mighty Rebels[7] rose,   20
Proud, and resolv'd that Empire to depose,
Angels fought first, but unsuccessful prov'd,
God kept the Conquest for his best Belov'd;[8]
At sight of such Omnipotence they fly,
Like Leaves before Autumnal Winds, and die.
All who before him[9] did ascend the Throne
Labour'd to draw three restiff[10] Nations on.
He boldly drives 'em forward without Pain,
They hear his Voice, and streight obey the Rein.
Such Terror speaks[11] him destin'd to command;   30
We worship *Jove* with Thunder in his hand;
But when his Mercy without Pow'r appears,
We slight his Altars, and neglect our Pray'rs.
How weak in Arms did Civil Discord shew! ⎫
Like *Saul* she struck with Fury at her Foe,[12] ⎬
When an Immortal Hand did ward the Blow. ⎭
Her Off-spring, made the Royal Hero's Scorn,
Like Sons of Earth, all fell as soon as born:
Yet let us boast, for sure it is our Pride,
When with their Blood our Neighbour Lands were dy'd,   40
Ireland's untainted Loyalty remain'd,
Her People guiltless, and her Fields unstain'd.[13]

---

4. i.e. of England and Ireland.
5. James, Duke of York (later James II), was one of Roscommon's patrons.
6. i.e. the faction-fighting of the English Civil Wars.
7. i.e. Satan and his angels.
8. i.e. Jesus.
9. The theory of the divine right of kings (understandably popular at this time) allowed royalists to suggest similarities between the divine nature of kingship as seen in an earthly king (Charles II) and the divine nature of kingship as exercised by the heavenly king (Jesus).
10. restive; i.e. England, Scotland and Ireland.
11. reveals.
12. I Samuel 20. 33.
13. Roscommon had proved his innocence and had been rewarded with the return of his own Irish lands and estates. However, the distribution and redistribution of land on the basis of acceptable or unacceptable behaviour during the interregnum was to be the largest problem faced by Charles II's administration in Ireland.

Prologue to *Pompey, A Tragedy*,

For the Theatre at *Dublin*, written by the Earl of *Roscomon* [1]

The mighty Rivals, whose destructive Rage
Did the whole World in Civil Arms engage,
Are now agreed, and make it both their Choice,
To have their Fates determin'd by your Voice. [2]
Cæsar [3] from none but You will hear his Doom,
He hates th'obsequious Flatteries of *Rome*:
He scorns, where once he rul'd, now to be try'd,
And he hath rul'd in all the World beside.
When he the *Thames*, the *Danube*, and the *Nile*
Had stain'd with Blood, Peace flourish'd in this Isle;   10
And you alone may Boast, you never saw
Cæsar till now, [4] and now can give him Law.

Great *Pompey*, too, comes as a suppliant here,
But sayes He cannot now begin to fear: [5]
He knows your equal Justice, and (to tell
A Roman Truth) [6] he knows himself too well.
Sucess, 'tis true, waited on *Cæsar*'s side,
But *Pompey* thinks he conquer'd when he dy'd.
His Fortune, when she prov'd the most unkind,
Chang'd his Condition, but not *Cato*'s [7] Mind.   20
Then of what Doubt can *Pompey*'s Cause admit,
Since here so many *Cato*'s Judging sit?

But you, bright Nymphs, [8] give *Cæsar* leave to woo
The greatest Wonder of the World, but you,

---

1. Later editions (e.g. London, 1717) have a fuller explanation: 'Translated by Mrs. *K. Philips* from the *French* of Monsieur *Corneille*, and Acted at the Theatre in *Dublin*'. Katherine Philips's translation of the play, first performed in the Smock Alley theatre in Dublin in 1663 (see headnote to Katherine Philips, p. 361), is set in Ptolemy's Egypt before, during and after the assassination of the noble Roman leader, Pompey the Great.
2. i.e. you [the audience] can praise them [with applause] or blame them [with hisses] during and after the performance.
3. Julius Cæsar, one of the characters in the play.
4. Though Cæsar's forces conquered Britain, mainland Europe and Egypt, they never came to Ireland.
5. i.e. he cannot be fearful now (before the play) since he showed no fear in life.
6. i.e. to tell you the honest truth . . .
7. severe judges – so called after Cato the Elder (234–149 BC), renowned for his strictness.
8. *Marginal note*: 'To the Ladies'. 'The greatest wonder of the world but you' was Cleopatra, who plays a major part in the play.

376

And hear a Muse,[9] who has that *Hero* taught
To speak as gen'rously, as e'er he fought,
Whose Eloquence from such a Theme deters
All Tongues but English, and all Pens but Hers.
By the just Fates your Sex is doubly blest,
You Conquer'd *Cæsar*, and you praise him best.   30

And You (Illustrious Sir)[10] receive as due,
A present Destiny reserv'd for You.
Rome, *France* and *England* join their Forces here,
To make a Poem worthy of your Ear.[11]
Accept it then, and on that *Pompey*'s Brow
Who gave so many Crowns, bestow one now.

from: An Essay on Translated Verse[1]

. . . When *France* had breath'd,[2] after intestine Broils,
And Peace, and Conquest crown'd her forreign Toils,
There (cultivated by a Royal Hand)[3]
Learning grew fast, and spread, and blest the Land;
The choicest Books, that *Rome,* or *Greece* have known,
Her excellent *Translators* made her own:
And *Europe* still considerably gains,
Both by their good *Example* and their *Pains*.
From hence our genrous Emulation came,
We[4] undertook, and we perform'd the same.   10
But now, *We* shew the world a nobler way,
And in *Translated Verse,* do more than *They*.

---

9. i.e. Katherine Philips.
10. *Marginal note*: 'To the Lord Lieutenant', i.e. the Duke of Ormond.
11. The story came from Rome, the tragedy was written by a Frenchman, the translation by
   an Englishwoman.

1. This important early Augustan poem, which was written about twenty years after the other
   poems by Roscommon included in this selection, reflects views on the writing of poetry
   which were first expounded by Horace, and later made popular in Europe in Nicholas
   Boileau's 1674 translation of *L'Art Poétique*. The ideas themselves may not be original,
   but Roscommon expresses them with grace and style. Alexander Pope was to recycle
   many of them in his *Essay on Criticism* (1711). This extract from the poem starts as
   Roscommon is praising the French for their pioneering work in translating classical texts.
2. i.e. was in a lull between wars.
3. That of Louis XIV (1638–1715); the king supported the arts most actively from 1660
   onwards.
4. i.e. the writers of England.

Serene, and clear, Harmonious *Horace* flows,
With sweetness not to be exprest in *Prose*.
Degrading *Prose* explains his meaning ill,
And shews the *Stuff*, but not the Workman's skill.
I (who have serv'd him more than twenty years)
Scarce know my Master as he there appears.
Vain are our *Neighbours Hopes,* and *Vain* their *Cares,*
The *Fault* is more their *Languages*, than theirs.   20
'Tis Courtly, florid, and abounds in words
Of softer sound than our[s] perhaps affords.
But who did ever in *French Authors* see
The Comprehensive, *English Energy*?
The weighty *Bullion*[5] of *One Sterling Line*,
Drawn to *French Wire*, would thro' whole *Pages* shine.
I speak my *private*, but *impartial sense*,
With *Freedom*, and (I hope) without *offence*:
For I'le Recant, when *France* can shew me *Wit*,
As strong as *Ours*, and as *succinctly Writ*.   30
Tis true, *Composing* is the *Nobler* Part,
But good *Translation* is no *easie* Art:
For tho *Materials* have long since been found,
Yet both your *fancy*, and your *Hands* are *bound*;
And by *Improving* what was writ *Before*;
Invention Labours *Less*, but *Judgment*, *more*.

The Soil intended for *Pierian seeds*[6]
Must be well *purg'd* from *rank Pedantick Weeds*.
Apollo starts, and all *Parnassus* shakes,
At the rude Rumbling *Baralipton*[7] makes.   40
For none have been with *Admiration*, read,
But who (beside their *Learning)* were *Well-bred*.

The first great work, (a Task perform'd by few)
Is, that *your self* may to *your self* be *True*:
No *Masque*, no *Tricks*, no *Favour*, no *Reserve*;
Dissect your Mind, examine ev'ry *Nerve*.
Whoever *Vainly* on his *strength* depends,
Begins like *Virgil*, but like *Mævius*[8] *Ends*.

5. gold. The idea is that the solid gold might be stretched out into a long, golden wire.
6. Pieria was the home of the Muses in classical mythology.
7. dry, logical writing. The term refers to a particular kind of syllogism.
8. The name given, by Horace, to a bad poet.

That wretch (in spight of his forgotten Rhymes)
Condemn'd to Live to all succeeding Times,   50
With *pompous Nonsense* and a *bellowing sound*
Sung *lofty Ilium*,[9] *Tumbling* to the *Ground*.
And (if my Muse can through past Ages see)
That *Noisy*, *Nauseous*, *Gaping Fool* was *He*;
Exploded, when with universal scorn,
The *Mountains Labour'd* and a *Mouse* was *Born*.[10]

Learn, learn, *Crotona*'s brawny Wrestler cryes
Audacious Mortals, and be *Timely* Wise!
'Tis I that call, remember *Milo*'s *End*,
Wedgd in that Timber which he strove to *Rend*.[11]   60

Each Poet, with a *different Talent* writes,
One *Praises*, One *Instructs*, Another *Bites*.
Horace did ne're aspire to *Epick Bays*,
Nor lofty *Maro*[12] stoop to *Lyrick Lays*.

Examine how your *Humour* is inclin'd,
And which the *Ruling Passion* of your Mind;
Then, seek a *Poet* who *your* way do's bend,
And chuse an *Author* as you chuse a *Friend*.
United by this *Sympathetic Bond*,
You grow *Familiar*, *Intimate* and *Fond*;   70
Your *thoughts*, your *Words*, your *Stiles*, your *Souls* agree,
No Longer his *Interpreter*, but *He*.

With how much ease is a *young Muse Betray'd*,
How *nice*[13] the *Reputation* of the *Maid*!
Your *early*, *kind*, *paternal* care appears,
By *chaste Instruction* of her *Tender Years*.
The *first Impression* in her *Infant* Breast
Will be the *deepest*, and should be the best.

---

9. Troy.
10. Horace himself first used this phrase: The mountains are in labour, a ridiculous mouse will be born. It refers to Æsop's fable of the mountain in labour.
11. Milo of Crotona was a famous athlete, renowned for his strength. It is said that one day, finding a tree which some woodcutters had partially split with a wedge, he attempted to pull it apart. But the wedge slipped and the tree closed on his hand, trapping him until wolves came and devoured him.
12. Virgil, whose name was Publius Virgilius Maro.
13. tender, delicate.

Let no Austerity breed servile *Fear*,
No *wanton* Sound offend her *Virgin-Ear*.   80
Secure from *foolish Pride's affected state*,
And *specious Flattery's more pernicious Bait*,
Habitual Innocence adorns her *Thoughts*
But your neglect must answer for her *Faults*.

Immodest words admit of no defence;
For want of *Decency* is want of *Sense*.
What mod'rate *Fop* would rake the *Park* or *Stews*,[14]
Who among Troops of *faultless Nymphs* may chuse?
Variety of *such* is to be found;
Take then a Subject, *proper* to expound: 90
But *Moral*, *Great*, and worth a *Poet's Voice*.
For Men of *sense* despise a *trivial Choice*:
And such *Applause* it must expect to meet,
As wou'd some Painter, busie in a Street,
To Copy *Bulls* and *Bears*, and ev'ry *Sign*
That calls the *staring Sots* to *nasty Wine*.

Yet 'tis not all to have a Subject *Good*,
It must *Delight* us when 'tis *understood*.
He that brings *fulsome*[15] *Objects* to my view,
(As many *Old* have done, and many *New*)   100
With *nauseous Images* my Fancy fills,
And all goes down like *Oxymel* of *Squils*.[16]
Instruct the list'ning world how *Maro* sings
Of *useful subjects*, and of *lofty Things*.
These will such true, such bright *Idea's* raise,
As merit *Gratitude*, as well as *Praise*,
But *foul Descriptions* are *offensive* still,
Either for being *Like*, or being *Ill*.
For who, without a *Qualm*, hath ever lookt,
On *Holy Garbage*, tho by *Homer Cookt*?   110
Whose *Rayling Hero's*, and whose *wounded Gods*,
Make some suspect, He *Snores*, as well as *Nods*.[17]

14. brothels. to rake = 1) to scour; 2) to behave in a rakish manner.
15. disgusting, offensive, obscene.
16. A (presumably disgusting) medicine made of honey, vinegar and powdered seashells.
17. The idea that even Homer nods (i.e. does not always write well) is common: this line is
a version of Horace's *Ars Poetica* 359.

But I offend – *Virgil* begins to *frown*,
And *Horace* looks with *Indignation* down;
My blushing Muse with *Conscious fear* retires,
And whom *They*[18] *like*, *Implicitely Admires*.

On *sure Foundations* let your *Fabrick Rise*,
And with attractive *Majesty* surprise,
Not by affected, *meritricious Arts*,
But strict *harmonious Symetry* of *Parts*,   120
Which through the *Whole*, insensibly must pass,
With vital Heat to animate the Mass.
A *pure*, an *Active*, an *Auspicious flame*,
And *bright* as *Heav'n*, from whence the *Blessing* came;
But few, oh few, Souls, præordain'd by *Fate*,
The Race of *Gods*, have reach'd that *envy'd Height* . . .
. . . How justly then will impious Mortals fall,
Whose *Pride* would soar to *Heav'n* without a *Call*?

Pride (of all others the most *dangerous* Fau't,)
Proceeds from want of *Sense* or want of *Thought*,   130
The Men, who *labour* and *digest* things *most*,
Will be much apter to *despond*, than *boast*.
For if your Author be *profoundly good*,
Twill cost you *dear* before he's *understood*.
How many Ages since has *Virgil* writ?
How few are they who understand him *yet*?
Approach his Altars with *religious Fear*,
No *vulgar Deity* inhabits *there*:
Heav'n shakes not more at *Jove's imperial Nod*,
Than *Poets* shou'd before their *Mantuan*[19] *God*.   140

Hail mighty MARO! may that Sacred Name
Kindle my Breast with *thy cœlestial Flame*;
Sublime Ideas,[20] and *apt Words* infuse.
The Muse instruct *my Voice* and *Thou* inspire the *Muse*! . . .

18. i.e. Virgil and Homer.
19. Virgil came from Mantua.
20. 'ideas' should be pronounced as having three syllables.

ANONYMOUS
(*c*.1663)

The restoration of Charles II in 1660 brought peace to Ireland and, for the first time for a generation, travellers intent on pleasure rather than on war or spoil – the first tourists, in fact – began to visit the country. One of the earliest accounts of such a visit is an indecent, burlesque account of a journey around Ireland undertaken by four mock-chivalresque English 'knights' – in reality, four rogues on the make – in the early 1660s. Many of the adventures which befall these scoundrels are reworkings of coarse *fablieux* – the type of material found throughout Europe in the later Middle Ages – but some sections of the poem contain interesting glimpses of life in Restoration Ireland. The first selection below begins as the 'knights', who have endured a terrible storm on their voyage from Holyhead to Dublin, finally reach land.

from: Iter Hibernicum[1]

from: Canto 15

. . . Knights who had given themselves for lost,
Beheld at last the Irish Coast,[2]
And much about the break of Day,
They Anchor cast in Dublin Bay:
And their arrivall they told anon,
By the loud Mouths of fifteen Canon.
To goe on Shore Knights were not loath,
Being glad to land at Hill of Hoath,
For they were sick of Sea, and tyred,
And there would fain have horses hired,   10
But that the Price did much disgust 'um,
Resolving to break their ill Custom:
For Knights, good-husbands,[3] were unwilling,
To give them[4] six pence, and seav'n Shilling,
For three poor Jades so small a Jorney.
They thought their conscience very horny,[5]

1. The Irish journey.
2. These rough rhyming tetrameters, later very common in Irish verse in English, make an early appearance here. They were to be Swift's favourite metre, as well as that of the author of the various versions of *The Irish Hudibras*. In the 1660s, they were the metrical form chosen by Charles Cotton for his Virgil travesties and for his 'Voyage to Ireland' (a poem first published in 1667 but not included in this volume because the author never actually reaches Ireland); most famously, they were used in Samuel Butler's *Hudibras* (1663).
3. i.e. men who manage their money with prudence.
4. i.e. those hiring the horses.
5. i.e. they thought those hiring the horses had a tough conscience . . .

Their Mony better than their Garrons,[6]
Away they went, and call'd them Carrons,[7]
Seav'n Miles a foot, and in Boots hobling,
Untill at last they got to Dublin: 20
Where being wondrous tir'd and weary,
They sent for Sack[8] to make them merry.
But throats of Knights seem'd very crusty,
They after Voyage were so thirsty,
They could not eate but were for all Drink,
Espetially the sharp, and small Drink,
Of which they fill'd their Bellies so full,
That they did get a Squirt most wofull,
Turning their Bumms o're side of low stool,
In which stood Pan instead of Close-stool,[9]   30
Each putting twenty times and twice in,
To their great Trouble e're Sun riseing.
But Knight of the black cap[10] was frollick,[11]
For he had brought a Cure for Collick.
What is't (quoth he) that doe I cannot?
With that, the Powder of Pomegrannat,
With hard loaf Sugar twice refined,
With grated Nutmegg he conjoyned:
This into Cows Milk, sweet not sower,
The learned Knight with Care doth Loure,[12]   40
Then let it boyle o're fire so long,
Till it grew very thick and strong.
This cur'd their shiteing in a trice,
For they had scarce eate of it twice,
But they found they should quickly doe well,
For it had glewed up their Tuell:[13]
For which they learned brother praysed,
Who them from Death of Shiteing raised.

---

6. i.e. the 'knights' liked their money better than the garrons (small horses: Ir. *gearrán*).
7. = carrion, vermin.
8. sherry, sweet wine.
9. A chamber pot enclosed in a box or stool.
10. The name of one of the four so-called 'knights', the others being the knight with the 'Muschatoes', Wilsero and Samsero, the latter also known as the knight of the velvet beaver (fur hat).
11. happy enough.
12. lower.
13. Tuell (probably) = tool – unrecorded with the meaning it obviously has here.

Like Ship made fine with Flaggs and Waistcloth,[14]
Knights shew'd being now drest in their best Cloaths,   50
As Ship is tallow'd, and drest in Harbour,
So Knights were trim'd and scrap'd by Barber.
Their Locks were curl'd, and finely kemed,[15]
Then powder'd, and Beards neatly trimmed.
Thus Knights together walk'd up and down,
To see, and to be seen, in Towne.
Apace they stalk like huffing Sinners,
Along High-Street, and row of Skinners,[16]
Then take a turn in Christ Church Walk,
And then to Coffie House to talk,   60
And thence to see all could be seen,
Saint Patrick's Church, St Stevens Green,
The Inns, the Toolsell,[17] and the Castle.
At signe of Morter, and of Pestle,[18]
With wandring tyr'd, they did not fail
To taist the best Dublinian Ale.
All they had seen was not worth a Louse,
Had they not gon to see the Play-Howse,
Where there appeared to their sight
Many a Lady fair and Knight.   70
But haveing there seen Dublin glories,
They went thence to drink Wine at Stories:[19]
Where still down Throat they so much shed,
They seldom went but drunk to Bed.
For all Ills still their Cure was Sack,
The drunken man doth nothing lack.
Like princes, Knights awhile thus swagger,
Spend much but seldom give to Begger:
But ere Days past were two times twenty,
Their Stock grew low, and Powches empty,   80

14. Waistcloths were coloured cloths hung about the upper part of a ship, sometimes for adornment, sometimes to screen men stationed there.
15. = combed.
16. Skinners' Row – soon to be the street where Dublin's printers and publishers plied their trade.
17. The tholsel or city hall.
18. According to Sir John Gilbert (*History of Dublin* (Dublin, 1978 ed.), I, 177), the landlord of the 'Pestill and Mortar' in Skinners' Row in 1662 was William Hill.
19. Though most taverns had typical names (e.g. the 'Pestill and Mortar'), the custom of distinguishing a drinking-place by the name of its proprietor, was already widespread in seventeenth-century Dublin.

And when they saw they were e'ne undone,[20]
They Bills drew of their Friends at London.
But Winds blew Cross for all their Rackett,
And for six weeks kept out the Packett.[21]
When Mony knights began to want,
Trust they had none, their Money scant,
They now began to be oppressed,
And walk about like Knights distressed.
But this was cunning Fortunes drift,[22]
This way to teach Knights how to shift,   90
For within a while they did avouch,
They could live without Coyne in Pouch,
And swore if they should Children have,
They'd send them there to learn to save,
To learn of cheating Tricks a Dozen,
To Lie, to Cogg, to Swear, to Cozen,[23]
To play, to rant, Debauch, to Whore,
And Pimp, with such like Virtues more:
In Christendom is not like School,
For to Commence[24] Wise Knave, or Fool . . .   100

from: Canto 16

Knights being recruted left off mourning,[1]
And 'gan to think now of returning,[2]
But the brave Knight of the Muschatoes
Did long to see how grew Potatoes,
And said that it would be great pitty,
Not to see Country as well as Citty,
For though they often had heard stories
Of the wild Irish, and of Tories,[3]

---

20. completely ruined.
21. i.e. the packet-boat (which would have brought notes of credit from the knights' friends in London) was prevented from sailing for six weeks by noisy, contrary winds.
22. purpose, aim.
23. to cog = to cheat; to cozen = to dupe, defraud.
24. to graduate, receive a university degree.

---

1. i.e. now that their purses had been replenished (recruited), the knights stopped mourning.
2. i.e. to England.
3. Dispossessed Irish who went on the run or took up arms against the English were known as 'raparees' or 'tories'. Ir. *tóraidhe* (a word which originally meant a pursuer rather than a hunted man).

As yet they had not seen their Fashons
Which did deserve much Commendations.   10
They then resolv'd to make a Sally
From their safe Castle in Smock-Ally,[4]
To see the Woods, the Hills, and Mountaines,
The Lakes, Wells, Rivers, Boggs, and Fountaines,[5]
In their smoak'd Cotts to broyle a Rasher,[6]
And with the Kerns in Straw to Coshar,[7]
To drink with them of Wigg[8] a Bolefull,
To hear them sing a Cronan[9] dolefull,
To hear their Lingua, and their Notes,
Which like the Welch comes from their Throats,   20
To see th'old Calloes[10] drink, and slabber
Soure Butter-milk, and Boneclabbor,[11]
That they might give to Gresham Colledg,[12]
The Irish Customs on their knowledg.
They hired then three Irish Garrons,
Which were but lean and ugly Carrons,[13]
These they procured of an Attornie,
To serv them in this little Jorney.
As soon as they had got their Tobies[14]
On th'outside of their little Hobbies,[15]   30
Away they rode into a Country
Where they saw not so much as one Tree,
But Mountain, Bogg, Furz, Heath, and Go[r]ss,
And now and then a wooden Cross;

---

4. The knights' lodging, close to Dublin Castle, was in the same street as John Ogilby's newly constructed theatre.
5. springs.
6. The Irish cottage, in which a fire was constantly burning but which had no chimney, was notoriously smoky.
7. kerns = Irishmen (usually armed), Ir. *ceithearn* ; to cosher = to lodge, or stay with, Ir. *cóisir*.
8. = whig, sour milk or a drink made with fermented whey, flavoured with herbs.
9. A song sung in the Irish manner. Ir. *crónán*.
10. cailleagh, old woman. Ir. *cailleach*.
11. bonnyclabber, thick naturally soured milk. Ir. *bainne clabair*.
12. The early meetings of the Royal Society – founded to promote 'physico-mathematicall experimental learning' (i.e. experimental science) in November 1660 – took place at Gresham College in London, and the term 'Gresham College' was often taken to mean the Royal Society or any gathering of those interested in the new science. Among papers submitted to the Royal Society were some describing primitive peoples.
13. See notes to lines 17 and 18 of Canto 15 above, see p. 383.
14. buttocks.
15. horses.

In every Hole and Nook a Chappell,
But without a Bell for to ring a Peel,
And planted in some corner privie[16]
The ruin'd Walls all hid with Ivie:
Which gave to travelling Knights this Notion,
'Thad been a land full of Divotion,   40
And that these Ruines were the Scarrs,
Of ancient, and late Civil Warrs.

But as the Knights on the Road were trouling,[17]
They heard a sad and grievious howling,
And on their right-hand they espied
A burial of one lately dy'd.
Such Shreeks, such Tunes, and dismall Singing
Beating their Breasts, and both Hands wringing,
Such tearless Crys, and hideous Roar,
Our Knights had never seen before,   50
And what to make of't could not tell
When first they heard the Irish Yell:[18]
But being at the length drawn nigher,
They could no[t] choose but to admire,
To see th'old Crones like madd to rave,
One or two, howling on each Grave,
Crying as if the Dead should heare,
But without shedding ever a Teare.
Such Irish Crones Knights ne'r saw untill
This time; with Kercheifs large, and Mantle.   60
But these Knights left, and on they ride,
When not far thence they had espied,
Foure Men at least unto one Plow,
Which to discribe I know not how,
For Horses Tails supply'd the Places
Of Collars, Harness, and of Traces.[19]
This they thought worthy to be noted,
That it here after might be quoted,

16. private.
17. trolling, strolling.
18. keening.
19. It is hard to determine whether the descriptions in this section are based on observation
    or are a retelling of generalised descriptions of Irish life in circulation at the time. There
    are, for instance, few reliable descriptions of ploughing by the tail, though almost every
    seventeenth-century commentator on Ireland mentions the custom as if he had seen it,
    and notes that it was prohibited by law.

Tho it by Statute Law was cancell'd.
Then Knights saw Cows and Horses spancell'd,[20]   70
Saw Sugans,[21] and their Women ride
Their Faces still to the wrong side,[22]
Their Cabbins full of Dirt and Smoak,
Enough an English Man to Choake,
Of which themselves doe take up halfe,
The rest serves Cow, Sow, Goat, and Calf,
Who around the Fire doe in Cold Weather,
Both eate their Meat and lie together.
Each Cabbin with two Dores is graced,
Like Squirrills 'gainst each other placed,   80
One still is stopp'd with Straw and Wattle[23]
When Wind on that side House doth rattle,
And when to th'other side it is shifted,
The Dore to th'other side is lifted.
Their Children naked as they're borne,
Live with Soure Milk, and parched[24] Corn,
Being bred like Beasts, and with worse fare
Than many Beasts in England are.
At these things Knights stood first, and gazed,
And seemed at them much amazed;   90
But Custom made't at last so Common,
That it was wonder'd at by no Man,
And Knights themselves (let us not wrong 'um)
Oft eate, and drank, and slept among 'um.

Knights thus amongst them Ten days dwellt
Until they like red herrings smellt,
Had Mutton eate with them, and Hogg,
And Butter buried in a Bogg,[25]
And drunk with them both sweet and soure Ale,
Eat Onyons, Shamrock, Leeks, and Sorrell,[26]   100

20. i.e. prevented from straying by having their front legs fettered together.
21. straw saddle. Ir. *súgán*.
22. Irish saddles were often designed to accommodate two people (see D.B. Quinn, *The Elizabethans and the Irish* (Ithaca, 1966), p. 98). This observation that women riding pillion faced 'the wrong way' or 'to the wrong side' (does this mean facing the horse's tail?) was also made by John Dunton in 1699 (Edward MacLysaght, *Life in Seventeenth-Century Ireland*, revised edition (Shannon, 1969), p. 373).
23. Branches of trees used as a windbreak.
24. lightly roasted.
25. Butter was sometimes stored in bogs in the Irish countryside.
26. Wood sorrel, a fairly common food, was sometimes called shamrock (Quinn, p. 66).

And that they might be to them pleasing,
Tobacco with them took, and sneesing:[27]
And saw them with no little Clutter
Make Boneclabbour, and churn Butter.
Th'old Crone with durty Hand first stirred,
The Cream which stood in Vessell furred,
Then without Apron blew, or Cassock,
She clapps her Breech upon an Hassock,[28]
To save her Coats (no lye I tell yee)
She rolls them up e'ne to her Bellie.   110
Betwixt her Thighs her Churn she places,
Not stands to churn like other Lasses,
For Churn being very low 'tis fitting
They churn, and make their Butter sitting:
And as the Cream by churning flys,
She catches it on her bare Thighs,
Then sweeping it from her foul Skin,
Into the Churn she putts it in.[29]
This is their great Frugalitie,
Their neat, and cleanly Huswifrie.   120
This and much more Knights did discern,
And of these Irish huswifes learn . . .

---

27. snuff.
28. i.e. sits on a stool.
29. This description of butter being churned by hand (including the lifting of the skirt and the scooping of cream from bare thighs) recurs in several texts, including that by Dunton (see MacLysaght, p. 332).

ANONYMOUS
(1663)

One of the most inventive and original Englishmen of the Commonwealth and Restoration periods, Sir William Petty (1623–87), lived in Ireland for considerable periods of time between 1652, when he arrived as physician to the parliamentary army and clerk to the Irish council, and 1685. While in Ireland, Petty amassed extensive estates and served both the Commonwealth and Restoration governments in a number of official positions. His most important contributions to Irish life were his accurate survey of the land of Ireland (the so-called 'Down' survey, mainly undertaken during the 1650s to assist in the redistribution of land under the Commonwealth) and his methodical, statistical analysis of Irish social data, published as *A Political Anatomy of Ireland* (written *c*. 1671, published 1691). This work demonstrates Petty's skill as a statistician and, in effect, establishes him as the founder of the modern science of economics. Petty was fascinated by the new experimental science and was a founding member of the Dublin Philosophical Society in 1684, as well as of the Royal Society in London in the early 1660s.

Petty was an indefatigable inventor and experimenter, whose achievements included a new suspension system for carriages, a method of purifying sea water and a 'double-bottomed boat' or catamaran. This invention seemed destined for a great future, particularly after promising early sea-trials in Dublin Bay and successful crossings of the Irish Sea; Petty won a wager of fifty pounds when the first large vessel he built, the thirty-ton *Invention II*, sailed from Dublin to Holyhead faster than the government packet-boat in July 1663. Later sailings were less successful, however, and Petty's second large double-bottomed ship, which had been named *The Experiment* by Charles II,[1] sank in the Bay of Biscay on a return voyage from Oporto.[2] The poem which follows seems to have been written when Petty was trying to persuade Irish sailors to venture on *Invention II* for the voyage to London, where it could be shown to the king. The poet's jocular name for the boat seems to have been the 'Castor and Pollux'.

The 'double-bottomed boat' was Petty's own favourite invention, but he was a man who made many enemies and the boat and its inventor were regarded as little more than comic diversion by the anonymous author of this burlesque. The use of a Latin title and of inflated heroic language are intended to invoke in the reader a sense of the absurdity of the whole project, and the poem concerns itself mainly with Petty's efforts to bribe sailors to serve on the ship. It seems likely (since the two poems were copied by the same hand at the same time into the same manuscript and exhibit many verbal and metrical similarities) that this poem and the previous one in this anthology are by the same author.

1. John Evelyn attended the launch on 22 December 1664. See *The Diary and Correspondence of John Evelyn*, ed. William Bray, 4 vols (London, 1857), I, 387. Samuel Pepys was also present.
2. Petty returned to the project in 1684 with a large vessel named *St Michael the Archangel*, built in Dublin. The sea-trials of this ship were a disaster.

In Laudem Navis Geminæ E Portu Dublinij ad Regem Carolum II^dum Missæ[3]

Let Fanshaw spend his Breath in Praise
Of the Escureal of the Seas,[4]
And Heathen Bards of Ship and Cargo
Of the old patched Vessell Argo.[5]
Let others talk of Spaine's Armado,
Which round by Scotland had Strapado,[6]
Or controvert till they are stark madd,
The Form of which Noah his Ark made.
Let others on their Fancy spie,
The Ship that saileth in the Skie: 10
Or sing the Vessell of Ulysses,
None of all which was such as this is,
Whose Birth, and Breeding I'le reherse,
To all the World in Burlesque Verse.

Then first of all this famous Model
Sprung from a mathematick Nodelle,[7]
Who Honour saw, alltho dim sighted,
And was for fair Inventions Knighted.[8]
He was one of those Learned Fellows,
That rais'd the Maiden from the Gallows,   20
To shew the Power of Phisicks Art,
When hang'd to make her live, and fart.[9]

---

3. In praise of the twin-hulled boat sent from the port of Dublin to King Charles II.

4. Sir Richard Fanshawe (1608–66) published his famous translation of the *Lusiads,* an epic account by Luis Vaz de Camões (1524–80) of the voyages of the great Portuguese explorer Vasco da Gama, in 1655. The reference seems to be to an important early passage in the *Lusiads* when da Gama's great ships are described sailing up the East African coast. Their size invokes comparison with the palace of Escorial near Madrid though, since Spain and Portugal were separate nations at the time of Vasco da Gama and of Camões, the comparison is misplaced. The equivalent vast palace in Portugal is at Mafra.

5. The name of the ship in which the mythological Jason set sail in search of the Golden Fleece.

6. 'Strapado' was a particularly vicious form of punishment or torture; the storm-tossed Spanish Armada of 1588 was viciously punished as its ships were wrecked on the rocks of Scotland and Ireland.

7. i.e. the 'noddle' or head of Sir William Petty.

8. Petty, who was notoriously short-sighted, was knighted in 1662.

9. Petty was famous for having restored to life a woman who had been executed for infanticide. According to John Evelyn, Petty 'bled her, put her to bed with a warm woman, and with spirits and other means, restor'd her to life'. (*The Diary and Correspondence of John Evelyn,* II, 95.)

He who had many Acres got,
By measuring of Land a Spot.[10]
How that should be the Art doth there lye,
For some doe say he measur'd fairly.

Who knows what Sciences lye lurking,
In Braines that allways are a Working,
Which will not lye still in their Urn,
But jogg'd about like Cream in Churn,   30
New Stuff arises from old Matter,
Like seperateing Earth from Water:
Sweet Butter's made by seperation,
And Cheese Curds by Coagulation,
And Vessells not kept clean by Labour
Convert sweet Milk to Boneclabor.[11]
By Eyes of Minde this thing being seen
He kept by Studdy his Brain-pan cleane,
Working on this, now on that Matter,
And compassing both Land and Water   40
By Mathematticks, and by Logick,
He goes about his famous Project.

Corruption's Generation's Mother,
One thing arises from another;
So Magotts spring from Cheese, and Meat,
These wee dispise, and those wee eate:[12]
So from luxurious fat of Witt,
The Brain new liveing Forms doth get,
And things will grow from Brains tho shallow,
As Weeds from Land that long lyes fallow.   50

Knight haveing compass'd whole Iland,
Surveying both the Boggs, and dry Land,
Lest Witt, to work on should want Matter,
Doth now project upon the Water.
But whilst his Brain's parturient,[13]
It's mid-wif'd by this Accident.

10. It was constantly asserted that Petty had gained his enormous estates in County Kerry by
    duplicity, though few questioned the accuracy of his maps of each Irish county.
11. bonnyclabber, thick naturally soured milk. Ir. *bainne clabair*.
12. It was widely believed that maggots were created in rotten meat and ripe cheese by spon-
    taneous generation. See also line 60 where it is asserted that beetles come from excrement.
13. giving birth.

Tho slight, doe not slight things dispise
Great Matters from small Things arise,
From a small Egge a flying Bird,
And liveing Beetles from dead Turd: 60
From Cabbage that doth stinke and rot,
Grows first a little green Magot,
From whose lean sides shortly there springs
Two little thin, and tender Wings,
To which Time gives a various die,
And formes a painted Butterfly.

This knight not full of twittle twattle,
But bookish as was Aristotle,
To gaine the Name of a Philosopher,
An hundred Books did turn and toss over,   70
And his cold Fingers ends did blow, soe
To become a Virtuosoe.[14]
In Studdy thus much Time he spent,
Some new unheard of thing t'invent;
A thing not found since the Creation,
A spicke-span new Art of Navigation.
But findeing now his Brains grow muddy,
With too much pouring in his Studdy,
He meant (his Spirits to recreate)
To goe to Coffie Howse and prate.   80
But as he went along the Street,
He many little Boys did meet,
Every one playing with this Toys,
For you must know they were but Boys.
And tho they were together mixt,
His carefull Eye on One he fixt,
Who with a peice of paper square,
Form'd divers Things both neat, and rare.
At first a Cock and Boat he made,
The Boy was skillfull at the Trade,   90
For with another fould or two
He form'd a Cock a Doodle doe.
But then behold a matter strange,
His Cock he to a Boat did change,

14. scientist, experimenter, learned person.

Then that to other Forms did pass,
A Book now, now a Looking-glass,
But at the last without much trouble,
He made a Boat with Bottom double,
A Mast he made with sprig of Fennell,
And set it swimming in the Kennell.[15]   100
The Knight as he 'gan to retire,
Did much the Witt of Boys admire,
He did not thinke this Boy was an Ass,
But rather taught by great Pythagoras.[16]
The Boat he saw in Kennell swimming,
He thought deserv'd a better trimming,
And went away with full Intention
For to improve the Boyes Invention.
Thus first of all, as I have hinted,
Was double Bottom Boats invented,   110
And little Children did, God bless 'um,
Teach wise Philosophers their Lesson.

The Magot biteing,[17] he takes Paper,
Now foulds it square, now long, now taper,
And with the Difficulty strugling,
From Forme to Form the Paper Juggling,
His Memory being jogg'd and jolted,
Th'Ideas, like Meal from Bran, was bolted,[18]
For he, it seems, haveing not forgot 'um,
Made Boat at last with double Bottom   120
Which with no little Joy, and clatter,
He launch'd into a Tub of Water.
But whilst that he was deeply thinking,
He found his Paper Frigot[19] sinking.
Therefore he thought it very good,
To make this new found Ship of Wood.
Which he at last made with much puther,[20]
And made it Masts, and Sailes, and Rudder,

15. gutter, drain.
16. The great mathematician of the ancient world.
17. maggot = whimsical fancy; to bite = to take a grip or hold.
18. to bolt or boult = to sift flour through a sieve, to examine something by sifting through
    it.
19. frigate.
20. = pother, bother.

And when he perceiv'd the Winde Western
He sail'd this Vessell in a Cisterne,[21]   130
And cause his Ship but softly crept on,
He himself did play the Neptune,
Tho not with Trident, yet with Ladle,
To make a rough Sea he did paddle.
It was fine sport to see the Vessell,
How it against the sides would jossle,
And swim in Cistern without rowing,
Knight, Æolus-like,[22] puffing and blowing;
For with his Breath he raised a storm
Yet to the Vessell could doe no harme,   140
For that over the Waves still jumping,
In spite of blowing, swam Tryumphing.

When he perceiv'd his Ship would doe,
His grand Designe he doth pursue,
By this he made another greater,
With Art, and every Way compleater,
Which he presented to the Colledg,[23]
Where dwell the Witts, and men of knowledg,
As I suppose with full Intention,
To be recorded for[24] th'Invention.   150
Now Knight at last, by deep Inspection,
Brings double Vessell to perfection,
A little Gemini[25] he built new,
And did intend to have her gilt too.
So strange a Thing was seen in no Age,
For she to Rings-end[26] made a Voyage.
But doe not think Knight such an Elf,
To venture in Her first himself,
For if he had, he had been doused,
And in salt Sea like Mackrell Soused,   160
For she (none knowing what's the matter)
Turn'd up her Arse above the Water.

---

21. water-tank, pond.
22. In Roman mythology, Æolus was god of the winds, Neptune of the seas.
23. i.e. Gresham College, the meeting place in London of the Royal Society.
24. credited with.
25. twin, i.e. twin-hulled boat.
26. The sea-side village where those disembarking from ships anchored in Dublin Bay were put ashore.

But this did nothing Knight dismay,
Rome was not built up in a Day.
A larger therefore he intended,
And to have all her faultes amended,
Cause her Bottoms hung down like Bollucks,
He named her Castor and Pollux.[27]
As from an Embrio in the Womb,
Into the World a Child doth come,   170
This Childe being nourish'd by Mam, and Dad,
Grows up to be a dapper Lad,
And (as 'tis dayly seen, and heard)
In time a Man, and weares a Beard.
So from a little paper Frigot,
Grew one of Wood, made of a Spigot;[28]
From thence a little bigger Toy,
Which could but hold a Man, and Boy,
Thence Castor and Pollux, with double Bum
Doth to its full Perfection come.   180
Thus from small Vessell in Tub swimming[29]
Is grown a Ship, with Sailes and trimming,
As bigg as other Ships, and able
To carry Masts, Anchor, and Cable,
And proudly sailing o'er the Billows,
Gan scud it faster than her Fellows.[30]

A tatling Gossip, Fame, they call her,
A very loud, and lying Brauler,
With Breath as bigg as any Thunder,
Blew over Seas this mighty Wonder.   190
They say She is a very Strumpet
And tells strange Stories with a Trumpet,
And would have thought her self quite undone
Had she not told this Tale at London,
To tell all Tales she cannt forbeare,
And blew them into every Eare,

27. The morning and evening stars, twin sons of Zeus and Leda, were special patrons of sailors in the ancient world. The phrase 'Castor and Pollux' was also used for anything doubled or twinned and is here applied jocularly to Petty's catamaran, the two hulls of which are likened to a set of testicles.
28. A wooden pin with a hole bored through it, used as part of a tap or faucet, particularly for liquor.
29. Petty had constructed two prototypes, one two-and-a-half feet long, the other of nearly two tons.
30. i.e. begins to sail more speedily than other boats.

Yet you must know it nought availes,
If they be true or lying Tales,
Or true or false she loud will blow them,
That all who have but Eares may know them.   200
The King (God bless him) at the last,
Did hear Fames loud, and foisting[31] Blast,
Who being a Lover of Navigation,
Making for Ships great preperation
To Ireland by post sent over,
To have this Ship sent round to Dover.

But Knight for Sea-Men being to seek,
Was forc'd to use his Rhetorick,
And with those Swabbers[32] often jangle,
'Cause none would sail his Finglefangle: 210
For at the pinch he found that Sailors,
Had hearts as little as any Tailors,
And tho to see to Lusty Swabbers,
Were yet but Cowards and fearfull Lubbers.[33]
But at the last with Mony, and bawlings
He did pick up some few Tarpaulings,[34]
Who being valiant made by Brandy,
Swore, if he would, they'd sail to Candy.[35]

But out alas! of the Misfortune,
Whilst he to haste did them importune,   220
And they on sleevless Errants[36] tarryed,
Their Wives heard on't (for they were marryed)
And like mad Furies they came runing,
From lousing of themselves, and suning,
Swareing they[37] should no strange Ship enter,
Nor first goe on so great Adventure.
Like Beldames[38] then the Knight they threaten,
Who did expect he should be beaten,

31. fraudulent.
32. low-ranking sailors (those who swab the decks).
33. i.e. and though to look at they were lusty swabbers, they were really cowards and frightened, clumsy fellows.
34. A nick-name for sailors (now 'tars').
35. A kingdom in seventeenth-century Ceylon; i.e. they would sail anywhere.
36. irrelevant, pointless errands.
37. i.e. their menfolk.
38. hags, viragos.

And allmost had bewraid his Breeches[39]
To hear their high outragious Speeches.   230
But at the last, standing on tiptoes,
And looking big without Muschatoes,[40]
He bid them cease awhile their bauling,
Their Furie, and their Catterwauling,
And he would satisfie their Grutches,[41]
Or put himself into their Clutches.
These Scolds haveing some little manners
Beleeving Knights were no Trapanners,[42]
But were, or should be, Men of Merrit,
Swore they would heare, tho' a[43] were a Spirit;   240
With that the Knight took up his Station,
And with loud voyce spake this Oration.

Fair Dames (quoth he) 'tis now or never,
That all of you'l be made for ever,
If you take what your Starrs doe offer,
And not refuse now their kinde proffer,
For you that are Wives of poor saylors,
As mean as Wives of Lousie Taylors,
I doe forsee it, very shortly,
You'l Gentlewomen be, and courtly.   250
In truth I will declare what may be,
Each one at least will be a Lady.
Your linsie woolsie will be loathed,
When you in Stuffs, and Silks are cloathed,[44]
Nor for your Raggs you'l care a Louse,
Not any more to keep an Alehouse:
Nor wash your Canns, nor wring the Spiggots,
When Husbands Captaines are of Frigots.
For tho' they're now cloath'd with Tarpauling[45]
(If you will cease and hold your bauling)   260

---

39. revealed his buttocks – expecting to be beaten (?)
40. mustachios, moustache or whiskers.
41. grouches.
42. trepanners, those who lure the unsuspecting into a trap.
43. he.
44. Linsey-woolsey was a dress material of coarse, inferior wool suitable for clothes of
    working women, while gentlewomen would be clothed in high-quality woven material
    (stuffs) and silks.
45. The waterproof material of which sailors' clothing was made.

And tho they stink of Pitch, and Tarr,
They'l Captaines be of Men of War,
For this their famous undertakeing,
And hold their heads as high as Rekeing.⁴⁶
The World won't for their Fames have stowage,⁴⁷
Who first in double Ship made Voyage,
And all Men of them shall more speake,
Than of Columbus, or Frank Drake,
They shall be talk'd of on th'Exchange,⁴⁸
For their Voyage so wonderous strange,   270
Their names prick'd down in Gresham Colledg,⁴⁹
For men of Fame, of Skill, and Knowledg,
In Brass ingrav'd with golden Letters.
Then you'l take place before your Betters.
And every one shall have a Jewell,
As big, and broad as any Trouell,⁵⁰
And Thimbles, curling Pinns, and Bodkinns,⁵¹
And Rings, and Braceletts, and such odd things,
And Pinns, and Gloves, and fine pin-cases,
And Knotts, Frizats,⁵² and long third lases,   280
With Forks, and silver handl'd Knives,
Fit presents for such worthy Wives,
That durst their Husbands first Adventure,
In double bottom'd Ship to enter,
Which our King sends for, for a tryall
To build by it a navie Royall,
Which must be done by my Direction,
Or else he'l ne'r bring't to Perfection,
And which he'l doe, when he doth finde,
It sayle quite blank against the Winde.   290
Besides I'le have a new device,
Some Peggs untrussing in a trice,
The Ship that's one with double Bum
Shall sever, and two Shipps become,

---

46. Obscure; the word might be connected with a 'reek' or stack of hay or turf.
47. i.e. the world will not be large enough to hold their fame.
48. The place where merchants met to buy and sell goods and stocks.
49. See above note to line 147. To prick = to mark off a name on a list.
50. Trouell (here) = a kitchen implement.
51. long pins used by women to fasten up their hair.
52. crisp curls on the head; i.e. you will have your hair done for you by others. 'lases' = laces, perhaps to draw a bodice tight or as an ornament in the hair.

And be as like to one another
As ever Sister was to Brother.
Will not this Project be a good one,
When Ships shall part thus on a sudden,
And fourty Sayle (which seem no more)
Shall presantly become fourescore?[53]   300
Oh how wee'l meet the Dutch and beat 'um,
When wee thus cuningly can cheat 'um.

Come Dames and now take Heart at Grace,[54]
Let every one stick up her Face,
For on my Word (beleev a Stranger)
To sail my Ship there is no danger,
For there they'l rest, and sleep their fill,
And be as safe as Mouse in Mill.
For if one Bottom should grow leakie,
When Ship is tost, and Sailes are reakie,[55]   310
And should too much of salt sea quaff,[56]
They may sail safe in t'other hafe.[57]
For so an ancient Poet sings,
Its good for Bows to have two Strings,
And as your selves may wisely note,
Two Oares belong still to one Boat.
Twould then concluded be at Gotham,[58]
One Ship is best with double Bottom.
For if one side on Rocks be staved,
They may in th'other still be saved.   320
It must indeed be wicked weather
If both the Bottoms sunk together.
You all must need confess that one
Legg, can't so fast as two Leggs run.
I thinke it is as plane a Case,
As is the very Nose of your Face.
Then gentle Dames be it your Will,
Under Correction, I ask it still,

---

53. i.e. if the two parts of the catamaran are separated and it becomes two ships, forty vessels
   can sudden
ly become eighty vessels.
54. i.e. at this concession.
55. = wreaky, damaged.
56. i.e. if one hull should take in too much sea water . . .
57. half.
58. A village near Nottingham renowned, proverbially, for the stupidity of its inhabitants.

To let your Husbands sail in this Vessell,
When fair Windes in her Poope shall whissle,   330
That they of poor, and worthless Wights,[59]
May captaines all be made, and Knights,
And you brave Ladys, and Gentlewomen,
Els for my sake beleev you no Men.

When they had heard what Knight had said,
They all were callm'd, their Wrath allay'd,
And every one incontinent,[60]
Gave Husbands leave with one Consent.
Then one of them among the rest,
A sooking[61] Dame as it was ghesst,   340
Of good strong Liquor took a Quart,
Here's to you (quoth she) with all my heart,
I am resolv'd to whet my whissle,
And drinke a good Voyage to the Vessell,
That wee, Sr Knight, the better may thrive all,
And she at London have safe arivall.
Straight to her Nose she setts the Stoop,[62]
And supp'd it off as round as a hoop.
With that the Knight call'd for a whole Barrell,
Which put an end to all their Quarrell,   350
For he with Cupps ply'd them so roundly,
Till they were all Drunk most profoundly.
Thus he at last did Sailors gett,
With Mony, good Words, good Ale, and Wit.
Castor and Pollux now's on the Ocean,
And the Knight gapeing for promotion,
Whose Fame shall everlasting be,
Whilst there is sailing on the Sea,
Whilst there are Men that love green Sallads,
Whilst there is burlisque Verse, or Ballads.   360

---

59. i.e. from being poor and worthless men . . .
60. *either* 1) unable to restrain themselves, *or* 2) immediately.
61. soaking, one who drinks immoderately.
62. stoup, drinking vessel, tankard.

AMBROSE WHITE
(*fl*.**1665**)

Almanacs were very popular in seventeenth-century Ireland, though they were so heavily used that few have survived. The astronomical information they contained was calculated for the city in which they were printed, and the body of the almanac contained information likely to be useful to those living in the area – the phases of the moon or the dates of fairs, for instance. Ambrose White's 1665 *An Almanack and Prognostication for the year of our Lord 1665 . . . calculated according to Art and referred to the Horizon of the Ancient and Renowned City of DUBLIN* also contained verses combining homely advice on domestic matters with basic agricultural information.

Verses for the year and for each month of 1665

'Tis you bright Stars, that in the fearful Sea[1]
Do guide the Pilot through his purpos'd way;
'Tis your direction that doth commerce give
With all those Men that through the World do live.

January 1665
Make much of them that labour sore.
Love well thy Wife, relieve the poor
To bed betimes, for being there,
It will both Wood and Candle spare.

February 1665
Spend not thy time in fruitless wooing,
Be sure to keep the Plough a going,   10
For thou wilt find they self more able,
By a Plough going than a Cradle.

March 1665
Now Sea and Land do will and wish,
For sparing Flesh to feed on Fish,
If Fish be scant and fruit of trees,
Supply that want with Butter and Cheese.

---

1. These introductory verses appear next to the general title.

April 1665

Let Cisley look well to her Dairy,
That Cheese be not tough nor Butter hairy
For though some count her office meanly,
It is a fine thing to be cleanly.   20

May 1665

Rise early now this Month of May
And walk the fields that be so gay,
To hear the Cuckow chant his lay,
The Nightingale and popping Jay.

June 1665

Whilst husband looks abroad what lacks,
Let Wife at home be mending sacks,
Though Ladies they may tear and rend,
Good Huswives make shift and mend.

July 1665

July thou art guilty of much evil,
Thy Hea-cocks make Men & Maids uncivil,   30
Better no Hay were, yea, nor no Horses,
Than that Maids should be Whores, and after turn nurses.

August 1665

Now with all hands your Harvest ply,
Cut down your Oats, reap Wheat & Rie,
Hook up your Pease, Mow down your Barly,
And ply thy work both late and early.

September 1665

Let Wife not gad, but keep at home,
For gadding Wife is worse than none,
Though man the best Husband be alive,
If Wife be bad, he scarce can thrive.   40

October 1665

If weather serve, thy business ply,
Be sure let not Plough idle lie,
For to get wealth is not amiss,
To use all means that lawful is.

November 1665

To quicken thy spirits and make thy self merry,
Drink now and then a cup of sherry,
But do not make it a common trade,
Lest things abused the worst are made.

December 1665

And to conclude this good old year,
Invite thy neighbours to good cheer,   50
Let Gates and Doores wide open be,
That rich and poor may enter free,
Let not the Cook or Butler rest,
And hang such churles as will not feast.

ANONYMOUS
(**1665**)

This scribbled manuscript verse is found in the National Library of Ireland copy of Ambrose White's 1665 Dublin almanac.

An Epitaph upon one Browne, an Irish Man

Here Browne, ye quondam Beggar,[1] lies
    Who counted by his tale,
Full six score winters, & above,
    Such vertue is in Ale.
Ale was his meat, his drinke, his cloth,
    Ale did his death reprieve.
And could hee still have drunke his Ale,
    Hee had been still alieve.

1. i.e. who was once a beggar.

JEREMY TAYLOR
(1613–*c*.**1665**–1667)

Jeremy Taylor, the famous Bishop of Down and Connor, is remembered as a fine preacher, and as the author of some of the most popular devotional works in the Anglican tradition, *The Rule and Exercises of Holy Living* (1650), *The Rule and Exercise of Holy Dying* (1651) and *The Worthy Communicant* (1660). He also published many volumes of controversy and of sermons. *The Golden Grove* (1655), a manual of belief and prayers, contains much of his verse. Taylor is justly praised as one of the finest prose stylist of his age, but his verse has been neglected.

Four Festival Hymns

I
A Hymn for Christmas Day

> Mysterious truth! that the self-same should be
> A Lamb, a Shepherd, and a Lion too!
> > Yet such was he
> > Whom first the shepherds knew,
> > When they themselves became
> > Sheep to the Shepherd-Lamb.
> Shepherd of men and angels, – Lamb of God, –
> Lion of Judah,[1] – by these titles keep
> The wolf from thy endangered sheep.
> > Bring all the world into thy fold;   10
> > > Let Jews and Gentiles hither come
> > In numbers great, that can't be told;
> > > And call thy lambs, that wander, home.
> > Glory be to God on high;
> All glories be to th' glorious Deity.

II
The second Hymn for Christmas Day; being a Dialogue between three Shepherds

> 1.   Where is this blessed Babe,
> > That hath made

---

1. One of the Old Testament names for God. The chosen people (the Jews) sometimes called themselves after Judah, one of the sons of Jacob. Jacob's blessing of his son includes the following: 'Judah is the lion's whelp; . . . he couched as a lion, and as an old lion' (Genesis 49. 9–10).

All the world so full of joy
  And expectation?
  That glorious boy,
  That crowns each nation
With a triumphant wreath of blessedness?

2. Where should he be but in the throng,
   And among
His angel-ministers, that sing   10
   And take wing
Just as may echo to his voice,
   And rejoice,
  When wing and tongue and all
  May so procure their happiness.

3. But he hath other waiters now;
   A poor cow,
An ox, and mule, stand and behold, –
   And wonder,
That a stable should enfold   20
   Him who can thunder.

Chorus: O what a gracious God have we!
How good, how great! ev'n as our misery.

III

A Hymn upon St. John's Day

This day
We sing
The friend of our eternal King,
  Who in his bosom lay,
  And kept the keys
Of his profound and glorious mysteries;
Which, to the world dispensed by his hand,
   Made it stand
Fix'd in amazement to behold that light,
   Which came   10
From the throne of the Lamb,
   To invite

Our wretched eyes (which nothing else could see
But fire, and sword, hunger, and misery)
    To anticipate, by their ravish'd sight,
    The beauty of celestial delight.
Mysterious God, regard me when I pray;
    And when this load of clay
      Shall fall away,
O let thy gracious hand conduct me up,   20
Where on the Lamb's rich viands[1] I may sup:
    And, in this last supper, I
May, with thy friend, in thy sweet bosom lie,
    For ever, in eternity.   Hallelujah.

IV

Upon the Day of the Holy Innocents[1]

Mournful Judah shrieks and cries
    At the obsequies
    Of their babes, that cry
More that they lose their paps,[2] than that they die.
    He, that came with life to all
    Brings the babes a funeral, –
    To redeem from slaughter him,
    Who did redeem us all from sin.
    They, like himself, went spotless hence,
    A sacrifice to innocence;   10
      Which now does ride
    Trampling upon Herod's pride;
Passing, from their fontinels[3] of clay,
To heaven a milky and a bloody way.
    All their tears and groans are dead,
    And they to rest and glory fled;
Lord, who wert pleas'd so many babes should fall,
Whilst each sword hop'd that ev'ry of them all
Was the desired King: make us to be
In innocence like them, – in glory, Thee. – Amen.   20

---

1. foods.

1. The church festival commemorating the children slaughtered by Herod in the expectation that one of them would be the infant Christ.
2. the breasts that give them suck.
3. fontanelles, the membranes that make up the skull of a new-born baby.

JO. BINCKES
(*fl*.*c*.**1669**)

Jo. Binckes, according to the prose explanation which accompanies this poem in the Ormond manuscript, had just returned from England where he had gone 'on purpose to shew his Matie A new devizd Weapon, ye use of wch I shall more fully declare, when I shall share it . . .' Binckes (about whom nothing is known) seems to have been an eccentric and (accurately) describes the following verse as a 'poor endeavour'. Though most of Binckes's poem is hard to understand, the following short passage of flattery makes its point in a clear if peculiar manner. Ormond received the poem on the eve of one of his departures from Ireland, probably in 1669 when he was recalled as lord lieutenant, to be replaced by the morose Lord Robartes.

from: An humble token of loyalty & sincere gratitude

The Lizards eyes the face of Man amazeth
Looking on w^ch, ye moor & moor it gazeth;[1]
When I yor heaven-infused graces view
My lord, my sense, Amazed, stares on you.
Heaven tempers so its gifts in you alone,
As y^t all graces seeme combind in on[e].
When I doe homage to nobility,
Streight on[e] doth declare your charity;
So earthly glory & y^t of heav'n begun
Makes you A glorious object like ye sun   10
W^ch darteth forth so many rayes of light
As y^t they dazll this my scantlinge[2] sight.
In you, great Junos[3] stately majesty
Is fraught with Christian Love and Charity.
What's Venus beauty to yr sacred face
W^ch is the Physyognomy of Grace . . .

---

1. The line seems to propose the unusual idea that the more a lizard looks at a man's face, the more astonished it becomes.
2. limited.
3. Juno, the wife of Jupiter, was the classical goddess of women and marriage, Venus the goddess of love.

ROGER BOYLE, EARL OF ORRERY (?) and ANONYMOUS
(*c*.**1670**)

The first two lines of this well-known verse were allegedly inscribed by the protestant Roger Boyle, first Earl of Orrery (1621–79) on the gates of Bandon Bridge some time in the 1660s – long before he abandoned secular writing for sacred verse (see p. 452). As the Countess of Cork and Orrery put it in her 1903 introduction to *The Orrery Papers* (p. xiii), 'A spirited and quick-witted R.C. capped these lines, during a dark night', by putting underneath them the second distich.

Lines allegedly written on the gates of Bandon Bridge

> Jew, Infidel, or Atheist
> May enter here, but not a Papist.

> Who wrote these words composed them well,
> The same are written on the Gates of Hell.

ANONYMOUS
(*c*.**1670**)

Burlesque verse and its closely related form, travesty – in which a serious work of literature is inverted and parodied so that it becomes the opposite of its true self and, often, a vehicle for political and social satire – were popular among the wits of the seventeenth century. The texts most commonly travestied were the Bible and the *Æneid* – the two best-known books in the western world at the time. The fashion for travesty, which started in France with Paul Scarron's *Le Virgile Travestie en Vers Burlesques* in 1648, had spread to England by the 1660s, when travesties of various books of Virgil appeared, the most memorable from the pen of Charles Cotton (1630–87). There is little doubt that the poem which follows was fashioned on these English travesties and influenced by *Hudibras*, the wildly popular verse attack by Samuel Butler (1612–80) on the extreme puritanism that had engulfed England during the previous generation. One way of attacking those you feared or disliked was to make them appear ridiculous in burlesque verse.

The extract which follows comes from one version of the only known Irish travesty of the *Æneid*; this work exists in three versions, two manuscripts – one the 'Purgatorium Hibernicum' and the other entitled 'The Fingallian Travesty' – and a printed text, *The Irish Hudibras* (London, 1689). It is hard to disentangle the relationship between these three texts, but the 'Purgatorium' seems to be the earliest, though the only surviving text of the poem is a careless, eighteenth-century copy of a lost original (NLI MS. 470).[1] The name 'Francis Taubman' is shown at the end of the manuscript, but it is not clear whether this indicates that he was the scribe of the manuscript or the author of the text. In any case, nothing is known of Taubman and scholars agree that this attribution is suspect; all three versions of the poem are best, for the moment, deemed anonymous. However, joint authorship is a real possibility and the poem may well be the work of a group of New English planters or landlords based in Fingal, the area north of Dublin known for its fertile soil and for the dialect of Hiberno-English spoken there until the eighteenth century – 'Fingallian'.[2] Whoever wrote the 'Purgatorium' wanted to make the native Irish – here represented by those of Irish extraction living in Fingal – and their catholic faith, seem absurd. Virgil's prince Æneas and his noble lover Dido are transformed into a bumbling young Fingallian called 'Prince' Nees (cf. also the Irish proper name Naois), and a coarse ex-nun named Dydy. The events of the sixth book of the *Æneid* – Æneas's descent into the underworld, his meeting with his father and the father's prophecy about the future greatness of the nation that Æneas would found – are transformed into Nees's descent into the cave at Saint Patrick's Purgatory and a prophecy by his father that Ireland would soon throw off the yoke of the mercantile English and return to the customs of Gaelic Ireland. The names of the characters are converted into 'mock' Irish forms, and the places mentioned in Virgil's text become places in Fingal. The poem is in rhyming tetrameters, the metre also used by Samuel Butler for his comic masterpiece and often known as 'Hudibrastics', and the speeches given to 'Prince' Nees are in broad – almost unintelligible – 'Fingallian' or, as the text describes it

---

1. This version of the text was probably written during the reign of Charles II, though it is hard to date it accurately, and some scholars have suggested a date as early as 1655; it seems unlikely, however, that the poem could be earlier than any of the travesties printed in England. More work needs to be done on this text and the date assigned to it here, 1670, should be considered provisional.
2. See Alan Bliss, *Spoken English in Ireland 1600–1740* (Dublin, 1979) for a full discussion of seventeenth-century Fingallian.

in 'Irish English hotch-potch'. The result, though somewhat tiresome for modern readers, is energetic and distinctive.

The authors of the 'Purgatorium' may have felt effortlessly superior to the culture they were burlesquing, but they thought enough of it to become familiar with it and its language. The text contains many words and phrases in Irish and the action of the poem is cleverly adapted from that in Virgil to fit the circumstances of seventeenth-century Ireland. The poem also includes many details of daily life – all of which, of course, are turned to ridicule. But the text does give the impression of being, at least to some extent, a serious exercise; the relevant lines of Virgil's Latin text are placed at the bottom of each page and the margins contain notes referring the reader to source works on Irish history in English, Latin and Irish. The evidence suggests, therefore, that the intended audience for this poem and its variants were well-educated, New English Fingallian settlers. Perhaps versions of the poem were circulated and amended within the group. At any rate, nearly twenty years after its first conception, with the fortunes of protestant settlers at a very low ebb, the poem was updated and put into print in the hope that it might undermine the credibility of the Irish catholic cause: the result was the 1689 printing of the text as *The Irish Hudibras*.

The extract below comes from about halfway through the 'Purgatorium' (ll. 1537–1644) and corresponds closely to *Æneid* vi 450–76. The Fingallian dialect of Hiberno-English used in this extract has been studied by Alan Bliss in *Spoken English in Ireland 1600–1740*, and the reader interested in the linguistic peculiarities of the text is referred to that book. I should like to thank Alan Harrison for his help with the annotations.

from: **Purgatorium Hibernicum,**

or, the sixth Booke of Virgills Æneis Travestie Burlesque a la mode de Fingaule[3]

> . . . Amongst this traine,[4] who (thinke you) espied he
> But his old mistres, Madam Dydy
> That pin'd to death, the fawneing strapp,[5]
> Some say for love, some of a Clapp,[6]
> When Nees from Lusk[7] turn'd helm alarbor[8]
> And tooke up quarters in his harbour.[9]

---

3. To make this difficult text more comprehensible, inverted commas have been inserted to indicate possessives and direct speech.
4. Nees is exploring the various levels of purgatory and has just seen 'a desperate troope of pinceing lovers' (accused, in a marginal note, of being 'Hemathrodites'), among whom he spies Dydy; 'pinceing', which is obscure, is replaced with the word 'whining' in the 1689 *Irish Hudibras*.
5. whore; cf. Ir. *straip*.
6. venereal disease.
7. A settlement in Fingal. But see note 9 to the couplet as a whole.
8. turned helm to larboard, i.e. turned round about.
9. This couplet makes little sense as it stands but, as Bliss notes (p. 332), NLI MS 470, from which this text is taken, is a carelessly written transcript. The corresponding passage in the 1689 printed text, *The Irish Hudibras*, is much clearer and explains that Dydy was pining because Nees had been unfaithful to her: 'When from her *Nees* turned Helm a Larbour, / To anchor in false *Jen*——'s Harbour' (p. 65).

Nees, glideing at her through the shade,
A sheep's eye cast from a calfe's head;[10]
Who soon the Prince's courage dashes,
For she did looke as pail as ashes,   10
Did pull him out on's[11] seaven sences.
'Sure, sure!' sayes Nees, 'dis me old vench[12] is!'
But when he drew more neare her qua[r]ters[13]
And knew her by her suggam[14] garters,
'Ful Dea, ro,[15] dou[16] unlucky jade,
I'll chance upon dee! Art thou dead?[17]
Fat devill vas be in dee, vench?
Vas he soe hot is cou'd no quench
De flame?'[18] 'Indeed, oh no!, but Nees chief
Occasion is of all dis mischeif.'   20
'But, be[19] de hand of Galarna,[20]
By fader's[21] sole, I tell de[e] true,
And be!,[22] more sure [I] tell dee still,
Avont avay against me vill,[23]
Comanded bee[24] superior powers,

---

10. 'To cast a sheep's eye at' was a proverbial phrase meaning 'to look amorously at'; the second part of the expression ('from a calfe's head') is used by Swift in *Polite Conversation* (*The Prose Works of Jonathan Swift*, ed. Herbert Davis (Oxford, 1957), IV, 141). The animals are reversed in the parallel line in *The Irish Hudibras*.

11. of his.

12. wench. See Bliss, pp. 230–1.

13. her hind quarters.

14. straw rope. cf. Ir. *súgán*.

15. = Ful Dea, ro = God's blood, sweetheart; cf. Ir. *fuil Dé, a rogha*. (*rogha* = choice.) The first word of this line is written 'Fut' in the manuscript – a scribal error for 'Ful'.

16. thou. For the substitution of 'd' for 'th' in Hiberno-English texts of this time – which occurs throughout this text – see Bliss, pp. 232–3.

17. i.e. 'I have chanced upon thee. Are you dead?' As in book vi of the *Æneid*, all those Nees sees in purgatory have died on earth.

18. A classic example of Nees's Fingallian speech. A 'translation' would be: 'What devil was in thee, wench? Was it so hot the flame could not be quenched?' The 'flame' is venereal disease.

19. by. See Bliss, p. 207.

20. = Gilarnoo, i.e. *Giolla na naomh mac Cuinn na mBocht*, or (in English) 'Servant of the saints, son of Conn of the poor'. This is an actual historical person, quoted by Conall Mac Geoghagan, seventeenth-century translator of the *Annals of Clonmacnoise*, as 'Gilnarnew of Cloniuchenos', one of the authors consulted during the compilation of the annals. The entry is under the year 1069.

21. [my] father's; see Bliss, pp. 232–3.

22. = and't be, if it be, indeed. cf. Ir. *muise* (mistakenly thought to come from Ir. *má sea*). See Bliss, p. 260.

23. = I went away against my will.

24. by.

Is make me h[a]unt dese donny bowers;[25]
And fate!,[26] and be!, I never tought
Mee company had ever trought[27]
Such after-clapps![28] Arra,[29] but stay!
Fat devill make it goe avay?   30
She cannot hold one touch, butt itching
She's after bee to run a bit[c]hing,[30]
Hold must the passe so vid her beares.
Nees is not see[31] soe many yeares.
If it be soe, dis good blad[32] first
I'le [* * *][33] my Deedy for a maid first.
Shall ne're be laid, me owne sait heart,[34]
Dat ve two shall with dry lips part.
Before dou goe, be me salvation,
Nees vill imploy dee occupation,   40
Untill ve take a little pastime –
A parting kisse: dis is de last time.'

The Prince's passion here was spent,
And rested in this complement;
But Dydy, like a sullen sow,
Fix't on the grownd her angry brow,
And noe more regards his balling[35]
Than shee were a rocke of Mabline;[36]

---

25. = which make me haunt these miserable bowers. For 'donny', cf. Ir. *donaí*.
26. faith. It is common for spelling in this text to reflect Hiberno-English pronunciation.
27. = brought.
28. i.e. such an attack of the clap (see note to line 4). In Irish, the prefix *iar-* = after-.
29. indeed. cf. Ir. *ara*.
30. This (probably indecent) passage is hard to explain: it may mean: 'she can not stay for even a short period (a 'touch') without itching to run looking for sexual partners; she must bravely contend like this with rough fellows.' The last line of the parallel passage in *The Irish Hudibras*, 'Shall never pass so vid her Bears' (p. 66) is equally incomprehensible. For an explanation of the use of the consuetudinal present tense of verbs in seventeenth-century Hiberno-English (e.g. 'after be'), see Bliss, pp. 292–4.
31. has not seen.
32. 1) fellow; 2) penis.
33. The single-syllable word is omitted in the manuscript.
34. Careless transcription: the line should read 'Shall nere be said, me owne suit heart' (i.e. sweetheart).
35. bawling – though the word could be 'babling' = babbling – depending on the rhyme needed.
36. A note at this point in *The Irish Hudibras* reads: 'In Fingaul'. There is no place in Fingal with this name, but the earliest recorded Irish name for the rocky islet off the coast now known as Rock-a-bill is *Cloch na mBilleán*, which could be represented in English as 'rock of Mabline'.

For, ever since the last crangore,[37]
An inward grudge to th'prince she boare,   50
For a small token he had lent her,
For ('twas without all peradventure
Belived by most) the active squire
Had set her lower roomes afire,[38]
Which caused her to suspect the sculline[39]
Had still a spice of the strangillin.[40]
Have you seen porks in yoalk of Luske,[41]
When they doe excer[c]ise theire tuske
Att trough, grunnt, foam, and seem to bee
Mov'd with impatience? – soe shee,   60
Chaffing and foaming att the mouth,
Did spite[42] her venom at the youth.

'I,[43] Nees,' sayes she in mighty snuffe,
'And be![44] is tink is varm enough,
If dou cam shance but to find out
Dee old consort to have a bout –
And den, fen dou has play'd de vagge,
To give mee, as before, de bagge![45]
Butt I will vatch de vales, Nees,
And putt foile on dee, dy dis chees.'[46]   70
Since which it to [a] proverbe grew,
When burne-breech hacknes will not doe.[47]

---

37. This word is unrecorded, but is probably the Ir. *crannchur*, something that has happened by chance.
38. These four lines refer to Nees's having infected Dydy with venereal disease.
39. scullion, wretch.
40. = strangullion, strangury; a disease of the urinary tract.
41. i.e. the pigs in the centre of (the town of) Lusk.
42. spit.
43. i.e. 'Ay, Nees,' she says, in a fit of great passion.
44. See note to line 23 above.
45. A rough paraphrase of these lines would be: And do you think it is warm enough (i.e. it is acceptable), if you can chance upon your old lover, to have a bout with her? And then, when you have played the wag (played truant) to dismiss me, as you did before?
46. 'dy' is an error for 'by'. The phrase 'watch the walls' may refer to the seventeenth-century proverb: 'Look on the wall and it will not bite you' which, according to John Ray in *A Collection of English Proverbs* (London 1670), was spoken in jest to such as are bitten with mustard (itself an obscure phrase but one which could, again, refer to venereal disease). The couplet seems to mean: But I will watch the walls, Nees, and frustrate your designs, by this cheese! The last oath is probably obscene.
47. A 'hackney' was a prostitute; 'burne-breech' probably means *either* infected with venereal disease (as used by Shakespeare), *or* exhibiting excessive sexual desire (cf. the slang phrase 'a brenten maid'); to 'do' was to please someone.

'And nowe in earnest let mee tell ho[w]
Dou art but an unvordy[48] fellow,
A tory Runagade and fo,[49]
To us[50] an honest voman so!'

'Sure, sure,' sayes Nees, 'she does but jeast,
It's not de nature of de beast;
Praise dee here,[51] mee joly rogue,
And gave de [me] one litle Poge[52]   80
For old acquaintance, for it's dee
Dat is mee only gra-ma-cree.'[53]

'Kiss mee? Poo! Fart upon dee, Nees!
Is[54] may as vel kisse my breast![55]
I know de[e] vell enough, and bee,
"Is de old hawke have de old Eye".[56]
Dou know de proverbe, Come noe neare!
De scald child, fate, is feare de fire.
And now I know de[e] for a Rogue,
I scorn de[e], as dirt of me brogue,'[57]   90
Belching an oyster[58] in her fist;
'I care not dis for all dee grist!'[59]
Soe fledd as nimble as the wind
(And bid the Prince to kisse behind)[60]
To Sichy, the old cuckold, nigh,
Where shee had other fish to fry.

48. unworthy.
49. i.e. an outlaw, renegade and foe . . .
50. use.
51. The equivalent line in *The Irish Hudibras* is 'Pree-dee come here, my pretty Rogue', i.e. pray thee . . .
52. kiss. cf. Ir. *póg*.
53. darling. Ir. *grá mó chroí*, 'love of my heart'.
54. = you.
55. The MS reads 'breast', but the word should be 'breech' – as it is in the equivalent line in *The Irish Hudibras* and as required by the rhyme.
56. This proverb, the meaning of which is obvious, is unrecorded. The proverb in line 88 is a version of 'The burnt child dreads the fire'.
57. brogue, shoe. Ir. *bróg*.
58. expectorating.
59. either = flattery (Bliss) or activity (Joseph Wright, *English Dialect Dictionary* (Oxford, 1898)).
60. cf. Ir. *póg mó thóin*.

'Swoop, swoop![61] a callagh,[62] oh!' sayes Nees,
'De Devill may dee coller spleece
'Twix me and Good and de hall door,[63]
Dou art a rotten rosted whore.   100
No vonder doit be deare, in trote,
Fen pole bushell is vort a groat,[64]
Fen beggars must be after chooseing!
Marry, comes up, my dirty cousin.[65]
I'le see her burne, and Devill have her,
'For I creep in her ——- for favour.
Fat, creep to her? to her? a turd she!
Since she is soe stout, I'le be soe sturdy!"[66] . . .

61. An oath or ejaculation unrecorded elsewhere, expressing derision. Perhaps = Ir. *suas, suas*.

62. old woman. cf. Ir. *cailleach*. The manuscript reads 'cattagh'.

63. spleece = splice = (here) split; 'Good' is a rare equivalent for 'God', found only in the Hiberno-English dialects of Forth and Bray and Fingal (see Bliss, pp. 319–20); hall = hell. The lines seem to mean 'The devil may split the bond between me and God and the door of hell'.

64. pole (probably) = whole. However, the passage (which does not occur in either of the other versions of this text) is obscure and may contain some mistranscription. As it stands, it seems to mean: 'When beggars must be choosers, no wonder a little bit ('doit' = a small quantity) is so expensive, in truth, when a whole bushel (i.e. a large quantity) is worth a groat (a coin of small value)'.

65. Joseph Wright recorded this strange expression, 'Marry come up, my dirty cousin' in his *English Dialect Dictionary*, and explained that it is used to those who are 'very fastidious or who assume a distinction to which they have no claim'. The saying was also used by Swift.

66. stout = proud; sturdy = obstinate.

417

AQUILA SMYTH
(*fl*.**1670**)

The first printed medical textbook written in Ireland in the English language was the work of an English doctor practising in Cork, James Wolveridge. His *Speculum Matricis Hybernicum; or the Irish Midwives Handmaid; catechistically composed* ... (London, 1670) is well-known to historians of medicine as one of the earliest works on midwifery in English, and as one of the most sensible of its time. Though his book draws heavily on Wolveridge's experience in Ireland – and though he is full of praise for fertility, fecundity and hardiness of the women of Ireland – the author thought of himself as an Englishman stationed in Cork, and wrote the book not for the Irish but for the edification of midwives working in the English countryside. This is why, he explains in the preface to his book, he wrote it in 'an English Dialect' rather than in Latin, and why he sent the manuscript to be printed in London though it was 'tossed by the impetuous waves of the Irish Seas e're it could set foot on the English-shore' ('The Author to the Reader'. sig. A3v).

As well as containing two poems by Wolveridge himself, the prefatory material to *Speculum Matricis Hybernicum* includes verses by four of Wolveridge's friends in Cork. Jonathan Ashe, a graduate of Oxford, contributed two poems, one in Latin and one in English, and Daniel Colman J.V.D. was the author of a poem in Latin which he signed '*Ex Musæolo meo in Suburbiis Borealibus Corcagiæ, Idibis Septembris, 1669*' ('From my writing room in the western suburbs of Cork, the Ides of September 1669'); Richard Sampson contributed a lamentably inept acrostic on the name JAMES WOLLVERIDGE and Aquila Smyth, M.D. sent in the ingenious (if in places only barely intelligible) poem which follows.

Nothing is known of Aquila Smyth except that he was a doctor living in Cork, and that, as a writer, he enjoyed finding double meanings in various terms from midwifery and evidently thought of himself as a wit. Smyth's poem is included here as an example of the type of verse which circulated in the medical community in Cork in the 1660s. Clearly, similar exchanges of verse must have taken place in professional coteries in the larger towns in Ireland as well as in Dublin at the time but, unfortunately, apart from the verses printed in *Speculum Matricis Hybernicum*, none of this material seems to have survived.

On the Praise, and happy delivery of *James Wolveridge*, Dr. of Physick, in his labours on the Labour of Women &c. Delivered by Aquila Smyth, M.D.

Here is the Key unlocks a Cabinet,[1]
So quick, so safe, by art not known as yet:
More friendly than the gourd o're *Jonas* head,[2]

---

1. i.e. Here is the key which unlocks the place where the secrets of midwifery have been kept out of sight – perhaps with overtones of the seventeenth-century low-life use of the word 'key' to mean a penis.
2. When the prophet Jonah, angry that God had saved the city of Nineveh, retired to the desert, God caused a gourd plant to 'come up over' him to protect him from the sun. Jonah was 'exceeding glad of the gourd'. (Jonah 4. 6.) The fast-growing gourd of the story is known as the 'Palma Christi' or the kiki plant.

It breaks the *Hymen*, and the Maidenhead.[3]
What shall I say! mysterious is thy art,
But so, that labour labours in no smart;[4]
Thy clouded Genius 'mid'st the Curtain foggs,[5]
Swallows thy worth in the *Hybernian* boggs;
Dismantle[6] then thy self, appear to be
Happy to all in thy delivery.
So the production of thy brain shall make
Midwives themselves produce; and for thy sake
Sol teeming thus, man-Midwives out a birth,
That is the product, to the globe and earth:[7]
But whilst thy brain doth labour, we do too
Bring but an Embrion out, though 't out do
Mountains (full gravidated, but produce
A mouse) when thou dost open natures sluce;
So riper seeds are sown on barren ground,
So th'Reaper hath a sickly harvest found.[8]
The pregnant *pia mater*[9] of thy brain
Doth settle in his place, the womb, again:
There is no *Mola*[10] in thy wit, what's here
Of truth is the effect and character.
Teeming[11] this nine moneths, we did surely look
That thou should'st be delivered of thy Book;
Prodigious Birth! who e're the like did know
A child brought forth, strait to a Midwife grow?

3. i.e. the book (which is more of a relief to its readers than the gourd was to the sunscorched Jonah) breaks down the barriers between the outside world and the mysteries of female generation.
4. i.e. but so mysterious that the 'labour' of producing it is painless.
5. the mists (of Ireland).
6. reveal yourself.
7. i.e. the sun brings forth its offspring thus, using a man midwife (Wolveridge) to assist in the birth (of this book) and so make it available to the whole world. The underlying meaning is that Wolveridge's book is approved by the sun – i.e. by nature herself.
8. It is not clear that the poet himself knew what he was trying to say in this complicated passage. A tentative interpretation is: But whilst your brain labours, we are at work as well, only bringing an embryo into the world; this, though it outdoes mountains (fully pregnant and in labour which produce only a mouse [a reference to Horace *De Arte Poetica* 139: *Parturiunt montes, nascetur ridiculus mus*. 'The mountains are in labour, a ridiculous mouse will be born']) when you open nature's sluice, (i.e. when the natural methods in your book are released on the world) will result in riper seeds being sown on barren soil (i.e. more fertility in women?) and a sickly harvest for death (i.e. lower rates of infant mortality?).
9. One of three delicate membranes which enclose the brain and spinal cord.
10. a false conception.
11. pregnant.

Cease nature, now, thy tyrannies in vain,
Here's one doth teach to mitigate a pain,
Sets open Natures Gate, so that the birth
Walks from the mother-womb to mother-earth:
No throws we have in this, no shreaks, no cryes,[12]
No Instruments, no Cupping of the thighes:
Here is an Art that after-age will boast,
And tell how *Wolv'ridge* hath deliver'd most
With ease, producing forth what's safe we see,
To which whole Colledges thy Gossips[13] be.

Your devoted Friend and Servant,
Aquila Smyth, M.D. Septemb. 9th. 1669. Cork.

---

12. i.e. we have in the birth of this book no writhing (in pain), no shrieks, no cries, no use of instruments, no bleeding of the thighs. 'Cupping' involved scarifying the skin so as to draw blood and then applying a heated cup to collect it.
13. sponsors; i.e. all the medical colleges will embrace and promote the ideas in this book.

ANONYMOUS
(1671)

Among many seventeenth-century Irish poems to be found in the manuscripts in the Bodleian Library Oxford, are three elegies commemorating members of Trinity College Dublin. All three died in 1671; two of them were fellows, Francis Usher and John Christian, and the other, John Nelson, was an undergraduate who died from smallpox at the age of eighteen. The poem commemorating Nelson is the most accomplished of the three.

Nelson was born in Ross, County Kerry, in about 1652 and was the son of an officer. He entered Trinity College on 27 March 1668 at the age of fifteen, and died three and a half years later, on 20 September 1671. The author of the poem on his death is not known.

On the death of Mʳ Jo. Nelson who Dyed of the Small Pox

Never than now did Death seem more a Hagg,[1]
    Who out of Envy has to him assign'd
Disease so loathsom, that we should not brag
    His Body was as spotless as his mind.
Thus have I seen a foaming Snail deface
A Thriving Plant, and leave a slimy Trace.

But sure 'tis rather Lust in Death, than Spite,
    That makes him like to Ravishers assault
Those most whose Graces temptingly invite,
    Force on, and after, half excuse the fault.   10
Base Ravisher! Unable to deface
The Inclosed Jewell, strok[2] the less priz'd Case.

Were't possible with leaves to wash his Urn
    And with lowd shrieks recall his former breath,
We should his joys to sudden sorrows turne,
    And for suppos'd give him a surer Death.
The Ancient Thracians did not vainly guess,
Death gives the lye of Life and Happiness.[3]

What though he young did to yᵉ untimely blow
    Of conquering Death his spotless soul resign,   20

1. An evil spirit: the word could refer to a man as well as to a woman.
2. i.e. struck. The 'jewel' was Nelson's mind, the 'case' his body.
3. The ancient inhabitants of Thrace (a country on the western shores of the Black Sea, now divided between Greece and Bulgaria) were noted for cruelty and barbarity, particularly for their habit of summarily sacrificing their enemies on the altars of their gods.

'Twas his discretion sooner thus to know
   Eternall Joyes, and Future Ills decline;
And more than others, this Advantage gains,
Reaps greater Wages, and for lesser Pains.

ANONYMOUS
(*c*.**1673**)

Sir William Petty entertained himself not only by writing verse – see below his poem under the year 1677 – but also by collecting it. The following piece, preserved in a manuscript volume in the British Library entitled 'Sir William Petty's Poetical Amusements', is clearly not by Petty himself, but must have been collected by him as it passed around his Dublin circle. Such poems about life in London are not particularly unusual since the persons mentioned were of general interest; this poem, however, seems to be the only verse survival containing details of the seamier side of life in Restoration Dublin. Though it might be unwise to assume that the upper classes in Restoration Dublin were quite as debauched as this poem suggests, a close reading of pages 56–65 of Edward MacLysaght's *Life in Seventeenth-Century Ireland* (revised ed., Shannon, 1969) shows that the city had a rather unsavoury reputation at times during the reign of Charles II.

Most of the men mentioned in the poem can be identified since they were noblemen or had university connections; the prostitutes, since they used pseudonyms, remain masked. It is interesting to note an apparently close connection between prostitution in London and in Dublin at the time, though it is possible, of course, that the whole thing is an elaborate hoax designed to embarrass respectable members of the Dublin elite. Whether the piece reflects fact or fantasy, however, someone clearly enjoyed writing it and, one presumes, Petty and his friends found it entertaining reading.

A Letter from a Missionary Bawd in Dublin, to her cheif in London
giveing an account of the propogation of lewdness and scandall in Ireland.

> Since I by your commission hold my place,
> 'Tis fit I let you know how matters pass.
> Love's mighty Empire has not in his Sphear
> A Collony more flourishing than here.
> We need no more recruits henceforth from you,
> Our harvest's great, our Reapers are not few;
> The Youths are sparkish,[1] Brisk, and lewd enough,
> The Women soft to love and scandall proof;
> But I touch things in breif, because you know
> The persons names and reputations too.   10
>
> Proud Margetson[2] whose beauty must give law,
> Because her looks strikes men with love and awe,

---

1. gallant.
2. Strange though it may seem, this might be a reference to Anne Margetson, only daughter of Dr James Margetson, Archbishop of Armagh. She married, on 11 July 1678, William, second Viscount Charlemont, a brother of the Jack Caulfeild mentioned on line 26 of this poem and eldest son of the Lord Charlemont mentioned at line 35. Despite this real-life connection, however, it seems more likely that the prostitutes in the poem affected the names of respectable members of society than that such people were really involved in the business described.

Amongst the crowd of her admiring Sparkes,
Sir William Talbot[3] for her cully marks;
She at ticktack[4] him often entertaines,
And through that spunge his Masters Guineys draines;
But they're agreed, for shee to him each day
Refunds in pleasure what she won at play.
The Mercinary Jilt has twice been sold,
She married first, and now she whores for gold.   20
Her husband, though he cannot ward the blow,
Rough as he is, has got a Mistress too.
The Vanity of rivalling his wife
Makes Bingham[5] grace his love & heal his greif.
He's of this freedom makeing use
Jack Cawfeild[6] to their Chambers introduce
Where he does ruffle them att hide and seek,
For Virgins in the dark ne're blush nor squeek.
The Lady Charlemount[7] is so religious
She turns the Church into a meeting house,   30
And there, when parson ends his exhortation,
Shee makes in pulpit an holy Assignation
And crys, when he hath held fourth all he can,
I have not [been] edify'd more by any man.
Her Bubled Lord[8] ne're thought of a surprize
Till he was caught by Lady Eley's[9] eyes,
Who like lewd Potiphar's wife[10] would haul him in
But he, like Joseph, cryes, Noe, tis a sin.
With tender caution and mature advice,
Tom Cawfeild[11] leaves his girles here with his Niece.   40
Green and unripe they come from Countrey farms,
But warm'd and chaf't in their kind kindred's Arms.

---

3. This is probably the Sir William Talbot who, at this time, rented Carton House, County Kildare, from the Fitzgerald family. He was a member of the junior branch of the family of Talbot of Malahide, and a baronet; cully = dupe, but the word can also mean a mate.
4. a kind of backgammon.
5. Possibly Sir George Bingham, who married twice and was an ancestor of the earls of Lucan.
6. One of the four sons of William Caulfeild, fifth Lord Charlemont. (The name was often spelt 'Cawfeild' at the time').
7. Sarah, second daughter of Viscount Drogheda, Jack Caulfeild's mother.
8. William, fifth Lord Charlemont, Jack Caulfeild's father and (from 1665) first Viscount Charlemont.
9. Jane née Lyndley, wife of Edward Loftus, second Viscount Loftus of Ely.
10. The story of Potiphar's wife and her attempted seduction of Joseph is told in Genesis 39. 7–20.
11. Fourth son of the fifth Lord Charlemont, and a younger brother of Jack Caulfeild.

Like fruit that's forct, they are so forward grown
That they will drop before they should be blown.[12]
Who evermore will trust a freind or son
As Steward, as[13] old Dillon has Sir John?[14]
Hee and his wanton mother sport and laugh,
Thinking that nothing can be ill that's safe:
'Tis sin and scandall when it gaines beliefe
But – who suspects a son for his father's wife?   50
Wise Chichester[15] brings not his spouse to town,
But keeps her for the healthfull country clown,
For since it must or here or there be done,
He swears hee'l have a wholesome butter'd bun.
Blainey,[16] twixt love and fear, has hurry'd hence,
Though seeing forraigne parts was his pretence;
And most men think the dreadfull Marrow's[17] armes
Did more perswade his flight than Arran's Charmes.
By day nor night Cuff's fiddlestrings ne're rests;
Oh heavens! Orpheus is among the beasts!   60
Where Biddy Nelson was the female drill,[18]
Still making ugly face and chattring still,
Lord Blessington presents the male Baboon,
Beating false time and scammering[19] at the tune.
Worth,[20] the tame ram, with inoffensive horne,
Sees his soft ewe by his head Pastor shorne.
By his languishing long ears, Dillany[21] may passe,
And horrid braying, for the fuller Asse.

---

12. i.e. like forced fruit, they will drop (from the plant) before they have attained perfection.
13. MS reads 'and'.
14. 'Old Dillon' is either Thomas, fourth Viscount Dillon, who died in 1673 at the age of 63, or Thomas, fifth Viscount Dillon, who died in 1674. 'Sir John' must have been the son of one of these noblemen (see l. 50).
15. Arthur Chichester, second earl of Donegal who married, on 9 March 1660, Jane Itchingham of Dunbrody, Co. Wexford.
16. Sir Edward Blayney had been created Lord Blayney in 1621, and this reference is to the fourth Baron Blaney. Details of the family between the first lord and the seventh lord, Cadwallader, who married in 1714, are sketchy.
17. No information can be discovered on Mesdames Marrow, Arran, Cuff or Nelson – but (on 'Arran') see the note to l. 69 below.
18. A West African baboon. Lord Blessington (who was presumably Ms. Nelson's friend) was Murrough Boyle (*b.* 1645), son of the archbishop of Armagh; the date of his elevation to a viscountcy was 23 August 1673. He attended Trinity College Dublin and the Middle Temple in London.
19. An unrecorded word, possibly connected with the verb 'to scamble', to stumble along.
20. Perhaps John Worth, son of the bishop of Killaloe, who entered Trinity College Dublin in 1662 and later became Dean of St Patrick's Cathedral, Dublin.
21. untraced.

Ardglass[22] alone of all the family
[line omitted in manuscript]   70
Till one nights ramble, by a sad mistake,
The Nymph was stung by Arran's poison'd snake.
Delhousy, proud that her sole charms have caught
The man whom Shrewsbury[23] so dearly bought,
Exposes blushing Bridges,[24] who would faine
Conceale the conquest which makes her so vaine.
Longford, that Elf, has had worse than ill luck,
And yet they say, she's right as ever struck,
For Smith's[25] fine pencill's every day employ'd
To draw her likeness in true flesh and blood.   80
Old Lady Cole, St Harrison[26] doth chuse,
Not so much for his doctrine as his use;
With holy lookes and tone he drew her in,
And so made godliness to pimp for sin.
Her Daughter Nicholl, on the world a skam,
Pretending kindred to her Stallion Cham;[27]
By this her crime we doubly do espy,
Since it adds incest to adultery.
Lean Droghedah does fret and pine away,
For being restrain'd from her belov'd Galmoy,[28]   90
Whose amorous fire shot through her does make
Her Lord's backbone as well as forehead ake.

22. Thomas Cromwell, sixth Baron and third Earl of Ardglass who married the daughter of
    Michael Boyle, archbishop of Dublin – but the reference may be to Lady Ardglass, 'the
    nymph' – or to a prostitute assuming her name. In either case, the 'Arran' of l. 72 is
    presumably a man, probably Richard Butler, earl of Arran, second son of the duke of
    Ormond. The reference to 'Arran' at l. 58 may also be to him.
23. Delhousie and Shrewsbury, two more of the ladies of the poem, are untraced.
24. Possibly John Bridges, who entered Trinity College Dublin in 1659, aged seventeen.
25. There were many young men named Smith in Dublin at this time, though none of them
    is known to have been an artist. Candidates include Isaac Smith (entered TCD 1664,
    aged seventeen), Samuel Smith (entered TCD 1658, aged fifteen) and William Smith
    (entered TCD 1659, aged sixteen).
26. Harrison might be Edward Harrison (entered TCD 1662, aged eighteen) or William
    Harrison (entered TCD 1662, aged sixteen). Lady Cole may be the wife of Sir John Cole
    of Newland, County Dublin, whose third daughter, Mary, married the earl of Drogheda
    in 1675. Longford (line 76) and Drogheda (line 89) seem to be names assumed by the
    prostitutes rather than references to the daughters of the real Lords Longford and
    Drogheda.
27. khan, ruler; also = champion. In this case it means her lover. 'Her Daughter Nicholl' is
    unidentified.
28. Piers Butler, third viscount Galmoye, later to serve as an officer on the side of King
    James at the battle of the Boyne, to be outlawed under King William and to follow James
    into exile in France.

Katty, with profferd spouse so often bob'd,
Is now resolv'd she will no more be fob'd;
The bait twitcht from her makes her pine and vext,
And swears (come on't what will) she'l take the next.
Her sister sprouts and blooms apace,
And of her Youth and Age, wont best an ace,[29]
But tells her father, though she young appears,
A maidenhead's a scandal at her years.   100
Stanley[30] does manage love with a good grace,
For shee and Purcell laugh in Stephen's face;
The good man, not suspitious in the least,
Laughs with them, for he's tickled at the jest.
Davyes is old, yet full of vanity,
Proud as the Tallents, indiscreet as Teigh,
Less handsome, though sillier by much
Than Yarner, and as impudent as Crouch.
Copley, that bawd, would fain prefer to me
Lord Blaney's sister and Montgomery.   110
Them once, for charity, I thought to take,
But seeming rusty Napps,[31] I turn'd them back.
Morris exalted now with double pride
Of being married, and with Child beside,
Looks with contempt or scorn on each young whore
That was her spleen and envy heretofore.
McDonnels house does hinder much my trade,
For all the Irish draps[32] do there parade.
Young Courcey, Lady Ellen, Mrs Hoar,
Tom Hacket's wife and fourty slatterns more.   120
Stephens and Jefferys are gone o're to you,
And so is Cheever and Frank Trevor too;
Although no virgins, I'll assure them sound,
And London in such flesh does not abound.
I pray make much of them upon my score,
And if you like them, I will send you more.

---

29. i.e. can not be beaten.
30. It is not possible to identify any of the prostitutes named in the next few lines.
31. 'A nap' was a slang term for a person infected with venereal disease; 'rusty' = 'sullen'.
32. = drab, prostitute.

DUDLEY LOFTUS (?)
(1619-**1675**-1695)

Some of those introduced to classical texts at school and university in the seventeenth century enjoyed the intellectual exercise of putting them into English so much that they continued translating throughout their lives. The author of the following version of Juvenal's famous tenth satire chose to hide his light under a bushel, however, and described himself on the title page of his periphrastic rendering of this rather unpleasant poem as 'a person, sometimes Fellow of Trin. Col. Dublin'. The poem, which carries a dedication to Lord Blessington, written by Edward Wetenhall, later Bishop of Cork, gives an account of how the translation came to be undertaken.

> Some perplext business drew him [the author] to the Terms [court sittings] at *Clonmel*, in which Journey, for diversion of Law thoughts and entertainment of time, which was not very capable of more serious studies, he took with him *Juvenal*, and his learned Translators, *Sir Robert Stapleton* and *Dr B. Holiday*, onely with the design of pleasing himself by the comparing the Original and Translations: a pleasure truly worthy of an ingenious mind, at once to view the product of Three so great Wits, employed on the same conceits. By the way at *Kilkenny*, making a short stay, a judicious Friend possest [suggested to] him, that *Juvenal* was the properest for a *Pindarick* Version, of any Authour of that nature. This induced him afterwards to try how he could think over *Juvenal's* thoughts that new way in *English*: which design he the rather cherished, because such kind of writing could not at all rival those great Names who had already done *Juvenal* so much justice in our Tongue. This occasion truly gave birth to this Poem.
>
> Returning home, he reviewed what he had done, and moved by the worth of the subject, gave three Copies to Persons of Quality, known by him to be addicted to Literature, (of whom your Lordship, by sending your Copy to the Press, not without great encouragement, made it known you were one) designing onely thereby, farther to invite them to the reading such old Books, which at once present much Wit, Learning and Morality. From the Press the Papers came to my hands; and I should neither do your Lordship nor my Friend justice, if from mine they did not return to yours.

As Tony Sweeney has pointed out, there was only one person in Ireland in the 1670s who was a sometime fellow of Trinity College Dublin, a lawyer who visited Clonmel on legal business and a classical scholar – Dudley Loftus. It is virtually certain, therefore, that Loftus wrote this translation.

Dudley Loftus was descended from Archbishop Adam Loftus, first provost of Trinity College. He himself entered Trinity College in 1635 and early established a reputation as a scholar; Sir James Ware asserted that he could translate from twenty languages by the time he was twenty. Loftus went on to become MP for Naas, for County Kildare and for County Wicklow in the Irish parliament and to become a distinguished lawyer, serving as deputy judge advocate, commissioner of revenue and judge of the Admiralty during the 1650s. He eventually became judge of the Prerogative Court. But his most lasting contribution was to learning. Loftus was a fine orientalist and, among other things, supplied the Ethiopic version of the New Testament in Walton's polyglot Bible of 1657. Among the many books he wrote were several of a legal nature, translations from various languages including Armenian and Greek, and an account of the ceremony of the consecration of the twelve bishops of the Church of Ireland in 1661. At the time of that ceremony, Loftus was vicar-general of the archdiocese of Dublin (a lay position), and pro-vice-chancellor of the university. Such a man might well have found light relief in paraphrasing Juvenal.

The connection with Clonmel comes through Loftus's extended involvement in the legal wrangle over the marriage ceremony which the twelve-year-old Lady Katherine Fitzgerald was forced to go though with the eight-year-old son of her guardian early in the 1670s. When Lady Katherine challenged the validity of the marriage ceremony and eloped with Edward Villiers, the matter went to court, some of the hearings being in Clonmel. Loftus published his long opinion on the case, dated October 1676, as *Digamias Adikia, or The First Marriage of Lady Katherine Fitzgerald ... with John Power, now Lord of Decies asserted ...* (London 1677).

Loftus's version of Juvenal's satire was printed in Dublin in 1675 with a full set of scholarly notes. The first of the two passages below (stanzas 32–8) is a 'dispraise' or disparaging description of old age, and the second (stanzas 48–52 and 56) considers the fate of good-looking boys in the days of the Roman Empire.

from: The Wish

being the Tenth Satyr of Juvenal Peraphrastically rendered in Pindarick Verse

[Old age]

32

Give length of age, good Jove, *give me more years,*
  This with an open face, you say;
   Your chief concern dwells in these pray'rs,
    They employ all your joys and fears,
  You speak 'em, pale as that 'gainst which you pray.[1]
  And yet old age rais'd to the heighth, you'd raise,
    Is fuller far of evils than of days;
   Let an old face be thoroughly descry'd,[2]
  Look at that *quondam* skin, curry'd by age, to hide;[3]
    Behold the hanging cheeks disgrace,   10
     It[4] cannot blush to think what 'twas,
  But in its way asham'd, seems to decline the face.[5]

---

1. *Original note*: 'Death, like which they looked, out of a concern and for fear of not obtaining their earnest and foolish request of a too long life.'
2. observed.
3. i.e. look at what once was skin, now tanned by age, [trying to] hide away ...
4. *Original note*: '*viz*: the bloodless cheek.'
5. *Original note*: 'By hanging down, as if it had a desire to quit its station.' [decline = turn away from].

Such wrinckles do indent the jaws,
As no Similies can essay,
But those i'th wood of *Tabracha*[6]
Where in cheek-pits the Grandam Ape does lose her paws.[7]

33

Young men from one another may be known,
This than that man fairer is,
T'other stronger much than this,
But Chaos-age has no distinction.   20
Eighty makes all alike,[8] there is no choice,
The limbs quaver like the voice,
The head's a perfect scull, no hair there grows,
All moisture in one current flows,
And the poor infant cannot rule his nose.
The teeth are fled,
And disarm'd gums are left to fight with bread;
Troublesome to his wife he well may grow,
And children, when t'himself he's so,
When the loath'd sight makes ev'n his flatt'rers spue.   30

34

All sense is gone, what signifies to eat?
You might as well remove the meat;
There is no provocation in grand Sallets,[9]
Wine's spilt upon the pavement of such pallats:[10]
He's chaste indeed, but that's no virtue, when
Nature leaves not the least remains of men:
As he tast[e]s, just so he hears:
Seleucus[11] self does sing in vain
So does the proudest of the golden train,[12]
All musick's lost to him that has no ears;   40

6. *Original note*: 'A wood near Tunis where there is great store of Apes.'
7. *Original note*: 'Great hollows in the cheek, resembling pits, so big that the old ape fears to lose her paws, or scarce able to reach their bottoms when she scratches, to which he compares the face of old men.'
8. *Original note*: 'Most people, about fourscore, are alike, at least no remarks of beauty remain to make the distinction.'
9. salads, i.e. not even attractive food stimulates the appetite.
10. *Original note*: 'Worn out, as the High-way by long usage, and as void of sense.' [pallats = palates].
11. *Original note*: 'A rare Musician in the Authour's time.'
12. *Original note*: 'Those that sung on the Stage to please the Spectators wore an embroidered garment called *lacerna*, termed golden, from the mixture of gold in the Embroidery.'

'Tis alike to him to sit
In the Gall'ry, or the pit,[13]
Mens voices well may be too weak,
He scarce can hear Cornets or Trumpets speak;
When he sends one t'enquire the hour,
He must the errand tell,
Just like the bell,
Must either ring it to him, or must louder roar.

35

Some cold blood the surviving coarse[14] retains,
Yet no heat at all it knows,   50
But what it to the Feaver owes.
Troops of diseases quarter[15] up and down the veins,
So many, if their names you'd have,
I must your pardons crave,
Might as soon that grand account adjust
Of all those *Hippia*[16] has betray'd to lust;
As soon unto you shew,
How many *Themison*[17] in one Autumn slew;
Count all th' Estates,
By *Basilus*[18] rook'd from our Confederates;   60
Or tell as soon
How many wards curst *Irus*[19] has undone;
Nay, I almost as soon might guess
What wealth that *Senator*[20] has,
Who once my Barber was,
Or count how many Farms his Honour does possess.

13. i.e. in the theatre.
14. corpse.
15. take up their lodgings.
16. *Original note*: 'A notorious Whore of that age, mentioned in his [Juvenal's] sixth Satyr.'
17. *Original note*: 'A famous Physician of that time.'
18. *Original note*: 'A Governour of a Province.' (This line seems to contain a veiled reference to the problems of Irish land settlement in the Restoration period.)
19. *Original note*: 'A notorious wicked Guardian in those dayes.' (This line may refer to the case of Lady Katherine Fitzgerald (on which Loftus delivered a long written judgment), the twelve-year-old heiress forced to go through a marriage ceremony with an eight-year-old boy by her guardian, later the Earl of Tyrone.)
20. *Original note*: 'Some call him *Tricinius*, some *Linnamus*, but all conclude he was first a Barber, afterwards a Senator, and vastly rich.' (Again, Loftus's readers would probably have recognised a wealthy tradesman turned parliamentarian in this line and its accompanying note.)

36

In age, nothing but Hospitals we find,
Here a useless shoulder lyes,
There feeble loins, there helpless thighs,
And here a wretch has lost both eyes,   70
And envies all that see, ev'n the purblind:[21]
Another with his pale lips stands,
And for his mouth's supply borrows another's hands;
T'other at the sight of meat,
Without a stomack, yawns a wish,
Gapes almost as young Swallows do,
(For whom the hungry Dam does seem to chew,)
But has no appetite to the dish,
He onely gapes to shew that he was wont to eat.

37

Their least of ills, though, lye in their disease;   80
Such losses in respect are gains;
What's hand, or eye, or head without the brains?
Dotage is more intol'rable than these.
Their memory's gone, all past things they disclaim,
They forget their Servant's name,
Their dearest Friend's forgotten quite,
Although he supp'd with them last night;
All thought of children's gone;
Those whom they got and bred, they are unknown;
And lest you this sad truth shou'd doubt,   90
Their wills can prov't, their names are there left out:
Lust they remember, and no more;
Perhaps their Testament is fill'd with an old whore.

38

But yet, allowing more than Nature will,
Say that their sense continues vig'rous still;
All they gain hence, is but to be
More sensible of misery.
Be their House ne're so num'rous grown,
They live to dwell alone;
See to close their children's eyes,   100

---

21. = blind in one eye or with defective vision.

> Hear all the dismal Funeral cryes,
> At Wive's and Sister's obsequies:
> Like rotten Oaks, forsaken, time's disgraces,
> As marks of ruine in those very places
> They singly stand, where once there stood
> Thousand fresh glories of a flour'shing wood;
> These are the onely benefits of years,
> To see beloved bodies burn,
> Whilst happy, you provide the Urn,
> And older grow in mourning and accustom'd tears . . .   110

[The fate of good-looking boys in the days of the Roman Empire]

48

> A Son too, if exceeding fair,
> Costs his parents double care
> In others love, in them he begets fear;
> One chaste and handsome we so seldom find,
> You'd think such bodies ne're did suit the mind.
> Though the House whence he took his blood,
> Be course and plain as the old *Sabines* were,[1]
> And gave him documents as severe;
> Nay though his disposition's good,
> Though Nature has done all she can,   10
> (Honest Nature far exceeding
> All the tricks and cheats of breeding)
> Though she bestows on him a modest look,
> The happy *Index* of a well writ Book,
> And with a Mint of blood[2] his face has lin'd,
> Ready in blushes to be coin'd;
> When she has giv'n him all this store,
> And she, though liberal, can give no more;
> After all this, O Beauty's curse!
> He shall Eunuch be or worse,   20
> The world will never suff'r him to live good, or man.

---

1. *Original note*: 'The *Sabines* were a chast[e] and rigid people and, in the beginning of the *Roman* State, embodied with them, *Numa Pompilius*, the great Emperor, was of that Nation.'
2. a lot of. The word 'mint' was used of a large amount of something costly.

49

So prodigal is lust to have it's end,
If the youth won't condescend,
So very impudent is gold,
'Twill with the parents correspondence hold:
To maintain a current trade,
The Father pander, Mother bawd is made.
Beauty does the youth destroy,
No Tyrant ever gelt[3] an ugly boy:
Nero no youth, though noble, e're thought meet   30
For Court, with swoln throat, or club feet,
Nor anyone that look'd as though
He was with child before and behind too.

50

Go, and rejoyce now in thy beauteous Son,
Who therefore has more wayes to be undone:
He'l be the common Town-bull, must receive
Whatever plagues the angry husbands give;
For he can be no happier than his star,[4]
And nets, you know, trapann'd[5] the God of war.
That punishment some greater find,   40
Than ever was by Law assign'd;[6]
Some men have spit'em,[7] others chose
To kill adult'rers with dry blows;
Some prolong their pain by Art,
And with a Mullet[8] clyster the back part.

51

But your choice Son shall have as choice a Dame:
Can that atone the crime, or bail the shame?
Or if it cou'd, it wou'd not do,
Who once adult'rer is, will twice be so;
He will not onely swallow baits   50
From those he loves, but those he hates;

---

3. gelded, castrated.
4. *Original note*: 'He (i.e. Juvenal) fancies him born under Mars, and alludes to the story in *Ovid*'s *Metamorphoses* where *Vulcan* catches *Mars* and *Venus* in a net.'
5. entrapped.
6. *Original note*: 'There were several Laws made against Adultery, yet the punishments inflicted by the abus'd Husband often surpass'd them all in severity.'
7. i.e. roasted them alive on a spit.
8. A kind of pincers or tweezers (*OED*); to clyster = to inject something into the rectum.

Money has charms almost as great as lust,
He can't afford always to sin on trust:
Servilia,[9] she is poor you know,
Very poor and ugly too;
Maugre[10] both ugliness and poverty,
She wants not baits for lechery.
Her Gallant she will have,
Though in pawn her cloaths she leave:
If she be naked, what cares she? 60
She is then as she wou'd be.
Most others are his own, and why?
The prodigal will give, the cov'tous buy:
Whether they breeding have or none.
On this account it is all one;
Be she the morosest creature,
She'l be complaisant, and yield to this ill good-nature.

52

But grant him chast[e], as chast[e] can be,
Grant him chast[e] as chastity;
He may be chast[e], safe he shall never be. 70
What signifi'd th'honest resolv'd intent
To *Hippolytus*[11] the fair?
Lust he avoided, not the snare;
He by *Phædra*[12] was accus'd
Of the incest he refus'd,
Suffred for being innocent,
He scap'd the sin, but cou'd not scape the punishment . . .

56

. . . Things going thus, you will be apt to say,
Why, then we must not pray;
Since ruine springs from our most holy cares, 80
What becomes then of Heav'n, and all it's train?
Either there's no such place, or 'tis in vain;

---

9. *Original note*: '*Servilia*, without offence to Commentators, may be fancied poor who, when her money was gone, gave away her clothes to maintain her lust.'
10. despite.
11. *Original note*: 'The Son of *Theseus*, banished by reason of a false accusation of his Mother-in-law who, missing her intent, wrought that revenge: he was torn in pieces by his Chariot-Horses going to exile.'
12. *Original note*: '*Hippolitus* his [i.e. Hippolitus's] Mother-in-law.'

435

We may as well want Gods as have no pray'rs.
'Tis true, but you of both may make fit use,
If good advice you don't refuse;
Ask not for friv'lous things, or if you do,
Be not concern'd your wishes don't ensue,
Leave your pray'rs to the Gods, and they will pray for you . . .

ZACHEUS ISHAM

(1651-**1675**-1705)

This dedicatory poem is printed in what purported to be a history of Ireland, Edmund Borlase's *The Reduction of Ireland to the Crown of England* . . . (London 1675). Like all seventeenth-century histories of Ireland, however, Borlase's history was a work of propaganda, in this case in defence of English and protestant rule in Ireland. Edmund Borlase (*d.* 1682) himself was born in Dublin some time in the 1620s, the son of Sir John Borlase (1576–1648), lord justice in the 1640s. He studied in Dublin and at Leyden where he qualified as a doctor of physic in 1650. Though his work contains specific references to diseases in Ireland, Borlase seems to have spent most of his professional life as a physician in Chester. However, his *Reduction of Ireland* was written to justify the conduct of the English and parliamentary forces in Ireland during the 1640s and to vindicate the reputation of his fathe, which needed some rescuing. He was remembered as a particularly brutal lord justice during his tenure of that office in the early 1640s, and was responsible for the racking of two respectable Irish catholics, Sir John Read and the elderly Patrick Barnewall, in 1641 and 1642.[1]

Zacheus Isham, the author of the poem, seems to have had no connection with Ireland apart from this poem. He was a clergyman in the Church of England who rose slowly through the ranks to become a canon of Canterbury cathedral. His only other publications were some sermons and a catechism. However, this poem is of interest as an indication of the way the Irish rebellion and its aftermath were being presented in Restoration London.

from: ## To his worthy and much honoured Friend
[Edmund Borlase]
Upon his History, entituled, The Reduction of IRELAND to the Crown of
ENGLAND

A Pindarique Ode

I

Ireland hath long in darkness layn,
With Time and Ignorance o'rcast:
Time, like a swelling Flood, had past
O'r all the Land, and laid it waste:
The Deluge every day new ground did gain:
Scarce any Track or Footstep there,
Scarce could the Mountains tops appear.
From hence the Monster *Ignorance* arose,
Of such a dreadful shape, and Birth, as those,

1. Sir John Borlase appears as the villainous 'Berosus' in Henry Burkhead's *Tragedy of Cola's Fury* (Kilkenny, 1646). See Patricia Coughlan, '"The Modell of its Sad Afflictions": Henry Burkhead's *Tragedy of Cola's Fury*', in Micheál Ó Siochrú (ed.), *Kingdoms in Crisis: Ireland in the 1640s: Essays in Honour of Donál Cregan* (Dublin, 2001), pp. 196, 202.

Which Nilus leaves when it o'rflows.[2]   10
Times sacred Reliques its blind malice rent;
And its devouring rage o'r all the Kingdom went:
But you, Sir, like the God of your own Art,
Have slain this Monster with an happy Dart:
And now with undisturbed peace you go
Through all the Realm, and unto others show,
What former Ages ne'r did know.
Ireland no longer barbarous seems, and rude;
Your fluent Pen her Glory hath renew'd.
What strong Disease can now your Art withstand;   20
Since you have given new Life to an expiring Land.

II

Her growing Fame from the first Rise you trace,
When she did English manners first embrace;
And her old barbarous Customs leave.
When with her Chains she did good Laws receive.
And thus by being conquered gained more
Than all her Victories did before.
Thus where the *Roman* conquer'd, 'twas his care
To plant good *Laws* and *Manners* there;
That even his vanquisht Foes might *Lawrels* wear[3]   30
From hence with wondrous Art and Diligence you
Guide us through unknown Paths, and there display
What ere's remarkable in the way . . .

IV

What a large share of Fame is won
By *Sidney*, *Chichester*, and *Grandison*?[4]
Lo! How brave *Mountjoy*[5] marches through the field,
And makes the astonish'd Rebels yield;
Covering the Kingdom with his shield?
With chained Foes his Chariot's compass'd round,
And his exalted head with Lawrel crown'd.   40
But who can mention calmly *Strafford*'s[6] name,
The Nations Glory, and Her shame?

---

2. It was believed that revolting creatures were left on the banks of the Nile after it had flooded.
3. Returning victors were crowned with a ceremonial wreath of laurel leaves.
4. Sir Henry Sidney (1529–86), Arthur Chichester, Baron Belfast (1563–1625) and Sir Oliver St John, Lord Grandison (1559–1630).
5. Charles Blount, Baron Mountjoy (1563–1606).
6. Thomas Wentworth, Earl of Strafford (1593–1641).

Lo! how he falls, a sacrifice to asswage
    The Peoples insolent Rage?
His Death his Princes Tragœdy doth presage.[7]
And for his Funeral fire the Kingdom's on a flame.
So when great *Cæsar* fell, the People thought,
    They could no more to slavery be brought.
But soon the Empire feels an heavier weight,
    Crush'd by the proud *Trium-virate*:   50
Till a young *Cæsar* sav'd the expiring State.
    How enviously the incensed Rout
    Still pick the fairest Victims out?
Like thunder the low Cottage they pass by,
But strike down Towers and Trees, which touch the skie:
And even the Lawrel can't escape, if that be rais'd too high.

V

Long did these Noble Persons[8] bless
The stubborn Realm with peace and happiness:
When lo! new storms compass the Kingdom round,
    And after a long calm an Earthquake rose;[9]   60
    Which Towns and Castles soon o'rthrows,
And with vast ruines covers all the ground.
Ireland now lost her old Renown,
And poisonous Creatures rag'd in every Town:
    Vipers in dreadful crouds did stand:
    Which their own Mothers Bowels tore,
    And wallowed in her gore.
Our Heroes[10] soon rescu'd the perishing Land:
    Their Conduct, Valour, and success
    Their Enemies proud fury did repress.   70
    Methinks amongst the rest I see
    Your Noble Father crown'd with Victory.[11]
    Lo! how be stops the rising flood,
And with his mighty Arms throws back the waves?
His Counsel and wise care the Kingdom saves,
    Which else had been o'rwhelm'd with blood.

---

7. i.e. the execution of Charles I in 1649.
8. i.e. the noblemen who had ruled Ireland up to and including Strafford.
9. The rising of 23 October 1641.
10. i.e. forces opposed to the rebels.
11. Sir John Borlase. See headnote.

Where e'r the loyal Troops were led,
With speed the trembling Rebels fled:
Thus were their Ancestors, the old Giants, chac't,[12]
When *Jove* did on their heads his thunder cast;   80
They threw their Mountains down, and ran away with haste.

VI

What dismal clouds, what dreadful vengeance hover'd
O'r this unhappy Realm, and cover'd
Her body o'r with blood and tears?
When her Sons arm'd with swords and spears,
Devoutly made Religion the pretence
To shake off all Obedience,
And even natural Innocence.
The Devil assumes the Prophets shape again;
And in a pious Garb deludes weak men.   90
His lying spirits through the Country went;
And with this new Divinity are sent.
Rebellion's but a name Fools to affright;
An Heretick to a Kingdom hath no right:
They now for God against their King must fight.
Thus are the People arm'd with Zeal,
Whose edge is keener than the sharpest steel.
And first Plots and Conspiracies they contrive;
And then with open force for their *Diana*[13] strive.
Their Zeal like Hell, was dark and hot;   100
And did as much torment the prey they got.
With thunder and with lightning they proclaim
Their Gospel, as the *Jews* receiv'd their Laws:
With *Mahomet*'s zeal they advance their Cause,
And to convert the Land, they set it on a flame.
Your Father soon to stop their fury came:
Lest all the Land should be to ashes turn'd:
But whilst he quench'd the fire, himself almost was burn'd.

VII

Now the blest smiles of Peace and Love,
All frowns and animosities remove.   110

---

12. chased.
13. Diana, one of the great goddesses of the classical world, here stands for the catholic church.

440

Nothing is left behind of War,
But here and there an ugly skar.
Great *Ormond*[14] was the *Augustus*, whose command
To perfect Loyalty and Peace reduced the Land.
Ormond, our great *Apollo* whose Renown
Did best deserve the Muses Crown.
Who rules in War and Peace with equal fame:
And all his faithful services justly claim
A loyal Subject's and true Patriot's Name.
Brave *Essex*[15] in his Power succeeds,   120
Fam'd for his own and his great Fathers deeds.
Whose gallant Death and Actions do inspire
His soul with such Heroick fire,
As flam'd in the young *Græcian*'s breast when he
Did a fam'd Generals Statue see.
So well this Hero fills his Princes Throne,
That he deserves to rule a Kingdom of his own . . .
Z. ISHAM

14. James Butler, Duke of Ormond (1610–88). Augustus Caesar (63 BC – AD 14) was considered the greatest Roman emperor.
15. Arthur Capel, Earl of Essex (1631–83), who assumed the lord lieutenancy of Ireland in May 1672.

WILLIAM MERCER
(*c*.1605–**1675**–*c*.1675)

William Mercer was a professional soldier who first came to Ireland in the royalist army in the 1640s. He rose to the rank of lieutenant colonel and must have managed to gain possession of an estate since he elected to settle in Ireland after the Restoration. Mercer was also a highly eccentric poet. When Lord Roberts, Baron Truro became lord lieutenant of Ireland in 1669, Mercer sent him a long poem of welcome which, in some ways, anticipates Dunton, Swift, Sterne and the post-modernists. The first section of the poem, entitled 'In Place of the Frontispiece', includes an engraving of an empty frame, inside which should have appeared – had Mercer been able to obtain it – a portrait of Lord Roberts. Since this was not forthcoming, Mercer left the frame unfilled, inviting the reader to fill it as he wished. Like *A Tale of a Tub*, the book includes an epistle dedicatory, essays to the curious reader, caveats, anagrams and prologues before the welcome itself, and its seven epistles. Mercer's other main publication – three dozen copies of which he presented to the mayor of Cork on his installation some time in the early 1670s – carries the title *The Moderate Cavalier or The Soldiers Description of Ireland and of the Country Disease, With receipts for the same . . . A Book fit for all* Protestants *houses in Ireland*.

This highly entertaining – but very peculiar – work is of value for the insight it gives into everyday life in Restoration Ireland, though the cures Mercer prescribes for certain Irish ailments are not recommended. The poem begins with extravagant praise of everything English in Ireland – he was an obsessive Anglophile – after which Mercer bewails the influence of the Irish in Ireland. The second poem below is one of the few 'echo' poems to have survived from seventeenth-century Ireland.

from: *The Moderate Cavalier, or The Soldiers Description of Ireland . . .*

> . . . Begin at *Dublin*, the chief Regal City,
> And mark how squares go there[1] (the more's the pitty).
> Though *English* be the Judges, *Irish* Clerkes
> Do there abound, with confidence like sparks[2]
> O' th' world they domineer: and who but they?
> With Cap in hand to them, brave Soldiers pray
> I' th' Court they will be seen; But goe to Church
> There *Teige* and *Dermot* leaves you in the Lurch.[3]
> In *Customes*, *Excise*, Offices for *Cloath*,
> *Leather*, *Measures*, *Chimneys* and to say troth   10
> In all *Money-matters*, they are *Projectors*,
> And most on end imploy'd to be *Collectors*.

1. how things go there.
2. bright, confident young men.
3. i.e. you will not find native Irishmen at (the protestant) church.

Let's down into the Countrey come and see
How all things there do goe; who's ever be
High Sherif, an *Irish* man is the Under;
Then, for the Bayliffs to be so's no wonder![4]
Apparatours[5] ith' Bishops Court, who're they
But *Irish*: and Who are *Atturneys* pray?
And *Proctours*,[6] are not they the very men?
For one *English*, of them is there not ten?[7]   20

Is not the Army stuff'd with such like trash?
They're *Alamode de France*, each one with's *Sash*,
A dirty *Crevate*, or a Fox-Furre *Muff*;
And some of them brave fellows are in Buffe,[8]
Booted and *Spurr'd*, have cast off their old *Broges*,
And wear great *Breeches*, that were *Trowz'd* like Rogues,[9]
With *Vest* and *Tunicke*, stead of *Blew Frize Jerkin*;[10]
Can now tell tales of *Madam* and her Rhyme toot – *Merkin*.[11]
An *Irish* man was seen in dayes of old
But with a *Skean*,[12] while now wee do behold   30
Him with a *Rapier* or a good *Back Sword*
A crosse his Arse, with *Damme* at ev'ry Word.
These are the Propps that now support this Nation:
God grant that they hold if e're come alteration.

All things thus order'd makes the *English* poore:
And poorer needs must be, while they're crow'd o're
By ev'ry *Snap*:[13] For th' *Irish* wait upon
Our Gentry, where they do but keep a man.[14]

Now here (perhaps) some would themselves excuse:
'Tis not for love, they do the *Irish* use   40

4. i.e. if the deputy sheriff is an Irishman, no wonder the bailiffs are so too.
5. apparitors, ushers or attendants at the ecclesiastical court.
6. proctors, stewards.
7. i.e. ten Irishmen.
8. Military coats made of dull, yellow leather. The colour 'buff' was often associated with particular army uniforms.
9. The contrast is between English-style loose breeches and close-fitting Irish trousers (Ir. *triús*), often worn by Irish rebels and outlaws.
10. A jerkin was a garment associated with the poor, and frieze was coarse woollen cloth or tweed.
11. toot = to it; Eric Partridge's definition of 'merkin', *The Routledge Dictionary of Historical Slang* (London, 1973), is 'an artificial vagina for lonely men'.
12. Ir. *scian*, knife.
13. cheat, pilferer.
14. i.e. even where only one servant is employed.

In all Imployments spoken of before,
But cause their knowledge is therein farre more
Than English have: But I say that surmise
Is false, and won't pass Muster with the wise,
Who know the little skill the Irish have
They learn'd it of the English; yet none (save
Some few of them) that are in any art
Their Crafts masters: although for th' botching part
Degenerate English, and their own nation
Will them imploy, 'gainst which there's no perswasion.   50

And here againe (methinks) I heare some grumbling
Against my last assertion, and much mumbling
Concerning Scholarship. All vulgar mouths
Are open affirming this Countrey youths
In Latine farre exceed our *English*. Who[15]
Feign Common consent, gave them long agoe
Preheminence; for School-Masters therefore
They will have *Irish*: oh! who, than we, more
Stupid? Good God! since this, so long hath past
For Current with most men, now at the last,   60
Help my blunt quill, and my duller braine
These foolish dreames and fictions to restraine
Amongst my Countrymen: open their eyes
And let them see, what they believ'd were lyes;
Remove that plague which doth so many seize-on
And grant they may at length be ruled by reason.

I say of Learning the Irish may not boast
For any thing yet seen in all their Coast.
No *Art* or *Science* have they yet found out,
No Treatise of Religion, and I doubt   70
No History or good Romance worth reading
Was yett by any of them writt, and spreading
In any part oth' world. What they doe call
Philosophy (wherein their boast's not small)
Is skill in Sophistry, wherewith to wrangle
They are well verst, who do for Trifles Jangle,[16]
And with a Pack of learned Cow-boys they
May with the world compare: none sayes them Nay.

15. i.e. those who . . .
16. i.e. who argue over unimportant matters in a loud and discordant way.

444

On th' other side, Whole Volumes, English Works
Through Christendom have gone – yea 'mongst the *Turks*.   80

'Tis true some *Irish* speak good Latine, though
The most of their Schoolmasters do not so;
But none of them can speak one word of *Greek*
Or *Hebrew*; in those tongues they are to seek;[17]
Where[18] all the English that do bear the name
Of Scholars, are good Linguists in the same . . .

. . . Nothing hath done more hurt to th' *English* Nation
Than *Irish* Schoolmasters, by all relation;
The *Fosterer*, the babes, the *Schools*, the youth
Do *English* turn to *Irish*, of a truth . . .   90

A Dialogue betwixt a *Soldier*, Author of this Book, and an *Echo*,

being a Summary Discourse of the Whole matter;[1] briefly resounded by the *Echo*.

Sold: Hark I heere an *Echo*; listen and hark;

Ech: *Hark*:	S: I will talk with it, shall I not now?
Ech: *Now*:	S: and tell the passages, and then mark
Ech: *Mark*:	S: what answer it makes: *Echo*, tell how?
Ech: *How*:	S: the *Irish* into Rebellion first
Ech: *First*:	S: gathered in a Riotous Rout?
Ech: *Rout*:	S: against Protestants, their fury burst
Ech: *Burst*:	S: for they were so full it needs must out;
Ech: *Out*:	S: of all measure was the cruel papist
Ech: *Papist*:	S: bloudy: a Murdrous Rogue was *Teige* 10
Ech: *Teige*:	S: and *Dermot* too, worse than a meer *Athist*[2]
Ech: *Athist*:	S: who Cov'nant keeps, there is no league
Ech: *League*	S: but the Pope does indulge to be broke
Ech: *Broke*	S: who to the Rebbells sent into Ireland
Ech: *Ireland*	S: a Bull,[3] that made the Kingdom smoak

---

17. i.e. they are lost.
18. i.e. whereas.

1. i.e. of the contents of Mercer's previous poem in this volume, *A Moderate Cavalier*.
2. atheist.
3. Since the Pope did not issue any written papal bulls in the 1640s, this may be a reference to Cardinal Rinuccini.

Ech: *Smoak*   S: and to burne, as if it were a fire-brand
Ech: *Fire-brand*   S: so stareing mad, the Bull was made
Ech: *Made*   S: so that the British should be pilled
Ech: *Pilled*   S: plundered, their Cattell stoln & prey'd
Ech: *Prey'd*   S: and ev'ry Protestant should be Killed   20
Ech: *Killed*   S: hanged, starved, to pitty no-man
Ech: *No-man*   S: that was of Brittish race, a child
Ech: *Child*   S: newly born, and ev'ry tender Woman
Ech: *Woman*   S: to put to th' Sword, he judg'd too mild
Ech: *Mild*   S: so was the Bull for the POWDER PLOT[4]
Ech: *Plot*   S: the *Lords Annoynted* must not be spared
Ech: *Spared*   S: then all his *Kingdoms* sure should not
Ech: *Not*   S: but the *Lord* (who for our safetyes cared
Ech: *Cared*   S: his *Name* alone be praised) then
Ech: *Then*   S: both the *King* and *State* preserved. We see   30
Ech: *See*   S: which should be a *warning* to all men
Ech: *Men*   S: *Watchfull* and *Carefull* always to be
Ech: *Be*   S: pondering these things and keeping sober
Ech: *Sober*   S: so that they may alwayes Remember
Ech: *Remember*   S: FORTY ONE the moneth OCTOBER
Ech: *October*   S: and the FIFTH day of NOVEMBER.
Ech: *NOVEMBER*[5].

---

4. This refers back to catholic involvement in the Gunpowder Plot of 1607 in London.
5. The dates of the outbreak of the Irish rising of 1641 and of the Gunpowder Plot.

SIR WILLIAM PETTY
(1623–**1677**–1687)

Sir William Petty (1623–87) maintained a life-long interest in Irish affairs and lived in Ireland for many years. (For some biographical details, see the headnote to the anonymous poem *In Laudem Navis Geminæ E Portu Dublinij ad Regem Carolum II^dum Missæ* 1663, p. 391.)

When the Duke of Ormond began his final term as lord lieutenant of Ireland in 1677, Petty sent him the following poem – an example of the ingenious verse-making common among the educated gentry of the age. Something of Petty's obsessive character can be gleaned from this text in which the multitude of specific terms (which make the poem seem, in places, a self-parody) tends to overwhelm the allegory.

A Navall Allegory

By the Register of the Admiralty of Ireland; To His Grace James Duke of Ormond as Grand Pilot of the good ship Ireland, upon his fourth expedition on that Bottome.[1]

What weather are we like to have? of what
Long voyage are we going that[2] you are at
The Helme this fourth time now, and take in hand
The whipstaffe[3] of the sword and Chiefe Command?

When first you took't, Boreas[4] Rebellion blew
An Ulster stress of wind which overthrew
Both Church and State, untill you sail'd close hall'd[5]
Into the smoothings, a Cessation call'd.

Next turne you took at Ireland's ticklish Helm[6]
Was when the Pope and 's Nuncio Plagu'd the Realme   10
With spirituall Frauds, and Bugbear fulmination
And when Rump[7] reign'd in carnall usurpation.

---

1. Technically, it was Ormond's third term of office, though it could be argued that he had been appointed twice by Charles I. bottom = base, foundation.
2. i.e. now that . . .
3. = 1) the handle of a whip; 2) a handle attached to the tiller of a small ship.
4. The north wind of the classical world. The wind of the 1641 rebellion blew from Ulster. Ormond's first term of office was from November 1643 to January 1646.
5. To sail close hauled is to sail near to the wind. smoothings = calm.
6. Ormond's second term of office was from September 1648 to December 1650; the reference is to Cardinal Rinuccini.
7. The earliest text of the poem has the word 'Noll' (i.e. Oliver Cromwell), but this was later erased and replaced by 'Rump'.

Then did you wisely lash the Helm a Lee[8]
And put the Ship atry, till you could see
What saile to make, you spoon'd away before[9]
The wind and sea, untill the storm was ore.
Without a knot of sail you drove twelve yeares
Tost with the floods of hope, and ebbs of Feares.[10]
Soe driven about with Tydes and Currents motion
And having crost a wide Atlantic Ocean[11]   20
You made the coast of Ireland, and then once more
You took the Helm, and steer'd in with the shore.[12]
A noble Pilotage! for tho the weather
Seem'd fair (the King restor'd) yet you had neither
Compass, nor card, nor running glass, nor line[13]
Yett stood the course your wisdome did Divine
Amidst a thousand Rocks. Here lay a Sand
Of Souldiers interest (Some in Command,
Some out); there ran a dangerous shelfe
Of vexd Adventurers and Men of Pelfe.[14]   30
Here a strong Tide of Innocents sett in
Which spoyled the fishing, Nocents were so thin.[15]
There Conaught Purchasers and Transplantees
Meeting a thousand sorts of bold grantees,
Made a grown[16] Sea. Here come a hazy fog
Of dark Provisoes, which the Acts did clog.
There arose clouds of severall sorts of men
(Whose names I cant remember, one of ten)

---

8. out of the wind, in shelter; atry = (of a ship) kept with her bows facing the sea during a gale.
9. to spoon = (of a ship) to run before the wind, to scud.
10. Ormond was exiled from Ireland from 1650 to 1662.
11. An allegorical ocean, since Ormond never crossed the real Atlantic.
12. Ormond's first term of office under Charles II was from February 1662 to May 1669.
13. card = chart; running-glass = hour glass (through which the sand runs); line = sounding line used to measure the depth of the sea.
14. money. An adventurer was a person who had subscribed money to support an army to suppress the rising of 1641 on the security of lands to be confiscated from Irish landlords. (See L. J. Arnold, *The Restoration Land Settlement in County Dublin, 1660–1688* (Dublin, 1993), pp. 17–19 for a glossary of the terms used in land settlement matters at this time.)
15. The court of claims would declare some catholics 'innocent' of any wrong-doing against Charles I or Charles II – in which case their claims to keep their land might be heard – or 'nocent' (guilty) – in which case they lost their land automatically.
16. rough. Those who lost their land in Munster or Leinster were likely to be 'transplanted' to Connacht, i.e. allocated land there.

Ensigne, Meromotu, men Reprisable,[17]
Nominees, and such as never yet were able   40
To set their foot on Land. All made a noise
Like sheet-flown sayles, the Court claim-swearing boyes
With Paraphrasd oaths, steeld with pretence of clause
In Act Explanatory and other Laws,
Begot a damned confusion, fore and aft.
Whilst some rejoycd, some fum'd, some cry'd, some laught,
Sometimes a flow of wind (or angry vote
of Parliament) would oversett your Boate.

All this while you (I mean Great Ormond you)
Stood right in with the Land, kept the Ship to   50
The King and Countryes Interest; and when a Puffe
Of other wind did blow, you kept your luffe[18]
And got to windward. Thus we all (tho late)
Came to an anchor in Certificate,[19]
Where having stopt a Tyde at length we went
All safe on th' shore of Letters call'd Patent.
Some of the Fleet stayd in the Bay Decree,
Some hull'd in th' open shore of Letterree.[20]
Thus landed all; The freight of Acreage paid
Yeares value, subsidy and chymny-aid.[21]   60
We went to sleep, & slept till Viscount Ranelagh,
Buzz'd by Sr James, that pretty Man a Law,

17. A 'Proviso-man' was one whose land was restored to him by special stipulation or proviso in the Act of Settlement. An 'Ensign' was someone who had served under the ensigns (banners) of Charles II in exile: ensigns' estates were restored to them in the Act of Settlement. 'Meromotu' is a coinage based on two Latin words, merus, 'unmixed or pure' and motu 'of motion': it refers to 'letterees' or persons restored to their estates by letters of Charles II. 'Men Reprisable' were those who had to be compensated for what they had lost. 'Nominees' were individuals named in the Royal Declaration of November 1660 or in the Acts of Settlement or Explanation as meriting royal favour: they were restored to their estates without further ado. Arnold (*op. cit.*) makes sense of this almost incomprehensible business.
18. sailed the ship close to the wind. windward = towards the wind.
19. After obtaining a decree of innocence from the court of claims, a claimant for an estate received a certificate containing a schedule of the lands he had been granted. This was confirmed in a letter patent (line 56) – though some of these were not issued for many years (Arnold, pp. 56, 111).
20. Some estates were allocated on the basis of royal decree, others on the basis of letters from the king. Those who obtained their estates by the latter manner were 'Letterees'.
21. By the allegory of the poem, the value of the goods in the ship was enough to pay taxes and expenses for a year.

Woke us agayne, & the green wax of Bees
Stung us to death with cursd Exchequer fees
And wild demands.[22] 'Oh King! is't your Intent
(After these scapes) the Hurricane Quitt rent
Should stave and sink's? Or that a Locust swarme
Of Pilfring Picaroons[23] should do us harme?'

'Noe (quoth the King) I'le rather make James goe
A fourth bout more for Ireland.' 'Let it be soe!'   70
Cryd one and all. Thus did with cheerful voyce
The whole ship's crew from stem to sterne rejoyce.

The Postscript

The greater was their Joy; because they all
Hop'd Ossory[24] (their Friend, Father, Admirall, –
Ossory the Great, the Honest, and the Stout)
Might by this meanes at Helm have t'other bout.[25]
'Were he' (quoth they) 'but Boatswaine, all were well.
Hee'd not the cables nor the anchors sell,
Make stayes nor shrouds of Rotten Ropes, nor lett
Harld Kenks[26] into the running Rigging[27] gett.   80
All sheeves[28] should in their Blocks run yare and clever,[29]
Capstans gyre[30] true, the Pumps of Justice never
Bee at fault, but allways fitt the Hold[31] to free
From what can dangerous or can noysome[32] bee.'

---

22. These few lines refer – rather confusingly since Petty gets carried away by his naval allegory – to a series of court intrigues against Ormond during the early 1670s. The main dispute to which they refer was between Ormond and the dishonest Richard Jones, Earl of Ranelagh, who had been chancellor of the Irish Exchequer during part of Ormond's previous vice-royalty. Despite the fact that Ormond's enemies had powerful friends, they failed to turn the king against him and, as the poem makes clear, Charles called on Ormond to take the lord lieutenancy of Ireland again in 1677.
23. rogues.
24. Thomas Butler, Earl of Ossory (1634–80), eldest son of the Duke of Ormond, widely respected as an honest man, a fine soldier and a promising statesman. Many poems, like this one, celebrate his worth. He died suddenly at the age of forty six in 1680.
25. Ormond had left Ossory as acting lord lieutenant when he had to visit England in 1664–5 and in 1668–9.
26. tangled kinks.
27. the ropes used to work or set sails.
28. pulleys.
29. quickly and easily.
30. turn on their axles.
31. the interior of a ship, below the waterline.
32. offensive.

Ormond and Ossory dont sail for wages,
They have great cargoes of their owne, and gages[33]
For Ireland's common interest still to be true,
And make the High pay to the Low their due.

Let's drink their Healths! Here's to 'em, my hearts of gold!
Ossory bee young and Ormond never old!   90

---

33. gauges; here, a gauge is the depth to which a vessel sinks with a full cargo.

ROGER BOYLE, EARL OF ORRERY
(1621–1679, pub.**1681**)

Roger Boyle, Baron Broghill and first Earl of Orrery, fifth son of the great Earl of Cork, was one of the best-known Irish writers of his day. After a colourful career as a soldier in Ireland throughout the 1640s and 1650s, starting as a royalist defending the Boyle estates during the 1641 rising, later serving under Cromwell, and finally being instrumental in the restoration of Charles II as king in Ireland, Boyle (who was created Earl of Orrery in 1660) was made President of Munster. He was known as a staunch protestant and a fine soldier.

Boyle was also a prolific dramatist, novelist and poet. He wrote several tragedies, two comedies and *Parthenissa*, a romance in the French style – the first published fiction by an Irish writer. His plays were widely read and some of them were performed in London; (Samuel Pepys comments on them in his diary.) Boyle was also a poet, though Dryden chided him for writing verse only when a fit of gout drew him from other duties.

Late in his life, Boyle turned to writing religious verse and, in the interesting introduction to his *Poems on most of the Festivals of the Church* (published posthumously in 1681), he explained what drew him to this material.

> God, of His Abundant Mercy, having Convinc'd Me, how much Precious Time I had cast away on Airy Verses; I Resolv'd to take a Final Leave of That Sort of Poetry; And in some Degree to repair the Unhappiness and Fault of what was past, to Dedicate my Muse in the Future, Entirely to Sacred Subjects . . .

> . . . The Handling of these Subjects in Verse, and Rhime, I was persuaded, would not be unpleasing to the less Studious, (who are those who most need such information) and since in poetry, there is a kind of Natural Musick, I imagined, that all Those, whose Souls were not quite out of Tune, might be affected with it.

> Besides, I found That Many who could hardly Repeat one verse of the Sacred Scripture, would yet say without Book, intire Psalms; even in the Unhappy Verses, and Rhimes, of Mr *Hopkins*, and Mr *Sternhold*;[1]. . . it seems to be the Inherent Prerogative of *Verse*, above *Prose*, To be better Fancied; To be easier Learn'd by Heart; and to be Longer Retain'd in the Memory . . .

Much of Boyle's secular verse is of little interest today, but he is credited with authorship of the first part of the double distich on the gates of Bandon earlier in this anthology. The two poems which follow come from *Poems on most of the Festivals of the Church*, the text of which was printed in Cork.

---

1. Thomas Sternhold (*d.* 1549) and John Hopkins (*d.* 1570) were the main authors of the metrical psalms (first ed. 1549?) used in the Churches of England and Ireland until Trinity College Dublin graduates Nahum Tate and Nicholas Brady produced *A New Version of the Psalms of David* in 1696.

To my Mother the Church of Christ in Ireland

Hail Sacred Mother! O do not Refuse
These the *First Fruits* of my Converted Muse;[2]
A Muse which in vain paths too long has trod
And now do's Consecrate her self to God.
This Change, O Muse, Most happy is for thee
Mount Sion now shall thy *Parnassus* bee
Thou never yet Could'st Sore to such a height
As that, from whence thou now begin'st thy flight;
The Spires of Airy Verse[3] climb not so high
As to the Feet of Sacred Poetry.   10

Mother Vouchsafe, My Influence to be
Now I thy Prodigall return to Thee.

On the Nativity of Our Blessed Lord and Saviour Commonly called Christmas Day

Hail Glorious Day which Miracles Adorn,
Since 'twas on Thee ETERNITY was Born.
Hail Glorious Day in which Mankind did View
The SAVIOUR *of the Old World* and the New.
Hail Glorious Day which Deifies man[1] Race,
Birth Day of JESUS and, through Him, *of Grace*.
In Thy Blest Light, the World at once did See
Proofs of His God-head and Humanity.
To prove him Man, He did from Woman come,
To prove him God, 'twas from a Virgins Wombe.   10
Man nere could faigne what his Strange Birth prov'd True,
For His Blest Mother was a Virgin too.
While as a Child He in the *Manger Cryes*,
Angells Proclaim His Godhead from the Skyes;
Hee, to So vile a Cradle did Submitt,
That Wee, through Faith in Him, on *Thrones* might Sit.

---

2. i.e. the first offerings. The phrase carries echoes of the payment of the first year's income (the 'First Fruits') required from incumbents in the established church when they took over a new benefice.
3. i.e. secular verse – as opposed to sacred poetry.

---

1. man's.

O Prodigie of Mercy, which did make
The God of Gods Our *Humane Nature* take!
And through Our Vaile of Flesh, His Glory Shine,
That Wee thereby, might Share *in the Divine*.   20
Hail Glorious Virgin whose Tryumphant Wombe
Blesses All Ages past and All to Come.
Thou more than Heal'st the Sin by *Adam's* Wife;
She brought in Death, but *Thou brought'st Endless Life*.
Noe greater Wonder in the World could bee,
Than Thou to Live in it, and *HEAV'N* in thee.

Heav'n does Thine own great prophesy Attest,
All Generations still shall Call Thee Blest.

To Thee that Title is most Justly paid
Since by Thy Son, Wee *Sons of God are made*.   30

ANONYMOUS
(1681)

Redmond O'Hanlon was the most famous Irish outlaw of the seventeenth century. Though the Ó hAnluains of County Armagh had, at various times, fought with as well as against English forces in Ireland, their lands were confiscated during the Cromwellian period and were not restored at the Restoration. As a result, Redmond O'Hanlon (as he was generally known) took to the hills in the late 1660s and, with his band of at least fifty men, fiercely harassed the army and protestant settlers throughout south-east Ulster, venturing also into Connacht and Leinster on daring raids. His courage and audacity were famous, as was his generosity to the poor – he was an Irish 'Robin Hood', in many ways – and he continued to be a threat to law and order until he was betrayed and killed in April 1681.

The ironic elegy which follows testifies to O'Hanlon's status as the cult hero of the day, fit to be likened (even mockingly) with the heroes of classical times.

An Elegy of the Modern Heroe, Redmond Ó Hanlan, Surnamed the Tory[1]

Come gentle Muse, assist my pen
To praise the worthiest of men,
With whom, your ancient Heroes put
In ballance, weigh not shell of Nut.[2]
As for great *Hanlan*'s reputation,
We shall evince by demonstration.

Of them, let *Jason*[3] first be nam'd,
For clean conveyance so much fam'd.
For whose each lock of Golden wooll,
Bold *Redmon* has a thousand stole.   10
Nor did their owners scape so cheap,
He often took both Fleece and Sheep.
Nay, *Mercury* himself, though made
A God, for his great skill i' th' trade[4]
Compar'd, would look like *Picaroon*[5]
To First-Rate Ship, or Star to Moon.

---

1. dispossessed Irish rebel; Ir. *tórai*.
2. i.e. the ancient heroes weigh less than a nutshell when balanced against Redmond O'Hanlon.
3. Jason, celebrated Grecian hero and leader of the Argonauts, who successfully rescued the Golden Fleece.
4. There were several ancient gods called Mercury, one of whom was patron of thieves and pickpockets.
5. (here) = privateer or corsair.

Next *Hercules*, about whose Club
Strange tales you tell, like those of Tub,[6]
Would the unequal combat shun,
O're-matched by his dead doing Gun.[7]   20
For if with Blunderbuss compar'd
Like all that met it, 'twould have feared.
The force of this *Achilles* hide,
Well tann'd as 'twas, wou'd ne'r abide,
Should lusty Blunder once assault him;
In spight of Fate, it would have maul'd him.[8]

Hector, that of the Greeks made spoyl,
(As you and Homer keep a coyl)[9]
Ne're bolder set upon his foes
Than he, who told them to their nose   30
'You must deliver up your Purse,
Or, by my Shoul, you'l fare the worse.'
Which said, if enemy seem'd stout,[10]
Soon half a dozen balls flew out,
And strait one Army fell to rout,[11]
Which if our party, no worse far'd
Than losing Prize, and being scar'd:
For th' famous Warrior was compleat
In all that makes a Generall great,
Knew when to fight, when to retreat;   40
In which no Mountains, Rocks, or Woods,
Cou'd stop his course, nor Bogs, nor Floods;
As oft he manifested when
Pursu'd by Floyd[12] and his six men

6. Hercules, the most famous of all classical heroes, was often shown wielding the olive-wood club with which he killed various monsters. 'A tale of a tub' was a cock-and-bull story, a meaningless romance.
7. i.e. Hercules, his club no match for Redmond O'Hanlon's death-dealing gun, would shun combat with him.
8. This complicated (and probably garbled) passage seems to mean: for if it [O'Hanlon's gun] were compared to a blunderbuss (like everyone did who met it), it would put fear into him. The strength of this Achilles' hide [Hercules is here called Achilles because he was impervious to danger, like Achilles], well tanned as it was, would never stand firm; should [O'Hanlon's] lusty blunderbuss assault him, in spite of fate, it would have seriously damaged him.
9. Hector was the Trojan hero whose tale is told in Homer's *Iliad*. to keep a coil = to make a disturbance, a noise.
10. i.e. if those who were being held up by O'Hanlon showed resistance . . .
11. i.e. and straightaway, one group retreated which, if it were our party . . .
12. The officer whose troop had been pursuing O'Hanlon.

Shewing a pair of heels so light
That some mistook it for plain flight.
But they are much mista'ne, alas!
And chiefly in the Miller's case:
For though his men and he retir'd
With speed, after the Mill was fir'd,   50
Yet none must think the *Count*[13] would run
From one old Miller and his son.
Attribute then, the haste was made
Only to fear of Ambuscade.

But death, although he ran so fast
Has got the heels of him at last,
For which the tears are numberless
That have been shed, as you may guess.
But to his friends, one comfort's left.
Although he be of life bereft,   60
He shan't partake the common fate;
For neither Redmon's limbs nor pate
Shall under sordid rubbish lye   ⎫
Forgot, but shall be plac'd on high,   ⎬
Monuments of his Chivalry.[14]   ⎭
Where, if his shining Beard and Hair,
Should like some new made Star appear,
(For Stars, in time past, *Heroes* were,)
To all that dare his Rivals be,
They will portend black destiny.   70

---

13. O'Hanlon was known as Count Hanlon on the Continent.
14. Despite the implications of this passage, O'Hanlon's head was not, according to contemporary pamphlets on his death, available to the authorities to impale, as was customary, on a spike over the entrance to Dublin Castle. It was removed from his body immediately after his death and secreted by his followers.

ANONYMOUS
(1681)

Few events connected with seventeenth-century Ireland inspired more verse than the sudden death, in London on 30 July 1680, of Thomas Butler, Earl of Ossory, eldest son of the Duke of Ormond. Ossory was universally regarded as a man of outstanding promise. He was a courageous soldier, a loyal courtier and an honest man, whose only folly seems to have been a love of gambling. He was widely seen as a worthy son of a worthy father and his unexpected death, at the age of forty-six, was considered a serious loss in both England and Ireland. Poets of all kinds rushed into print in both countries to lament his death, and several poems were also sent, in manuscript, to his grieving parents; these are among the Ormond poems at Yale.

The simple poem which follows is from the Ormond collection, and though it is far less impressive on the surface than some of the printed poetic effusions on Ossory's death – such as the majestic Pindaric ode by Thomas Flatman (Dublin and London, 1680) – it draws on its author's personal experience of Ossory and contains some vivid and unexpected details.

from: Upon the Earle of Ossory's dying of a Feaver

To the Dutchesse of Ormond
Your Son's true worth (whom we lament as dead),
Has drawne these verses from my heart, not head;
They are a plaine true Narrative of what
All men allow; no feigning what was not.
I never thought you pleas'd with flattering fiction,
Nor that such stuffe was proper in affliction.
I seldome rhyme, though there be seasons, when
The Grav'st and hollyest, have so used their pen.
Who onely writes on such as Ossory
Perhapps needn't write twice more, before he dy.   10

1. The best siz'd Pillar of the fairest Pile,
That has of late been built on Ireland's I'le
Is fall'n; some were too short, others too long,
Some are too old, and others much too young.

2. His numerous Name[1] being like a towne too wide
To be well mann'd or fully fortified:
He was their Cittadell within; Their mote[2]
Without, their force which on the sea did flote;

1. family, clan, people – here, apparently, intended to include not just the Butlers but the people of Ireland.
2. embankment, surrounding fortification.

458

At land their Army, nothing being more
Ready to fight, upon the Sea or Shore.   10

3. He didn't grasp commands to scrape up Gold.
When he was Cheif, all offices were sold,
'Tis true: for what d'y thinke? For skill in Armes,
For vigilance and Courage; These only Charmes
Wrought on his soule; He that could pay good store
Of Sterling merrit, needed pay no more.

4. Who knew him well, could not believe that ever
He mean't to dy thus tamely of a Feaver.
The Fates did disappoint him; It was their Checke[3]
Hee had not dy'd upon a Blood-smeared Decke,   20
Or Storming, fell downe from a Scaling Ladder,
First by Granadoes[4] rent; or, what is sadder,
Some Royal ship, his Coffin should have been,
Stranded in fight, where tall rocks might be seen
To shew the sea-faring Crew, where Ossory
Fought for the Laws, and for the king did dy.

5. What, must wee weep? No; Let no muses whine
Nor verse be wett with metaphorick brine.
His Names not dead, who stands enshrined wth Glory
Embalm'd by fame, with Monuments and Story.   30
Cannons, go weep out flames; culverins[5] go cry
And roare, from every Ship and Battery
That Ossory's gone. Gone? Whither? To share Jove's thunder[6]
And try what powers can make him fear or wonder . . .

7. Rather than weep, Frett, that the king, the Nation,
Ireland, his house, and the whole confederation
Of worthy men, his children, and his wife,
Were all treppann'd and couzn'd[7] of his life.

---

3. (probably) a term from hawking meaning the action of a hawk which forsakes her proper
   quarry for lower game. Here the implication is that Ossory should have been honoured
   with a noble death (as detailed later in the verse) rather than the one he did receive.
4. grenades.
5. large cannons.
6. Jove was god of war.
7. cheated and defrauded.

For hee (who Fire and ball was proof) with Ice
Was burnt, and with a Peach shott in a trice[8] . . .   40

13. How many wronged wretches (poor & blind)
Will grope in vaine their remedyes to find?[9]
What will the lame-maimed Seamen doe? Whose Chest
Was Patron Ossory's most munificent Brest?
The sound (instead of Songs of Drinke and Lasse)
Will sing his name at Helme (Each his watch Glasse)
And on the Deck, fancy the starry Trayne
They see, is Ossory up in Charls his wayne;[10]
But singing, sigh that Ossory is no more,
Shall make'm fight at Sea, nor drink at Shore.   50
What Lamentacions will this blow so sharp
Cause to be sett upon the Irish harp?

14. All hands to worke. Let every faculty
Come help to soften this calamity.
Come you Divines! more than deserve the faire
Preferments you have had, Beat not the aire
In Pulpits, but let your inspired Arts
Preach Balsams to the bruised Ormond-Hearts.
Enlarge on Job, and Branch on every head
That David spake, when Bash'ba's son was dead.[11]   60

15. Where are the Opticks[12] I have often had
That could reduce a Shape, tho ne're so bad
Deform'd & ugly, to a handsome Hew?
Help now to make things hideous and true
Looke faire, tho false; Make Ormonds house beleeve
They may their Ossory, & their son retreeve;
Give of those Optick Instruments to each
Of his Name one, To valiant Soldiers reach

---

8. Ossory's final sickness started when he was taken ill at the sheriffs' dinner at
   Fishmongers' Hall in London on the evening of 26 July 1680. Was he eating a confection
   made of peaches and ice at the time?
9. Ossory was famed for his charity.
10. The constellation now known as the Great Bear was sometimes known as 'Charles's
    Wain' – the 'wain' being a chariot or cart and 'Charles' being either Charlemagne or a
    churl or farmer.
11. The references are to the book of Job and to II Samuel 12. 15–23. 'branch on every head'
    means expand on, explain every point.
12. lenses, optical instruments.

One a Peece more, and then (for fear of failer)
Give two a peece, to every fighting Sailer;   70
Thus by refractions and contriv'd reflections,
Dilude all these,[13] and temper their affections.

16. Palliat this sore (sore Æsculapian[14] hand)!
Till dozing time can cicatrize it,[15] and
Beget new hopes, untill new measures be taken
And old designs off from our minds be shaken.

17. Now tell me (Heavn's favourit) when shall I
Leave off to mourne? When? Not till thou dy.
You are in Paradise, we know right well,
You have already conquered Death & Hell;   80
Send me a pass-port from the place of Blisse,
And lett me your exalted feet goe kisse;
Soe shall your shineing face, all my tears dry
Like Summers-Sunn. Oh Let me goe, I'le dy.

---

13. Altered in a contemporary manuscript hand to 'his freinds'.
14. Æsculapius was god of medicine and healing in the ancient world.
15. heal, enable it to develop a scar (a cicatrice).

ANONYMOUS
(1682)

Since most English protestants of the late seventeenth century thought that the terms 'Irish' and 'catholic' were synonymous, it is not surprising that the anti-catholic hysteria of the Popish Plot (1678–81) aroused considerable anti-Irish feeling. The Irish were seen as traitors and perjurers, a threat to the English state and to the English way of life. The verses which follow, from a broadsheet printed in London in 1682, reflect the general English view of the 'rebel' Irish at the time of the plot, presenting them as the cause of every ill to have befallen England since the Reformation, from the Gunpowder Plot to the Great Fire of London. The speaker in the song is an Irish catholic.

A Looking-Glass for a Tory;[1]
or the Bogg-Trotter's Glory

To the Tune of Hey Boys up Go We.

The Devil and we have done brave things,
No age can match the same;
We have disturb'd the best of Kings,
Set *England* in a flame.[2]
We've made his Subjects almost mad,
A man that's blind may see
And yet we have escaped a gad[3]
Such crafty Knaves are we.

We swear this Hour and next deny
What we before had Sworn;   10
Both God and Conscience we defie,
Religion we do Scorn:[4]
If we confess, the Priests forgive,
What sins so e're they be:
Like Devils on earth we mean to live,
Such Perjur'd Knaves are we.

We make new Plots to hide the old,
And thus we please the Pope;

---

1. dispossessed Irish rebel; Ir. *tórai.*
2. i.e. set England ablaze and plotted against the king, as alleged by Titus Oates and the other Popish Plot perjurers.
3. noose. Ir. *gad*, a rope made of thick fibres or of willow saplings.
4. Perjury was a particular hallmark of the trials associated with the Popish Plot.

Let us but have the Roman Gold,
Wee'l never fear a Rope.   20
Wee'l make old *Tony Cooper*[5] know,
That we such pranks can play,
As shall give him a gentle blow,
The clean contrary way.

An Oath in Bonny-clapper[6] dipt,
Goes nimbly down our throats:
Wee'l venture to be hang'd or whipt,
For sixpence or two groats.[7]
We fear no collours red nor blue,[8]
Our wits are gone astray,   30
We go to Heaven (give us our due)
The clean contrary way.

Oh Cram a Chree[9] the times are hard,
We know not how to live;
If that our Oaths should be debarr'd,
And Pope no Money give,
Why fait and trote *dear Joy* we must
Without Potatoes play,[10]
And the English would preserve our dust,
The clean contrary way.   40

But, by my Gossips, had a *gra,*[11]
Our Priests have spurr'd us on,
And we will try to stretch the Law,
Before we will be gone;
Wee'l swear for shooes and throw our brogues
To the Devil on New-years day:

5. Anthony Ashley Cooper, first Earl of Shaftesbury, leader of the opposition in the English parliament, a fervent opponent of the succession of James Duke of York, and of everything catholic.
6. A typically Irish drink of thick, soured milk. Ir. *bainne clabair.* See Alan Bliss, *Spoken English in Ireland 1600–1740* (Dublin, 1979), pp. 271–2.
7. A groat was a coin worth four pence.
8. (probably) = redcoats or bluecoats, i.e. English soldiers or sailors.
9. = *gra-ma-cree,* darling. Ir. *grá mó chroí,* 'love of my heart'.
10. Common examples of exaggerated Hiberno-English pronunciation 'fait' and 'troat', and of the stereotyped English perception of the Irish as potato-eaters; also an early use of the phrase 'Dear Joys' applied to native Irishmen.
11. Ir. *grá,* love. The line might be paraphrased: But, by my godfathers! we had a liking for it (i.e. for the uttering of false oaths, as in the previous stanza).

We know that none will count us Rogues
The clean contrary way.

A Testimony Maker[12] may
Spring up within a night,   50
We know that many a man will say,
A Mushroom's[13] come in sight:
But let them rail and slight us now,
They shall our glory see,
The Devil and Pope our Trades allow,[14]
Sing hey boys up go we.

If we could swear the Pope again,
Unto the British Shore,
And see the English Rascals slain,
And tumbling in their gore;   60
Then every Teague would get his Land,
Rebels of each degree;
And we might with our Swords in hand
Sing hey boys up we go.

Now by Saint *Patrick* let us try[15]
What man can swear the best,
A Pox upon a Common lye,
Let's swear above the rest.
Let's swear that every Protestant,
Their sacred King would slay,   70
And we shall rise let who will want,
The clean contrary way.

Let's swear the Papists ne're did ill,
Since Mass was first in fashion,
That they had neither pow'r nor will
To hurt the English Nation:

---

12. A giver of false information, a false witness.
13. i.e. a new, previously unknown conspiracy.
14. i.e. they allow us to sin (since they give us absolution afterwards – a common protestant jibe).
15. In this verse and the one that follows, the speaker urges his Irish catholic friends to compete with each other to see who can tell the best lies or commit the most convincing perjuries. In lines 68–70, for instance, the reader knows that it is catholics, not protestants, who are said to want to kill the king.

That they're as harmless as a child,
Which ev'ry man may see.
And when our Oaths have them beguil'd
Then hey boys up go we.   80

Let's swear that *Godfrey*[16] hang'd himself,
Because he could not wed;
And then he forfeits all his wealth,
And the Plot will all lye dead.
Let's Swear that these *Morocco* blades,
Brought Oats but tother day
Upon their pretty *Barbary* Jades,[17]
Though the clean contrary way.

Let's Swear with all our force and might,
There was no Powder Treason,[18]   90
And then one fasting day take flight,
You know it is but reason.
Let's Swear the City ne're was burn'd
By Papists that did flee,[19]
And then the stream will soon be turn'd[20]
And hey boys up go we.

16. The murder of Sir Edmund Godfrey, a zealous protestant magistrate, in 1678, was the
    event which precipitated Oates's perjuries and the hysteria of the Popish Plot. The
    catholics executed for Godfrey's murder were convicted on the basis of perjury. These
    lines propose that it should be asserted that Godfrey committed suicide; if this were true,
    his property would have been forfeit and there would have been no basis for the Popish
    Plot.
17. These lines seem to refer to the rumours (rife in the autumn of 1678) that thousands of
    catholics had landed secretly on deserted beaches around England, and were riding
    through the countryside by night. As John Kenyon notes, the rumours of these 'night
    riders' are an interesting example of crowd hysteria. John Kenyon, *The Popish Plot*
    (London, 1972), p. 101.
18. A reference to the Gunpowder Plot of 1607.
19. It was widely believed that the Great Fire of London had been deliberately started by
    catholics.
20. i.e. the present anti-catholic, anti-Irish tide will soon be turned, and we shall go 'up'.

JOHN WILSON
(1627-**1682**-1696)

Elegies lamenting the deaths of virtuous men, as well as odes celebrating the coming and going of lord lieutenants, flowed from the pens of Dublin poets with depressing regularity during the reigns of Charles II and James II. Most of these effusions are deservedly forgotten. However, 'To his Excellence, Richard Earle of Arran' has some interest because, adjoining the printed copy of the poem in the British Library is an anonymous, manuscript answer. The tired banality of John Wilson's almost incomprehensible ode is neatly ridiculed by the attacker, whose poem also sheds some light on the world of Dublin poetasters inside and outside the court in the early 1680s.[1]

John Wilson, a lawyer who was appointed recorder of Londonderry in 1681, wrote legal texts and plays as well as odes of welcome and congratulation. Though several of his plays were well received on the stage and a collected edition (edited by J. Maidment and W.H. Logan) was published in 1874, all have since sunk without trace. The occasion of Wilson's poem to Lord Arran is explained in its lengthy title.

To his Excellence, Richard Earle of Arran &c., Lord Deputy of Ireland,
ON THE OCCASION OF HIS GRACE JAMES DUKE OF ORMONDE &C. LORD LIEUTENANT OF THE SAME (HIS FATHER'S) GOING FOR ENGLAND, AND LEAVING THE GOVERNMENT TO HIM.

Hence the nice Witts that are so squeamish grown,
Nothing will down with them, but what's their own;
It has been said (yet tax'd) I *freeze*, and *burn*
At the same instant, both *rejoice* and *mourn*:[2]
And why (I pray) mayn't different notes agree?
Take away discord, there's the Harmony!

Both are met here: we mourn one *Sun* gone *East*,
And joy another rising in the West:[3]
Such – such, as had the Antient *Persian*
View'd the *Parelia*, this double *Sun*,   10
Had made him stagger at the smart surprise,
Not yet resolv'd, divide his sacrifice.[4]

---

1. I am grateful to Raymond Gillespie for alerting me to this manuscript response to Wilson's poem.
2. A reference to the paradoxes common in Elizabethan and metaphysical verse. yet taxed = although challenged.
3. i.e. Ormond has gone to England, Arran has come to Dublin from the west of Ireland.
4. This obscure reference seems linked to a sun-worshipper of ancient Persia (Darius?) who, if presented with the problem of two suns of equal strength ('Parelia' seems to be

'Tis now past twenty times since th' Ormonde stem
First brancht it self in such a Princely Beam:[5]
And may it yet encrease, and multiply
It's scatter'd Rayes into a *Galaxy*.

Spread-Eagles joyn in body:[6] *Lucifer*
And *Vesper* are the same alternate Star:[7]
The Eleventh, *Castor* and *Pollux* too,
Relieve each other, and in that, still new.[8]   20

Nature had never made a second day,
Without a night's repose: that short allay
Stampt us another, and that timely care
Stept in, and sav'd the Infant-World's despair.

And now, 'tis but a day from Sun to Sun:
The one takes up, the other holds it on;
Seasons to Seasons give a fresh supply:
The year absolv'd, comes the *Epiphany*.[9]

Such your most noble Father (*Sir*'s) with you;
He closes one, and you begin the new: 30
And, be his Motions[10] yours, I'll boldly say,
The *Sun* withdrew, and yet *We* lost no day.

---

from Latin *parilis*, equal), would have to divide his intended sacrifice in two. The oddity of the reference is noted at line 15 of the next poem (see p. 468).

5. Wilson's arithmetic if is hard to follow and must be somehow linked to the fact that the Duke of Ormond, who was twelfth Earl of Ormond, had four sons, of whom the Earl of Arran was the third.

6. A representation of an eagle with body, wings and legs displayed, in heraldry or as a emblem. The Butler crest includes a falcon – but it is not 'spread-eagled'.

7. The planet Venus which appears as both the morning star (when it is often called Lucifer, the bringer of light) and as the evening star (often called Hesperus, the western star).

8. There were only eleven signs in the zodiac of the ancient world, the eleventh of which, Pisces, was represented by the double image of two fish. Though Castor and Pollux (the twin sons of Leda) were often used to represent anything doubled or twinned, the two were also said to have been placed in the sky as 'The Twins', or the morning and the evening star. Wilson probably expects his reader to be aware of both associations.

9. i.e. the feast of the Epiphany (6 January) comes after the old year has been absolved or cleared away.

10. = 1) actions; 2) movements of the sun.

ANONYMOUS
(1682)

On Mr Wilson's admirable Copy of Verses dedicated to his Ex: the Earle of Arran[1]

Hence the nice Witts that are so squeamish grown,
Nothing will down with them, but what's their own;

'Twas wholesome Counsell, and 'twas fairely done,
To tell them their dull fare before they come.
Their puney Stomachs never would Digest
This Nauseous stuff of thine, this porters feast.[2]
But yett methinks, 'twas prodigall to rime
Out of that slender, shallow stock of thine;
Thy name in preface might have done as well:
'Here little Wilson, here doth dulness dwell.'
For who the devill with appetite would look
On such a dish, & drest by such a Cook?   10
Who can endure, dos't think, to see thee run
For an old threadbeare simile to the Sunn?
A thing the very Phillis-fooles[3] dispise,
And far more bright, see the faire Cælia's eyes.
But thus from thy 'Parelia' to fall
To Lucifer and Vespers, worst of all!
To hail[4] thy prince with scraps pickt here & there,
From sacred Lilly and the famous Hare,[5]
Tell me for sure thou did'st it out of sport
To show thy worst – or was't compos'd at Court?   20
Was[6] then that Latin Cub of thine brought forth
To boast thy haughty ignorance in both?
By Heaven, were I in 's Excellency's case,
I'd hang the wretch that did pen[7] this disgrace.

---

1. see headnote to previous poem.
2. i.e. food for mere door-keepers. 'prodigall' (l. 5) = recklessly extravagant.
3. i.e. writers of conventional love-poems to 'Phyllis' or (next line) 'Celia'.
4. MS reads 'heal'.
5. William Lilly (1602–81), author of annual almanacs and (probably) John Hare (*fl.* 1640s), author of *The Marine Mercury* (1642).
6. MS reads 'where'.
7. Conjectural reading: the manuscript is illegible, and the word could be 'send'.

'Tis true indeed the style may serve to shew
When Sun's in Cancer, when in Scorpio,
To help a wretched Almanack's dull sale,
And Martyrdome of Christmas pyes bewayle;[8]
But never, sure, did flattering poet kiss
The hands of prince in such style as this,   30
A style whose panegyrick is abuse,
Which nothing but his madness can Excuse.
For madd he is, at least hee is possest,
The fiend Belphegar[9] heaves within his breast.

8. The reference is impossible to clarify. (Scrap paper was used to line pie-dishes – and the pies could be said to be 'martyred' when eaten – or was there a popular rhyme about Christmas pies?)
9. Wilson had written a tragi-comedy entitled *Belphegor, or The marriage of the devil*. The work was printed nine years later in London.

ANONYMOUS
(1683)

This lampoon on the senior fellows of Trinity College Dublin is heavily influenced by Dryden's famous satire *MacFlecknoe* (London, 1682); in that poem, Dryden ridiculed the poet Thomas Shadwell, imagining him being formally invested with the mantle of dullness by his dull 'father' poet, Richard Flecknoe. The introit to this poem describes one of the senior fellows of Trinity College, William Palliser (later Archbishop of Cashel), falling in love and getting married. Since the college did not, at this time, permit married fellows, Palliser had to resign his fellowship and leave the college. He was replaced as a senior fellow, on 24 February 1683, by Dives Downes (later Bishop of Cork and Lismore), the ceremony of whose installation is scurrilously and irreverently parodied in the poem. The seven senior fellows ('that Wicked Synod') are described meeting to give praise to 'high Debauchery', and the extract below begins as Dives Downes is about to be installed as a senior member of the club. The fact that senior fellows of Trinity College were required to be celibate, ordained priests of the Church of Ireland, and that most of them went on to become bishops, adds to the irony of the imaginary, unsavoury, satanic events described below.

The poem comes from the important, four-volume poetical miscellany, 'A Whimsical Medley', compiled by Theophilus, Lord Newtown Butler who was a student at Trinity College from 1686 to 1689. Although most of the material in this manuscript collection dates from Newtown Butler's time in Trinity – and later – this particular poem comes from the early months of 1683. It is just possible that it is the work of John Jones, whose scandalous Tripos speech of 1688 (the text of which is also in 'The Whimsical Medley') led to his temporary suspension from the college; Jones, who later became a famous schoolmaster, had entered Trinity College in May 1681. (See below p. 511).

from: A Lampoon on the Senior Fellowes of Dublin Colledge

> . . . But now 'tis time, you'll say, that I relate
> The Ceremonious manner of the State
> For this Installment. Fancy now you see
> Some darksome Place design'd for K[n]avery,
> Where Thieves resort to share their illgott prey,
> Where doors are bolted, & where tell tale day
> Finds no Admittance; Where no Busie Ear
> Nor Listning Mortalls, their ill deeds can hear.
> In such a Place, for such a Councill fitt
> See in what Apelike State the Brethren sit.   10
>
> His Reverend Dullness[1] fills the Upper Place;
> Pedantick Majesty adorns his Face.

---

1. Narcissus Marsh (1638–1713), provost of the college 1679–83, later archbishop of Cashel, Dublin and Armagh.

Next him the Sage his Sister,[2] without whom
Nothing of Consequence was ever done;
A Crown of Rue[3] was placed upon her head,
Her glowing Nose was more than usual red:
A Branch of Savine[4] in her hand she bore,
A Holy Robe of Bible work she Wore;
On it was Wrought Hammen & Tamar's strife
And Cain's soft dalliance with his Sister Wife.   20
The Lustfull David from the Turrett spyes
The Naked Barshebah, and bless'd his Eyes.[5]

There Lott's two daughters, whom their Country's Fame
Cou'd ne're perswade to leave their pleasing game
Contending for their feeble Father lay,
While the Good Man seems tickled att the Play.[6]
Due to his Meritts, the next place was Foy's;[7]
Mercer[8] the next, as 'twas his place, Enjoys.
Scarce was He cured of the Clap, Yet he
Must needs crawl out to this Solemnity.   30
Next him satt Acton's Belly,[9] bigg as Tun,[10]
He with design of being drunk was come.
Brown's Politicks the next place did claim,[11]
Podmore[12] satt last, tho' not the least in fame.

Scarce were they seated when a sudden Flame
Of Lightning Downs's[13] Comeing did proclaim.
Extorsion, Fraud and Penury with Him,
And a whole Troop of Friends came Crowding in.
To whom Foy riseing, for it was his Place
To speak for all the rest, with sullen Grace   40

2. Deborah Marsh.
3. an evergreen shrub, a symbol of sorrow or distress.
4. sabine, juniper, the juice of which is reputed to be an abortifacient.
5. Old Testament stories of lust; for Amnon and Tamar, see II Samuel 13. 1–19; for Cain, see Genesis 4 (though the incestuous relationship is spurious); for David and Bathsheba, see II Samuel 2–3.
6. For the story of Lot and his daughters, see Genesis 19. 30–8.
7. Nathaniel Foy (1648–1707), later Bishop of Waterford and Lismore.
8. George Mercer (*b. c.* 1648), later vice-provost, but removed from the position for being married in June 1687.
9. Richard Acton (*c.* 1645–89), vice-provost 1687–9.
10. barrel.
11. George Browne (1649–99), provost 1695–9.
12. John Padmore or Podmore (1653–85), fellow 1675–85.
13. Dive or Dives Downes (1652–1709), senior fellow, installed 24 February 1682–3.

Thus Spoke: 'Sir, since at last your happy Fate
And Meritts call you [to] the Helm of State,
Renounce that trifling Thing call'd God, for He
With our Affairs will never well agree;
Leave Heaven to Beggars Sir, (be bold and Cheat),
Justice to Fools; be damn'd, and then be Great;
And let it not seem Strange, if We to Those
Conditions, now Enjoyned, One more Impose.
For as the Church of Rome has thought it fitt,
That He in Sex-discerning Chair should sitt   50
Who stands Elected Pope,[14] so you must try
On Beauteous Deborah here Your Faculty.'
Scarce had he spoke when Downs, without remorse,
To her old Bones with Stomach of an horse
Perform'd the Loathsome Task without a pause.
The Fiends all Clapp'd their hands, with Loud Applause.

Then haveing quite forsaken all that's just
Sworn to be true, and sacred to his Trust,
Brown Takes the Sacred Viol,[15] and does shed
The Drops of Mystick Wine upon his head.   60
Samuell att Rama thus Anointed Saul;[16]
In this, fond Brown, too well I see thy fall.
Thy Glories fade, Thy Politicks outdone,
The Stars loose lustre by the Riseing Sun:
Thus foolish Samuell gave the Pow'r away.

See with what Joy they meet the newborn day,
How nimble does the Gratefull health go round;
Dives's health on ev'ry tongue does sound.
Marsh between Wine and Joy seems allmost dead;
Deborah, haveing spent her Moisture, shed   70
Kind Tears of Joy while Mercer Loudly swore,
And Foy's Exalted Mind was for a Whore.
Brown kissed all the Assembled Brethren round;
Acton and Podmore Wallow'd on the Ground.

14. Anti-catholic propaganda asserted that a female (Pope Joan) had been pope in the ninth
century and that, since that time, anyone elected pope had to submit himself to scrutiny
by selected cardinals, before being crowned, so that the cardinals could certify that he
was indeed a man. The commode-like chair allegedly used for this examination is here
referred to as the 'Sex-discerning chair'.
15. vial or phial.
16. I Samuel 10. 1.

In dismall Note the Raven and the Owl[17]
Sing their Loud Praises, Lowd the Furys howl;
The Wanton Fiends about their Feet did play:
The Devill was drunk, & Hell kept Holy-Day.

[17]. birds of ill omen and darkness.

LUKE WADDING
(*c*.1628–**1684**–1691)

Luke Wadding was born in Wexford into a well-known Old English family. He left Ireland for France in 1651 and studied at the Sorbonne. He was ordained into the catholic church and returned to Ireland in 1668 as vicar-general of the diocese of Ferns. He soon became known as a kindly, learned and effective representative of his church, and was well respected by his protestant neighbours. Wadding weathered the storm of the Popish Plot scare in Ireland, and was allowed to remain in the country. In 1671, he was appointed Bishop of Ferns. During the Jacobite period, Wadding was granted a pension of £150 per annum, but he was forced to flee Wexford when the town fell to the Williamites in 1690, and he died soon afterwards.

Wadding left a fascinating diary in which he lists, *inter alia*, the contents of his impressive library. Among the volumes of verse in his collection were carol books, ballads (of which Wadding was very fond) and the works of Crashawe, Herbert, Dryden, Quarles, Carew, Butler and Donne. Wadding also notes that he gave away at least ten dozen copies of his own book, *A Smale Garland of Pious and Godly Songs*, to members of his congregation.[1]

This little book of poems collected by Wadding gives a unique insight into the world inhabited by catholics in Ireland during the 1670s and 1680s. It contains not only the earliest printed versions of some of the famous Wexford carols, but also poems specifically written to give solace to catholics during the difficult days of the Popish Plot scare, and to comfort those facing exile or the disruption of their lives because of the enforcement of anti-catholic legislation.[2]

On *Christmas* Day the Yeere 1678,
when the Clergy were Banish'd in the Time of the Plot[3]

> This is our *Christmass* Day,
> The day of *Christ's* birth,
> Yet we are far from Joy
> And far from *Christmass* Mirth;
> On *Christmass* to have no Mass
> Is our great discontent;

---

1. See Patrick J. Corish, 'Bishop Wadding's Notebook', *Archivium Hibernicum*, vol. 29 (1970), pp. 49–114.
2. Although most poems in the book date from the 1670s and are almost certainly by Wadding himself, others (the Wexford carols, for instance, which first appear in print here) were probably traditional hymns.
3. The Popish Plot, which plunged England into a mood of hysterical anti-catholicism from the middle of 1678 until 1681, also sent shock waves through Ireland where the authorities closed catholic schools and churches, arrested catholic priests and, in general, enforced the anti-catholic legislation which was on the statute books. Some Irish catholics, including Father Wadding, vigorously asserted their innocence of any desire to plot against the state, and reaffirmed their loyalty to the crown. This poem reflects this point of view, as well as being a lament for the state of desolation which the authorities' reaction to the Popish Plot had brought upon the church.

That without Mass this Day shou'd pass
Doth cause us to lament.

The name of Christmass
Must chang'd and alter'd be,   10
For since we have no Mass,
No Christmasse now have we.
It's therefore we do mourn,
With grief our Hearts Are prest,
With tears our Eyes do Run,
Our Mind and Thoughts want rest.

As *Jeremy* sadly sat,[4]
With tears for to lament,
The Temple desolate,
Her Gold and Glory spent,   20
So we doe grieve and mourn,
To see no Priest at Mass,
No light on Altars Burn,
This Day of Christmass.

No Mass heard this great Day,
No Mattins sung last Night,
No Bells to call to pray,
No Lamps, no taper Light,
No Chalice, no rich Robes,
No Church, no Chappel Drest,   30
No Vestments, precious Coapes,
No Holy Water blest.

King *David* in his Days,
Before the Ark did Dance
With Musick and with praise,
Its honour to advance;[5]
But we our sad Eyes fix
To see laid on the ground
Our Ark, our Crucifix,
Our Tabernacle down.   40

4. See the Old Testament book The Lamentations of Jeremiah.
5. II Samuel 6. 14.

Our Pictures daily open,
As books before our eyes,
To read what we hear spoken
Of Sacred Mysteries;
They now are laid aside,
And cast out of their place,
Themselves from us they hide,
In darkness and disgrace.

But if Church Walls cou'd speak,
And old times to us tell,   50
If dead those graves could break,
Where thousand years they dwell;
If that they could arise
To preach what practis'd was,
We should have Priests always,
Our Altars and our Mass.

Most pure and precious things
Were given in these times
By Emperors, Queens, and Kings,
With gold and silver shrines.   60
They deem'd nothing too rich
That through their Hands could pass
To Beautify the Church,
And to set forth the Mass.

What those first Christians left us,
Written by their pen,
What learned Fathers taught us,
Great Saints and holy Men,
What in their times was done,
And practis'd in each place,   70
As clear as shines the Sun,
Doth show they still had Mass.

But good old Times are past,
And new bad times are come;
And worser times make haste,
And hasten to us soon.

Therefore in frights and fears,
Those holy Days we pass,
In sorrow and in teares,
We spend our Christmass.   80

Some News each Post doth bring,
Of *Jesuits* and their Plots,
Against our sacred King,
Discovered first by Oates.[6]
Such Plotters we may curse
With Bell and Book[7] at Mass;
By them the time is worse
Then e're we felt it was.

God bless our King and Queen,
Long may they live in Peace;   90
Long may their Days be seen,
Long may their Joys Increase.
And those who do not pray
That *Charles* in Peace may reign,
I wish they never may
See Priest nor Mass again.

Lines Presented to a Freind in her Garden, which Formerly was a Large Chapple[1]

To the Tune of *What Time the Groves were Clad in Green*, &c.

In silent Sadness I sat down
    On new green banks of grass
With Cherry Trees environ'd round,
    Where once a Chapple was;
A holy, blessed, sacred place,
    Of vertues and good deeds,
Lay wholy changed before my Face
    To a Garden full of Weeds.

---

6. Titus Oates (1649–1705), the man who concocted the Popish Plot.
7. The full phrase is 'bell, book and candle' and refers to the service of excommunication at the end of which, when the sentence of excommunication has been read, a bell is rung, a book is closed and a candle extinguished.

---

1. This poem comes from a section of the book entitled: 'A Smale Garland: A Posie Presented to a *Mary* in her own Garden, on St. *Mary's-Day*'.

Here formerly great Numbers came
    At all hours of the Day,
Our Christians then did fear no blame
    On bended knees to pray.
Here I now daily walk alone
    As in a Wilderness,
Sad change of Times I do bemoan,
    In silent Pensiveness.

As *Jeremy*, I cry'd and mourn'd
    At this most strange Event;
God's House into a Garden turn'd,
    Did cause me to lament.
My Teare like Water down did fall,
    My Heart for to pour out,
With lifted Hands then did I call
    To all the Heavens about.

I pray'd the Heavens for to behold
    This Ark[2] lay'd on the Ground;
I ask'd of them who was so bold
    As Lyon to pull down;[3]
All her Buildings high and low
    Are trodden under Feet,
The Stones in her sanctuary
    Are scatter'd in the Street.

Our Altars valu'd more than Gold
    Were deck'd for Holiness;
Adorn'd with objects to behold
    And moove to godliness;
Now Trees growe where those Altars stood
    For Priests to sacrifice
And offer up that precious Blood,
    Which our Souls purifies.

Our Priestly Vestments white and red,
    Our Violet and our Green,
The Black which we keep for the Dead,
    Are no more to be seen;

10

20

30

40

2. The holiest part of the Tabernacle in the temple of the Old Testament – so, the altar
   (literally or figuratively) of a Christian church.
3. i.e. pull it down.

No Pulpit for the sacred Word,
    To give the spiritual Bread,
Our Preachers which did that afford
    Are sent away or Dead.

Our Bells no more are heard to ring
    To call us to the Quier,   50
No Organs left to help us sing,
    No Incense for our fyer;[4]
No Silver Lamps now left to Shine,
    No Tapers to give Light,
No Mass by day here can we find,
    Nor Mattins here by night.

Good God, look on our Misery,
    Look on our woful state,
Forget us not eternally,
    Thy mercy's ne're too late.   60
And tho' our grievous Sins deserve
    Thy wrath and rage at us,
See not thy Holy Things that serve
    Thy Church disposed thus.

The Banish'd Man Lamenteth the 20th of November, the Day of his Parting drawing near.[1]

To the Tune of *Farewell fair Armedia &c.*

Behold I am speechless, my lips are grown weak,
My Tongue without motion wants Language to speak;
My heart drown'd with sadness, sighs only affords,
My eyes with their Tears do weep with my words.
I grieve and I mourn, I cry and lament,
Again to return to my banishment.
To part with my country, my kindred and friends,
And with all the comforts that on them attends.

---

4. fire.

---

1. Wadding himself was not banished in the 1670s or early 1680s, but he may have written this poem and its sequel for his friend 'S.G.', master of the school at New Ross (see poem on pp. 482–5).

Adieu my dear Country, poor friends, all farewell,
My Heart's grief in parting, my Tongue cannot tell,   10
I should be more happy with you to remain,
To share of your sufferings, partake of your pain;
To drink of your Vinegar, taste of your Gall,[2]
Condoling your ruins, lamenting your fall,
And wher e'er I go, my Heart (that's not steel),
These Thorns that do pierce you, with pity must feel.

Why twice I was banisht, this cause is most true,
For rendring to GOD and to *Cæsar* their due,
When first I was banisht no cause could they bring,
But I was Subject to Charles my King;   20
What for him I suffer'd, the cause gave content,
'Twas for him and with him away I was sent;[3]
For suffering with him I cou'd not complain,
One thought of his sufferings did ease all my pain.

Again to be banisht, the cause as they saith,
Is the Old Religion, my God and my Faith;
For God and my Faith, I must be content
Again from my Country away to be sent.
And for my Religion, if suffer I must,
My comfort is great, the cause being just.   30
To suffer for Justice, great Blessings there are;
With Joy then I'll suffer, in hope to have share.

I am not then speechless, my lips are not weak,
My tongue hath its motion and language to speak;
My Heart, free from sadness, smiles only affords,
My eyes and my looks do laugh with my words.
I shall neither Mourn, nor Cry, nor Lament
Again to return to my Banishment.
For God I most freely leave Country and Friends,
And part with all Comforts that on them attends.   40

2. bitterness.
3. This implies that the subject had been banished to France during the Commonwealth period.

The Banish'd Man's Adieu to his Country[1]

To the Tune of *Since Cælia's my Foe*

Dear Country Adieu, tho' faithful and true,
Tomorrow, with sorrow, I must part with you.
Without more delay, this is my last Day,
Remember, *November* doth force me away.
Yet I cannot well tell how to bid you farewell,
My parting is smarting more painful than Hell,
More inflamed than Fire, I burn with desire
That my Death its last breath at home may expire.

In strange countrys unkind, I shall never find
New faces, new places to pleasure my mind;   10
Where ever I go, I am certain to know
A stranger, a ranger, shall never want woe.
I would part with the gain of *France* and of *Spain*,
Their pleasures and treasures, at home to remain,
But if I must be gone, with my self all alone,
In some Cave, near my Grave, I'll make my sad moan.

In the long *Winter* nights it shall be my delight
With displeasure at leisure to tell my sad plight,
In the *Summer* and *Spring*, to the Vallies I'll sing
My complaints their plaints Ecchoes shall ring.   20
In black I'll appear all the days of the Year
My Cries the Skies and Heavens all shall hear,
From the Heavens I will crave this Blessing to have
That I may die with my Friends near my grave.

---

[1]. The use of internal assonance in this poem suggests the influence of the Irish *amhrán* metre.

The Lamentation of the Scholars Presented to their Master, *S.G.*, at the Dissolving of the Schools in *Ross*[1]

To the Tune of *Fortune my Foe*, &c.

Must our *Apollo* from us now be gone?[2]
And all our Muses leave their Hellicon?
Must they forsake their new Parnassus Hill,
And leave no taste of Aganippeas well?

They must depart, we can no more desire
One flame or spark of their Poetick Fire;
Our Lyrick strains, and Tuneful Odes must turn
To grunting, sad complaints of those who mourn.

When they are gone, then must we fear that we
(By *Ovid*'s Rule) must Metamorphos'd be,[3]   10
And that our Souls by Transmigration pass
Unto the Bodies of an Ox, an Ass.

When they depart, nothing is left that's fit
To cloath and beautify our naked Wit;
Without them, we can only feed and feast
And sleep and rest, and live as doth the Beast.

Raise then your Voices up unto the Skies,
And fill the Vallies with your woful Cries,
More sad than mourners of a funeral,
Make our laments be known to great and small.   20

---

1. Two of the poems in *A Smale Garland* are verse letters from Wadding to his friend 'S.G.', master of the famous Jesuit school near New Ross, County Wexford. 'S.G.' was forced to leave the country after his school was closed by the authorities during the Popish Plot. Though the poem which follows may have been written by the dispersed schoolboys (as it purports to be), it is more likely the work of Wadding himself – though if so, it is perhaps surprising to find him employing only secular, classical references in the text.

2. Apollo was the classical god not only of prophecy and learning but also of the arts and music. The schoolmaster at New Ross is, half-humorously, likened to this powerful, senior deity. Helicon and Parnasses were mountains sacred to the Muses, as was the fountain of Aganippe, at the foot of Mount Helicon.

3. The *Metamorphoses* of Ovid (43 BC – AD 17) were, like the works of his contemporaries Virgil and Horace, familiar to every seventeenth-century schoolboy.

Let mournful *Cypres* wreaths[4] adorn our Head,
And with our sad complaints awake the Dead,
With doleful, bawling sounds let us now sing
And waste ourselves away, our woes to ring.

Orpheus like, we'l speak to Trees and Stones,[5]
To Hills and Vallies part our woful moans,
That all that doth in Heaven and Earth appear,
May shew their pity, our laments to hear.

Rivers which from themselves do run away
To hear our plaints, will stop and make some stay,[6]   30
Receive our Tears that have more bitter taste
Than brackish Seas, to which they make such haste.

The gliding streams which thro' Meddows travel
With grief doe toss their Silver, shining channel;
The whispering Brooks and the gentle Spring
Their Discontents against their bankes do ring.

Æolus[7] with his boisterous blasts doth tell
That all the Winds that in his Cave do dwell
Are sent abroad to drownd all Ships that may
Apollo with our Muses bear away.[8]   40

The Seas do foam their Anger out apace,
And will not have our Muses leave this place;
What Ship attempts to carry them away
Will be more fatal than the *Horse* of *Troy*.[9]

The struting[10] fish is happy in this deluge,
For sorrow, she hath her most safe refuge,
Yet in her troubled Element, she spyes
Her watry bed to dim her bleared Eyes.

---

4. signs of mourning.
5. Orpheus, who had received his lyre from Apollo, could calm wild beasts and nature itself with the beauty of his playing.
6. pause.
7. The ruler of the winds in classical mythology.
8. The reference is to the storm at the beginning of book I of the *Æneid* – for which, see the translation by Richard Stanihurst on pp. 70–2 – and to the fact that 'S.G.' will be taken into exile on a ship.
9. For the story of the Trojan horse, see *Æneid* II, 14–354.
10. = strutting, swollen, distended – but what the word means here is not clear. deluge = the sea.

The Beasts most sad in humble Vallies feed
And from the lofty Hills run down with speed   50
Into the thickest Groves, where they may stay
When that our learned muses must away.

The pleasant fruitful, and the barren, Tree,
Bend down their Heads and underneath them see
How in their Shades we sit in heaviness,
And give their sucking Roots but bitterness.

The damask Rose, the white and blushing red,
Look pale to see us thus disordered,
The pretty Pansey and the gentle Pink
Conform their Colours to our darkest Ink.   60

The five Leaf'd Blossom,[11] and the Mary-gold
Lie closely shut, not willing to behold
With open Eyes how our *Apollo*'s sent
With all her[12] Muses, into banishment.

The Lilly fair, the Iasinth[13] purpled red,
The courtly Tulips droope their hanging Heads,
Gardens and Meddows are with Mourners drest,
And helps us how our griefs may be exprest.

The chattering Birds which on the Trees do sit,
Their tuneful, warbling Notes do now omit,   70
And with sad murmuring noise, they only sing
To welcome our next, sad, approaching Spring.

The Airy Regions kindly melt away
And with their heavy Clouds weep our decay;
With drooping showers and pow'ring floods of rain
They shew their sorrows for their woeful pain.

The bearded commets[14] and the ranging stars
Foretel us nothing but of Death and Wars,

---

11. cinquefoil or potentilla.
12. i.e. belonging to one of the flowers?
13. hyacinth – according to Ovid, a deep red or purple lily.
14. comets with tails.

Plannets their Anger with their Influence breath,
And cast dark Humours on us here beneath.[15]   80

Iris,[16] cast off thy colour'd streaming Rays,
Clad thee in black to mourn our dismal Days,
Put off thy blue, thy scarlet and thy green,
To our sad Eyes not pleasant to be seen.

Cynthia,[17] the Luster of our Darker Skie,
With clouds eclips'd, let thy Face mask'd lie,
Let not thy borrowed brightness more appear
Or shine again on this our Hemi-sphere.

Phœbus,[18] most swift, make haste from us away,
Stay not to see the scenes of our sad Play,   90
Hide thy bright Cheeks with dark and cloudy light,
Send not thy purer beams to our sad sight.

Let total Nature into sadness turn,
And each created thing assist to mourn,
Let Shrub and Cæder, all things great and small,
Help us with Swans to sing our funeral.

Clotho,[19] make haste, *Lachesis* take thy turn,
Atropos cut our Thread, it is too long spun,
Since we have lost the Masters of our Wit,
Pray let us Die, to Live we are unfit.   100

Æolus to you this Verse is due by right,
Which doleful Pen with dismal Ink did write;
Accept our Legacy and where e'er you go,
Sing to the Tune of Fortune was my Foe.[20]

---

15. A reference to the medieval belief in the influence of the planets on the 'humours' of humans.
16. goddess of the rainbow.
17. The moon.
18. The sun.
19. Clotho, Lachesis and Atropos were three powerful goddesses said to preside over the birth and life of man: Clotho presided over birth and Lachesis over life, while Atropos had the power to cut the thread of life with her scissors.
20. The tune to which this song is to be sung.

ANONYMOUS
(1684)

This poem dates from the spring of 1684. Once the Popish Plot was over, Charles II began to make arrangements to bring Irish affairs more directly under his own control. He appointed Lawrence Hyde, Earl of Rochester (1641–1711) lord lieutenant, and announced that control of the army in Ireland would be taken away from the lord lieutenant and given to a general appointed by the king. As an initial move, Charles proposed the sending to Ireland of a regiment commanded by a catholic, Colonel Justin MacCarthy.

Irish protestants, who felt that their security could only be guaranteed by the presence of an exclusively protestant army, were, understandably, alarmed by this clear sign of a shift in the balance of power towards catholics, and one of them circulated the following, energetic little poem, a copy of which was kept among Ormond's papers. Protestants in both England and Ireland were particularly suspicions of the king's motives at this time, since it was generally expected that he would shortly declare himself a catholic (see lines 5–6).

To all Protestants in England, Scotland & Ireland

New Comissions are com ore
for ten Papist Captains more.[1]
Our Millitia is slow,
their two Graces say:[2] Bee't soe.
Flatter not y^{r}selves, ye King
is a Papist too, within.
Doth not his old French Caball
stand untoucht?[3] Hee swears they shall.
Proclamations seem sevear,
but I'le war'nt yee not an hair   10
of a Lord or Priest shall fall –
hee'l find means to save them all.
Thus by Governers betrayd,
blame us not to be afrayd.

---

1. Presumably a rumour that commissions would be sent from London to enable catholics to become officers in regiments such as that commanded by Colonel MacCarthy.
2. One of the excuses for the king's taking control of the Irish army was said to be the fact that the Irish militia, made up of protestant volunteers, would be slow to respond to a crisis. The 'two graces' were presumably his Grace the Earl of Sunderland and his Grace the Duke of York, the two chief supporters of the king's plan.
3. In the early 1670s, Charles II's desire to develop strong links with France was forwarded by the five lords who made up the a committee of the privy council known as the 'Committee for Foreign Affairs'. When a treaty was signed with France in 1673, it was noticed that the initials of the five lords who signed it spelled the word CABAL – by which this powerful, personal cabinet was known. The members of Charles's unpopular, pro-French Cabal were Lords Clifford, Arlington, Buckingham, Ashley and Lauderdale.

Arme then, Arme, ye Plott's on foot
after all they have done too't.
Papists yet will cut our throts,
notwithstanding all ye Votes,
if we rise not, One & All,
& that way prevent our fall.   20

'J.H.'
(*fl.*1684)

Though Wentworth Dillon, fourth Earl of Roscommon (1637–85), had been writing occasional verse since the early 1660s (see pp. 374–81), his *magum opus*, *An Essay on Translated Verse*, was not published until 1684. Its appearance was greeted by this anonymous poem, which is of interest for its critical assessment of his work and for the fact that it hails Roscommon as an Irish writer, linking him with the man who had tutored him in his youth, James Ussher, Archbishop of Armagh (1581–1656). The text comes from a poem in a manuscript in the Bodleian Library where it is attributed to 'J.H.'

Upon the Earl of Roscommon's poems being publish'd

You blooming youth[1] of the inspired Train,
As e're, you hope to have the happy vein,
Tho you already Testimonials bring,
A muse stood gossip[2] at your Christening;
If with the best success you'd learn to write,
Behold the choicest Auction for your Wit.

   You elder heads to whom is paid just praise,
Who long without controul[3] have wore the Bays,
And may imagine that th'Applause you've got
Is not by Time itself to be wore out,   10
Would you perpetuate[4] and ensure your fame,
At this Eternal Lamp renew your flame.
You ill natur'd Criticks, who no sooner spy
But run to quench the flames of Poetry,
To tare the Beauty's of the Building out,
Canvas[5] each line, toss every word about,
Weigh each pointing[6] in the nicest scales,
Here nor your Malice nor your Skill prevails.
Roscomon gives such just and Generous Rules
As all your awkerd[7] censures ridicules: 20

1. Roscommon was forty-seven years old when this poem was written.
2. godparent.
3. i.e. before the appearance of Roscommon's poem – which will teach poets how to 'control' their verses.
4. i.e. if you want to perpetuate . . .
5. entangle in a net – a term from hawking.
6. piece of punctuation.
7. awkward.

Who different Methods do's at once disclose
Both to translate the best, and to compose.
He only could comunicate to us,
Flaccus and Maro's mightier Genius:[8]
Make every stroak of Excelence appear
And truly show in English what they are.
Let Ireland boast of this prodigious Birth }
That she has in one century brought fforth }
Two of the finish't[9] worthys upon Earth: }
Armagh's deep Learning first thro Europe ran,   30
That Primate Usher'd in this Nobleman.

8. Flaccus = Horace; Maro = Virgil.
9. Corrected from 'choicest' which is in turn corrected from 'first-rate'.

PART V

1685–1701
Jacobite and Williamite Ireland

ANONYMOUS
(1685)

The year 1685 was a momentous one for Ireland. Charles II died unexpectedly in February and his catholic brother, the Duke of York, ascended the throne as James II; within six months, James removed the Duke of Ormond from his position as lord lieutenant of Ireland, and replaced him with Henry Hyde, Earl of Clarendon. Though Clarendon was a protestant, he was more tolerant of catholics than Ormond, and Irish protestants, whose security depended on the maintenance of the Cromwellian land settlement and on a stable, vigorously protestant government, were alarmed at the change. Indeed, they had reason to be; as was widely acknowledged, the new king was heavily influenced by his old friend Richard Talbot (now ennobled as the Earl of Tyrconnell), a vehement supporter of the Irish catholic cause in general and of the dispossessed Old English catholic landowners in particular. Tyrconnell was put in charge of the Irish army and everyone could see that radical change was on the way. Protestants realised that their control of the army, the judiciary, the administration and the church was about to end.

The author of this anonymous broadside, though he recognised that Ormond's departure marked the end of an era, expressed the vain hope that James might yet see how valuable Ormond had been to him in Ireland, and reappoint him as lord lieutenant. In fact, it was barely eighteen months before James replaced Clarendon with the one man Irish protestants did not want as their governor, the Earl of Tyrconnell.

To his Grace the Duke of Ormond,
upon his Leaving the Government and Kingdom of *IRELAND*

> Have we a further Trouble yet in store?
> And can our Destiny afflict us more?
> To lose our Prince We thought too great a blow,
> And must we lose his glorious Image too?
> *Ireland* for more than thrice seven years[1] has been
> Envy'd without, for being so blest within;
> While Plague, Fire, Famine, War abroad has reign'd,
> This only was the safe and happy Land;
> Which Happiness, *Great Sir*, to You we owe,
> Next to the God above, and God below.[2]   10
>
> The *Irish Harp*, Which long abus'd had lain,
> Your skilful Hand first brought in Tune again.
> And when some others by our King were sent
> To play upon the Noble Instrument,

1. i.e. since Ormond's first appointment after the Restoration, in 1662.
2. The theory of the divine right of kings allowed poets to refer to the king as a direct representative of God on earth.

Such was their Ignorance, or their Errours such,
They prov'd but Foils to your Melodious Touch.
Into Your Hands then, which before it grac'd,
The Noble Instrument again was plac'd;
On which, a long, soft Tune, again You play'd,
When jarring Discord did all else invade.   20
And we rejoyc'd to think you wou'd play on —
But Heav'ns and our King's Will must still be done:
We submit humbly to that Soveraign Pow'r,
Which can the Bliss it takes away, restore;
More we can't have, nor do we wish for more.
Adieu then, much-lov'd Prince ——
(With mournful Hearts we make this Pray'r for you)
Greatest and Best of Un-Crown'd Heads, adieu.

And since You must go hence ——,
O're you shall fly, a steddy Gale of Pray'rs,   30
And under roll an humble Sea of Tears,
All the amends which for Your mighty Toil
Can be return'd by a poor Widdow-Isle:

Such now, alas! she is, and ne're till now,
That *ORMOND*'s Noble House do's wholly from her go,
Not leaving, to support her fainting Mind,
An *ARRAN,* or an *OSSORY* behind.[3]

May Heav'ns choice Blessings on them all attend,
And bring them to a Calm and Glorious End.
Glorious and Calm may all their Passage be,   40
As was the Hour in which they put to Sea
And landed; wheresoe're her *ORMOND* goes,
May *England* doat on him, as *Ireland* does.
To whose great King, due Homage having done,
His Councils Honour'd, and secur'd his Throne,
Let Him Return His VICEROY here again:
May Heav'ns and *England*'s Monarch say, *Amen.*

[3]. Twice during his term as lord lieutenant, Ormond had been forced to leave Ireland for a period; each time he left one of his sons, the Earl of Ossory or the Earl of Arran, as his deputy.

ANONYMOUS
(*c*.1686)

When he was appointed lieutenant-general of the Irish army early in 1686, the Earl of Tyrconnell's first task was to purge it of protestants. He acted with dispatch and, by September of that year, most of the privates and just under half the officers were catholics. Word of the changes soon spread and catholics flocked to Dublin from the countryside eager to join up or to gain commissions; some of them found themselves, as J.G. Simms put it, 'jeered at by the Protestant proletariat, who derided their imperfect English'.[1]

Such derision lies behind the poem below, clearly the work of a Dublin protestant wit of the day. The Hiberno-English purported to be spoken by the ingenuous 'Cromach O Rough' – probably a deliberate distortion of a typically west of Ireland native Irish name such as Cormac O'Rourke – is extreme but not unintelligible and includes authentic verb-forms and prosodic features, vocabulary and idiom. Anyone who enjoyed the verse would not only be familiar with the type of gullible character burlesqued but would also realise that the Teague O'Regan mentioned in line 17, far from driving a plough near Enniskillen around the time of the poem, was a colourful officer in the French army on the Continent; O'Regan would shortly arrive back in Ireland where he would be knighted and become the famous defender of Charlemont and of Sligo.

The poem probably originated in the same Dublin circle as the 'Purgatorium Hibernicum', *The Irish Hudibras*, the ballad on Redmond O'Hanlon and other similar poems – a circle of young, New English landlords or merchants frightened by the rising power of catholics and determined to try and make them seem ridiculous. Where necessary in this text, 'd' or 't' should be read as 'th', and 'sh' as 's' or 't'.

To his Onor de Rit Onorable Richard Earle of Tyroincol [*sic*]

De Devil tauke me my Lord if I would not be
Ash stout ash[2] S[t] Patric ag[t] Heresy.
O shoul, I hate it ash worse ash[3] a Toad;
My Leggs would not be after Carry[4] his Load.[5]
Tis your Onor Protects us from Protestant Atheists
Or else by de Virgin dey would ruin de Papists;

---

1. J.G. Simms, *Jacobite Ireland 1685–91* (London and Toronto, 1969), p. 24. The evidence is in *Historical Manuscripts Commission Report*, *Ormonde MSS* new series (1920), viii, 346.
2. as stout (firm) as . . .
3. O soul! I hate it as worse as . . . The last phrase is a Malapropism introduced to indicate the speaker's unfamiliarity with correct English usage.
4. For a full discussion of the common Hiberno-English verbal construction known as 'the *after write* construction', see Alan Bliss, *Spoken English in Ireland 1600–1740* (Dublin, 1979), pp. 301–3.
5. This line is obscure but seems to mean: My legs would not have been able to carry his load (i.e. the load of reptiles [or heretics] St Patrick carried out of Ireland as he banished them).

For Dey are grown so Proud wid deir upstart Religion, ⎫
Dey think to make us ash fearfull ash a Pidgeon; ⎬
But fait, dey are full ash foollish as a widgeon.⁶ ⎭
For yoʳ Onor in de end will show dem a Trick, 10
And out of dish Kingdom deir schisms will Kick,
And fitt up de army wid true Catholicks
Wᶜʰ I hope will destroy all de Hereticks.
I hope too yoʳ Worship will not Dishdain ⎫
To make me a Dragoon who will take much Pain ⎬
De Pope and yoʳ Lordship's Rit⁷ to Maintain. ⎭
Dere ish Teague o Regan who did drive de Plow
At Enny Schilling not long ago,
Ish now a fine Offisher; why am not I
That not only in fighting skill'd but Poetry? 20
Dou shom⁸ say no body is Unculpable,
Not God in you to find a fault ish able;⁹
De Pope den you ish not more Infallible.
Den I hope you will Consider Dish humble Petishion,
And turn to an offish¹⁰ de sad Condishion
Of Cromach o Rough, Born in dish Nashion
Teacher in Philosophy and Argumentashion.

---

6. a wild duck.
7. right.
8. some.
9. i.e. even God can find no fault in you.
10. i.e. turn into an officer.

EDMUND ARWACKER
(*c*.1655–**1686**–*c*.1710)

Edmund Arwacker was educated at Kilkenny College and Trinity College Dublin, and was ordained into the Church of Ireland. He was chaplain to the Duke of Ormond and, later, Archdeacon of Armagh. Arwacker was not only the most prolific Irish poet of his age but incomparably the worst. His endless effusions in praise of the notables of the day plumb depths of almost unimaginable banality. One of the less absurd offerings from his pen is a poem of enthusiastic greeting for the invention of a device for distilling sea water and so making it drinkable – an invention which, it was thought, would greatly improve life on board ship, and so enable the British to conquer the most distant nations. The patent for this invention had been taken out by a nephew of the scientist Robert Boyle, Captain Robert Fitzgerald, in 1683, and Arwacker's poem apparently celebrates the endorsement of the invention by Boyle and the Royal College of Physicians in London. *Fons Perennis* is also dedicated to the new king, James II, which may explain its inordinate length – twenty-two pages in quarto. In the following extract, Arwacker addresses the members of the College of Physicians with his customary high-flown hyperbole.

from: Fons Perennis,

A Poem on the Excellent and Useful Invention of Making Sea-water Fresh

. . . Great Sons of Heav'n, Props of our Humane State,
Whose Skill maintains the Life Heav'n did create!
The Wonders, which in our Defence you shew,
Preserve our beings, and your Mem'ries too:
Since for our Safety they but seldom fail,
Sure for your Glory they must still prevail.
You who from Death's grim Jaws his Prey reprieve,
And with a Breath make ev'n the Dying Live,
Be deathless still, as you on us bestow
Almost an Immortality below,   10
And from the Mouth of the devouring Grave,
Whole Lands at once with one Prescription save.[1]
Nor is the Blessing Life your Gift alone,
You give us all that tends to make it one;[2]
You the Twin Charms of Youth and Beauty give,
A Bliss that few are willing to out-live.
In those soft Streams, distilling from the Sea,
To whose first Knowledge you prepar'd the Way,

---

1. The implication is that lands which are now uninhabitable because they lack fresh water will become open to colonisation once drinking water can be obtained from the sea.
2. This convoluted couplet means: Nor is the only blessing you give us the gift of life; you also give us all that tends to make it a blessing.

The Rough-dull Skin grows smooth and clear as they.
The Sea thus happily improv'd by you,   20
Does ev'ry day a rising *Venus* shew.
Here the soft Charmers of our easie Hearts,
Whose Pow'r alone out-braves your healing Arts,
Heighten those Beauties which the World enslave,
And make you perish by the Darts you gave.[3]
No more our Ladies to the *Spaw*[4] shall go,
Who to your Streams may greater Blessings owe . . .

. . . The Sailer now to farthest Shores may go,
Since in his Road[5] these lasting Fountains flow;
The Sea, corrected by this wondrous Pow'r,   30
Preserves those now whom it destroyed before:
No more with Thirst the Feav'rish Sea-man dyes,
The Briny Waves afford him fresh Supplies.
The mighty *Boyle*[6] does by his pow'rful Art,
The Ocean to a Well of Life convert;
Whose fame had *Israel*'s thirsty Monarch heard,
He had these Springs to *Bethel*'s Well preferr'd;
And their Diviner Vertue had (if known)
Excus'd the Risque he made *three Worthies* run:[7]
Had these in *Naaman*'s Days been understood,   40
Jordan's famed Stream had scarce been thought so Good;
Nor wou'd their Influence, more truely Great,
Require he shou'd the Healing Bath repeat.[8]
Boyle, our good Angel, stirs the Sov'reign Pool,
That makes the Hydropic-Leprous[9] Seamen whole,
And now, who first shall put to Sea, they strive,
Since safer there, than on the Shore they live;
And, when to Coasts remote they boldly steer,
Proclaim the Worth of their Preserver there . . .

---

3. i.e. Cupid's darts.
4. spa (pronounced 'spaw' in the eighteenth century).
5. road = any way from one place to another; (so here) = the sea over which the ship passes.
6. The Hon. Robert Boyle (1627–91), son of the great Earl of Cork and the most famous scientist or natural philosopher of his day.
7. Three mighty men broke through the ranks of the encircling Philistines to bring King David water from the well of Bethlehem. He did not drink the water but offered it to God saying: 'Is not this the blood of the men that went in jeopardy of their lives?' II Samuel 23. 15–17.
8. The prophet Elisha instructed Naaman, who wanted to be cured of his leprosy, to bathe himself seven times in the river Jordan. Naaman did so and was healed. II Kings 5.
9. hydropic = having a insatiable thirst; leprous = afflicted with leprosy.

ANONYMOUS
(*c*.**1687**)

The Royal College of Physicians in Ireland, founded in 1654, was always closely connected with Trinity College and, therefore, likely to attract the cynical attention of student poets. The verse which follows was collected, probably when he was a student at Trinity in the 1680s, by Lord Newtown Butler for his manuscript collection of verse, the 'Whimsical Medley'. Sir William Petty, incidentally, was famous for having performed the same feat of reviving an executed criminal in England; in his case, the woman he rescued was allowed to survive, to marry and, reputedly, to produce a large family.

On the College of Physicians in Dublin
who, haveing brought to life a malefactor that was given from the Gallows to be Dissected, Redelivered him to the Sherif to be Executed

> Whoe'er wou'd Life preserve, Let him beware
> How he confides in Dublin Doctors Care.
>
> Taught by me, lett him banefull Physick hate,
> The Vile Dissectors shun, as his own Fate.
>
> Spar'd by the Rope, and Hangman's cruell hand,
> My Life I lost by Gallen's[1] Guessing Band,
>
> And to their shame, lett after Ages say,
> That those the Gallows save, the Doctors slay.

1. Claudius Galenus (*b. c.* 130 AD), the most celebrated medical writer of antiquity.

ANONYMOUS
(1687)

During 1686 and 1687, Tyrconnell's grip on Ireland grew steadily more effective: catholic judges, army officers and officials replaced protestant ones throughout the country, and in June 1687 the king sent Tyrconnell a royal warrant which empowered him to grant new charters to cities and corporate towns. Irish towns and corporations had returned almost exclusively protestant members to the Irish parliament during the reign of Charles II, and the new charters were intended to upset that arrangement. With new rules for selecting members of parliament, towns dominated by catholics would start to return catholic MPs, and as soon as these catholics secured a majority in parliament, that body could be expected to overturn the Cromwellian and Restoration land settlements. This would open the door to the return of Irish land to its ancient catholic proprietors and thus begin the process of the overthrow of protestant Ireland.

Tyrconnell arranged to meet the king at Chester in August 1687 to report on progress and to receive royal approval; the king endorsed his policies and the lord deputy returned to Ireland with his authority enhanced. The following mischievously ironic poem celebrating Tyrconnell's meeting with the king was circulating in Dublin on his return.

from: A Congratulatory Poem on the arrival of his Sacred Majesty at the City of Chester, August the 27ᵗʰ 1687

> Haste, haste! Let the free sound of winged Fame
> Proclaim our joyes, and our old Sorrows tame;
> We have no room for sadness: all our bliss
> Centers in present welcom Happiness.
> The *Dolphins* peep above our sandy Barr,
> *Mermaids* cut capers in the serene Air,
> Bells ring alone, the silver Trumpets sound,
> *Swans* sing, and *Moles* appear above the Ground.
> Here Royal *James* shewes his imperial Eye,
> As full of love as awefull Majesty . . .   10
>
> . . . Even they who are not willing to obey
> Blush, unto him, Observance not to pay:
> Decrepid Age his Crutches throwes aside,
> Matrons look spruce as a new married Bride.
> Boys gallop, all our girls with nimble feet
> And speaking Eyes, contend their Prince to meet.
> Even they who on our Altars live, compose
> Te Deums new, and seem well pleas'd as those:

Dull sighs are banisht, fears disperst, and wit
Stands all a *Tipto* for this Triumph fit. . .   20

. . . And to confirm our Easiness the more,
Loyal and brave *Tyrconnel* is come o'er,
Dear to his Prince, and naturally fit
For Royal Trust; *this was a lucky hit*:
With him, the Irish nobles hopefull are,
Their king may Dublin see, and Mollingar¹ . . .

1. Mullingar. As S. Ó Seanóir and M. Pollard point out in their article "'A Great Deal of
Good Verse": Commencement Entertainments in the 1680s', *Hermathena*, nos. cxxx
and cxxxi (1981), pp. 7–36, (p. 35, n. 61), the phrase 'Until the king should come to
Mullingar' was used – certainly in the nineteenth century – to mean that something was
never expected to happen. They quote the entry for Mullingar in the 1843 *Gazetteer of
Ireland*: 'This mode of expressing a thing improbable has grown into very general use in
the town . . . Thus, several leases of land and houses are granted on supposed actual
perpetuity: that is until the King should come to Mullingar.'

ANONYMOUS
(1687)

During the 1680s, at Trinity College Dublin (as at Oxford and Cambridge universities), ribald and irreverent speeches were delivered during the ceremony of 'commencements' (the conferring of degrees) by the *terrae filius* – a student permitted to play the role of fool or jester for the day. Three of these speeches were recorded, one in full (that for 1688) by the young Lord Newtown Butler (see below the poem by John Jones, pp. 511–2), and the others (those for 1686 and 1687) in part by a student named John Rochford. Though the tripos speeches Rochford recorded are not particularly lively, his transcription includes some entertaining poems – presumably they were circulating among the students at Trinity at the time – the most interesting of which is the one which follows. It is a response to a rumour, current in the early months of 1687, that the poet and dramatist John Dryden (1631–1700), who had just converted to catholicism, was to be appointed provost of Trinity College.[1] If Dryden had come over from London to Dublin, he would have been greeted with ferocious animosity – as indeed would any catholic sent as provost; in fact, the next poem in the Rochford manuscript promises that, if Dryden should come to Dublin, 'We'el dog thy coming from the Eucharist, / And kick thy gutts till thou disgorge thy Christ'.

On Doctor Dryden's coming over to the provost of Trinity College

Haile, Rhyming Atheist! May thy passage be
As boystrous as thy ranting poetry.
May the just God who doth command the seas
Pickle in briny waves thy wither'd bayes,
Whilst the resenting seas conspire thy fall,
And in thy fate, serve theire great Admirall.
But if the milder god preserve thy breath,
Doom'd to be lost by a dry, hempen death,[2]
At thy approach, let raging whirlewinds rise,
And dismall lightening fill the troubl'd skies;   10
Such omen should attend a libertine:
For[3] thou mightest brave the gods like Maximin,[4]
Hurle pointed daggers at the starry throne,
And lowdly tell the trembling gods their owne –
But with this difference:

1. For a review of the evidence on this, see Roswell G. Ham, 'Dryden and the Colleges', *Modern Language Notes*, vol. 49 (1934), pp. 324–32.
2. i.e. Dryden really deserves to be hanged.
3. MS illegible: conjectural reading.
4. The reference is to a scene in Dryden's tragedy *Tyrannick Love, or The Royal Martyr*, the main character of which is Maximin, 'Tyrant of Rome'.

He o're his quarrell with the harmless skies
Treated the hungry gods with sacrifice;
Thou never would'st admit a deity;
A manly Atheist in thy infancy.
But if the partiall gods doe yet refuse   20
To drowne, or tempest-tosse thy turncoat Muse,
And calmer gales attend thee, may it be
Only to drive thee to some forraine sea.
Goe with thy Cortez to the Indian shore
There be presented to the emperour.[5]
The fourth time change thy noe religion there,
Lest to thy prince[6] ungratefull thou appeare;
For should some kindness there to thee be showne,
'Twere sin in thee not to adore the sun.
When there thou landest, th'affrighted blacks will see   30
A double monster – both by ship and thee;[7]
But if whilst wee in vaine against thee strive,
Safely to th'Irish coast thou do'st arrive,
May brawny Shadwells[8] ne're be wanting here
To pull thy sacred lawrells and thy haire;
May drubs of College-green afflict thee more
Than those smart blows thou in Rose-ally bore.[9]

---

5. Cortez is a character in Dryden's tragedy *The Indian Emperor, or The Conquest of Mexico*. The emperor is Montezuma.
6. i.e. James II. Protestant enemies of Dryden accused him of changing religion merely to keep on the right side of the new king.
7. In a passage towards the end of Act I scene ii of *The Indian Emperor*, Montezuma describes the arriving Spanish ships as 'divine monsters'.
8. Thomas Shadwell was the poet ridiculed by Dryden in *MacFlecknoe* (1682). Shadwell was a large man – 'corpulent' might be a fair word to describe him – but not brawny. However, see the following note.
9. On 18 December 1679, Dryden was attacked and beaten senseless by three thugs in an alleyway named Rose Alley not far from his home in London. The event became the talking point of the town and, though it was generally agreed that the thugs were sent by someone whom Dryden had attacked in a satire, the identity of the person responsible for the incident was never discovered. drubs = those who beat or 'drub' someone with cudgels; 'College-green' is the street in front of Trinity College in Dublin.

ANONYMOUS
(1687)

Though he laid an energetic claim to them as soon as they appeared, it is impossible to believe that the words of this famous – or infamous – song were the work of Thomas Wharton, first Marquis of Wharton (1648–1715). This notorious English politician was certainly vehemently opposed to catholicism and to James II, but he had little connection with Ireland before he landed at Ringsend as incoming lord lieutenant on 21 April 1709, more than twenty years after this song appeared on the streets of London. One of the earliest broadsheet versions of the song calls it 'A New Song lately come from Ireland', a claim likely to be true; its contents, language and idiom make it clear that whoever wrote it had a sharp ear for Hiberno-English and a good grasp of Irish attitudes to current events. It also refers to Ireland as 'here'. The song bears remarkable similarities, in vocabulary, idiom and representation of the pronunciation of spoken Hiberno-English, to other Dublin anti-catholic verses in this anthology, the 'Cromach O Rough' piece, for example (see p. 495). It is a clever piece of mimicry, entirely possible to produce in Dublin the late 1680s, but a most unlikely performance from the pen of an English politician not known to have written anything else.

The speakers in the first ten stanzas of the first part of the song are two Irish catholics rejoicing at the impending arrival of Tyrconnell as lord deputy, while the last two stanzas of the first part (which are in 'standard' English) are more objective.[1] The second part of the song, which is a slightly later composition and clearly written to capitalise on the popularity of the first part, is another dialogue, this time between two Irishmen living in England. Where appropriate in both songs, 'd' should be read as 'th', 'sh' as 's', and 'au' as 'a'.

Lilliburlero

Ho! brother *Teague*, dost hear de Decree,
  Lilli Burlero Bullen a la;[2]
Dat we shall have a new Debittie,[3]
  Lilli Burlero Bullen a la,
Lero, Lero, Lero, Lero, Lilli Burlero Bullen a la,
Lero, Lero, Lero, Lero, Lilli Burlero, Bullen a la.

---

1. The last two stanzas of the first part do not appear in some early printings of the poem.
2. Meaningless sounds arranged in rhythmic patterns are a feature of working songs (in the Scottish highlands, 'waulking' songs, sung by teams of women waulking (beating and shrinking) cloth together), and it could be argued that the first part of 'Lilliburlero' is a marching song, the 'refrain' of which is its main point (to enable the troops to march in step); the 'verses', far from being formally 'written' by anyone, could be seen as improvised texts commenting on contemporary politics which were 'collected' for broadsheet publication. For a recent article on the poem, see Breandán Ó Buachalla, 'Lilliburlero agus Eile', *Comhar*, vol. 46, part I (Márta 1987), pp. 13–15; part II (Aibreán 1987), pp. 27–9. For the origin of such songs, see Adam Fox, *Oral and Literate Culture in England 1500–1700* (Oxford, 2000), *passim*.
3. Tyrconnell (whose surname was Talbot) was appointed lord deputy of Ireland on 8 January 1687. The position of lord deputy was an inferior one to that of lord lieutenant and, theoretically, carried less power.

Ho! by my Shoul[4] it is a T[albo]t,
  Lilli Burlero, &c.
And he will cut all the English throat,[5]
  Lilli, &c. 10

Though by my shoul de *Inglish* do Prat,[6]
  Lilli, &c.
De Law's on Dare side, and *Chreist* knows what,
  Lilli, &c.

But if Dispence[7] do Come from de Pope,
  Lilli, &c.
Weel hang *Magno Carto*[8] & demselves in a Rope,
  Lilli. &c.

And the good T[albo]t is made a Lord,
  Lilli, &c. 20
And he with brave Lads is coming aboard,
  Lilli. &c.

Who all in *France* have taken a swear,[9]
  Lilli, &c.
Dat dey will have no Protestant h[ei]r,
  Lilli. &c.

O! but why does he stay behind?
  Lilli, &c.
Ho by my shoul 'tis a Protestant wind,[10]
  Lilli, &c. 30

Now T[yrconnel]l is come a-shore,
  Lilli, &c.
And we shall have Commissions gillore,[11]
  Lilli, &c.

---

4. soul.
5. A reference to the common view of Englishmen in Ireland that Irishmen were always about to massacre them (as they believed had happened in 1641).
6. prate.
7. dispensation.
8. Magna Carta (1215), the charter of liberties granted to the English people by King John.
9. This verbal construction is linked to the Irish idiom discussed by Alan Bliss, *Spoken English in Ireland 1600–1740* (Dublin, 1979), pp. 304–5.
10. A westerly gale delayed Tyrconnell at Holyhead on his way to take up the position of lord deputy early in 1687. The wind is 'protestant' not because of its direction but because it frustrates catholic hopes.
11. galore (from Ir. *go leor*, plenty); i.e. large numbers of commissions for catholic officers in the army.

And he dat will not go to M[a]ss
    Lilli, &c.
Shall turn out[12] and look like an Ass,
    Lilli, &c.

Now, now de Heretics all go down,[13]
    Lilli, &c.   40
By *Chreist* and *St. Patrick* the Nation's our own,
    Lilli, &c.[14]

There was an old prophecy found in a bog,
    Lilli, &c.
That Ireland should be rul'd by an ass and a dog:
    Lilli, &c.

And now this prophecy is come to pass,
    Lilli, &c.
For Talbot's the dog, and Tyrconnell's the ass,[15]
    Lilli, &c.   50

The second part of Lilliburlero[16]

By Creish, my dear Morish,[17] vat maukes de sho shad?
    Lilli, &c.
De hereticks jeer us, and mauke me mad
    Lilli, &c.

Plaugue tauke me, dear Teague, but I am in a Raage,
    Lilli, &c.
Poo-oo, what Impudence is in dis Age!
    Lilli, &c.

12. i.e. be turned out. Before Tyrconnell's command, all those in the Irish army had to prove themselves protestants; under Tyrconnell, the poet hopes, those who do not go to mass will be turned out.
13. i.e. the heretic English will become the underdogs.
14. The last two (later) stanzas of the first part of the song and the whole of the second part are taken from Thomas Crofton Croker's edition of the text in *The Historical Songs of Ireland* (London, 1841).
15. Tyrconnell's brother, Peter Talbot (1620–80) was catholic Archbishop of Dublin; thus the two brothers are satirised as the 'rulers' of catholic Ireland.
16. This addition dates from 1688 when a wave of anti-catholic feeling swept through England after James II's flight from England to France.
17. Maurice, Ir. *Muiris*, another generic (satirically motivated) name for an Irishman; cf. Teague.

Dey shay dat Tyrconnels a Friend to de Mash,
    Lilli, &c.   60
For which he's a Traytor, a Dog and an Ass.
    Lilli, &c.

Ara![18] Plaugue tauke me now, I mauke a Sware,[19]
    Lilli, &c.
I, to Shaint Tyburn[20] will mauke a great Pray'r.
    Lilli, &c.

O, I will pray for to Saint Patrick's Frock,[21]
    Lilli, &c.
Or to Loretto's sacred Smock.[22]
    Lilli, &c.   70

Now a Plaugue tauke me, what dost dow tink?
    Lilli, &c.
De English Confusion to Popery drink,
    Lilli, &c.

And by my Shoul de Mash-house pull down
    Lilli, &c.
While dey were swearing de mayor of de Town.[23]
    Lilli, &c.

O Fait and be![24] I'll make a Decree
    Lilli, &c.   80
And swaare by the Chancellor's Modesty
    Lilli, &c.

Dat I no longer in English[25] will stay,
    Lilli, &c.

18. indeed; Ir. *ara*.
19. For this construction (known as the 'make right' construction), see Bliss, pp. 305–6.
20. A jibe at the supposed ignorance and superstition of the Irish in England; Tyburn was the site of the main gallows in London.
21. tunic, cassock.
22. There is no 'smock' associated with Loreto. It is a town in Italy, a place of pilgrimage on account of the 'holy house' – said to be the house in which the Virgin Mary was brought up which was miraculously transported, by angels, from Nazareth to Loreto in 1291.
23. i.e. the first thing the townsfolk do, even as they are swearing in a new mayor, is pull down the mass-house.
24. 'Faith' was a minor oath of the time: 'and be' = 'if it be' (cf. Ir. *má 'seadh*); see Bliss, p. 260.
25. England.

For by Gode dey will hang us out of de way.
    Lilli, &c.

Vat if de Dush[26] should come as dey hope,
    Lilli, &c.
To up hang us for all de Difense of de Pope.
    Lilli, &c.   90

26. What if the Dutch . . .

ANONYMOUS
(*c*.**1688**)

This poem is a satire on a young lawyer who came to Dublin from the west of Ireland, probably in 1686 or 1687, to work in the office of the chief baron. Though his name is not known, the victim of the satire clearly possessed not only a substantial girth and a 'ponderous jaw' but also sufficient musical skill to be able to join the musicians employed at Dublin Castle in performing both as a singer and on the fiddle. He was also an Irish-speaker whose command of English, it is implied, was hardly adequate for him to plead cases in court. Though the poet does not say so, the victim may well have been a catholic: James II appointed three catholic judges in 1686, and catholic lawyers (like catholics of other professions) were now making their way to Dublin and gaining employment. The satire which follows is, however, more of a personal than a political or sectarian attack.

An Elegy of the Pig that Followed the Ld Chief Baron Henn[1] and Baron Worth[2] from Connaught to Dublin

Here a well-travel'd Pig does Lye,
Who did forsake his Native Stye,
To Waddle in good Company;
With Loss of Sows soft dalliance,
For Travel sake he did dispence.
If he had liv'd he'd gone to France.[3]
When Pig his Journy did begin,
Wading in Puddle up t' th' Chin,
He follow'd the Laws thro' thick and thin.
The People ran with nimble feet,   10
The Judges, as some thought, to meet;
But 'twas th'approaching Pig to greet.
To Pig each Sheriff bow'd his Rod,
When first on Country Bounds he trod,

1. Henry Henn was an Englishman who was called to the bar in 1658 and practised in London. He came to Ireland in 1669 and rose through the legal ranks until he was appointed chief baron in 1680. He also acted as a justice of assize on the Connacht circuit from 1680 until 1687 when he was superseded and returned to England. (Francis Elrington Ball, *The Judges in Ireland 1221–1921*, 2 vols. (London, 1926), I, 354).
2. William Worth, son of Edward Worth, Bishop of Killaloe, was born in Cork and entered Trinity College in 1661 at the age of fourteen. He was called to the Irish bar 1669 and became baron of the Exchequer.
3. In February 1688, two of the newly appointed catholic judges, Thomas Nugent, Baron Riverston, and Sir Stephen Rice, were sent by Tyrconnell to France with proposals for legislation. The line implies that the victim of the satire would have travelled with them if he had lived longer.

Which he receiv'd with gracious Nod.[4]
He cou'd not Plead, Yet Men of Sense,
Did give this reason in his defence,
It was for want of Utterance.
'Twas ponderous Jaw that made his head
Hang down like Bencher over read;[5]   20
But now alas! young Plowden's dead.[6]
Being one of those that trot o're Bog:
'Twas want of English made this Hog
Upon his Tongue to wear a Brogue.[7]
Your Connaught Pigs talk Irish best;
Therefore they speak true English least,
For these are Wide[8] as East from West.
How often did Pig the Fiddle grace,
Kept Consort with Tom Tollet's[9] Face,
And to the Treble Grunt a Base?   30
Lament Lament ye Tunefull Throats
Your Brother's Fall with mournfull Notes,
Poor Pig hath Eat up all his Oates.
Let Modern Witts his death Express
In Songs, for he like them did place
In Palate all his happiness.
Mourn Judge, Attorneys, Council, Clark,
Let Sows Grunt, Cats mew, and Mastiffs bark,
For Pig, that dy'd e'er he was Peark.[10]

---

4. Judges on circuit were formally greeted at the circuit boundaries by the appropriate legal officers.
5. i.e. like one of the senior members of the legal profession (a 'bencher') who had read too many books.
6. Edmund Plowden (1518–85), author of several authoritative legal textbooks. 'Young' Plowden therefore means a young jurist following in Plowden's footsteps.
7. An unusual (and early) use of 'brogue' to mean both a rough shoe (Ir. *bróg*) and an Irish way of speaking English.
8. i.e. the Irish language (or, perhaps, Hiberno-English speech) is as far apart from English as . . .
9. *Original note*: 'One of the Castle Musick.' He was probably the father of the Charles Tollett employed as a state musician in 1717. (Brian Boydell, *A Dublin Musical Calendar 1700–60* (Dublin, 1988), p. 291.)
10. Possibly a pun on 'pork'. The word 'perk' means self-assertive or smart; but it is also short for 'perquisites', one of the meanings of which is the emoluments for any office. Although dictionaries record 'perks' as a short form of 'perquisites' only from 1824, it seems to have that meaning here. Thus the line could mean that the victim had died before he had reached his prime and before he had received any salary or any 'perks' (i.e. extra payments) from his office – also before he was old enough to become 'pork'.

JOHN JONES AND OTHERS
(1688)

The fellows of Trinity College Dublin who were present at the commencements ceremony in 1688 were sufficiently shocked by the content and tone of the tripos – a mixture of ribald speech and bawdy dramatisations ridiculing staff and students which was traditionally permitted as part of the day's events – to demand that the man largely responsible for it, John Jones, the *terrae filius* for the year, be suspended from the college. Jones's suspension was soon lifted and he went on to become a doctor of divinity and a highly respected Dublin schoolmaster. But the text of the tripos which he assembled for the occasion – it would be wrong to say he 'wrote' it since the text was probably composed and acted by a group of students, with Jones as prime mover and master of ceremonies – was copied by Theophilus Butler, Lord Newtown Butler into his manuscript 'Whimsical Medley' and, thus, it survived.

Much of the text, which is partly in English and partly in dog-Latin, is tedious to modern ears but one of its poems gives an energetic picture (or an energetically imagined picture) of the lifestyle of a foppish Trinity student of the time. Thomas Weaver was a Dubliner who had been in the college since 1678 and who received the degree of MA at the ceremony at which he was ridiculed. The poem about him suggests that, surprisingly, life in Trinity College and, indeed in Dublin itself, during the Jacobite period, was comparatively untouched by the frenzied political and military activity taking place in the country as a whole. The business of the day in Trinity was the conferring of degrees and the ridiculing of staff and students.[1]

[Verses on Thomas Weaver]

There's scarce a well-drest Coxcomb[2] but will own
Tommy's the prittiest Spark[3] about the town.
This all the Tribe of Fringe and Feather[4] say,
Because He Nicely moves by Algebra,[5]
And does with Method Tie his Cravat string,
Takes Snuff with Art, and shows his sparkling Ring,

---

1. James Woolley has pointed out ('John Barrett, "The Whimsical Medley", and Swift's Poems', in *Eighteenth-Century Contexts: Historical Inquiries in Honor of Phillip Harth*, ed. Howard D. Weinbrot, Peter J. Schakel and Stephen E. Karian (Madison and London, 2001), pp. 147–70, (160–1) that, though this poem was printed in Peter Anthony Motteux's London periodical, the *Gentleman's Journal*, in the 1690s, the text came to Motteux from a Dublin source; there seems no reason to doubt that it was indeed spoken in Trinity in 1688. The poem is one of many which have been attributed to Swift, a classmate of Jones; but there is no hard evidence to link it with Swift and it was certainly associated with Jones.
2. A conceited, showy person.
3. fop.
4. i.e. the women (whose clothing is adorned with fringes and feathers).
5. This reference is impossible to understand fully. Mathematics was one of the subjects taught at Trinity in the 1680s, and the reference may be to how algebra was taught; in the next line, 'with method' may have something to do with the teaching of logic.

Can sett his Fore Top,[6] Manage well his Wigg,
Can Act a Proverb, and can dance a Jigg,
Does sing French Songs, can Rhime and furnish Chatt
T' Inquisitive Miss, from Letter or Gazett;[7]   10
Knows the Affairs of Cock Pitt and the Race,
And who were Conquerors att either Place;
If Crop or Trotter took the Prize away,
And who a Fortune gain'd the other day,[8]
He swings Fringe Gloves, sees Plays, writes Billedeux[9]
Fill'd up with Beauty, Love, Oaths, Lyes and Vows,
Does scent his Eybrows, perfum'd Comfitts[10] eat,
And smells like Phœnix Nest, or like Civet cat,[11]
Does shave with Pumice Stone,[12] compose his Face,
And Rowls his Stockings by a Looking Glass;[13]   20
Accomplish'd thus, Tommy, you'll grant, I hope,
A pritty Spark att least, if not a Fop.

---

6. A lock of hair at the front of the head, or a corresponding lock on a wig.
7. Two Dublin newspapers of the 1680s were *The News-Letter* and *The Dublin Gazette*. The line means that Weaver reads the papers and can pass on pieces of news to an 'inquisitive Miss'.
8. The main cockpit in seventeenth-century Dublin was in Cork Hill where considerable sums were wagered on the cock fights. Horse-racing took place at the Curragh and, again, large sums were wagered, particularly on the outcome of the annual King's Plate. 'Crop' and 'Trotter' have the distinction of being probably the only horses involved in early racing in Ireland (i.e. before about 1750) whose names are known. (See Tony Sweeney, *The Sweeney Guide to the Irish Turf* (Dublin, 2002), pp. 46–9).
9. billets-doux, love-letters.
10. sweetmeats.
11. Civet, a substance with a strong, musky smell, derived from a tropical animal named a civet cat, was used in perfumery in the early modern period. The phœnix was a mythical bird which was said to burn itself on its nest every six hundred years, emerging from the ashes with renewed youth. The usage here is obscure.
12. A piece of lava used to rub something smooth.
13. Rowls = rolls; Tommy presumably does this so that he can admire his own legs.

TWO BROADSIDES CALUMNIATING IRISH PAPISTS
(1689)

For many Englishmen, 1688 was an *annus mirabilis*; the flight of James II and the assumption of the English throne by William of Orange and his wife Mary were seen as a victory of protestantism and the rule of law over catholicism and tyranny. England had been saved from the unspeakable horrors of catholic despotism as practised on the Continent. Ireland, still catholic and loyal to James, remained a threat to be overcome; one simple way of whipping up anti-Irish and anti-catholic fervour was to circulate broadsheets ridiculing the Irish catholics. Samuel Pepys collected many such broadsheets, including the two which follow, on the streets of London.

Here, Here, Here is Pig and Pork:
or,
(A Catholick Tradition)
shewing

How a lustful Roman Bore[1]
Made a delicate Piggin Riggin a Catholick Whore;
Whereby you may see, if you are not stark blind,
That the Priests will never Marry while some Wives are so kind.

Giving an Account of Father *Wisely*, the Popish Bishop of *Kildare* in *Ireland*,[2] and a Shop-keeper's Wife in *High-street*, *Dublin*

In *Dublin* was play'd such a Prank,
the like was never seen,
Between a full fed Priest
and bonny black *Ishabeen*.[3]

He enjoin'd the Sinner a Pennance
for some notorious Sin,
And made poor *Bessee* uncase,
unto her naked Skin;

And when she naked was
he laid on many a stroak,   10
With his fat brawny Fist
untill he made her back-side smoak.

---

1. boar.
2. Edward Wesley, appointed Bishop of Kildare in July 1683; he died in 1691.
3. 'black' (probably) = wicked (i.e. she was a sinner); 'Ishabeen' is obscure.

But when Confession was ended,
he did as he was used;
He fell to kissing and tickling,
and playing with her Shoes,

Untill his Catholic Engine was rais'd,
then flat on the Bed, on her Back
He laid her, and gave her Instructions,
till he made the Cords to crack.   20

But a curse on the Heretick Noise,
her Husband came in on the Alarm,
And found his Wife enclos'd
[in] the Reverend Fathers Arms.

And now the warm Game begun,
he threatn'd the Priest with his Stones,[4]
And with a good Cudgel belabour'd
his Ghostly Reverend Bones.

Thus having disabl'd the Stallion,
and somewhat abated his Rage,   30
He thought to put up[5] the Matter
and not bring his Name on the Stage,

But dismist the lustfull Priest,
after his Oath by the Mass,
Of his silence and future Forbearance
of what had come to pass.

Now you Catholick Bigots beware,
it is high time for you to reform,
Seeing the Priests be as other Men are,
they are flesh and blood and full as warm.   40

Do you think they can lead chast[e] Lives,
who are pamper'd and idle and fat?
To be sure they lye with your Wives,
their Confession is in order to that.[6]

4. i.e. threatened to castrate him.
5. forget.
6. i.e. they plan to lie with your wives when they have heard their confession.

For this Song is plain Matter of Fact,
and every one of your Cases may be,
And if you will not for Religion,
yet [for] th'hate of Cuckolding, flye Popery.

The Lusty Friar of Dublin

With an Account how He was Catch'd a Bed with another Man's Wife, and for
that Cause was Adjudg'd to Part with his Codlings to his Great Grief.

There was an old Fryar of late,
that liv'd in *Dublin* City,
And hard by the Castle great gate,
now pray now attend to this Ditty.
He lodg'd at the House of a Squire,
whose Lady wou'd often presume,
To suffer this bald-pated Fryar,
to put his old Pope into Rome.
This was an Irish Friar,
This was an Irish Friar,   10
Who every day the Wanton did play
And Cuckold his Landlord the Squire.

His Landlord one Morning did fetch
a Walk which he lov'd as his life,
Returning again he did catch
the Friar a Bed with his Wife.
He run to the Co[n]vent, behold!
this Friar in hopes to degrade,
And there a sad Story he told,
how he a poor Cuckold was made.   20
This was an Irish Friar, etc.

His brethren all by Consent,
this Friar they there did bestave,[1]
Allotting his that Punishment
the Squire[2] would covet or crave.
The Landlord couragious and stout,

---

1. beat him with staves.
2. landlord.

declar'd to the Friary crew,
That both his Stones³ should be cut out,
that he no more mischief might do.
This was an Irish Friar, etc.   30

They strait for a Surgeon did send,
and gave him an hundred Pound
That he might the Friar befriend ,
and smother this terrible Wound:⁴
For though he⁵ astray then did run,
such things we must often excuse,
For surely he wou'd be undone,
if he should those Play-fellows loose.
This was an Irish Friar, etc.

'That day, that you must do the thing,   40
we in the next Room will abide,
A pair of Dog-stones⁶ you may bring,
the which will the Mystery hide.
He must on a Table be bound,
and while you this work are about,
Tho' you never give him a Wound,
yet order him then to cry out.'
This was an Irish Friar, etc.

The Landlord began to draw near,
when they had bid the Surgeon prove true;   50
'And tho' he's a Friar, ne'er fear,⁷
to make him an Eunuch too.
Here take up your hundred pound,
here['s] Silver Guineas gullore;'⁸
His Landlord said, 'I will be bound,
when done, to give half as much more.'
This was an Irish friar, etc.

The day being come, he was ty'd
fast down with a strong hempen-band,

---

3. testicles.
4. i.e. the friars bribed the surgeon to feign carrying out the castration.
5. i.e. the friar.
6. dog's testicles.
7. These lines are spoken by the landlord.
8. galore, cf. Ir. *go leor.*

516

His Arms and his Legs open wide,   60
he could not stir head, foot or hand.
The Friars, and Landlord likewise,
sate waiting all in the next Room,
To hear the most horrible crye,
when Guelding was to be his Doom.
This was an Irish Friar, etc.

The Friar no fear had at all,
but there did most patiently lye,
And oft to the Surgeon did call,
to Counsel when he should cry.   70
The Surgeon he thus did reply,
'You need not to keep such a rout,[9]
I'll warrant you by and by,
you'll find when 'tis time to cry out.'
This was an Irish Friar, etc.

The Friar was never at rest,
but still would be acting of Groanes,
He counted they were but in jest,
but the Surgeon strait whipt off his Stones.
As soon as this mischief befel him,   80
though he was both lusty and stout,
The Surgeon, he need not to tell him,
he found it was time to cry out.
This was an Irish Friar, etc.

The Friars all running with speed,
as soon as his Crys they did hear,
And seeing their Brother to bleed,
the Rogues they did tremble for fear.
The Surgeon said, 'twas but Discretion,
to Gueld all, were there many more,   90
The Lasses might come to Confession,
and they not debauch them no more.
The Friar he cursed the Knife,
The Friar he cursed the Knife;
He sighs and he groans for the loss of his Stones,
He had rather have parted with Life.

9. make such a fuss.

ANONYMOUS
(1689)

The Irish Hudibras, which was published in the early summer of 1689, is a much amended version of the 'Purgatorium Hibernicum'.[1] The most interesting difference between the two texts lies in the political references which have been updated, in the *Hudibras*, to include events in the reign of James II up to and including the arrival in England of William of Orange. Like the 'Purgatorium', the *Hudibras* travesties the sixth book of the *Æneid* and follows the Fingallian hero, Nees, in his adventures in the Irish underworld. The perspective of the author (or authors) is, again, that of the bigoted protestant, determined to show Nees and his native Irish companions to be superstitious, ignorant and uncivilised. As before, the text is accompanied at the foot of the page by samples from Virgil's text as they are translated and, in the margin, by scholarly notes explaining unusual words and giving references to source books of Irish history in English, Latin and Irish. Although the poem was published in London, it was clearly written in or near Dublin, probably over a considerable period of time, and probably as a collaborative effort by several New English protestant landlords.[2] For the 1689 publication, the author(s) provided an explanatory preface and a glossary of 'Fingallian Words' and 'Irish Phrases' which might be unintelligible to an English reader. For a full analysis of the language of *The Irish Hudibras*, see Alan Bliss, *Spoken English in Ireland 1600–1740, passim.*

A key scene in this text, as in its Virgillian counterpart, is that in which the hero's father, whom he encounters in the underworld, foretells the future of his race. In the case of *The Irish Hudibras*, much of the 'prophesy' is a retelling of events which had already happened before the date of its publication as if they were a prophesy. Throughout the seventeenth century, Irish catholics gained much of their self-confidence in opposing the English from prophesies, in verse and prose, which assured them that they would, eventually, prevail. The prophesy in *The Irish Hudibras* is, thus, a cruel joke; Nees, like his countrymen, would expect to hear great things in it and yet the text, having the benefit of hindsight, can assert that James II is to lose the throne of England and that it is highly likely that he, Tyrconnell and the Irish will lose any war they engage in against the English and the Dutch.

The first extract comes as Nees's father, Anchees, is prefacing a 'prophesy' of the future of the Irish race with a brief account of events in Ireland and England from the Elizabethan wars to the end of the reign of Charles I; the text begins just after Charles's head has been brought 'to th' Block'.

---

1. For a discussion of the significance of these texts, see the headnote to the 'Purgatorium Hibernicum' (p. 412 above).
2. Though the name Francis Taubman is associated with the 'Purgatorium' – the words 'By Francis Taubman' occur at the end of the NLI manuscript of the poem – and that of James Farewell with *The Irish Hudibras* – Anthony à Wood attributed it to him (*Athenæ Oxoniensis* (Oxford, 1721), col. 837) – it seems unlikely that either man was the 'author' – in the normal sense of the word – of either version of the poem. See Bliss, pp. 47–8 and 56–7.

from: The Irish Hudibras

... Thus shall he[3] fall, and to his Son
He shall bequeath an empty Throne:
Which e're he fills, must banisht, Toyl
For Laurels in a Foreign Soyl:[4]
Thence, with Majestick Glory born,
With greater Triumph shall return;
Whose Restauration-Day, the Head
Of Rump and Regicides do dread:[5]
And though poor *Ireland* hopes in vain,
'Twill ne're be Ours, while He does Reign.   10
A *Court of Claiming* he shall call,[6]
Poor *Teague* again is out of All:
His Claim rejected, and his Lands
Restor'd into the *English* hands.
Nor dare a Nocent-Rebel once stir,
In *Ulster*, *Connaught*, *Mead*,[7] or *Munster*;
The *Irish* Glory so departed,
And poor *Enees* so quite dead-hearted;
That he has hardly left a Groat,
To pay for cutting *English*-Throat.   20
The Hereticks shall sit at helm,
And rule (while he[8] does Reign) the Realm;
Shall bear on Breast the Royal Stamp,
All Offices in Court and Camp,
So that poor *Nees* shall not be able,
To put in for a Cones-table:[9]

---

3. Charles I. Anchees does not speak Fingallian like his son Nees because, according to the prefatory note, he had been a soldier in the Low Countries where he would have been exposed to English as spoken by native speakers. For examples of seventeenth-century Fingallian speech, see the extract from the 'Purgatorium Hibernicum' above.
4. A reference to Charles II's exile between the death of his father and his own restoration.
5. Members of the Rump parliament and those who had signed Charles I's death warrant had reason to expect to be prosecuted by the incoming Restoration administration.
6. The Act of Settlement of 1662 set up a 'court of claims' to arbitrate on land ownership. Claimants (whether catholic or protestant) were judged either 'innocent' of wrongdoing, in which case their claims were usually met, or 'nocent', in which case their claim was rejected. No one was satisfied with the outcome.
7. Meath, one of the five provinces of ancient Ireland.
8. Charles II.
9. i.e. every warrant for a civil or military appointment will have the royal stamp on it (and require an oath of allegiance) so that an Irishman can not even apply for the position of a constable.

But still to make his own Life easie,
He shall do all he can to please ye;
Who was, had he *Teagues* Cause maintain'd,
The best of Kings that ever Reign'd.[10]   30

He dead, his Brother[11] mounts the Throne,
And once more *Ireland* is our own.
He *Petre*[12] now shall bear the sway,
And Popery shall come in play:
He shall new model all the Nation,
From College unto Corporation:
To former plight[13] he shall transplant us,
By *Mandats*, *Briefs*, and *Quo Warranto's*.[14]
Gospel and Law[15] shall trample o're,
By a Supreme-Dispensing Power: 40
If any jealous Lord oppose it,
Shall purge in Inquisition Closet;
And by his Will, which is his Law,
Shall keep the Hereticks in awe:
In spite of Law, shall do his best[16]
To take off *Penal*, and the *Test*;
And for the Freedom of our Nation,
Shall make an *Act of Toleration*;[17]
Where all may have their Liberty
To go to Hell as well as Thee.   50
Shall turn the Nobles in disgrace,
For *Teague* and *Rory* to make place;[18]
Turning, (*Ill omen* of his Fall)
'Till he himself turn out[19] of all:

---

10. A reference to Charles II's well-known sympathy for the catholic cause.
11. James II.
12. James II's confessor (and a man widely thought to have great influence over him) was a Jesuit, Father Edward Petre (1631–99).
13. position (an example of the legal terminology in the poem).
14. legal documents; a 'mandate' is a legally enforceable command, a 'brief' is a royal mandate and a 'quo warranto' is a writ requiring someone to show by what authority he is acting. The last was used against protestant corporations in 1687. See J.G. Simms, *Jacobite Ireland 1685–91* (London, 1969), p. 35.
15. i.e. protestant gospel and English law.
16. i.e. James II will do his best to remove the penal laws and the Test Act (prohibiting non-Anglicans from holding official office).
17. James II always claimed to favour freedom of religion for his subjects, and one of his first actions on reaching Dublin Castle in March 1689 was to issue a proclamation on the matter.
18. Generic names for native Irishmen, cf. the Irish names *Teig* and *Ruiari*.
19. i.e. is turned out of all, a reference to James II's flight from England.

Of Promise-making-Kings the best,
Till over-ridden by the Priest;
Which turn'd the Helm into a *Paddle*[20]
And threw great *J[ame]s* out of the Saddle. . . .

Like most Irish protestants, the author(s) of *The Irish Hudibras* had a particularly strong aversion to the Earl of Tyrconnell. Tyrconnell was from a landowning Old English family; his father, Sir William Talbot, had been member of parliament for County Kildare in the parliament of 1613 and Tyrconnell himself had become close friends with James II while they were on the Continent in the early 1650s. To treat the swash-buckling, womanising Tyrconnell, scion of a respectable Old English family, as if he were an uneducated 'native' Irishman raised in the bogs, was an insult of the highest order. But, in the passage which follows, Nees's father, 'prophesying' the rise and fall of Tyrconnell, does just that.

. . . Then clapping hands, as sign of wonder,
'Behold (says he) that Son of Thunder,
Tyrconnel, with his Spoils possest,
The bravest King of all the rest.
His Haughtiness bred in the Bogs,
Shall call his Betters, Rogues and Dogs.
From Butchers Bratt,[1] rais'd to a Peer,
To be a K[ing] in *Shamrogshire*!

This Devil[2] shall do that which no Man
Cou'd yet effect, restore the *Roman*;   10
And in his time establish Popery,
Which *Curse ye Meroz*[3] calls a Foppery.
Chappels shall up, the Churches down,[4]
And all the Land shall be our own.
He shall secure our Title[5] here,
By a Rebellion in each Sheir,[6]

20. *Original note*: 'Helm.' The note is confusing. The lines seem to mean: 'Which (= who i.e. the priests) transformed what had been the means for guiding the ship of state (the helm) into a stick which turned great James out of his saddle'.

1. A slur: Tyrconnell's father was not a butcher. See headnote. 'Shamrogshire' is a disparaging name for Ireland.
2. i.e. Tyrconnell.
3. Sir Thomas Meres (1635–1715) had introduced a bill into the English House of Commons in 1685 which would have compelled all foreigners settled in England to become members of the Church of England.
4. Catholic chapels and protestant churches.
5. Documents proving ownership of land.
6. shire, country.

An Army shall Collect the Rent,
Confirm our Rights by *Parliament*.
The *Act of Settlement* shall bate,[7]
And *Nees* shall get his own Estate,   20
If by the *Monsieur* not supplanted,
Who for a Sum has Covenanted;
And both their Interests be not lost
By the prevailing *British* Host.[8]
He shall subdue the *Heretick*,
To bring in trusty *Catholick*.
Humble the Peer, Exault the Peasant,
Without Assize of damage-Feisant.[9]
And shall advance the meanest sort
To highest place of Camp and Court: 30
All shall be common as before;
No more shall Justices, no more
Shall Court of Claims, or Council-Table,
Or Formidon,[10] be formidable.
Drink down Excise, know no Committe,[11]
But Routs and Riots in each City;
Cut Throats; in Massacre skill'd well;
And Plunder, tho' it were in Hell.
Thus shall he rule the Rebel Rout,
Till by the *Monsieur*[12] josled out;   40
Reduc'd to such a low Condition,
He shan't to Curse have a Commission . . .'

7. i.e. shall cease to have force. The reference is to the 1662 Act of Settlement.
8. These lines suggest that there are three claimants to 'Nees's' estate: Nees himself (the old proprietor), 'Monsieur' (probably Louis XIV who financed James II and might be granted land in return) and, if the British forces continue to 'prevail', a new, English owner.
9. = 'damage-feasant', a term used of a stranger's cattle found trespassing and doing damage on one's land. Here the 'assize of damage-feasant' is an ironic reference to the Restoration courts.
10. The court of claims administered the restoration land settlement; the 'council-table' was the Irish Privy Council; a 'formidon' was a writ for claiming property.
11. i.e. pay no attention to regulations promulgated by excise authorities or any other committee . . .
12. This either refers to the Comte d'Avaux, a French diplomat who accompanied James from France to Ireland and had some influence over him, or to Louis XIV.

Nees's father proceeds to 'prophesy' the collapse of the Jacobite cause and the end of Tyrconnell.

> ... But now the Night, like thickning Smoak
> That dwells in *Crates*,[1] possession took
> O'th'Firmament, when he begun,
> With weeping, thus t' advise his Son.
>
> Oh *Nees*, poor *Nees*, do not importune,
> To know thy Countrey-mens misfortune,
> That will befal them by Adventurers,
> By *English*, *Dutch*, and *Scotch* Debentures:[2]
> Our Lands possest, we put to rout,
> By two Brigades of Horse and Foot: 10
> Transported some, and some Transplanted,
> Whilst the prevailing party Ranted.
> Till he's[3] restor'd, with all his Train;
> But here's the Devil on't again;
> The Fates will only shew his Reign,
> To hope for more, is but in vain. ...
> And truly, *Nees*, there's ne'er a one
> For us to crack of,[4] when he's[5] gone;
> Not one, like Him, will e'er appear
> Again, to grow in *Shamrogeshire*. ...   20
> *Lilli-bo-lero, lero* sing,[6]
> *Tyrconnel* is no longer K[ing]. ...

1. Irish cabins – always full of smoke because they lacked chimneys. cf. Ir. *creat(a)*, frame of a house or roof.
2. Mercenary soldiers issued not with pay but with debentures (vouchers certifying that they were owed money) to be exchanged for land in Ireland.
3. James II.
4. boast about.
5. Tyrconnell.
6. It is the author(s) of the poem who sing this triumphalist, protestant song, not Nees.

ANONYMOUS
(1689)

The following verses come from a song entitled 'The Court of England or the Preparation for the Happy Coronation of King William and Queen Mary' which found its way into English songbooks in the eighteenth century. An Englishman asserts the glorious potential of England now it is rid of Jesuits and Jacobites, and he is answered by a Welshman (Taffy), an Irishman (Teague), a Scotsman (Sawny), a Frenchman (Monsieur) and a Dutchman (Myn-heer), each of whom puts his country's view on the Williamite succession in the broken English assumed to be spoken by the natives of that country. The original version of the song can be dated to the spring of 1689, while Tyrconnell was still in charge of the Irish army and before the coronation of William and Mary in London on 11 April. The poem repeats the often asserted claim that Irish soldiers were enticed to England during the reign of James II by promises of the great wealth they would be able to accumulate. The text is in exaggerated Hiberno-English: for 'd' read 'th', for 't' read 'th', for 'sh' read 'ch' or 's', for 'w' read 'v', for 'aa' read 'a', etc., as appropriate.

from: The Court of England . . .

[Teague's Response to the Accession of King William]

Bub a boo! bub! Oh hone![1]
The Broder of the Son,
And de Shild of mee Moder de poor Teague undone!
Pull down Mass-House and Altar,
And burn Virgin Psalter,
And make hang upon[2] Priest, and no Friend cut de Halter
of poor Jesuit.

When *Teague* first came o'er,
To de *Engeland* shore,
Wid Six, Seven, Eight Thousand *Irish* Lads, all and more: 10
Teague was promist good Fashion
Great Estate in de Nation
Wid all *London* in his Pocket, upon me Shaulwashion
by de Jesuit.

---

1. Conventional expressions of regret in Irish. cf. Ir. *abhó* and *o hone*, both meaning 'alas'. For a full analysis of Hiberno-English of the time, see Alan Bliss, *Spoken English in Ireland 1600–1740* (Dublin, 1979), *passim*.
2. For this type of verbal periphrastic construction, see Bliss, pp. 305–8.

But when de boor[3] *Dutch*
Got *Teague* in his Clutch
Stead of make great Estate, and Chrees[4] knows what much,
Damn'd Heretick Dogue
Made *Teague* a poor Rogue,
Turn'd him home to make starve, widout Shoe or Broge   20
                    for de Jesuit.

But I'll beg Captain's Plaash[5]
Of de sweet Eyes and Faash
Of mee Dear-Joy[6] *Tyrconnel*, his Majesties Graash;
And fight like a *Hero*
By me Shaul a *Mack-Nero*[7]
Cut Troat for Shaint *Patrick*, and sing *Lilliburlero*
                    for de Jesuit.[8]

---

3. boorish or perhaps 'poor'.
4. For a note on this spelling, see Bliss, p. 249.
5. place. For this solution to problems, see the poem by 'Cromach O Rough' above, p. 495.
6. = my friend; also used of Irishmen by Englishmen from about 1685 to 1700, see Bliss, p. 265.
7. This unusual phrase occurs in at least three anti-Irish poems of the period 1688–9; a son of Nero would be a follower of a leader of barbarous and vicious habits, i.e. James II, in the eyes of the writer of this piece.
8. A remark meant to show the stupidity of the speaker since 'Lilliburlero' is an anti-catholic song.

FIVE BROADSIDES ON THE IRISH WAR
(1689–1691)

In the late 1690s, with the Williamite troops on active service in Ireland, the streets of London were full of news-sheets and broadsides on Irish affairs. Samuel Pepys was able to collect scores of ballads inspired by the situation in Ireland between the departure of the troops in the autumn of 1689 and their return after the Siege of Limerick in the autumn of 1691. Though most of the ballads celebrate English military valour and accuse the Irish of cowardice, many display a surprising sympathy for the plight of the Irish soldiers, blaming the Jesuits and the French for leading them into defeat.

A small selection from the many broadside ballads of the period is included below. The first song is of particular interest because it repeats imagery and wording found in a salacious Dublin-printed poem of 1689, written in a barbarous mixture of English and dog-Latin, entitled *A Cruel and Bloody Declaration Publish'd by the Cardinals at Rome, against Great-Britain, and Ireland.* That text, which, with a translation, is printed in *Verse in English from Eighteenth-Century Ireland*, pp. 39–42, is one of the liveliest of the period; its English-language companion, printed below, may be less salacious and less vigorous, but it seems to be based on the same – presumably lost – satirical original. Both poems show the virulence that characterised protestant attacks on the catholic church and its beliefs at this time.

News from London-Derry in a packet of advice from Room

It was sent over by the Pope, to the Earl of Tyrconnel; late Commander of the Catholick Army: Containing many Wonderful Lyes, Damnable Cheats, and False Promises, to the Protestants of England[1]

> You *Protestants* of *England*
> you greatly are to blame;
> For slighting of your *Mother Church*,
> and bringing her to shame.
> *But a Cursing we will goe, will goe, will goe,*
> *and a Cursing we will goe.*
>
> We sent you o'er a *Popish* Queen,
> a *Hocus Prince* of *Wales*:[2]
> But all our Projects seem to you,
> but Idle Tricks and Tales;   10
> *But a Cursing we will goe, &c.*

---

1. The poem purports to be the contents of a letter from the cardinals in Rome addressed to English protestants.
2. Mary of Modena, James II's second wife and her infant son, the Prince of Wales (later the Young Pretender).

But would the *English* Noble-men,
with all their Gentry goe,
And stoop unto *His Highness*,[3]
and Kiss his Little Toe.
Then a Blessing we would come, &c.

We'll send you o're to *England*
both Relicks, Pardons, Beads;
A Bushel of St. *Peter*'s Teeth,
and Twenty of his Heads.[4]   20
And a Blessing we will come, &c.

We'll Sell you sweet Indulgences,
and by the Beat of Drum,
We'll Pardon your Iniquities,
past, present, and to come.
And a Blessing we will come, &c.

Then you may Drink, and you may Swear,
both Murder, Steal and Whore;
And the Devil is within the Rogue
that can desire for more.   30
And a Blessing we will come, &c.

And if your friends have been detain'd
in Purgatory long;
We'll set them free for Twenty pence,
and save them by a Song,
And a Singing we will goe, &c.

We'll teach you Bestiality,
to *Pater Noster* say,
The use of *Holy Water*, and
to *Images* to Pray,   40
And a Conjuring we will come, &c.

We'll show you how you may exceed,
all *Herreticks*, by odds;

---

3. i.e. the Pope.
4. The central portion of the poem contains exaggerated references to catholic beliefs and
   practices – particularly those despised by protestants as superstitious.

And make of one small Loaf of Bread,
a pound of *Popish Gods*,
And a Lying we will come, &c.

But if you'll not do what the Pope
so humbly doth require,
He'll come and plead his Interest,
with Faggot and with Fire.   50
And a Burning we will come, &c.

The Bonny *Clabbor-Cut-Throats*,
that's cruel, and far worse,
Will muster up an Army,
of *Bog-trotting* Horse,[5]
And a Fighting we will come, &c.

Then every sweet and *Dear Joy*,
with *Patrick* and with *Teague*,
Will batter down the *London*-Walls,
and level quite the *Hague*.[6]   60
And a Plundering we will goe, &c.

Then take advice, and bow before
His Holiness's Feet;
Both Hug and Kiss them with poor Lips
tho' Sweaty still they're Sweet.
And a Kissing we will goe, &c.

And quickly send a Post to Rome,
that *Catholicks* may know,
If any that are *English* men
will stoop before his Toe,   70
And a Stooping they must goe, must goe, must goe,
and a Stooping they must goe.

---

5. This probably refers to the regiments of Irish soldiers sent to England by Tyrconnell in 1688 (Simms, *Jacobite Ireland*, pp. 45–8). They caused considerable trouble among the English and were disbanded after William's arrival late in 1688. Bonny-clabber (Ir. *bainne clabair*, thick, soured milk), like 'bog-trotting' and 'Dear Joys', was used widely in the broadsheets of the time to indicate Irishness.

6. The fear was that if the Irish troops got to London, they would batter down its walls and then, victorious, continue to the Hague – capital of the United Provinces of which William of Orange was also ruler (*stadholder*).

Poor Teague in Distress

or, The French and Irish Army Routed. Together with the Flight of the Duke of
Berwick, *Fitz-James*,[1] *Tyrconnel*, and the rest of the Head Leaders, to FRANCE.[2]

Good Tydings I bring, from *William* our King,
The Glory of *Protestant* Soldiers shall ring,
While the *French* and *Teagues,* for their cruel Intreagues
Are forced to scowre and run many Leagues,
Being Routed.

De *English* Boy, dey vill us destroy,[3]
Where shall we go hide our selves now, my Dear-Joy?
Our Leaders are fled, which fills us with dread,
Be Chreest, dey vill hang up poor *Teague* till he's dead,
Being Routed.   10

It is de *French* Crew dat makes us to rue,
For dem we are forc'd to sing *Hub bub bub boo*;
Had dey not come o're, to our Native Shore,
We then would have turn'd to King *William* before[4]
We were Routed.

Begar, says *Monsieur*,[5] when first I came here,
Dey tell me of having five hundred a year;[6]
But here me find none, but de broken Bone,
An Army dispers'd, and quite overthrown,
Being Routed.   20

The *Teagues* straight reply'd, it can't be deny'd,
You sent o're to *France* our Gold, Silver beside;[7]
And Cattle consume, so sad is our Doom,
We have nothing left here but Brass in the room,
Now we're Routed.

1. James Fitz-James, Duke of Berwick (1670–1734), the elder of James II's two natural sons. Tyrconnell and some of the French forces left Ireland in September 1690.
2. The poem has three speakers: an English protestant (stanza 1), an Irishman, and a French officer (whose dialogue makes up the rest of the poem).
3. Since stanzas 2 and 3 are spoken by an Irishman, they are in exaggerated Hiberno-English: read 'th' for 'd', 'w' for 'v', etc.
4. Many Irishmen, including Tyrconnell himself, considered making terms with William after his accession to the English throne.
5. 'Monsieur' is a French officer: 'begar' is a imagined French oath – probably 'By God'.
6. i.e. an income of five hundred pounds a year.
7. The rumour that the wealth of Ireland had been shipped to France was partly true (Simms, p. 49).

We came to help you, a Cowardly Crew,
Therefore all that ever ye have is our due:
Begar, speak a word, me draw out my Sword,
To Kill you, so presently scamper abroad,
Being Routed.   30

With that they did part, but *Teague* griev'd at heart,
A thousand times wish'd he had kept Plow and Cart;
And ne'r mounted Horse, for by *Patrick's* Cross,
We *Irish* are beaten, and suffer the loss,
Being Routed.

De *English* did Fight, and put us to flight,
We could not endure to behold 'um in sight:
As they did Advance, to Run was our chance,
Dear-Joy, we did lead them a delicate Dance,
Being Routed.   40

In midst of the Fray, we run, by my Fay,[8]
But 'twas our good Officers taught us the way;
By help of our Brogues, we took to the Boggs,
For fear they would thump us, and thrash us like Dogs
Being Routed.

My Friends I did Trace, but could not keep pace,
With Noble *Tyrconnel,* his Majesties Grace:
He cannot deny, but while we did flye,
His speed was so swift, he run faster than I,
Being Routed.   50

The *French Brigadeer,* he scowr'd for fear,
He knew it not safe for to stay longer here:
With dexterous skill, he rid Vales and Hill,
And left the poor *Teagues* to be Hang'd if they will,
Being Routed.

When *Berwick* did find *Fitz-James* in the mind,
To follow their Leaders, and ne'r look behind;

8. faith.

The *Monsieur D'Louson*, and Noble Lord *Powis*,[9]
They'r all gone to tell a sad Story to *Lewis*,[10]
Being Routed.   60

Be Chreest, let them go, 'tis certain, we know
A Friend we shall find of a *Protestant* Foe,
Our Joys to compleat, therefore we'll Retreat,
And fall down for Mercy at King *Williams* Feet,
He will Save us.

The Bogg-Trotters March

Old *James* with his Rascally Rabble of Rogues,
    he drew up his Army pretending to stand;
But as they march'd they must trust to their Brogues,
    the Dee'l take the hindmost was his Command:
He had a Ditty he mumbl'd along,
    it went in the Tune of *Lilli borlero*;[1]
But we will follow them close with a Song
    of March Boys, march, Boys, Tan ta ra ra ro:
March Boys, march Boys, merry, merry march, Boys,
    Teague's but a Mushroom to a Man, Boys,   10
See how they fly, how they run, how they dye,
    whilst Conquering *William* leads us on, Boys.

Thus *Teague* with his Loyalty, Mettle, and Pride,
    Resolves to maintain his Natural Prince;
Who the Plague blames him, so nearly Ally'd
    in Truth, Religion, Wit and Sence;
He quits his Crowns, they Surrender his Towns,
    if he plays the Fool, they all do the same, Sir;
Lose or win, or get it all again soon;
    thus they play the Factions-Game, Sir,   20

---

9. Antonin de Caumont, Comte de Lauzun (1632–1723), a French courtier who escorted
  James II's wife, Mary of Modena, to exile and later commanded French forces at the
  battle of the Boyne. William Herbert, Duke of Powis (1617–96), an English Jacobite
  who accompanied James to Ireland in March 1689.
10. Louis XIV.

---

1. An ironic comment, since 'Lilliburlero' is an anti-catholic song.

Game Sir, Game Sir, Ninny, Ninny, tame Sir;
    see what a Monster they have made thee;
Shave, shave thy Pate, Drown thy Wife, Poyson *Kate*[2]
    be Chreest and St. *Patrick* they've all betray'd thee.

The *Irish* Nation was carry'd to Pawn,
    for Money, the Catholick War to maintain;
As soon as King *William* a Sword he had drawn,
    his Conquering Army redeem'd it again;
Now *Monsieur*, Begar,[3] he may hang himself,
    they scamper'd and left the whole Kingdom behind 'em,   30
But still we will follow the Hect'ring-Elf,[4]
    in *France*, in *France*, we hope to find 'em.
Charge Boys, Charge Boys, rally, rally, charge Boys,
    like noble Lads with warlike Thunder;
Pursue them amain,[5] in retreat they are slain,
    their Troops and their Ranks we'll break in sunder.

Loud Cannons did roar, and the Trumpets did sound,
    the which Warlike-Musick soon fill'd 'em with fear;
The Devil a Teague of 'em all stood their ground,
    nor likewise the prodigal-Huff, *Monsieur*;[6]   40
For, like nimble Deer, they all took their flight,
    not only the *French*, but the Catholic-Tory;[7]
And still in their running they bid us Good-night,
    and thus brave *Nassau*[8] gained glory:
Sound Boys, sound Boys, let the Trumpet sound, Boys,
    we were resolved they should restore us
Towns which we won, whilst the Catholicks run,
    and thus did we Conquer all before us.

Poor Teague with a sigh and a sorrowful face,
    with crossing his Breast, to the Saints he did cry,   50
In spight of *Tyrconnel*, his Majesties Grace,
    we're forc'd to the Bogs and the Mountains to fly:

2. This list echoes of refrains from popular English songs.
3. See note to line 16 of 'Poor Teague in Distress' above.
4. malicious bully, i.e. James II.
5. without delay.
6. prodigal-Huff = extravagant bully; *Monsieur* = the French forces in Ireland.
7. catholic outlaws, i.e. anyone against the Williamites.
8. William of Orange was also Prince of Nassau.

When none did resist we conquer'd a Deal,
    the greatest part of the Irish Nation;
But Fait[9] it has prov'd like a slippery Eel,
    we are forc'd to surrender at discretion:
Nassau, Nassau, with his valiant Army,
    fought and pursu'd us all together;
Rather than dye, we did bid them good-bye,
    for our Brogues they were made of running Leather.   60

Old Jemmy our Master[10] is scamper'd to France
    and we wou'd have follow'd as fast as we could;
But ere we cou'd out of the Nation advance,
    like sorrowful Tories we all were fool'd:
Many that ventur'd to fight were Kill'd,
    but, for my own part, I was fearful to fire:
Be Chreest in my running I was well skill'd,
    and therefore in time I did retire:
Charge Boys, charge Boys, still they follow'd, Charge Boys,
    fearful I was that they wou'd find me;   70
But as I run, I did throw down my Gun,
    and never so much as look'd behind me.

Teague the Irish Trooper,

being his Sorrowful Lamentation to his Cousin *Agra*,[1] and the rest of his fellow
Soldiers, recounting their Misfortunes in the most remarkable Fights, from the
River BOYNE, to the Surrender of LIMERICK, their last Hope.

Dear Cousin *Agra*, and my Friends now attend
To this doleful Ditty, which poor *Teague* has penn'd:
The *Irish* Nation be[2] Chreest now is lost,
In [all] our designs we are utterly crost:
We still have been forc'd to Surrender and Yield,
To K.[3] William's *Army who Conquers the Field*.

When first his vast Army set foot on the Land,
Against them we marcht, yet not able to stand:

---

9. faith – an oath, but also implying, here, our cause.
10. James II.

1. A proper name made from the Ir. *a ghrá*, my dear.
2. by. For the reasons for this Hiberno-English usage, see Alan Bliss, *Spoken English in Ireland 1600–1740* (Dublin, 1979), pp. 193–4.
3. King.

For they did with Courage and Conduct appear,
Which caused us streightways to tremble for fear: 10
When e're they drew near, we were forced to Yield,
To K. William's *Army who Conquer'd the Field.*

Remember the Fight at the *Boyne,* my dear Joy,
How they did our Army and Forces destroy;
Through Fire and Water they marched amain,[4]
And vow'd that the Kingdom they soon would regain:
That day we were forc'd to Surrender and Yield,
To K. William's *Army, which Conquer'd the Field.*

They threaten to put then the Kill upon[5] *Teague,*
Therefore by my shoul[6] we run one, two, three League,   20
Too many for us they have been all along,
Which makes me to sing this sorrowful Song;
As being compell'd to Surrender and Yield,
To K. William's *Army which Conquers the Field.*

There's fair *Drogheda,* nay, and *Dublin* too,
This Conquering Army in short did subdue;
While we to the Bogs, and the Mountains did fly,
Dear Cousin, cause *Teague* was unwilling to dye:
Thus were we constrain'd to Surrender and Yield,
To K. William's *Army, which Conquers the Field.*   30

Then famous *Athlone* we resolv'd to defend,
The which then was taken by storm in the end:[7]
And *Galloway* likewise Surrender'd also,[8]
Be Chreest then our game did begin to run low,
And forced we were to Surrender and Yield,
To K. William's *Army, which Conquers the Field.*

The Fight at fair *Agram*[9] I'd like to forgot,
Where so many Thousands were slain on the spot;

---

4. at full speed.
5. For an explanation of this construction, see Bliss, p. 304.
6. soul.
7. Athlone, County Westmeath, fell to the Williamites on 30 June 1691.
8. Galway surrendered in August 1691.
9. Aughrim, County Galway, scene of the most decisive battle of the war (12 July 1691), at which the Irish and French forces were defeated by Williamite forces, the French commander St Ruth was killed and up to 7,000 Irish soldiers were slaughtered.

My Father and Brother were kill'd in the Fray,
My heart now is ready to break Cousin *Gray*,[10]   40
And still we are forc'd to Surrender and Yield,
To King William's *Army, which Conquers the Field.*

There's great *Collonel Sarsefield*[11] did swagger and bost,
That he would soon down with the Protestant Host;
But now to our sorrow by Chreest we have found,
That they have like Tygers encompast us round:
And famous fair Limerick *is forced to Yield,*
To K. William's *Army which Conquers the Field.*

In that very City our hopes we did place,
And now we are all in a sorrowful case;   50
For why their great Cannons against us they play'd,
At which Warlike Thunder we all were afraid,
And Limerick *at length now is forced to Yield,*[12]
To K. William's *Army which Conquers the Field.*

Be Chreest Brother Tory when we Salli'd out,
Like Souldiers of courage both Valliant and Stout,
The Governour Monsieur did bar up the Gate,
The which is a sorrowful tale to relate;[13]
For there Teague was slaughter'd and forced to Yield,
To K. William's *Army which Conquers the Field.*   60

I put on my Shack-boots,[14] and left Cart and Plow,
And thought to have been a Commander e're now,
But I must return like a poor tatter'd Rogue,
Without e'er a Shirt, Coat, nay Stocking, or Brogue,
Since famous fair Limerick *is forced to Yield,*
To K. William's *Army, who Conquers the Field.*

A curse on the French would they ne'er had come here,
By them our sorrows has been most severe;

---

10. i.e. dear cousin – another proper name from the Ir. *a ghrá*, my dear.
11. Patrick Sarsfield, Earl of Lucan (*d.* 1693), the most distinguished commander on the Jacobite side.
12. In September 1691. The Treaty of Limerick was signed on 3 October 1691.
13. Whether this happened or not, the charge is typical of those directed by the Irish against the French at the time.
14. = jackboots, strong, high boots, usually worn by cavalry soldiers.

But seeing we find how we have been misled,
Great *William* for ever shall now be our head;   70
To His Royal Power and Conduct we'll Yield,
Where ever he goes let him Conquer the Field.

Teague the Irish Soldier

or His Lamentation for the bad Success in the loss of Lymerick,
and his resolution to quit the Wars.

Now, now we are lost, by my Shoul,[1] all undone,
We dare not approach to *France* or to *Rome;*
The Monsieur[2] hath need of his Money and Men,
And Swears that begar, he'l ne'r trust us agen:
Since *Lymerick's* lost, we're debarr'd from all hope,
And I fear the Church Cause will end in a Rope.

Ah Hone, Brother, *Sarsefield*, come, come let's away,
The Devil shall tauke me if longer I stay:
Father-Priest, my Dear-Joy, have on us put Cheat,[3]
With future Rewards of a Heavenly Seat;   10
Estates here on Earth by his promise I know,
But *Lymerick's* lost, and what shall we do now?

Our Prophets Unlucky, the Truth still have mist,
Henceforth I'll believe them no more, no by Chreest;
They told us brave things which at length we should find
And yet may prove true when the Devil is blind:
But for all they can do, we may now make our moan,
Since *Lymerick's* Taken as well as *Athlone.*

Six Thousand tall Lads, sent to second the Cause,
Ship'd over to *France-Land* in spight of the Laws;[4]   20
Like bold Sons of *Mars*, we protested, that all
The *Hereticks* Lands betwixt us must fall;

1. soul. Throughout this text, read 's' for 'sh'.
2. Louis XIV. 'begar' in the next line is the standard oath which Frenchmen were thought to utter.
3. See Bliss, *Spoken English in Ireland 1600–1740*, p. 304.
4. Under the terms of the Treaty of Limerick, the Irish army, under Patrick Sarsfield, was permitted to go to France. It is estimated that 12,000 Irish soldiers went to France in the autumn of 1691 (Simms, *Jacobite Ireland*, p. 260).

But *Teagueland* Sings now, *Hallow-loo*, and makes moan,
Since *Lymerick* has yielded as well as *Athlone*.

Tyrconnel in Heav'n, be his Majesties Grauce,
Promis'd each a Reward, or an Officers plauce;
But Monsieur came in, and carry'd the Prey
Whilst I poor *Pillgarlick*[5] receiv'd the Brass pay;
But still we expected a much better Fate,
But the Taking of *Lymerick* ends all the debate.   30

This Town we secur'd to make sure of the Game,
But a pox o' the Devil, he ow'd us a shame:
At the first of the Onset we quitted the Fray;
Our Arms we threw down, then to Heels and away;
Since *Lymerick* is lost, now what Fort shall we choose?
Poor Teague and the Monsieur may hang in a Noose.

The *Shannon* with ecchoes doth loudly repeat
Our Howls and our Cries for *Lym'ricks* Defeat;
Our Fortress and Shelter in times of distress,
And to cry now by Chreest, how can I do less: 40
Bold *Ginckle*,[6] tho' 'bove we make Prayers and Complaints
With the *English*, out-does all our Legions of Saints.

I'll no more on a Steed with Holster and Boot,
Nor be ty'd to a Sword, nor with Pistol will Shoot;
On a *Galloway* Tit[7] I'll trot it away,
With Bridle and Cropper of Thumbrope of Hay:[8]
In a Cot[9] daub'd with Cow-turd, I'll lie me down warm,
In my Bed with each Feather as long as my Arm.[10]

---

5. i.e. 'poor me'. James II had debased copper coinage issued in Ireland while, it was commonly thought, the gold and silver was shipped to France.
6. Godard van Reede, Baron Ginkel, first Earl of Athlone (1630–1703), a native of Utrecht, left in command of the Williamite forces in Ireland by William III in 1690. Commanded the Williamites at Aughrim and in the siege of Limerick.
7. 'Galloway' = (here) Galway; a 'tit' was a small horse or a nag.
8. i.e. a bridle and crupper (a rope secured to the back of the saddle and passing under the horse's tail) made of a rope formed (by thumb-pressure) out of straw – a 'sougawn' rope; (Ir. *súgán*, straw rope).
9. cottage. The walls of Irish country dwellings were sometimes strengthened with cow-dung.
10. Expensive mattresses were filled with soft, small, downy feathers: large feathers went into cheap bedding.

Le' Zune long since left us, St. *Ruth* he is Slain,[11]
Tyrconnel is dead, and my King o're the Maine;   50
Now, now good St. *Patrick* come in with a blow,
And give it them home,[12] as thy Saintship knows how;
For poor Teague and I have quite done our best,
And now by my Shoul, thou must e'n do the rest.

11. Antonin de Caumont, Comte de Lauzun (1632–1723) commander of French forces at the battle of the Boyne. Charles Chaumont, Marquis de St. Ruhe or Ruth, commander of French forces at the battle of Aughrim, where he was killed. Tyrconnell died on 14 August 1691.
12. i.e. give them an effective blow.

GEORGE FARQUHAR
(1677–**1691**?–1707)

George Farquhar, the son of a clergyman, was born in Derry. It has often been asserted that he fought on the Williamite side at the battle of the Boyne; if so, he would have been only thirteen years old at the time. The Pindaric ode which follows, though it was not published until later, must have been written in the early 1690s, when Farquhar was no more than fourteen or fifteen. The purpose of the ode was not to reflect any experiences Farquhar might have had at the Boyne but (like Swift's 'Ode to the King' which follows this poem), to bring his name to the attention of the Williamite leaders after the event, perhaps so that he could be considered for a post in the Williamite administration in Ireland. However, Farquhar received no recognition for this ode, and proceeded to Trinity College Dublin in 1694. He left the university without taking a degree and went to London where he became a successful playwright and actor. He later rejoined the army, but died at the age of thirty in 1707.

The ode, with its extravagant similes and abstruse references, makes an interesting companion piece to Swift's almost contemporary 'Ode to the King', the next poem in this anthology.

On the Death of General *Schomberg* kill'd at the *Boyn*
A Pindarick

I

What dismal Damp has overspread the War?
The Victor grieves more than the Conquer'd fears;
The Streams of Blood are lost in Floods of Tears,
And *Victory* with dropping Wings comes flagging from afar.

II

The *Brittish* Lyon roars
Along the fatal Shores;
The *Hibernian* Harp in mournful Strains,
Mixt with the *Eccho* of the Floud, complains,
Round whose reflecting Banks[1] the grieving Voice,
Shakes with a trembling Noise,
As if afraid to tell
How the great, Martial, Godlike *Schomberg* fell.

10

III

Gods! How he stood,
All terrible in Bloud,

1. i.e. the shores of Ireland.

539

Stopping the Torrent of his Foes, and Current of the Floud.
He, *Moses* like, with Sword, instead of Wand,
This redder Sea of Gore cou'd strait command;
But not like *Moses*, to secure his Flight,
But spight of Waves and Tides to meet, and fight.[2]

IV

The labouring Guns oppos'd his Passage o're   20
With Throws tormented[3] on the Shore,
Of which delivered, they start back, and roar,
As frighted at the Monster which they bore.
The furious Offspring[4] swath'd in curling Smoak
And wrapt in Bands of Fire,
Hot with it's Parent's sulphurous Ire,
And wing'd with Death, flies hissing to the Stroak.

V

Like some great rugged *Tower*,
The Ancient Seat of Power,
Bending with Age it's venerable Halls,   30
With old and craggy Wrinkles on its Walls,
The Neighbours Terrour whilst it stands, and Ruin when it falls,
Thus mighty *Schomberg* fell –
Spreading with Ruines o're the Ground,
With Desolation all around,
Crushing with destructive Weight
The Foes that undermin'd his Seat;
Whilst *Victory*, that always sped,
With towring Pinions o're his Army's Head,
Making his Banner still her Lure,   40
Like *Marius*'s Vultures,[5] to make Conquest sure,
Seeing the spacious Downfal so bemoan'd,
Perch'd on the Ruines, clapt her Wings, and groan'd.

2. Exodus 14 tells how Moses lifted up his rod and stretched it over the Red Sea which divided so that the Children of Israel could escape the Egyptians by passing through it on dry land. The sea then returned and killed the pursuing Egyptians.
3. A 'torment' was an 'engine of war worked by torsion for hurling stone, darts etc.' (*OED*). The line seems to mean: 'with shells or bombs fired onto the shore' – with 'shore' being an echo of the previous image of the Jews and the Red Sea.
4. i.e. the shell or bomb fired by the torment.
5. Gaius Marius (157–86 BC) reformed the Roman army and ordained (according to Pliny) that Roman legions should bear only the figure of an eagle (not a vulture) on the standard born before them into battle. The standard not only 'lured' soldiers to keep close to it in the fray, but encouraged them to victory.

VI

Thus *Israel's* Heroe[6] 'twixt the Pillars sat,
The *Ne plus Ultra* of his Fate
These *Columns* which upheld his Name,
Much longer by their Fall,
Than those erected strong and tall,
The standing Limits of *Alcides's*[7] Fame.
He sat depriv'd of Sight,   50
Like a black rowling Cloud involv'd in Night,
Conceiving *Thunder* in it's swelling Womb,
Big with surprising Fate, and introduced the rushing Doom:
No Flash the sudden Bolt must here disclose,
The Lightning of his Eyes extinguish'd by his Foes,
His Foes, industrious in their juggling Fate;
Him slavishly enchain'd we see,
To what must set him free,
And them, his cheated Keepers, captivate.
He shook his Chains with such a Noise,   60
The trembling Rout,
Amidst their Joys,
Gaz'd all about,
And heard the real *Sampson* in the Voice:
They saw him too, 'twas *Sampson* all,
Who by his thundring Fall
Gave the loud dread Alarm,
Dragging a Train of Vengeance by each *Gyant* Arm.
Their chilling fears did such amazement Frame,
They seem'd all stiff and dead before the Ruin came.   70
The Ruine! only such unto his Foes;
From thence his glorious Monument arose;
But *Time*'s corroding Teeth in spight of Stone
Has eat thro' all, and even the very Ruine's gone:[8]
But *Schomberg*'s Monument shall ne'er decay;
The gliding *Boyn*
Time never can disjoyn,

---

6. *Original note*: 'Sampson'. This stanza is based on the story of Samson, blinded and in chains but still possessed of amazing strength, who destroyed a house crowded with mocking Philistines by pulling down the columns which supported the roof; see Judges 13. *Ne plus ultra* (Latin for 'not further beyond') = the highest thing which can be attained.
7. Another name for Hercules, linked to his reputation for strength.
8. i.e. the very ruin of the house destroyed by Samson.

Nor on it's Flouds impose his Laws;
They slide, untoucht, from his devouring Jaws,
And always running, yet must ever stay. 80

VII

Hark! how the *Trumpets* hollow Clangours sound;
The Army has receiv'd an universal Wound;
The Death of *Schomberg* hung
On every faultring Tongue,
Whilst pallid Grief did place
A sympathizing Death in every Soldiers Face.
But hold, ye mighty Chiefs,
Suspend your needless Griefs,
And let victorious Joy your Arms adorn;
The mighty Warriour's *Ghost* 90
Upon the *Stygian* Coast[9]
Your Sorrows, more than his own Fate, do's mourn;
He scorns to be lamented so,
Moving in stately *Triumph* to the Shades below.
Behold the Sprites[10] that lately felt the Blow
Of his commanding warlike Arm,
They shivering all start wide,[11] and even more fleeting[12] grow,
As if the powerful Hand
That cou'd their Grossest[13] Shapes alive command,
Had Power to dissolve their Airy Form. 100

VIII

Then let not funeral Plaints his Trophies wrong;
Let Spoils and Pageants march his Hearse along,
And shout his *Conclamatum*[14] in Triumphal Song.
All baleful *Cypress* must be here deny'd,
But Lawrel Wreaths fix in their blooming Pride:
For as he conquer'd living, so he conquering dy'd.

9. The banks of the Styx, the river over which the dead must cross to enter the underworld in classical mythology.
10. spirits, i.e. the 'shades' of those killed at the battle of the Boyne, now about to enter the underworld.
11. awake suddenly.
12. transitory, unstable.
13. most solid; the bulk of living bodies is compared with the insubstantial, airy nature of spirits.
14. acclamation, but also the calling of a dead person in lamentation. In the ancient world, laurel wreaths were a sign of victory and cypress wreaths a sign of mourning.

JONATHAN SWIFT
(1667–**1691**–1745)

This peculiar ode, with its outlandish images, is very much a product of its time, as comparison with Farquhar's almost contemporary 'On the Death of General *Schomberg* Kill'd at the *Boyn*' makes clear. Until recently, it was thought that the first appearance of Swift's ode was in the fourth volume of *Miscellanies* issued by the Dublin printer Samuel Fairbrother in 1735. However, James Woolley has recently unearthed a unique copy of the Dublin 1691 printing of this poem, which establishes the text of the first edition and, since it states that the poem was 'presented to His Majesty [William III] upon His departure from Ireland', opens several interesting possibilities for biographers of Swift. See James Woolley, 'The Ode to the King' in ed. H.J. Real et al, *Reading Swift: Papers from the Fourth Münster Symposium on Jonathan Swift* (Munich, 2003), pp. 265–83.

After a youth spent mostly in Ireland and graduation from Trinity College Dublin, Swift had become attached to the household of Sir William Temple at Moor Park in Surrey in 1689. On Temple's recommendation, he returned to Ireland in 1690 with the Williamite entourage, hoping to be able to find some paid employment. This poem was probably his first major literary effort, and its purpose was, primarily, to bring him to the notice of William and his advisers. The irregular or 'Cowleyan' ode – consisting of stanzas of varying lengths with rhyming lines of varying lengths, loosely based on the type of ode written by the classical Greek poet Pindar – was made fashionable by Abraham Cowley (1618–67) in the 1650s. It was widely used for formal and funerary verse throughout the second half of the seventeenth century and, in using the form here, Swift was writing in what was at the time a 'fashionable' form. However, as the text which follows makes clear, the Pindaric ode was not a form which suited Swift's poetic temperament.

ODE to the KING
On His IRISH Expedition,

And the Success of his Arms in general,
Presented to His Majesty upon His departure from Ireland

I

Sure there's some Wondrous Joy in *Doing Good*;
Immortal Joy, that suffers no Allay[1] from Fears,
Nor dreads the tyranny of years,
By none but its Possessors to be understood:
Else where's the Gain in being *Great?*
Kings would indeed be Victims of the State;
What can the Poet's humble Praise?
What can the Poet's humble Bays?

---

1. abatement, lessening.

(We Poets oft our Bays allow,
Transplanted[2] to the Hero's Brow)   10
Add to the Victor's Happiness?
What do the Scepter, Crown and Ball,[3]
(Rattles for Infant Royalty to play withal)
But serve t'adorn the Baby-dress
Of one poor Coronation-day,
To make the Pageant gay:
A three hours Scene of empty Pride,
And then the Toys are thrown aside.

II

But the Delight of *Doing Good*
Is fix't like Fate among the Stars,   20
And Deifi'd in Verse;
'Tis the best Gemm in Royalty,
The Great Distinguisher of Blood,
Parent of Valour and of Fame,
Which makes a Godhead of a Name,
And is Cotemporary to Eternity.
This made the Ancient Romans to afford
To *Valour* and to *Virtue* the *same Word*:[4]
To shew the Paths of both must be together trod,
Before the *Hero* can commence *a God*.   30

III

These are the ways
By which our happy Prince[5] carves out his Bays;
Thus he has fix'd His Name
First, in the mighty List of Fame,
And thus He did the Airy Goddess[6] Court,
He sought Her out in Fight,
And like a Bold Romantick Knight[7]
Rescu'd Her from the Giant's Fort:
The Tyrant Death lay crouching down,
Waiting for Orders at his feet,   40

---

2. i.e. to be transplanted.
3. orb.
4. The Latin word *virtus* means both 'valour' and 'virtue'.
5. i.e. William III.
6. According to Ovid (*Metamorphoses* XII, 390), the classical goddess Fame lived on the top of a mountain.
7. a knight in a romance.

Spoil'd of his Leaden Crown;
He trampled on this Haughty *Bajazet*,[8]
Made him his Footstool in the War,
And a Grim Slave to wait on his Triumphal Car.

IV

And now I in the Spirit see
(The Spirit of Exalted Poetry)
I see the *Fatal Fight*[9] begin;
And, lo! where a Destroying Angel stands,
(By all but Heaven and Me unseen,)
With Lightning in his eyes, and Thunder in his hands;   50
In vain (said He) *does* Utmost Thule[10] *boast*
No poys'nous Herb[11] *will in Her breed,*
Or no Infectious Weed,
When she sends forth such a malignant Birth,
When Man himself's the Vermin *of Her Earth;*
When Treason *there* in person *seems to stand,*
And Rebel *is the* growth *and* manufacture *of the Land.*[12]
He spake, and a dark Cloud flung o're his light,
And hid him from Poetick sight,
And (I believe) began himself the Fight   60
For strait I saw the Field maintain'd,
And what I us'd to laugh at in *Romance*,
And thought too great ev'n for effects of Chance,
The Battel almost by *Great William*'s single Valour gain'd;
The *Angel* (doubtless) kept th' Eternal gate,
And stood 'twixt Him and every Fate;
And all those flying deaths that aim'd him from the field,
(Th' impartial deaths[13] which come
Like Love, wrapt up in fire;
And like that too, make every breast their home)   70
Broke on his everlasting shield.

---

8. Bajazet, ruler of the Ottoman empire (1389–1402); he appears as a character in Marlowe's *Tamburlaine the Great* (1590) and was later to be used by Nicholas Rowe as a representation of Louis XIV in his tragedy *Tamerlane* (1702).
9. i.e. the battle of the Boyne.
10. i.e. Ireland. Thule was the name given in the ancient world to the most northerly regions known to man.
11. In later editions (Fairbrother 1735 and later) the word 'Herb' is replaced with 'Beast'.
12. The classic English view – that Ireland produced nothing but rebels.
13. i.e. bullets (flying deaths) not aimed at anyone in particular.

How vainly (Sir) did Your Fond *Enemy*[14] try
Upon *a rubbish heap of broken Laws*[15]
To climb at Victory
Without the Footing of a *Cause*;
His Lawrel now must only be a Cypress Wreath,[16]
And His best Victory a Noble Death;
His scrap of Life is but a heap of miseries,
The remnant of a falling snuff,[17]
Which hardly wants another puff,   80
And needs must *stink* when e're it dies;
Whilst at Your Victorious Light
All lesser ones expire,
Consume,[18] and perish from our sight,
Just as the Sun puts out a Fire;
And every foolish *Flye* that dares to aim
To buzz about the mighty flame;
The wretched insects singe their wings, and fall,
And humbly at the bottom[19] crawl.

VI

The *Giddy Brittish Populace*,   90
The Usurping Robbers of our Peace[20]
Who guard Her[21] like a Prey;
And keep Her for a sacrifice,
And must be sung, like *Argus*,[22] into *ease*
Before this *Milk-white Heifer* can be stole away,
Our *Mighty Prince*[23] has charm'd its many hundred Eyes;

14. foolish enemy (i.e. James II); in Fairbrother 1735 and later editions, stanzas V and VI are printed in reverse order.
15. This is not an impartial comment. Which were 'valid' laws and which were 'broken' ones depended only on the outcome of the battle.
16. See note to l. 103 of the previous poem.
17. 'Snuff' is the wick of a candle after it is burned; if it is not regularly trimmed and cut short, it can smoke and (line 81) stink as the candle sputters out.
18. burn away.
19. i.e. of the candle-stick (?).
20. Fairbrother 1735 and later editions read: 'That *Tyrant-Guard* on *Peace*, / Who watch Her like a Prey;'
21. i.e. peace.
22. In Ovid's *Metamorphoses*, Argus was a jealous husband who had a hundred eyes to see if his wife, Io, was deceiving him; Mercury charmed him to sleep with the music of his lyre and then killed him.
23. Fairbrother 1735 and later editions have 'Our *Prince*'.

Has lull'd the Monster in a deep
And (I hope) an Eternal Sleep,
And has at last redeem'd the *Mighty Prize*.
The *Scots* themselves, that Discontented Brood,   100
Who always loudest for *Religion* bawl,[24]
(*As those still do wh'have none at all*)
Who claim so many Titles to be *Jews*,
(But, surely such whom God did never for *his people* chuse)
Still murmuring in *their wilderness* for *food*,[25]
Who pine us[26] like a *Chronical Disease*;
And one would think 'twere past Omnipotence to please;
Your Presence all their *Native Stubborness* controuls,
And for a while unbends their contradicting souls:
As in old Fabulous Hell,   110
When some Patrician God would visit the Immortal Jayl
The very brightness of His face
Suspended every Horror of the place,
The Gyants under *Ætna* ceas'd to groan,[27]
And *Sisiphus* lay sleeping on his stone.[28]
Thus has our Prince compleated every Victory,
And glad *Ierne*[29] now may see
Her Sister Isles are *conquered* too as well as She.

VII

That *Restless Tyrant*[30] who of late
Is grown so Impudently Great,   120
That Tennis-ball of Fate;
This Gilded Meteor which flyes
As if it meant to touch the Skies;
For all its boasted height,
For all its Plagiary[31] Light,
Took its first Growth and Birth
From the worst excrements of earth;[32]

24. Swift had a life-long dislike and mistrust of the Scots.
25. The reference is to Exodus 26 and 27.
26. torment us.
27. In classical mythology, Jupiter crushed the giant Typhœus under Mount Etna, in Sicily.
28. Sisyphus, king of Corinth, had to roll a huge stone up a hill, though it always rolled back again.
29. Ireland.
30. Louis XIV.
31. stolen.
32. It was widely rumoured that Louis XIV was born out of wedlock.

Stay but a little while and down again 'twill come,
And end as it began, in Vapour, Stink, and Scumm.
    Or has he, like some fearful Star, appear'd,   130
Long dreaded for his *Bloody Tail* and Fiery Beard,
    Transcending Nature's Ordinary Laws,
    Sent by Just Heaven to threaten Earth
    With War, and Pestilence, and Dearth,
Of which it is at once the Prophet and the Cause?[33]
    Howe're it be, the Pride of *France*
    Has finish'd its short Race of Chance,
    And all Her boasted Influences[34] are
    Rapt in the *Vortex*[35] of the Brittish Star;
Her *Tyrant* too an unexpected wound shall feel   140
    In the last wretched remnant of his days;
Our Prince has hit Him, like *Achilles*, in the *Heel*,[36]
    The poys'nous Dart has made him reel,
    Giddy he grows, and down is hurl'd,
    And as a Moral to his *Vile Disease*,[37]
Falls sick in the *Posteriors* of the World.

---

33. Comets were still popularly considered portents of evil.
34. The stars were thought to influence men through an invisible, ethereal fluid which flowed from them to the earth.
35. The whirlpool-like effect in the solar system in which objects are attracted into the swirling rotation of another object – in this case, a star, or rather the 'Brittish' star of King William.
36. Achilles was invulnerable to injury except in the heel.
37. Fairbrother 1735 and later editions have: 'And as a Mortal to his *true Disease*, / Falls sick in the *Posteriors* of the World.' The reference is (rather surprisingly) to an anal ulcer.

ELLIS WALKER
(*fl*.1677–99, **1692**)

Although it is sometimes asserted that Ellis Walker was from Derry and that he was the son of the famous defender of that city, Rev. George Walker (1618–90), the evidence points to his being originally from England. The records of Trinity College Dublin show that he entered the university in 1677 at the age of sixteen, and was the son of an Oswald Walker of Yorkshire. He became a scholar in 1679 and was awarded his BA in 1682. Walker probably remained at Trinity studying for an MA throughout the 1680s but fled Ireland 'for shelter' in 1689 at the onset of 'the present Troubles' and went for refuge to the house of his uncle Samuel Walker in York.[1] There he worked on his verse translation of Epictetus, the publication of which was licensed in August 1691. Between that date and its actual publication in 1692, Walker made friends in both Oxford and Cambridge; his translation contains commendatory verses by poets resident in both universities in September and October 1691. Since he is styled MA on the title page, Walker probably received that degree *ad eundem* from one of the English universities (as did Swift).

After his translation of Epictetus came out (and it was a commercial success, running to three printings in London and one in Dublin before 1700), Walker returned to Ireland where he is recorded as headmaster of the Drogheda Grammar School from 1694 to 1701. His pupils at Drogheda performed 'a Latin play out of Terence' in 1698.[2] Nothing further is known of him, though his translation was widely used until superseded by that of Elizabeth Carter in 1758. Epictetus (*b. c.* AD 60), the author of the *Enchiridion* (or 'Handbook') and the most famous of the Stoic philosophers, was widely respected for the high sense of morality he recommended to his followers as well as for the practical nature of his advice. In the passage which follows, Epictetus is concerned with how a man should regard his possessions.

from: *Epicteti Enchiridion* made English

XI

Be not transported with too great a sense
Of any outward object's excellence.
For should the pamper'd Courser[3] which you feed,
Of swiftest heels, and of the noblest breed,
Through sense of vigour, strength of Oats and Hay,
From his full Manger turn his head, and say,
'Am I not beautiful, and sleek, and gay?'
'Twere to be born in him, the speech might suit[4]
The Parts and Education of the Brute:
But when with too much pleasure you admire   10

---

1. *Epicteti Enchiridion Made English ... by Ellis Walker* (London, 1695), 'To my Honoured Unkle Mr Samuel Walker of York', sig A2.
2. W.B. Stanford, *Ireland and the Classical Tradition* (Dublin, 1976), p. 24.
3. A racing horse or a stallion.
4. i.e. if the sentiment had been born in the horse himself, this remark might suit ...

Your Horses worth, and vainly boasts his fire,
And tire us out with endless idle prate
About his crest, his colour, or his gate,⁵
'Tis plain, you think his Owner fortunate.
You're proud he's your's, and vainly claim as due
What to the Beast belongs, and not to you.
Too plainly is your selfish folly shewn,
Adding your Horses vertues to your own.
Well then, perhaps, you'l ask what's yours of these
Dear outward things, that seem so much to please?   20
Why nothing but the use: if then you choose
What's truly good, what is not so refuse,⁶
If the well chosen good you rightly use,
As Nature's light informs you, then alone
You may rejoyce in something of your own.

XII

As in a Voyage, when you at Anchor ride,
You go on shore fresh water to provide,
And perhaps gather what you chance to find,
Shelfish or Roots of palatable kind;
Yet still you ought to fix your greatest care   30
Upon your ship, upon your business there:
Still thoughtful, lest perhaps the Master call,
Which if he do, then you must part with all
Those darling trifles, that retard your hast,⁷
Lest, bound like Sheep, you by constraint are cast
Into the Hold. Thus in your course of Life,
Suppose you a lovely Son, or beauteous Wife,
Instead of those forementioned trinkets find,
And bless your Stars, and think your fortune kind;
Yet, still be ready, if the Master call,   40
To cast your burden down, and part with all.
Forsake the beauteous Wife, and lovely Son,
Run to your Ship; without reluctance run;
Nor look behind, but if grown old and gray,
Keep always near your Ship, and never stay
To stoop for worthless lumber on the way.

---

5. gate = gait. crest = the ridge of the neck of a horse.
6. i.e. refuse what is not truly good.
7. hast = haste.

Short is the time allow'd to make your coast,
Which must not for such tast[e]less joy be lost.
Your reverend play-things will but ill appear, ⎫
Besides you'l find they'l cost you very dear: ⎬   50
'Tis well if Age can it's own weakness bear.   ⎭
Unman'd with dotage, when you're call'd upon,
How will you drag the tiresome luggage on?
With Tears and Sighs, much folly you'l betray,
And crawle with pain undecently away.

XIII

Wish not that things not in your power may run
As you would have them, wish them as they're done,
Wish them just as they are, just as you see;
Thus shall you never disappointed be.
You seem some sharp disease to undergo,   60
Alas 'tis vain to wish it were not so:
'Tis but the Bodies pain, a surly ill,
Which may impede the body, not the will:
For all the Actions of th'obsequious mind,
Are in your power, to your own choice confin'd.
Thus strength and vigour may your nerves forsake ⎫
And lameness from your Feet all motion take,   ⎬
But can in thee not the least hindrance make.   ⎭
'Tis in thy power to resolve not to go,
Judge if it be an hinderance or no,   70
You on your Feet may an embargo lay,[8]
As well as chance or natural decay.
Consider thus, in all things else you'l find
Nothing can hinder, or confine the mind;
In spite of every accident, you're free;
Those hinder something else, but cannot thee.

---

8. i.e. you can forbid your feet to venture forth.

ANONYMOUS
(c.1692)

Mock-litanies were a popular satiric form in the late seventeenth and early eighteenth centuries. The one which follows fits the circumstances of young 'gentlemen at large' – Englishmen of gentle birth who were attached to the Dublin court, but were not assigned specific duties. The text is modelled on two similar poems in *A Third Collection of the Newest and Most Ingenious Poems . . . against Popery and Tyranny . . .* (London, 1689), a popular songbook of the day. This poem, like others from the same period, shows that life in the court in Dublin Castle resumed its wonted way early in the 1690s.

The Gentlemen at Larges Litany

From leaving fair England, that goodly old seat,
And comeing to Ireland to serve for our meat
In hopes of being made all verry great
                        Libera nos Domine.[1]

From staying at Dublin till we have spent
Our ready Coine all in following the s[c]ent
Of what we could never catch – Preferment,
                        Libera nos Domine.

From liveing upon one short meale a day
Without bit of breakfast our stomach to stay,   10
Or supper to drive the long night away,
                        Libera nos Domine.

From dwelling where folks to prayers doe fall
Thrice for each meal, and where they doe call
To the Chappell oftner than to the Hall,
                        Libera nos Domine.

From drinking and whoreing and staying [out late]
And being locked out of the Castle gate,
And returning again to the bonny Kate,
                        Libera nos Domine.   20

1. Preserve us, O Lord.

From lying all night with a Lowsie whore,
And bringing away from her the Glandore[2]
And running with Monsieur Roboe on the score,[3]
                    Libera nos Domine.

From quarrelling amongst our selves, without
Some body to hold us from goeing out,
From handling cold iron[4] being stout,
                    Libera nos Domine.

From playing Cards in the room above stairs
And loosing our mony with a bon[5] air,   30
To gratifie the Lady thats not verry fair,
                    Libera nos Domine.

From the Stewards rebukes and Controllers[6] smile,
Bestow'd with a grace enough to beguile
One out of his way a Yorkshire mile,[7]
                    Libera nos Domine.

From turning Tory[8] or Highwaymen
And leaveing our bones near Stephens green,[9]
Now let us all say I pray God Amen,
                    Libera nos Domine.   40

This Litany would have been Longer but that the Author knew those
Gentlemens Constitutions, can as ill endure long as frequent Prayers.

---

2. An infectious disease, in horses and men, marked by unpleasant swellings and discharge.
3. 'on the score' = on credit; Monsieur Roboe is untraced.
4. a sword; stout = brave. The stanza means: Lord deliver us from quarrelling among ourselves when there's no one to stop us going out, in a fit of bravado, and drawing our swords . . .
5. good (affected use of French?)
6. The court official in charge of accounts.
7. More than a mile – since Yorkshiremen had a reputation for trickery.
8. outlaw.
9. The main gallows in Dublin were situated near St Stephen's Green.

CHARLES HOPKINS
(*c* . 1 6 6 4 – **1 6 9 4** – *c* . 1 7 0 0)

Charles Hopkins was the eldest son of the learned bishop of Derry, Ezekiel Hopkins (1634–90). He was educated at Trinity College Dublin and at Cambridge. He is said to have distressed his father greatly by joining 'the rebels' in Ireland in 1689; his father died in 1690 and Charles subsequently went to London where he made a considerable reputation for himself as poet and playwright, becoming friendly with many of the writers active in the city. Dryden once described Hopkins as 'a poet who writes good verses without knowing how, or why; I mean he writes naturally well, without art or learning, or good sence'.[1] Certainly, Hopkins wrote easily and fluently, and it seems clear that he would have become a considerable figure on the English literary landscape but for his fondness for strong drink and, according to Giles Jacob in his *Poetical Register* (London, 1719–20), 'a too passionate fondness for the fair sex' which, apparently, was the cause of his death. As Jacob put it, Hopkins died 'a martyr to the cause'.

The passage that follows, which is from Hopkins's witty verse paraphrase of scenes from Ovid, provides him with an opportunity to express his admiration for female beauty; Perseus comes upon the fair Andromeda, chained naked to a rock. The passage ends with a couplet expressing a rather sardonic view of 'desire'.

from: The Story of Perseus and Andromeda,
in Imitation of part of that in the Fourth Book of OVID's Metamorphoses[2]

<blockquote>

Propitious chance led Perseus once to view
The fairest Piece that ever Nature drew;
Chain'd on a rocky Shore, the Virgin stood,
Naked, and whiter than the foaming Flood;
Whom, as he cours'd the confines of the Sky, ⎫
Amaz'd he saw; and kept his wond'ring Eye ⎬
So fix'd, he had almost forgot to fly. ⎭
Had not the Winds dispers'd her flowing Hair,
And held it waving in the liquid Air;
Or had not streams of Tears apace roll'd down   10
Her lovely Cheeks, he would have thought her Stone.
Strait he precipitates his hasty flight,
Impatient to attain a nearer sight.
Now, all at once, he feels the raging Fires,
Sees all the Maid, and all he sees, admires.
With awe and wonder, mixt with love and fear,
He stands as motionless as shame made her.

</blockquote>

1. Dryden to Mrs Steward, 7 November [1699], quoted in James Anderson Winn, *John Dryden and his World* (New Haven, 1987), p. 16.
2. Ovid *Metamorphoses* 4, fable 16.

Urg'd on at last, but still by slow degrees,
Loth to offend, he draws³ to what he sees.
Oh! Why, he cryes, most matchless Fair-one, why   20
Are you thus us'd? Can you be doom'd to dye?
Have you done any Guilt? that guilt relate.
How can such Beauty merit such a Fate?
I am thy Champion, and espouse thy Cause;
In thy defence, the Thund'rer's Off-spring draws.⁴
Say, if thou'rt rescued by the Son of Jove,
Say, for thy Life, wilt thou return thy Love?
The bashful Virgin no return affords,
But sends ten thousand Sighs, instead of Words:
With Grief, redoubled with her Shame, she mourns,   30
She weeps, he joys, she blushes, and he burns.
In Chains extended at her length she lay,
While he with transport took a full survey.
Fain would her Hands her conscious Blushes hide,
But that the Fetters which they wore, deny'd.
What could she do? all that she could, she did;
For drown'd in floods of Tears, her Eyes she hid.
Much urg'd to speak, she turn'd her bashful look
Far as she could aside, and trembling spoke:
My mother, conscious of her Beauty, strove   40
(Alas! too conscious) with the Wife of Jove:
Who by a cruel and unjust Decree,
To punish her, takes this revenge on me.⁵
Here am I doom'd a dreadful Monster's prey,
Who now, now, now is issuing from the Sea.
Haste, generous Youth, our common Foe subdue;
And if you save my Life, I live for you.
Thus spoke the Maid, half dying with her fears,
When lo! the Monster from the Sea appears.
The dauntless Heröe mounts his flying Horse,   50
And o'er the Waves directs his airy course.
Let him, alone, his Victory pursue;
For dreadful War has nothing here to do.

---

3. draws near.
4. Perseus was a son of Jupiter, the majestic king of the gods, one of whose attributes was to be god of thunder and thunderbolts.
5. Cassiope, Andromeda's mother, had boasted that she was more beautiful than Juno, queen of the gods and wife of Jupiter. As a punishment for this rashness, the land of Andromeda's father was flooded and it was decreed that Andromeda herself was to be chained to a rock to be the victim of a ravening sea-monster.

This short Account will Love-sick Swains suffice;
He slew his Foe, and strait receiv'd his Prize.
Thrice happy Youth, too fortunately blest;
Who only came, and conquer'd, and possest.
None of the pangs of Love your bliss annoy'd;
You but beheld, admir'd, and so enjoy'd.

Desire

All other Lovers longer Toils sustain: 60
Desires, Hopes, Jealousies, an endless Train.

NAHUM TATE
(1652–**1694**–1715)

Nahum Tate, the son of Faithfull Teate (see pp. 321–45), was born in Dublin. He changed his name from Teate to Tate when he was at Trinity College, from which he graduated in 1672. He later moved to London where he knew all the literary figures of the day and collaborated with Dryden on the second part of *Absalom and Achitiophel* (1682). Tate made a living as a poet and dramatist and became poet laureate in 1692. Though he has often been ridiculed for adapting *King Lear* to give the play a happy ending, Tate was by no means as much of a dunce as later literary critics (most of whom have never bothered to read his work) have made him out to be. His better verse deserves to be reprinted.

The first poem below, which was presumably commissioned by the fellows of Trinity College Dublin, celebrates the centenary of the foundation of the university where Tate himself was educated. It stands up well to comparison with similar poems by Dryden. The second and third poems come from an interesting and underrated collection of Tate's poems, *Miscellanea Sacra, or Poems on Divine & Moral Subjects Vol I*, in which Tate explores various religious themes with sensitivity and skill.[1]

An Ode upon the 9th of January 1694,

the Anniversary of the University of Dublin being One Hundred Years since
their Foundation by Queen Elizabeth,
compos'd by Mr N. Tate, sett to Musick by Mr Henry Purcell

> Great Parent,[2] Hail! All hail to Thee,
> Who hast from last Distress surviv'd
> To see this Joyfull Year arriv'd
> The Muses Second Jubilee.[3]
>
> Another Century Commencing
> No decay in Thee can trace;
> Time with his own Laws dispencing
> Adds new Charms to Ev'ry Grace.
>
> After War's Alarms repeated,
> And a circling Age compleated,   10
> Vig'rous Offspring Thou dost raise;
> Such as to Hierne's[4] Praise

---

1. Tate had intended to produce an annual volume of sacred verse, but this 1696 volume was the only one which appeared.
2. i.e. the university itself. The 'last distress' of the second line is the war of 1689–91.
3. A jubilee is the fiftieth anniversary of an event.
4. Probably a variant of Ierne's, i.e. of Ireland. Ierne (also written 'Iren' and 'Ierna'), a poetic name for Ireland, came originally from Ir. *Éirinn*.

Shall Liffee make as proud a Name
As that of Isis or of Cam.[5]

Awfull Matron,[6] take thy Seat
To Celebrate this Festival;
The Learn'd Assembly well to treat
Blest Eliza's[7] Days Recall.
The Wonder of her Reign recount
In Songs that Mortal Strains surmount,   20
Songs for Phœbus to Repeat.

'Twas she who did at first inspire
And strung the mute Hybernian Lyre;
Whose deathless Memory
(The Song of Harmony)
Still animates the Vocal Quire.

Succeeding Princes next recite![8]
With never dying Verse requite[9]
These Favours they did Show'r;
'Tis that alone can do 'em right   30
To save 'em from Oblivion's Night
Is only in the Muses Power.

But chiefly recommend to Fame
Great William's and Maria's Name,
For surely no Hybernian Muse
(Who's Isle to Him her Freedom owes)
Can Her Restorer's Praise refuse,
While Boyne or Shannon flows.

Thy Royall Patrons sung, repair
To Illustrious Ormond's Tomb:[10]   40
Living He made thee his care;
Give him next Thy Cæsars Room.

5. The river Thames is known as the Isis as it passes through Oxford and the river Cam
flows through Cambridge.
6. aweful = inspiring respect or admiration. The 'Great Parent' of line 1 is now addressed
respectfully as 'Matron'.
7. Queen Elizabeth I.
8. This line is addressed to the poet himself.
9. repay.
10. The first Duke of Ormond had been made chancellor of the university at the Restoration.
Following his death in 1688, the university was now paying court to his grandson, the
new duke (lines 43–7).

Then a Second Ormond's Story
Let Astonisht Fame recite.
But She'll wrong the Hero's Glory
Till with equal Flame she write
To that which he displays in Fight.

Chorus

With Themes like these, Ye Sons of Art,
Treat this Auspicious Day,
To bribe the Minutes, e'ere they part,   50
Those Blessings to bequeath that may
Long, long remain your Kindness to Repay.

The Blessed *Virgin*'s Expostulation,

when our *Saviour* at Twelve Years of Age had withdrawn himself[1]

Tell me, some pitying Angel, quickly say
Where does my Soul's sweet Darling stray,
In Tygers, or more cruel *Herod*'s Way?[2]
O! rather let his tender Foot-steps press
  Unguarded through the Wilderness,
  Where milder Salvages[3] resort;
The Desart's safer than a Tyrant's Court;
  Why, fairest Object of my Love,
Why dost Thou from my longing Eyes remove?
Was it a waking Dream that did foretel   10
Thy wondrous Birth? No Vision from Above?
Where's *Gabriel* now that visited my Cell?[4]
I call – He comes not – flatt'ring Hopes, Farewel.
  Me *Judah*'s Daughters once Caress'd,[5]
  Call'd me of Mother's the most Blest;
Now (fatal Change!) of Mothers, most distress'd!
  How shall my Soul its Motions guide,

---

1. For the story of the twelve-year-old Jesus staying behind in Jerusalem after Mary and Joseph had set out for Nazareth, see Luke 2. 42–50.
2. For the story of Herod's slaughter of the innocents, see Matthew 2. 16.
3. savages.
4. For the story of the annunciation by the angel Gabriel to the Virgin Mary, see Luke 1. 26–38.
5. i.e. I was once honoured by the Jewish women . . .

How shall I stem the various Tide,
Whilst Faith and Doubt my lab'ring Thoughts divide?
For whilst of thy Dear Sight I am beguil'd,   20
I Trust the God! – But oh! I fear the *Child*.

Upon the sight of an anatomy[1]

1

Nay, start not at that *Skeleton*,
'Tis your own Picture which you shun;
Alive it did resemble Thee,
And thou, when dead, like that shalt be:
Converse with it, and you will say,
You cannot better spend the Day;
You little think how you'll admire
The Language of those *Bones* and *Wire*.

2

The *Tongue* is gone, but yet each Joint
Reads Lectures, and can speak to th'Point.   10
When all your Moralists are read,
You'll find no Tutors like the Dead.

3

If in Truth's Paths those *Feet* have trod,
'Tis all one whether bare or shod:
If us'd to travel to the Door
Of the Afflicted Sick and Poor,
Though to the Dance they were estrang'd,
And ne'er their own rude Motion chang'd;[2]
Those Feet, now wing'd, may upwards fly,
And tread the Palace of the Sky.   20

4

Those *Hands*, if ne'er with Murther stain'd,
Nor fill'd with Wealth unjustly gain'd,
Nor greedily at Honours graspt,
But to the *Poor-Man*'s Cry unclaspt;

1. A human skeleton with the bones wired together – such as was used for anatomy classes
in a medical school.
2. i.e. even if they were never accustomed to dancing, and never moved elegantly . . .

560

It matters not, if in the Myne
They delv'd, or did with Rubies shine.

5

Here grew the *Lips*, and in that Place,
Where now appears a vacant space,
Was fix'd the *Tongue*, an Organ, still
Employ'd extreamly well or ill;   30
I know not if it cou'd retort,
If vers'd i'th' Language of the Court;
But this I safely can aver,
That if it was no Flatterer;
If it traduc'd no Man's Repute,[3]
But, where it cou'd not Praise, was Mute:
If no false Promises it made,
If it sung Anthems, if it Pray'd,
'Twas a blest *Tongue*, and will prevail
When Wit and Eloquence shall fail.   40

6

If Wise as *Socrates*, that *Skull*,
Had ever been, 'tis now as dull
As *Mydas*'s;[4] or if its Wit
To that of *Mydas* did submit
'Tis now as full of Plot and Skill,
As is the Head of *Matchiavel*:
Proud Laurels once might shade that Brow,
Where not so much as Hair grows now.

7

Prime Instances of Nature's Skill,
The *Eyes*, did once those Hollows fill: 50
Were they quick-sighted, sparkling, clear,
(As those of Hawks and Eagles are,)
Or say they did with Moisture swim,
And were distorted, blear'd, and dim;
Yet if they were from Envy free,
Nor lov'd to gaze on Vanity;

---

3. i.e. if it did not slander anyone . . .
4. Socrates was famed for his wisdom, Midas for his stupid request that everything he
touched might be turned to gold, and Machiavelli for his political scheming.

If none with scorn they did behold,
With no lascivious Glances rowl'd:
Those Eyes, more bright and piercing grown,
Shall view the Great Creator's Throne;   60
They shall behold th' *Invisible*,
And on Eternal Glories dwell.

8

See! not the least Remains appear
To shew where Nature plac'd the *Ear*!
Who knows if it were Musical,
Or could not judge of Sounds at all?
Yet if it were to Council bent,[5]
To Caution and Reproof attent,
When the shrill Trump shall rouse the Dead,
And others hear their Sentence read;   70
That *Ear* shall with these Sounds be blest,
Well done, and *Enter into Rest*.

5. i.e. if it listened to wise advice . . .

ANONYMOUS
(1698)

The eccentric London bookseller John Dunton (1659–1733) left two accounts of his visit to Ireland in 1698. One, entitled *The Dublin Scuffle*, was published in 1699 but the other, which Dunton called 'Teague Land, or A Merry Ramble to the Wild Irish', remained partially in manuscript until recently.[1] In this second text, Dunton gave an account of the speech of the people of Fingal[2] which he described as 'a sort of jargon speech, peculiar to themselves'. As a sample, he recorded the words of an assonantal lamentation made by a mother over the grave of her son who had been, apparently, 'a greate fischer & huntsman'. The strange, half-remembered, barely coherent verse is an interesting survival – the remnants of a seventeenth-century keen or lament in Hiberno-English.

Ribeen a Roon

Ribeen a Roon, Ribbeen mourneen,[3]
thoo ware good for loand, stroand and mounteen,
for rig a tool and roast a whiteen,
reddy tha taakle,
gather tha baarnacks,
drink a grote at nauny hapennys.

1. The most recent edition of *The Dublin Scuffle* is ed. Andrew Carpenter (Dublin: Four Courts Press, 2000); an edition of *Teague Land*, with the same editor and publisher, appeared in 2003.
2. For a discussion of the significance of seventeenth-century Fingallian and references, see the headnote to the 'Purgatorium Hibernicum', pp. 411–7, and Alan Bliss, *Spoken English in Ireland 1600–1740* (Dublin, 1979), pp. 27–8.
3. A rough and tentative paraphrase of this text would be: Robin my love, Robin my dear, you were good on the land, on the strand, on the mountain: for making things, for roasting a whiting; get your things together, gather the bannocks (soda bread loaves), have a drink at Nanny Halfpenny's (an ale house?).

JOSEPH AICKIN
(*fl*. **1699**)

Little is known of Joseph Aickin or Aicken. In *The Poets of Ireland* (Dublin, 1912) (p. 6), D.J. O'Donoghue suggests (without giving any evidence) that he was 'a medical man', but it seems more likely that he was the master of a private school near Essex Bridge in Dublin. This Joseph Aickin wrote *An English Grammar* (Dublin, 1694), *The Mysteries of the Counterfeiting of the Coin of the Realm, fully Detected* (Dublin, 1696) and *An Address to the Magistrates, Clergy and Learned Gentlemen of the City* (Dublin, 1698); in this last book, Aickin recommended his own 'rational and expeditious' method of teaching languages. Almost certainly it was this schoolmaster who set himself the task of celebrating, in simple verse, one of the great events of his time – from a protestant point of view – the siege of Derry in 1689.

This poem was published twice, once in Dublin in 1699 and again in *Derriana*, a collection of documents relating to the siege of Derry edited and published by the Derry bookseller, George Douglas, in 1790. Douglas described the text as being 'from the pen of an illiterate but amusing poet' and stated that it had been copied from 'a homely manuscript said to be found in a gentleman's library at Armagh about thirty years ago'; if this is true, it seems that Aickin's poem had been circulating in manuscript as well as in printed form throughout the eighteenth century. The poem, which is of epic bulk and which appeared in the 1790 printing under the grandiose title of 'Londeriados', is divided into four substantial books, each of which contains between fourteen and twenty-two sections. This is a serious poem (one which a nineteenth-century editor described as pervaded by 'an air of truth')[1] and not – though the reader might sometimes be forgiven for suspecting that it was – a parody.

from: Londerias, or A Narrative of the Siege of London-Derry

from: Book I, section 1

I sing the Men, who *Derry* did restore
To the condition as it was before.
They taught the French that Cities might withstand
Their Storms and Bombs under a good command.
Why should Heroick Deeds in Silence be,
Since Poets are of the Fraternity?
Assist me Muse! Whilst I the Siege do sing
Into my *mem'ry* all the matter bring.
Inspire my tongue! When I the causes tell
How the *dire War*, how this *fam'd Siege* befell,   10
How the *Town stands*, how the proud foe advance,
How they're repuls'd, and who great fame enhanse . . .

---

1. John Graham, *A History of the Siege of Londonderry* . . . (Dublin, 1829), p. 105.

from: Book III, section 6,

General Hamilton takes Colonel Murray's father prisoner and sends him to move
his son to quit the town

Now Hamilton[1] had got intelligence
That Murray's[2] father liv'd not far from hence,
Aged above eighty years; for him he sent
And brought the old man captive to his tent.
Pray, said the sage, your business with me tell.
Your son, said he, Sir, ventures to rebel
Against his king.[3] He holds that city out,
Him you may counsel better without doubt.
On yon tall gibbet reaching to the sky,
Your bones shall hang if he does not comply, }   10
And yield the town, – go tell him so, or die;
And here you must your sacred honour pawn,
To bring the answer e'er to-morrow's dawn.
Old Murray answers, he will not disown
His due allegiance to King William's throne;
But, as I must obey you, I will try[4]
If with such cruel terms he will comply:
I found my son, Sir, from his early youth
A paragon of steadiness and truth;
A scion worthy of his ancient line, }   20
Respecting law both human and divine,
Form'd, mind and body, for some great design. }

In haste the vet'ran's guarded to the town,[5]
And meets his son then cover'd with renown,
As on the street the youthful hero stood,
His steel still reeking with the Frenchman's blood.[6]
Son, said the sire, this Bible in my hand
Must give due sanction to my last command;
Swear now, I charge you, that in town or field
To James's power you will never yield; 30

1. Richard Hamilton, commander of the Jacobite forces besieging Derry.
2. Colonel Adam Murray, a Scottish settler and one of the two 'amateurs' defending Derry,
   the other being the militant Church of Ireland clergyman, George Walker.
3. i.e. against James II – at the time of the siege, an ex-king from the protestant point of
   view, the rightful king of Ireland from a catholic point of view.
4. put to the test.
5. i.e. to Derry.
6. General Maumont. See note to line 57.

That for our faith you'll spend your latest[7] breath,
And choose with me sweet liberty or death.
Father, says Murray, as he dropp'd a tear,
That voice I love so dearly wounds my ear,
Imputing treachery or slavish fear.
The deeds I do, I cannot stoop to tell,
But all my gallant friends here know me well;
Why then, through dangers, have you made such speed,
To give me counsel which I do not need?
Adam, said he, I never could have meant   40
Such imputation, but I have been sent
By Hamilton, to tell you I must die,
Unless with his commands you now comply,
Give up the town or from its ramparts fly.
But now my long lov'd son, my darling child,
Who on my knee so oft have sweetly smil'd,
Cheering a father's and a mother's heart,
I've made my last request, and I depart;
Hamilcar's task was mine, and now I go
To meet like Regulus an angry foe,[8]   50
He may command my instant execution,
But Murray's blood will seal the revolution.
In such a case I could die ten times o'er,
And count it gain to bleed at eighty-four.
Stay, said a voice, stay Murray, with your son,
His race of glory is but just begun;
Maumont's career arrested by his steel,[9]
His sword's sharp edge this Hamilton shall feel.
Ill fare the man whose cunning could engage
In such a task your venerable age.   60
No, no, said he, not thus is glory won,
My word is pledg'd, a soldier's course I run,
Take honour from me and my life is done.
Then peals of thund'ring cannon rend the air,
And warlike trumpets from the city bear
Defiance to the foe's detested arts,
As for the camp the veteran departs.

7. last.
8. Hamilcar Barca (*d*. 229 BC) is said to have made his nine-year-old son Hannibal swear an oath never to be a friend to Rome. Regulus (*d*. 251 BC) met an excruciating death at the hands of the bloodthirsty Carthaginians.
9. In a skirmish during a sortie from the city, Colonel Murray had personally killed the French army general who commanded the cavalry, General Maumont.

The gallant Hamilton[10] forgives the fraud,
If such it was, and ventures to applaud
Without reserve, a more than Spartan deed,   70
Which well became the Murrays of the Tweed;[11]
From Philiphaugh this hero's fathers came,
A line long known in rolls of Scottish fame.
No longer forc'd through hostile bands to roam,
A guard of honour guides the old man home;
Where he was suffer'd undisturb'd to dwell,
Though by his son the Irish army fell.

10. This poem, unlike most accounts of the siege, regularly praises the Jacobite forces for
    gallantry.
11. The Murray family came from Philiphaugh on the banks of the Tweed, on the border
    between Scotland and England.

JOHN HOPKINS
(*c*.1675–**1699**–*c*.1700)

John Hopkins was the younger brother of Charles Hopkins and second son of Ezekiel Hopkins, the bishop of Derry. Little is known of his life, though he maintained, in the introduction to his translation of Ovid, that he and his brother were in different kingdoms when they were, independently, translating Ovid during the 1690s; since Charles was in England at this time, the remark suggests that John was in Ireland, and the records of Trinity College Dublin do show a John Hopkins in residence there in the 1690s.

Hopkins was a prolific poet and, like his brother, seems to have favoured subjects of a mildly salacious nature. (Both brothers, for instance, translated with considerable relish Ovid's story about the ivory statue of a naked virgin which comes to life in Pygmalion's arms. John's translation is the second of his poems printed below.) Though he afterwards seems to have regretted undertaking the task, Hopkins also turned three books of Milton's *Paradise Lost* into rhyming verse, an early example, if a peculiar one, of enthusiastic admiration for the poem. In the passage that follows – from near the beginning of Hopkins's very free 'imitation' of the temptation scene in Book IX – Adam has just finished his exhortation to Eve to resist temptation; with his permission, she sets off to wander in the garden.

from: The Fall of Man
being an Imitation of the 9th Book of Milton's Paradise Lost

> . . . With thy Permission, then, says *Eve*, I Go,
> Doubt not, my Love, I shall resist the Foe.
> Then softly drawing from his Hand Her own,
> She smiling Leaves him, so Secure she's Grown.
> Quickly, he crys, ah! quickly, *Eve*, return,
> With great concern I shall thy absence Mourn.
> Well pleas'd, She Promises to see Him Soon,
> And in the Bow'r to wait¹ him, e'er 'tis noon.
> With ardent Looks he views Her on Her way,
> Delighted much, but Wishing more Her stay.   10
> Still does he Gaze while the Dear form he sees,
> But soon No more perceives Her, hid by Trees.
> Lost, and Unblest, he must Alas! no more
> Behold a guiltless Bride all Charming as before.
> Thro' fragrant shades of Roses does She go,
> The Roses now in deeper Blushes Glow.
> Superfluous leafs, which grew Deform'd, She crops
> And slender Stalks of drooping Flow'rs she Props.

1. await.

But of her self, (fair Flow'r!) She takes no care,
Tho' storms are nigh, and She from Succour far. 20
At length the Serpent ranges thro' the Fields,
He comes, He tempts, and as He temp[t]s, She yields.[2]
And now Perswaded by a long Dispute,
She boldly Tastes of the forbidden Fruit.
Rashly she Eats, then to Debate she fell,
Nor knows she yet has she done Ill or well.
Now she resolves, what e'er the Danger be,
Adam shall Taste the Fruit, made Guilty too as she.
In words, like these, she does her Fondness show, ⎫
Adam shall share with me in Bliss, or Woe, ⎬ 30
To Life, or Death, we shall together Go. ⎭
Should he not Taste, and I by Doom not Live,
He would be wedded to another Eve.
Then would his Second Fair my Guilt approve,
'Tis death to think he should a Second Love.
So saying, strait to *Adam* she repairs,
Contriving reasons to Subdue his fears.
Impatient grown, He had a Garland made,
Of choicest Flow'rs to Crown her lovely Head
Whom lost he finds, and in Amazement stands, 40
To see a bough held Brandish'd in her Hands.
Eve with excuses tells what She has done, ⎫
Urges that he should Equall Hazzard run, ⎬
And bids him not such Proffer'd Blessings shun. ⎭
With brisk, alluring Air her Spouse she Warms,
Alas! what Woman wants Prevailing Charms!
She guilds her Crime with Thousand reasons giv'n,
And Damns him with large promises of Heav'n.[3]
Flushing she Spoke, her Cheeks such Blushes wore,
As the fair Fruit which in her Hands she bore. 50
Adam awhile, Astonish'd, and amaz'd,
Stood speechless by, and on the apples Gaz'd.
From his slack Hand the falling Garland shed
The faded Roses, which now lost their Red.
At length, all Trembling, silence thus he breaks,
And to his Fatall, but Lov'd *Eve*, he speaks.

---

2. This passage, in which the poet condenses the magnificence of the great climax of
Milton's poem into a single line of banality and bathos, has drawn particular scorn from
critics.
3. i.e. her alluring pictures of heaven tempt him to do something which damns him.

How late,[4] vain fair one, Didst thou idly Boast,
Yet art thou Lost, yes, on a Suddain, Lost.
Defac'd, deflowr'd, robb'd of thy Blooming store,
Just like those Roses faded ——   60
Never! ah, never to be Beauteous more.
Doom'd, and Condemn'd, Death must thy Sentence be,
Death be it then to both ——
For thou hast Curst they self, and with thee, Me . . .

Pigmalion and his Iv'ry Statue[1]

In a lewd Age *Pigmalion* spent his times,
Women debauch'd themselves with Monstrous Crimes.
No vertuous Virgin in his Days was known,
All the Chast, Female Modesty was gone,
Therefore a long, long time he lived alone.
An Iv'ry Statue now at last he Frames,
And from the Maid he form'd, he gathers Flames.
In every part, the Virgin did excel,
Which Limb was best, the Artist could not tell,
It was all Lovely, and he Lov'd it well.   10
Curious her shape, so sparkling were her Eyes,
Such quick, such glancing brightness in them lies,
They would have roll'd, but that her shame denies.
Such lively strokes he to the Maid did give,
That, tho' a Statue, she appear'd to live.
The Artist's self that she had Life believ'd,[2]
And fondly was by his own Art deceiv'd.
He felt her flesh, for he suppos'd it such,
And fear'd to hurt her, with too rude a touch.
Often he Kiss'd her, while he madly burn'd,   20
And fancy'd now, how she the like return'd.
He Wooes her, Sighs, and her fair Hands does press,
And tells his Passion in a Dear Address,
Till at the last, his Notions grew so vain,
That he believ'd she sigh'd, and prest again.
He sends her presents, Gums, and precious Stones,
The choicest Bracelets, and bright, glitt'ring Zones,[3]

---

4. lately.

---

1. Imitated from Ovid *Metamorphoses* 10, fable 9.
2. i.e. the artist himself believed that she was alive.
3. girdles, belts.

Soft singing Birds, which flutt'ring all around,
With pretty Notes, rais'd a delightful sound;
Rich Pendants, Rings and Gums he sends the Maid,   30
With Wreaths of flow'rs adorns her Lovely Head,
And lays her now, soft on a Downy Bed.
In Pompous[4] robes he does his Idol dress;
Much so she Charms, but not, when naked, less.
Now was the time, when *Venus*[5] kept her Feast,
And Love-sick Youths to her fam'd Temple prest.
There, to be offer'd,[6] Snowy Heifers come,
And the rich altar smoaks with pretious gum.
Among the Crowd, the hopeless Lover goes,
Tho' no Just-reason, or Pretence he knows.   40
Before the Altar now he, weeping, stands,
And Bows, with Off'rings in his careful hands.
Fiercer, and Fiercer his desires grow there,
And rise more furious, from his wild Despair.
A long, long time, does he forbear to pray,
And still his doubts deny'd his Speech the way,
Yet wish'd (altho' he knew not why) to stay.
At last, his fearful silence now he Breaks,
And thus, but still in mighty fear, he speaks.
If you, Love's Beauteous, Charming Goddess, have,   50
And can bestow what Mortal suppliants Crave,
Shew now your Pow'r, on me your Blessings shed,
Grant me the Wife I wish, one like, he said,
(But durst not say, grant me) my *Iv'ry Maid*.
This done, he thrice percieves the flashing Fires,
The happy Omen blest his fond desires,
And to the Maid he now with doubtful Joy retires.
With wond'rous longings he in haste returns,
And now, more fiercely than before, he burns,
Closely he claspt her to his panting breast,   60
And felt her softer still, the more he prest.
Now, all at once, with a surprize of bliss,
He finds her Lips grow warmer with his Kiss,
He finds them Moist, and Soft, and Red as his.
Her throbbing Breasts heav'd now, and gently swell'd,
While he with wonder the Lov'd sight beheld.

4. magnificent.
5. i.e. the goddess Venus, patroness of love.
6. i.e. offered as sacrifices.

The Maid, now Fairer, in his Arms he bore,
Tho' fram'd of Iv'ry, polish'd fine before.
Let none henceforth of wish'd success Despair,[7]
When Statues soften'd by our Passions are.   70
The happy Artist, now perceives his Wife
With beating Pulses, and with perfect Life,
And, for a while, as Motionless he stood,
As she had done, e'er she grew Flesh and Blood.
Her Lover first she with the light descrys,[8]
For which she Checks,[9] and turns her bashful Eyes,   }
While in her blooming Face her Beauteous Blushes rise. }

7. i.e. in future, let no one despair of gaining what he wishes . . .
8. sees.
9. i.e. because of which she stops short.

THREE POEMS FROM DUBLIN CASTLE
(1699–1700)

JONATHAN SWIFT

After spending the early 1690s as secretary to the distinguished, retired diplomat Sir William Temple, at Moor Park in Surrey, Swift was ordained into the Church of Ireland in 1695 and appointed prebendary of Kilroot in the north of Ireland. He only remained at Kilroot for about fourteen months, however, and in May 1696 returned to the civilised delights of Moor Park and the company of Temple's household. Here he remained until Temple's death early in 1699, shortly after which he was appointed chaplain to Charles Berkeley, Earl Berkeley (1649–1710), one of the newly appointed lords justices of Ireland whose wife, Frances, was a niece of Sir William Temple. Swift travelled to Dublin with the Berkeley entourage in August 1699 and lived in Dublin Castle from that time until Berkeley was recalled in April 1701.

The poem below was written immediately after Swift's arrival in Dublin in 1699. Before coming to Ireland, he had thought that he would hold the position of Berkeley's secretary as well as that of his chaplain and was very annoyed to discover that a young man named Arthur Bushe had outmanoeuvred him and taken the secretaryship himself. The poem gives an idea of the air of political intrigue which existed in Dublin Castle at the time and shows how absurd such intrigue can be made to look.

The Discovery

When wise Lord B[erkeley] first came here,
We Irish Folks expected wonders,
Nor thought to find so great a Peer
E'er a week pas't committing Blunders:

Till on a Day cut out by Fate,
When Folks came thick to make their Court,
Out slipp't a Mystery of State
To give the Town and Country Sport.

Now Enter Bush with new State-Airs,
His Lordship's premier Ministre,[1]   10
And who in all profound Affairs
Is held as needfull as His Glyster;[2]

1. This French term was soon to be replaced by the English 'prime minister'.
2. clyster; an enema or the instrument used to inject it.

With Head reclining on his Shoulder,
He deals, and Hears mysterious Chat ;
While every ignorant Beholder
Asks of his Neighbor; Who is that?

With this, He putt up to[3] My L[or]d;
The Courtiers kept their Distance due,
He twitcht his sleeve, and stole a word,
Then to a Corner both withdrew.   20

Imagine now My L[or]d and Bush
Whisp'ring in Junto[4] most profound,
Like good King Phys and good King Ush,[5]
While all the rest stood gaping round.

At length, a spark[6] not too well bred
Of forward Face, and Ear acute,
Advanc't on tiptoe, lean'd his Head
To overheare the grand Dispute

To learn what Northern Kings design,
Or from Whitehall some new Express,   30
Papists disarm'd, or Fall of Coin,[7]
For sure (thought He) it can't be less.

My Lord, said Bush, a Friend and I
Disguis'd in two old thredbare Coats
Ere Mornings dawn, stole out to spy
How Markets went for Hey and Oats

With that he draws two Handfulls out,
The one was Oats, the other Hay,
Putts This to's Excellency's Snout,
And begs, He would the other weigh.   40

3. Meaning uncertain: (probably) = addressed himself to.
4. A word (adapted from the Spanish *junta*, together) used at the time to mean the group of Whig lords in power in England.
5. Phiz and Ush, two usurping kings in the Duke of Buckingham's play *The Rehearsal* (1672), a parody of contemporary tragedy (see note 10).
6. smart young man.
7. devaluation of coinage.

My Lord seems pleas'd, but still directs
By all means to bring down the Rates,[8]
Then with a Congee circumflex[9]
Bush smiling round on all, retreats.

Our Listner stood a while confus'd,
But gath'ring spirits, wisely ran for't,
Enrag'd to see the World abus'd
By two such whisp'ring Kings of Branford.[10]

ANONYMOUS

This verse, listing of the attributes of some of the courtiers attached to Dublin Castle in 1699–1700, is a variant of a poem bearing the same title but concerned with members of London society which is found in 'The Whimsical Medley', Lord Newtown Butler's manuscript collection of contemporary verse.[1] Miscellanies of the age frequently contain such poems, sometimes offering 'Advice to a Painter' who, if he wanted to draw a belle or a beau, should make a composite figure taking *such* a quality from *such* a person. In this case, the composite picture is of an Irish court beau.

The Picture of a Beau

As he that would a perfect Picture make,
From differing faces must the features take,
So he that would the Character designe
Of a staunch Coxcomb[2] must together join
The differing Qualetys of each Fop and Beau
That all the Play, the Strand and Castle show.[3]
He that like Blessington[4] writes, like Villiers[5] walks,

---

8. This probably means the price Lord Berkeley would pay for hay and straw.

9. congee = a low, ceremonial bow; circumflex = sharply bent (in this case at the waist).

10. i.e. Phiz and Ush, the two kings in Buckingham's burlesque *Rehearsal*; see note to line 23 above. The two characters, who are always whispering to each other, are kings of Brentford. In changing 'Brentford' (a town in Essex) to 'Branford', Swift is probably playing on the fact that 'bran' is made of the husks of oats (among other types of corn).

1. TCD MS. 879, I, f.36.

2. A conceited, showy person.

3. Three fashionable places in Dublin, the playhouse, the strand at Dollymount and Dublin Castle.

4. Murrough Boyle, Viscount Blessington (*d.* 1718), one of the lords justices of Ireland in 1696 during the illness of the lord deputy, Henry Lord Capell.

5. Probably not Edward Villiers, Viscount Villiers and Earl of Jersey (1656–1711) who, though one of the lords justices from May 1697 to April 1699, does not seem to have come to Ireland at the time. More likely the reference is to the young George Villiers, Viscount Grandison, still a minor at the time of this poem.

Dances like Lanesborough[6] and like Upton[7] talks,
Whose sprightly parts like Orrarys[8] does shine
Like Kingland's[9] wise, like Chidly Coot[10] is fine,   10
Like Lord Moore[11] witty, like Jack Eyrs[12] Brave,
Generous like Hill,[13] like Captain Southwell[14] grave,
Like Coll. Cunningham[15] learnd speeches makes,
Reasons like Tennison,[16] like Purcil[17] speakes,
Like Worth[18] a Patriot, like Allen Brodrick[19] Just,
And like the Speaker, faithfull to his Trust;
Ikerin[20] like belles letters understands,
Well bred like Bligh,[21] well shap'd like Sir J. Sands,[22]

6. Sir James Lane, second Viscount Lanesborough (d. 1724). He was the son of George Lane, secretary for many years to the first Duke of Ormond.

7. Anthony Upton (d. 1718 by his own hand), Justice of the Common Pleas from 1702.

8. Lionel, third Earl of Orrery (d. 1703), grandson of Roger Boyle, the dramatist and poet.

9. Nicholas Barnewall, third Viscount Kingsland (d. 1725). He had been a captain in the Earl of Limerick's dragoons, fighting on the Jacobite side in the wars of 1689–91, and was outlawed as a result. However, he was reinstated under the Treaty of Limerick and swore the necessary oath of allegiance in 1692.

10. Chidley Coote (fl. 1660–1700) was a grandson of the famous Sir Charles Coote the elder, remembered for his ferocity in the war following the rising of 1641. Chidley Coote was attainted by the Jacobite parliament which sat in Dublin in 1689 by the name of Chidley-Coote Fitz-Chidley Esq. He had risen to the rank of general in the Irish army by the time he was mentioned in this poem.

11. Henry Hamilton Moore, third Earl of Drogheda (c. 1650–1714), one of the lords justices of Ireland 1701–2.

12. Possibly John Eyre (d.1709) of Eyrescourt Castle, County Galway, grandson of a Colonel John Eyre who had come to Ireland with Cromwell.

13. Unidentified.

14. Probably Edward Southwell (1671–1730), son of Sir Robert Southwell, secretary of state for Ireland from 1690 until his death in 1702. Edward was to succeed his father in the position.

15. Possibly the army officer recorded as Captain Alexander Coningham of Letterkenny in 1696 when his son entered Trinity College Dublin.

16. Probably Henry Tenison, son of the Bishop of Killala, who entered Trinity College Dublin in 1682. He became member of parliament for Monaghan in 1695 and was also one of the Commissioners of the Revenue.

17. Perhaps John Percivall, MP for Granard, County Longford.

18. William Worth (c.1646–1721) a distinguished Irish lawyer, eldest son of the Bishop of Killaloe.

19. Alan Broderick, Viscount Middleton (c.1656–1728), later attorney general for Ireland, speaker of the Irish House of Commons and a friend of Jonathan Swift.

20. Pierce Butler, fourth Viscount Ikerrin (d.1710), a member of the Ormond clan. Lord Blessington was his father-in-law.

21. The Right Hon. Thomas Bligh (1654–1710), a member of the privy council.

22. Probably William Sandes, of Carrigafoyle, County Kerry, MP in the parliament of 1697.

Like Hartstong[23] loves, and like old Jerom[24] looks
Dresses like Welch,[25] and like Sir Thomas F——cks. . . .[26]   20

JONATHAN SWIFT

Although Swift wrote 'Mrs Harris's Petition', as the following poem is usually known, early in 1701, it circulated in manuscript for nearly ten years before appearing in an unauthorised printing in London. From the moment of its composition, it has been appreciated as one of the most vibrant and spontaneous poems of the age; Ireland has not produced a finer comic presentation of character in verse.

Swift's wry glimpse into ordinary life in Dublin Castle comes at a key moment in Irish life, when a long period of turmoil, war and social disruption was giving way to one of relative calm; 'Mrs Harris's Petition' is, in fact, the last poem of note to come from the turbulent world of Stuart Ireland and, as such, is the last poem in this book.

TO THEIR EXCELLENCIES THE *Lords Justices of* IRELAND

The Humble Petition of Frances Harris,[1]
Who must Starve, and Die a Maid if it miscarries

THAT I went to warm my self in Lady *Betty*'s[2] Chamber, because I
    was cold,
And I had in a Purse, seven Pounds, four Shillings and six Pence,
    besides Farthings, in Money, and Gold;
So because I had been buying things for my *Lady* last Night,
I was resolved to tell[3] my Money, to see if it was right:

23. Probably Standish Hartstonge, MP for Kilkenny. He was a son of Sir Standish Hartstonge, a baron of the Irish Exchequer; his brother was John Hartstonge (1654–1717) who had been consecrated Bishop of Ossory in 1693.
24. Unidentified.
25. Possibly the Rev. Philip Walsh, chaplain to Michael Boyle, Archbishop of Armagh (who served as lord justice and was well known at court).
26. The transcript from which this text was taken suggests that there are two further (presumably indecent) lines in the poem, but since the volume from which the transcript was made is not now available, it is impossible to verify this. The parallel poem in the 'Whimsical Medley' is rounded off with a couplet likely to have been replicated in the Dublin poem, with appropriate amendments: 'May in the Mall, Hide Park, and Boxes shew / And lawfully commence an Accomplish'd Beau.'

1. The title is a parody of the formula used in real-life petitions to the lords justices or similar authorities. The justices at the time were the Earl of Berkeley and Henri de Massue de Ruvigny, Earl of Galway (1648–1720), a Huguenot general who had fought at the battle of the Boyne. Frances Harris was one of Lady Berkeley's gentlewomen.
2. Lady Betty Berkeley (later Germain) (1680–1769), daughter of Lord Berkeley and a long-standing friend of Swift.
3. count.

Now you must know, because my Trunk has a very bad Lock,

Therefore all the Money, I have, which, *God* knows, is a very small
    Stock,

I keep in a Pocket[4] ty'd about my Middle, next my Smock.

So when I went to put up my Purse, as *God* would have it,
    my Smock was unript,

And, instead of putting it into my Pocket, down it slipt:

Then the Bell rung, and I went down to put my *Lady* to Bed,   10

And, *God* knows, I thought my Money was as safe as
    my Maidenhead.

So when I came up again, I found my Pocket feel very light,

But when I search'd, and miss'd my Purse, *Lord!* I thought I should
    have sunk outright:

Lord! Madam, says *Mary*,[5] how d'ye do? Indeed, says I, never worse;

But pray, *Mary*, can you tell what I have done with my Purse!

Lord help me, said *Mary*, I never stirr'd out of this Place!

Nay, said I, I had it in Lady *Betty*'s Chamber, that's a plain Case.

So *Mary* got me to Bed, and cover'd me up warm,

However, she stole away my Garters, that I might do my self no Harm:

So I tumbl'd and toss'd all Night, as you may very well think,   20

But hardly ever set my Eyes together, or slept a Wink.

So I was a-dream'd, methought, that we went and search'd the
    Folks round,

And in a Corner of Mrs. *Dukes*'s[6] Box, ty'd in a Rag, the Money
    was found.

So next Morning we told *Whittle*,[7] and he fell a Swearing;

Then my Dame *Wadgar*[8] came, and she, you know, is thick of Hearing;

Dame, said I, as loud as I could bawl, do you know what a Loss
    I have had?

Nay, said she, my Lord *Collway*'s[9] Folks are all very sad,

For my Lord *Dromedary*[10] comes a *Tuesday* without fail;

Pugh! said I, but that's not the Business that I ail.

---

4. A small bag or pouch for money, normally carried outside the garments at this time.
5. another servant.
6. *Original note*: 'One of the footmen's wives'.
7. The Earl of Berkeley's valet.
8. The old, deaf housekeeper.
9. i.e. Lord Galway's. Part of the comic effect is in these mispronounced names.
10. *Original note*: 'Drogheda, who with the primate were to succeed the two Earls'. Henry
    Hamilton Moore, Earl of Drogheda (*c*. 1650–1714) and Narcissus Marsh (1638–1713),
    Archbishop of Armagh, succeeded as lord justices in 1701. The point of the line is that
    Lord Galway's retainers would have to leave Dublin Castle when they were replaced by
    those of the incoming lord lieutenant.

Says *Cary*,[11] says he, I have been a Servant this Five and
    Twenty Years, come Spring,   30
And in all the Places I liv'd, I never heard of such a Thing.
Yes, says the *Steward*,[12] I remember when I was at my Lady
    Shrewsbury's,[13]
Such a thing as this happen'd, just about the time of *Goosberries*.
So I went to the Party[14] suspected, and I found her full of Grief;
(Now you must know, of all Things in the World, I hate a Thief.)
However, I was resolv'd to bring the Discourse slily about,
Mrs. *Dukes*, said I, here's an ugly Accident has happen'd out;
'Tis not that I value the Money three Skips of a Louse,[15]
But the Thing I stand upon, is the Credit of the House;
'Tis true, seven Pound, four Shillings, and six Pence, makes a
    great Hole in my Wages,   40
Besides, as they say, Service is no Inheritance in these Ages.
Now, Mrs. *Dukes*, you know, and every Body under-stands,
That tho' 'tis hard to judge, yet Money can't go without Hands.
The *Devil* take me, said she, (blessing her self,) if I ever saw't!
So she roar'd like a *Bedlam*,[16] as tho' I had call'd her all to naught;
So you know, what could I say to her any more,
I e'en left her, and came away as wise as I was before.
Well: But then they would have had me gone to the Cunning Man;[17]
No, said I, 'tis the same Thing, the *Chaplain*[18] will be here anon.
So the *Chaplain* came in; now the Servants say, he is my
    Sweet-heart,   50
Because he's always in my Chamber, and I always take his Part;
So, as the *Devil* would have it, before I was aware, out I blunder'd,
Parson, said I, can you cast a *Nativity*,[19] when a Body's plunder'd?
(Now you must know, he hates to be call'd *Parson*, like the *Devil*.)

---

11. Clerk of the kitchen.
12. A man named Ferris whom Swift called (in the *Journal to Stella*, 21 December, 1710) 'that beast'.
13. As Pat Rogers points out (*Jonathan Swift: The Complete Poems* (Harmondsworth, 1983), p. 623), this was the dowager Lady Shrewsbury, widow of the fourteenth earl; she died in 1702.
14. person (a mock-legal term).
15. This is a proverbial saying, like others in the next few lines; Swift returned to the use of proverbs as an indication of character in *Polite Conversation*, *A Dialogue in Hybernian Stile* and elsewhere.
16. An inmate of the lunatic asylum in London, the 'Bethlehem'; 'to call someone all to naught' meant to abuse them.
17. The fortune-teller or someone able to discover the location of stolen goods.
18. i.e. Swift himself, chaplain to Lord Berkeley at the time.
19. draw up a prediction, cast a horoscope – like a fortune-teller.

Truly, says he, Mrs. *Nab*, it might become you to be more civil:
If your Money be gone, as a Learned *Divine*[20] says, d' ye see,
You are no *Text* for my Handling, so take that from me:
I was never taken for a *Conjurer* before, I'd have you to know.
Lord, said I, don't be angry, I'm sure I never thought you so;
You know, I honour the Cloth,[21] I design to be a *Parson*'s Wife,   60
I never took one in *Your Coat* for a *Conjurer* in all my Life.
With that, he twisted his Girdle at me like a Rope, as who should say,
Now you may go hang your self for me, and so went away.
Well; I thought I should have swoon'd; *Lord*, said I, what shall I do?
I have lost my *Money*, and shall lose my *True-Love* too.
Then my *Lord*[22] call'd me; *Harry*, said my *Lord,* don't cry,
I'll give something towards thy Loss; and says my *Lady*, so will I.
Oh but, said I, what if after all the Chaplain won't *come to*?[23]
For that, he said, (an't please your *Excellencies*) I must Petition You.

The Premises tenderly consider'd,[24] I desire your *Excellencies*
   Protection,   70
And that I may have a Share in next *Sunday's* Collection:[25]
And over and above, that I may have your *Excellencies* Letter,
With an Order for the *Chaplain* aforesaid; or instead of Him, a Better:[26]
And then your poor *Petitioner*, both Night and Day,
Or the *Chaplain*, (for 'tis his *Trade*) as in Duty bound, shall ever *Pray*.[27]

20. Some critics have identified this phrase as a reference to Dr John Bolton, who had just received a preferment (the Deanery of Derry) which Swift thought should have come to him.
21. A reference to the distinctive clothes worn by the clergy. 'Your coat' in the next line also refers to clerical garb. 'design' = intend.
22. Lord Berkeley. There is a note against the word '*Harry*': 'A Cant Word of my Lord and Lady to Mrs Harris'; i.e. their usual familiar name for her. cf. Swift's calling her 'Mrs Nab' (line 55).
23. to come around, after being in a bad mood, to a pleasant one.
24. This last paragraph, like the poem's title, is a parody of the language of official petitions.
25. The offertory money collected at the church service.
26. An 'order' could be a written instruction to someone (in this case the chaplain) to pay money to someone else (in this case Mrs Harris).
27. 1) pray to God, as does a clergyman; 2) pray to a senior official, as does a petitioner.

Sources of the texts

Part I   1485–1603: Verse from Tudor Ireland

John Butler, Mayor of Waterford, and others
from: 'Letter sent by the Mayor and Inhabitants of the Citie of Waterford . . .', *Popular Songs of Ireland* ed. Thomas Crofton Croker (London, 1886 ed.), pp. 300–12; transcribed by Crofton Croker from papers now in the Public Record Office, London (SP.63/214), The Hanmer Papers.

Henry Howard, Earl of Surrey
'Description and praise of his love Geraldine', *Songes and Sonettes, written by the ryght honorable Lord Henry Haward late Earle of Surrey . . .* (London, 1557) (Tottel's *Miscellany*), sig. B1r.

Andrew Boorde
'I am an Iryshe man . . .', verse on Ireland from the third chapter of *The First Boke of the Introduction of Knowledge* (London, 1547?), Early English Text Society edition by F.J. Furnivall (London, 1870), pp. 131–2.

John Bale
'Edward 6 *vel* Quene Marie', BL Add. MS. 20091, p. 227.

Francis Edderman(?)
from: 'A most pithi and plesant history whear in is the destrouction of Troye gethered togethere of all the chyfeste autores turned unto Englyshe myttere' (Dublin, *c.* 1558), transcription from ESTC on-line.

Song on Queen Elizabeth, 'The Annals of Ireland: the Reign of Queen Elizabeth' in *The Works of Sir James Ware* (Dublin, 1705), pp. 4–5 of the 'Annals'.

Barnaby Rich
'An Epitaph upon the death of Syr William Drury . . .', *The Paradise of Dainty Devices* (1576–1606), ed. Hyder Edward Rollins (Cambridge, Mass., 1927), pp. 121–4.

Thomas Churchyard
(i) from: 'Of the unquietnesse of Ireland', *The Miserie of Flanders, Calamatie of Fraunce, Misfortune of Portugall, Unquietnesse of Ireland, Troubles of Scotlande: and the Blessed State of England* (London, 1579), sigs D1r–D2r. (ii) from: 'A Letter sent from the Noble Earl of Ormond's house at Kilkennie to the Honourable Sir Henry Sidney . . . at Cork . . .', *A Generall Rehearsall of Warres, called Churchyards Choice* (London, 1579), sigs 2D4v–2E1r.

'You and I will go to Fingall', *Calendar of State Papers Ireland 1601–1603* (London, 1912), pp. 681–2.

John Derricke
from: *The Image of Irelande, with a discoverie of Woodkarne, wherein is more lively expressed, the Nature, and qualities of the said wilde Irishe Woodkarne . . .* ed. John Small (Edinburgh, 1883).

Lord Gerald Fitzgerald, Lord Baron of Offaly
'A Penitent Sonnet', Richard Stanyhurst, *Translation of the first Four Books of the Æneis of P. Publius Maro . . .* ed. Edward Arber, The English Scholar's Library of Old and Modern Texts Series (London, 1895), pp. 153–4.

581

Richard Stanihurst

(i) 'Upon thee death of thee right honourable and his moste deere coosen, thee lord Baron of Louth', Richard Stanyhurst, *Translation of the first Four Books of the Æneis of P. Publius Maro*... ed. Edward Arber, The English Scholar's Library of Old and Modern Texts Series (London, 1895), pp. 150–1. (ii) 'An Endevored Description of his Mystresse', ed. Arber, pp. 141–2. (iii) from: *Thee First Four Bookes of Virgil, his Aeneis translated intoo English heroical verse*, ed. Arber, pp. 20–1.

Barnaby Googe

['A good horse described'], Conrad Heresbach, *Foure Bookes of Husbandrie* ... (translated by Googe) (London, 1577), ff. 115v–116.

Ludowick Bryskett

from: 'The mourning Muse of Thestylis', *Colin Clouts Come Home Againe* (London, 1611), sigs. B3r–B4v. The poem was printed with Spenser's *Colin Clouts Come Home Againe* and elegies on Sidney by Spenser, Ralegh and Grevill in *Astrophel* (London, 1595). This text from 1595 with amendments from the 1611 printing.

Edmund Spenser

(i) from: *Colin Clouts Come Home Againe* (London, 1611). (ii) from: *Epithalamion* (London, 1611). (iii) from: *The Faerie Queene*, Book VII, the Mutability Cantos (Canto vi, stanzas 36-55) (London, 1611).

Sir John Harington

'Of the warres in Ireland', from *The most witty and elegant epigrames by Sir J.H.* (London, 1618).

J.G.E (Anthony Nixon?)

from: *England's Hope against Irish Hate* (London, 1600).

Gervase Markham

from: 'The Newe Metamorphosis', BL. Add MS. 14824, ff. 25r–25v and 21r.

Ralph Birchensa

from: *A Discourse occasioned upon the late defeat, given to the arch-rebels, Tyrone and ODonnel, by ... Lord Mountjoy ... the 24 of December 1601 ... and the yeelding up of Kinsale shortly after by Don John to his lordship* (London, 1602), sigs. B4v–C3r and D2r–D3r.

from: 'A joyfull new ballad of the late Victory obtain'd by my Lord *Mount-Joy* ...', *The Roxburgh Ballads* ed. J. Woodfall Ebsworth, Volume VIII (Hertford, 1897), part 2, pp. xi***–xiii***.

Richard Bourke, Earl of Clanricard

'Of the last Queene', Bodleian Library MS Douce *c*. 54, fol. 7v.

Part II   1603–41: Early Stuart Verse

Richard Nugent
Four sonnets from *Rich: Nugents Cynthia. Containing direfull sonnets, madrigalls, and passionate intercourses, describing his repudiate affections expressed in loves owne language* (London, 1604).

Thomas Scot(?)
'An Irish Banquet or the Mayors Feast of Youghall', Thomas Scot, gent., *Phylomythie or Phylomythologie* (London, 1616), from the section entitled *Certaine Pieces of this Age Paraboliz'd* ...

Sir John Davies
'On the Deputy of Ireland his Child', *Poems of Sir John Davies*, ed. Robert Krueger (Oxford, 1975), p. 303.

George Wither
[Poem for the marriage of Sir Francis Willoughby and Lady Cassandra Ridgeway], *The Continuation of the History of the Willoughby Family* by Cassandra Duchess of Chandos (1679–1735), ed. A.C. Wood (Eton: The Shakespeare Head Press, 1958, for the University of Nottingham), pp. 82–4.

Sir Parr Lane
from: 'Newes from the Holy Ile', TCD MS 786 (re-editing of text transcribed by Alan Ford and printed as 'Parr Lane, "Newes from the Holy Ile"' by Alan Ford, *Proceedings of the Royal Irish Academy*, Vol. 99C, 115–56 (1999)).

The Lamentable Burning of the City of Corke (in the province of Munster in Ireland) by Lightning: which happened the Last of May, 1622. After a prodigious Battell of the Stares which Fought most strangely over and neere that Citty, the 12. and 14. of May. 1621. (London?, 1622?).

Edward Bletso
Dialogus inter viatorem & Heremitam in obitum Armigeri validissimi Owen O'Hara August 10 1622 [A dialogue between a traveller and a hermit on the death of the worthy knight, Owen O'Hara, August 10 1622]. Bodleian Library: MS. Rawl. poet. 152, f. 248r.

Thomas Pestell
'Verses on a bible presented to the Lady K[atherine] C[ork]', *The Poems of Thomas Pestell*, ed. Hannah Buchan (Oxford, 1940), pp. 2–3.

Richard Bellings
All selections from *A Sixth Booke to the Countesse of Pembrokes Arcadia written by R[ichard] B[ellings] Esq.* (Dublin 1624). (i) Agelastus's reflections on fate and honour', pp. 96–8; (ii) 'The Description of a Tempest', sig. P1r-P1v; (iii) 'Directions to a Painter to draw his Mistris', sig O3r-O4v.

W. Martin
'To his approved friend the Author', Richard Bellings, *A Sixth Booke to the Countesse of Pembrokes Arcadia* (Dublin, 1624), sig. A4r.

Lady Ann Southwell
'An Elegie written by the Lady A: S: to the Countesse of London Derrye. supposeinge hir to be dead by hir long silence', Folger Shakespeare Library MS. V. b. 198, ff. 19v–20v; this text taken from the transcription in *The Southwell-Sibthorp Commonplace Book*, ed. Jean Klene (Medieval and Renaissance Texts and Studies, vol. 147, Tempe, Arizona, 1997), pp. 24–7.

Inscription on the tomb of Sir Arthur Chichester, first Baron of Belfast. Text taken from the tomb in St Nicholas's Church, Carrickfergus.

Alexander Spicer
from: *An Elegie on the much lamented death of the right Honourable Sir Arthur Chichester Knight, Lo. Baron of Belfast . . .* by Alex. Spicer. April 12. Printed in the yeare of mourning. 1643 (London, 1643). This is a 1643 reprint of the poem first published in 1625.

Mount Taraghs Triumph Broadside (Dublin, 5 July 1626).

Francis Quarles
(i) from: *Argalus and Parthenia* (London, 1629). This text taken from the old-spelling critical edition by David Freeman (Folger Books, [Cranbury (New Jersey), London (England) and Mississauga (Ontario, Canada), Associated University Presses for the Renaissance English Text Society], 1986), pp. 90–4. (ii) 'Like to the Damaske Rose', *Argalus and Parthenia*, ed. Freeman, p. 180.

Dudley Boswell
'A Theologicall description of the divine rapture and extasie that the blessed soule of this Countesse [i.e. Catherine Boyle, Countess of Cork] was in at it's separation from the body', *Musarum Lachrymæ* (Dublin, 1630), sigs. B4r–B4v.

George Brady
'An Elegie upon the death of the right noble and vertuous Lady, the La: Katherine Countesse of Corke', *Musarum Lachrymæ* (Dublin, 1630) sigs. A3r–B2r.

John Shank(?)
['The Irish Exile's Song'], Bodleian Library, MS. Rawl D 398, f. 242.

Michael Kearney
Passages in English verse from Kearney's translation of Geoffrey Keating's *Foras Feasa ar Éirinn*, Royal Irish Academy MS. 24 G 16.

'Ye merry Boys all that live in Fingaule', British Library, Sloane MS 900, ff. 54–5.

James Shirley
(i) 'A Prologue there to the *Irish Gent.*', *Poems &c. by James Shirley, including Narcissus or the Self-lover, Prologues and Epilogues and the Triumph of Beautie* (London, 1646), pp. 38–9. (ii) 'A Prologue to another of Master Fletcher's Playes there', *Poems &c.* (London, 1646), pp. 41–3. (iii) 'A Prologue to a Play there; Call'd, *No wit to a Womans*', *Poems &c.* (London, 1646), pp. 40–1.

Andrew Cooper
'Upon Mr James Shirley his Comedy, called The Royal Master', *The Dramatic Works and*

Poems of James Shirley ed. William Gifford and Alexander Dyce, 6 vols (London, 1833, reprint New York, 1966), I, lxxxiv.

'The Life and Death of John Atherton, Lord Bishop of Waterford and Lysmore . . .' (London, 1641).

Part III   1641–60: From the Rising to the Restoration

Anonymous political poems from the 1640s
(i) Verse prophesy about the Irish, *A Bloody Irish Almanack* (London, 1641). (ii) 'Verse written by the Irish Confederates', *Bellum Hybernicale*: or, IRELAND'S WARRE Astrologically demonstrated, from the late Celestiall-congresse . . . . by Capt. GEO: WHARTON, Student in Astronomy. Printed in the Yeere, 1647 p. 28 [main text by Sir George Wharton (1617–81)]. (iii) Elegy on the Death of Sir Charles Coote, Beinecke Library, Yale University, Osborn MS Fb 228 #19. (iv) Anagram on Charles Coote (the younger), Beinecke Library, Yale University, Osborn MS Fb 228 #26(c). (v) from: 'On the breach of the peace', Beinecke Library, Yale University, Osborn MS Fb 228 #25. (vi) Stanza from *A New Ballad called a review of the Rebellion in three parts.* (London (June 15) 1647). (vii) Anagram on Michael Jones, Beinecke Library, Yale University, Osborn MS Fb 228 #26.

Cornelius Mahony(?)
'A kind of a Ballad . . .', *A Relation of the Sundry Occurrences in Ireland* . . . (London, 1642).

George Web
'On the Renovation of the Bishops of Ireland, happily effected by the Piety and Ingenuity of the most Learned Sir James Ware, Knight', *A Commentary on the Prelates of Ireland* . . . (1705 Dublin ed. of the works of Sir James Ware), sig. π 4.

'An Account of an Irish Quarter', [also known as 'A Banter made upon an Irish Sheriff, on the Account of an Entertainment he gave to two gentlemen belonging to the Life Guard of Ireland, when the Duke of O. was Lord Lieutenant there, viz. about the Year 1643, called, The Irish Entertainment']; this text from *Songs and Poems of Love and Drollery* [edited by] T[homas] W[eaver] (London, 1654), pp. 79–84.

from: *A Looking-Glasse of the World, or, the Plundered Man in Ireland: His Voyage, his Observation of the Beasts of the Field, of the Fishes of the Sea, of the Fowles of the Aire, of the Severall Professions of Men &c.* (London, 1644).

Payne Fisher
(i) 'On a dangerous Voyage twixt Mazarine and Montjoy', British Library Add. MS 19863, ff. 23v–25. (ii) 'Newes from Lough-Bagge alias the Church-Iland upon the first discovery and fortifying of it', BL. Add. MS 19863, ff. 18–20. (iii) 'A March', BL. Add. MS 19863, ff. 32–34v.

Inscription on a monument in the church at Gowran, Co. Kilkenny, William Carrigan, *The History and Antiquities of the Diocese of Ossory*, 4 vols (Dublin, 1905), III, 406.

John Booker
'The explanation of the frontispeece', *A Bloody Irish Almanack . . .* (London, 1646).

John Watson
'To the excellent and most noble Lord, the Lord Marquis of Ormond, James Butler', Beinecke Library, Yale University, Osborn MS Fb 228 #16.

Sir Edmund Butler
'Arise distracted land', Beinecke Library, Yale University, Osborn MS Fb 228 #15.

from: *Hyberniæ Lachrymæ, or, a sad contemplation on the bleeding condition of Ireland.* (London, 1648).

William Smith
(i) 'To Ireland', Beinecke Library, Yale University, Osborn MS Fb 228 #14. (ii) Inscription on monument in St Mickle's Church, Damagh, Co. Kilkenny, William Carrigan, *The History and Antiquities of the Diocese of Ossory*, 4 vols (Dublin, 1905), III, 444.

'The Loyall Subjects Jubilee, or *Cromwels* Farewell to *England*, being a Poem on his advancing to *Ireland, July* the 11. 1649' (London, 1649).

George Wither
from: *Carmen Eucharisticon: a private thank-oblation exhibited to the Glory of the Lord of Hosts*, for the timely and wonderfull Deliverance, vouchsafed to this Nation, in the routing of a numerous Army of Irish Rebells before *Dublin*, by the Sword of his valiant Servant, Michael Jones, Lieutenant-Generall for the Parliament of England. Composed by *Geo. Wither* Esquire, August 29, 1649 (London, 1649).

'Ormondes Breakfast or a True Relation of the Salley and Skirmish performed by Colonel Michael Jones . . .' (Dublin, 1649).

Edward Calver
from: *Zion's Thankfull Ecchoes from the Clifts of Ireland, Or the little Church of Christ in Ireland, warbling out her humble and gratefull addresses to her Elder Sister in England: And in particular, To the Parliament, to his Excellency, and to his Army, or that part assigned to her assistance, now in her low, yet hopefull Condition* (London, 1649).

Thomas Cobbes
'A Poeme uppon Cromuell and his Archtrayterous Rabble of Rebellious Racailles and England's Jaole-birds, levelled and arranged nowe together, with a compendious runninge over of Great Britaine's present deplorable state, and a more ample description of Irelande's auncient, late, more moderne and nowe imminent condition, if the Inhabitants thereof (as beneath exhorted) doe not unanimously and seriously addresse themselves to defend their auncient Religion, theire Kinge, theire countrey, the pristine Rights, Lawes and customes of their countrey, their wives, their children and their owne lands and Personall estates . . .', Beinecke Library, Yale University, Osborn MS Fb 228 #27.

'The Fingallian Dance', British Library MS Sloane 900.

'On the Protector', Beinecke Library, Yale University, Osborn MS Fb 228 #28.

['The Irish'], a verse from 'A Medley of the Nations' in *A Collection of Loyal Songs written against the Rump Parliament between the years 1639 and 1661*, 2 vols (London, 1731).

William Wheeler
'To the Honorable Commissioners for Assesments, The Complaint of the South Suburbs of Corke' (Cork, 1656).

William Wright
'A Preparative to a Pacification betwixt The *South*, and *North*, Suburbs of *Corke*. For Mr William Wheeler' (Cork, 1656).

Faithfull Teate
(i) from: *Ter Tria: or the Doctrine of the Three Sacred Persons, Father, Son, & Spirit. Principal Graces, Faith, Hope, and Love. Main Duties, Prayer, Hearing, and Meditation. Summarily digested for the pleasure and profit of the Pious and Ingenious Reader*. By Faithfull Teate, Preacher of the Word at Sudbury in Suffolk (London, 1658). This text taken from 2nd edition (London, 1669). (ii) from: 'Hope', *Ter Tria* (London, 1669 ed.), pp. 130–45.

John Perrot
from: 'A Song for that Assembly' i.e. the Assembly of Megiddon, in *A Sea of the Seed's Sufferings, Through which Runs A River of Rich Rejoycing . . .Written in the Year 1659, in Rome-Prison of Mad-Men, By the extream Suffering Servant of the Lord, John* (London, 1661), pp. 10–14.

Part IV   1660–85. The Reign of Charles II

The Corporation of Belfast
'Verses sent to Generall Monck by the Corporation of Belfast', *The Town Book of the Corporation of Belfast 1613–1816*, ed. Robert M. Young (Belfast, 1892), p. 79.

William Fuller
'An Antheme Sung at the Consecration of the Arch bishops and Bishops of Ireland, on Sunday the 27 of January 1660 [i.e. 1661], at St Patrick's in Dublin' (Dublin, 1661?). [This version of the text from the Thomason tracts 669f.26.(61)].

from: 'To his Grace James Duke of Ormond . . . upon his returne to this Kingdom and Government', Beinecke Library, Yale University, Osborn MS Fb 228 #36.

'On the Act of Settlement', Beinecke Library, Yale University, Osborn MS Fb 228 #32.

Katherine Philips
(i) 'To the Lady E[lizabeth]. Boyl', *The Collected Works of Katherine Philips, the Matchless Orinda*, ed. Patrick Thomas (3 vols., Stump Cross, Essex): I, *Poems* (1990), 221–2. (ii) 'To the Lady Mary Butler at her marriage with the Lord Cavendish, October 1662', *Works of Philips* . . . ed. Thomas, I, 250–1. (iii) 'To the Countess of Roscomon, with a copy of *Pompey*', *Poems by the deservedly admired Mrs K[atherine] P[hilips], The Matchless Orinda. (*London, 1667), pp. 151–2. (See also *Works of Philips* . . . ed. Thomas, I, 223–4). (iv) 'The Irish Greyhound', *Works of Philips* . . . ed. Thomas I, 195–6.

'Philo-Philippa'
'To the Excellent Orinda', *Poems by the most deservedly Admired Mrs K[atherine] P[hilips]*. . . (London, 1667), sigs. C2r–D2r.

Wentworth Dillon, Earl of Roscommon
(i) 'Epilogue to *Alexander the Great* when acted at the Theatre in Dublin', *Poems by the Earl of Roscommon*. . . (London, 1717), pp. 140–3. (ii) 'Prologue to *Pompey, A Tragedy*, Translated by Mrs. K. Philips from the French of Monsieur Corneille, and Acted at the Theatre in Dublin', *Poems by the deservedly admired Mrs K[atherine] P[hilips], The Matchless Orinda*. (London, 1667) sigs. 3G1r-3G1v. (iii) from: *An Essay on Translated Verse* (London, 1685).

from: 'Iter Hibernicum', British Library MS. Sloane 360, pp. 104–110.

'In Laudem Navis Geminæ E Portu Dublinij ad Regem Carolum IIdum Missæ', British Library MS. Sloane 360, pp. 73–80.

Ambrose White
Verses for the year and for each month of 1665, *An Almanack and Prognostication for the year of our Lord 1665 . . . calculated according to Art and referred to the Horizon of the Ancient and Renowned City of DUBLIN*, by Ambrose White (Dublin, 1665).

'An Epitaph upon one Browne, an Irish man', manuscript note in the National Library of Ireland copy of *An Almanack and Prognostication for the year of our Lord 1665 . . . calculated according to Art and referred to the Horizon of the Ancient and Renowned City of DUBLIN*, by Ambrose White (Dublin, 1665).

Jeremy Taylor
Four Festival Hymns, *The Whole Works of Jeremy Taylor*, ed. Reginald Herber, 15 vols (London, 1822), XV, 78–80.

Jo. Binckes
from: 'An humble token of loyalty & sincere gratitude', Beinecke Library, Yale University, Osborn MS Fb 228 #35.

'Lines allegedly written on the gates of Bandon Bridge', *The Orrery Papers*, ed. the Countess of Cork and Orrery, 2 vols (London, 1903), I, xiii.

from: 'Purgatorium Hibernicum', National Library of Ireland MS 470.

Aquila Smyth
'On the Praise, and the happy delivery of James Wolveridge . . .', James Wolveridge, *Speculum Matricis Hybernicum; or, the Irish Midwives Handmaid* . . . (London, 1670), sigs. A1r–A2r.

'On the death of Mr Jo. Nelson who dyed of the small pox September 20 1671', Bodleian Library, MS Rawl poet 127.

'A Letter from a Missionary Bawd in Dublin, to her cheif in London gieving an account of the propogation of lewdness and scandall in Ireland', British Library Add. MS 72899 ('Sir William Petty's Poetical Amusements') ff. 158–9.

Dudley Loftus(?)
from: *The Wish, being the Tenth Satyr of Juvenal Periphrastically rendered in Pindarick Verse*. By a person, sometimes Fellow of Trin. Col. DUBLIN (Dublin, 1675).

Zacheus Isham
from: 'To his worthy and much honoured Friend [Edmund Borlase] . . .' an ode prefaced to Edmund Borlase's *The Reduction of Ireland to the Crown of England* . . . (London, 1675).

William Mercer
(i) from *The Moderate Cavalier or the Soldiers description of Ireland and of the Country Disease* . . . (Cork, 1675). (ii) 'A Dialogue betwixt a *Soldier*, Author of this Book, and an *Echo*, being a Summary Discourse of the Whole matter; briefly resounded by the *Echo*', *Moderate Cavalier*, pp. 35–6.

Sir William Petty
'A Navall Allegory', British Library Add MS. 72899.

Roger Boyle, Earl of Orrery
Two poems from *Poems on most of the Festivals of the Church* . . . (London, 1681). The text of this work was printed by William Smith in Cork.

An Elegy of the Modern Heroe, Redmond Ó Hanlan, Surnamed the Tory. Broadside (Dublin, 1681).

from: 'Upon the Earl of Ossory's dying of a Feaver', Beinecke Library, Yale University, Osborn MS Fb 228 #45.

A Looking-glass for a Tory; or the Bogg-trotter's Glory Broadside (London, 1682).

John Wilson
To his Excellence, Richard Earle of Arran &c., Lord Deputy of Ireland . . . Broadside (Dublin, 1682). British Library 807.g.5 (28).

'On Mr Wilson's admirable Copy of Verses dedicated to his Ex: the Earle of Arran', manuscript response to the previous poem; bound in a volume of Dublin-printed broadsides from the 1680s, British Library 807.g.5 (29).

from: 'A Lampoon on the Senior Fellowes of Dublin Colledge', Trinity College Dublin MS. 879, I, ff. 39–49

Luke Wadding
All texts from *A Smale Garland of Pious and Godly Songs* (Gant, 1684).

'To all protestants in England, Scotland & Ireland', Beinecke Library, Yale University, Osborn MS Fb 228 #51.

'J. H.'
'Upon the Earl of Roscommon's poems being publish'd', Bodleian Library MS Don. c. 55, ff. 21–22.

Part V   1685–1701: Jacobite and Williamite Ireland

To His Grace the Duke of Ormond Upon his leaving the Government and Kingdom of Ireland. Broadside (Dublin and London, 1685?).

'To his Onor de Rit Onorable Richard Earle of Tyroincol (*sic*)', Bodleian Library, MS. Don e. 23, ff. 75v–76.

Edmund Arwacker
from: *Fons Perennis: A poem on the excellent and useful invention of making sea-water fresh* . . . (London, 1686).

'On the College of Physicians in Dublin who, haveing brought to life a malefactor that was given from the Gallows to be dissected, Redelivered him to the Sherif to be Executed', Trinity College Dublin MS 879, I, 186.

from: *A Congratulatory Poem on the arrival of His Sacred Majesty at the City of Chester, August the 27th 1687*. Broadside (Dublin?, 1687), British Library 807.g.5 (46).

'On Doctor Dryden's coming over to the provost of Trinity College', British Library Add MS. 38671, f. 32v.

'Lilliburlero'; first part from *A New Song*, Broadsheet (London, 1687) (Pepys V, 33); second part from *The Historical Songs of Ireland* . . . ed. T. Crofton Croker (London, 1841), pp. 6–9.

'An Elegy of the Pig that followed the Ld Chief Baron Henn and Baron Worth from Connaught to Dublin', Trinity College Dublin MS. 879. I, ff. 183–183v.

John Jones and others
['Verses on Thomas Weaver'] Trinity College Dublin MS. 879. I, ff. 73v–74.

Here, Here, here is Pig and Pork: or (a Catholic Tradition) . . . Broadside (London, 1689?) Pepys II, 315.

The Lusty Friar of Dublin, Broadside (London, 1689?) Pepys III, 43.

from: *The Irish Hudibras* (London, 1689), pp. 127–31, 144–6, 148–51.

['Teague's response to the accession of King William'] *The Musical Miscellany*, 6 vols (London, 1729-31), III, 36.

News from London-Derry in a packet of Advice from Room, Broadside (London, 1689?) Pepys V, 45.

Poor Teague in distress, Broadside (London, 1690?) Pepys II, 304.

The Bogg-Trotters March, Broadside (London, 1690?) Pepys V, 54.

Teague the Irish Trooper, Broadside (London, 1690?) Pepys II, 360.

Teague the Irish Soldier, Broadside (London, 1691?) Pepys V, 72.

George Farquhar
'On the Death of General *Schomberg*: a Pindarick', *The Complete Works of George Farquhar*, ed. Charles Stonehill, 2 vols (London, 1930), II, 309–12.

Jonathan Swift
Ode to the King on his Irish Expedition . . . Broadside (Dublin, 1691).

Ellis Walker
from: *Epicteti Enchiridion made English in a poetical paraphrase* (London, 1695).

'The Gentlemen at Larges Litany', text from a transcription in a (now lost) copy of Harwards's *Prognostication for the year of Our Lord 1666* . . . *[for] the Kingdom of Ireland* . . . (Dublin, 1666); see *The Poems of Jonathan Swift* ed. Harold Williams, 2nd ed. (London, 1958), pp. 1063–4.

Charles Hopkins
'The Story of Perseus and Andromeda', *The History of Love* (London, 1699).

Nahum Tate
(i) 'An Ode upon the 9th of January 1694', Trinity College Dublin MS. 879, I, f. 199. (ii) 'The Blessed *Virgin*'s Expostulation, when our *Saviour* at Twelve Years of Age had withdrawn himself', *Miscellanea Sacra: or, Poems on Divine and Moral Subjects*, vol I (all published) (London, 1696), pp. 30–1. (iii) 'Upon the Sight of an Anatomy', *Miscellanea Sacra*, pp. 40–4.

'Ribeen a Roon', Bodleian Library, MS Rawl D 71.

Joseph Aickin
from: *Londerias: or a Narrative of the Siege of London-Derry* . . . (Dublin, 1699).

John Hopkins
(i) from: *The Fall of Man* (London, 1699). (ii) 'Pigmalion and his Iv'ry Statue', *Amasia* (London, 1700) [from the section 'Metamorphosis of Love', pp. 37–40].

Jonathan Swift
'The Discovery', *The Poems of Jonathan Swift*, ed. Harold Williams, 2nd ed. (London, 1958), pp. 61–4.

'The Picture of a Beau', *The Poems of Jonathan Swift* ed. Williams, p. 1071. Williams transcribed the text some time in the 1930s from a (now lost) copy of Michael Harward's *Prognostication for the year of Our Lord 1666* . . . *[for] the Kingdom of Ireland* . . . (Dublin, 1666). A similar text appears at Trinity College Dublin MS. 879, I, f.36. The poem is not by Swift.

Jonathan Swift
'The Humble Petition of Frances Harris', *Miscellanies in Prose and Verse*, 2nd ed. (London, 1713), pp. 351–8. There is a transcription of this poem (taken from a pirated, printed text) in TCD MS 879, II, 368.

INDEX OF TITLES AND FIRST LINES[1]

---

1. Titles are in italics, first lines in roman type.

INDEX OF AUTHORS